(Continued on back endsheets)

Dictionary of Literary Biography • Volume One Hundred One

British Prose Writers, 1660-1800
First Series

Surry Community College LRC
P. O. Box 304
Dobson, NC 27017

WITHDRAWN

LIBRARY USE ONLY

Dictionary of Literary Biography • Volume One Hundred One

British Prose Writers, 1660-1800
First Series

Edited by
Donald T. Siebert
University of South Carolina

A Bruccoli Clark Layman Book
Gale Research Inc.
Detroit, New York, London

Advisory Board for
DICTIONARY OF LITERARY BIOGRAPHY

John Baker
William Cagle
Jane Christensen
Patrick O'Connor
Peter S. Prescott

Matthew J. Bruccoli and Richard Layman, *Editorial Directors*
C. E. Frazer Clark, Jr., *Managing Editor*

Printed in the United States of America

Published simultaneously in the United Kingdom
by Gale Research International Limited
(An affiliated company of Gale Research Inc.)

S#91-587

The paper used in this publication meets the minimum requirements
of American National Standard for Information Sciences—Permanence
Paper for Printed Library Materials, ANSI Z39.48-1984.   ∞™

Copyright © 1991
Gale Research Inc.
835 Penobscot Bldg.
Detroit, MI 48226-4094

ISBN 0-8103-4581-1
90-44215 CIP

To the memory of my wife,

Joan Markham Siebert

. . . in sickness and in health . . .

Contents

Plan of the Series

. . . Almost the most prodigious asset of a country, and perhaps its most precious possession, is its native literary product—when that product is fine and noble and enduring.

Mark Twain*

The advisory board, the editors, and the publisher of the *Dictionary of Literary Biography* are joined in endorsing Mark Twain's declaration. The literature of a nation provides an inexhaustible resource of permanent worth. We intend to make literature and its creators better understood and more accessible to students and the reading public, while satisfying the standards of teachers and scholars.

To meet these requirements, *literary biography* has been construed in terms of the author's achievement. The most important thing about a writer is his writing. Accordingly, the entries in *DLB* are career biographies, tracing the development of the author's canon and the evolution of his reputation.

The purpose of *DLB* is not only to provide reliable information in a convenient format but also to place the figures in the larger perspective of literary history and to offer appraisals of their accomplishments by qualified scholars.

The publication plan for *DLB* resulted from two years of preparation. The project was proposed to Bruccoli Clark by Frederick G. Ruffner, president of the Gale Research Company, in November 1975. After specimen entries were prepared and typeset, an advisory board was formed to refine the entry format and develop the series rationale. In meetings held during 1976, the publisher, series editors, and advisory board approved the scheme for a comprehensive biographical dictionary of persons who contributed to North American literature. Editorial work on the first volume began in January 1977, and it was published in 1978. In order to make *DLB* more than a reference tool and to compile volumes that individually have claim to status as lit-

erary history, it was decided to organize volumes by topic, period, or genre. Each of these freestanding volumes provides a biographical-bibliographical guide and overview for a particular area of literature. We are convinced that this organization—as opposed to a single alphabet method—constitutes a valuable innovation in the presentation of reference material. The volume plan necessarily requires many decisions for the placement and treatment of authors who might properly be included in two or three volumes. In some instances a major figure will be included in separate volumes, but with different entries emphasizing the aspect of his career appropriate to each volume. Ernest Hemingway, for example, is represented in *American Writers in Paris, 1920-1939* by an entry focusing on his expatriate apprenticeship; he is also in *American Novelists, 1910-1945* with an entry surveying his entire career. Each volume includes a cumulative index of subject authors and articles. Comprehensive indexes to the entire series are planned.

With volume ten in 1982 it was decided to enlarge the scope of *DLB*. By the end of 1986 twenty-one volumes treating British literature had been published, and volumes for Commonwealth and Modern European literature were in progress. The series has been further augmented by the *DLB Yearbooks* (since 1981) which update published entries and add new entries to keep the *DLB* current with contemporary activity. There have also been *DLB Documentary Series* volumes which provide biographical and critical source materials for figures whose work is judged to have particular interest for students. One of these companion volumes is entirely devoted to Tennessee Williams.

We define literature as the *intellectual commerce of a nation:* not merely as belles lettres but as that ample and complex process by which ideas are generated, shaped, and transmitted. *DLB* entries are not limited to "creative writers" but extend to other figures who in their time and in their way influenced the mind of a people. Thus the series encompasses historians, journalists, publishers, and screenwriters. By this means readers of *DLB* may be aided to perceive litera-

*From an unpublished section of Mark Twain's autobiography, copyright © by the Mark Twain Company.

ture not as cult scripture in the keeping of intellectual high priests but firmly positioned at the center of a nation's life.

DLB includes the major writers appropriate to each volume and those standing in the ranks immediately behind them. Scholarly and critical counsel has been sought in deciding which minor figures to include and how full their entries should be. Wherever possible, useful references are made to figures who do not warrant separate entries.

Each *DLB* volume has a volume editor responsible for planning the volume, selecting the figures for inclusion, and assigning the entries. Volume editors are also responsible for preparing, where appropriate, appendices surveying the major periodicals and literary and intellectual movements for their volumes, as well as lists of further readings. Work on the series as a whole is coordinated at the Bruccoli Clark Layman editorial center in Columbia, South Carolina, where the editorial staff is responsible for accuracy of the published volumes.

One feature that distinguishes *DLB* is the illustration policy–its concern with the iconography of literature. Just as an author is influenced by his surroundings, so is the reader's understanding of the author enhanced by a knowledge of his environment. Therefore *DLB* volumes include not only drawings, paintings, and photographs of authors, often depicting them at various stages in their careers, but also illustrations of their families and places where they lived. Title pages are regularly reproduced in facsimile along with dust jackets for modern authors. The dust jackets are a special feature of *DLB* because they often document better than anything else the way in which an author's work was perceived in its own time. Specimens of the writers' manuscripts are included when feasible.

Samuel Johnson rightly decreed that "The chief glory of every people arises from its authors." The purpose of the *Dictionary of Literary Biography* is to compile literary history in the surest way available to us–by accurate and comprehensive treatment of the lives and work of those who contributed to it.

The *DLB* Advisory Board

Foreword

Diversity marks the writers included in this volume, just as diversity characterizes the intellectual and artistic achievement of their whole age in the British Isles, an age traditionally spanning a century and a half, from the Restoration through the eighteenth century. It was an age of the multifaceted individual, an age when literary people were involved in affairs of state and extended their interests, and in many cases their expertise as well, into the other arts—painting, music, architecture, landscape gardening, for instance—and into fields such as science: it was a time when the notion of two cultures, one of science and the other of art, could not have been comprehended. Nor did the typical writer specialize. It is not atypical that the great dramatist and poet John Dryden was also the first great English critic; nor that the great poet Alexander Pope also wrote distinguished prose—including the informal essay, the familiar letter, and literary criticism—besides practicing both painting and landscape gardening with skill. No one would have thought it unusual that the great philosopher David Hume would also have written essays on everything from manners, fine taste, and tragedy, to economics, or that he would also have written a voluminous *History of England* (1754-1762) that would be the standard history well into the next century. The nineteenth-century historian Thomas Babington Macaulay characterized Sir William Temple in this manner: "a man of the world among men of letters, a man of letters among men of the world. Mere scholars were dazzled by the Ambassador, and Cabinet councillor; mere politicians by the Essayist and Historian." Temple was no doubt as wonderfully versatile as Macaulay says, but the wonder that he might have excited among his contemporaries would have derived only from the *brilliance* of his performance in these two arenas, certainly not from the possibility that he would have been both effective statesman and elegant writer.

Thus in the *Dictionary of Literary Biography* some writers represented in the two volumes covering Restoration-and-eighteenth-century nonfiction prose also appear in the volumes variously de-voted to drama, poetry, and the novel. Swift, for instance, appears in the volumes on novel, poetry, and nonfiction prose, while Oliver Goldsmith, perhaps not always given his due as a major writer, appears in the volumes on drama, poetry, and the novel, as well as nonfiction prose: the contributions that each made in the various literary kinds were considerable.

Such multiple inclusions may result in some degree of overlapping, most obviously in the biography itself, and also in the treatment of works, for a biography appearing in a volume on nonfiction prose demands the mention of the poetry, plays, or novels of the writer, and even some mention of the purpose, reception, and value of those works. Yet this multiple representation has advantages. Viewing an author from several perspectives—and often from the varying perspectives of different scholars—employing different generic emphases, illuminates that author's achievement more completely than any single perspective could, for in such an approach we view a writer's contribution to a single kind of writing, all in the context of a life, while remembering at the same time that there were other dimensions of an individual talent.

Not only did many writers of this age work effectively in a variety of principal genres, but they also did so in genres that in the twentieth century we may not normally think of as "literary" forms. The diary or journal, memoirs or autobiography, and the familiar letter are prominent examples. Indeed, the letter stands out in particular, for when Alexander Pope managed (with some trickery) to get his personal correspondence published, that literary event seems to have initiated a new and necessary form of literature, certainly in eighteenth-century England, a form that every writer would henceforth regard as a necessary accomplishment. After Pope it is rare to discover a distinguished writer in major genres who did not leave a body of correspondence well worth reading, both for what it reveals about the writer's life and times and for its high level of writing per se.

The familiar letter is related to an assumption about life itself that one could argue is fundamental to eighteenth-century culture. We think of this age as one in which polite and worldly values predominated—a stereotype in fact of elaborate costumes, powdered wigs, witty repartee, indeed an overall pattern of highly stylized behavior, whether in the elaboration of minuets, duels, levees, or even in the salutes and exchanges of the most ordinary personal relations: "I am, Sir, your most obedient and humble servant." There is some degree of truth in this popular image, but perhaps more of untruth. The vast majority of the population never had the chance to indulge themselves so, nor did they have any direct connection with letters and the arts, much less with high life. Moreover, could we revisit those times, we might be shocked at the repellent grossness and social ineptitude of many a lord or lady.

Still, the image does suggest something that rightly belongs to the literature of the age: namely, the assumption that life, at least ideally, should be cultivated as a fine art in itself. Thus a great deal of eighteenth-century writing is biographical in the broad sense of the term, as if it were an age of the "how-to" manual in the art of living. History in Lord Clarendon and Bishop Burnet begins as autobiography and remains almost fixated on the biographical. In David Hume the "character" of any significant historical figure serves to make sense of that figure's actions, to be sure, but such an analysis remains of great interest in and of itself: what lessons are there, Hume implies, about how best to live? Samuel Johnson freely admitted that the biographical part of literature was what he loved most. Moreover, he maintained that even the life of a relatively obscure man, if well told, would have immense value. In a letter to a friend he notes, "[Your uncle's] art of life certainly deserves to be known and studied. He lived in plenty and elegance upon an income which to many would appear indigent and to most, scanty. How he lived therefore every man has an interest in knowing." And in Johnson's *Lives of the Poets* (1779-1781) the long critical biographies (say of Alexander Pope or Joseph Addison) have the "character" at their very center. The biographical first part leads into the "character," and the critical examination of the works follows it; the "character" becomes in a sense both the moral encapsulation of a life and the determinant of a writer's achievement. The same central concern about how best to live might be found throughout the nonfiction writing of this period, whether it be sermons, philosophical or political discourses, periodical essays, literary criticism, satire, or even hack journalism. The diary and the letter are but the most obvious manifestations.

If the writers represented in this volume are somewhat different from those of more recent times in their typical range and emphases, however, they are much more similar to modern writers than to their predecessors in the Renaissance in one important respect—prose style. One has only to contrast the elaborately wrought sentences, learned diction, and formal tone of Sir Thomas Browne or John Donne (in his sermons) with the relaxed and offhand critical remarks of John Dryden, as if he were sitting cross-legged with gentlemanly ease in his armchair at Will's Coffeehouse, to realize that a revolution in prose style had occurred. That is not to say that everyone in this period wrote with some version of the colloquial plain style. Samuel Johnson's prose in *The Rambler* (1750-1752) might be characterized as almost baroque, though years later in his *Lives of the Poets* he wrote in much shorter, less formally structured sentences, and chose more ordinary words. Nonetheless, if it is difficult to find many examples of plain style in the prose of the earlier seventeenth century, it is equally difficult to find a great deal of formally structured prose in the later seventeenth century and into the following century.

What brought about this revolution? One standard explanation is the influence of the New Philosophy—that is to say the revolution in thought spurred by adoption in England of Baconian empiricism as the method of science. Induction rather than Aristotelian, or more properly neo-Aristotelian, deductive logic was to be the way to discovering the so-called laws of nature, and thereby what we know as the scientific method was born. Charles II chartered the Royal Society in 1662, and the progress in scientific knowledge made under its auspices was the talk of all informed people and hailed, for instance, by two rather different writers represented in this volume—John Dryden and Samuel Pepys. Certainly the facile optimism, implicit materialism, and occasionally ridiculous experimentation evident in the Society evoked the satiric scorn of conservatives such as Jonathan Swift, but it is notable that Swift himself wrote in a plainer style than did his mentor Sir William Temple, who, for all his allegiance to the ancients in preference to the moderns, wrote in a plainer, much more gentlemanly style than did his forebears in the Renaissance.

The locus classicus for the association of scientific thinking and plain style is Bishop Thomas Sprat's *History of the Royal Society* (1667). It is Sprat who insists, while praising the new approaches to science made possible by Baconian assumptions, that such liberating thinking must be expressed in a prose that avoids the pitfalls laid by figurative language and rhetoric, a fanciness of style that distracts the reader and obscures truth:

> How many rewards, which are due to more profitable, and difficult Arts, have been still snatch'd away by the easie vanity of *fine speaking*? . . . And, in few words, I dare say; that of all the Studies of men, nothing may be sooner obtain'd, than this vicious abundance of *Phrase*, this trick of *Metaphor*, this volubility of *Tongue*, which makes so great a noise in the World. . . .
>
> [The members of the Royal Society] have therefore been most rigorous in putting in execution, the only Remedy, that can be found for this *extravagance*: and that has been, a constant Resolution, to reject all the amplifications, digressions, and swellings of style: to return back to the primitive purity, and shortness, when men deliver'd so many *things*, almost in an equal number of *words*. They have exacted from all their members, a close, naked, natural way of speaking; positive expressions; clear senses; a native easiness: bringing all things as near the Mathematical plainness, as they can: and preferring the language of Artizans, Countrymen, and Merchants, before that of Wits, or Scholars.

To be sure, there is naïveté in the assumption that prose style might be as plain as mathematical language, although Sprat is by no means as extreme in his prescription as his colleague in the Royal Society, John Wilkins, who in an *Essay Towards a Real Character and a Philosophical Language* (1668), actually did recommend a style so plain that there would be an almost literal word-for-thing exactness—a goal whose absurdity was justly ridiculed by Swift in the third part of *Gulliver's Travels* (1726). Nevertheless, in Sprat's words we can observe an approximate description, at least in respect to its conversational easiness, of that plain style that would become the norm of belletristic writers as well as of scientists.

One would have to cite Joseph Addison as the exemplar of this ideal. In the following well-known passage from *Spectator* number 10 (12 March 1711), an essay announcing Mr. Specta-

tor's aims, consider both his point and the way in which he phrases it: "It was said of *Socrates*, that he brought Philosophy down from Heaven, to inhabit among Men; and I shall be ambitious to have it said of me, that I have brought Philosophy out of Closets and Libraries, Schools and Colleges, to dwell in Clubs and Assemblies, at Tea-Tables and in Coffee-Houses." How unfashionable bookishness in general and pedantic style in particular have become, at least in Addison's mind. The cadences of his sentence belong not to the pulpit or lecture hall, but of course, as he indicates, to the tea table and coffeehouse. One will find few long and periodic sentences in Addison. Rather, the well-bred, informal talk of fashionable society has become the goal, even of learned discourse. Later in the century Johnson, himself not always a practitioner of the Addisonian manner, points to the essence of this great stylist's achievement:

> His prose is the model of the middle style; on grave subjects not formal, on light occasions not groveling; pure without scrupulosity, and exact without apparent elaboration; always equable, and always easy, without glowing words or pointed sentences. Addison never deviates from his track to snatch a grace; he seeks no ambitious ornaments, and tries no hazardous innovations. His page is always luminous, but never blazes in unexpected splendour. . . . Whoever wishes to attain an English style, familiar but not coarse, and elegant but not ostentatious, must give his days and nights to the volumes of Addison.

Many aspiring stylists probably tried to do just that, for the number of Addison's admirers and would-be imitators must be legion in the eighteenth century. Benjamin Franklin, for instance, as he recounts in his *Autobiography*, fashioned his own style by reading a *Spectator* paper, shutting the book, then trying to reproduce the essay as nearly as possible, and finally using the original as a critique of his own efforts.

That easy style that Addison so well exemplifies implies an attitude about learned discourse itself: it need not be difficult to read; philosophy should descend not only from heaven to earth, but also and especially to the coffeehouse. Addison's sentence becomes almost a topos in eighteenth-century thought. That fashionable philosopher Lord Shaftesbury opines that "to philosophize is but to carry good-breeding a step higher. . . ." And that much less fashionable (at least in his own day) and more difficult philosopher David Hume adopted what is essentially the same attitude. After his bold and seminal *Treatise of Human Nature* (1739, 1740) "fell *dead-born from the Press*," as he puts it in his autobiography, he then devoted most of his philosophical writing to making the ideas of that challenging work more accessible in terms of style: "I had always entertained a notion, that my want of success in publishing the Treatise . . . had proceeded more from the manner than the matter." In any event, few writers in the eighteenth century wanted to be identified as pedants or metaphysicians, and what better way to avoid this invidious identification than to avoid sounding like one?

One last generalization comes to mind in this survey of the Restoration-and-eighteenth-century prose of ideas. (Undoubtedly a preface such as this will necessarily run too close to sweeping pronouncements to which there must be numerous exceptions.) In many respects a down-to-earth style is the vehicle of down-to-earth ideas, and one might hazard without too much risk the argument that the prose of ideas in this period was devoted in the main to the practical, the obviously useful, whether it be the examination of one's personal life and how it might best be understood and lived—the moral dimension, broadly conceived—or the pursuit of those means by which it might be materially improved—the political on the one hand, and the scientific and technological on the other. Once again the spirit of the empirical and the utilitarian is pervasive among the writers represented here. That great French encyclopedist Denis Diderot might be cited in this regard, because it is well to remember that the phenomenon being considered is not limited to Great Britain; it is one of the hallmarks of the Enlightenment:

> Place on one side of the scales the actual advantages of the most sublime sciences and the most honored arts, and on the other side the advantages of the mechanical arts, and you will find that esteem has not been accorded to the one and to the other in just proportion to the benefits they bring. . . . How strangely we judge! We expect everyone to pass his time in a useful manner, and we disdain useful men. . . . Let us finally render artists [that is, artisans] the justice that is their due. The liberal arts have sung their own praise long enough; they should now raise their voice in praise of the mechanical arts.

Perhaps in this statement and indeed in many assumptions about the purpose and style of writ-

ing, covered in this preface, we see the essential modernity of the intellectual prose of the Restoration and eighteenth century.

The reader of this volume might ask what dictated the inclusion of the writers treated here. Why is Thomas Rymer included but not Thomas Sprat, an author quoted above? One might well think of such interesting writers as the following, important in a special sense, who might have been part of this volume: John Aubrey, Richard Bentley, Colley Cibber, John Evelyn, Lord Halifax, Sir Roger L'Estrange, Joseph Spence, and divines such as Francis Atterbury, Isaac Barrow, Robert South, or John Tillotson—and of course many, many more.

In planning such a project, especially one limited by the constraints of volume size, an editor has to be selective. Clearly there is not room for a hundred authors, however interesting they might be in some special sense. In determining inclusion, I have asked myself the following questions as a rationale of selection: (1) has the writer produced a considerable body of significant or distinguished nonfiction prose—significant intellectually (that is, in being innovative or seminal), or otherwise distinguished by its enduring quality and effectiveness as literature (despite how meaningless a term such as "literature" might be regarded in so-called postmodern criticism); (2) has the writer been widely quoted or otherwise recognized by contemporaries or by later readers, critics, and scholars? A reasonably strong affirmative to either question might justify including the author. Sprat, then, is a writer about whom one might answer in the weak affirmative to both questions (much more faintly "yes" to the first), but so weakly as to preclude his selection.

But one has to admit that others might determine differently, whether about Sprat or about other possibilities. And of course, who can be sure that our judgments have any real validity? In his otherwise incisive essay "Of the Standard of Taste" (1757), Hume poses the rhetorical question of who in his right mind could prefer John Bunyan to Joseph Addison, and among Hume's contemporaries anyone who might have preferred Bunyan would have deserved a place in the Hospital of St. Mary of Bethlehem—that is to say, Bedlam. Yet one notices in recent decades that at least as much appreciative criticism has been devoted to Bunyan as to Addison.

—*Donald T. Siebert*

Acknowledgments

This book was produced by Bruccoli Clark Layman, Inc. Karen L. Rood, senior editor for the *Dictionary of Literary Biography* series, was the in-house editor.

Production coordinator is James W. Hipp. Systems manager is Charles D. Brower. Photography editor is Susan Brennen Todd. Permissions editor is Jean W. Ross. Layout and graphics supervisor is Penney L. Haughton. Copyediting supervisor is Bill Adams. Typesetting supervisor is Kathleen M. Flanagan. Information systems analyst is George F. Dodge. Charles Lee Egleston is editorial associate. The production staff includes Rowena Betts, Polly Brown, Teresa Chaney, Patricia Coate, Sarah A. Estes, Mary L. Goodwin, David Marshall James, Ellen McCracken, Kathy Lawler Merlette, Laura Garren Moore, John Myrick, Gina D. Peterman, Cathy J. Reese, Edward Scott, Laurrè Sinckler, Maxine K. Smalls, John C. Stone III, and Betsy L. Weinberg.

Walter W. Ross did the library research with the assistance of the following librarians at the Thomas Cooper Library of the University of South Carolina: Gwen Baxter, Daniel Boice, Faye Chadwell, Cathy Eckman, Gary Geer, Cathie Gottlieb, David L. Haggard, Jens Holley, Jackie Kinder, Thomas Marcil, Marcia Martin, Laurie Preston, Jean Rhyne, Carol Tobin, and Virginia Weathers.

Dictionary of Literary Biography • Volume One Hundred One

British Prose Writers, 1660-1800
First Series

Dictionary of Literary Biography

Joseph Addison
(1 May 1672 - 17 June 1719)

Lillian D. Bloom
Research Scholar, Henry E. Huntington Library and Art Gallery

BOOKS: *Nova philosophia veteri praeferenda. In Theatri oxoniensis encaenia: sive comitia philologica 1693 celebrata* (Oxford: e Theatro Sheldoniano, 1693);

A Poem to His Majesty, Presented to the Lord Keeper (London: Printed for J. Tonson, 1695);

The Campaign, A Poem, To His Grace the Duke of Marlborough (London: Printed for Jacob Tonson, 1705);

Remarks on Several Parts of Italy, &c. in the years, 1701, 1702, 1703 (London: Printed for Jacob Tonson, 1705; revised, 1718);

Rosamond: An Opera, humbly inscribed to her Grace the Duchess of Marlborough (London: Printed for J. Tonson, 1707);

The Present State of the War and the Necessity of an Augmentation Consider'd (London: Printed & sold by J. Morphew, 1708);

The Tatler. By Isaac Bickerstaff, Esq., nos. 1-271, by Addison and Richard Steele (London: Printed by John Nutt for John Morphew, 12 April 1709 - 2 January 1711);

The Whig Examiner, nos. 1-5 (London: Sold by A. Baldwin, 14 September - 12 October 1710);

The Spectator, nos. 1-555, by Addison and Steele (London: Printed for Samuel Buckley & Jacob Tonson & sold by A. Baldwin, 1 March 1711 - 6 December 1712); second series, nos. 556-635, by Addison (London: Printed for Samuel Buckley & Jacob Tonson & sold by A. Baldwin, 18 June - 20 December 1714);

The Guardian, nos. 1-175, by Addison, Steele, and others (London: Printed for J. Tonson, 12 March - 1 October 1713);

Cato: A tragedy, as it is acted at the Theatre-Royal in Drury Lane (London: Printed for J. Tonson, 1713);

The Late Tryal and Conviction of Count Tariff (London: Printed for A. Baldwin, 1713);

The Lover. By Marmaduke Myrtle, Gent., 40 nos., nos. 10 and 39 by Addison, others by Steele (London: Printed & sold by Ferd, Burleigh, 25 February - 27 March 1714);

The Free-holder, nos. 1-55 (London: Printed & sold by S. Gray, 23 December 1715 - 29 June 1716);

The Drummer; or, The Haunted House. A Comedy. As it is acted at the Theatre-Royal in Drury-Lane (London: Printed for Jacob Tonson, 1716);

To Her Royal Highness the Princess of Wales, with the tragedy of Cato. Nov. 1714. To Sir Godfrey Kneller on his Picture of the King (London: Printed for J. Tonson, 1716);

A Dissertation upon the Most Celebrated Roman Poets. Written originally in Latin by Joseph Addison, Esq.; Made English by Christopher Hayes, Esq. [Latin and English texts] (London: Printed for E. Curll, 1718);

Two Poems, viz. I. On the Deluge, Paradise, the Burning of the World, and of the New Heavens and New Earth. An Ode to Dr. Burnett. II. In Praise of Physic and Poetry. An Ode to Dr. Hannes [Latin texts followed by English translations

Joseph Addison (portrait by Sir Godfrey Kneller; by permission of the National Portrait Gallery, London)

by Thomas Newcomb] (London: Printed for E. Curll, 1718);

The Resurrection. A Poem. Written by Mr. Addison [Latin text followed by an English translation by Nicholas Amhurst] (London: Printed for E. Curll, 1718);

Poems on Several Occasions, With A Dissertation Upon the Roman Poets (London: Printed for E. Curll, 1719);

The Old Whig, nos. 1 and 2 (London: Sold by J. Roberts & A. Dodd, 19 March and 2 April 1719);

Notes upon the twelve books of Paradise Lost (London: Printed for Jacob Tonson, 1719);

Miscellanies, in Verse and Prose (London: Printed for E. Curll, 1725);

The Christian Poet. A Miscellany of Divine Poems (London: Printed for E. Curll, 1728);

The Evidences of the Christian Religion (London: Printed for J. Tonson, 1730);

A Discourse on Antient and Modern Learning (London: Printed for T. Osborne, 1734);

The Poems of Addison, volume 23 of *The Works of the English Poets*, edited by Samuel Johnson (London: H. Baldwin, 1781).

Editions: *The Works of the Right Honourable Joseph Addison*, 4 volumes, edited by Thomas Tickell (London: Printed for Jacob Tonson, 1721)—includes the first printings of "Dialogues upon the Usefulness of Ancient Medals, Especially in Relation to Latin and Greek Poets" and "Of the Christian Religion";

Miscellaneous Works in Verse and Prose, 3 volumes (London: Printed for Jacob Tonson, 1726);

The Works of the Right Honourable Joseph Addison, A New Edition, 6 volumes, notes by Richard Hurd (London: Printed for T. Cadell & W. Davies, 1811);

The Miscellaneous Works of Joseph Addison, 2 volumes, edited by A. C. Guthkelch (London: Bell, 1914);

The Spectator, 5 volumes, edited by Donald F. Bond (Oxford: Clarendon Press, 1965);

The Freeholder, edited by James Leheny (Oxford: Clarendon Press, 1979);

The Guardian, edited by John Calhoun Stephens (Lexington: University Press of Kentucky, 1982);

The Tatler, 3 volumes, edited by Bond (Oxford: Clarendon Press, 1987).

PLAY PRODUCTIONS: *Rosamond*, libretto by Addison and music by Thomas Clayton, London, Theatre Royal, Drury Lane, 4 March 1707;

Cato, London, Theatre Royal, Drury Lane, 14 April 1713;

The Drummer, London, Theatre Royal, Drury Lane, 10 March 1716.

OTHER: "Tityrus et Mopsus" ("Hic inter corylos"), in *Vota Oxoniensia pro serenissimis Guilhelmo rege et Maria regina M. Britanniæ . . . Nuncupata* (Oxford: e Theatro Sheldoniano, 1689);

"Gratulatio" ("Cum Domini"), in *Academiæ Oxoniensis Gratulatio pro exoptato serenissimi regis Guilielmo ex Hibernia reditu* (Oxford: e Theatro Sheldoniano, 1690);

"To Mr. Dryden," in *Examen Poeticum: Being the third Part of Miscellany Poems*, dedication signed by John Dryden (London: Printed by R. E. for Jacob Tonson, 1693);

"Virgil's Fourth Georgic" (translation), "A Song for St. Cecilia's Day at Oxford," "The Story of Salmacis and Hermaphroditus" (translation, from Ovid's *Metamorphoses*, book 4), and "An Account of the Greatest English Poets," in *The Annual Miscellany: for the Year 1694. Being the Fourth Part of Miscellany Poems* (London: Printed by R. E. for Jacob Tonson, 1694);

"An Essay on Virgil's Georgics," in *The Works of Virgil: Containing His Pastorals, Georgics, Æneis. Translated into English Verse; By Mr. Dryden* (London: Printed for Jacob Tonson, 1697);

"Sphæristerium," "Resurrectio Delineata ad altare Col. Magd.," "Machinæ gesticulantes,

Anglicè A Puppet-Show," "Insignissimo Viro Thomæ Burnet D.D. Theoriæ Sacræ Telluris Autori," "Barometri descriptio," "Prælium inter pygmæ & grues commissum," and "Ad medicum et poetam ingeniosum" [anonymous], unauthorized versions, in *Examen Poeticum Duplex: sive musarum anglicanarum delectus alter* (London: Impensis Ric. Wellington, 1698); authorized versions published in *Musarum Anglicanarum Analecta*, volume 2 (1699);

"Ad D. D. Hannes, Insignissimum Medicum et Poetam," "Pax Gulielmi Auspiciis Europæ redditta, 1697," and "Honoratissimo Viro Carolo Montagu, Armigero, Scaccharii Cancellario, Ærarii præfecto, Regi à Secretioribus Consiliis, &c." [dedication], in *Musarum Anglicanarum Analecta: sive poemata quædam melioris notæ, seu hactenus inedita, seu sparsim edita*, volume 2 (Oxford: e Theatro Sheldoniano, impensis John Crosley, 1699);

"A Letter from Italy, to the Right Honourable Charles Lord Hallifax," "Milton's Stile Imitated," and translations, with notes, from Ovid's *Metamorphoses*, books 2 and 3, in *Poetical Miscellanies: the fifth Part*, edited by John Dryden [and Nicholas Rowe] (London: Printed for Jacob Tonson, 1704);

Prologue to *The Tender Husband, or, The Accomplish'd Fools*, by Richard Steele (London: Printed for Jacob Tonson, 1705);

George Granville, Baron Lansdowne, *The British Enchanters: or, No Magick like Love. A Tragedy*, epilogue by Addison (London: Printed for Jacob Tonson, 1706);

Prologue to *Phædra and Hippolitus. A Tragedy*, by Edmund Smith (London: Printed for Bernard Lintott, 1709);

"Epilogue Spoken at Censorium on the King's Birthday," in *Town-Talk*, by Steele, no. 4 (London: Printed by R. Burleigh & sold by Burleigh, Anne Dodd, James Roberts & J. Graves, 6 January 1716);

"Verses written for the Toasting Glasses of the Kit-Kat Club in the Year 1703" and "Lady Manchester," in *The First [-Sixth] Part of Miscellany Poems. Containing Variety of New Translations of the Ancient Poets: Together with Several Original Poems* (London: Printed for Jacob Tonson, 1716);

Sir Samuel Garth, ed., *Ovid's Metamorphoses in Fifteen Books. Translated by the most Eminent Hands*, includes translations by Addison,

Dryden, and others (London: Printed for Jacob Tonson, 1717).

Nathan Drake keened in 1805 that Joseph Addison for all his literary achievement and "moral dominion" frustrated biographers, who stood helpless before his reticence and distrust of self-revelation. Time and scholarship have not made the private individual more accessible. *The Letters of Joseph Addison*, for example, scrupulously gathered and edited by Walter Graham for publication in 1941, exposed a cinematic "Thin Man," a largely nonexistent personality clothed and bewigged. Almost as if his personal papers had been censored, not a single piece of correspondence between him and his family has been preserved. Peter Smithers's second edition of a full-scale biography (1968) unearthed few significant clues to Addisonian uniqueness. Only surface details about the public figure, who apparently forfeited depth for appearance and impact, have been perpetuated.

A mélange of paradoxes, he made his artistic life fuel his political career so that a rapid symbiotic association developed between artistry and politics. He began by composing poetry, not because his mind teemed with images but because his was a poetic age, and he had no quarrel with its conventions. From start to finish—from 1689 ("Tityrus et Mopsus") to 1716 ("To Sir Godfrey Kneller")—his poetry lacked an imaginative passion, a reflection perhaps of the peace he made with the uninterrupted containment of his own mind. He experimented with several genres of drama: opera, tragedy, and comedy. Unable to write a fifth act for *Cato* when he had presumably plotted it in 1699 at Magdalen, he nonetheless finished it in little more than a week's time to satisfy the importunate pleadings of the Whigs about a decade later. *Cato* (1713) became the most controversial theatrical success of the first half of the eighteenth century.

A dull, hesitant speaker among strangers, Addison was purportedly mute among superiors. Yet in the course of a relatively few years, from 1710 to 1719, he devised a prose style that suggested uncluttered, good-humored talk. The fact that he presented little of his buried self gave a pleasurable dimension to his periodical writing, particularly to the essays of *The Spectator* (1711-1712, 1714). Such an abeyance of ego forced no new complications or intimacy onto his audience. Indeed, no barriers of angst stood between author and reader; each responded to the

other in a near-perfect rapport of measured empathy. Addison's genius finally found itself in the undefined art of popular journalism.

He was born on May Day 1672 in the rectory at Milston, Wiltshire. He nurtured through time and inner necessity a dignified restraint which Alexander Pope later denigrated as a "stiff sort of silence," presumably an even tenor of disciplined emotion that gave little away and so protected the armored individual. Throughout his life, he cultivated prudence, recoiled from financial pressure, and usually agreed to any offer of "employment" with an annual stipend. He accepted his ambition and a corollary quest for acclaim. He depended on "great men" because they were great; he could be useful to them and they to him. The point remains that he wore many masks as he tempered personality to the moment, and who the man really was has evaded definition.

Much of this expedient latency he absorbed from his father, Lancelot, who had been granted a B.A. at Queen's College, Oxford. Once ordained, the elder Addison responded to money problems with political sensitivity; he accepted his first clerical appointment among Royalist families in Sussex. Shortly after the Restoration, he secured, perhaps as a royal reward, the chaplaincy of the British garrison at Dunkirk. Serving there and then in Tangier from 1661 to 1670, he returned to England, married Jane Gulston, and settled down in the village rectory. No simple country priest ready for a remote parish in southwestern England, Lancelot Addison—a scholar, writer, and traveler—identified himself as "a Chaplain in Ordinary to his Majesty" on the title page of his first book, *West Barbary, or a Short Narrative of the Revolutions of the Kingdoms of Fez and Morocco* (1671).

The Addisons' first child died in infancy. Their second, Joseph, wailed so piteously that he was baptized on the day of his birth. But he survived, and several more siblings followed him. Lancelot Addison in the meanwhile maneuvered for a place within the ecclesiastical hierarchy; in 1683 he became dean of Lichfield Cathedral. Because of his father's elevation, the eleven-year-old Joseph without demur enrolled at the Lichfield Grammar School, an institution in the Midlands that grounded its pupils in the classics. The school helped the bashful but precocious boy to stock his mind with knowledge, to think in terms of a career, and to plan on political preferment

Portrait of Addison by W. Sonmans, probably painted at Oxford before 1700 (Collection of Viscount Devonport)

by advertising his talents among powerful men in government.

In 1686 Lancelot Addison, now the holder of four offices in the Church, took his son out of what he dismissed as a provincial grammar school and sent the withdrawn adolescent to Charterhouse in London. Here the "gentleman scholar" stayed for a year, just time enough to meet Richard Steele, a "poor scholar" from Ireland. According to the speculative, if exaggerated, reconstruction of Thomas Babington Macaulay, Joseph Addison, aged fifteen, had the classical expertise of "a Master of Arts." Apparently Lancelot recognized his son's scholarly nimbleness, felt that it had been little encouraged or challenged, even at Charterhouse. Again the boy was

moved, this time to Oxford, where without choice he matriculated at his father's college (Queen's) on 18 May 1687.

He found quick collegiate distinction with a Latin verse dialogue, "Tityrus et Mopsus," published in *Vota Oxoniensia pro serenissimis Guilhelmo rege et Maria regina M. Britanniæ* (1689), a compendium of encomia on the royal couple's Protestant triumph over James, the Old Pretender. The dialogue, Addison's first extant composition, offers insight into the deftness of his political timing: it voices his allegiance to a dominant party and especially to its establishment, a loyalty that marked his authorship until the last publication in his lifetime, *The Old Whig*, in March and April 1719. The dialogue probably nailed down his election as a demy (a foundation scholar) at Magdalen College on 30 July 1689 with its small stipend and promise of a fellowship to come.

At Oxford, where he took his B.A. on 6 May 1691, he enjoyed the reputation of being a fluent Latin poet. Yet he doffed his hat to the new scientific spirit. At the encaenia on 7 July 1693, with the relaxed stance of an avant-garde intellectual, he delivered an oration using a gerundive imperative, "Nova Philosophia Veteri præferenda est" (that is, the new philosophy or science must be chosen over an outdated scholastic methodology). At Magdalen, particularly, he "fashioned" an adult personality. He was tactful, financially alert, obedient to the political order both in the university and in the wider reaches of the state. He realized that his search for identity and reward had to continue despite a want of brashness, a hesitance to talk and push himself forward. He accepted such a conflict of psyche, came to terms with it, and inched his way upward.

On 14 February 1693, when he took his M.A., he calculated the limits of his current life. Comfortable as he was at Magdalen, he felt driven to prove himself with more than imitative Latin verse and to pledge fealty to patrons beyond college walls. He consequently tried his hand at English couplets addressed "To Mr. Dryden." Casting aside subtlety as counter to his purpose, he lauded the elder poet's "sacred Lays," "poetick Heat," and holy "Rage." The sledgehammer praise did not embarrass the recipient; rather, John Dryden printed it in his *Examen Poeticum: Being the third Part of Miscellany Poems* (1693).

Goaded by a desire for attention, if only to the extent that his name be echoed in literary conversation, Addison found space for four other poetic orts in *The Annual Miscellany: for the Year 1694*. Of these only "An Account of the Greatest English Poets" adds to the biography, providing a clue to his reading and taste. Like his contemporaries, he admired Abraham Cowley, William Congreve, and Edmund Waller. Atypically, however, he asserted the epic greatness of John Milton but immediately thereafter used his own literary affirmation for a political statement. While Miltonic verse scanned "serene and bright," the poet's republicanism—unlike Addisonian adherence to the Revolution Settlement—"Betray[ed] a bottom odious to the Sight." Textually the last of the "Greatest English Poets" was the Whig minister Charles Montagu, Baron Halifax, who presumptively suppressed his art of "negligent grace" for

service in "*Nassau*'s secret councils." From this time onward Addison recognized that he could not make his way alone: that for himself no separation existed between art and a commitment to faction, that talent and propaganda were indivisible, and that even as an artist he required party sanctuary.

In 1695 he searched for a new patron in the Whig hierarchy, one even more powerful than Halifax. He dedicated *A Poem to His Majesty* to John Somers, Lord Keeper of the Great Seal, whom he entreated to "receive the present of a Muse Unknown." Addison piled flattery on flattery to etch the portrait of Somers, "the great man" who dispenses favor and office. "On You, my Lord, with anxious Fear I wait, / And from your Judgment must expect my Fate." With the entreaty versified, a subtheme in the poem proper cautiously emerged. The accomplishments of William's ministry, led by Somers, called for a publicist's muse to sing "in daring numbers" the subtle, understated glories of king and party.

The flattery and proposal worked well together. Somers sent for Addison who, when only twenty-four, had access to the two most stalwart Whigs in England. His deference paid off: it secured the fellowship at Magdalen he had long anticipated; it made possible the publication of the second volume of *Musarum Anglicanarum Analecta* (1699), for which he wrote the dedication and edited sixteen pieces, eight of them his own. The edition advertised the Whig poet whose subdued glibness rarely jarred or antagonized. As a literary experience it merited, according to Samuel Johnson, "particular praise," possibly because it borrowed words and styles from no one classical source but from many, all judiciously interwoven and attuned to matters meaningful in 1699.

If Addison's patrons gave him a leg up at Oxford, they also pushed him away from Magdalen's cloisters and shady walks. Aware of his literary potential and political adroitness, Halifax and Somers arranged for him to receive a treasury grant for travel abroad. By the late summer of 1699 he had crossed the Channel. The push that forced his vagrancy, antithetical to the stability of the "middle condition" he admired, was a pragmatic foresight which insisted on an end to penny-pinching. He saw his travels as an assignment that ideally would serve the king and his ministers but, more immediately, would insure a paid "employment." The assignment, he knew, specified tasks from the menial (perhaps even reprehensible) to the elegant. Since he traveled under

Charles Montagu, Baron Halifax (later first Earl of Halifax), circa 1703-1710 (portrait by Sir Godfrey Kneller; by permission of the National Portrait Gallery, London). Halifax and another powerful Whig, John Somers, arranged a treasury grant to subsidize Addison's travels on the Continent in 1699-1703.

the patronage of the crown's chief ministers, he had entry into diplomatic missions. His tasks multiplied, imposing on the young man the technique of sophisticated watchfulness. For his sponsors he had to ferret out the names of friends and enemies abroad; for himself he had to eradicate hints of parochial behavior with a diplomat's polished caution.

Addison journeyed on the Continent for almost four years, from 1699 through 1703. However far from home, he never lost sight of political friendships or the opportunity to celebrate those friendships. Allegedly while crossing snow-covered Mount Cenis in the early winter of 1701, he reworked the formula of *A Poem to His Majesty*. He roughed out his new effort and entitled

it—while yet in manuscript—"A Letter from Italy," addressing it to Charles, Lord Halifax.

In both poems the persona continues unchanged since the poet and his circumstances have not substantively altered: both are humble, diffident men, chosen celebrants of English "Liberty," the catchword of Whig polemic. Both are "ravish'd" pleaders. "A Letter" apostrophizes Halifax as one hallowed by sacrifice. The second paragraph of the poem in manuscript at the Bodleian Library (MS. Rawl. Poet. 17.) in a rhetoric of omission limns a statesman idled during a Parliamentary investigation. The charges leveled against him in the spring of 1701 are poetically unvoiced. Instead the poet relies on a series of polarities to emphasize the wasted greatness of a great

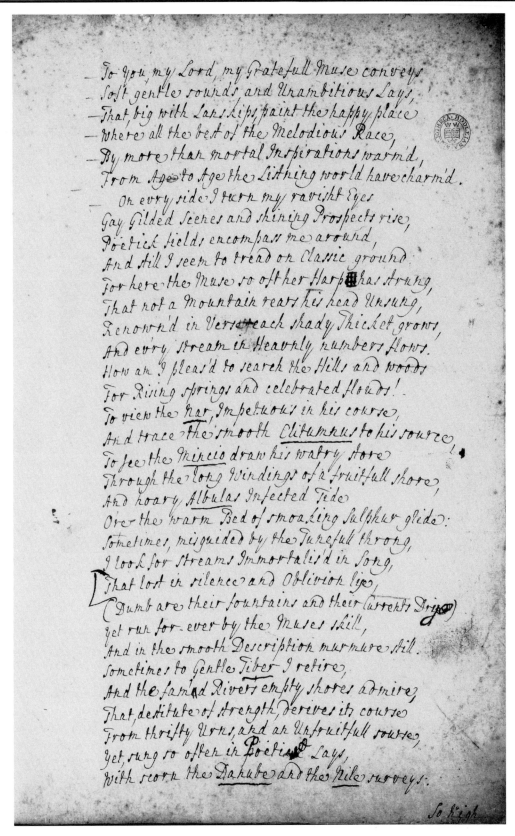

Page from the manuscript for "A Letter from Italy," written in winter 1701 and addressed to Charles Montagu, Baron Halifax
(MS. Rawl. Poet. 17; by permission of the Curators of the Bodleian Library, Oxford)

man. The persona therefore stands dwarfed alongside the fallen leader whose contributions to government deserve what he had never received: the grandeur of "Advent'rous song" and "Majestic Lays."

The bibliographical history of "A Letter from Italy" and the poem's place in the biography require reconstruction. Dating the manuscript poem "From Italy / 19 February 1702," Addison, temporarily housed in Geneva, sent it to Edward Wortley, who passed it to their mutual friends at court and to Wortley's relative baron Halifax, still a shadowy manipulator of the king's diplomatic appointments. The poet had set his political hopes not on a printed text but on a handwritten copy. (Indeed, "A Letter from Italy" was first published in December 1703 in the elder Jacob Tonson's *Poetical Miscellanies: the fifth Part*, with the year 1704 on its title page.) Revealed to William by a courtier—more likely by Halifax himself—the manuscript reminded the monarch of the young versifier and his eagerness for assignment. But before Addison could be named officially field secretary to Prince Eugene, the imperial commander readying for an Italian campaign, William died unexpectedly on 8 March 1702, and the Whigs, confronted by a suspicious Queen Anne, seemed disarrayed.

Addison must have been distressed at losing a diplomatic post of value, one that could have led to a safe and permanent secretaryship in an English embassy. More dependent than ever on his dwindling grant from the royal treasury, he played out his role as a reluctant Ulysses. At the same time he translated his travel notes into a book padded with familiar quotations drawn from Virgil, Ovid, Silius Italicus, or whoever else rated a place in schoolboy texts. Concerned with places—a kind of classical tourism—rather than with people, he did not seek originality in his descriptions but a conventional resonance that reminded readers subliminally and comfortably of what they already knew. Published by Tonson, the book, a prose parallel to "A Letter from Italy," appeared circa 22 November 1705 as *Remarks on Several Parts of Italy, &c. in the years, 1701, 1702, 1703*. Ambiguously dated in the title and never clarified, even in the revised edition of 1718, this volume—perhaps the first of the two projected—spun an impersonal travelogue that began 12 December 1699 in medias res ("Monaco and Genoa"); it ended precipitously some vague years later with the narrator "coasting"

through the "Tirol, Inspruck, Hall, &c.," never, at least in the text, to find his way homeward.

Addison came home in either February or March 1704. If his travels did nothing else, they strengthened the confidence that sometimes accompanies self-awareness. He had established several things about himself: he could write poems of flattery that lulled an audience of hardened politicians, and he could move with inconspicuous ease in diplomatic circles. No longer tempted by a collegiate refuge, he gambled on a Haymarket garret near government offices in Whitehall and waited for an appointment with official status. In the meanwhile he took his seat among the Whigs in the Kit-Cat Club and in congenial coffeehouses, such as St. James's. The London milieu, however, did not alleviate his financial anxiety. Thrift was an ever-present familiar. In his mind he at first equated political employment with survival, only later with the quiet wealth and status he craved.

Unexpectedly, foreign affairs rescued Addison. In August 1704—some eight days after the battle on the thirteenth—all London learned of the triumph at Blenheim in Bavaria. Halifax, mindful of a patron's duty toward a disciple, thought a poetic celebration in order even when sponsored by a Tory ministry. He suggested as much to Sidney, Lord Godolphin, the lord treasurer, who was unfettered by precise party designation and who was probably one of the closest friends of John Churchill, the great Duke of Marlborough. The idea of an ode moved through ministerial channels until Henry Boyle, the chancellor of the exchequer, asked Addison to poetize the victory over France. The request was honored, a rough draft rather quickly turned over to Godolphin who, satisfied with it, appointed the no-longer "ravish'd" pleader a commissioner of appeal in excise with a yearly stipend of two hundred pounds.

The Campaign was published by Jacob Tonson on 14 December, soon enough for the event to animate conversation and yet retrospective enough for the talkers to perceive its significance. The poem further captured a serendipitous moment with its appearance on the day that Marlborough landed at Greenwich with his prisoners, almost forty high-ranking French officers. *The Campaign* is both an overt paean and a muted dirge, cast loosely as a moral exercise with Marlborough the hero and Tallard the villain in a struggle for the souls and bodies of British troops. Refining a method that he had tried in

John Churchill, first Duke of Marlborough, whose military triumph at Blenheim is the subject of Addison's poem The Campaign, *and his wife, Sarah (portraits attributed to J. Closterman [left] and after Sir Godfrey Kneller [right]; by permission of the National Portrait Gallery, London)*

his earlier political poems, Addison does not appropriate detailed fact or historical perspective: rather he generalizes an incontrovertible truth that young men, victims of the patriotic moment, died for military gain; he glorifies and so renders null a possible source of shame, Marlborough's scorched-earth policy in Bavaria.

Cleansed of potential improprieties, the English general, "Calm and serene" amid the carnage of "the furious blast," functions poetically like a brilliant integer within a scheme, "th' Almighty's orders to perform." Addison projects the metaphor of a "god-like leader" who rode *alone* across the front and gave the order to sound the charge. Within this metaphor of apotheosis there is no room for others such as John Cutts, Richard Ingoldsby, and William, Earl of Cadogan, all of whom had leadership roles in the struggle; even Prince Eugene carries off "Only the second honours of the day."

In *The Campaign* history undergoes no substantive distortion to the extent that the victory at Blenheim happened. But certain telling details are either minimized or set aside because they undercut what Addison intends as the theme of his Virgilian song: the military brilliance of Marlborough, who tightly controlled the battle in all its

stages, who turned a tattered army into a unique weapon of high morale and single-minded pursuit. Unmentioned, for example, is Marshal Camille Tallard's accidental capture by some Hessian troops, who led him to the nearest allied camp, Marlborough's. The surrender, purposely not dramatized in the text, becomes the unvoiced climax of the poem, the abbreviated instant of Tallard's ruin and Marlborough's exaltation.

Similarly, to enhance the ethical dimension of British troops at Blenheim, Addison likens them to "martyrs that in exile groan'd," marching through "various realms" of inspirational nomenclature, an implicit *via dolorosa*. While he sounds the muffled beat of "Confed'rate drums" vaguely "terrible from far," he obscures the reality of a polyglot fighting force (some fifty thousand) of whom not more than nine thousand were British. Since the allied armies have no place within the context of the poem, he can celebrate the campaign as a British venture in heroism and pious commitment.

He does not romanticize the "gore" of victory. He does not use the term as a poetic euphemism for dung and slime smeared with blood. The connotations of filth in clotted blood are present in his frequent repetition of the word. He does not gloss over images that catch the indiscriminate butchery of war, even at Blenheim, where "Nations with nations mix'd confus'dly die, / And lost in one promiscuous carnage lye." But he concentrates mainly on "the Gallic squadrons" in rout, pushed into the Danube. Here whole cavalry regiments perished, men and horses alike, the mangled bodies of beast and master, intermingled, swept away in "floods of gore" that mock the presumed dignity of death. Still, since he writes as a publicist, he cunningly subsumes the moment of mourning for fallen Britons—like "the noble Dormer"—by narrating the poem as a series of "wond'rous ... exploits ... divinely bright," much like a fairy "tale" with an unusual happy ending.

Jealous of Addison as "The Towring Youth" who had never known either "Envy or Party Spleen," Daniel Defoe, a ministerial hireling, in *The Double Welcome* (1705) excoriated *The Campaign* and denounced Addison as a servile hack before whom "Maecenas" (Halifax) dangled not a paltry carrot but a "Pension":

> Let *Addison* our Modern *Virgil* sing,
> For he's a Poet fitted for a King;
> No Hero will his mighty Flight disdain,
> The first, as thou *the Last* of the Inspir'd Train;
> Maecenas has his Modern Fancy strung,
> And fix'd his Pension first, or he had never sung.
> . . . .
> The Towring Youth with high Success aspires,
> And sings as one whose Song the World admires.

Such naysayers were few in 1705. Known for its larger-than-life portrait of Marlborough, *The Campaign* won applause for more than two centuries with at least two authorized editions in Addison's lifetime. Joseph Warton in his *Essay on the Writings and Genius of Pope* (1756) might have tried to question its success as a mere "Gazette in Rhyme," but for the most part its drumbeat of selective history and crisp heroic couplets depicted a romantic notion of battle. Yet the idealized images of poetry shrank before the stark realities of modern warfare early on in the twentieth century. No longer wholly credible is the portrayal of fearless military composure within sound of the "dreadful burst of cannon" and of a near-mythic leader marked, in the words of Samuel Johnson, by "deliberate intrepidity, a calm command of his passions ... in the midst of danger."

Addison's life as a Whig publicist became busier than ever with the continuation of the War of the Spanish Succession. In November 1707 he wrote *The Present State of the War* and saw it published early in the next year. The pamphlet was his first journalistic commitment to the Anglo-French struggle, a logical successor to *The Campaign*, which focused on a single battle and its preliminary skirmishes. The format itself served him well: it let him work in a genre which he had not tried before but which gave a happy boldness to political editorializing. Designed for a large, mixed audience, the pamphlet commanded rapid composition at the expense of nuance. It therefore encouraged the anonymous Addison to speak paradoxically in propria persona and to argue for a party platform more openly than he could in simulated verse epic or in any government publication, such as the *London Gazette*. Finally it gave him the chance to treat a single subject with persuasive intimacy, as he would do later in *The Spectator*.

The Present State of the War deals with material no longer pertinent to twentieth-century readers. What does give it interest today is Addison's out-and-out emergence as a propagandist. Like the fictive undeviating patriot of *The Campaign*, the pamphlet's persona or Addison himself, the two having merged intellectual identities, assumes a ramrod militarism that stifles controversy: the war against France has not only to be prosecuted but "augmented." The organization of the pamphlet, its emotional logic of cause and effect, is Addison's contrivance, but its policy had been hammered out by the Whig junto. Nowhere in the pamphlet, however, does he speak of party because he wants the theme philosophically enlarged, freed from the bickering and self-interest of faction. The pamphleteer promises to set before British patriots, and therefore people of his own mind, data which offer a rationale for the war and, more to the point, for its escalation. "Let it not ... enter into the heart of any one, that hath the least zeal for his religion, or love of liberty ... to think of peace with *France*, till the *Spanish* monarchy be entirely torn from it, and the house of *Bourbon* disabled from ever giving the law to Europe." His presentation—direct, repetitive, and flag-waving in a rousing wind—tacitly phrases a question: who but a traitor would look to peace? The answer is self-evident.

Early in his tract Addison asserts certain a priori premises, that the War of the Spanish Succession, specifically the conflict with "the Gallic Tyranny," is a live-or-die contest for England and so beyond negotiation. Still, some Britons in 1707 muttered about the desirability of peace. They be-

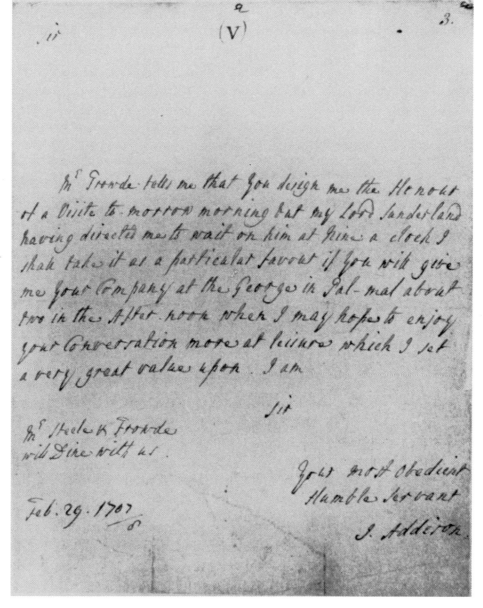

Letter from Addison to Jonathan Swift (Add. MS. 4804; by permission of the Trustees of the British Library)

lieved that the military objectives of the 1701 Treaty of Grand Alliance had been fulfilled: that France's fleet had been virtually destroyed, her troops ousted from Italy and the Spanish Netherlands. Apparently dismissive of the peace-mongers and their arguments, Addison heard not the voice of the turtledove but only that of Whig councils that dreaded "the evil empire" of an insatiable France and her Jacobite allies in Scotland. What the pamphlet holds out to its readers is the prophecy of Whig merchants and their dream visions of Britain's untold wealth accumulated from and during conflict.

The war placed a halo on greed and beatified it with respectability. The Addison who mourned the dead in 1704 now accepted war itself as so many investments, whether of men or of bullion, as so many cautious risks when weighed against the financial gains that victory brought. "It may be necessary," he confessed, insensitive to his bloodletting analogy, "for a person languishing under an ill habit of body to lose several ounces of blood, notwithstanding it will weaken him for a time, in order to put a new ferment into the remaining mass, and draw into it fresh supplies."

Several years later—perhaps in 1718—Addison considered his pamphlet a successful foray in a paper war since he authorized Thomas Tickell to include it in his edition. Never republished before then, it has not withstood time's obliteration, in part because it wants the moral substance and goodwill of issue that perpetuate political writing; it wants the vibrancy that he projected in certain *Freeholder* essays. If the pamphlet occupies little space in the Addisonian canon today, it did in its time satisfy the martial determination of Whiggish Britons, prepared to gamble on the prospect of a mercantile empire.

The Present State of the War was, in November 1707, written to order by a polemicist impervious to war as a threat to social and moral order. For some forty-four pages he suggests the energy and rhetoric of a zealot calling for violence in the name of principle. "The only means therefore for bringing *France* to our conditions, and what appears to me, in all human probability, a sure and infallible expedient, is to throw in multitudes upon them, and overpower them with numbers . . . and in one summer overset the whole power of *France*." What his optimistic timetable deliberately obscures is a new scheme for replacing costly foreign mercenaries with native conscripts, for dehumanizing British lives as an "expedient," as so many "multitudes" and "numbers."

The year 1708 was a good one for Joseph Addison. He proved his loyalty to the Whigs as a poet, a pamphleteer, and an able civil servant. His political rise depended upon himself and his push but also upon circumstances. In February of that same year the Whigs and moderate Tories called for the dismissal of Robert Harley, secretary of state for the northern department, who had leaked secrets to France. Queen Anne, despite misgivings, acceded to their politely couched imperative. When Parliament was dissolved on 4 April, Whig candidates—Addison among them—faced the polls with jauntiness. He probably wanted elected office as another forward movement in his career: one that made his name as familiar as his literary output and enhanced his reputation as an administrator and a "man of business." In the spring of 1708 he sought the Parliamentary seat of Lostwithiel, which lay in a strong Tory landscape in Cornwall. When the contest ended and the declaration was announced on 17 May, Addison came in one of the winners with thirteen votes. Too Whiggish for minuscule Tory Lostwithiel, he willy-nilly became the target of several recall petitions. Not

ready to surrender what he considered rightly his, he was nevertheless unseated more than a year later, on 20 December 1709.

Visibly unperturbed by this defeat, he had in late 1708 won a grander prize as secretary to Thomas, Lord Wharton, Lord Lieutenant of Ireland. Other employments followed inevitably from this association: he represented Cavan in the Irish House of Commons from 1709 to 1713; he became a privy councillor in Ireland and the keeper of records in Dublin Castle. On 11 March 1710 he was returned to the English Parliament on Lord Wharton's interest at a by-election for Malmesbury, a seat which he held until his death.

But to move back to 1709. Planning a London holiday, Addison arrived there in September and found that Richard Steele had already launched *The Tatler* on 12 April. Printed on both sides of a folio half-sheet, it offered a journalistic grab bag of political news, social gossip, wit, and unobtrusive tutoring. The first issue of *The Tatler* or *The Lucubrations of Isaac Bickerstaff* (as some later editions were titled) explained the diversity of each number and hence its fragmented format. "*All Accounts of* " genteel amusement "*shall be under the Article of* White's Chocolate-house"; poetry from Will's Coffee-house; learning from the Græcian; "Foreign *and* Domestick News, *you will have from St.* James's Coffee-house; *and what else I have to offer on any other subject, shall be dated from my own Apartment.*" In its beginnings *The Tatler* was considered another miscellany in the style of the *Mercure Gallant* and the *Gentleman's Journal*.

Even before Addison's arrival in London, *The Tatler* had become politically suspect, guilty by association with the former editor of the *London Gazette* and with Sidney, Lord Godolphin, who had from time to time allied himself with the Whigs, offended Queen Anne, and the Church of England. Tory Grubeans stood ready to attack the new periodical, but they could not anticipate the variable and transparent fictions through which Bickerstaff or the author's surrogate sounded political principle without party label. For example, in number 4, dated 19 April 1709, Steele presents the parable of "*Felicia*, an Island in *America*" recovering from the "Death of [its] late glorious King." Felicia is of course Great Britain, whose "Chief Minister has enter'd into a Firm League with the ablest and best Men of the Nation [obviously members of the Whig junto], to carry on the Cause of Liberty, to the Encouragement of Religion, Virtue, and Honour." Before the end of its second week, then, *The Tatler* made the late King William its mythic protector and the Revolution Settlement its talismanic rule of law.

Steele relished the challenge of outwitting Tory propagandists. But the thrice-weekly publication of the journal exacted a heavy price of concentration and ingenuity. As soon as he could, he bamboozled or begged contributions from friends and especially from Addison, who appreciated the maneuverability of *The Tatler* as a party vehicle with the further flair of authorial anonymity.

Just when he first contributed to *The Tatler* remains unsure; debatable, too, is the precise number of his contributions (about sixty-nine in whole or part). Even what he wrote or suggested for it cannot be absolutely determined. An exegesis of the papers during his English visits (September or October 1709 to April 1710 and 19 August to the close of the journal) suggests that in these months the full-length essay became the favored form, that the characters of Tom Folio, Ned Softly, Sir Timothy Tittle, and "the Political Upholsterer" are in all likelihood his creations. Whatever Addison's effort in *The Tatler*, Steele admitted in the preface to volume 4 of the collected essays that his part-time collaborator "performed with such Force of Genius, Humour, Wit, and Learning, that I fared like a distressed Prince who calls in a powerful Neighbour to his aid; I was undone by my Auxiliary; when I had once called him in, I could not subsist without Dependance on him."

The Tatler ran for 271 numbers, ending on 2 January 1711, perhaps because Tory journalists had by now zeroed in on its political slant and perhaps because the collaborators had already contemplated the start of *The Spectator*. However clouded the "Auxiliary" contribution is to *The Tatler*, John Gay in *The Present State of Wit* (dated 3 May 1711) wondered at the nature of a personality "who refuse[d] to have his Name set before those Pieces which the greatest Pens in England would be Proud to own." Trying to second-guess the reasons for Addison's self-effacement, Gay instead identified his essays with vague accuracy: "I am assur'd, from good hands, That all the Visions, and other Tracts in that way of Writing, with a very great number of the most exquisite Pieces of Wit and Raillery throughout the Lucubrations are entirely of this Gentleman's Composing: which may, in some Measure, account for that different Genius, which appears in the Winter Papers, from those of the Summer; at which

time the Examiner often hinted, this Friend of Mr. Steele's was in Ireland."

Despite Gay's appreciation of Addison's performance in *The Tatler*, the periodical itself served as an adjunct of Whiggery. Almost from its introduction, the editors used their skill on and off, directly or indirectly, to frustrate the propaganda machine of Robert Harley (later Earl of Oxford) and Henry St. John (later Viscount Bolingbroke), who supported—according to *Tatler* 92—a "low Race" of scribblers (by implication, Tories) in their war against "great and heroic Spirits" (by reversal, Whigs).

Unlike Steele, who accepted the inevitable scars of editorial jousting, Addison resented journalistic assault or, indeed, any kind of censure. He particularly despised the opponent of *The Tatler*, the weekly *Examiner*, which St. John founded on 3 August to disseminate the Tory advocacy of peace while it hacked away at Whig warmongering. Then—between 2 November 1710 and 14 June 1711 (nos. 13-45)—Jonathan Swift edited the papers, which depicted the City Whigs as cannibalistic republicans whose fingers dripped with "the gore" of British lives spent in futile battle.

Not by accident, Addison in 1710 met Arthur Maynwaring, the Whig junto's chief propagandist, who presumably "could not suffer [*The Examiner's*] insolence to pass, without animadversion." As a consequence of this meeting, Addison published *The Whig Examiner*, whose title defined its purpose: from its very first number "to give all persons a rehearing, who have suffered under any unjust sentence of *The Examiner*. As that author has hitherto proceeded his paper would have been more properly entitled the *Executioner*. At least, his examination is like that which is made by the rack and wheel."

In terms of the image which he manufactured, Addison saw himself as a victim, destined to unmask the primitive brutality of *The Examiner*. His strategy, to laugh the Tories into oblivion, derived from confidence in his sense of comedy and timing, but in this case he fulfilled neither the strategy nor the assignment. For a short time *The Whig Examiner* stumbled on without vigor or direction. Perhaps Addison was too fastidious for sustained name-calling or for the dirty game of political invective. Perhaps his genius needed a cloak of invisibility, not the well-bruited secret of his authorship. Whatever the reasons for Addisonian inadequacy, the periodical

Robert Harley, first Earl of Oxford, who supported Tory journalists in their campaign against The Tatler
(portrait after Sir Godfrey Kneller; by permission of the National Portrait Gallery, London)

failed, historically askew with the moment of publication.

Between *The Present State of the War* and the ditto-like *Whig Examiner* Addison foundered as a Whig journalist. He could not humanize the slogan of "No Peace without Spain" which thematically framed both works. He could not make less predatory his Exchange-minded intimation that Britain's new plenty rose proportionately to the depletion of allied wealth. The truth is that *The Whig Examiner* did not excite a people tired of rations, high taxes, casualty lists, and, as he later wrote in *Spectator* 26, of "uninhabited Monuments." Addison's periodical in 1710 satisfied a handful of "new" men, of Whig merchants engaged in international commerce. But they required no more satisfaction than their bank accounts, their "fleets," and inventories.

Without the rage and manic sarcasm of *The Examiner, The Whig Examiner* became its own

worst enemy. Too finicky for effectiveness, it left only a faint smudge in the paper war. For five numbers—from start to close—from 14 September to 12 October, Addison intuited the journal's end, since the cause it espoused had already tottered. Whether indifferent to or bored by *The Whig Examiner*'s repetition of stale material and its deadly awful sameness, Addison committed a journalistic sin. He left unmentioned one of the reasons for the periodical's being: to promote the Whig cause at the Parliamentary election ordered by the queen for October. Such neglect stunned Maynwaring, especially in view of the Parliamentary campaign begun by the third *Examiner* in late summer.

He quickly realized Addison's lack of editorial belligerence, the rapid-fire attack that was called for in a crisis year. He understood that it would not do to match the "rack and wheel" techniques of *The Examiner* with the gentle and gen-

17

LIBRARY USE ONLY

Surry Community College LRC
P. O. Box 304
Dobson, NC 27017

teel defense of Samuel Garth's poetry or Tory calumny with an analysis of the clichés, passive obedience and nonresistance. Involved himself in writing some portions of *The Whig Examiner*, Maynwaring had to question himself: why would a reading public, eager for plowshares and pruning hooks, rise in anger when *The Whig Examiner* mocked its opponent's misuse of classical allusions, mixed metaphors, and improprieties of speech? The propagandist, who suffered no sentimentality, permitted Addison's periodical to die without an obituary; he simply supplanted it with another, *The Medley* (5 October 1710 - 6 August 1711). But like its predecessor this effort contradicted historical inevitability, and it too died, or as Swift wrote in the *Journal to Stella*, "Grub Street is dead." A Tory peace, in spirit, if not in actuality, broke out in 1711.

The Tatler, as we have seen, closed down on 2 January 1711. For the next two months Addison and Steele undoubtedly planned the character and makeup of another periodical to be printed and sold by Samuel Buckley and Jacob Tonson the younger, as well as distributed by Anne Baldwin in Warwick Lane and (somewhat later) by Charles Lillie, "Perfumer," in the Strand. *The Spectator* immediately distanced itself from the earlier journal by an avowal of political objectivity, an "exact Neutrality between Whigs and Tories" (number 1). Indeed, in several other numbers (16, 262, 556) Addison repeated his persona's disclaimer of partisanship. Forbearance became a lighthearted mode of deception operative on need. Almost as if to test the quick of his audience, he drafted the third number to intimate a party affiliation; that is, he mocked what he judged a bizarre Tory whim to capture the directorship of the Bank of England, which had been established in 1694 through the economic foresight of Charles Montagu. To emphasize the incongruity of the aspiration, he created a dream allegory that centered on the further incongruity of the romance figure, Public Credit.

Unlike the squat, leaden "Old Lady of Threadneedle Street," the allegory's young heroine sat on a gold throne in the Great Hall of the Bank. As mysterious as she was "infinitely timorous [that is, conservative] in all her Behaviour," she nonetheless decorated her salon with the Magna Carta and the Act of Settlement, with the Acts of Toleration and Uniformity. Suddenly Public Credit faced three pairs of mismatched dancing phantoms: Tyranny and Anarchy; Bigotry and Atheism; and the last couple, the Genius of the Commonwealth hand in hand with a young man, probably the Stuart Pretender. Brandishing a sponge and sword, he began to erase the documents that protected Britain's heritage of liberty. At this moment of crisis Public Credit did what any genteel maiden would do—at least in the masculine vision of international banking. She fainted, and her moneybags, demurely inconspicuous behind the throne, flattened.

In the nick of melodramatic time, predictably, "a second Dance of Apparitions very agreeably matched together" tiptoed into the Great Hall. "The first Pair was Liberty, with Monarchy at her right Hand: The second was Moderation leading in Religion"; and the third was the Hanoverian heir with the Genius of Great Britain. What had once seemed desolate, now revived: "the Bags swell'd to their former Bulk, the Piles of Faggots and Heaps of Paper changed into Pyramids of Guineas." Public Credit assumed once more her role of chaste mistress to Great Britain's wealth. Within a few days after the introduction of *The Spectator*, then, Addison chanced and won a Whig controversy without strident ado. The journal immediately thereafter resumed its posture of neutrality, and the readership grew.

The Spectator also differed from *The Tatler* in that it rejected a medley format for its papers. Probably at Addison's insistence, the new periodical offered a single unified essay in each number. The format itself projected a oneness of thematic purpose whereby the essayist would enlighten both men and women while he painlessly entertained them. He realized that his intention needed a lightness of touch. To achieve such delicacy in "distinct Sheets" published "as it were by Piece-meal," he would eschew mere descriptive prose and laboring digression, would instead "immediately fall into our Subject and treat every part of it in a lively Manner." He would reduce the material of his papers—no matter what its scope or profundity—"to their Quintessence" (124). All this he would "endeavour" to do within a folio half sheet, printed on both sides, two columns to the page, with advertisements filling the whole or part of the last column.

The Spectator built upon the reputation of *The Tatler*, and so it began with a ready-made audience of possibly "Three Thousand" disciples, "with Twenty Readers to every Paper" sold. During the first year of publication Addison repeated that the "Demand for my Papers has encreased every Month since their first Appearance in the World" (10, 124, 262). He emphasized the circulation figures to puff *The Spectator*, to sweeten his bitter recollection of *The Whig Examiner*, and to reassure an ego momentarily rattled but not muddled in the early years of the St. John-Harley ministry (later the Lords Bolingbroke-Oxford ministry until the summer of 1714).

The first series of *The Spectator*, the collaboration of Addison and Steele, consisted of 555 numbers, printed in sheets and distributed daily (Sundays excepted) from March 1711 to December 1712 and later collected in seven volumes. Of the 555, Addison wrote 202 independent essays with no help from others; Steele only 89. Hence Macaulay's mathematically just panegyric: "Addison is the Spectator." The continuation of *The Spectator*, or the second series (556-635), was Addison's with assistance from Eustace Budgell, Thomas Tickell, and others. It appeared three times a week from June to December 1714 and later as volume 8. Of the 79 essays, 25 were written by Addison, who in August had been named secretary to the Lords Justices (the Regents), about 10 by Budgell in whole or in part, and about 26 by Tickell.

To suggest the coherence of the journal's 635 papers the writers in the first series emphasize a few themes. So Steele and Addison in 1711 and 1712—Steele more than his former "Auxiliary"—delineated the world of London, "this great City," as they reacted to it. Still another theme—this time an Addisonian offering—concerns literary criticism, an unexpectedly popular feature of the periodical. The essays number about sixty, divisible into four groups: English tragedy (39, 40, 42, 44, and 548); true and false wit (58-63); "The Pleasures of the Imagination or Fancy" (411-421); the eighteen Saturday papers on *Paradise Lost* that begin with number 267; scattered essays on ballads (70, 74, 85), Sappho (223 and 229), humor (35, 47, 249), modern poetry (523). What these critical papers give to a spectatorial audience is a tidy package of fashionable criticism without either condescension or pedantry.

Fortifying the semblance of thematic wholeness are the Saturday issues on philosophy and devotion, formulated as lay sermons prefatory to weekend or Sunday meditation. Very much the contribution of Addison, they serve both a pragmatic and religious intention. They document the time-tested rational arguments for divine existence (459, 465); they give preference to natural religion over faith and therefore espouse a rational Anglicanism attuned to moderate government. The Saturday papers also deal with specific subjects such as immorality (111), zeal (185), atheism (186), enthusiasm and superstition (201, 458), with their implications of republicanism, on the one hand, and arbitrary government on the other; the nature of prayer (207); good intentions (213); God in nature, or cheerfulness as a "kind of worship to the great Author of Nature" (393); the scale of being (519); the divine attributes (531). To give these and other lessons in piety a charisma of their own, Addison composed five hymns (441, 453, 465, 489, 519), most of them a reworking of favorite psalms in *The Book of Common Prayer*.

Dependent in part on the repetition of certain themes, the journal's unity is further manipulated by the presence of seven type figures who meet twice a week as members of the Spectator Club: the silent, featureless Mr. Spectator, whose voice blends with both Steele's and Addison's; Will Honeycomb; the Templar; the Clergyman; Sir Andrew Freeport; and Sir Roger de Coverley. The club provides a congenial narrative in support of the putative political and consequent social neutrality of the periodical.

Despite the persona's flim-flam promise to give each "Rank or Degree" of society a hearing, the journal deliberately cultivates a myopic perspective of classes, but deepens it into a narrative symbolism by the friendly conflict between the squire Sir Roger de Coverley and the international merchant Sir Andrew Freeport. By knighting the two men and making them clubbable—hence equal, or almost so, in a social hierarchy—Addison and Steele predicate an accommodation between "the landed" and "the money" interests in which each shares or exchanges benefits, "their just Rights and Privileges" (34).

Addison preferred Sir Andrew to all the other club members since he had already proved himself a person of accomplishment, a doer, who saw that his ships blown home from every "Point in the Compass" profited the public as well as himself. The preference is muted so that, like the others, Sir Andrew plays a comic role. What elevates him above jest is the fact that he "made his Fortunes himself" and his "Notions of Trade" (perhaps his only "Notions") are "noble and generous."

Contrasted with him is Sir Roger, who, "the descendant of worthy ancestors," has pride of place in the club's roster of membership. When Steele introduces him, he is a hearty bachelor, but out of step with the world of London in his rustic Toryism and even with himself in his showy

Addison in 1716 (portrait by Sir Godfrey Kneller; by permission of the Yale University Library)

parade of old-fashioned manners and clothing. Given more space and detail than Sir Andrew, the figure of "the good old Knight" is constructed upon a series of interconnecting polarities.

The squire's virtues both nourish and feed upon his eccentricities. When, for example, he and Mr. Spectator traveled from London to the country, they did "not so much as bait at a Whig Inn. . . . for we were not so inquisitive about the Inn as the Inn-keeper, and provided our Landlord's Principles were sound, did not take any Notice of the Staleness of his Provisions" (126). Yet in the essay just previous to this mockery of the squire's blinkered Toryism, Mr. Spectator stresses Sir Roger's "Reflections on the Mischief that Parties do in the Country; how they spoil good Neighbourhood, and make honest Gentlemen hate one another." Ultimately the squire's capacity for

friendship transcends bigotry and the "Malice of Parties." He loves Sir Andrew, although he suspects that the merchant holds "Republican Doctrines" and even has "a Hand in the Pope's Procession," which the Tory ministry in 1711 cited as an example of "Presbyterian" subversion (269).

Even Sir Roger's death reveals the split within the personality. At once selfless and vain, he "caught his Death at the last County Sessions, when he would go to see Justice done to a poor Widow Woman, and her Fatherless Children that had been wronged by a Neighbouring Gentleman" (517). Addison perforce killed him off because Sir Roger had no place to go; figuratively he clung to his ancestry much like a limpet to a rock. In a society that gauged everyone on performance, he did not perform. In a time of enterprise, he bustled about to have antlers hung on the walls of his estate and a patchwork of fox

Addison in 1719 (portrait by Michael Dahl; by permission of the National Portrait Gallery, London)

noses on the stable doors (112). Addison enjoyed the knight's garrulous, if naïf, goodness; he respected his sense of a vital past. He knew, as he later stated in *Guardian* 137, that "a Man of Merit [and certainly the squire is such], who is derived from an Illustrious Line, is very justly to be regarded more than a Man of equal Merit who has no Claim to Hereditary Honours."

Unlike Sir Roger, Sir Andrew Freeport, whose very name risibly allies him to mercantilist theory, did not die. When the latter makes his final appearance in *Spectator* 549, he feels comfortable with himself; he contemplates a life well spent in an "abundance of those lucky Hits, which at another time he would have called pieces of Good Fortune," and a retirement well earned. In withdrawing from the City to a rural estate, he insinuates that the time has come to cap his career and convert energy into a canny investment "in Substantial Acres and Tenements." In

fact, he has the last realistic word in the survey and judgment of his life. There is really no more to be said on the subject. "I remember," he comments, "an excellent Saying . . . *Finis coronat opus*. You know best whether it be in *Virgil* or in *Horace*, it is my business to apply it." That the "Saying" comes from Ovid's *Heroides* in no way diminishes the old man's strength or subtracts from his "Acres and Tenements."

The year 1713 was a time of shuttling literary activity for Addison. In that spring he composed, as we have seen, a fifth act for *Cato* and from a side box or backstage watched its first performance. That night and the drama's extraordinary reception brought him all the handclapping he ever desired and possibly a bit he preferred to shun. Whatever its reputation today, his one tragic verse drama made history in the first half of the eighteenth century. The reasons for such acclaim are atextual, lying not in spectacular or innovative dramaturgy but in its partisan theme.

But what is its "message"? When he hastily drafted the first four acts of *Cato*, he could not plot a conclusion and therefore could not conceive a thematic intent. While he had already turned out successful political verse, he probably had not affiliated a large and costly enterprise like the drama with faction's support. Wasting nothing, he continued to struggle with it intermittently and dully, unable to finish what had begun as an academic exercise contrary to his slowly emerging comic talent. He contrived a last act only in 1713, written—said Steele in a "Dedication" to *The Drummer*—"in less than a Week's time."

In preparation for the election of 1713, Addison was prodded to see in *Cato* the latent political texture which, with honing, could be made apparent to an audience set up for it. Lady Mary Wortley Montagu thought it deserved a place on the stage. So did the actress Anne Oldfield, wise in the ways of the theater and, as the former mistress of Arthur Maynwaring, experienced in the techniques of thought control. Other Whigs urged that the playwright complete the tragedy quickly, that he flesh out the declamatory figure of Marcus Porcius Cato of Utica, the stoic peculiarly unrestrained in his denunciation of Julius Caesar's tyranny.

Several individuals convinced Addison that the drama called for production as both a literary and party investment. Once committed by wishful thinking to assurances of *Cato*'s alleged theatricality, he enhanced its twofold function. When he added the lines on the necessity of civil freedom, he hoped that an audience would recall buried memories of 1688, how the Whigs upheld the Revolution Settlement against Tory attacks. When he "flung" in "the love part," he capitulated to popular taste.

Whatever changes Addison made to *Cato* before 14 April 1713, he seemed compulsively eager to escape the charge of political bias for himself and his tragedy. He therefore approached Alexander Pope, an ambivalent Tory or a Whig, for an opinion of the play. Pope reported that certain lines had poetical merit but that the piece as a whole suffered from dramatic stasis. Addison seemingly agreed with this verdict but admitted "that some particular friends of his whom he could not disoblige insisted on its being acted."

Fostering his own "insistence" was a tangle of motives and pressures: his hope for literary adu-

lation accompanied by financial advantage, his slow recognition of *Cato* as pointed dramatic propaganda, and above all, his determination that no infighting among parties detract from a box-office success in whose proceeds he would share. Nonetheless, when with Pope—and with Swift as well—he assumed the part of an anxiety-ridden dramatist who wished that the Lords Bolingbroke and Oxford would reject any invidious rumor that *Cato* was a "party play." In truth, he wanted the play understood precisely as such but as a "party play" that offended no party, especially the "opposite faction." At first he had it his way. Steele's crew, adroitly spaced throughout the pit, cheered every mention of the word "Liberty," while several of the queen's advisers were ostentatiously seated at the Drury Lane on Tuesday, 14 April, during Easter week.

Before that Tuesday, interest in the play—at least to Swift—was one of amused tolerance. He saw no party involvement in it. *Cato*'s debut, however, silenced Swift's forbearance and disciplined the response of faction. In a letter to John Caryll, dated 30 April, Pope described the event: "The numerous and violent claps of the Whig party on one side of the Theatre, were echoed back by the Tories on the other, while the author sweated behind the scenes with concern to find their applause proceeded more [from] the hand than the head."

In the first year of its run, *Cato* was unstoppable. It played in London some twenty times. After 1713 it became a standard repertory piece presented every season until 1750 and staged about 234 times by 1797. (It was printed with and without the love scenes some 111 times between 1713 and 1799.) Long before the end of the century, Voltaire in his *Letters concerning the English Nation* (1733) dismissed the love scenes as distasteful artifice but credited Addison with being "the first *English* writer who compos'd a Regular Tragedy thro' every part of it." By the time of the Regency, nearly a hundred years after the first night, it became the closet drama that Pope had initially said it was. Maynard Mack, in the spirit of a Popean biographer, recently described it as a "vast echoing museum filled with plaster casts."

After the triumph of *Cato*, Addison faced new literary demands but experienced few winning moments except perhaps as a "man of business." While he busied himself with the play at Drury Lane, Steele had begun *The Guardian*, which lasted for 175 numbers from 12 March to

Addison late in life (portrait by Sir Godfrey Kneller; from Peter Smithers, **The Life of Joseph Addison,** *second edition, 1968)*

1 October 1713 under the fictive editorship of Nestor Ironside, whose relatives in the Lizard family occasionally helped him with journalistic chores. Addison made his first contribution to *The Guardian* on 28 May with number 67. Presumably during July he oversaw the periodical when Steele readied himself for the hustings and the seat at Stockbridge which he won on 25 August 1713.

As overseer, Addison sought to moderate Whig pugnacity in *The Guardian* with a series of playful essays on a lady's tucker, the "ruffle around the uppermost Verge of the Woman's Stays" (100, 109), on the parodic antics of lions and jackals (71), on a lion's head for a postbox at Button's (98). Even with these essays he could not give the fledgling journal an aura of neutrality. Clearly by August, Steele again set its tone by publishing on the seventh his combative number 128 on Dunkirk, an attack on the Tory ministry for not forcing the French "demolition" of the har-

bor there, as the Peace of Utrecht specified.

The spring and summer of 1713 involved Addison in a fever of politico-literary composition. He could not escape the ubiquitous *Cato* with its coupling of Whiggism and "Liberty" or Toryism and "Tyranny." Yet just before he substituted for Steele on *The Guardian*, he made a blatant offering to the Whig platform. This time it was *The Late Tryal and Conviction of Count Tariff*, a pamphlet allegory which broadcast England's maritime trading victory over the French and, more significantly, the Parliamentary defeat of the eighth and ninth articles of the Tory-sponsored Treaty of Navigation between Great Britain and France. He wrote the allegory speedily between 18 and 28 June, saw to its publication on the last day of the month. He did not disguise its intention: its economic patriotism was designed as rhetoric for the Whigs. If it survived only as long as

23

the issue which produced it, that was the necessary exorbitancy of to-the-moment journalism. Addison did not fantasize its place in literary history. Nor did he overstate the artistry of *The Guardian*, which, unlike *The Spectator* and even *The Tatler*, thought of itself as a partisan periodical. He watched *The Guardian* blaze into faction and consume itself. Unlike the phoenix, however, it died, a sacrifice to party. He could do nothing more for Nestor Ironside and the Lizards. He had contributed some fifty-two or fifty-three essays to the periodical, about thirty percent of the total number.

After Queen Anne died on 1 August 1714, England looked to George's arrival from Hanover on 18 September and his coronation on 20 October. In that interval authority lodged in a Regency. On Halifax's recommendation, Addison drew on 3 August an appointment as secretary to this governing committee. He accepted the stop-gap employment as he did most others during his political lifetime. But in a period of burgeoning hope, he anticipated one of the several high offices of government. He had, he confessed, serious "pretensions to the Board of Trade." But passed over, he suffered a bitter autumn—he wrote in carefully measured petulance to Lord Halifax on 30 October 1714—and felt weighted down like "an old sergeant or corporal." With the coming of the new year and for months thereafter, he swallowed "resentment," stood hat in hand, watching for a royal nod and a place that fulfilled "pretensions."

George in the first year of his reign presented an unpopular Germanic figure, reclusive and almost speechless if only because he knew so little English. His ministry set about gathering middle-of-the-road opinion on his behalf while shredding the Jacobite image of James as the legitimate monarch of Great Britain. They therefore turned to a publicist whose modulated voice carried conviction without intemperance. They asked Addison to create a Whig journal with a large circulation, one that could assuage extremes and bring them nearer to the center, purportedly to George. Almost as if in advance payment, he was named on 20 December 1715 a member of a significant trade commission with an annual salary of one thousand pounds. Three days later, the first number of the thrice-weekly *Freeholder* had been printed and readied for sale by Samuel Gray, publisher of the *Daily Courant*.

The fifty-five numbers of *The Freeholder* ran a sustained advertisement of the Whigs—their great men, their quasiphilosophical policies, and their Parliamentary programs. It circulated from 23 December 1715 (the day after James Stuart landed in Scotland) to 29 June 1716 (three days after Parliament rose). The reasons for its birth were several, both personal and political. Throughout most of 1715 Addison had searched for advantage. Before he agreed to undertake the journal as a solo enterprise, he demanded and received—as we have already noted—a position on the commission for trade and plantations, which brought him early information on profitable exports and imports. He also stayed with the periodical out of an indebtedness to party, those "particular friends of his whom he could not disoblige." Finally, *The Freeholder* arose from his own creative urgency. For many years he had submitted to the fact that his fate, tied to the vagaries of Whig fortune, left him little time for serious composition, free of a propagandist's concern with the state of the parties. He had to grab at whatever opportunity came along, and the journal in 1715 promised such an opportunity. Hence, he considered it an artistic effort in which each essay, polished and complete, made a statement "upon Government, but with a View to the present Situation of affairs in *Great Britain*," endangered by "unnatural Rebellion" (55).

For a little more than six months, Addison touched upon or gave over entire numbers to Parliamentary problems: for example, to the suspension of habeas corpus (16), the passage of the Septennial Act (25, 28), and the increase in the Land Tax (20). With greater success, however—at least for today's readers—he wrote about the structure of the state: the principle of natural law and the doctrine of consent, their assimilation into the unwritten British constitution and the near-subversion of that framework by the Jacobites or the Tory High Fliers who screened their revolutionary motives behind the pietistic slogan, "the Church is in danger" (32, 37). Addison probed these matters Whiggishly but usually without "that Mixture of Violence and Passion, which so often creeps into the Works of Political Writers" (55).

He was undeniably one of those "Political Writers" who regarded *The Freeholder* as a supplement to his office in the commission of trade and plantations. As meaningful as the journal was to him, he remained conscious of his audience for whom he would lighten sobriety and enliven the dry materials of theory, polemic, and legalistic proceedings with witty equivalents of short fiction and characterization. He "sacrificed to the Graces" with what he called "proper Scenes and Decorations" (45), with the transmutation of political clichés into a narrative of stock figures—the Tory Fox Hunter and his Inn-keeper, Second Sighted Sawney, "Stateswomen" whose tuckers did them no good since their "Stays [were] ready to burst with Sedition" (26). The satire which energizes these types forfeited fine-tuning but never compromised criticism with belittlement or with invective.

Addison accepted the reality of party journalism even as he had become, on the death of Arthur Maynwaring in November 1712, a covert manager or an untitled director of Whig propaganda. For several years he recruited, advised, wined, and housed his hirelings. He himself enjoyed anonymity as a participant in paper wars, but even without anonymity he seldom retreated from a position or sought shelter behind the walls of the Cockpit. Rather he stayed in the field as long as he could. Almost three years after the last *Freeholder*, when he was dying, he took part in a journalistic contretemps over the peerage bill, an internecine crisis that camouflaged a struggle for leadership within the Whig party. From his couch in the spring of 1719 he actively organized an impressive group of pamphleteers and dictated *The Old Whig* (19 March and 2 April) in defense of the Whig establishment led by Charles Spencer, Earl of Sunderland, and James, Earl Stanhope. In the course of the verbal feints that followed, Addison's journal confronted *The Plebeian* (14 March - 6 April), written in four numbers by Steele in support of Robert Walpole and progressive Whiggism. The bill, never important except to a handful of aggressive politicians, failed of final passage. Indeed, the whole war of words has relevance only as a biographical moment, as a squabble between onetime collaborators whose friendship began some three decades earlier at Charterhouse. And that too was the price of political journalism.

In the last five years of his life little happened to Addison except that he married and died—but not necessarily effect from cause. On 9 August 1716 he celebrated his wedding to Charlotte, the widow of Edward Rich, the tempestuous sixth Earl of Warwick. While the match probably did not do much for his emotional life, it gave him access to the splendors of Holland House in Kensington, particularly to the library and galleries there. It probably brought him one of the great offices of government. On 6 April

1717 Lord Sunderland named him secretary of state for the southern department. Even some who were Whig-shy cheered the appointment. In a letter dated 9 July 1717, Swift congratulated the new secretary with an ironical caveat: "I am only a little concerned to see you stand single, for it is a prodigious singularity in any Court to owe ones Rise entirely to Merit."

Having deferred to party superiors for so long, Addison had little time to be "a great man." He suffered from a degenerative heart condition and dropsy, wrongly diagnosed from the symptoms of a cough and shortness of breath as asthma. By March 1718 he reluctantly retired with an annual pension of £1,500. Perhaps brooding on his physical decline—despite the birth of his only child, Charlotte, on 30 January 1719—he had few doubts about his literary immortality. In his will, signed 14 May 1719, he bequeathed his literary remains to James Craggs the younger (his successor as one of the principal secretaries of state) but assigned the task of editing them to Thomas Tickell, a professional Whig protégé. In the last month of his life he kept tight control of his emotions by contemplating and deciding on the order of his collected works to be published posthumously. The ultimate choice was his. He worked with whatever energy a self-employment demanded or the gasping for breath permitted. On 17 June 1719 he died at Holland House. The funeral, if he could have stage-managed it from a side box or the wings, was all he desired for himself, the fifth act in a life dedicated to the pursuit of fame and reward. He lay in state in the Jerusalem Chamber of Westminster Abbey during the day of 26 June. That night he was interred in King Henry VII's Chapel in the Albemarle vault "next [his] lov'd Montagu," according to Tickell's "Dirge."

The Addisonian personality has remained aloof, perhaps as secretive as the man who has always seemed a prepared surface with invisible, well-manned defenses. But the artist deliberately left behind a record of performance—how he wished to be known and remembered. The best of his art is *The Spectator*, a collaboration which by comparative test pinpoints the nature of his achievement. Steele buttonholed his audience with an ingratiating openness and a hint—real or invented—of troubled immediacy: he "stumbled and got up again and got into jail and out again, and sinned and repented." In such a manner William Makepeace Thackeray synthesized his appreciation of "this amiable creature"

*Charlotte Myddelton of Chirk (later Countess of Warwick), who married Addison on 9 August 1716
(Collection of Col. R. Myddelton at Chirk Castle)*

in *The English Humourists of the Eighteenth Century* (1853). Indeed, he urged all "to think gently of one who was so gentle . . . [to] speak kindly of one whose own breast exuberated with human kindness."

What Thackeray missed in the interest of descriptive parallelism is the fact that Addison had greater perspective and comic instinct, greater agility of mind than did Steele. The "Auxiliary" brought the range of topics to *The Spectator* in language that approximates the easy drift of rational conversation. He perfected a "middle style," the verbal equivalent of his journalistic ethos. He wrote much like a literate reporter who never lost sight of his general audience. He was for the most part comfortable with the spectatorial world and its values. He did not ignore the truth that folly existed there, that time and effort, paradoxically, nurtured the trivial, the silly, and the downright nasty. Far from being the best of all possible worlds, it nonetheless allowed him

sufficient space and privacy for a hidden spirit that had to be embattled. Because he lived in intimacy with this fictional world—possibly the only intimacy he required—he managed to catch the defining qualities of the age of Anne as few others could do.

Addison created a new journalism, one which painlessly ensnared and projected the ideas and sentiments of his readers. In a rhetoric that muffles the assertions of opinion and commitment—although both are there—he identified with his readers even as they identified with the pied-piper persuasiveness of his delicately crafted *Spectator* essays. Finally, author and audience possessed a mutuality of taste, which he articulated as a first step in a melioristic process of refinement—but he made no guarantee.

Letters:

The Letters of Joseph Addison, edited by Walter Graham (Oxford: Clarendon Press, 1941);

The Correspondence of Richard Steele, edited by Rae Blanchard (Oxford: Oxford University Press, 1941; reprinted, with a new appendix, Oxford: Clarendon Press, 1968).

Bibliographies:

Samuel J. Rogal, "Joseph Addison (1672-1719): A Check List of Works and Major Scholarship," *Bulletin of the New York Public Library*, 77 (Winter 1974): 236-250;

Robin Carfrae Alston, *A Check List of the Works of Joseph Addison* (Leeds: Printed by the compiler for private circulation, 1976).

Biographies:

G. J. [Giles Jacob], *Memoirs of the Life and Writings of the Right Honourable Joseph Addison esq., with his Character by Sir Richard Steele, and a true Copy of his Last Will and Testament* (London: Printed for E. Curll, 1719);

[T. Birch and J. Lockman], *The Life of J. Addison, Esq. extracted from No. III. and IV. of the General Dictionary, Historical and Critical To which is prefixed the Life of Dr. Lancelot Addison, Dean of Litchfield, his Father* (London: Printed for N. Prevost, 1733);

John Campbell, "Addison," in *Biographia Britannica* (London: Printed for W. Innys, W. Meadows, J. Walthoe, T. Cox, A. Ward & others, 1747);

Samuel Johnson, "Addison," in his *Lives of the English Poets* (1781), edited by George Birkbeck Hill, 3 volumes (Oxford: Clarendon Press, 1905), II: 79-158;

[Thomas Tyers], *An Historical Essay on Mr. Addison* (London: Printed by J. Nichols for the author, 1783);

Richard Phillips, *Addisoniana*, 2 volumes (London: Printed for Richard Phillips by T. Davison, 1803);

Nathan Drake, *Essays, Biographical, Critical, and Historical, illustrative of the "Tatler," "Spectator" and "Guardian,"* 3 volumes (London: Printed by C. Whittingham for J. Sharpe, 1805);

Joseph Spence, *Observations, Anecdotes, and Characters of Books and Men* (1820), edited by James M. Osborn, 2 volumes (Oxford: Clarendon Press, 1966);

Nathaniel Ogle, *The Life of Addison* (London: Printed by Thomas Davison, 1826);

Lucy Aikin, *The Life of Joseph Addison*, 2 volumes (London: Longman, Brown, Green & Longmans, 1843);

Thomas Babington Macaulay, "Life and Writings of Addison," review of *The Life of Joseph Addison*, by Lucy Aikin, *Edinburgh Review*, 78 (July 1843): 193-260;

Arthur L. Cooke, "Addison's Aristocratic Wife," *PMLA*, 72, part 1 (June 1957): 373-389;

Peter Smithers, *The Life of Joseph Addison*, second edition, revised (Oxford: Clarendon Press, 1968);

James L. Battersby, "Johnson and Shiels: Biographers of Addison," *Studies in English Literature*, 9 (1969): 521-537.

References:

George A. Aitkin, *The Life of Richard Steele*, 2 volumes (London: William Isbister, 1889);

J. D. Alsop, "New Light on Joseph Addison," *Modern Philology*, 80 (August 1982): 13-34;

P. B. Anderson, "Addison's Letter from Italy," *Modern Language Notes*, 47 (May 1932): 318;

Norman Ault, "Pope and Addison," in his *New Light on Pope* (London: Methuen, 1949), pp. 101-127;

Edward A. and Lillian D. Bloom, *Joseph Addison's Sociable Animal* (Providence: Brown University Press, 1971);

Edward A. and Lillian D. Bloom, eds., *Addison and Steele: The Critical Heritage* (London, Boston & Henley: Routledge & Kegan Paul, 1980);

Edward A. and Lillian D. Bloom, and Edmund Leites, *Educating an Audience: Addison, Steele, and Eighteenth-Century Culture* (Los Angeles: William Andrews Clark Memorial Library, 1984);

Lillian D. Bloom, "Addison's Popular Aesthetic: the Rhetoric of the 'Paradise Lost' Papers," in *The Author in his Work*, edited by Louis L. Martz and Aubrey Williams (New Haven & London: Yale University Press, 1978), pp. 263-281;

Donald F. Bond, "Addison in Perspective," *Modern Philology*, 54 (November 1956): 124-128;

Richmond P. Bond, *The Tatler. The Making of a Literary Journal* (Cambridge, Mass.: Harvard University Press, 1971);

Leicester Bradner, "The Composition and Publication of Addison's *Latin* Poems," *Modern Philology*, 35 (May 1938): 353-367;

Bradner, *Musae Anglicanae / A History of Anglo-Latin Poetry / 1925-1950* (New York: Modern

Language Society of America / London: Oxford University Press, 1940);

Daniel Defoe, *The Double Welcome. A Poem to the Duke of Marlbro* (London: Printed & sold by B. Bragg, 1705);

John Dennis, *Remarks upon Cato, A Tragedy* (London: Printed for B. Lintot, 1713);

Bonamy Dobrée, *English Literature in the Early Eighteenth Century 1700-1740* (Oxford: Clarendon Press, 1959), pp. 102-120;

Dobrée, "The First Victorian," in his *Essays in Biography* (Oxford: Clarendon Press, 1925), pp. 201-345;

Irvin Ehrenpreis, *Swift the Man, His Works, and The Age*, 3 volumes (Cambridge, Mass.: Harvard University Press / London: Methuen, 1967-1983);

Lee Andrew Elioseff, *The Cultural Milieu of Addison's Literary Criticism* (Austin: University of Texas Press, 1963);

Albert Furtwangler, "Mr. Spectator, Sir Roger and Good Humour," *University of Toronto Quarterly*, 46 (Fall 1976): 31-50;

John Gay, *The Present State of Wit* (London, 1711); edited by Donald F. Bond in *Publications of the Augustan Reprint Society*, series 1, no. 3 (May 1947);

Bertrand A. Goldgar, *The Curse of Party. Swift's Relations with Addison and Steele* (Lincoln: University of Nebraska Press, 1961);

Robert Halsband, "Addison's *Cato* and Lady Mary Wortley Montagu," *PMLA*, 65 (December 1950): 1122-1129;

Donald Kay, *Short Fiction in "The Spectator"* (Tuscaloosa: University of Alabama Press, 1975);

Michael G. Ketcham, *Transparent Designs: Reading, Performance, and Form in the "Spectator" Papers* (Athens: University of Georgia Press, 1985);

C. S. Lewis, "Addison," in *Essays on the Eighteenth Century Presented to David Nichol Smith in Honour of His Seventieth Birthday* (Oxford: Clarendon Press, 1945), pp. 1-14;

Maynard Mack, *Alexander Pope / A Life* (New Haven & London: Yale University Press / New York & London: W. W. Norton, 1985);

Brian McCrea, *Addison and Steele Are Dead* (Newark: University of Delaware Press / London & Toronto: Associated University Presses, 1990);

Allan Ramsay, *Richy and Sandy, A Pastoral on the Death of Mr. Joseph Addison* (Edinburgh, 1719);

Robert W. Rogers, *The Major Satires of Alexander Pope* (Urbana: University of Illinois Press, 1955);

George Sherburn, *The Early Career of Alexander Pope* (Oxford: Clarendon Press, 1934);

Sherburn, ed., *The Correspondence of Alexander Pope*, 5 volumes (Oxford: Clarendon Press, 1956);

Sir Richard Steele, "Epistle Dedicatory to Mr. Congreve—occasioned by Mr. Tickell's Preface to the four volumes of Mr. Addison's Works," in *The Drummer*, second edition (London: Printed for John Darby & sold by J. Roberts, 1722);

James Sutherland, "The Last Years of Joseph Addison," in his *Background for Queen Anne* (London: Methuen, 1939), pp. 127-144;

Jonathan Swift, *Journal to Stella* (1784), edited by Harold Williams, 2 volumes (Oxford: Clarendon Press, 1948);

William Makepeace Thackeray, *The English Humourists of the Eighteenth Century* (London: Smith, Elder, 1853);

Calhoun Winton, *Captain Steele: The Early Career of Richard Steele* (Baltimore: Johns Hopkins University Press, 1964);

Winton, *Sir Richard Steele, M.P.: The Later Career* (Baltimore & London: Johns Hopkins University Press, 1970).

John Arbuthnot

(April 1667 - 27 February 1735)

Claudia Newel Thomas
Wake Forest University

BOOKS: *Of the Laws of Chance* (London: Printed by B. Motte & sold by R. Taylor, 1692);

An Examination of Dr. Woodward's Account of the Deluge (London: Printed for C. Bateman, 1697);

An Essay on the Usefulness of Mathematical Learning, in a Letter from a Gentleman in the City to His Friend in Oxford (Oxford: Printed at the theater for A. Peisley, 1701);

Tables of the Grecian, Roman and Jewish Measures, Weights and Coins; reduc'd to the English Standard (London: Printed for R. Smith, 1705); expanded as *Tables of Ancient Coins, Weights and Measures, explain'd and exemplify'd in several Dissertations* (London: Printed for J. Tonson, 1727);

A Sermon preach'd to the People at the Mercat-Cross of Edinburgh on the Subject of the Union (Edinburgh, 1706);

Law is a Bottomless-Pit (London: Printed for J. Morphew, 1712);

John Bull in His Senses (London: Printed for J. Morphew, 1712);

John Bull Still in His Senses (London: Printed for J. Morphew, 1712);

An Appendix to John Bull Still in His Senses; or, Law is a Bottomless-Pit (London: Printed for J. Morphew, 1712);

Lewis Baboon turned Honest, and John Bull Politician (London: Printed for J. Morphew, 1712);

Proposals for printing a very Curious Discourse, in Two Volumes in Quarto, Intitled Ψευδολογια Πολιτικη or A Treatise of the Art of Political Lying, with an Abstract of the First Volume of the said Treatise (London: Printed for J. Morphew, 1712);

To the Right Honourable The Mayor and Aldermen of the City of London: The Humble Petition of the Colliers, Cooks, Cook-Maids, Blacksmiths, Jackmakers, Brasiers, and others [single sheet] (London: Printed for J. Roberts, 1716);

Reasons humbly offer'd by the Company exercising the Trade and Mystery of Upholders (London: Printed for J. Roberts, 1724);

Oratio Anniversaria Harvaeana (London: Printed for J. Tonson, 1727);

A Brief Account of Mr. John Ginglicutt's Treatise concerning the Altercation or Scolding of the Ancients (London: Printed for J. Roberts, 1731);

An Essay Concerning the Nature of Aliments, and the choice of them, according to the different Constitutions of Human Bodies (London: Printed for J. Tonson, 1731);

Practical Rules of Diet in the Various Constitutions and Diseases of Human Bodies, volume 2 of *An Essay Concerning the Nature of Aliments* (London: Printed for J. Tonson, 1732);

An Essay Concerning the Effects of Air on Human Bodies (London: Printed for J. Tonson, 1733);

Γνωθι σεαυτον. Know Yourself. A Poem (London: Printed for J. Tonson, 1734).

Editions: *The History of John Bull*, in *Miscellanies. The Second Volume*, edited by Alexander Pope and Jonathan Swift (London: Printed for B. Motte, 1727);

The Miscellaneous Works of the Late Dr. Arbuthnot, 2 volumes (Glasgow: Printed for J. Carlisle, 1751);

The History of John Bull, edited by Herman Teerink (Amsterdam: H. J. Paris, 1925);

Memoirs of the Extraordinary Life, Works, and Discoveries of Martinus Scriblerus, by Arbuthnot, Pope, Swift, John Gay, Thomas Parnell, and Robert Harley, Earl of Oxford; edited by Charles Kerby-Miller (New Haven: Published for Wellesley College by Yale University Press, 1950);

"A Critical Edition of the Satires of John Arbuthnot," 2 volumes, edited by Robert Allen Erickson, Ph.D. dissertation, Yale University, 1967;

The History of John Bull, edited by Alan W. Bower and Robert A. Erickson (Oxford: Clarendon Press, 1976).

OTHER: "An Argument for Divine Providence, taken from the constant regularity observed

John Arbuthnot (dubiously attributed to Charles Jervas; by permission of the Wellcome Institute Medical Museum, London)

in the Births of both Sexes," *Philosophical Transactions*, 27 (1710): 186;

Three Hours after Marriage, A Comedy, by John Gay, with the assistance of Arbuthnot and Alexander Pope (London: Printed for B. Lintot, 1717);

"Virgilius Restauratus: seu Martini Scriblerus Summi Critici Castigationum in Aeneidum Specimen," in *The Dunciad Variorum*, by Pope (London: Printed for A. Dodd, 1729), pp. 99-103;

"An Epitaph on Francis Charteris," *London Magazine* (April 1732);

"An Essay of the Learned Martinus Scriblerus, Concerning the Origin of Sciences. Written to the Most Learned Dr. F. R. S., from the Deserts of Nubia," in *Miscellanies. The Third Volume*, edited by Pope and Jonathan Swift (London: Printed for Benj. Motte & Lawton Gilliver, 1732);

Memoirs of the Extraordinary Life, Works, and Discoveries of Martinus Scriblerus, by Arbuthnot, Pope, Swift, Gay, Thomas Parnell, and Robert Harley, Earl of Oxford; in *The Works of Mr. Alexander Pope, In Prose*, volume 2 (London: Printed for J. & P. Knapton, C. Bathurst, and R. Dodsley, 1741).

So careless of his literary reputation that he permitted his children to make paper kites of his manuscripts, Dr. John Arbuthnot nevertheless achieved renown as a member of the Scriblerus club and as creator of the British national character, John Bull. A distinguished physician, Arbuthnot was highly regarded as a mathematician and philosopher by his contemporaries. Convivial, a lover of food, wine, cards, and music, he attracted friends among the most distinguished men and women of his era. His conservative principles and keen wit inspired, in Alexander Pope's words, "raillery / on every learned sot" and on many Whigs, while he shared his scientific interests in essays on ancient coins, on diet, and on the effects of air. Yet Arbuthnot often published anonymously, and his association with Jonathan Swift, Pope, and John Gay led to misattributions of his work by early readers and editors. As a result, his canon is still disputed, and may never be fixed.

John Arbuthnot was christened on 29 April 1667, the son of the Reverend Alexander and Margaret Lammy Arbuthnott of Kincardineshire, Scotland. The Reverend Alexander Arbuthnott's patron and kinsman, Robert, Lord Arbuthnott, presided over the parish named for his family. The eldest of eight children, John was sent to Marischal College in Aberdeen and received his master's degree in 1685. In 1689 his Jacobite father was forced to retire after refusing to conform to the newly reinstated Presbyterian church. He died in February 1691, but burial was delayed until John returned to the Kirk the session book that his father had taken with him when he retired. Lord Arbuthnott further stipulated that no epitaph critical of government policy or the current incumbent would be permitted over the grave. Young John seems to have declined raising any monument under these conditions, and left Scotland soon afterward to seek his career in London. There, he appears to have boarded with William Pate, an erudite woolen merchant, and to have supported himself by teaching mathematics.

Of Arbuthnot's early career, little is known, although his first publication reflected his intellectual interests as well as his favorite entertainment. *Of the Laws of Chance* (1692) chiefly translated Christiaan Huygens's *De rationiis in ludo Aleae*, a demonstration to laymen of the laws of probability, applied to dice and card games. In 1694 he enrolled at University College, Oxford, evidently as companion and tutor to Edward Jef-

freys, son of an M.P. While there, he made lasting friendships with such learned men as Dr. Arthur Charlett, Master of University College, and Dr. David Gregory, Savilian Professor of Astronomy. By 1696, however, young Jeffreys's "unsteddiness" made Arbuthnot "resolv'd on some other course of life," and he proceeded to St. Andrews University, where after examination he was awarded a Doctor of Medicine degree. By 1697 Arbuthnot was back in London and soon married Margaret, of whom little is known but her Christian name. The couple eventually had four children who survived to adulthood—George (1703), Charles (1705), Margaret, and Anne—and six who died. Arbuthnot soon established himself as a wit and scholar as well as a physician. His second publication, *An Examination of Dr. Woodward's Account of the Deluge* (1697), indicated Arbuthnot's relish for intellectual controversy. He wittily exposed the illogic of John Woodward's hypotheses that Noah's flood had been caused by water erupting from the earth's center, and that fossils were the remains of life before the flood, dissolved and drawn to various strata by gravity. Arbuthnot graciously acknowledged Woodward's achievement, but his objections led to years of conflict with the doctor and his partisans.

Arbuthnot also participated in the nascent vogue for what Richard Steele called bringing philosophy to the tea table. *An Essay on the Usefulness of Mathematical Learning* (1701) is a "letter" recommending the study of mathematics to young gentlemen at Oxford, not only as the basis of most scientific and professional pursuits, but also to acquire "a vigorous constitution of mind." Arbuthnot's *Tables of the Grecian, Roman and Jewish Measures, Weights and Coins* (1705; expanded in 1727) similarly seeks to digest recent scholarship in philology and antiquity for the use of "young Gentlemen." "An Argument for Divine Providence, taken from the constant regularity observed in the Births of both Sexes" (*Philosophical Transactions*, 1710) draws on earlier studies of the Bills of Mortality, concluding that the proportion of males to females consistently defies the laws of probability, and thus must be the work of God. Arbuthnot's use of statistics was not original, but reflected the interest in philosophical-theological speculation characteristic of intellectuals such as Sir Isaac Newton and Woodward. For such works, and for his growing medical reputation, Arbuthnot was named a fellow of the Royal Society in 1704. There, he served on two controversial

This portrait of Arbuthnot, by Sir Godfrey Kneller, once hung in the home of Alexander Pope (by permission of the Hunterian Art Gallery, Glasgow)

committees. The first, organized in late 1704 and including Newton and Sir Christopher Wren, was directed to supervise publication of the Astronomer Royal's catalogue of the stars. Unfortunately, the Astronomer Royal, Rev. John Flamsteed, despised Newton, and Arbuthnot's role as go-between in the ensuing conflict deteriorated, leaving Flamsteed permanently resentful. The other committee was formed in 1712 to declare whether Newton or Gottfried Wilhelm Leibniz had invented infinitesimal calculus. The committee, mostly Newton's colleagues, soon concluded in his favor.

Arbuthnot's career as political satirist

evolved from his appointment as Physician Extraordinary to Queen Anne in 1705. According to tradition, the doctor had treated Prince George at Epsom. Another tradition suggests that Arbuthnot was already physician to the queen's children. His service was evidently successful, for after the prince's death, Arbuthnot was named Physician Ordinary to Queen Anne in 1709. His Tory opinions and loyalty to the British rulers were by then firmly established. In 1706 he had published *A Sermon preach'd to the People at the Mercat-Cross*, eloquently persuading the Scottish people of the advantages of the Act of

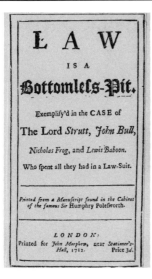

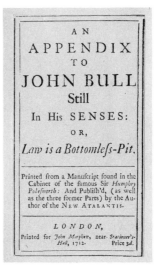

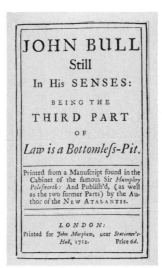

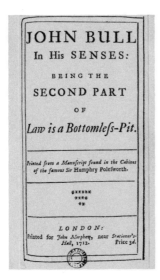

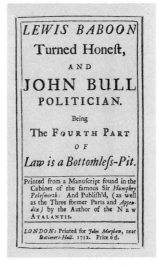

Title pages for the five pamphlets that were later collected as Arbuthnot's History of John Bull

Union. By 1711 Arbuthnot was associated with Robert Harley, Lord Oxford's ministry, and had reputed influence, through Mrs. Abigail Masham, on the queen. At about this time he became friends with Jonathan Swift, an association that propelled him to the center of political controversy and into a bond with the greatest Tory writers of his day. Their intimacy grew throughout the duration of the Brothers Club, Henry St. John, Viscount Bolingbroke's rival to the Whig Kit-Cat Club. Swift evidently encouraged Arbuthnot's taste for humorous satire and for literary pranks, such as tricking the maids of honor into subscribing to a nonexistent book.

Swift, however, was involved in a crucial project: the defense of Oxford's ministry as the Tories sought to end the War of the Spanish Succession. In December 1711 John Churchill, Duke of Marlborough's effort to prolong the war nearly prevailed when the Whigs persuaded Daniel Finch, Earl of Nottingham, a High-Church Tory, to move the House of Lords' support for the war in exchange for their support of the Act of Occasional Conformity. Only the Queen's last-minute creation of twelve Tory peers preserved the ministry and its majority. Swift, Harley's propagandist in *The Examiner*, now produced *The Conduct of the Allies* (November 1711, with 1712 on its title page) and *Some Remarks on the Barrier-Treaty* (February 1712), accusing Marlborough and the former Whig ministry of mismanagement and deceit in their pursuit of the war. He undoubtedly encouraged Arbuthnot's contribution to the peace effort, a series of five pamphlets which appeared from March to July 1712, *The History of John Bull*. *The History of John Bull* is not only Arbuthnot's most sustained literary achievement, but also, according to Thomas Babington Macaulay, in his *History of England* (1848-1861), "the most ingenious and humorous political satire extant in our language." In his tale of John Bull's lawsuit with his neighbors against Lewis Baboon, Arbuthnot captured the essence of British national identity and of British prejudices against Europeans. He also managed to present potentially controversial behavior, such as the Tory ministry's neglect of Britain's allies in the peace negotiations, as wise policy.

The first John Bull pamphlet, *Law is a Bottomless-Pit*, appeared on 4 March 1712. *John Bull in His Senses* followed on 17 March, *John Bull Still in His Senses* on 16 April, and *An Appendix to John Bull Still in His Senses* on 9 May. The final pamphlet, *Lewis Baboon turned Honest, and John Bull Politician*, was published on 31 July. Each pamphlet develops the analogy, suggested in various contemporary essays, between Britain's involvement in the European war and a legal dispute among neighbors over an estate. Arbuthnot skillfully manipulates seemingly disparate aspects of British political dissension, weaving them into the story of John Bull's domestic and legal woes.

In *Law is a Bottomless-Pit*, John Bull (the British), a clothier, and Nicholas Frog (the Dutch), a linen merchant, joined in a lawsuit against Philip Baboon, Lord Strutt (King Philip of Spain), when young Strutt inherited his estate and neglected his family's traditional drapers, preferring the wares of his grandfather, wealthy and crafty Lewis Baboon (Louis XIV, Bourbon King of France). Supported by various other tradesmen representing allied states, and by Esquire South (Austria), Bull and Frog employed Humphrey Hocus (Marlborough) as their attorney. As Arbuthnot interpreted recent events, John Bull finally "came to his senses" and realized that his wife (the recent Whig ministry) and Hocus were lovers. After her death, he acquired a wise new wife (Oxford's ministry), examined his accounts, and reached an agreement with Lewis at the Salutation Tavern (Utrecht) despite the objections of Frog. Arbuthnot also portrays the Act of Union as John's reconciliation with his sister, Peg (Scotland). His tale about Peg's lover Jack (the Dissenters) exposes the religious controversies of the past decade as political manipulation.

Thus, while some early critics thought the episodes of Peg and Jack destroyed the "unity" of the John Bull pamphlets, their story contributes to Arbuthnot's argument that the long war was responsible for a wide range of economic, political, and religious troubles. In fact, the chief distinction of Arbuthnot's allegory is his manner of drawing together disparate techniques and materials into a coherent narrative. His style, for example, reflects several devices popular among political propagandists: the allegory, the beast fable, and the "secret history." His personifications represent persons, institutions, and nations, yet appear as credible actors in Bull's disputes. Arbuthnot's material encompasses facts and rumors, past events and projected conclusions, combined into a defense of current policy. Most clever, perhaps, is his reduction of complex issues to a mundane scenario, persuasive in its deceptive clarity. The characters' brisk, colloquial speech renders the intricate negotiations between Britain and France as the plain dealing of two experienced merchants:

> *L. Baboon*: I know of no particular Mark of Veracity, amongst us Tradesmen, but Interest; and it is manifestly mine not to deceive you at this time; you may safely trust me, I can assure you.
> *J. Bull*: The Trust I give is in short this, I must have something in hand before I make the Bargain, and the rest before it is concluded.
> *L. Baboon*: To shew you I deal fairly, name your Something.

The tale's national characters personify British prejudices—the Dutch are selfish and frugal; the French, sly and fickle—but Arbuthnot makes lively, even plausible, neighbors of his caricatures. In each case, he gives the nation its due: Frog is a more diligent merchant than Bull; Baboon excels his younger neighbors in vitality, so that the tale is not merely xenophobic. In Peg, Arbuthnot created a Scottish character of some complexity, psychologically plausible in her demand for deferential treatment. John Bull himself, of course, has lived on in the British imagination as the epitome of their collective personality. He is described in the first pamphlet:

> Bull, in the main, was an honest plain-dealing Fellow, Cholerick, Bold, and of a very unconstant Temper, he dreaded not Old *Lewis* either at Back-Sword, single Faulchion, or Cudgel-play; but then he was very apt to quarrel with his best Friends, especially if they pretended to govern him: If you flatter'd him, you might lead him like a Child.

With their intriguingly detailed fable, revealed in *John Bull Still in His Senses* as the "private Memoirs" of "the famous Sir *Humphrey Polesworth*," the John Bull pamphlets were immediately reprinted, "Key'd," answered, and imitated. Arbuthnot soon contributed another piece, a mock-proposal for *A Treatise of the Art of Political Lying* (1712). In this pamphlet, Arbuthnot outlines the eleven chapters of the first volume of the treatise, defining political lying as "the art of convincing the people of salutory falsehoods, for some good end." As might be expected, the Whigs excel in this art, for "we could not have carried on the war so long without several of these salutory falsehoods."

In 1713 Swift included Arbuthnot in a select club dedicated to his friend Alexander Pope's plan for a periodical burlesquing the works of the learned. John Gay, Thomas Parnell, and Lord Treasurer Oxford also participated. The group's chief project, *Memoirs of Martinus Scriblerus*, was not published until 1741, and then a severely edited version appeared in volume two of Pope's prose works. Many scholars credit Arbuthnot as the chief inspirer of the Scriblerian's tale of an eccentric pedant who, in Pope's words, "had dipped into every art and science, but injudiciously in each." With his erudition and amused scorn of "learned sots," Arbuthnot was the logical source of such episodes in Martin's life as his father Cornelius's provision of "ancient" playthings and musical instruments, and his attempts to convey philosophy to Martin and his companion, Conrad Crambe. In an obvious allusion to Arbuthnot's old nemesis, Cornelius chose to "exhibit" his infant son on a rusty "ancient" shield suspiciously like the famous artifact long claimed as a "votive shield" by Woodward. When a housemaid scoured the rust of his beloved shield, Cornelius dropped both shield and infant, exclaiming, "Where, where is the Crust that cover'd thee so long? . . . where all those beautiful obscurities, the cause of so much delightful disputation, where doubt and curiosity went hand in hand, and eternally exercised the speculations of the learned?"

Although the death of Queen Anne on 1 August 1714 scattered the short-lived club, Arbuthnot's association with Pope, Swift, and Gay continued, as he collaborated with, and contributed to the works of, his fellow Scriblerians. John Gay's play *Three Hours After Marriage* (1717) brought a torrent of critical abuse upon Gay, Arbuthnot, and Pope, particularly for the play's thinly disguised parody of Dr. Woodward as the credulous Dr. Fossile. In 1727 Pope and Swift included the John Bull series and *The Art of Political Lying* in their second volume of *Miscellanies*, *The History of John Bull* in a version that Pope seems to have edited to render the pamphlets a coherent narrative. Arbuthnot evidently helped Pope assemble his *Peri Bathous; or, the Art of Sinking in Poetry* (1727), a satire of modern (mostly Whig) poetry. Later, after *Peri Bathous* had wrung from Pope's antagonists the responses he edited to annotate his *Dunciad*, Arbuthnot contributed an appendix to *The Dunciad Variorum* (1729). "Virgilius Restauratus" parodies Lewis Theobald's style and method in *Shakespeare Restored* (1726), the work exposing Pope's inadequacies as Shakespearean editor that earned "Tibbald" his title of King Dunce. A final piece, "An Essay of the Learned Martinus Scriblerus, Concerning the Origin of Sciences," ap-

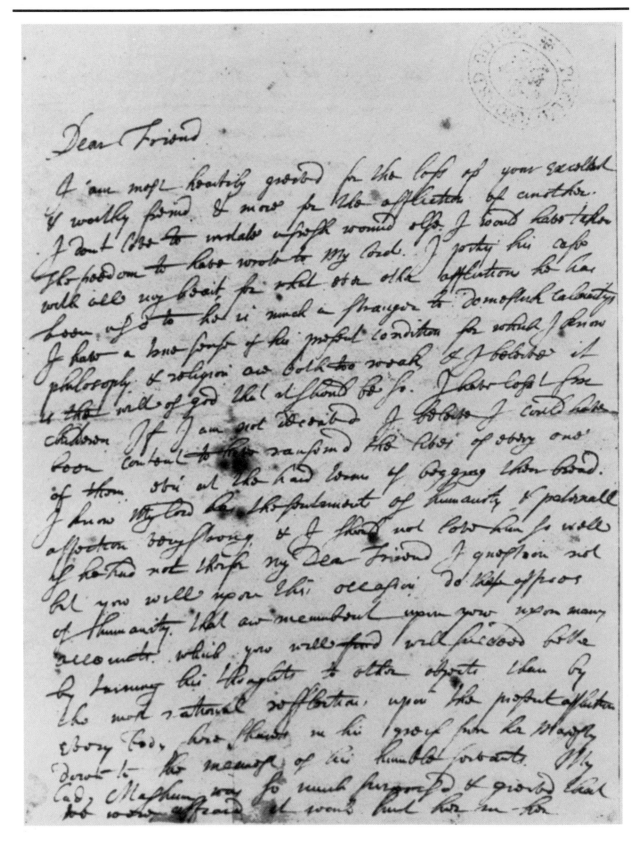

Letter from Arbuthnot to Jonathan Swift (November 1713), written after the death of Elizabeth Harley, Marchioness of Carmarthen, daughter of Robert Harley, Earl of Oxford (Public Record Office, London)

present condition. I am glad I did not know my Lady Carmarthen's will as you but I know enough to believe her a most valuable person I have nothing left to wish for my Lord in a fortune in this case but that you would prosper the loss of the poor child to be some comfort to him I believe it will not be a good way for my Lord to keep up but to appear as soon as possible again in his business I know by experience that the best cure is by diverting the thoughts. I hope we may see you here next Saturday. You friend, to remember you kindly I am

Dear Sir

Your affectionate Brother
& most humble servant

Jo. Arbuthnott

I take your opportunity to make my compliments to My Lord. I am truly praying to him & I have the vanity to think he would do for me upon such an occasion.

peared in the so-called third volume of Pope and Swift's *Miscellanies* (1732), which was actually the fourth. Martinus reported from the Nubian desert that he had traced the arts and sciences back to an ancient tribe of pygmies.

After Anne's death, Arbuthnot lost his post as Royal Physician. He moved from his rooms at St. James's, first to Piccadilly (1714), later to Burlington Gardens (circa 1728). Although no longer at the center of political events, he continued his intellectual and literary pursuits as well as his medical practice, and maintained his large circle of friends. His brothers Robert (a Rouen banker) and George were by then agents of the Old Pretender (James Francis Edward Stuart, the only son of James II), their activities monitored by the new ministry, but Arbuthnot's loyalty to the Hanoverians was never seriously questioned. He continued his humorous attacks on the "excesses" of modern science and its inventions. *The Humble Petition of the Colliers, Cooks, Cook-Maids, Blacksmiths, Jack-makers, Brasiers, and others* (1716) bemoans the virtuosi's invention of "catoptrical" lenses to harness solar heat and light. "Catoptrical victuallers" could ruin those whose livelihoods depended on conventional cooking methods. In 1719 a medical debate erupted over the proper treatment of smallpox. While Dr. John Freind championed purgation, Dr. Woodward recommended emetics. Contemporaries attributed two ribald pamphlets on the conflict, *An Account of the Sickness and Death of Dr. W-dw-d* and *The Life and Adventures of Don Bilioso de l'Estomac*, to Arbuthnot. And in *Reasons humbly offer'd by the Company exercising the Trade and Mystery of Upholders* (1724), Arbuthnot supported the physicians' request for a bill forbidding apothecaries to dispense medicine without prescriptions. In that pamphlet, London's undertakers complained that the bill would bankrupt them.

Meanwhile, Arbuthnot's career, and his other interests, flourished. In 1723 the Royal College of Physicians named him Second Censor; in 1727, an Elect. The latter honor stipulated delivery of the annual Harvean oration. Arbuthnot's, in October 1727, was an elegant classical recapitulation of the medical profession. Arbuthnot also continued his attacks on Whig policies. He is often credited with "The Quidnunki's" (1724), a tetrameter ballad that represents the endless cycle of political vice as the antics of a tribe of Indian monkeys. In *A Brief Account of Mr. John Ginglicutt's Treatise* (1731), the son of a City fishmonger defends "the calling of names" among politicians as "true Greek and Roman eloquence." Arbuthnot's final political comment, however, is his most bitter. His "Epitaph on Francis Charteris" (*London Magazine*, April 1732) denounces the debauched colonel as "Proof and example / Of how small estimation is exorbitant wealth / In the sight of God, by his bestowing it on / The most unworthy of all mortals." Because of his close association with Sir Robert Walpole, Charteris seemed to Arbuthnot and the Scriblerians the epitome of twisted Whig values.

Dr. Arbuthnot suffered from asthma, gout, and chronic kidney stones throughout his last years. His wife, Margaret, died in 1730, and his youngest son, Charles, in 1731. An added sorrow was Gay's death in 1732, after Arbuthnot's attendance at his deathbed. Throughout these losses, however, Arbuthnot continued to write on various topics. His *Essay Concerning the Nature of Aliments* (1731) and *Essay Concerning the Effects of Air on Human Bodies* (1733) consider the importance of diet and climate to human health. A final poem, *Gnothi Seauton. Know Yourself* (1734), echoed Pope's *Essay on Man* (1732-1734) in its reflections on humanity's place in the creation: "In vain thou hop'st for bliss on this poor clod, / Return, and seek thy father, and thy God." On 27 February 1735, Arbuthnot died from a painful abcess of the bowels. He had long considered his illness fatal, telling Swift and Pope that he asked only for a peaceful death. Not long after Arbuthnot died, Pope wrote to the doctor's son George, "There can be but one happy of your whole Family at this hour. I doubt not He is so."

Arbuthnot's canon has never been defined. Some pamphlets included in the first collection of his works (1751) are almost certainly not his. On the other hand, Swift has been credited with such works as *The History of John Bull* by early editors and some modern scholars. Because Arbuthnot rarely acknowledged his publications, scholars are still discovering and analyzing works for possible inclusion in the canon. As for *The Memoirs of Martinus Scriblerus*, the extent of Arbuthnot's contribution may never be ascertained.

But Arbuthnot's reputation, like his life, is characterized by resilience. On his deathbed, he inspired Pope's "Epistle to Dr. Arbuthnot" when he wrote his friend a moving letter asking the poet to continue his campaign against vice, but in less personal, less dangerous language. In the resulting poem, Pope celebrated Arbuthnot as "Friend to my Life, (which did not you prolong, / The World had wanted many an idle Song.)" Despite

John Arbuthnot (portrait by William Robinson; by permission of the Trustees of the National Museums of Scotland)

his friendships with such noted Tories as Harley, Bolingbroke, Swift, and Pope, Arbuthnot retained his name for candor among people of both parties. For example, Lady Mary Wortley Montagu turned to Arbuthnot for assistance when stung by Pope's satire. He was esteemed as a mathematician and philosopher, although he disclaimed any pretension to rigorous scholarship. He gave abundant hints and assistance to his friends, heedless of his own manuscripts (a modern editor described his very handwriting as careless); yet he survives in most accounts as the leading spirit among the Scriblerians. His serious medical and scientific treatises long ago lost their

value, but John Bull lives on in the British imagination. When Samuel Johnson refers to Arbuthnot in his *Life of Pope* (1781) as "able to animate his mass of knowledge by a bright and active imagination," he perhaps best describes Arbuthnot's gift, the source of his lasting achievement.

Letters:

"The Correspondence of Dr. John Arbuthnot," edited by Angus Ross, Ph.D. dissertation, Cambridge University, 1956;

The Correspondence of Alexander Pope, 5 volumes, edited by George Sherburn (Oxford: Clarendon Press, 1956);

The Correspondence of Jonathan Swift, 5 volumes, edited by Harold Williams (Oxford: Clarendon Press, 1963-1965).

Biography:
George A. Aitken, *The Life and Works of John Arbuthnot* (Oxford: Clarendon Press, 1892).

References:
Lester M. Beattie, *John Arbuthnot: Mathematician and Satirist* (Cambridge, Mass.: Harvard University Press, 1935);

Patricia Köster, "Swift, Arbuthnot, and the Law," *American Notes and Queries*, 7 (February 1969): 83-84;

Köster, ed., *Arbuthnotiana*, Augustan Reprint Society Publication, no. 154 (Los Angeles: William A. Clark Memorial Library, 1972);

Köster, ed., "Arbuthnot's Use of Quotation and Parody in His Account of the Sacheverell Affair," *Philological Quarterly*, 48 (April 1969): 201-211;

Joseph A. Levine, *Dr. Woodward's Shield: History, Science, and Satire in Augustan England* (Berkeley: University of California Press, 1977);

Thomas F. Mayo, "The Authorship of the History of John Bull," *PMLA*, 45 (March 1930): 274-282;

Wolfgang Michael, "Who is John Bull?" *Contemporary Review*, 144 (September 1933): 314-319;

Angus Ross, "Notes on the Letters of Dr. Arbuthnot," *The Scriblerian*, 2 (Autumn 1969): 1-2;

Robert C. Steensma, *Dr. John Arbuthnot* (Boston: Twayne, 1979);

Dennis Todd, "New Evidence for Dr. Arbuthnot's Authorship of 'The Rabbit-Man-Midwife,'" *Studies in Bibliography*, 41 (1988): 247-267.

Papers:
Papers relating to Arbuthnot remain in private collections throughout England. In his biography, George Aitken cites the British Museum, the Bodleian Library, and the Advocates' Library as sources.

George Berkeley

(12 March 1685 - 14 January 1753)

Kenneth P. Winkler
Wellesley College

See also "Eighteenth-Century Background: George Berkeley," in *DLB 31: American Colonial Writers, 1735-1781*.

BOOKS: *Arithmetica absque algebra aut Euclide demonstrata* and *Miscellanea Mathemetica* (London: Typis J. Matthews, impensis A. & J. Churchill and J. Pepyat, Dublin, 1707);

An Essay towards a New Theory of Vision (Dublin: Printed by A. Rhames for J. Pepyat, 1709; revised, 1709); revised again and published with *Alciphron*, volume 2 (London: Printed for J. Tonson, 1732; revised again, 1732);

A Treatise concerning the Principles of Human Knowledge. Part I. Wherein the chief causes of error and difficulty in the sciences, with the grounds of scepticism, atheism, and irreligion, are inquir'd into (Dublin: Printed by A. Rhames for J. Pepyat, 1710); revised and published with *Three Dialogues between Hylas and Philonous* (London: Printed for J. Tonson, 1734);

Passive Obedience, or the Christian doctrine of not resisting the supreme power, proved and vindicated upon the principle of the law of nature. In a discourse deliver'd at the College-chappel (Dublin: Printed by F. Dickson for J. Pepyat, 1712; London: Printed for H. Clements, 1712);

Three Dialogues between Hylas and Philonous. The design of which is plainly to demonstrate the reality and perfection of humane knowledge, the incorporeal nature of the soul, and the immediate providence of a deity: in opposition to sceptics and atheists. Also, to open a method for rendering the sciences more easy, useful, and compendious (London: Printed by G. James for Henry Clements, 1713); revised and published with *A Treatise Concerning the Principles of Human Knowledge*, 2 volumes (London: Printed for J. Tonson, 1734);

Advice to the Tories Who Have Taken the Oaths (London: Printed by R. Baldwin & sold by R. Burleigh, 1715);

De Motu: sive, de motus principio & natura, et de causa communicationis mottum (London: Impensis J. Tonson, 1721);

An Essay towards Preventing the ruine of Great Britain (London: Sold by J. Roberts, 1721);

A Proposal for the Better Supplying of Churches in our Foreign Plantations, and for converting the Savage Americans to Christianity (London: Printed by H. Woodfall, 1724; revised, 1725);

A Sermon preached before the Incorporated Society for the Propagation of the Gospel in Foreign Parts (London: Printed by J. Downing, 1732);

Alciphron: or, the Minute Philosopher. In seven dialogues. Containing an apology for the Christian religion, against those who are called free-thinkers, 2 volumes [includes *An Essay Towards a New Theory of Vision*] (London: Printed for J. Tonson, 1732; revised, 1732); revised again and republished without *A New Theory of Vision*, 1 volume (London: Printed for J. & R. Tonson & S. Draper, 1752; New Haven: Increase, Cooke & Co., 1803);

The Theory of Vision, or Visual Language, shewing the immediate presence and providence of a deity, vindicated and explained (London: Printed for J. Tonson, 1733);

The Analyst: or, a discourse addressed to an infidel mathematician. Wherein it is examined whether the object, principles, and inferences of the modern analysis are more distinctly conceived, or more evidently deduced, than religious mysteries and points of faith (London: Printed for J. Tonson, 1734);

A Defence of Free-Thinking in Mathematics. In answer to a pamphlet of Philalethes Cantabrigiensis, intituled, Geometry no friend to infidelity, or a defence of Sir Isaac Newton, and the British mathematicians. Also an appendix concerning Mr. Walton's Vindication of the principle of fluxions against the objections contained in the ANALYST. Wherein it is attempted to put this controversy in such a light as that every reader may be able to judge thereof. By the author of The mi-

George Berkeley circa 1729 (portrait by John Smibert; by permission of the Massachusetts Historical Society)

nute *philosopher.* (Dublin: Printed by M. Rhames for R. Gunne, 1735; London: Printed for J. Tonson, 1735);

Reasons for not replying to Mr. Walton's full Answer in a letter to P. T. P. (Dublin: Printed by M. Rhames for R. Gunne, 1735);

The Querist, containing several queries, proposed to the consideration of the public, Part I (Dublin: Printed by R. Reilly for G. Risk, G. Ewing & W. Smith, 1735; London: Printed for J. Roberts, 1736); Part II (Dublin: Printed by R. Reilly for G. Risk, G. Ewing & W. Smith, 1736; London: Printed for J. Roberts, 1736); Part III (Dublin: Printed by R. Reilly for Jos. Leathley, 1737; London: Printed for J. Roberts, 1736); revised edition, Parts I-III (Dublin: Printed by G. Faulkner, 1750);

Queries relating to a National Bank, Extracted from the Querist. Also a Letter containing a plan or sketch of such a bank (Dublin: Printed & sold by George Faulkner, 1737);

A Discourse Addressed to Magistrates and Men in Authority (Dublin: Printed by George Faulkner, 1738);

Siris: a chain of philosophical reflexions and inquiries concerning the virtues of tar-water, and divers other subjects connected together and arising one from another (Dublin: Printed by M. Rhames for R. Gunne, 1744; London: Printed for C. Hitch & C. Davis, 1744; revised edition, Dublin: Printed by M. Rhames for R. Gunne, 1744; London: Printed for Innys, Hitch & Davis, 1744);

A Letter to T----- P----, Esq.; From the Author of Siris. Containing Some Farther Remarks on the Virtues

Kilkenny College, where Berkeley was enrolled in 1696 (engraving by Greig circa 1795, after a drawing by G. Holmes). Other distinguished alumni of the school include Jonathan Swift and William Congreve, who graduated in the 1680s.

of Tar-Water (Dublin: Printed by George Faulkner, 1744);

Two Letters from the Right Reverend Dr. George Berkeley . . . The One to Thomas Prior Esq. Concerning the usefulness of Tar-Water in the Plague. . . . The Other to the Rev. Dr. Hales, on the Benefit of Tar-Water in Fevers (London: Printed for W. Innys, C. Hitch & M. Cooper, and C. Davis, 1747);

A Word to the Wise; Or, An Exhortation to the Roman Catholic Clergy of Ireland (Dublin: Printed by George Faulkner, 1749; Boston: Printed & sold by S. Kneeland, 1750);

Maxims Concerning Patriotism. By a Lady (Dublin, 1750);

A miscellany, containing several tracts on various subjects (Dublin: Printed by G. Faulkner, 1752).

Editions: *The Works of George Berkeley*, 2 volumes (Dublin: Printed by John Exshaw, 1784);

The Works of George Berkeley, 4 volumes, edited by A. C. Fraser (Oxford: Clarendon Press, 1871; revised, 1901);

Berkeley's Commonplace Book, edited by G. A. Johnston (London: Faber & Faber, 1930);

Philosophical Commentaries, Generally Called the Commonplace Book, edited by A. A. Luce (London & New York: Nelson, 1944);

The Works of George Berkeley, Bishop of Cloyne, 9 volumes, edited by A. A. Luce and T. E. Jessop (London: Nelson, 1948-1957);

Philosophical Commentaries, edited by George H. Thomas (Alliance, Ohio, 1976; reprinted, New York: Garland, 1989);

The Notebooks of George Berkeley, edited by Desireé Park (Oxford: Alden Press, 1984)—a facsimile of British Library Add. MS. 39305;

George Berkeley's Manuscript Introduction, edited by Bertil Belfrage (Oxford: Doxa, 1987).

George Berkeley is best known for his denial of matter and for a series of arguments which, according to David Hume, "*admit of no answer and produce no conviction.*" James Boswell offered a similar assessment: "though we are satisfied [Berkeley's] doctrine is not true," he said to Samuel Johnson, "it is impossible to refute it."

He reported that Johnson disagreed: "I never shall forget the alacrity with which Johnson answered, striking his foot with mighty force against a large stone, till he rebounded from it,—'I refute it *thus*.'" Boswell interpreted Johnson's gesture as a "stout exemplification" of the first truths or original principles without which, Boswell insisted, "we can no more argue in metaphysicks, than we can argue in mathematicks without axioms." But any axiom can safely be expressed in words, and in choosing to act rather than argue, Johnson may have been suggesting that some truths, unlike axioms, are best left unarticulated. Whatever his intention, Johnson's "refutation" dominates our memory of Berkeley: for many Berkeley is the clearest example of an abstract thinker no longer at home in the everyday, the philosopher unable to remember he is still a man. But when his philosophical writings are placed alongside his books and pamphlets on psychology, politics, physics, the Christian religion, mathematics, economics, and public health, and when all of these are seen in the context of his life, the man who emerges is marked not by inhumane abstraction, but by a passionate absorption in the concrete.

George Berkeley, the first son of William and Eliza Berkeley, was born on 12 March 1685 at Kilkenny, Ireland. "I was distrustful," George confessed in his notebooks, "at 8 years old." He entered Kilkenny College, where Jonathan Swift and William Congreve had been students, in 1696, a few months after his eleventh birthday. There is no record of his studies at Kilkenny, but "A Description of the Cave of Dunmore," written from memory in 1706 (probably for delivery to a philosophical society in Dublin), records a visit to the cave with schoolmates in 1699. The manuscript describes the rocks in the cave's ceilings and walls, as well as the bones Berkeley discovered at the bottom of a spring-fed pool. "I have every where endeavoured," its author explains, "to raise in yr imagination the same ideas I had myself when I saw it as far as I could call to mind at the distance of almost seven years." He was later to urge the reader of his *Treatise concerning the Principles of Human Knowledge* (1710) to "make my words the occasion of his own thinking, and endeavour to attain the same train of thoughts in reading, that I had in writing them."

In March of 1700 Berkeley entered Trinity College, Dublin. John Locke's *Essay concerning Human Understanding*, published in 1690, was already being read by some of the students there.

The presence of Locke's essay at the college was largely the work of William Molyneux, the leading Irish scientist of his day, whose own book on optics—the first on the subject in the English language—influenced Berkeley's work on vision.

Berkeley received his bachelor's degree in 1704. He remained at the college to compete for a fellowship, and he won one in June of 1707. It was then that he began to fill the notebooks now known as the *Philosophical Commentaries*.

Berkeley's notebooks were discovered in the nineteenth century but properly edited—in successively more accurate versions by G. A. Johnston, A. A. Luce, and George H. Thomas—only in the twentieth. The nearly nine hundred entries are a record of immaterialism in embryo. They chart Berkeley's study of Locke, Nicolas Malebranche, Isaac Newton, and René Descartes, and the liberating discovery of what he called "the Principle": "Existere is percipi or percipere" (or as he later added in a facing-page correction, "or velle i:e agere"): to be is to be perceived or to perceive (or to will, i:e., to act). The principle divided all of reality into two categories: the active minds who perceive and will, and the passive objects of perception—the ideas—whose existence depends on the thoughts and operations of mind or spirit.

Berkeley's first important publication, *An Essay towards a New Theory of Vision*, published in 1709, was a contribution to what is now called cognitive psychology—an attempt to explain how we perceive by sight the distance, magnitude, and situation of objects. Although Berkeley had already embraced immaterialism, he wrote as if the objects of touch have an existence independent of the mind. "Not that to suppose that vulgar error, was necessary for establishing the notion therein laid down"; he later explained, "but because it was beside my purpose to examine and refute it in a discourse concerning *vision*."

The treatment of distance served as a model for magnitude and situation. Berkeley followed Descartes, Malebranche, and Molyneux in assuming that distance is not seen directly. It must therefore be seen by means of something else. Earlier writers had suggested that when objects are relatively close, we compute their distance by an innate or natural geometry. The optic axes—the lines drawn from each eye to the object—form a larger angle when the object is near, and a smaller angle when the object is distant. We judge the distance, they proposed, by considering the size of the angle, just as a blind man, in an illustration made famous by Descartes, judges the distance of an object by the size of the angle formed by the sticks he uses to touch it. The same writers suggested that we also make use of nongeometrical distance cues: the fuzziness of the object (which suggests greater distance), our past experience of objects of the same sort, and the apparent size of the objects in their environment.

Berkeley's own theory dispensed entirely with computation and innate geometry. He suggested that we rely on visual cues contingently connected with distance, cues whose value can be determined only by experience. The cues or signs he emphasized were the sensation of the disposition or "turn" of the eyes, the fuzziness of the object, and the strain we feel as we struggle to keep the object in focus. The first cue is reminiscent of the blind man's sticks, but Berkeley insisted that geometrical principles play no role. We simply learn to associate a certain feeling with a certain distance. There is no necessary connection between the feeling and what it signifies, and no way of discovering a priori that one goes along with the other.

Berkeley held that distance is immediately perceived only by touch. To *see* distance is to coordinate ideas of vision with the objects of touch, which include one's own body and its movements. The "outwardness" of a visual idea is the result of its habitual association with bodily movements and other tactual objects.

The contingent connection between the objects of sight and touch supplied Berkeley with an answer to "Molyneux's Question," a question first posed by Molyneux in a letter to Locke, who quoted it in the second edition (1694) of the *Essay concerning Human Understanding*: would a man born blind, suddenly made to see, be able to tell, without touching, which of two objects was the cube and which the sphere? Locke and Molyneux were sure that the answer is no; Berkeley thought he could explain why they were right. Because there is no necessary connection between the objects of sight and touch—no connection permitting us to say, a priori, that one object is the mark or sign of another—the blind man, denied the relevant experience, can do no more than guess.

Because the ideas of vision are arbitrary signs of the objects of touch, Berkeley viewed them as a language, a visual language in which the Author of Nature speaks to us of the tactual objects to come. The world is not a machine, blindly obeying laws long ago laid down by a now-indifferent God. It is a text or speech, renewed and extended at every moment, and bespeaking a continuing providence. Like a text or speech, its signs have no real power over what they signify. They are useful to us not because of what they bring about, but because of the divine intentions they communicate.

As a junior fellow at Trinity Berkeley held a series of annual academic and administrative appointments, among them librarian (1709), junior dean (1710, 1711), and junior Greek lecturer (1712). He preached his first sermon at the college chapel in 1708, and he was ordained an Anglican priest in the spring of 1710. In the same year he published his most important work, *A Treatise concerning the Principles of Human Knowledge*.

Berkeley's medium as a philosopher was argument or debate, and the *Principles* is relentlessly argumentative. In the first thirty-three numbered paragraphs or sections, Berkeley develops at least six different arguments for immaterialism. He devotes the next fifty sections to a give-and-take with imaginary interlocutors. He then examines the consequences of immaterialism for skepticism, science, mathematics, and belief in God.

Berkeley's first argument for immaterialism turns on the meaning of the word *exist*, when applied to sensible things: "The table I write on, I say, exists, that is, I see and feel it; and if I were out of my study I should say it existed, meaning thereby that if I was in my study I might perceive it, or that some other spirit actually does perceive it." The existence of sensible objects is thereby reduced to its lived meaning. The reduction testifies to Berkeley's absorption in the concrete, his impatience with claims that cannot be cashed out in life.

A second argument joins the commonsense conviction that we perceive objects such as houses, mountains, and rivers to the philosophical discovery that we perceive only our own ideas. It follows, Berkeley argues, that ordinary objects can be nothing but ideas. An obvious objection is that we need to distinguish between direct and indirect perception: ideas are the only objects of direct or immediate perception, but houses, mountains, and rivers are perceived indirectly, by means of the ideas that represent them. But Berkeley argues that there is no relation by which ideas can represent external objects.

A third argument replies to the distinction between primary and secondary qualities. Berkeley's materialist opponents believed that every

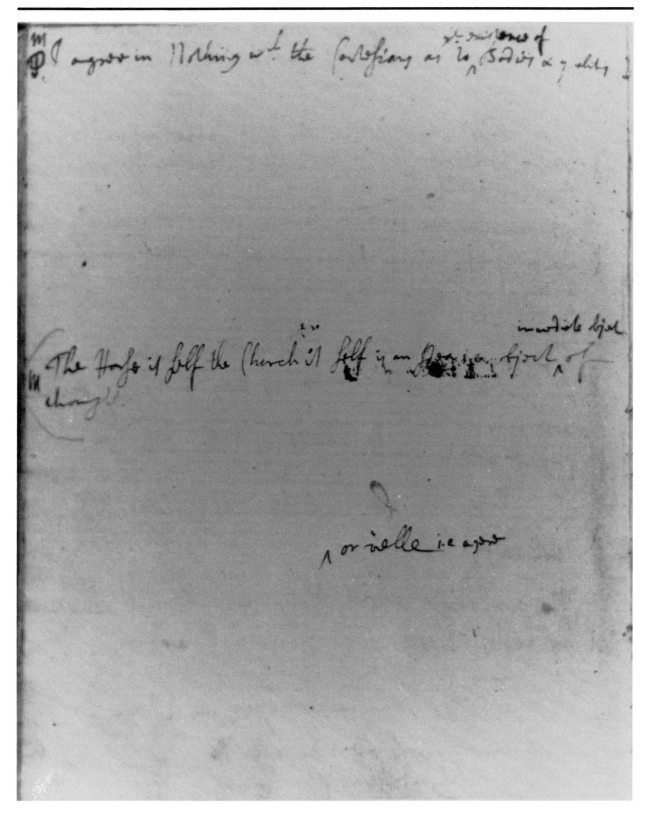

Pages from one of the notebooks Berkeley began keeping at Trinity College, Dublin (Add. MS. 39305, folios 7ᵛ and 8ʳ; by permission of the Trustees of the British Library)

+
y ... his arguments do not
seem to prove against Space, but only
against Bodies.

+ Aristotle as good a man as Euclid but
+ He may be allow'd to have been mistaken.

x Lines not proper for Demonstration

⊕m We see the House it self, the Church it
self ▪▪▪▪▪▪▪▪▪▪ it being an Idea & nothing more.

x Instead of injuring our Doctrine much
Benefits Geometry.

E Existere is percipi or percipere the horse
is in the stable, the Books are in the study as
before.

n In Psyfiques ... a vast view of things
soluble hereby but have not ...

n Hyps & such like unaccountable things
confirm my Doctrine.

The earliest known portrait of Berkeley, painted by John Smibert circa 1720, probably during Berkeley's
second trip to Italy (Collection of Mrs. Maurice Berkeley)

physical object is a fabric or system of *corpuscles*, tiny pieces of matter too small to be seen or felt. Corpuscles are endowed with what Locke called the primary qualities: extension, size, shape, motion or rest, and number. Locke and others contended that secondary qualities—qualities such as color, taste, or smell—exist in objects only as powers to bring about sensations or ideas. Objects owe these powers to their corpuscular constitutions, but neither the corpuscles nor the objects themselves contain anything resembling our sensations. Some writers based the primary/secondary quality distinction on arguments from perceptual relativity: because the color we perceive varies with our position and state, it cannot belong to the object, which remains unchanged. Berkeley had doubts about this form of argument, and

pointed out that if it works at all, it works equally well for primary qualities such as size and shape. His main objection to the distinction is that extension, figure, and motion cannot be conceived apart from all secondary qualities. Corpuscularian matter is simply inconceivable; anyone who believes in it suffers from an illusion of understanding.

Many of Berkeley's arguments express his suspicion of abstract ideas, and in the introduction to the *Principles* he tries to transmit this suspicion to his readers. According to the doctrine of abstraction, the limits of thought lie beyond the limits of the world: we can frame an idea of color, for example, apart from extension, even though color cannot exist apart from extension, and we can frame an idea of a general triangle which is neither equilateral, isosceles, nor scalene, even though every actual triangle must be one of the three. Berkeley held that the limits of thought and the world coincide: we cannot conceive, he argues, of what cannot possibly exist. Matter or material substance is one more abstract idea. We have the ability to *consider* extension, figure, and motion apart from all of the secondary qualities, but any idea we contemplate includes some secondary quality or other, even if we are (for the sake of doing physics, perhaps) attending only to the primary. Berkeley traced the doctrine of abstraction to the mistaken assumption that every meaningful word stands for a distinct idea. General thinking is possible, he proposes, not because we can contemplate abstract ideas, but because we can treat a particular idea as the representative of an entire class. The communication of ideas is not, in any case, "the chief and only end of language." "There are other ends, such as the raising of some passion, the exciting to, or deterring from an action, the putting the mind in some particular disposition."

From his arguments against matter Berkeley infers that mind is the only substance. Yet we ourselves, he observes, are not the cause of our sensations or ideas of sense. There must therefore be some other spirit who causes and perceives them, a spirit Berkeley identifies with God. God's wisdom and goodness can be measured by the complexity and beauty of the system of ideas he creates. The test of an idea's reality is its liveliness or strength, and its coherence with other ideas. Science is reinterpreted as a search for more useful or powerful signs, rather than as a search for causes. The scientist, the grammarian of the language of nature, extends our prospect beyond the present.

The *Principles* was published as "Part I," and even in 1734, when Berkeley published a second edition, "Part I" appears in the running heads. Part II was meant to be about mind, God, and freedom of the will, but Berkeley lost the manuscript while traveling in Italy, probably in 1714, and he never found the time, he told a friend, to write twice on the same subject.

Berkeley was disappointed in the reception of the *Principles*. His friend John Percival wrote from London on 26 August 1710 that

a physician of my acquaintance undertook to describe your person, and argued you must needs be mad, and that you ought to take remedies. A Bishop pitied you that a desire and vanity of start-

ing something new should put you on such an undertaking. . . . My wife, who has all the good esteem and opinion of you that is possible from your just notions of marriage-happiness, desires to know if there be nothing but spirit and ideas, what you make of that part of the six days' creation which preceded man.

In another letter, dated 30 October of the same year, Percival reported that William Whiston and Samuel Clarke "look on you as an extraordinary genius, and profess a value for you, but say they wished you had employed your thoughts less on metaphysics, ranking you with Father Malebranche, [John] Norris, and another whose name I have forgot, all whom they think extraordinary men, but of a particular turn, and their labours of little use to mankind for their abstruseness." Berkeley wrote the *Three Dialogues between Hylas and Philonous* (1713) to turn such readers around. He carried the manuscript of these dialogues with him to London in January of 1713.

In 1712, before leaving Dublin for London, Berkeley wrote *Passive Obedience*, a short book based on three sermons delivered at the Trinity College Chapel earlier in the year. The text of the sermons was Romans 13.2: "Whosoever resisteth the power, resisteth the ordinance of God," and *Passive Obedience* is an argument for an "absolute unlimited non-resistance or passive obedience due to the supreme civil power wherever placed in any nation." One should obey the laws, or, if obedience is inconsistent with reason or conscience, one should patiently submit to whatever penalties the supreme power has annexed to disobedience. (This means that passive obedience covers some of what is now known as civil disobedience.) This obedience—Berkeley calls it *loyalty*—is a natural or moral duty. It cannot be violated even if violation would attain the greatest good, or deliver us from the greatest evil.

It is evident by the light of nature, Berkeley argues, that there is a supreme spirit, and evident too that the end he proposes is good. This good has to be that of his creatures, "the general well-being of all men." Berkeley's view seems to be that reason can discern the content of the moral law by looking toward this end, but the binding character of the law depends essentially on God's will. Berkeley thereby combines rationalism with voluntarism.

What is the method for attaining the end God has proposed? Should we cast rules aside and seek to maximize the good whenever we can? Berkeley's answer is no: we should observe

Berkeley circa 1727 (portrait sometimes attributed to John Smibert; location unknown; from Raymond W. Houghton, David Berman, and Maureen T. Lapan, Images of Berkeley, *1986)*

those laws which, "if universally practised, have, from the nature of things, an essential fitness to procure the well-being of mankind; though in their particular application they are sometimes, through untoward accidents and the perverse irregularity of human wills, the occasions of great sufferings and misfortunes ... to very many good men." This is the earliest statement of an important moral theory now known as *rule-utilitarianism*. It is worse, Berkeley admits, for the person who has supreme power to abuse it than it is for a subject to rebel, but he offers little consolation to the person seeking a justification for rebellion. "Sit still," he urges, "and pray for better times."

The argument that loyalty is a duty without exceptions turns on the miseries of anarchy. Locke had asked, with reference to Thomas Hobbes, whether mankind would be foolish enough "to take care to avoid what Mischiefs may be done them by *Pole-Cats*, or *Foxes*, [yet be] content, nay think it Safety, to be devoured by *Lions*." Here Berkeley sides with Hobbes: "a man had better be exposed to the absolute irresistible decrees even of one single person, whose own and posterity's true interests it is to preserve him in peace and plenty," Berkeley writes, "than remain an open prey to the rage and avarice of every wicked man upon earth, who either exceeds him in strength, or takes him at any advantage."

In January 1713 Berkeley arrived in London, where he met Joseph Addison, Richard Steele, Alexander Pope, John Arbuthnot, and Jonathan Swift. He wrote a series of essays on free-thinking for *The Guardian*. In one essay, written under the name of "Ulysses Cosmopolita," he re- counts an out-of-body voyage (made possible by a "philosophical snuff ") into the pineal gland of a freethinker. There Ulysses finds a "cold and comfortless" imagination, a loud mob of passions, and in the storehouse of ideas "a great number of lifeless notions confusedly thrown together."

Berkeley's most important publication dur- ing his stay in London was *Three Dialogues between Hylas and Philonous*, which appeared in May of 1713. Berkeley's spokesman, Philonous, tries to convince Hylas that immaterialism is not only less skeptical than materialism, but more faithful to common sense. In the first dialogue Philonous of- fers several arguments from perceptual relativity. His aim is not to show that there is no color or ex- tension in things themselves, but that the color and extension *we immediately perceive* are ideas in the mind. Hylas, his opponent, clings to a material- ist standard of reality, according to which a qual- ity can be real only if it exists outside the mind. The relativity arguments therefore force Hylas to admit that we do not immediately perceive real qualities. Philonous can say that we do, because real qualities are merely ideas that meet the stan- dards of strength and coherence laid down in the *Principles*. New to the *Three Dialogues* is an impor- tant discussion of creation, in which Berkeley an- swers the question raised by Lady Percival. Cre- ation consists in perceptibility, and so the Mosaic story is no threat to Berkeley's view.

In the *Principles* Berkeley had said that we have no idea of spirit, because a passive idea can- not resemble an active being. In the second edition of the *Principles*, which was published together with a revised edition of the *Three Dia- logues* in 1734, Berkeley claimed that we nonethe- less have a *notion* of spirit. In the accompanying edition of *Three Dialogues*, Hylas asks Phi- lonous whether this is fair: "You admit . . . that there is spiritual substance, although you have no idea of it; while you deny there can be such a thing as material substance, because you have no notion or idea of it. Is this fair dealing? To act con- sistently, you must either admit matter or reject spirit." Philonous argues at length that there is "no parity of case between spirit and matter," but his argument has left many readers unconvinced.

Berkeley took his first tour of the Conti- nent, as secretary to Lord Peterborough, between October 1713 and August 1714. After his return he lived mostly in England until a second tour in the fall of 1716, when he traveled to Europe as tutor to the son of the bishop of Clogher. It was

in Lyons, on a slow journey home, that Berkeley composed *De Motu*, which he entered, unsuccess- fully, in a prize competition sponsored by the Royal Academy of Sciences at Paris. Berkeley ar- rived in London in the late fall of 1720; *De Motu* was published in London in 1721.

De Motu: sive, de motus principio & natura, et de causa communicationis mottum (On motion: or, the principle and nature of motion, and the cause of the communication of motions) is the full- est statement of Berkeley's philosophy of science. Physical force, he argues, is merely a mathemati- cal hypothesis. Scientific theories are instruments of prediction, tools for the anticipation of experi- ence. As such they are neither true nor false, or if they are sometimes true or false, it is only be- cause they can be translated without loss into ex- periential terms. The only true force or cause is spiritual, and it is the province not of physics but of metaphysics.

For a year after his return to England Berke- ley apparently lived in London, still on leave from Trinity College. In 1721 he published *An Essay towards Preventing the ruine of Great Britain*. The essay, an attack on get-rich-quick schemes and the sophistication of freethinkers, was occa- sioned by the bursting of the South Sea Bubble. It is a plea—often priggish and humorless—for religion, industry, frugality, and public spirit: "Other nations have been wicked, but we are the first who have been wicked upon principle." Berkeley proposes public buildings and monu- ments as a way of focusing public spirit—as a strat- egy for making its object more concrete.

In August of 1721 Berkeley was introduced to Charles Fitzroy, Duke of Grafton, who later be- came lord lieutenant of Ireland. With a promise from the duke that he would recommend him for preferment, Berkeley returned to Trinity Col- lege in September 1721. He had been advanced to senior fellow in his absence. He took the de- grees of B.D. and D.D. in November 1721, and later served as both senior proctor and Hebrew lecturer. He was named dean of Derry in May of 1724, and in that month he resigned his fellow- ship.

Berkeley used the income from his dean- ery—£1,250 annually—to finance his campaign to found a college in Bermuda, a project he had conceived in May of 1722. His plan was to edu- cate not only the sons of settlers but also Native Americans, who would return to their tribes as missionaries. Bermuda was chosen because it was convenient to the colonies, yet free of their cor-

Whitehall, Berkeley's house in Middletown, Rhode Island, where he lived during the years 1729-1732 while waiting without avail for the arrival of the funds he needed to start a college in Bermuda

John Smibert's second, larger portrait of the group associated with Berkeley's Bermuda plan: Smibert, Richard Dalton of Lincoln-shire, John Wainwright, Miss Handcock (perhaps the daughter of William Handcock), John James of Bury St. Edmunds, Mrs. Anne Berkeley (holding the Berkeleys' first child, Henry), and George Berkeley. The painting was probably completed in 1739, seven years after Berkeley had abandoned the project (by permission of Yale University Art Gallery; gift of Isaac Lothrop of Plymouth, Massachusetts).

rupting influence. Berkeley expressed his hopes for the New World in the closing stanzas of his "Verses on the Prospect of Planting Arts and Learning in America," written in 1726:

There shall be sung another golden Age,
  The rise of Empire and of Arts,
The Good and Great inspiring epic Rage,
  The wisest Heads and noblest Hearts.

Not such as *Europe* breeds in her decay;
  Such as she bred when fresh and young,
When heav'nly Flame did animate her Clay,
  But future Poets shall be sung.

Westward the Course of Empire takes its Way;
  The four first Acts already past,
A fifth shall close the Drama with the Day;
  Time's noblest Offspring is the last.

With the charter of St. Paul's College, with private subscriptions, and with a promise from Parliament of twenty thousand pounds, Berkeley sailed to America in September of 1728, one month after his marriage to Anne Forster. In January of 1729 he arrived in Newport, Rhode Island, where he waited three years for the funds Sir Robert Walpole proved unwilling to release. While in America Berkeley met Samuel Johnson, a former tutor at Yale who later became the first president of Columbia University. Johnson was Berkeley's most prominent disciple. In a series of letters published in Luce and Jessop's edition as "Philosophical Correspondence between Berkeley and Johnson," Johnson pressed Berkeley on several important topics, among them the nature of time and the relationship between our ideas and their archetypes in the mind of God.

Berkeley returned to London in 1732 with the manuscript for *Alciphron: or, the Minute Philosopher*, a series of seven dialogues. Berkeley's champion is Euphranor, a studious farmer. Euphranor goes to the home of Crito to meet two visiting freethinkers, Alciphron and Lysicles. The first dialogue raises the central question of the following two: are religious and moral beliefs necessary for the general good of mankind? In dialogue 2 Lysicles (who believes that happiness lies in the pleasures of sense) offers an argument, modeled on Bernard Mandeville's, that vice does more to promote the general good than virtue does. In dialogue 3 Alciphron defends an atheistic moral sense theory modeled on that of Anthony Ashley Cooper, Third Earl of Shaftesbury. We are moved not by sensual plea-

sure, Alciphron argues, but by the beauty of virtue itself. Euphranor argues against both views.

In dialogue 4 Euphranor sketches Berkeley's theory of vision, which he uses to show that we have at least as much right to infer the existence of God as we have to infer the existence of other, finite minds. Our visual experience is a divine language, Euphranor explains, and speech is our best evidence for the existence of other minds. In dialogue 5 Euphranor argues for the utility of the Christian religion, and in dialogue 6 he defends the status of scripture as revelation. The seventh dialogue is a reply to philosophical objections to Christianity. Alciphron argues that the word *grace* is meaningless. Euphranor replies that a word need not stand for a distinct idea in order to be meaningful. Meaning, he suggests, sometimes arises from a word's place in a language or system; he cites the "force" of the physicist and the imaginary numbers of the mathematician. Euphranor also defends the freedom of the will, and its compatibility with God's foreknowledge of our actions.

Berkeley lived in London for two-and-a-half years after his return from America. On 19 May 1734 he was consecrated bishop of Cloyne. On his way to Cloyne Berkeley visited Dublin, and it was probably there that he wrote *The Analyst* (1734). Berkeley objected to the authority assumed by mathematicians (such as Edmund Halley) in matters of religion. *The Analyst* tries to undercut that authority by bringing to the surface the mysteries in Newton's doctrine of "fluxions" or instantaneous velocities—the differential calculus. Newton's followers took lines to be generated by the motions of points, planes by the motions of lines, and solids by the motions of planes. The higher the point's velocity, the larger the line it generates in a given span of time. In England instantaneous increments in quantity were known as moments; on the Continent, where Gottfried Wilhelm Leibniz's version of the calculus was preferred, these increments were known as differences. A fluxion was then defined as the velocity of a moment or difference. Berkeley argues that we have no clear idea of such a thing. At times a fluxion is taken to be finite (though vanishingly small); at other times it is taken to be nothing. There is no consistent treatment, and true or useful results are reached by compensating errors. Berkeley concludes that analysis furnished "a strong *argumentum ad hominem* against the philomathematical infidels of these times."

This portrait, painted by James Latham circa 1737-1738, is thought to be the last portrait of Berkeley painted during his lifetime (by permission of the Board of Trinity College, Dublin)

Berkeley lived in Cloyne for nearly twenty years, and his two main publications during this last period of his life dealt with problems he faced as bishop. *The Querist* (1735-1737) is a series of several hundred questions on the poverty of Ireland. Its immediate cause, Berkeley argues, is the laziness and drunkenness of the Irish people, but their behavior, he contends, is rooted in turn in their poverty, which deadens their wants and ambition. The economy of Ireland cannot be healthy unless these people live decently. Only someone with food in his belly and clothes on his back can have wants as opposed to needs; wants encourage industry, and industry brings wealth. Wealth is not a matter of the gold or silver a country holds, but a matter of how much is produced. Money does not represent amounts of gold and silver; it is a counter whose significance lies in the

claim it enables one to make on the labor and resources of those who honor it. (Here there is a striking parallel with Berkeley's views on the meanings of words.) Berkeley makes several practical suggestions. A national bank is necessary to assist the flow of money. There should be an academy of design to improve Irish linen. There should be sumptuary laws to prevent the spending of money that does nothing for the common people—money that leaves the country when it could be encouraging industry at home.

The most striking themes in Berkeley's economic writings are psychological. Wealth depends on labor, which depends on wants. Needs are such that their frustration leaves one listless—without wants—so they must be met first of all.

Siris, published in 1744, may be the only work of philosophy that begins with a recipe: to

Letter to Dr. Brackstone including a recipe for tar water, which Berkeley had recommended in his 1744 book Siris *as a cure for a variety of ailments (by permission of the Board of Trinity College, Dublin)*

make tar water, the curative potion whose powers the book celebrates and investigates, add a gallon of cold water to a quart of pine tar, stir for three or four minutes, let stand for forty-eight hours, and pour off the clear water. The most volatile parts of the tar enter the water, creating a mixture which, though powerful, is mild. Berkeley recommends it for a variety of ailments, as both prevention and cure, and he appeals throughout to his own experience. He does not claim that tar water is a panacea, but he suspects that it is one, and so far experience has not disappointed him. It is effective, he thinks, against most if not all diseases, but only time and trial will tell how effective it is.

Berkeley speculates on the powers of tar water. His thoughts are drawn to air, from air to fire or ether (the most volatile part of the air), and from fire or ether to the supreme spirit, the source of the power to heal and soothe. *Siris* is not a tightly argued treatise but a meditation, in which Berkeley's thoughts are drawn upward not by argumentative necessity, but by the gentle coercion of association.

In 1752 Berkeley moved his family to Oxford, where he hoped to supervise the education of his son George. Berkeley died there on 14 January 1753. His will asks that his body remain above ground for five days "or longer, even till it grow offensive by the cadaverous smell." He was buried in the chapel of Christ Church on 20 January.

In the closing sentence of an essay on "projectors," Johnson writes that "those who have attempted much, have seldom failed to perform more than those who never deviate from the common roads of action: many valuable preparations of chemistry, are supposed to have risen from unsuccessful inquiries after the grand elixir: it is, therefore, just to encourage those, who endeavour to enlarge the power of art, since they often succeed beyond expectation; and when they fail, may sometimes benefit the world even by their miscarriages." Tar water was no panacea; Berkeley never reached Bermuda; and he won few converts to immaterialism. But he enlarged not only the powers of philosophy but its problems.

Letters:

Life and Letters of George Berkeley, D.D., volume 4 of *The Works of George Berkeley*, 4 volumes, edited by A. C. Fraser (Oxford: Clarendon Press, 1871; revised, 1901);

Berkeley and Percival: The Correspondence of George Berkeley, afterwards Bishop of Cloyne, and Sir John Percival, afterwards Earl of Egmont, edited by Benjamin Rand (Cambridge: Cambridge University Press, 1914);

Letters, edited by A. A. Luce (London: Nelson, 1956); volume 8 of *The Works of George Berkeley, Bishop of Cloyne*, 9 volumes, edited by Luce and T. E. Jessop (London: Nelson, 1948-1957).

Bibliographies:

T. E. Jessop, *A Bibliography of George Berkeley* (London: Oxford University Press, 1934; revised edition, The Hague: Nijhoff, 1973);

C. M. Turbayne and Robert Ware, "A Bibliography of George Berkeley, 1933-1962," *Journal of Philosophy*, 60 (January 1963): 93-112;

Geoffrey Keynes, *A Bibliography of George Berkeley* (Oxford: Clarendon Press, 1976);

C. M. Turbayne and R. Appelbaum, "A Bibliography of George Berkeley, 1963-1974," *Journal of the History of Philosophy*, 15 (January 1977): 83-95;

Colin M. Turbayne, "A Bibliography of George Berkeley, 1963-79," in *Berkeley: Critical and Interpretive Essays*, edited by Turbayne (Minneapolis: University of Minnesota Press, 1982), pp. 313-329;

"A Bibliography of George Berkeley, 1980-85," in *Essays on the Philosophy of George Berkeley*, edited by Ernest Sosa (Dordrecht, The Netherlands: D. Reidel, 1987), pp. 243-260.

Biographies:

Joseph Stock, *An Account of the Life of George Berkeley D.D. late Bishop of Cloyne in Ireland, with notes containing strictures upon his works* (London: Printed for J. Murray, 1776);

A. C. Fraser, *Life and Letters of George Berkeley, D.D.*, volume 4 of *The Works of George Berkeley*, 4 volumes, edited by Fraser (Oxford: Clarendon Press, 1871; revised, 1901);

A. A. Luce, *The Life of George Berkeley, Bishop of Cloyne* (London: Nelson, 1949);

Edwin S. Gaustad, *George Berkeley in America* (New Haven & London: Yale University Press, 1979).

References:

David M. Armstrong, *Berkeley's Theory of Vision* (Parkville: Melbourne University Press, 1960; New York: Garland, 1988);

Margaret Atherton, *Berkeley's Revolution in Vision* (Ithaca, N.Y.: Cornell University Press, 1990);

Jonathan Bennett, *Locke, Berkeley, Hume: Central Themes* (Oxford: Clarendon Press, 1971);

David Berman, *George Berkeley: Essays and Replies* (Dublin: Irish Academic Press, 1986);

Harry M. Bracken, *Berkeley* (London: Macmillan, 1974);

Bracken, *The Early Reception of Berkeley's Immaterialism, 1710-1733*, revised edition (The Hague: Nijhoff, 1965);

Richard J. Brook, *Berkeley's Philosophy of Science* (The Hague: Nijhoff, 1973);

Jonathan Dancy, *Berkeley: An Introduction* (Oxford: Blackwell, 1987);

Willis Doney, *Berkeley on Abstraction and Abstract Ideas* (New York: Garland, 1988);

Daniel Flage, *Berkeley's Doctrine of Notions* (London: Croom Helm, 1986);

John Foster and Howard Robinson, eds., *Essays on Berkeley: A Tercentennial Celebration* (Oxford: Clarendon Press, 1985);

Anthony Grayling, *Berkeley: The Central Arguments* (London: Duckworth, 1986; La Salle, Ill.: Open Court, 1986);

G. Dawes Hicks, *Berkeley* (London: Benn, 1932);

G. A. Johnston, *The Development of Berkeley's Philosophy* (London: Macmillan, 1923);

A. A. Luce, *Berkeley and Malebranche* (London: Oxford University Press, 1934);

Luce, *Berkeley's Immaterialism* (London: Nelson, 1945);

Luce, *The Dialectic of Immaterialism* (London: Hodder & Stoughton, 1963);

Gabriel Moked, *Particles and Ideas: Bishop Berkeley's Corpuscularian Philosophy* (Oxford: Clarendon Press, 1988);

Paul J. Olscamp, *The Moral Philosophy of George Berkeley* (The Hague: Nijhoff, 1970);

Stephen C. Pepper, Karl Aschenbrenner, and Benson Mates, eds., *George Berkeley*, University of California Publications in Philosophy, volume 29 (Berkeley & Los Angeles: University of California Press, 1957);

George Pitcher, *Berkeley* (London: Routledge & Kegan Paul, 1977);

John J. Richetti, *Philosophical Writing: Locke, Berkeley, Hume* (Cambridge: Harvard University Press, 1983);

Ernest Sosa, ed., *Essays on the Philosophy of George Berkeley* (Dordrecht: D. Reidel, 1987);

I. C. Tipton, *Berkeley: The Philosophy of Immaterialism* (London: Methuen, 1974);

Colin M. Turbayne, *The Myth of Metaphor* (New Haven: Yale University Press, 1962; revised edition, Columbia: University of South Carolina Press, 1970);

Turbayne, ed., *Berkeley: Critical and Interpretive Essays* (Minneapolis: University of Minnesota Press, 1982);

J. O. Urmson, *Berkeley* (Oxford: Oxford University Press, 1982);

G. J. Warnock, *Berkeley*, third edition, revised (Oxford: Blackwell, 1982);

Julius Weinberg, "The Nominalism of Berkeley and Hume," in his *Abstraction, Relation and Induction* (Madison: University of Wisconsin Press, 1965);

John Wild, *George Berkeley: A Study of His Life and Philosophy* (Cambridge, Mass.: Harvard University Press, 1936);

Kenneth P. Winkler, *Berkeley: An Interpretation* (Oxford: Clarendon Press, 1989).

Papers:

There are important collections of Berkeley's papers and letters at the British Library and at Trinity College, Dublin.

Henry St. John, Viscount Bolingbroke

(16 September 1678 - 12 December 1751)

Claudia Newel Thomas
Wake Forest University

BOOKS: *A Letter to the Examiner* (London, 1710);

The Representation of the Right Honourable the Lord Viscount Bolingbroke (London: Printed for J. Morphew, 1715);

A genuine letter of advice and consolation, written from Paris by the Lord Viscount Bolingbroke (London: Printed for A. Boulter, 1715);

The Occasional Writer, nos. 1-3 (London: Printed for A. Moore, 1727);

The Craftsman Extraordinary: Containing an answer to the Defense of the Enquiry into the Reasons of the Conduct of Great Britain (London: Printed for R. Francklin, 1729);

Observations on the publick affairs of Great-Britain (London: Printed for the Author, 1729);

The Second Craftsman Extraordinary: Being farther remarks on a pamphlet lately publish'd, entitled, Observations on the conduct of Great Britain (London: Printed for R. F., 1729);

A Letter to Caleb D'Anvers, Esq.; concerning the state of affairs in Europe (London: Printed for R. Francklin, 1730);

The Case of Dunkirk Faithfully Stated and Impartially Considered (London: Printed for A. Moore, 1730);

The Monumental Inscription on the Column at Blenheim-House, Erected to the Immortal Memory of the late Duke of Marlborough (London: Printed for W. Hinchcliffe, 1731);

A Final Answer to the Remarks on the Craftsman's Vindication (London: Printed for R. Francklin, 1731);

The Freeholder's Political Catechism (London: Printed for J. Roberts, 1733; New London, Conn.: Printed & sold by T. Green, 1769);

A Dissertation upon Parties (London: Printed by H. Haines at R. Francklin's, 1735);

Letters to a Young Nobleman on the Study and Use of History (London: Privately printed, 1738); republished as *Letters on the Study and Use of History*, 2 volumes (London: Printed for A. Millar, 1752);

The Idea of a Patriot King (London: Printed for T. C., 1740?);

Remarks on the History of England, from the minutes of Humphrey Oldcastle, Esq. (London: Printed for R. Francklin, 1743);

A Collection of Political Tracts (London: Printed for R. Francklin, 1748);

Letters; On the Spirit of Patriotism: On the Idea of a Patriot King: and On the State of Parties, at the Accession of King George the First (London: Printed for A. Millar, 1749; Philadelphia: Printed & sold by B. Franklin & D. Hall, 1749);

A Familiar Epistle to the Most Impudent Man Living (London: Printed for J. Millan, 1749);

Reflections Concerning Innate Moral Principles (London: Printed for S. Bladon, 1752);

A Letter to Sir William Windham. II. Some Reflections on the Present State of the Nation. III. A Letter to Mr. Pope (London: Printed for A. Millar, 1753).

Editions: *The Works of the Late Honorable Henry St. John, Lord Viscount Bolingbroke*, 5 volumes, edited by David Mallet (London, 1754);

The Works of Lord Bolingbroke, 4 volumes (London: Bohn, 1844);

Historical Writings, edited by Isaac Kramnick (Chicago: University of Chicago Press, 1972);

Contributions to the Craftsman, edited by Simon Varey (Oxford: Clarendon Press, 1982).

Henry St. John, Viscount Bolingbroke, dazzled and perplexed his contemporaries. Alexander Pope and Jonathan Swift revered his eloquence and charm, while Sir Robert Walpole despised his hypocrisy and untrammeled ambition. His precocious rise and precipitous fall in Parliament, his sustained opposition campaign studded with rash misjudgments, his political expediency clothed in uncompromising principles: Bolingbroke's contradictions perpetuate dispute over his achievements. Whether an idealist or an opportunist, however, Bolingbroke consistently expressed the yearnings of contemporary Tories for a return to government by the landed interest. Despite his preference for an end to parties,

Henry St. John, circa 1705 (mezzotint by G. White, after a portrait by T. Murray)

he instituted the notion of a "loyal opposition." His *Craftsman* essays and occasional writings inspired Swift, Pope, and John Gay to create satiric masterpieces. And his style still merits analysis as a rhetorical exposition of conservative ideology, although political scientists may no longer agree with John Adams that "there is nothing so profound, correct, and perfect on the subject of government."

Henry St. John was born on 16 September 1678 into a family situation that exacerbated his mercurial temperament. His mother, Mary Rich, died in his infancy. His father, Henry St. John, Sr., was a Restoration rake for whom Bolingbroke had little respect. Soon after his birth, St. John was sent from the family seat at Lydiard Tregoze, Wiltshire, to his paternal grandparents' manor at Battersea. There, he was raised by his grandmother, Lady Johanna St. John, a strict dis-

senter. Tradition differs as to whether young Henry was educated at Eton or, more probably, a dissenting academy, and whether he attended Christ Church, Oxford. St. John's education concluded with a grand tour of Europe from 1698 to 1700, during which he perfected his knowledge of European languages, politics, and religions, confiding his insights in letters to Sir William Trumbull, retired Tory secretary of state. He also indulged in drinking and whoring, favorite activities that eventually undermined his career despite his aspirations to statesmanship and philosophy.

By 1701 St. John was back in England, and in February he won election to Parliament representing the family borough of Wooton Bassett. In 1700 he had married Frances Winchcombe, a Berkshire heiress, in an arranged match; St. John's neglect of her soon became notorious. His

A satirical Whig print showing Bolingbroke (in the picture at left) writing dispatches to France while in bed with his mistress, possibly Anna Maria Gumley, who later married Bolingbroke's political ally William Pulteney

Parliamentary debut, however, was brilliant. With energy and eloquence, he joined the backbench Tories in their efforts to dismantle the Whig junto. As the War of the Spanish Succession mandated cooperation under Whig guidance, St. John eventually moderated his behavior and drifted toward Robert Harley's Court Tories, angling for a ministerial position. In 1704, when Daniel Finch, Earl of Nottingham's faction-torn coalition collapsed and Harley took over as secretary of state, Henry St. John became secretary of war in the new, moderate coalition ministry. For the next four years, he worked zealously to supply John Churchill, Duke of Marlborough's campaigns, even after he began to doubt the wisdom of continuing the war. After 1706, however, Tory support for the war deteriorated, and Marlborough and Sidney, Earl of Godolphin, turned increasingly to the Whigs. In 1708 St. John fol-

lowed Harley out of office rather than cling to power in a hostile, Whig-dominated ministry. After a Whig resurgence in the 1708 elections, St. John had to wait two years for another opportunity to hold office.

The years of Harley's ministry, from 1710 to 1714, bounded St. John's brief rise to eminence and his irrevocable fall. By 1710 Harley had succeeded in toppling Godolphin's ministry. He took over as lord treasurer, and reluctantly named St. John secretary of state for the Northern Department. Once in office, St. John worked vigorously to extend his power and push forward Tory peace negotiations. His ambition was so great, however, that he continually overreached himself. In March 1711, for example, Antoine de Guiscard, an accused traitor, attempted to assassinate Harley during an interrogation. While Harley recovered from knife wounds, St. John at-

Bolingbroke dressed in viscount's robes for the coronation of George I, 20 October 1714 (portrait by an unknown artist; by permission of the National Portrait Gallery, London)

tempted to take his place in the House of Commons, insinuating that he had been Guiscard's real target. St. John's blundering efforts to control Commons merely exposed his own lack of followers and increased Harley's suspicion of his rivalry. During Harley's absence, moreover, St. John discovered that he had been kept ignorant of secret peace negotiations with France. Furious, he set about wresting control over the process from Harley, replacing cautious moves toward a unilateral peace with a bold thrust for peace on British terms.

To muster support for peace, Harley and St. John turned to the public, a policy that influenced the rest of St. John's career. In August 1710 he helped Harley establish a pro-Tory paper, *The Examiner*. Among his early essays, he contributed *A Letter to the Examiner* denouncing the opposition Whigs as a "Factious Cabal," anxious to prolong the war against the Queen's wishes. Arguing what became a theme of propeace propaganda, St. John accused Britain's allies of "bubbling" her of men and money for their own national ambitions. Thanks to the Whigs, Britain was now "a Farm to the *Bank*, a Province of *Holland*, and a Jest to the whole World." After November 1710, when Swift took over *The Examiner*, such accusations would flow steadily from the press, culminating in Swift's *The Conduct of the Allies* (1711) and in Dr. John Arbuthnot's *The History of John Bull* (1712). By cultivating friendships with men such as Swift, Arbuthnot, and Matthew Prior (all of whom were members of his "Brothers Club," a social effort to extend his influence that endured from 1711 to 1713), St. John established himself as a patron of Tory writers. He also established the tactics of his long, extra-Parliamentary career as a political journalist.

Late in 1711, Queen Anne salvaged Harley's majority, insuring his peace initiative, when she created twelve Tory peers to break Whig opposition to a peace without allied control of Spain. She dismissed Marlborough soon afterward. As negotiations progressed, however, the rivalry between Harley (since 1711, earl of Oxford) and St. John erupted into war. In July 1712, when created viscount Bolingbroke, St. John regarded his elevation as an Oxford-inspired affront. Sent to Paris to aid the negotiations, Bolingbroke basked in his own importance, foolishly appearing at the opera when the Pretender (James Francis Edward Stuart, only son of James II) was in the audience, and exceeding his instructions at the peace talks. The Treaty of Utrecht, signed in 1713, finally reflected Oxford's cool, tortuous negotiations more than Bolingbroke's rash demands. But as the ministry remained torn by conflict even after the treaty was concluded, Bolingbroke felt justified in contesting once more for party leadership.

Anne's successor was a chief source of Tory dissension. Unlike the Whigs, united in favor of the Hanoverians, Tories were split between adherence to the Hanoverian Settlement and loyalty to the Stuart Pretender. Oxford, Bolingbroke, and other leading Tories negotiated secretly with both sides, demanding that the Pretender convert to at least nominal Anglicanism before taking the throne. While his party wavered in its preference, Bolingbroke wished to meet either successor firmly established in Parliament with an all-Tory ministry. A solid Tory victory in the 1713 election augured well for his plan, and by summer 1714 Bolingbroke had undermined Oxford's influence in Parliament. He had even won Queen Anne's ear, if not her confidence, through his influence over her favorite, Mrs. Abigail Masham. By 17 July Bolingbroke had convinced the queen to dismiss Harley, but she refused to bestow the lord treasurership on a man she considered immoral. Worse, she fell mortally ill, leaving Bolingbroke to negotiate with the Whigs in the face of an imminent Hanoverian succession. By 1 August Queen Anne was dead, and Bolingbroke's career shattered. "What a world is this and how does Fortune banter us," he wrote to Swift. In March 1715, fearful for his life after

the Whigs seized his papers, he fled to France.

Bolingbroke's flight might seem the greatest mistake of his career, if he had not agreed to serve as secretary to the Pretender soon after assuring the British minister to Paris of his loyalty. Later, he alleged despair of clearing his name as his incentive for joining the Jacobites. In his new position he aided final preparations for the Pretender's disastrous invasion of 1715. Afterward the Pretender dismissed Bolingbroke, blaming him for the expedition's disorganization. Disabused at last of the Jacobites' prospects, Bolingbroke began to plan his return to power as the head of a renovated Tory party. While negotiating his pardon with various British ministers, he composed two essays. "Reflections upon Exile" (written in 1716) announced his Senecan acceptance of fate and his happiness due to reduced expectations. Despite its obvious inadequacy as a description of Bolingbroke's attitude, the essay reflects his yearning for contentment with solitude and intellectual pursuits. Bolingbroke also expressed his faith in reason and his respect for natural law, themes he would reiterate throughout his writings, and particularly in the four long epistles he dedicated to Alexander Pope (written circa 1730-1735 but unpublished until 1754). More pragmatic, however, was *A Letter to Sir William Windham* (circulated among his friends in late 1717 and published in 1753). Designed to palliate his own culpability in serving the Pretender while demanding that all Tories abjure the Jacobite cause, this letter blamed partisan politics for the Tories' failure under Queen Anne, while Bolingbroke promised to devote himself to national rather than party concerns. The letter, an attempt to shift blame from Bolingbroke to the Jacobites and Whigs, circulated among Tory leaders but failed to win their favor.

Bolingbroke accommodated himself to life in exile. His personal charm and command of French won him entrance to the salons of aristocratic intellectuals and scholars, such as Voltaire and the Abbe Conti. He studied philosophy with Levesque de Pouilly and history with Pierre Joseph Alary. In both pursuits, he learned to apply the new attitudes of the Enlightenment—of such empiricists as Sir Isaac Newton and John Locke—in defense of conservative principles. In *Reflections Concerning Innate Moral Principles* (written in 1724), Bolingbroke contested the notion of innate benevolence, arguing that in fact self-love is innate and must be guided by education and experience to love for others. Although Bolingbroke's

First page from a seven-page letter to Voltaire in which Bolingbroke compared the fostering of heart and spirit to the cultivation of a garden, a metaphor Voltaire was later to use at the end of Candide *(auctioned by Sotheby & Co., 11 June 1968). Bolingbroke is credited with inspiring Voltaire to reject the a priori reasoning of René Descartes in favor of the empiricism of John Locke, whose* Essay Concerning Human Understanding *is recommended in this letter.*

philosophical theories were derivative, they enabled him to reformulate aspects of conservative ideology, such as the Great Chain of Being, in a manner attractive to Gay, Pope, and even Swift, despite his reservations about Deism. Meanwhile, his wife's death in 1718 left Bolingbroke free to marry his mistress, Marie-Claire de Marcilly, Marquise de Villette, in a private ceremony early in 1719. He leased with her the Château de la Source, dividing his time between their country retreat and the intellectual Club de l'Entresol in Paris. Throughout his exile, he never ceased intriguing for reinstatement in Britain, even permitting his wife to bribe George I's mistress, Countess Ehrengard Melusina von der Schulenberg, Duchess of Kendal, to win the king's favor. At last, despite Robert Walpole's reiterated enmity, he won a royal pardon in 1723 and a restoration of his property rights in 1724. Although, at Walpole's instigation, Bolingbroke's bill of restoration stipulated that he could never again serve the Crown, he returned to England in June 1725, convinced that he could still win back political power.

Bolingbroke worked for the next ten years to forge a unified party of opposition to Walpole, proselytizing Tories and dissident Whigs. His base was a Middlesex estate which he renamed Dawley Farm after decorating his hall with murals of farm implements. On this ferme ornée, Bolingbroke celebrated the virtues of Horatian retirement with friends such as Pope, while supervising his campaign to regain Parliament. He forged an alliance with William Pulteney, an ambitious Whig whose resistance to Walpole had resulted in dismissal from office. Pulteney, assisted by Bolingbroke's old Tory ally Sir William Windham, was Bolingbroke's Parliamentary spokesman. Outside the House, Bolingbroke sought to establish a rationale and program for his opposition. Walpole, after the South Sea stock debacle of 1720, had entrenched himself as no minister before him had done. By winning Queen Caroline's confidence and engrossing all the avenues to royal patronage, Sir Robert initiated the Whig ascendancy that lasted until the French Revolution. To undermine Sir Robert's authority, Bolingbroke accused him of controlling the government on behalf of the monied interest— the same incorrigible faction he had blamed for the Spanish war. On behalf of the gentry who had financed that war through the land tax, but had now lost their hereditary right to direct the nation, Bolingbroke waged war against Walpole.

His chief weapon, founded with Pulteney in 1726, was *The Craftsman*.

Although Bolingbroke contributed many essays to *The Craftsman*, as well as three *Occasional Writer* pamphlets (1727) and other essays supporting its opinions, two series stand out among his efforts. Throughout 1730-1731, he published twenty-four essays in *The Craftsman*, which were later gathered as *Remarks on the History of England* (1743). These pieces, presented as the ruminations of Humphrey Oldcastle among his club of philosophers, review British history as a continual battle between the spirit of liberty and the quest for power. According to Bolingbroke, Britons have traditionally been a free people, living according to "original rights, conditions of original contracts, co-equal with prerogative, and coeval with our government." Each reign witnessed the struggle of the people (by whom Bolingbroke usually means the hereditary landowners) to preserve their ancient constitutional rights against the encroachments of the monarch. He extolled the ideal of a balanced government based on separate but cooperative King, Lords, and Commons, insinuating a current imbalance in favor of the crown. Bolingbroke concentrated on Elizabeth I as the exemplary monarch. She won her people's hearts, dominated her government, and was frugal with taxes. Implicit was a contrast with George II, ruled by Caroline and Walpole, and demanding stipends while doing little as the nation's representative. Bolingbroke presented Elizabeth's policies as appropriate for an island nation: minimal involvement on the Continent to maintain the balance of power and concentration on the sea and navy as natural barriers. When Bolingbroke turned to James I, he discovered a corrupt monarch analogous to George II. Vain, profligate, disdainful, and dominated by George Villiers, first Duke of Buckingham, James initiated policies that led to civil war. Bolingbroke's implied warning was clear; his estimate of the current government, harsh (his printer was twice arrested during publication of the series). Although Walpole subsidized several periodicals to combat such criticism, Bolingbroke's rhetorical ability and superior knowledge of British history made proministerial responses difficult.

Bolingbroke's second memorable series was the nineteen-letter *A Dissertation upon Parties* (published in *The Craftsman* during 1733-1734 and as a pamphlet in 1735). By this time Walpole had survived the Excise Crisis, but years of journalistic denunciation and Parliamentary opposition had

*Henry St. John, Viscount Bolingbroke, circa 1730 (portrait attributed to Jonathan Richardson;
by permission of the National Portrait Gallery, London)*

weakened him. Looking toward the 1734 general election, Bolingbroke composed his rhetorical masterpiece to inculcate a desire for union in the national interest. Bringing his version of British history up to date, Bolingbroke seized every opportunity to suggest that Walpole and George II embodied James I's and Charles I's threats to liberty, while their rule lacked even the dubious advantages of Charles II's reign. *A Dissertation upon Parties* climaxes with a description of Britain corrupted and enervated by the "art of stockjobbing" and controlled by a heartless "ministerial jobber." Royal power, exercised by Walpole, has finally destroyed the constitutional balance, as well as the entire social structure, now pervaded by the passion for money. To counter this frightful vision British freeholders must rise up and elect representatives impervious to Walpole's machinations. Only a national party imbued with the "spirit of public benevolence" could heal the constitution and the society. Unfortunately, while producing these impassioned essays, Bolingbroke subsidized his opposition campaign with a pension from the French government. When enough of this relationship reached the ministry, Bolingbroke's campaign evaporated. When Pulteney rose in 1734 to protest Walpole's influence over the approaching elections, the prime minister responded with a devastating speech against Bolingbroke, characterizing the "anti minister" as "void of all faith or honour, and betraying every master he ever served." Bolingbroke hung on until after the disappointing elections, but neither Pulteney nor the other opposition Whigs trusted him. In a tacit admission of failure, he retreated again to France in May 1735.

At Chanteloup, Bolingbroke resumed the life of a country gentleman and his investigations of philosophy and history. "Of the True Use of Retirement and Study" (probably written in 1736), addressed to Allen, Lord Bathurst, celebrated again the wisdom of withdrawal from the world of politics. From Chanteloup he also addressed his *Letters on the Study and Use of History*, which caused a scandal when it was publicly published in 1752. The letters were ostensibly to prepare young Henry Hyde, Viscount Cornbury, to serve his country. For this purpose, Bolingbroke found ancient accounts nearly useless, compounded of legends. Even scripture—this criticism most enraged his early readers—was unreliable, abounding in contradictions. A responsible modern, seeking guidance for the political role ordained by his social status, should concentrate on history since the sixteenth century, for which ample records survived. After thorough study, past actions and decisions would emerge as patterns for modern conduct. Bolingbroke called this "philosophy teaching by examples" rather than by abstract injunctions. *Letters on the Study and Use of History* reviewed European history from 1500, culminating in the heroic efforts of Queen Anne and the Tories to extricate Britain from the Spanish war. He concluded by blaming the Whigs for the perplexities of contemporary foreign policy: "A rage of warring possessed a party in our nation till the death of the late queen: a rage of negotiating has possessed the same party, ever since." He advised his lordship to draw the conclusions of more than two centuries of British diplomacy: "We must always remember, that we are not part of the continent, but we must never forget that we are neighbors to it."

In 1736 Bolingbroke moved again, to Argeville, where he lived until 1744, making lengthy visits to England to sell Dawley (1738-1739), to visit old friends such as Pope, and to settle his inheritance (1742, 1743-1744). In Argeville during 1736 he composed four last essays for *The Craftsman*, criticizing ministerial peace negotiations although he privately conceded their relative success. His failure to defeat Walpole haunted him, and he set out once again to justify his opposition principles to a new generation. In *A Letter on the Spirit of Patriotism* (written in 1736), he rallied Lord Cornbury and the "Boy Patriots" to unceasing struggle against Walpole's policies, recommending for their emulation the classical orators Demosthenes and Cicero. Like these statesmen and, by implication, like himself, they must mount a systematic campaign of resistance, exhorting the nation to rise up in moral outrage against the prime minister and his monied henchmen. When the king realized this national disgust, he would dismiss Walpole. Bolingbroke's faith in national moral reform now seems hopelessly idealistic, but this letter has been described as the first call for a regular "loyal opposition" in Parliament.

Meanwhile, Bolingbroke centered his more practical efforts in the enmity between George II and Frederick, Prince of Wales. When he visited England in 1738, he perceived that Walpole's power had declined since the death of Queen Caroline. A group of "patriots" clustered around the crown prince, preaching freedom under his aegis, might rally the people to Bolingbroke's cause. Throughout his visit, Bolingbroke encouraged a spate of literature exhorting Frederick to defend liberty, ranging from Gay's *Fables: Volume the Second* (1738) and Pope's *One Thousand Seven Hundred and Forty* to David Mallet's *Alfred: A Masque* (1740). Finally, he composed his own contribution, a treatise in the humanist tradition of a manual for a prince. *The Idea of a Patriot King* (written in 1738-1739) was hailed by his adherents as a masterpiece; Pope begged permission to print a half-dozen copies when the original manuscript became dog-eared from circulation among friends. Today, the work has been either condemned as foolishly naive, or analyzed as deliberately ironic rhetoric. In fact, Bolingbroke acknowledged that a patriot king was "the most uncommon of all phenomena in the physical or moral world," but he seems to have believed that only an attempt by Frederick to emulate this prodigy could cleanse the government. The patriot king embodied all of Bolingbroke's cherished ideals: a philosopher, the king would realize that only by serving the national interest could God's natural law be fulfilled. Accordingly, he would dismiss all ministers corrupted by factionalism and choose honest, disinterested patriots for his counselors. There would be no parties because there could be only one national interest. Traditional social distinctions would once again flourish, because money could no longer purchase power. Whether naive or ironic, *The Idea of a Patriot King* marked the end of Bolingbroke's hope to lead a unified opposition to the defeat of Walpole. Only a new king, in a new reign, might accomplish that feat.

In addition to *The Idea of a Patriot King*, Bolingbroke contributed one final essay to the opposi-

The Château de la Source, near Orléans (top), where Bolingbroke spent the last five years of his exile in France, and an engraving of the Uxbridge, Middlesex, estate (bottom) that he bought in 1733, after a royal pardon and restoration of his property rights made possible his return to England in 1725

tion. "On the State of Parties at the Accession of King George the First" (written in 1739) once again excoriates the Whigs and the earl of Oxford for creating the dissension which led to the present state of affairs. Only Bolingbroke himself had foreseen the danger, but his advice had gone unheeded. As Bolingbroke penned this last warning against faction, Walpole's power at last began to decline. Over Walpole's objections, Britain finally declared war on Spain after months of opposition agitation. In Parliament, however, the opposition itself remained divided and behaved indecisively. Sir William Wyndham, long Bolingbroke's spokesman and head of the Tories, died in 1740. Bereft of any effective leadership, some opposition allies drifted toward accommodation with the ministry, while others disputed the form a new ministry might take. When Walpole finally fell, early in 1742, his lieutenants were able to keep his government relatively intact. Bolingbroke was forced to admit the failure of his efforts. After attending Pope's deathbed, he and his wife retired permanently to the estate at Battersea where he had lived as a child. There, he continued to ply succeeding administrations with advice, most of which was ignored. When a new opposition arose around Prince Frederick, he was no longer among its leaders. In 1749 he wrote "Some Reflections on the Present State of the Nation," rehearsing once again Britain's decline into corruption at the hands of monied upstarts and power-hungry ministers. Again he expressed his hope for a patriot king. But his lingering hopes were dashed by Frederick's death in 1751. His wife had died in 1750, and Bolingbroke himself succumbed to a painful cancer on 12 December 1751.

Bolingbroke's reputation declined rapidly after his death. In his last years, he had become embroiled with William Warburton, Pope's officious literary executor, in a public squabble over Pope's character. Shortly after the poet's death, Bolingbroke had discovered a 1500-copy edition of The Idea of a Patriot King, no doubt authorized by his friend as an adulatory gesture. Bolingbroke, however, regarded the edition as a breach of trust and burned the copies. Earlier, he had suppressed some verses about "Atossa" intended for the final version of Pope's Of the Characters of Women, suspecting they described the still-living duchess of Marlborough rather than, more probably, the duchess of Buckingham. Bolingbroke said nothing publicly until 1745, when he released a pamphlet including the verses and accus-

ing Pope of deceit for preserving them. The pamphlet was evidently a warning to Warburton, rumored to be composing a biography of Pope with severe reflections on Bolingbroke. Warburton refrained, and Bolingbroke published no more about Pope until 1749, when excerpts from The Idea of a Patriot King, evidently from Pope's text, began appearing in The London Journal. Enraged, Bolingbroke published a correct version, prefaced by an "Advertisement" revealing Pope's perfidy. Writers such as Warburton and Joseph Spence promptly defended the poet's memory, and Bolingbroke found himself in the midst of a pamphlet war. Bolingbroke's role in the imbroglio has often been condemned, but he evidently regarded Pope's surreptitious edition as an inexcusable breach of friendship.

The "Advertisement" to The Idea of a Patriot King caused more discussion than the text itself. But when Bolingbroke's works began to be published after his death, his essays aroused scandalized criticism of their Deism and hypocritical self-justification. When David Mallet published a five-volume edition of Bolingbroke's works in 1754, Samuel Johnson denounced him as "a scoundrel, for charging a blunderbuss against religion and morality; a coward, because he had not resolution to fire it off himself, but left half a crown to a beggarly Scotchman, to draw the trigger after his death!" Two years later, Edmund Burke parodied Bolingbroke's style in A Vindication of Natural Society, and later asked, "Who now reads Bolingbroke, who ever read him through?" Today, historians and literary scholars are again reading Bolingbroke, acknowledging his rhetorical mastery as a political journalist, his inspiration of the great Tory satirists, and his plea for a genteel hegemony fast slipping from the grasp of the conservative squirearchy.

Letters:

The Letters and Correspondence of Henry St. John, Lord Viscount Bolingbroke, 4 volumes, edited by Gilbert Park (London: Printed for G. G. & J. Robinson, 1798);

Lettres Historiques, Politiques, Philosophiques et Particulières de Henri St. John, Lord Vicomte Bolingbroke, 3 volumes, edited by H. P. Grimoard (Paris: Dentu, 1808);

"Letters of Henry St. John to James Brydges," edited by Godfrey Davies and Marion Tinling, *Huntington Library Bulletin*, 8 (October 1935): 153-170;

Lettres Inedités de Bolingbroke à Lord Stair 1716-1720, edited by Paul Baratier (Trévoux: Imprimerie de Trévoux, 1939);

"Letters from Bolingbroke to James Grahme," edited by H. T. Dickinson, *Transactions Cumberland and Westmoreland Antiquarian and Archaeological Society*, new series 48 (1988).

Bibliography:

Giles Barber, "Some Uncollected Authors XLI: Henry Saint John, Viscount Bolingbroke, 1678-1751," *Book Collector*, 14 (Winter 1965): 528-537.

Biographies:

Walter Sichel, *Bolingbroke and His Times*, 2 volumes (London: James Nisbet, 1901, 1902);

H. T. Dickinson, *Bolingbroke* (London: Constable, 1970).

References:

Bertrand A. Goldgar, *Walpole and the Wits: the Relation of Politics to Literature, 1722-1742* (Lincoln: University of Nebraska Press, 1976);

Brean S. Hammond, *Pope and Bolingbroke: A Study of Friendship and Influence* (Columbia: University of Missouri Press, 1984);

Jeffrey Hart, *Viscount Bolingbroke: Tory Humanist* (London: Routledge & Kegan Paul, 1965);

Sydney W. Jackman, *Man of Mercury: An Appreciation of the Mind of Henry St. John, Viscount Bolingbroke* (London: Pall Mall Press, 1965);

D. G. James, *The Life of Reason: Hobbes, Locke, Bolingbroke* (London: Longmans, Green, 1949);

Isaac Kramnick, "An Augustan Reply to Locke: Bolingbroke on Natural Law and the Origin of Government," *Political Science Quarterly*, 82 (December 1967): 571-594;

Kramnick, *Bolingbroke and His Circle: The Politics of Nostalgia in the Age of Walpole* (Cambridge, Mass.: Harvard University Press, 1968);

Harvey C. Mansfield, *Statesmanship and Party Government: A Study of Burke and Bolingbroke* (Chicago: University of Chicago Press, 1965);

Walter McIntosh Merrill, *From Statesman to Philosopher: A Study in Bolingbroke's Deism* (New York: Philosophical Library, 1949);

George H. Nadel, "New Light on Bolingbroke's Letters on History," *Journal of the History of Ideas*, 23 (October-December 1962): 550-557;

Pat Rogers, "Swift and Bolingbroke on Faction," *Journal of British Studies*, 9 (May 1970): 71-101;

Frank T. Smallwood, "Bolingbroke *vs.* Alexander Pope: The Publication of the *Patriot King*," *Papers of the Bibliographical Society of America*, 65 (1971): 225-241;

Simon Varey, *Henry St. John, Viscount Bolingbroke* (Boston: Twayne, 1984).

Papers:

Bolingbroke manuscripts are held throughout Great Britain, Europe, and the United States. Some important collections are in the British Library, the Public Record Office, and the New York Public Library. H. T. Dickinson includes a list of manuscript sources in his biography of Bolingbroke.

Gilbert Burnet
(18 September 1643 - 17 March 1715)

Martine Watson Brownley
Emory University

SELECTED BOOKS: *A Discourse on the Memory of that Rare and truely virtuous person Sir Robert Fletcher of Saltoun* (Edinburgh, 1665);

The Memoires of the Lives and Actions of James and William, Dukes of Hamilton and Castleherald, &c. (London: Printed by J. Grover for R. Royston, 1677);

The History of the Reformation of the Church of England, 3 volumes (volumes 1 and 2, London: Printed by T. H. Richard Chiswell, 1679, 1681; volume 3, London: Printed for J. Churchill, 1715);

Some Passages of the Life and Death of the Right Honourable John, Earl of Rochester (London: Printed for R. Chiswell, 1680);

The Life and Death of Sir Matthew Hale, Kt., Sometime Lord Chief Justice of His Majesties Court of King's Bench (London: Printed for William Shrowsbery, 1682);

The History of the Rights of Princes in the Disposing of Ecclesiastical Benefices and Church-Lands (London: Printed by J. D. for Richard Chiswell, 1682);

An Answer to Animadversions on the History of the Rights of Princes (London: Printed for Richard Chiswell, 1682);

The Life of William Bedell, D.D., Bishop of Kilmore in Ireland (London: Printed for John Southby, 1685);

Some Letters Containing An Account of what seemed most remarkable in Switzerland, Italy, &c. (Amsterdam, 1686);

Reflections on Mr. Varillas's History of the Revolutions that Have Happened in Europe in Matters of Religion. And more particularly on his ninth book that relates to England (Amsterdam [London?], 1686; London, 1689);

A Supplement to Dr. Burnet's Letter Relating to His Travels through Switzerland, Italy, Germany &c. (Rotterdam: Printed by A. Acher, 1687);

A Defence of the Reflections on the Ninth Book of the first Volume of Mr. Varillas's History of Heresies. Being a reply to his answer (Amsterdam: Printed for J. S., 1687);

A Continuation of Reflections on Mr. Varillas's History of Heresies. Particularly on that which relates to English Affairs in his third and fourth tomes (Amsterdam: Printed for J. S., 1687);

Three Letters concerning the Present State of Italy, written in the year 1687 . . . Being a supplement to Dr. Burnet's Letters (N.p., 1688);

Reflections on the Relation of the English Reformation, lately printed at Oxford, 2 parts (Amsterdam: Printed for P. Bleau, 1688; London: Printed for R. Chiswell, 1689);

A Sermon Preached at the Coronation of William III and Mary II (London: Printed for J. Starkey & R. Chiswell, 1689);

A Discourse of the Pastoral Care (London: Printed for Richard Chiswell, 1692);

A Sermon Preached at the Funeral of the Honourable Robert Boyle; at St. Martins in the Fields, January 7, 1691/2 (London: Printed for Richard Chiswell, 1692);

An Essay on the Memory of the Late Queen (London: Printed for Richard Chiswell, 1695);

An Exposition of the Thirty-nine Articles of the Church of England (London: Printed by R. Roberts for R. Chiswell, 1699);

Bishop Burnet's History of His Own Time, 2 volumes (volume 1, London: Printed for Thomas, Ward, 1724; volume 2, London: Printed for the editor by J. Downing & H. Woodfall, 1734);

Thoughts on Education. Now first printed from an original manuscript (London: Printed for D. Watson, 1741).

Editions: *Bishop Burnet's History of His Own Time,* 6 volumes, edited by M. J. Routh, second edition, enlarged (Oxford: Oxford University Press, 1833);

History of the Reformation of the Church of England, 7 volumes, edited by Nicholas Pocock (Oxford: Clarendon Press, 1865);

Burnet's History of My Own Time: Part I: The Reign of Charles the Second, 2 volumes, edited by Osmund Airy (Oxford: Clarendon Press, 1897, 1900);

The Right Reverend Gilbert Burnet, Lord Bishop of Salisbury (engraving by G. B. Shaw, after John Riley)

A Supplement to Burnet's History of My Own Time, edited by H. C. Foxcroft (Oxford: Clarendon Press, 1902).

OTHER: *Utopia: Written in Latin by Sir Thomas More, Chancellor of England: Translated into English*, translated by Burnet (London: Printed for Richard Chiswell, 1684).

Gilbert Burnet's inexhaustible energy is nowhere better shown than by the amount of literary work he managed to accomplish in the midst of a varied and tumultuous career in Church and State. As a divine he published more than fifty sermons and several important theological and devotional works. An able and indefatigable controversialist and propagandist, he produced numerous

tracts on the political and religious issues of his times. Among his miscellaneous writings are several translations, including one of Sir Thomas More's *Utopia*, a discourse on education, a travel book, and many letters and speeches. But despite his voluminous output, as a literary figure Burnet is best known for his work as a biographer and historian.

Burnet was born in Edinburgh on 18 September 1643. His mother was a strict and zealous Presbyterian, the sister of Archibald Johnston of Warriston, the fanatic Convenanter; his father, Robert Burnet, a successful lawyer, was a moderate Episcopalian, thoroughly Royalist and Erastian, who was forced into exile on the Continent three times for refusing to take the Covenant. Growing up in such a household undoubtedly contributed a great deal to fostering the tolerance and moderation characteristic of Burnet throughout his life. His background gave him a broad personal understanding of the religious and political issues that split both Scotland and England repeatedly for well over half a century. But with his wide and humane viewpoint, Burnet, like many moderates in all periods of history, throughout his career often found himself a man in the middle, the object of suspicion and attack by both sides. In his later life the English would always distrust him as a Scot and accuse him of Presbyterian leanings; the Scots in their turn would despise him as a renegade, a deserter to English and Anglican principles.

A very precocious child, Burnet entered the Marishal College of Aberdeen at the age of ten and by fourteen became master of arts. After several more years of intensive reading in law, history, and theology, he entered the church. His conscientiousness as a young clergyman in Saltoun, his first parish, presaged the diligence and energy that would make him one of the ablest bishops of the age, just as his first published work, *A Discourse on the Memory of that Rare and truely virtuous person Sir Robert Fletcher of Saltoun* (1665), written to commemorate the death of the man who had presented him with the living, reflected the predilection for biography that would mark much of his best writing. In addition, the personal traits that would repeatedly make friends for Burnet and then too often turn those friends into enemies were equally apparent.

Along with his learning and intelligence, Burnet possessed good looks and considerable personal charm. He was also a warm and generous man, always eager to assist others. But the form that his assistance took was in many cases the revelation or assertion of truths extremely unpleasant to the recipient; Burnet's fearless honesty perpetually combined with his naive self-confidence and problematical judgment to produce a tactlessness at best obtuse. At twenty-one he vehemently criticized Scottish ecclesiastical policy to the powerful John Maitland, Duke of Lauderdale. Two years later, he drafted a memorial to the Scottish bishops protesting episcopal abuses, and subsequently stood his ground under their fierce counterattacks, including the threat of excommunication. In both cases Burnet's objections were amply justified, as they generally were throughout his career; the problem was that his efficacy as a reformer was repeatedly undermined by his meth-

ods and approaches. In later years he would upbraid Charles II for personal immorality and urge William III to alter his cold and reserved manners. As troublesome as his temerity and impudence was his limitless curiosity and almost total lack of reticence, for Burnet, like James Boswell after him, was indefatigable not only in searching out information about others but also in purveying it widely.

As a young man Burnet spent time in England and also lived and traveled on the Continent in Holland and France. The liberal atmosphere of Holland encouraged his own broad religious sympathies, while the absolutism and Catholicism of France stimulated his commitment to Protestantism, law, and liberty. In England he became a confidant of Lauderdale and a friend of James, Duke of York (later James II), while Charles II appointed him a royal chaplain. In Scotland he played an increasingly important role in ecclesiastical affairs, and in 1669 he was named professor of divinity at the University of Glasgow. By the time he was thirty he had refused four Scottish bishoprics, received the offer of yet another, and had been promised the first vacant archbishopric. Nevertheless, by 1674, in one of the reversals of favor that recurred throughout Burnet's career, he had so alienated Lauderdale that he decided that safety dictated permanent residence in England.

In London for the next decade, Burnet busily immersed himself in the tumultuous politics of the time, continually moving in and out of court favor as he alternately pleased or outraged various powerful figures or factions. A gifted and popular preacher, he became chaplain to the Rolls Chapel and also received the lectureship to St. Clement's. In addition to various controversial pieces, Burnet's first historical work, *The Memoires of the Lives and Actions of James and William, Dukes of Hamilton and Castleherald, &c.*, which he had completed in 1673, was published finally in 1677. Sir Charles Firth in his *Essays Historical and Literary* (1938) describes the *Memoires* as the "first political biography of the modern type," and in it Burnet employs biographical methods to produce a historical perspective for an entire era. Focusing on the problematical careers of the two dukes and also on the Scottish transactions of King Charles I, Burnet covers the period from 1625 to 1652, with the origin and development of the civil wars in Scotland. The *Memoires* contains much valuable material; the duchess of Hamilton had given Burnet access to the family papers, and his close friend Sir Robert Moray had convinced him to replace his original narrative account with extensive quotations from and reproduction of documents. Its title reflects the combining of genres characteristic of most of Burnet's best historical writing.

About a year after the *Memoires* appeared, as hysteria over the Popish Plot mounted, Burnet published the first volume of his *History of the Reformation of the Church of England*, a major scholarly treatment of events from the reign of Henry VIII to that of Elizabeth. For this work Burnet received wide popular acclaim and public thanks from both Houses of Parliament. Even with his strong Protestant biases, Burnet managed to evolve a broad overview for *The History of the Reformation*, which he had gone to a good deal of effort to research. Always a hasty writer, however, he was too often extremely careless in reproducing material which he had laboriously assembled. Despite its many faults, commentators generally consider *The History of the Reformation* as a pioneering work in ecclesiastical history, both in the comprehensiveness of its treatment and also in its extensive inclusion of authentic sources. Until well into the nineteenth century it remained the standard history of the subject. A second volume was published in 1681, with a final volume of supporting documents in 1715.

Burnet strongly defended the first Catholic victim of the Popish Plot and worked tirelessly for moderation during the Exclusion Crisis. But he increasingly alienated both Charles II and James, and as royal dislike of him grew, he retired in 1681 from action to contemplation, studying algebra and philosophy and constructing a laboratory for chemical pursuits. Burnet had always enjoyed friendships across a wide political spectrum; at this time his closest friends were George Savile, Marquis of Halifax; Lord William Russell; and Arthur Capel, Earl of Essex; and the involvement of the latter two in the Rye House Plot in 1683 only heightened the court's suspicion and disaffection.

Amid the political and religious turmoil of the early 1680s, Burnet also produced several biographies. Traditionally considered a branch of history, biography by the middle and late seventeenth century was beginning to evolve as a separate genre. The prefaces to Burnet's biographies show his recognition of many of the elements that were crippling life writing at the time, particularly its serious factual deficiencies and tendencies to flattery and panegyric. However, his own

commitment to inculcate morality in all of his works led him to some of the same exemplary and inspirational emphases that made too many early biographies dull and lifeless. Mainly for this reason, Burnet's accomplishments in the development of English biography have generally been somewhat undervalued, although his works show considerable experimentation with the formal possibilities of the genre.

Among Burnet's biographies are lives of Sir Matthew Hale (1682) and Bishop William Bedell (1685), but his best known is the sensational *Some Passages of the Life and Death of the Right Honourable John, Earl of Rochester* (1680). The churchman and the rake had met during the last year of Rochester's life, and in the biography, which Rochester had urged him to write, Burnet recounted in detail the conversations on morality and religion that culminated in Rochester's deathbed conversion. Although Boswell quotes Samuel Johnson's conversational remark in 1777 that in Burnet's biography "We have a good *Death*: there is not much *Life*," Johnson's comment in his own treatment of Rochester in the *Lives of the Poets* (1779-1781) that the biography is one "which the critick ought to read for its elegance, the philosopher for its arguments, and the saint for its piety" succinctly summarizes the strengths of one of Burnet's most-popular and best-known works. Despite minor structural weaknesses, it is by literary standards generally considered his most impressive work, and it was often republished through the nineteenth century.

After his accession to the throne James II refused to receive Burnet at court, but granted permission for him to leave England. Burnet's commentary on his subsequent travels on the Continent appeared in 1686 as *Some Letters Containing An Account of what seemed most remarkable in Switzerland, Italy, &c.*, in the form of a series of letters to his friend Robert Boyle. He emphasized that in writing it he deliberately avoided material found in ordinary travel books, and as a result the information included is diverse, ranging from the kinds of fish found in Lake Geneva to a discussion of the readings of a disputed passage in the Gospel of John available in Continental libraries. He also effectively manipulated the genre of the travel book for polemical purposes, never foregoing any opportunity to contrast Catholicism unfavorably with Protestantism or to oppose absolutism in government. The work was extremely popular among Burnet's contemporaries, and it was republished several

Frontispiece and title page for Burnet's best-known biography, which focuses so much on Rochester's final year and his deathbed conversion that Samuel Johnson said of the book, "We have a good Death: *there is not much* Life."

times in the eighteenth century.

Early in his travels Burnet had bypassed Holland because of the many English political exiles in the country, but when he journeyed to Utrecht in the following year, he found letters of invitation to the court of the prince of Orange at The Hague. William and Mary warmly welcomed Burnet, and with his many contacts in England and his extensive knowledge of the English political and ecclesiastical situation, he soon became a valued adviser to both. He produced polemical pamphlets and also rendered more personal services to the prince and princess, warning them of a French plot to kidnap William and convincing Mary that she should immediately inform William of her intention of placing total authority in his hands should they reign in England. James's outrage at Burnet's influence finally led William

to bar him officially from court, but correspondence via William Bentinck (later earl of Portland) kept him in constant touch with the prince and princess. James ultimately sought to prosecute Burnet on capital charges in Scotland, and by the summer of 1687 he was in danger from English and French plots to kill or abduct him. As William's chaplain, he sailed in the first ship with the prince on the expedition to England.

After the revolution Burnet was named a royal chaplain and clerk of the Royal Closet. In a few months he became chancellor of the Garter, and then was appointed bishop of Salisbury. William left to the queen the major role in dealing with ecclesiastical affairs, and through his close friendship with her Burnet exerted substantial influence in this area. Throughout the reign he remained a key figure in ecclesiastical policy, working ceaselessly for toleration in the State and reform in the Church. He was a model bishop, tireless in supervising and serving his diocese. At the urging of the queen, John Tillotson, Archbishop of Canterbury, and others, he composed various influential religious and theological works, such as *A Discourse of the Pastoral Care* (1692) and *An Exposition of the Thirty-nine Articles of the Church of England* (1699). From the time of his sermon in Exeter Cathedral after William's landing, he was constantly called on to preach during the reign; his funeral sermon for his friend Boyle is generally considered one of his finest efforts (1692). An equally powerful piece of character drawing is his *Essay on the Memory of the Late Queen* (1695). One of his characteristic generic mixtures, in this case a combination of biography, sermon, essay, memoir, and character sketch, it is a moving memorial that conveys the fervent respect and admiration Burnet always felt for Mary.

Characteristically, Burnet raced from William's deathbed to be the first to inform Anne that she had become queen. After her accession he preached the first sermon before her, but he never exerted the influence with Anne that he had with Mary and, to a lesser extent, with William. He remained tireless in his episcopal work and also in his duties in the House of Lords, where he had always been an active participant. In addition, the plan for increasing the revenues of poor livings instituted in 1704 as Queen Anne's Bounty had originated in one of his proposals to William years before. A firm supporter of the Hanoverian succession, Burnet lived to preach before King George I, to whom the last volume of his *History of the Reformation* is dedicated (1715).

Burnet's most important work appeared posthumously. In 1724 his son published the first volume of his father's *History of My Own Time*, and a second followed in 1734. Burnet had begun what he described as his "secret history" in 1683, adding to it over the years and revising it several times. Long awaited and eagerly devoured by a wide audience, this history was as controversial as its author had been. Its scope is wide, covering portions of Scottish and English history from before the civil wars to the Treaty of Utrecht. In depth the work is more variable. Although it remains a crucial source for William's invasion and various other events to which Burnet had been an eyewitness, in many other sections coverage is sketchy. But Burnet had never intended to be comprehensive, explaining in his

preface to the work that his "chief design in writing was to give a true view of men and of counsels, leaving public transactions to gazettes and the public historians of the times." More seriously, his lifelong problems with accuracy, along with his characteristic credulity and prejudices, mar the work. Thus in the *History of My Own Time* worthless gossip and scandal mingle promiscuously with invaluable firsthand information available in no other source. With its colorful anecdotes and fascinating details, the value of the work as entertainment is high, even if the reliability of its information is not always at the same level.

The *History of My Own Time* is written in Burnet's characteristic loose, flexible style, with few literary embellishments. Jonathan Swift and some contemporaries vehemently condemned Burnet's stylistic infelicities and carelessness, but other contemporaries and later readers found its ease and colloquial directness a refreshing change from the stilted diction and overblown rhetoric that too often characterize the historical writing of the period. The inevitable literary comparisons with Edward Hyde, Earl of Clarendon's majestic *History of the Rebellion* (1702-1704) have from the beginning functioned somewhat unfairly to Burnet's disadvantage, for Clarendon's was a very different kind of work in intention, approach, and execution. Like most of Burnet's writings, the *History of My Own Time* is a generic amalgam, containing elements of autobiography, essay, memoir, sermon, and biography as well as actual history. A highlight is its character sketches, for with his insatiable curiosity Burnet had closely observed his contemporaries, and he could be an astute judge of human personality. He had read extensively in classical, English, and Continental character writers, and many of his earlier works had given him substantial practice in depicting men and women. Though like most of Burnet's writing his character sketches lack formal symmetry and polish, their wealth of telling small detail adroitly deployed gives them an immediacy and realism unusual in historical depictions of character during the period. Particularly notable are his characters of Lauderdale; Robert Leighton, Archbishop of Glasgow; Charles II; James II; and, naturally enough, William and Mary.

Although many angry contemporary readers dismissed the *History of My Own Time* as a worthless farrago of anecdote, libel, and polemic, later eighteenth- and nineteenth-century readers from Johnson to Thomas Babington Macaulay praised its entertaining narrative. Modern historians, while condemning Burnet's lack of judgment, have emphasized that his errors were in most cases comparatively venial ones and that he never deliberately misrepresented his material. Every historian of the period continues to draw on Burnet's work, but its popular audience in the twentieth century has been negligible. Despite its many obvious defects, however, the central role of Burnet's *History of My Own Time* as a primary source of information about the period it covers and its considerable literary interest make it the most important historical work written in England between those of Clarendon and David Hume.

Among his enemies Burnet numbered the ablest writers of his times, and posterity's view of him has generally been shaped accordingly, from John Dryden's depiction of him as the Buzzard in *The Hind and the Panther* (1687) to Alexander Pope and John Gay's parody in the *Memoirs of P. P., Clerk of This Parish* (1727). In comparison to Burnet, even the hapless Thomas Shadwell seems fairly lucky. That Burnet as a person provided ample satirical fuel is incontestable, just as various structural and stylistic weaknesses offered valid grounds for serious objections to his writings. But ridicule of Burnet the man has often tended to color assessments of him as a writer and has sometimes overshadowed his literary and historical accomplishments. Burnet's various generic experimentations in history and biography played a role in preparing for the great later eighteenth-century achievements in both fields, a contribution that has been inadequately evaluated by later critics. Nor have his writings been readily available to a general audience; although many of his works continued to be republished well into the nineteenth century, there are no modern editions of any of them.

Letters:

H. C. Foxcroft, "Some Unpublished Letters of Gilbert Burnet the Historian," *The Camden Miscellany*, third series 13 (London: Royal Historical Society, 1907), pp. 5-45.

Bibliographies:

T. E. S. Clarke and H. C. Foxcroft, *A Life of Gilbert Burnet, Bishop of Salisbury* (Cambridge: Cambridge University Press, 1907), Appendix II, pp. 522-556;

Clarke and Foxcroft, "List of Letters from Gilbert Burnet Known to be Extant," in *A Life of Gilbert Burnet, Bishop of Salisbury*, Appendix III, pp. 557-566;

Ralph Hebgen, "A Checklist of Secondary Literature on Gilbert Burnet, Bishop of Salisbury, 1643-1715," *Anglican and Episcopal History*, 58 (June 1989): 213-224.

Biography:

T. E. S. Clarke and H. C. Foxcroft, *A Life of Gilbert Burnet, Bishop of Salisbury* (Cambridge: Cambridge University Press, 1907).

References:

Sir George Clark, "Gilbert Burnet, 1643-1715," *Aberdeen University Review*, 37 (Autumn 1957): 113-124;

H. W. C. Davis, "Gilbert Burnet," in *Typical English Churchmen from Parker to Maurice*, edited by William Edward Collins (London: S.P.C.K., 1902), pp. 149-191;

Mary Delorme, "Gilbert Burnet, Bishop and Historian," *History Today*, 29 (September 1979): 594-609;

John Drabble, "Gilbert Burnet and the History of the English Reformation," *Journal of Religious History*, 12 (December 1983): 351-363;

Sir Charles Firth, "Burnet as an Historian," in his *Essays Historical and Literary* (Oxford: Clarendon Press, 1938), pp. 174-209;

G. P. Gooch, "Burnet and the Stuart Kings" and "Burnet and William III," in *Courts and Cabinets* (New York: Knopf, 1946), pp. 70-101;

K. C. Hamilton, "Two Restoration Prose-writers— Burnet and Halifax," in *Restoration Literature: Critical Approaches*, edited by Harold Love (London: Methuen, 1972), pp. 205-223.

Papers:

Miscellaneous Burnet manuscripts are scattered among English and Scottish libraries. Among the major works, manuscripts for the *History of My Own Time* are held by both the Bodleian Library (MSS. Add. D. 18-21) and the British Library (MS. Harley 6584), while the British Library has two manuscripts for the *Memoires of the Dukes of Hamilton* (MS. Add. 33,259; MS. Sloane 1007).

Samuel Butler

(February 1613 - 25 September 1680)

William C. Horne
Salisbury State University

BOOKS: *Hudibras. The First Part. Written in the time of the late Wars* (London: Printed by J. G. for Richard Marriott, 1663);

Hudibras. The Second Part. By the Author of the First (London: Printed by T. R. for John Martyn & James Allestry, 1664);

To the Memory of the Most Renowned Du-Vall: A Pindarick Ode (London: Printed for H. Brome, 1671);

Two Letters, One from John Audland, a Quaker, to William Prynne. The Other, William Prynnes Answer by the Author of Hudibras (London: Printed for Jonathan Edwin, 1672);

Hudibras. The First and Second Parts. Written in the time of the Late Wars. Corrected and Amended, with Several Additions and Annotations (London: Printed by T. N. for John Martyn & Henry Herringman, 1674);

Hudibras. The Third and Last Part. Written by the Author of the First and Second Parts (London: Printed for Simon Miller, 1678);

The Plagiary Exposed: or an Old Answer to a Newly Revived Calumny against the Memory of King Charles I (London: Printed for Thom. Bennet, 1691).

Editions: *Hudibras in Three Parts . . . with Large Annotations, and a Preface,* 2 volumes, edited by Zachery Grey (Cambridge: Printed by J. Bentham for W. Innys, A. Ward, and others, in London, 1744);

The Genuine Remains in Verse and Prose of Mr. Samuel Butler, 2 volumes, edited by Robert Thyer (London: Printed for J. & R. Tonson, 1759);

Hudibras, 3 volumes, edited by Treadway Russel Nash (London: Printed by T. Rickaby for B. & J. White, 1793);

Satires and Miscellaneous Poetry and Prose, edited by René Lamar (Cambridge: Cambridge University Press, 1928);

Hudibras, edited by John Wilders (Oxford: Clarendon Press, 1967);

Characters, edited by Charles W. Daves (Cleveland: Press of Case Western Reserve University, 1970);

Prose Observations, edited by Hugh De Quehen (Oxford: Clarendon Press, 1979).

As the author of *Hudibras* (1663-1678), a poetic monster of grotesque comic/satiric proportions, Samuel Butler has achieved legendary status as a monster maker. Previous to this century, Butler was mainly known as an anti-Puritan satirist who broadly followed the model of Miguel de Cervantes's *Don Quixote* (1605) in creating the perfect hypocrite, Sir Hudibras the Presbyterian Knight. *Hudibras,* a poem in double and triple rhyming iambic-pentameter couplets, longer than John Milton's *Paradise Lost* (1667), is not simply identifiable as burlesque, mock epic, parody, or allegory. It is, like the Butler of legend, an unclassifiable eccentricity, a true original in English literature.

Recent criticism of Samuel Butler has attempted to replace the Butler of legend with a Butler whose literary creations are more humanly recognizable, more understandable in terms of the contexts in which he worked. The problem of providing detail in the portrait of Samuel Butler has been hampered by sketchy biographical facts which offer minimal illumination of some parts of his life, while others remain hazy, if not entirely dark. Because of the lack of information, twentieth-century criticism has frequently turned to Butler's writings other than *Hudibras.* Paying attention to Butler's occasional verse, his political pamphlets, and his numerous prose characters has helped us better understand Butler's literary contexts. The view of Butler as a one-poem author has changed as Butler's other compositions, especially his prose characters, have gained a literary status in their own right. These compete in at least a few critics' judgments with *Hudibras* for precedence. Careful readings of Butler's prose observations in his notebooks have shifted the image of Butler from the eccentric anti-Puritan

Samuel Butler (engraving by P. Thomson, after the portrait by Gerard Soest)

satirist to the skeptical rationalist or empiricist with a wide-ranging intellect. We have discovered that Butler had a voracious curiosity, especially about nature (both in the sense of the natural world and human nature).

The reliable facts about Butler's life tend to cluster around two periods: the poet's early years in Worcestershire and his period of fame after the publication of the first part of *Hudibras* in late 1662 (with 1663 on its title page). The best recent summary of Butler's life is provided by John Wilders in his 1967 Clarendon Press edition of *Hudibras*.

Butler's ancestors were yeoman farmers who lived in the vicinity of Worcester in the very small village of Strensham, where their farm was leased from the Russell family. Samuel and Mary Butler's fifth child of eight, Samuel the poet was

baptized on 14 February 1613. By 1621 the family may have been living at Barbourne in the parish of Claines, where they owned a house. In 1626, when Butler's father died, the family was again leasing a farm from the Russells at Defford, which was near Strensham. At this time Butler evidently attended King's School, Worcester.

The will of Samuel Butler, Sr., shows that the father was neither impoverished nor illiterate. To his son the future poet, he left "all my Lawe and Latine bookes of Logicke, Rhetoricke, Philosophy, Poesy, phisicke, my great Dodaneus Herball, and all my lattine and greeke bookes whatsoever." In the will the father had arranged for his son to be bound apprentice, though in 1628 at age fifteen the son still held family land and the house at Barbourne, which he had inher-

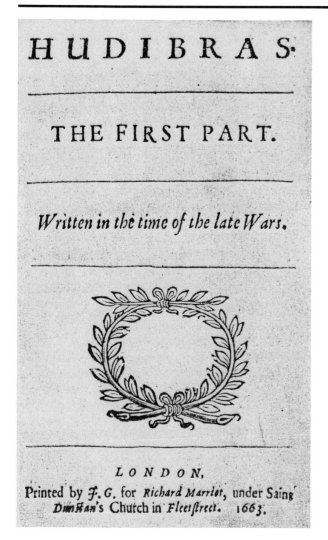

HUDIBRAS.

THE FIRST PART.

Written in the time of the late Wars.

LONDON,
Printed by *J. G.* for *Richard Marriot*, under Saint
Dunstan's Church in *Fleetstreet*. 1663.

Title page for Butler's satiric "Accot of y^e Ridiculous folly & Knavery of ye Presbiterian & Independent Factions" during the English civil war

ited. It seems probable that Butler soon after forsook the life of a farmer for employment as a clerk in various wealthy households, first close to and then distant from Worcestershire. Though Anthony à Wood reports that Butler was at Cambridge for a time, Michael Wilding finds it unlikely that Butler's recently widowed mother with her eight children would have had the money to send her scholarly son to the university.

Butler may have left the farm, but the farm did not leave Butler. During his employments Butler evidently had access to private libraries, and as a compulsive and rather undisciplined reader, he filled his mind with recondite and abstruse learning. Underlying this accumulation, however, is an unvarnished sense of English farm life, not the idealized bucolic world of the pastoral, but the world of leeks and cabbages, gridirons and fry-

ing pans, saddles and cruppers, "tainted Beef" and "Gangrene in stale Pork," clover grass and the rumps of horses and cows.

One of Butler's early biographers, in the preface to the 1744 edition of *Hudibras*, says that his first employment was in the household of a "Mr. Jeffreys of Earls-Croom," described as "an eminent justice of the peace for that county." It is more likely that Butler worked as a clerk for the son, who was not so "eminent."

John Aubrey, Butler's most trustworthy biographer, places Butler next in the service of "the Countess of Kent" for "severall yeares." Wilders tells us that "the Dowager Countess of Kent, whose husband, the Earl died in 1639, lived at Wrest Park in Bedfordshire, and was a friend and patroness of Selden the antiquary." Butler's reading may have been influenced by his friendship with John Selden, and in the countess's employment Butler probably also first became acquainted with another of the countess's protégés, the miniaturist Samuel Cooper (who later painted Butler's portrait). During this time, according to Aubrey, Butler extended his interests beyond reading (and possibly writing) to include painting, drawing, and also music.

Untrustworthy early sources assert that Butler next was in the service of Sir Samuel Luke, "of an ancient Family in Bedfordshire," and that Luke was the model for the character of Hudibras. Luke, who was a true-blue Presbyterian, an important officer in the Parliament's army, a member of Parliament, and committeeman, has many of the identifying features of Butler's Presbyterian knight, and his name fills in the blank by rhyming with "valiant *Mamaluke*" in *Hudibras*, I.i.896-897; here Butler playfully seems to identify the personage on whom his hero is modeled. Later commentators question this identification as well as Butler's association with Luke.

The best piece of external evidence suggests another model for the character of Hudibras. In a recently uncovered letter by Butler dated 19 March 1663, shortly after the publication of the first part of *Hudibras*, the poet informs his correspondent, Sir George Oxenden, president of the East India Company, that the original of Hudibras was a "West Countrey Kn^t then a Coll: in the Parliament Army & Com^{te} man wth whom I became Acquainted Lodging in ye same house wth him in Holbourne." Butler says that this gentleman's disputes on religion with his clerk, the model for Ralpho, delighted him so much that he fell into a "way of Scribling wch I was never Guilty of before nor since." Hudibras's encounter with the bearbaiting mob is evidently based on a lawsuit between this West Country knight and a fiddler, which the knight lost and which forced him to come up to London in humiliation. In spite of the hint Butler gives concerning the models for Hudibras and Ralpho, he generally opposes the efforts of commentators to find the identity of important personages in the characters of the poem. He writes to Oxenden that his "chiefe designe was onely to give ye world a Just Accot of ye Ridiculous folly & Knavery of ye Presbiterian & Independent Factions then in power. . . ."

Butler's statement of his design in his letter to Sir George Oxenden provides a basis for critical discussion of Butler's intention in *Hudibras*, especially for most modern critics, who argue that Butler's satire hits targets broader than "ye Presbiterian & Independent Factions then in power." In addition, the letter by Richard Oxenden (covering Butler's letter) locates the poet as a habitué of Grays Inn Walk at the time he was friendly with Sir George, probably during Oxenden's latest visit to England between 1659 and 1662. Butler is also identified as living at Grays Inn by Aubrey, who says that Butler "had a Clubb every night" with the metaphysical poet John Cleveland.

Butler's connections with Grays Inn, either formal or informal, account for his familiarity with the law and lawyers whom he satirizes both in *Hudibras* III.iii and in his characters of "A Lawyer," "A Corrupt Judge," "A Justice of the Peace," and "A Juror." Butler's friendship with Cleveland is likewise significant, for Cleveland's overdone metaphysical wit with its recondite allusions and farfetched conceits no doubt influenced the burlesque wit in *Hudibras*, the minor poetry, and the characters.

The publication of the first part of *Hudibras* very late in 1662 was a watershed in Butler's life. At almost fifty years of age, Butler produced a poem that was, according to Wood, "not only taken into his majesty's hands, and read by him with great delight, but also by all courtiers, loyal scholars and gentlemen, to the great profit of the author and bookseller." Wilders notes nine editions published in the first year, some of them pirated and one spurious. Samuel Pepys's laughable efforts to appreciate *Hudibras*, even after he judged it in his diary "so silly an abuse of the Presbyter Knight going to warrs, that [he was]

ashamed of it" (26 December 1662), is one good contemporary indicator of Butler's popularity.

Butler must have ridden high on the crest of his fame, though it apparently did not last too long. The reputed failure of Charles II and Edward Hyde, Earl of Clarendon, to acknowledge Butler's service turned the author of *Hudibras* into the unrewarded poet of legend, a legend perpetuated by several Restoration and eighteenth-century authors. Though there were several small gifts and a pension of one hundred pounds awarded to Butler late in his life, the poet may have furthered the legend himself, possibly with some justification. Butler was first lionized as a politically fashionable poet and later ignored as an antiquated wit. He in turn did not seem to embrace any age as his own. Though in *Hudibras* he had converted the religious and political conflicts of the civil wars and the Commonwealth era into undignified brawl over a prostitute, he was not, as a consequence, delighted by the Restoration and its lecherous power elite. His acid criticisms are expressed in his notebooks and in his verse "Satyr upon the Licentious Age of Charles the 2nd."

Immediately after the Restoration in 1661, Butler had held the post of steward of Ludlow Castle for Richard Vaughan, Earl of Carberry, who was at that time lord president of Wales. With the fame that accompanied the publication of the first part of *Hudibras*, Butler gave up the post, though he did not completely sever his connection with Carberry, even after he came down to London. The 1660s were a productive period for Butler. In early 1664 a second part of *Hudibras* appeared; the period between 1667 and 1669 saw composition of most of his prose characters; and, as Hugh De Quehen has determined, the bulk of his prose observations was recorded in his notebooks in the later 1660s.

By 1670 Butler had been taken into the service of George Villiers, Duke of Buckingham, and in the summer of 1670, as Norma E. Bentley first proved, Butler was part of Buckingham's entourage on a diplomatic mission to France. Charles Sackville, Lord Buckhurst, Sir Charles Sedley, the Royal Society historian Thomas Sprat, and the comedian Joe Haines were also in the group. As Butler's observations on France and the French transcribed in William Longueville's commonplace book demonstrate, Butler the son of a yeoman farmer was not much of a Francophile.

First page of Butler's observations on France and the French, as transcribed by William Longueville in his commonplace book
(f. i^r; by permission of the Rosenbach Museum & Library)

One wonders how comfortable Butler was in his dependent association with the duke of Buckingham. Butler was serving as Buckingham's secretary in June of 1673, when the duke was chancellor of the University of Cambridge. Wood says that Butler assisted Buckingham in the composition of *The Rehearsal* (1672). Butler, however, attacked Buckingham for his self-indulgent, libertine life-style in his character of "A Duke of Bucks," a satire whose hostility to the excesses of aristocratic conduct are similar to those in "Satyr upon the Licentious Age of Charles 2nd."

Hugh De Quehen places the composition of Butler's shorter verse satires in the early 1670s. "The Elephant in the Moon" and other attacks on Royal Society virtuosi probably date from this period, and these works as well as Butler's annotated edition of the first and second parts of *Hudibras* in 1674 draw on earlier notebook entries. E. S. De Beer suggests that during the late 1660s Butler may have done some writing for the stage, though the evidence is quite scanty. The verse satires of the early 1670s may, however, represent Butler's effort to assimilate the styles of witty dialogue and repartee that the major writers of Restoration comedy had mastered so brilliantly. Such an effort may also be evident in the third part of *Hudibras* (published in late 1677 with 1678 on its title page), especially in the "marriage debate" between the libertine-sounding widow and the Presbyterian knight or in Hudibras's consultation with the lawyer. Butler's poetic genius worked in narrow channels, and his success in his verse satires and the third part of *Hudibras* is not of the same order as John Dryden, William Wycherley, or Sir George Etherege in their comedies.

By the late 1670s, Butler, by then in his sixties, may have come in his public image to approximate the character of the antiquated wit from the previous age whom the great Restoration playwrights mocked in their comedies. A graphic description of Butler two years before his death is offered by James Yonge, a physician from Plymouth: "I saw the famous old Mr. Butler, a old paralytick claret drinker, a morose surly man, except elevated with claret, when he became very brisk and incomparable company."

After being confined by gout to his room in Rose Alley, Covent Garden, for more than six months, Butler died there on 25 September 1680. His pallbearers included famous men, but he had died in poverty in a mean neighborhood. Butler was buried at the expense of his friend William Longueville, who owned Butler's manuscripts in the early eighteenth century.

Aubrey described Butler as having "leonine-coloured haire, sanguino-cholerique, middle sized, strong; a severe and sound judgment, high couloured; a good fellowe." Capturing Butler's character more tellingly than Yonge, Aubrey observed: "Satyricall Witts disoblige whom they converse with; and consequently make to themselves many Enemies and few Friends; and this was his manner and case."

Butler's prose pamphlets, such as *Two Letters, One from John Audland, a Quaker, to William Prynne. The Other, William Prynnes Answer* (1672) and *The Plagiary Exposed* (1691), have a limited interest to the modern reader. They serve as indicators of Butler's development as a topical satirist. Another topical piece, "An Occasional Reflection of Dr. Charlton's Feeling a Dog's Pulse at Gresham-College. By R. B. Esq.," is a charming addition to Butler's verse attacks on Royal Society virtuosi. Butler's primary reputation in the prose medium rests with his prose observations recorded in his notebooks and, preeminently, with his characters.

Edited by Hugh De Quehen in 1979, *Prose Observations* offers entries from Butler's holograph manuscript in the British Library "according to the order and foldings in which Butler accumulated them." De Quehen also makes available for the first time most of Butler's observations transcribed by William Longueville in the commonplace book owned by the Rosenbach Museum & Library in Philadelphia.

In De Quehen's edition the prose from the holograph manuscript is comprised of 146 pages of observations classified under the headings of "Learning and Knowledge," "Truth and Falsehood," "Religion," "Wit and Folly," "Ignorance," "Reason," "Virtue and Vice," "Opinion," "Nature," "History," "Physique," "Princes and Government," and "Criticismes upon Books and Authors." Following these are approximately one hundred pages of unclassified entries, variously labeled "Contradictions" and "Inconsistant Opinions." The main items in Longueville's commonplace book are an English-French dictionary in Butler's hand (not included in De Quehen's edition), a self-revealing series of observations on France and the French, and assorted entries under headings such as "Wisdome," "Learning," "The Soule," and "Confidence."

If, as Samuel Johnson said, "Curiosity is one of the permanent and certain characteristics of a vigorous mind," then Butler's mind must have

A page from the "Criticismes upon Books and Authors" section of the manuscript Butler bequeathed to William Longueville, with marginal notes by Longueville and crosses made during the 1750s by Robert Thyer to mark his selections for The Genuine Remains in Verse and Prose of Mr. Samuel Butler *(Add. MS. 32625, f. 202ᵛ; by permission of the Trustees of the British Library)*

been violently active during most of his life. His concerns include matters as diverse as the nature of probability, the differences between heroical poetry and burlesque, the role of heresies in the propagation of the early Christian church, the difficulty of harmonizing wit and judgment, the English habit of imitating French fashions, the equivocal generation of insects and vermin, the first historical instance of a man hanged, drawn, and quartered, the quackery of surgeons who pretend to cut kidney stones from men's bladders, the effect of bad governments administered by good hands, and the limited usefulness of allegories.

It is not just the heterogeneity and breadth of Butler's observations that make them interesting, but Butler's fascination with patterns of similitude and dissimilitude. Throughout the prose observations, we discover, as Hugh De Quehen puts it, Butler's "collection of analogical material: anecdotes and observations which, while not necessarily true or consistent in themselves, will realize satiric truth when yoked as similes to the plain topical states of a poem or a Character." Butler enjoyed linking two unlike spheres of activity in a new and revealing relationship. "An Humorist is the same thing in Civility and Conversation, as a Cross-knave is in Bus'nes, and it is equally troublesome to have any thing to do with the one as the other." He also liked to break apart conventional associations and expose the unexpected incongruities: "Incontinence is a less Scandalous sin in Clergy-men then Drinking, because it is manag'd with greater Privacy, then the other Iniquity, which is apt to expose them to greater Freedom, and tempt them naturally to venture too far, without their Necessary Guard of Hypocrisy. . . ." In Butler's characters and his poetry, witty similitude overrides dissimilitude to produce simile, metaphor, and paradox. Conversely, his use of dissimilitude breaks down similitude into its discrete parts and yields antithesis or plain analysis.

Most critics employ Butler's prose observations to gloss their readings of *Hudibras*, the verse satires, or the characters. In contrast, Dan Gibson, Jr., uses all of Butler's writings, including his prose observations, to summarize Butler's intellectual views under the headings of "Society and Morals," "State," "Church," "Science," and "Literary Criticism." The thrust of Gibson's effort is toward the abstraction and classification of Butler's thought.

Ricardo Quintana in "Samuel Butler: A Restoration Figure in a Modern Light" is one of the few critics of Butler to focus exclusively on the prose observations, at least for a large part of an essay. Quintana sees them as the key to Butler's intellectual system and goes a long way to making him into a consistent thinker. Quintana's Butler "falls within the spirit of the English enlightenment." He is rationalistic, empirical, anti-Aristotelian, and Baconian. He is a moral observer strongly tinged by rational Protestantism, but not a deist; he is both anti-Puritan and anti-Papist. In political theory, he is conservative by instinct, but neither a Hobbesian nor an anti-Hobbesian liberal. Quintana may work more closely than Gibson with the substance of the prose observations, but the thrust of his effort is also toward abstraction and classification. Both critics do not pay enough attention to textual repetitions and inconsistencies and to the literary pattern of Butler's thought, especially to what De Quehen calls his "analogical" habit of mind.

Next to *Hudibras*, Butler's literary reputation rests on his prose characters, which were not published during his lifetime. Robert Thyer printed 120 of them in *The Genuine Remains in Verse and Prose* (1759), and Dr. Charles W. Daves brought the number to 196 in his edition of 1970. In *Prose Observations* De Quehen included two more for the first time and four for the first time in their original form. Butler's characters, some of them quite lengthy, are a late addition to the tradition of character writing, which flourished in England in the early seventeenth century. The character as it was composed by Joseph Hall, Thomas Overbury, and John Earle was initially Theophrastan in its emphasis on classification of various social and ethical types, but as the century progressed, character writing became progressively more polemical and satirical. In the characters of writers such as Richard Flecknoe and John Cleveland (done in the 1640s and 1650s), we see the culmination of the tendency to use the character for political and ideological propaganda, a tendency which had already begun to manifest itself in the earlier writers.

Butler's characters are almost entirely satiric, never exemplary in mode, and though they frequently hit partisan targets connected with the civil wars and Commonwealth, the range of Butler's satire carries him far beyond the Roundheads and the "Good Old Cause." The breadth of Butler's attack is suggested by the encyclopedic spectrum of hypocritical fools and knaves he treats. If *Hudibras* is an anatomy of hypocrisy, attacking the divorce between speech and action in the Presbyterian knight's roles as soldier, justice

Butler's "Character of a Bankrupt," from the manuscript he left to William Longueville (Add. MS. 32625, f. 235ʳ; by permission of the Trustees of the British Library)

of the peace, committeeman, lover, orator, debater, logician, patron of an astrologer, and plaintiff-at-law, the characters provide a much more comprehensive analysis of hypocrisy as it operates in a legion of human types and social roles. As Ian Jack has suggested, if Butler had continued *Hudibras*, he would eventually have dramatized Hudibras's behavior in every role treated in the characters. For most of the headings in Butler's classified prose observations, one can find several characters. For example, the observations on

"Religion" provide material for "A Fifth-Monarchy-Man," "A Popish Priest," "A Catholic," "A Proselite," "A Quaker," "An Anabaptist," and "A Silenc'd Presbyterian." "Wit and Folly" furnishes suggestions for the characters of "A Small Poet," "An Epigrammist," "A Quibbler," "A Tedious Man," "A Modern Critic," "A City-wit," "A Drole," "A Fool," "A Lampooner," and several others.

As with Butler's prose observations, Butler's characters are filled with recondite learning and curious lore. More so than the prose observations, the characters are populated with what Richard Garnett has called a "museum of particulars": strange objects, out-of-the-way allusions, and difficult-to-pronounce abstractions that take on a palpable existence. In "An Hermetic Philosopher" we find, to note a few examples, "Sloughs and Ditches," "toasted Cheese and Bacon," "lost Maidenheads," "the Liver of a Camelion," "*Whittington*'s Bells," "a *Pittacorum Regio*," "*horary Questions*," and "*Monades, Triades* and *Decades*."

Butler's wit is inherently excessive, a "Work of Supererrogation" as Butler himself put it in "A Small Poet." Butler cannot resist stringing out the plain description of a character with hard words and epithets, obscure terms of art, wretched puns, and difficult and farfetched metaphors and similes. If Butler was haunted by "the demon of analogy," as Ian Jack said, that demon manifests itself even more strongly in the characters than it does in *Hudibras*. Reading through the first few sentences of any character, we almost always encounter enough forcibly clever similes, metaphors, and diminishing comparisons to make us say with Ms. Millamant in William Congreve's *The Way of the World* (1700): "Truce with your similitudes." We are delighted by Butler at the same time we are exhausted by him.

Butler's characters have received some critical attention over the years, especially as part of broader studies of the character tradition. Considered, however, in comparison to the attention paid to *Hudibras*, the characters, in effect, have been neglected. Charles F. Totten in an article and an unpublished dissertation uncovers unifying satiric patterns in groups of characters and in the whole body of them. Viewed in their entirety, Butler's characters, according to Totten, "constitute an anatomy of a world of madness and folly, and reveal a satiric hierarchy in which the highest places go to the basest hypocrites." Other critics such as K. M. P. Burton and Arnold Asrelsky have argued that the characters embody the general satiric point of *Hudibras* more sharply and in greater variety than Butler's famous poem.

Butler's characters, as Totten points out, are the last collection of prose characters written in England "sufficiently large to be designated a Character book." As such, Butler's influence on later character writers is obviously minimal. The satiric particularity of Butler's prose does, however, influence later satirists such as Jonathan Swift. More broadly it serves as a basis for characterization within the English comic novel, especially in the work of Henry Fielding, Laurence Sterne, and Tobias Smollett.

Most critics would grant that in Butler's canon the characters are right below *Hudibras* in importance. Few critics, however, have tried to say why this is so. An even more significant omission is the lack of an integrated examination of Butler's canon, one which establishes formal and thematic relationships among *Hudibras*, the prose observations, the minor verse, the prose pamphlets, and the characters. Butler's final importance is not simply as a well-known poet or a somewhat lesser-known character writer, as an intellect of breadth or a satirist of awesome energy. Critics need to show that he is all of these in combination and that Butler's accomplishment in its totality is greater than the sum of its parts.

Bibliographies:

James L. Thorson, "Samuel Butler (1612-1680): A Bibliography," *Bulletin of Bibliography*, 30 (January-March 1973): 34-39;

George Wasserman, *Samuel Butler and the Earl of Rochester: A Reference Guide* (Boston: G. K. Hall, 1986).

Biographies:

Anthony à Wood, *Athenae Oxonienses*, 4 volumes, edited by Philip Bliss (London: F. C. & J. Rivington and others, 1813-1820), III: 875-876;

John Aubrey, "Samuel Butler," in *Brief Lives, Chiefly of Contemporaries*, 2 volumes, edited by Andrew Clark (Oxford: Clarendon Press, 1898), I: 135-136;

Rene Lamar, "Du nouveau sur l'auteur d'Hudibras," *Revue anglo-americaine*, 1 (1924): 213-227;

E. S. De Beer, "The Later Life of Samuel Butler," *Review of English Studies*, 4 (April 1928): 159-166;

Norma E. Bentley, " 'Hudibras' Butler Abroad," *Modern Language Notes*, 60 (April 1945): 254-259;

Michael Wilding, "Samuel Butler at Barbourne," *Notes and Queries*, 211 (January 1966): 15-19;

John Wilders, Introduction to *Hudibras*, edited by Wilders (Oxford: Clarendon Press, 1967), pp. xv-xxi.

References:

Arnold Asrelsky, "The Forgotten Augustan: A Critical Study of the Works of Samuel Butler (1612-1680)," Ph.D. dissertation, New York University, 1971;

K. M. P. Burton, "Samuel Butler," in her *Restoration Literature* (London: Hutchinson, 1958), pp. 118-126;

Charles W. Daves, Introduction to *Characters*, edited by Daves (Cleveland: Press of Case Western Reserve University, 1970), pp. 1-27;

Hugh De Quehen, Introduction to *Prose Observations*, edited by De Quehen (Oxford: Clarendon Press, 1979), pp. xvii-xxxviii;

Dan Gibson, Jr., "Samuel Butler," in *Seventeenth Century Studies*, edited by Robert Shafer (Princeton: Princeton University Press, 1933), pp. 277-335;

Ian Jack, *Augustan Satire: Intention & Idiom in English Poetry 1660-1750* (Oxford: Clarendon Press, 1952);

Ricardo Quintana, "Samuel Butler: A Restoration Figure in a Modern Light," *English Literary History*, 18 (March 1951): 7-31;

Charles F. Totten, "Hypocrisy and Corruption in Four Characters of Samuel Butler," *Essays in Literature*, 2 (Fall 1975): 164-170;

Totten, "The Prose Characters of Samuel Butler (1612-1680): A Critical Study," Ph.D. dissertation, Wayne State University, 1972;

George Wasserman, *Samuel "Hudibras" Butler* (Boston: Twayne, 1976).

Papers:

No manuscript version of *Hudibras* is known to exist. Butler's holograph manuscript in the British Library (B.L. Add. MS. 32625) is the main source for his prose observations, many of his characters, and his minor verse satires. The British Library also has the transcriptions of Robert Thyer (B.L. Add. MS. 32626), also a source for prose characters and minor verse. William Longueville's commonplace book in the Rosenbach Museum & Library in Philadelphia preserves some prose observations and a few characters, not in Butler's hand.

Edward Hyde, Earl of Clarendon

(18 February 1609 - 11 December 1674)

Martine Watson Brownley
Emory University

BOOKS: *An Answer to a Pamphlet, entit'led, A Declaration of the Commons of England in Parliament assembled, expressing their Reasons and Grounds of passing the late Resolutions touching no further Address or Application to be made to the King* (N. p., 1648);

A Full Answer to an Infamous and Trayterous Pamphlet, Entituled, A Declaration of the Commons of England in Parliament assembled, expressing their Reasons and Grounds of passing the late Resolutions touching no further Addresse or Application to be made to the King (London: Printed for R. Royston, 1648);

A Letter From a True and Lawfull Member of Parliament, And One faithfully engaged with it, from the beginning of the War to the end (London, 1656);

Animadversions Upon a Book, Intituled, Fanaticism Fanatically Imputed to the Catholick Church, By D^r. Stillingfleet, And The Imputation Refuted and Retorted by S. C. (London: Printed for R. Royston, 1673);

A Brief View and Survey of the Dangerous and pernicious Errors to Church and State, in Mr. Hobbes's Book, Entitled Leviathan (Oxford: Printed at the Theater, 1676);

The History of the Rebellion and Civil Wars in England, 3 volumes (Oxford: Printed at the Theater, 1702-1704);

The History of the Rebellion and Civil Wars in Ireland (Dublin: Printed for P. Dugan, 1719/20);

A Collection of Several Tracts of the Right Honorable Edward, Earl of Clarendon (London: Printed for T. Woodward & J. Peele, 1727); republished as *A Compleat Collection of Tracts, By That Eminent Statesman The Right Honourable Edward, Earl of Clarendon* (London: Printed for C. Davis and others, 1747); republished as *The Miscellaneous Works of the Right Honourable Edward Earl of Clarendon, Lord High Chancellor of England* (London: Printed for Samuel Paterson, 1751);

The Life of Edward Earl of Clarendon, Lord High Chancellor of England, and Chancellor of the Uni-

versity of Oxford (Oxford: Clarendon Printing-House, 1759);

Religion and Policy and the Countenance and Assistance Each Should Give to the Other, 2 volumes (Oxford: Clarendon Press, 1811).

Editions: *The History of the Rebellion and Civil Wars in England*, 8 volumes, edited by Bulkeley Bandinel (Oxford: Clarendon Press, 1826);

The History of the Rebellion and Civil Wars in England, 6 volumes, edited by W. Dunn Macray (Oxford: Clarendon Press, 1888);

Two Dialogues: Of the Want of Respect due to Age and Concerning Education, introduction by Martine Watson Brownley, Augustan Reprint Society, nos. 227 and 228 (Los Angeles: William Andrews Clark Memorial Library, 1984).

OTHER: Commendatory verses, in *The Tragedy of Alboivne, King of the Lombards*, by Sir William Davenant (London: Printed by F. Kingston for R. Moore, 1629);

Elegy on John Donne, in *Deaths Duell, or, A Consolation to the Soule, against the Dying Life, and Living Death of the Body. In a Sermon*, by Donne (London: Printed by T. Harper for R. Redmer & B. Fisher, 1632); Hyde's elegy republished in *Poems, by J. D. With elegies on the authors death* (London: Printed by M. Flesher for J. Marriot, 1633);

The Difference and Disparity Between the Estates and Conditions of George Duke of Buckingham, and Robert Earl of Essex, in *Relinquiae Wottonianae*, by Sir Henry Wotton (London: Printed by Thomas Maxey for R. Mariot, 1651), pp. 37-70.

As a politician and a historian, Edward Hyde, first Earl of Clarendon, played a vital role in shaping both the events of his time and the perceptions of these events by his contemporaries and posterity. A proponent of reform early in the Long Parliament, he later wrote propaganda for King Charles I and became chancellor of the

Edward Hyde, Earl of Clarendon (portrait after Adriaen Hanneman; by permission of the National Portrait Gallery, London)

Exchequer; ultimately emerging as Charles II's chief adviser during the Interregnum, he played a key Royalist role in negotiating the Restoration of the Stuarts and served as lord chancellor of England from 1660 to 1667. Clarendon's writings, entirely in prose except for two early poems, are integrally connected with his immersion in the life and issues of his era. Although he was a prolific author who produced works on a variety of subjects, Clarendon's literary fame is based primarily on his *History of the Rebellion and Civil Wars in England*, a magisterial treatment of the tumultuous period through which he lived.

Hyde was born on 18 February 1609, the third son of Henry and Mary Langford Hyde, in a prosperous Wiltshire family of country gentry. Educated by a local schoolmaster under the super-

vision of his father, he entered Magdalen College, Oxford, in 1622, at the age of thirteen, receiving the B.A. degree in 1626. His father had intended a career for him in the church, but after the deaths of his two older brothers he entered the Middle Temple to study law. His uncle Nicholas Hyde, Lord Chief Justice of the King's Bench, supervised his legal studies. However, his writings and records of his reading throughout his life show that he maintained a strong interest in religious and theological issues.

Hyde initially preferred polite learning and history. He cultivated various literary men, particularly Ben Jonson and his circle; in 1628 he shared his chambers at the Temple with William Davenant. One of his two youthful forays into poetry was commendatory verses printed before

Notes taken by Clarendon, probably from army records, for use in writing his History of the Rebellion *(by permission of the Pierpont Morgan Library)*

Davenant's play *The Tragedy of Albovine, King of the Lombards* (1629). Three years later he wrote an elegy on John Donne that appeared in the first edition of *Deaths Duell* (1632) and was republished in Donne's 1633 *Poems*. Hyde's poems are competent but uninspired; neither suggests that his decision to limit himself to prose in subsequent works was a mistake. In February 1634 he served on the committee that arranged a spectacular and expensive production of James Shirley's new play *The Triumph of Peace*, staged by the Inns of Court for the king and queen to atone for their fellow barrister William Prynne's violent attack on the drama in *Histriomastix* (1633).

The mixture of literary and artistic concerns with legal and political ones that marked the production of *The Triumph of Peace* is emblematic of Hyde's gradual transition during the early 1630s from belletristic to professional endeavors. As he became more involved in legal studies and practice, he first made time at night and during vacations for what he termed "polite learning," but business increasingly predominated. His brief marriage in 1629 to Anne Ayliffe, who died of smallpox after only six months as his wife, had given him connections with the Villiers family, and he successfully cultivated other powerful men who could assist him, among them William Laud, Archbishop of Canterbury. An advantageous second marriage on 10 July 1634 to Frances Aylesbury, whose father was a Master of Requests and also Master of the Mint, accelerated Hyde's already rapid rise; his appointment as Keeper of the Writs and Roles of the Common Pleas came six months later.

Hyde himself dated his wholehearted commitment to the law from the time of his second marriage. His ties with the Jonson circle lapsed, except with John Selden, whose constitutional and antiquarian knowledge was an important influence on Hyde as both a politician and a historian. Significantly, however, Hyde maintained his associations with Lucius Cary, Viscount Falkland, and the circle who gathered at his homes at Burford and especially at Great Tew, which Hyde would eulogize years later in *The History of the Rebellion* as "a college situated in a purer air" and "a university bound in a lesser volume." In this atmosphere divines mingled with scholars and poets; the various pursuits of men such as William Chillingworth, John Hales of Eton, Gilbert Sheldon, Sidney Godolphin, John Earle, George Morley, and William Waller reflected the range of Hyde's mature concerns. He would retain an in-

terest in literature even as his major focus changed to legal, religious, and political activities; amid a life increasingly devoted to action, he would maintain a deep commitment to study and contemplation.

Election to both the Short Parliament (which served for three weeks in 1640) and the Long Parliament (which was summoned in November 1640 and sat until December 1648) interrupted Hyde's prosperous legal career and comfortable life. In the deepening crisis he devoted himself entirely to public affairs, assiduously attending both the House of Commons itself and many committees. Initially he worked with those seeking to curb the abuses of royal power that had occurred while Charles I had ruled without Parliament. His maiden speech attacking the Earl Marshal's Court attracted some attention; he also took leading roles in investigating other prerogative courts and preparing charges against the judges, particularly in the case of ship money. However, although his commitment to constitutionalism and the rule of law had led him to cooperate with more radical reformers early in the Long Parliament, Hyde was actually a moderate in the great English tradition of those who reform in order to preserve rather than destroy. He was also devoted to the Church of England, and when John Pym and his party began to move against episcopacy, Hyde opposed them. He fought the Root and Branch Bill and after voting against the Grand Remonstrance, strongly objected to its publication.

As Pym and his followers pursued increasingly radical courses, many moderates like Hyde found themselves shifting toward the king's side. Charles I had noted Hyde's actions in Parliament and summoned him personally to thank him, particularly for his support of the Church. Later an answer that Hyde composed to the Grand Remonstrance was brought to the king's attention by Lord George Digby and was published by Charles as his own response. In January 1642, when Hyde's friends Falkland and Sir John Colepeper joined the government, Hyde was offered the position of solicitor general. Although at that time he felt he could best serve the king by refusing the position, he agreed to work closely with Falkland and Colepeper to advance the royal cause in Parliament. Later Charles asked him to compose replies to various Parliamentary declarations and addresses. Hyde sent his drafts to the king at York, who, before submitting them to his council for approval and publica-

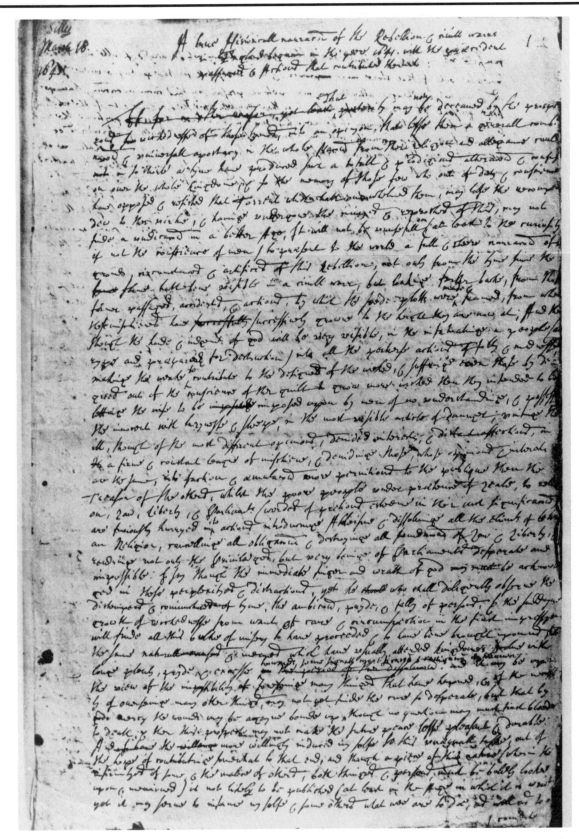

First page from the manuscript for Clarendon's History of the Rebellion *(by permission of the Curators of the Bodleian Library, Oxford)*

tion, copied them out in his own hand in order to protect Hyde's increasingly perilous position with the Parliament and its leaders. As Parliamentary suspicion and surveillance of him mounted, in May 1642 Hyde left London to join the king at York, traveling for safety on the back roads with his old friend Chillingworth as his guide.

First at York and then at Oxford from October 1642 to March 1645, Hyde continued to advise the king informally and to draft almost all royal declarations. The constitutionalism and appeals to law that mark Hyde's many manifestos played a major role in rallying a party for Charles in the "paper skirmishes" preceding the outbreak of fighting and in promoting the king's cause throughout the early years of the war. Although the detailed point-by-point refutation of opponents characteristic of seventeenth-century polemic makes many of his works dull reading for modern tastes, he was an extremely effective propagandist for his party. Some of his satiric attacks and also his forgeries written to create dissension among enemies show the range of his polemical styles.

On 22 February 1643 Hyde was knighted and sworn in as a member of the Privy Council; on 3 March he was named chancellor of the Exchequer, a position he held until 1660. In addition to financial matters, he played a key role in various negotiations for peace, from discussions in Oxford with the English and with the Scots in early 1643 to the conference at Uxbridge in 1645. His indefatigable energy, loyalty, and devotion to duty made him in many ways a useful royal servant. Unfortunately, the basic problem with Hyde's political position during these years—and a recurring problem throughout his career—was that the king he served did not actually share either his constitutionalism or his moderation. Charles I found Hyde's articulation of such stances invaluable for propagandistic purposes, but again and again he turned to others with fewer legal, moral, or Anglican scruples, whose advice more satisfactorily suited his own predilections. When he decided to send the Prince of Wales with an advisory council to the west of England in March of 1645, he chose Hyde for that service.

Hyde's year in the west was marked by the constant quarreling of the prince's council with Royalist military commanders in the area. As the king's armies were pushed steadily westward by the victorious Parliamentarians, to insure the prince's safety the council retreated first to the Scilly Islands (4 March 1646) and then, after Parliamentary warships threatened those islands (17 April 1646), to Jersey. Queen Henrietta Maria ordered her son to join her in Paris, and although Hyde and the council, fearing French and Catholic influences, delayed as long as possible, Charles ultimately obeyed in July 1646. Hyde chose not to attend the prince into France and remained behind on Jersey, ultimately staying with the governor in Elizabeth Castle.

Hyde settled with pleasure into a life of reading and writing, in which, according to his own account in *The Life of Edward Earl of Clarendon* (1759), he "seldom spent less than ten Hours in the Day." He began to write commentaries on the Psalms and also some essays. When Parliament on 15 January 1648 voted to make no more addresses to the king and published a declaration explaining the action by detailing Charles's past misdeeds, Hyde returned to his role as Royalist polemicist. First in a brief pamphlet (13 pages) and then in an exhaustive treatment (172 pages) that was later translated into Latin, he refuted the Parliamentary allegations. Hyde also continued a more important work. On 18 March 1646 in the Scilly Islands, he had begun a history of the war, and on Jersey he set to work on it enthusiastically. Isolated from the centers of Royalist power, he could do little directly to advance the king's cause. But he envisioned his history as potentially a vital contribution, a way once again to help his party and to assert the ideals that he believed were crucial for the English nation. He planned to include political instruction as well as vindication; in addition to preserving the truth about the past, he felt the history could contribute to the future and help shape the peace that would one day come by showing him and others what they should do, even as it comforted them for what they had already done in vain. Because he was determined to write fully and frankly, avoiding both apologia and polemic, he expected that the work as a whole would not be publishable, but he hoped that parts from it could eventually be collected for the general public.

Hyde's situation on Jersey was hardly propitious for historical composition. Despite all he could relate from his personal experiences, there were many things that he had no way of knowing, and he had taken no materials with him when he left England. Although he conscientiously solicited information from others and although the king personally supported his efforts, he received very little of what he requested. Typi-

Clarendon in 1662 (medal by Abraham and Thomas Simon; by permission of the Trustees of the British Museum)

cally undaunted, for he was always a sanguine man, Hyde wrote on. By early March of 1648, two years after beginning the history, he had finished six books, which chronicled events from the death of King James I through March of 1644. These six books compose about three fourths of the first seven books of the final version of *The History of the Rebellion*, while those seven books, in their turn, constitute a little over half of the entire work. He had started on the next book when the queen and prince summoned him to Paris in mid May as an adviser.

Hyde left Jersey at the end of June 1648, and, after a series of perambulations and adventures, including capture by an Ostend privateer, he finally joined Prince Charles at The Hague in September. Amid the bitter feuds and constant intrigues of the Royalists abroad, Hyde sought principled policies and money, two commodities that were to continue in extremely short supply for the duration of the exile. After the execution of Charles I, as courtiers and counselors debated the merits of Scottish and Irish alternatives for

Charles II, Hyde became increasingly dispirited, and when Francis, Lord Cottington, proposed an embassy to seek Spanish aid for the new king, he was happy to participate. On 29 September 1649 the two set out from Paris, arriving in Madrid on 26 November. The cool reception that the ambassadors immediately encountered presaged the frustration and difficulties they would experience for well over a year of futile effort in Spain. Their presence proved an embarrassment to the Spanish government, which was primarily concerned over relations with the Commonwealth. An already awkward situation was exacerbated in late May 1650 when one of the ambassador's servants was involved in the murder of Anthony Ascham, the Parliamentary envoy to Spain. While on the embassy Hyde turned once again to intellectual pursuits, studying the Spanish language, history, and government. He continued the commentaries on the Psalms that he had begun on Jersey and also started a study of the Papacy.

Leaving Spain in March of 1651, Hyde stopped in Paris to see the queen and was reunited with his family in Antwerp in June. As soon as Charles II escaped to the Continent after the battle of Worcester, he summoned Hyde to him in Paris. From this time on, despite various attempts to undermine his position, Hyde increasingly assumed the role of the king's chief adviser. He handled the secretary of state's duties for Sir Edward Nicholas until 1654, and in January of 1658 was named lord chancellor and lord keeper. Throughout this period he was at the center of Royalist operations abroad, coordinating efforts in England and on the Continent through voluminous correspondence and personal negotiations. In 1656 he returned briefly to polemical writing with one of his most effective forgeries, *A Letter From a True and Lawfull Member of Parliament*, which denounced Oliver Cromwell's punitive policies against the English Royalists in late 1655. Adjudicating internecine feuds, begging money, instructing agents and diplomats, commiserating with friends and placating foes, Hyde counseled patience and stood firmly for a restoration by English and Protestant means, one that would protect the rights of the monarch, the Parliament, and the Anglican church. As the chief architect of the Restoration on the Royalist side, he played a key role in the negotiations in the spring of 1660 and also penned the Declaration of Breda, with its masterful deferral of the conditions of a final settlement to the approval of a free Parliament.

Hyde returned to England with Charles II and the triumphant Royalists and continued to manage almost all of the king's public business. As speaker of the House of Lords and presiding officer of the Court of Chancery, in addition to his pivotal role in the Privy Council and its most powerful committees, he functioned in key legislative, judicial, and executive positions. On 3 November 1660 he joined the peerage as baron Hyde of Hindon, and that same month Oxford installed him as its chancellor. At Charles II's coronation he became viscount Cornbury and earl of Clarendon. He seemed the most powerful man in the country other than the king himself; in reality, he managed to maintain his position for only seven years.

An early shock in the fall of 1660 had been the revelation of his daughter Anne's secret contract of marriage with James, Duke of York (later James II), and her subsequent pregnancy by him. Despite strong opposition from most members of the royal family, the king supported the union and the furor subsided. Other problems proved

more intractable. In working out practical details of the Restoration settlement, Clarendon provoked a great deal of enmity among all elements in the country. Both he and the king supported indemnity for all except the regicides, but Clarendon bore the brunt of widespread anger over the thwarting of Cavalier attempts at more widely distributed punishments. Problems over redistribution of lands, official appointments, and settlement of the Scottish and Irish governments further exacerbated the growing dislike of the chief minister. Ecclesiastical affairs produced yet more difficulties. Clarendon personally was a deeply religious man, steeped in the liberal theological ideas espoused by the Great Tew group and dedicated also to the Anglican church in its political role in the state. His exact position on various ecclesiastical issues remains obscure at crucial points after the Restoration, but in general, he preferred comprehension within the established church rather than toleration for the Presbyterians and others. He was not responsible for the harsh legislation against the Dissenters that came to be known as the "Clarendon Code," but his opposition to toleration angered both Charles II and Dissenters of all groups.

Clarendon's unpopularity was such that by May of 1663 his fall was generally predicted, but an abortive attack by his former friend Digby, now earl of Bristol, charging him with high treason (10 July 1663) failed utterly. However, Charles II, like his father, did not share Clarendon's dedication to constitutionalism and the English law; in addition, he found his chancellor's frequent lectures decrying his lack of attention to public business and his riotous private life more and more annoying. Clarendon had for many years proved indispensable to the king because of his experience and indefatigability in conducting royal business, but after the Restoration his methods and approaches proved increasingly inadequate. Accustomed to sole responsibility, he disliked delegating authority and proved incapable of managing the growing governmental bureaucracy. In the press of business he too often neglected vital areas such as Parliamentary liaison.

In foreign as well as domestic affairs Clarendon bore the brunt of popular dissatisfaction with policies that in many cases he had opposed in Council. When the king's marriage produced no heir, Clarendon was unfairly accused of having foreknowledge of the queen's barrenness and of arranging the union so that his daughter Anne's children would inherit the crown. He was widely blamed for the sale of Dunkirk to France in late 1662. Above all, popular opinion held him responsible for the second Anglo-Dutch war, a conflict that he strongly opposed but was pressured into by merchants and the duke of York.

After the disasters of the war culminated in the Dutch attack on Chatham in June 1667, popular fury rose to fever pitch. Clarendon was the most visible and vulnerable target; over the seven years since the king's return, he had become a symbol of the inefficiency and corruption of Charles II's government. Ambitious courtiers and politicians chafed under his power, the worst envying the amount of it while the best deplored his lack of administrative skills in employing it. More frivolous members of the court, particularly Charles's mistress, Barbara Villiers Palmer, Lady Castlemaine, disliked Clarendon for his formality, which could verge on pomposity, and for his stern morality, which could become self-righteousness. Believing in a balance of power between monarch and Parliament, Clarendon had opposed various attempts by Parliament to extend its jurisdiction in response to problems during the Dutch war and thus had alienated the House of Commons.

During the summer of 1667, George Villiers, Duke of Buckingham; Sir William Coventry; and others convinced Charles that his only hope of dealing with the country at large and particularly with Parliament when it met in October was to remove Clarendon. The king hoped for a voluntary resignation; Clarendon's refusal forced him to send Sir William Morrice to demand the seals of his office (30 August 1667). Unsatisfied, Clarendon's enemies moved to arraign him for high treason when Parliament reconvened. A committee of the Commons produced seventeen charges against him, but the vagueness of the accusations led the House of Lords to refuse to commit Clarendon into custody when they received the impeachment. As neither house would give in to the other, pressure mounted on Clarendon to leave the country. Determined to prove his innocence, he initially refused, but the king's desire for his departure, along with the threat of a special trial by a jury of his enemies among the peers, finally impelled him to flee. On the night of 29 November he departed England for France, leaving behind a vindication of his conduct for the Lords. The two houses agreed on the burning of his vindication and on an act banishing him, making his return to England high

treason and requiring Parliamentary consent for any pardon.

Because of contrary winds, Clarendon's journey to Calais ultimately required three days. The delay was only the first of a series of misfortunes and frustrations experienced in his first months abroad. He moved frequently, initially traveling to Rouen (25 December 1667) and then returning to Calais (21 January 1668), where he spent three months seriously ill. During this period Louis XIV repeatedly ordered him to leave France in order to please the English government, but the conclusion of the Triple Alliance changed the French attitude toward his residency. On his way to the baths at Bourbon, a group of English mercenaries who blamed him for the nonpayment of their arrears attacked him at Evreux (23 April 1668), pillaging his belongings, wounding some of his servants, and stunning him with a blow to his head. The authorities intervened as the sailors were carrying him outside to kill him, and he stayed for some time at Bourbon to recuperate. In the middle of June he reached Avignon and finally settled in July at Montpellier.

Once again forced from action to contemplation, Clarendon settled in, initially with sadness and reluctance but soon enough with genuine pleasure, to study, read, and write. On 23 July 1669 he began to compose *The Life of Edward Earl of Clarendon, From His Birth to the Restoration of Royal Family in the Year 1660.* Although scholars of autobiography correctly praise the *Life* as one of the finest seventeenth-century examples of the genre, Clarendon's basic commitment was to historical writing. However, banished in the south of France, with his papers left behind in England, and his friends and associates legally forbidden to communicate with him, history was not at that point an option. That the *Life* was a way of compensating for his inability to write history is clear from both its objective and impersonal narrative stance and the materials he included. An opening section on Clarendon's early life and career focuses on his friends almost as much as on himself, and it also includes a general survey of the European political situation in 1639. In the account of the 1640s, history constantly displaces autobiography in the *Life.* The work is focused on Clarendon the public servant rather than Clarendon the private man. Although personal vindication was unquestionably part of his motivation for writing the *Life,* the fact that on the day after beginning the autobiography he started to compose a separate vindication of his political conduct suggests his concern to keep the two tasks at least somewhat distinct.

In less than two years Clarendon completed the *Life* (1 August 1670). His astonishing literary energy is clear from the number and variety of other works that he was writing simultaneously. While composing the *Life* he also completed his essays, commentaries on the Psalms, a refutation of Thomas Hobbes, and probably his dialogues.

Of Clarendon's twenty-five essays, two were written while he was on Jersey, one at Moulins, and four are undated. The rest were produced at Montpellier between 1668 and 1670. Most are on conventional topics ("Of Pride," "Of Industry," "Of Friendship"), although his long essay comparing the active and contemplative lives includes an interesting section on historical writing, and parts of "Of the Reverence due to Antiquity" show certain Baconian predilections as Clarendon makes a case for the moderns against the ancients. In general, Clarendon is not at his best in the essay form. The capaciousness of his style and thought requires more space than it allows, and he lacks the suggestive brevity and epigrammatic originality characteristic of the best examples of the genre. Similar problems mark the *Contemplations and Reflections Upon the Psalms of David*, which he had begun on Jersey (through Psalm 8) and continued in Spain (through Psalm 67) and at Antwerp (Psalm 68). On 13 December 1668 he took up the work again at the seventy-first Psalm and finished on 27 February 1670. He indicates that in composing the *Contemplations*, he did not use earlier commentators nor did he eschew repetition, and neither procedure encouraged depth in his work. The major interest of the *Contemplations* is psychological rather than literary or theological. Indirectly they reveal Clarendon's attempts to come to terms with various political and personal situations he faced during his three periods of retreat from active involvement in affairs. They also show the deep personal religious faith that sustained him throughout his life.

Another product of his first years of exile was *A Brief View and Survey of the Dangerous and pernicious Errors to Church and State, in Mr. Hobbes's Book, Entitled Leviathan*. Although Hobbes was an old friend, Clarendon had been appalled at the political tenets espoused in the *Leviathan* (1668) and had long wanted a refutation published. His own manuscript was completed in April 1670, but it did not appear until 1676, with a dedicatory epistle to Charles II dated 10 May 1673. The *Brief*

View and Survey demolishes each of Hobbes's arguments exhaustively in the point-by-point procedure characteristic of all Clarendon's polemical work. He fulminates against Hobbes's politics as a philosophical system constructed by abstract reason divorced from practical experience and history.

Two final literary productions, probably written in the early years of Clarendon's banishment, were his two dialogues. In the first, five older men—a Courtier, a Lawyer, a Soldier, a Country Gentleman, and an Alderman—discuss the "Want of Respect due to Age," while a Bishop joins them for the second dialogue on education. As a serious-minded older person upholding traditional values among the often impudent and unruly young men and women of the Restoration court, Clarendon had experienced incessant ridicule as well as dangerous political opposition. In the dialogue on old age, however, despite flashes of anger at the behavior of the young, more balanced views reflecting the moderation generally characteristic of Clarendon prevail. As chancellor of Oxford he had been actively concerned about education, and in his second dialogue he joins the many seventeenth-century writers from Francis Bacon to John Locke who considered educational reform. He offers a conservative view of the strengths and weaknesses of English educational institutions, which ranges widely enough to conclude with a discussion of drama. Like most English writers, Clarendon uses Cicero's expository form as a model for his dialogues; although they lack the drama of the Platonic dialogue, they have a freshness and liveliness lacking in many of his other works.

In June 1671 Clarendon's second son, Laurence, was finally allowed to visit him, and Clarendon moved from Montpellier to Moulins. At his father's request Laurence brought various papers, including the manuscript for the original history that Clarendon had written on Jersey more than two decades before. He turned immediately to complete this work, to which he sacrificed the *Life* that he had recently finished. He combined parts of the original history from Jersey with sections of the *Life* and also added some new material. From this conflation emerged the final *History of the Rebellion*. The entire process seems to have taken about a year, for in June 1672 he began the *Continuation of the Life*.

The History of the Rebellion is the most important of the many treatments of the civil wars produced by contemporaries. Not since Sir Walter

Portrait of Clarendon in his Lord Chancellor's robes published as the frontispiece in the first edition of his
History of the Rebellion *(engraving by R. White, after Sir Peter Lely)*

Raleigh's magnificently baroque *History of the World* (1614) had a seventeenth-century writer produced a historical work comparable in literary stature to Clarendon's. The *History* is not without significant flaws, for there are problems of proportion, and its factual accuracy is extremely uneven. In addition, combining the original history and the *Life* created certain difficulties, and awkward transitions and repetitions show that Clarendon could be negligent in his editing. Nevertheless, from his disparate materials he managed to create an amalgam of public history, private apologia, state documents, memoir, polemical vindication, eyewitness accounts, and political analyses—a strange and brilliant synthesis that in many ways tested the boundaries of traditional seventeenth-century historical narrative.

Like his materials, Clarendon's approach to history was eclectic, encompassing all of the major traditions of historical writing of his era. In addition to Providential elements, his work incorporated the classical and Renaissance conceptions of history as moral and ethical instructor, as well as more recent views of history as a guide to statecraft. Clarendon also recognized the historiographical advances made by the seventeenth-century antiquarians and did his best to include documentary evidence, although the conditions under which he wrote hampered his efforts. He considered his own role in events as one of his primary qualifications for writing history, because he shared the classical and Renaissance belief that historians should have participated in the political affairs and events they describe. The inevitable resulting bias was in Clarendon's case offset by certain unusual circumstances of his state service. He had begun his political career in the Parliamentary opposition, and even after becoming a Royalist, he had constantly opposed powerful elements in his own party: Digby and less constitutional courtiers under Charles I, the queen and her circle in the Louvre during the Interregnum, ambitious politicians and Charles II's cronies in the Restoration court, and, above all, the two Stuart kings whose beliefs never entirely accorded with his. For Clarendon, these political differences combined with the detachment encouraged by his periods of exile from active service to produce perspective extremely useful for historical writing. The capaciousness of his historical vision was also enhanced by his wide intellectual interests, particularly his readings in classical and Continental historians, in theological controversy, and in law and literature. Finally, the circumstances of its composition widened the point of view in the final *History*. The more exact and detailed accounts in the original history, written about the recent past, combined with the more generalized and anecdotal overviews in the *Life*, composed twenty years later, to offer both depth and breadth of perspective.

Integral to Clarendon's achievement in *The History of the Rebellion* is the fact that at a time when formal concerns were generally neglected in English historical writing, he managed to make his account a work of literature. By the mid seventeenth century, a reaction against various rhetorical excesses characteristic of the humanist historians, along with the emphasis placed on content to the exclusion of form by the antiquarian movement, had combined with Baconian empiricism and a growing distrust of the imagination and poetry to undermine seriously the stylistic level of English historical works. Clarendon's early belletristic endeavors and the literary associations he maintained throughout his life had given him an understanding of literary style and an appreciation of its importance. Like the capacious overview he evolved for the *History*, his prose in it combines elements of the various styles of the age, from the rich and rolling Ciceronean periods of the opening sentence echoing Richard Hooker to

the informal loose style usually employed for narrative and the Senecan point that adds sting to the irony that enlivens his text. Clarendon was at no time a man of few words, and some of his long sentences sprawl out of control. Nevertheless, the majestic formality of the style and the sense of intellectual process that it conveys make it in the context of the era an impressive and effective prose for historical writing.

In narrative, too, Clarendon evolved various techniques that were considerably more sophisticated than those of his predecessors. He carefully structured the narrative perspective of the *History*. Author and narrator are kept separate—references to himself within the account are in the third person—and he uses variable internal focalization to shift the point of view adroitly as events develop. Clarendon also integrated related literary forms into the *History*, tailoring each genre to serve historical purposes. His account of the Spanish embassy is basically a travelogue; similarly, many of his extended political analyses function in effect as essays. But in generic terms his greatest narrative triumph in the *History* comes in the character sketch. From classical times character sketches had been conventional in histories, but Clarendon enormously expanded their literary role in historical writing.

The seventeenth century in England was a great age of character portrayals, from Theophrastan sketches and Jonsonian humor characters early in the century to the polemical characters produced during the civil wars and the summary characters that were becoming conventional at the end of histories of single reigns and biographies. Clarendon had long been interested in drawing characters. One of his earliest works, *The Difference and Disparity Between the Estates and Conditions of George Duke of Buckingham, and Robert Earl of Essex* (1651), is a comparison on the Plutarchan model which refutes Sir Henry Wotton's *Parallel* (1641) between the two courtiers. Traditionally it has been connected with Buckingham's assassination and considered Hyde's earliest historical work, but various references in it that seem to reflect the period of the civil wars may indicate either composition or revision during the 1640s. In his commonplace book Clarendon excerpted from Tacitus, Plutarch, and other classical portrayers of character; among contemporaries he knew Jonson and also John Earle in Falkland's group at Great Tew, the best of the English Theophrastan writers. Clarendon's experiences had given him rich and varied exposure to human character, and both his letters and polemical writings during the Royalist exile show his abilities to understand and portray individuals. His fascination with character depiction is shown by several extended sketches of various enemies that he wrote early in his final exile in France, independent characters apparently produced simply for the pleasure of exploring and delineating these figures. But it was in his history that Clarendon's literary skill in the character sketch appears at its most distinguished.

An acute observer of his contemporaries, in *The History of the Rebellion* Clarendon portrayed them for posterity with remarkable psychological realism. Particularly notable are the portraits of Oliver Cromwell and John Hampden, which highlight his ability to be fair in depicting opponents, and the extended comparison of Henry Wilmot and George Goring, a comic masterpiece. Above all, his masterpiece is the long character of Falkland, a moving tribute to the uncompromising idealism and integrity of his closest friend. The tendency to excerpt these sketches and publish them separately has misrepresented the scope of Clarendon's achievement in them, for they function as integral parts of his narrative. Because he saw individuals as one of the crucial determinants in shaping events, he uses character sketches for causal explanation. While such sketches directly advance the story, others regulate the narrative pace, translate thematic concerns into concrete particulars, or move the narrative focus from physical to psychological action. As in the *History* itself, Clarendon's achievement in the character sketch is not without flaws. Bias marks some sketches, while his obituary characters of the Royalists killed in battle tend often to be vague types rather than individuals. Nevertheless, Clarendon's sketches in *The History of the Rebellion* are the finest historical characters produced during the century and remain among the best in all of English historical writing.

Having completed his *History*, Clarendon on 8 June 1672 began the *Continuation of the Life of Edward Earl of Clarendon*. This long work, covering his service as lord chancellor and the early years of his exile, contains much interesting material, but it is substantially less satisfactory as either history or autobiography than the *Life*. More narrowly focused, it is primarily a detailed defense of his conduct of affairs. The *Continuation* is also disappointing in literary terms, for both his prose style and his narrative show some of the same defects as his polemical works.

Two other works that Clarendon completed in his final exile focus on religion and its proper role in the state. In *Animadversions Upon a Book, Intituled, Fanaticism Fanatically Imputed to the Catholick Church, By D^r. Stillingfleet*, he defends Falkland and the ideals of the Great Tew against the attacks of Hugh Cressy, a member of Falkland's circle who subsequently became a Roman Catholic priest and after the Restoration accused his former associates of Socinianism. The work was published anonymously in 1673. *Religion and Policy and the Countenance and Assistance Each Should Give to the Other*, begun in Spain and dated at the end 12 February 1674 from Moulins, is a lengthy scholarly survey of papal claims to temporal power. Clarendon shows his biographical orientation by organizing the study as a successive examination of the lives of all the popes, but his repetitious refutations of papal supremacy throughout the work seriously mar its literary value.

At various times during his exile Clarendon had written to the king and also to the duke of York begging permission to return home, but he received no replies. In the late spring of 1674, he left Moulins for Rouen, perhaps to be closer to England in case he was finally allowed back. In August 1674 he wrote once more to the king, the queen, and the duke, again with no result. Clarendon died at Rouen on 11 December 1674. His body was interred in Westminster Abbey on 4 January 1675, in Henry VII's chapel in an unmarked grave.

The bulk of Clarendon's writings published during his lifetime are polemical pieces. His sons waited almost thirty years to print *The History of the Rebellion*, the first of his major works to appear posthumously, and its appearance in three handsome volumes from 1702 to 1704 caused a sensation. It was widely acclaimed as a literary masterpiece, a judgment that has stood with few challenges for almost three hundred years. But the high Tory politics of Clarendon's son Laurence, by then earl of Rochester, and of his associates who helped him prepare the work for the press insured that the *History* would ignite fierce controversy from the beginning. Clarendon and his work played an important role in the bitter battles between Whigs and Tories during the eighteenth century and continued to excite partisan commentary well into the nineteenth. In contrast, the early twentieth century showed a diminished interest in the *History*, although it remained a central source for historians. Recently it has begun to receive more extended literary analysis, as opposed to the conventional appreciative accolades characteristic of earlier periods.

None of Clarendon's other works approached the popularity of *The History of the Rebellion*, which went through at least twenty editions during the eighteenth and nineteenth centuries. His essays, dialogues, and commentaries on the Psalms, first published in 1727, were each republished at least twice in the eighteenth century, but have never received much attention. The *Life* and the *Continuation* were not published until 1759; unlike the *History*, their sale was very slow. From the beginning, limited access to the *Life* as a whole blunted its impact; it has never been printed in full as Clarendon composed it. Although critics have recognized its excellence and its importance among early English autobiographies, a major difficulty in dealing with this work continues to be the lack of a complete and accurate text. *Religion and Policy*, Clarendon's last work, did not appear until 1811. Of Clarendon's nonhistorical works, only the *Brief View and Survey* has received some modern attention as an important contribution to the debate inaugurated by Hobbes.

As both a maker and writer of history, Clarendon became a central figure in seventeenth-century England. But ironic reversals marked his story after death just as in life. He died in banishment, disgraced and largely forgotten, but the incompetence and corruption of the politicians who supplanted him provided contrasts that allowed his integrity and devotion to constitutionalism to emerge more clearly in retrospect. Increasingly eclipsed under Charles II and seriously threatened by James II, the Anglican principles for which he stood triumphed in the reigns of William and Mary and particularly of Anne—appropriately enough, for the two queens were his granddaughters, the only surviving children of the marriage of James II and Clarendon's daughter Anne. A literary figure almost in spite of himself, for his preference was always for action rather than contemplation, at a time when history and literature were splitting apart, Clarendon reclaimed Clio for the Muses with his most enduring work, *The History of the Rebellion*.

Letters:

State Papers Collected by Edward, Earl of Clarendon, 3 volumes, edited by Richard Scrope and Thomas Monkhouse (Oxford: Clarendon Printing-House, 1767-1786);

T. H. Lister, ed., *Letters and Papers*, volume 3 of *Life and Administration of Edward, First Earl of Clarendon; with Original Correspondence and Authentic Papers Never Before Published* (London: Longman, Orme, Brown, Green & Longmans, 1837).

Bibliography:

Graham Roebuck, *Clarendon and Cultural Continuity: A Bibliographical Study* (New York & London: Garland, 1981).

Biographies:

T. H. Lister, *Life and Administration of Edward, First Earl of Clarendon; with Original Correspondence and Authentic Papers Never Before Published* (London: Longman, Orme, Brown, Green & Longmans, 1837);

Sir Henry Craik, *The Life of Edward Earl of Clarendon, Lord High Chancellor of England*, 2 volumes (London: Smith, Elder, 1911);

R. W. Harris, *Clarendon and the English Revolution* (London: Chatto & Windus, 1983; Stanford, Cal.: Stanford University Press, 1983).

References:

Martine Watson Brownley, *Clarendon and the Rhetoric of Historical Form* (Philadelphia: University of Pennsylvania Press, 1985);

Irene Coltman, *Private Men and Public Causes: Philosophy and Politics in the English Civil War* (London: Faber & Faber, 1962);

C. H. Firth, "Clarendon's 'History of the Rebellion,'" *English Historical Review*, 19 (January 1904): 26-54; (April 1904): 246-262; (July 1904): 464-483;

Sir Charles Firth, "Edward Hyde, Earl of Clarendon, as Statesman, Historian, and Chancellor of the University," in his *Essays Historical and Literary* (Oxford: Clarendon Press, 1938), pp. 103-128;

Robin Gibson, *Catalogue of Portraits in the Collection of the Earl of Clarendon* (Waldrop, Hampshire: BAS Printers, 1977);

P. H. Hardacre, "Portrait of a Bibliophile I: Edward Hyde, Earl of Clarendon, 1609-1674," *Book Collector*, 7 (Winter 1958): 361-368;

Christopher Hill, "Clarendon and the Civil War," *History Today*, 3 (October 1953): 695-703; reprinted as "Lord Clarendon and the Puritan Revolution," in *Puritanism and Revolution* (London: Secker & Warburg, 1958), pp. 199-214;

Ronald Hutton, "Clarendon's *History of the Rebellion*," *English Historical Review*, 97 (January 1982): 70-88;

Percy Lewis Kaye, *English Colonial Administration Under Lord Clarendon, 1660-1667*, Johns Hopkins University Studies in Historical and Political Science, series 27, 5-6 (Baltimore: Johns Hopkins University Press, 1905);

Royce MacGillivray, *Restoration Historians and the English Civil War* (The Hague: Martinus Nijhoff, 1974), pp. 197-225;

George E. Miller, *Edward Hyde, Earl of Clarendon* (Boston: Twayne, 1983);

Thomas H. Robinson, "Lord Clarendon's Moral Thought," *Huntington Library Quarterly*, 43 (Winter 1979): 37-59;

H. R. Trevor-Roper, "Clarendon and the Practice of History," in *Milton and Clarendon* (Los Angeles: William Andrews Clark Memorial Library, 1965);

Trevor-Roper, *Edward Hyde, Earl of Clarendon* (Oxford: Clarendon Press, 1975);

B. H. G. Wormald, *Clarendon: Politics, History and Religion, 1640-1660* (Cambridge: Cambridge University Press, 1951).

Papers:

The Bodleian Library, Oxford University, holds the bulk of Clarendon's extant papers. More than 150 volumes of Clarendon manuscripts include his letters, state and family papers, commonplace books, copies of certain of his works, including holographs of *The History of the Rebellion* and the *Life*, and many other miscellaneous materials. For details on the collection, see Falconer Madan, *A Summary Catalogue of Western Manuscripts in the Bodleian Library at Oxford* (Oxford: Clarendon Press, 1895), III: 557-574, and also the *Calendar of the Clarendon State Papers Preserved in the Bodleian Library*, 5 volumes, edited by Octavius Ogle and others (Oxford: Clarendon Press, 1869-1970).

Daniel Defoe
(1660? - 24 April 1731)

Paula R. Backscheider
University of Rochester

See also the Defoe entries in *DLB 39: British Novelists, 1660-1800* and *DLB 95: Eighteenth-Century British Poets, First Series.*

SELECTED BOOKS: *A Letter to a Dissenter from His Friend at The Hague* (The Hague [i.e., London]: Printed by Hans Verdraeght [pseud.], [1688]);

Reflections upon the Late Great Revolution (London: Printed for Ric. Chiswell, 1689);

An Essay upon Projects (London: Printed by R. R. for Tho. Cockerill, 1697);

The Poor Man's Plea . . . for a Reformation of Manners and Suppressing Immorality in the Nation (London, 1698);

The True-Born Englishman: A Satyr (London, 1700);

[Legion's Memorial] ([London, 1701]);

The History of the Kentish Petition (London, 1701);

The Original Power of the Collective Body of the People of England, Examined and Asserted (London, 1702);

An Enquiry into Occasional Conformity (London, 1702);

The Shortest Way with the Dissenters (London, 1702); republished as *The Shortest Way With the Dissenters. [Taken from Dr. Sach[evere]ll's Sermon, and Others]* (London: Printed & sold by the booksellers, [1703]);

The Opinion of a Known Dissenter on the Bill for Preventing Occasional Conformity (London, 1703);

A Brief Explanation of a late Pamphlet, Entituled, The Shortest Way with the Dissenters (London, [1703]);

A Hymn to the Pillory (London, 1703);

A Review of the Affairs of France: and of all Europe, 9 volumes (London, 19 February 1704 - 11 June 1713)—several name changes, including *A Review of the State of the British Nation* and simply *The Review* for the last volume;

A Serious Inquiry into This Grand Question; Whether a Law to prevent the Occasional Conformity of Dissenters, Would not be Inconsistent with the Act of Toleration (London, 1704);

The Storm: Or, A Collection of the most Remarkable Casualties And Disasters Which happen'd in the Late Dreadful Tempest, Both by Sea and Land (London: Printed for G. Sawbridge & sold by J. Nutt, 1704);

The Double Welcome. A Poem To the Duke of Marlbro' (London: Printed & sold by B. Bragg, 1705);

The Consolidator (London: Printed & sold by Benj. Bragg, 1705);

An Essay at Removing National Prejudices against a Union with Scotland (London, 1706);

Jure Divino: A Satyr in Twelve Books (London, 1706);

Caledonia: A Poem in Honour of Scotland, and the Scots Nation (Edinburgh: Printed by the Heirs and Successors of Andrew Anderson, 1706; London: Printed by J. Mathews & sold by John Morphew, 1707);

A Brief History of the Poor Palatine Refugees (London: Printed & sold by J. Baker, 1709);

The History of the Union of Great Britain (Edinburgh: Printed by the Heirs and Successors of Andrew Anderson, 1709);

A Speech without Doors (London: Printed for A. Baldwin, 1710);

Instructions from Rome (London: Printed & sold by J. Baker, [1710]);

An Essay upon Publick Credit (London: Printed & sold by the Booksellers, 1710);

Reasons Why This Nation Ought to Put a Speedy End to This Expensive War (London: Printed for J. Baker, 1711);

Reasons Why a Party among Us, and also among the Confederates, are Obstinately Bent against a Treaty of Peace ([London]: Printed for John Baker, 1711);

An Essay at a Plain Exposition of that Difficult Phrase a Good Peace ([London]: Printed for J. Baker, 1711);

An Essay on the History of Parties, and Persecution in Britain (London: Printed for J. Baker, 1711);

Frontispiece for A True Collection of the Writings Of The Author of The True Born English-man,
the 1703 authorized collection of Defoe's works

No Queen; Or, No General (London: Printed & sold by the Booksellers of London & Westminster, 1712);

The Conduct of Parties in England (London, 1712);

Peace, or Poverty (London: Printed & sold by John Morphew, 1712);

The Present State of the Parties in Great Britain (London: Sold by J. Baker, 1712);

An Enquiry into the Danger and Consequences of a War with the Dutch (London: Printed for J. Baker, 1712);

And What if the Pretender Should Come? (London: Sold by J. Baker, 1713);

An Essay on the Treaty of Commerce with France (London: Printed for J. Baker, 1713);

Mercator, 26 May 1713 - 20 July 1714;

A General History of Trade, 4 parts (London: Printed for J. Baker, 1713);

Memoirs of Count Tariff (London: Printed for John Morphew, 1713);

Memoirs of John, Duke of Melfort (London: Printed for J. Moor, 1714);

The Secret History of the White Staff: Being an Account of Affairs under the Conduct of Some Late Ministers (London: Printed for J. Baker, 1714);

Advice to the People of Great Britain (London: Printed for J. Baker, 1714);

Hanover or Rome (London: Printed for J. Roberts, 1715);

The Fears of the Pretender Turn'd into the Fears of Debauchery (London: Printed and sold by S. Keimer, 1715);

An Appeal to Honour and Justice (London: Printed for J. Baker, 1715);

The Family Instructor, in Three Parts (London: Sold by Eman. Matthews & Jo. Button, in Newcastle upon Tine, 1715);

An Account of the Conduct of Robert Earl of Oxford (London, 1715);

An Account of the Proceedings against the Rebels (London: Printed for J. Baker & Tho. Warner, 1716);

A True Account of the Proceedings at Perth (London: Printed for J. Baker, 1716);

Fair Payment No Spunge: Or Some Considerations on the Unreasonableness of Refusing to Receive Back Money Lent on Publick Securities (London: Sold by J. Brotherton & W. Meddows, and J. Roberts, 1717);

The Question Fairly Stated, Whether Now is Not the Time to do Justice to the Friends of the Government as well as to its Enemies? (London: Printed for J. Roberts, J. Harrison & A. Dodd, 1717);

Memoirs of the Church of Scotland (London: Printed for Eman. Matthews & T. Warner, 1717);

Considerations on the Present State of Affairs in Great-Britain (London: Printed for J. Roberts, 1718);

Memoirs of the Life and Eminent Conduct of that Learned and Reverend Divine Daniel Williams DD. (London: Printed for E. Curll, 1718);

Memoirs of Publick Transactions in the Life and Ministry of his Grace the D. of Shrewsbury (London: Printed for Tho. Warner, 1718);

The Family Instructor. In Two Parts (London: Printed for Emman. Matthews, 1718);

A Continuation of Letters Written by a Turkish Spy at Paris (London: Printed for W. Taylor, 1718);

The Memoirs of Majr. Alexander Ramkins (London: Printed for R. King & W. Boreham, 1719);

The Life and Strange Surprizing Adventures of Robinson Crusoe (London: Printed for W. Taylor, 1719);

The Anatomy of Exchange-Alley: Or a System of Stock-Jobbing (London: Printed for E. Smith, 1719);

The Farther Adventures of Robinson Crusoe (London: Printed for W. Taylor, 1719);

A Brief State of the Question, between the Printed and Painted Callicoes and the Woollen and Silk Manu-

facture (London: Printed for W. Boreham, 1719);

Manufacturer, 30 October 1719 - 17 February 1720;

The King of Pirates: Being an Account of the Famous Enterprises of Captain Avery (London: Printed for A. Bettesworth, C. King, J. Brotherton & W. Meadows, W. Chetwood, and sold by W. Boreham, 1720);

Memoirs of a Cavalier (London: Printed for A. Bell, J. Osborn, W. Taylor & T. Warner, [1720]);

The Life, Adventures and Pyracies of the Famous Captain Singleton (London: Printed for J. Brotherton, J. Graves, A. Dodd & T. Warner, 1720);

Serious Reflections during the Life and Surprising Adventures of Robinson Crusoe (London: Printed for W. Taylor, 1720);

The South-Sea Scheme Examin'd (London: Printed for J. Roberts, 1720);

The Fortunes and Misfortunes of the Famous Moll Flanders (London: Printed for & sold by W. Chetwood & T. Edling, 1721);

Due Preparations for the Plague as Well for Soul as Body (London: Printed for E. Matthews, 1722);

Religious Courtship (London: Printed for E. Matthews & A. Bettesworth, J. Brotherton & W. Meadows, 1722);

A Journal of the Plague Year (London: Printed for E. Nutt, J. Roberts, A. Dodd & J. Graves, 1722);

The History and Remarkable Life of the Truly Honourable Col. Jacque (London: Printed & sold by J. Brotherton, T. Payne, W. Mears, A. Dodd, W. Chetwood, J. Graves, S. Chapman, & J. Stagg, 1723);

The Fortunate Mistress: Or, A History Of The Life and Vast Variety of Fortunes Of Mademoiselle de Beleau. . . . Being the Person known by the Name of the Lady Roxana, in the time of King Charles II (London: Printed for T. Warner, W. Meadows, W. Pepper, S. Harding & T. Edlin, 1724);

The Great Law of Subordination Consider'd (London: Sold by S. Harding, W. Lewis, T. Worrall, A. Bettesworth, W. Meadows & T. Edlin, 1724);

A Tour thro' the Whole Island of Great Britain, 3 volumes (London: Sold by G. Strahan, W. Mears, and others, 1724, 1725, 1727);

The Royal Progress (London: Printed by John Darby & sold by J. Roberts, J. Brotherton & A. Dodd, 1724);

A Narrative of All the Robberies, Escapes &c. of John Sheppard (London: Printed & sold by John Applebee, 1724);

The History of the Remarkable Life of John Sheppard (London: Printed & sold by John Applebee, J. Isted & the Booksellers of London and Westminster, [1724]);

Every-body's Business, Is No-body's Business (London: Sold by T. Warner, A. Dodd & E. Nutt, 1725);

A General History of Discoveries and Improvements, 4 parts (London: Printed for J. Roberts, 1725-1726);

The Complete English Tradesman, 2 volumes (London: Printed for Charles Rivington, 1726; with supplement, 1727);

A Brief Historical Account of the Lives of the Six Notorious Street-Robbers, Executed at Kingston (London: Printed for A. Moore, 1726);

The Political History of the Devil (London: Printed for T. Warner, 1726);

Some Considerations upon Street-Walkers (London: Printed for A. Moore, [1726]);

The Protestant Monastery: Or, A Complaint against the Brutality of the Present Age (London: Printed for W. Meadows, 1727);

A System of Magick (London: Sold by J. Roberts, 1727);

Conjugal Lewdness: Or, Matrimonial Whoredom (London: Printed for T. Warner, 1727);

A Brief Deduction of the Original, Progress, and Immense Greatness of the British Woollen Manufacture (London: Sold by J. Roberts & A. Dodd, 1727);

An Essay on the History and Reality of Apparitions (London: Printed & sold by J. Roberts, 1727);

A New Family Instructor; In Familiar Discourses between a Father and his Children (London: Printed for T. Warner, 1727);

Parochial Tyranny (London: Printed & sold by J. Roberts, [1727]);

Augusta Triumphans: Or, The Way to Make London the Most Flourishing City in the Universe (London: Printed for J. Roberts & sold by E. Nutt, A. Dodd, N. Blandford & A. Stagg, 1728);

A Plan of the English Commerce (London: Printed for Charles Rivington, 1728);

Atlas Maritimus & Commercialis: Or, A General View of the World, so far as it relates to Trade and Navigation (London: Printed for James & John Knapton; William & John Innys; John Darby; Arthur Bettesworth, John Osborn &

Thomas Longman; John Senex; Edward Symon; Andrew Johnston; and the Executors of William Taylor, 1728);

Second Thoughts are Best (London: Printed for W. Meadows & sold by J. Roberts, 1729);

An Humble Proposal To The People of England, For the Encrease of Their Trade, And Encouragement of their Manufactures (London: Printed for Charles Rivington, 1729);

The Advantages of Peace and Commerce (London: Printed for J. Brotherton & Tho. Cox, and sold by A. Dodd, 1729);

An Effectual Scheme for the Immediate Preventing of Street Robberies (London: Printed for J. Wilford, 1731);

The Compleat English Gentleman, edited by Karl D. Bülbring (London: David Nutt, 1890).

Today Daniel Defoe is known as the author of great novels—*Robinson Crusoe* (1719), *Moll Flanders* (1721), *A Journal of the Plague Year* (1722), *Roxana* (1724), and others less well known. In his own time, however, his reputation was based on his nonfiction prose. The undisputed premier journalist of the early eighteenth century, he earned the title given him by the *Moderator,* "The Goliath of a party." At his death, his obituaries paid tribute to "Mr. Daniel Defoe, sen. a person well known for his numerous and various writings. He had a great natural genius; and understood very well the trade and interest of this Kingdom." None mentioned *Robinson Crusoe,* but his sacrifices for "civil and religious liberty" attracted notice.

Nineteenth-century writers consistently paid tribute to the man who was among the first to write "the doctrine on which . . . all free political constitutions rest." They acknowledged "the debt which the people . . . owe, not simply for the pleasure afforded by his incomparable works of imagination, but because of the long years of suffering which he endured on account of the . . . heroic efforts that he made to place our religious and political freedom upon a true and lasting basis." We may have forgotten pamphlets like *The Original Power of the Collective Body of the People of England* (1702), but they were enthusiastically and frequently quoted for two centuries and echoes of them exist in, for instance, the United States Constitution.

Probably born in 1660, Defoe was the son of a City of London tallow chandler, James Foe, and his wife, Alice. Educated for the Nonconformist ministry at Charles Morton's respected

Title page for an unauthorized edition of Defoe's 1706 satiric poem, with a caricature of Defoe in the pillory

Newington Green Academy, he decided to enter trade and became a hose factor. On 1 January 1684, he married the daughter of a wealthy cooper, Mary Tuffley, who brought him a £3,700 dowry. The next year, he fought with James Scott, Duke of Monmouth, in the unsuccessful rebellion to establish a Protestant monarchy. Back in London, he expanded his business interests, which included investments in a diving bell, civet cats, international shipping, and land in Essex. By 1691 he was bankrupt. He settled with his creditors and slowly established a successful brick and tile works. In 1700 he published *The True-Born Englishman*, a poem that ridiculed those who rejected King William because he was Dutch. Defoe described the English as a mongrel race, the prod-

uct of wave after wave of immigrants. He concluded, "A *True Born Englishman*'s a Contradiction, / In Speech an Irony, in Fact a Fiction" and " 'Tis Personal Virtue only makes us great." The most popular poem of the Restoration and early eighteenth century, it went through ten authorized and at least twelve pirated editions in the first year and appeared in fifty editions by midcentury.

Defoe continued to write poetry and began to write political pamphlets. In 1702 he published *The Shortest Way with the Dissenters*, the pamphlet that led to his conviction for seditious libel and his pillory sentence. Because of his continued weaknesses as a businessman and the year (1703) he spent as a fugitive and then a prisoner

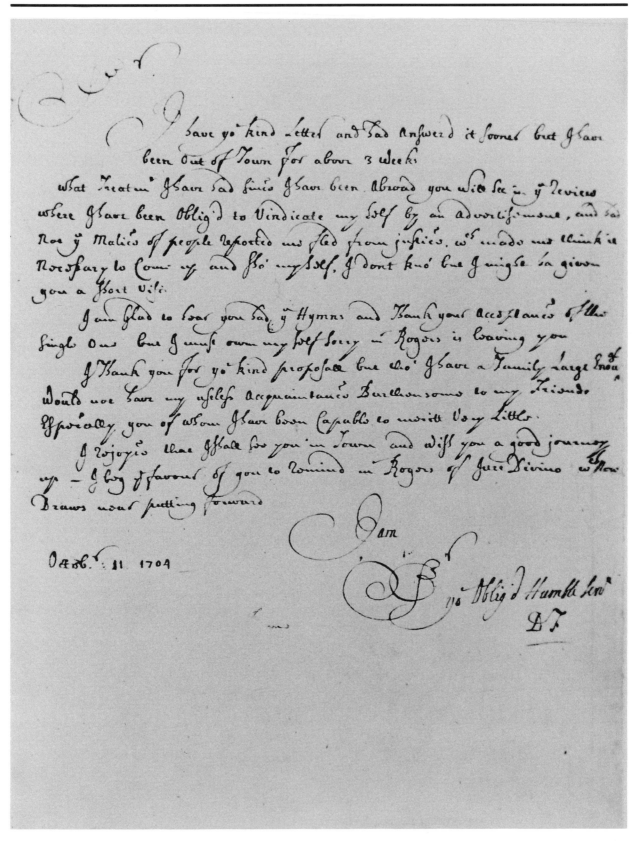

Letter probably written to Samuel Elisha, a Shrewsbury burgess and practitioner of law with whom Defoe stayed during his travels
as a propagandist for Robert Harley (MA 788; by permission of the Pierpont Morgan Library)

in Newgate, he went bankrupt again. Robert Harley, secretary of state for the Northern Department, effected his release from prison in November 1703, and Defoe expected to become one of his agents. Employment from Harley was slow in coming, and, in order to support himself, his wife, and seven children, he began to write for money. His major effort was the *Review*, a periodical he wrote alone for nine years (19 February 1704 - 11 June 1713). Soon he reached an agreement with Harley. He traveled as a propagandist and opinion sampler for Harley in 1704 and 1705 and, in 1706, went to Scotland to work for the proposed union of England and Scotland.

He spent most of the next four years there and part of 1710-1712. During this time, he became the most prolific and feared propagandist of the century. With the accession of George I in 1714 and the more tranquil Hanoverian years, he largely turned from controversy to other kinds of writing. In April of 1719 he published *Robinson Crusoe*, and four editions of it sold before *The Farther Adventures of Robinson Crusoe* was published that August. In 1722 he produced *Moll Flanders, A Journal of the Plague Year*, and *Col. Jack*. His last novel, *The Fortunate Mistress*, the novel we call *Roxana*, came out in 1724. In the last fifteen years of his life, he published millions of words: histories, travel books, biographies, and proposals for improving society, morals, and the economy. He died on 24 April 1731 in his lodgings on Rope Maker's Alley, in the heart of the city he loved.

Exactly how much nonfiction prose Defoe wrote, we shall probably never know. Some of what has been attributed to him is disputed, and other things are surely skillful compilations rather than entirely original compositions. In 1981 Frank Bastian made a case for adding twenty-nine pieces, some long rejected by other Defoe experts, and, beginning in 1986, P. N. Furbank and W. R. Owens have pointed out the inadequately argued attributions of other works. Careful cases for the exclusion of individual items have been made by J. A. Downie, Rodney Baine, Henry Snyder, and Pat Rogers. During the same years, others, most notably Maximillian E. Novak, have attributed or identified substantial works by Defoe. Novak, for instance, located the manuscript for the 1682 *Historical Collections* in the William Andrews Clark Library at the University of California, Los Angeles.

What it is safe to say is that Defoe, whose entry is the longest in the *New Cambridge Bibliography of English Literature*, is surely a contender for the distinction of having been the most prolific nonfiction prose writer in all of British and American literature. Although few can name any of these pieces except, perhaps, *The Shortest Way with the Dissenters*, during his entire life Defoe was more famous for his nonfiction than he was for his novels. Reputedly, his nonfiction writings are characteristically brief and journalistic. His periodical the *Review* and his political propaganda, much of it written in the years during which Jonathan Swift wrote *The Examiner* (1710-1711) and *The Conduct of the Allies* (1711), come to mind. This conception is wrong. Defoe's nonfiction pieces *average* nearly two hundred pages, and it would be as accurate to think of him as the writer of history, economics, and practical divinity as of political journalism.

It was Defoe's religion that drew him into writing. He was a Nonconformist, a Protestant "Dissenter" who refused the sacraments and membership in the Church of England. His earliest known pamphlet and his first published poem championed what he saw as the "Protestant interest." The pamphlet, *A Letter to a Dissenter from his Friend at the Hague* (1688), was part of the literature warning Dissenters that James II's Declaration of Indulgence was hypocritically manipulative and coercive. Defoe insisted that the true beneficiaries of the declaration would be Catholics and used insinuation to raise suspicion. He wrote, "There are many things which would make a wise man suspect that there is some farther Design than Liberty of Conscience in all this zeal for repealing the Penal Laws and Test."

From this time on, Defoe wrote numerous pamphlets each time significant legislation regarding the Dissenters came before Parliament. The majority of these pamphlets, then, cluster around 1702 (the time of the introduction of the Occasional Conformity Bill), 1710 (the time before its passage), 1714 (the passage of the Schism Bill), and 1717 (when Parliament considered restoring full rights to Dissenters).

Defoe's first criminal arrest resulted from these writings. Queen Anne began her reign in 1702 with several speeches asserting her desire to strengthen the Church of England. Commons responded with the Occasional Conformity Bill, and Defoe quickly published three pamphlets on the subject. *An Enquiry into Occasional Conformity* and *The Opinion of a Known Dissenter on the Bill for Preventing Occasional Conformity* argue that the bill is a matter of indifference to Dissenters because

The portrait of Defoe published as the frontispiece in the authorized edition of his Jure Divino
(engraving by Michael Vandergucht, after a portrait by Jeremiah Taverner)

no true Dissenter is an Occasional Conformist. Defoe bluntly calls Occasional Conformity a sin, accuses those who practice it of "prostituting" their religion, and asks, "And how can you take it as a Civil Action in one place and a Religious Act in another? This is playing *Bo peep* with God Almighty. . . ."

Defoe published the notorious pamphlet, *The Shortest Way with the Dissenters*, to coincide with the House of Lords' debate on the Occasional Conformity Bill in December. *The Shortest Way with the Dissenters* imitated the immoderate language of High Church sermons and pamphlets. In this mock-sermon, the High Church persona argued that England should eliminate the Dissenters for the good of posterity and that the time was right; the metaphors, again taken from High Church rhetoric, described the Dissenters as butchers, rats, snakes, poison, weeds, and wounds. Unfortu-

nately for Defoe the pamphlet was taken at face value by many people and acclaimed and quoted by the High Church. Soon the Tories who had approved so enthusiastically of *The Shortest Way with the Dissenters* learned that they had been tricked; they had been lured into revealing their fanaticism, and, as Defoe said later, "these Gentlemen are satyrs on themselves, by fixing the Characters, as things which must be suitable, since the likeness was such they could not know themselves from a Stranger."

The House of Commons ordered the pamphlet burned, and, in a separate criminal action, Defoe was indicted for seditious libel. As soon as he realized the effect of his satire, he tried to pacify the angry parties. *A Brief Explanation of a late Pamphlet* appeared in the first week of January 1703, and he wrote eight more essays and poems on the subject in the next year. One of these pamphlets pointed explicitly to his sources: *The Shortest Way With the Dissenters. [Taken from Dr. Sach[evere]ll's Sermon, and Others.]* These pamphlets of 1703 usefully explain many of Defoe's opinions about Nonconformity and show him developing sensitivity to the complex relationships between government and press, politics and journalism.

Each time the Bill for Preventing Occasional Conformity came up for debate, Defoe contributed to the paper wars. Although these tracts continued to defend his own character and to explain *The Shortest Way with the Dissenters*, they were quite different from his pre-pillory ones. Now Defoe described the loyalty of the Dissenters in detail and argued the advantages of "peace and union" between the Protestant sects. For instance, *A Serious Inquiry into This Grand Question; Whether a Law to prevent the Occasional Conformity of Dissenters, Would not be Inconsistent with the Act of Toleration* (1704) contradicted the earlier pamphlets by admitting that Dissenters had "publickly declar'd" that "Occasional Communion [was] Lawful in it self" and insisted that the Bill was unjust and unreasonable, that it would deprive the Dissenters of their civil rights, and would have seriously deleterious effects on his people. These pamphlets showed increasing control of argument and diction and the development of a subtle range of tones and points of view. At this time, too, he began to experiment with more elaborate fictions. *The Consolidator* (1705), written in the form of an imaginary lunar voyage, developed some of the ideas he no longer expressed openly. Through an allegorical history of England, he presented his views on, for example, parliamentary monarchy, standing armies, occasional conformity, and the War of Spanish Succession. In a typical section Defoe dramatized the conflict between the Crolians (Dissenters) and the Solunarians (High Church). The Crolians formed a federation with considerable political and economic power.

Defoe was an early participant in almost every religious controversy, political or doctrinal. Large numbers of his pamphlets defend the civil rights of Dissenters. Others attack the Jacobites, those Englishmen who supported the Stuarts and hoped for the return of James or his son, and yet others are part of the Sacheverell, Bangorian, and Salters' Hall controversies. Some of Defoe's most creative work can be found in these writings, and some serve as apprentice pieces for his fiction. During the Jacobite agitation and rebel-

lion that occurred after Queen Anne's death in 1714, for instance, Defoe published extensively. In some of these works, such as *A True Account of the Proceedings at Perth* (1716), he tried to reduce the resentment against the Scots in the hope of fostering harmony and unity within the nation as a whole. He depicted the ordinary Scot as brave but deluded and betrayed by a few powerful leaders. In other works, including *Hanover or Rome* (1715), he urged his countrymen to support the king's efforts to end the Jacobite threat permanently.

Defoe also discouraged the increase of Jacobitism by describing the human and financial losses the Jacobites suffered and by depicting them as objects of satire or contemptuous pity. *The Memoirs of Major Alexander Ramkins* (published in late 1718 but dated 1719), an important precursor to his novels, for instance, tells the story of a Jacobite who repeatedly gave up promising opportunities only to end up destitute and imprisoned. Ramkins's disillusioned reflections are the vehicle for the exposure of French duplicity. He asks, "Were not 300000 Men driven like Sheep from the Banks of the *Boyne* [in Ireland] for want of Arms, while what would have furnish'd a Million of Men, were Rusting in the Magazines of *France*?" Defoe, the master propagandist, reduces thirty years of Jacobite invasions into the history of France's need for diversionary attacks on the English coast.

Before Defoe died, he had written more than sixty-five individual works on issues affecting the Dissenters and another fifty or so on the recurrent threat of the Jacobites. The other large group of pamphlets he wrote was in the service of three monarchs, and his religion influenced them as well. These pamphlets commented on almost every political issue. For William, he wrote on the succession, standing armies, and the war with France. During Anne's reign, he advocated such policies as moderation, union with Scotland, support of public credit, and peace with France. A firm supporter of the Protestant succession, he condemned the Jacobite riots and praised George I, then wrote about the measures Walpole took to stabilize the government and hasten economic recovery.

It was common in the nineteenth century to see Defoe as a great spokesman for the branch of the Whig party most clearly associated with what had come to be called "revolution principles." These "principles," based on an interpretation of the Revolution Settlement that had brought Wil-

"Daniel De Foe and the Devil at Leap-Frog," a caricature by one of Defoe's contemporaries

liam to the throne in 1688, vested supreme power in the people. Defoe's great statement of this position is *The Original Power of the Collective Body of the People of England* (1702). Addressed to the Houses of Lords and Commons, it was, in Defoe's opinion, "The Vindication of the Original Right of all Men to the Government of themselves." He told the members of Parliament, "You may Die, but the People remain; you may be Dissolved . . . Power may have its Intervals, and Crowns their *Interregnum*; but Original Power endures to the same Eternity the World endures to. . . . Nor have I advanced any new Doctrine, nothing but what is as ancient as Nature, and born into the World with our Reason. . . ."

This ringing statement grew out of the pamphlets such as *Reflections upon the Late Great Revolution* (1689) written to defend William's accession to the throne after James II fled to France and especially out of the incident involving the "Kentish petitioners" in 1701. Five men from Kent, the county closest to France, brought a petition from the justices, grand jury, and other leading citizens to Commons. In it, they asked that English military forces be increased for their protection;

as they said, they had begun to fear "That they had sow'd their Corn, and the *French* were a coming to Reap it." Commons invoked the 1664 Act against Tumultuous Petitionings, declared the petition "Insolent" and "Seditious," and imprisoned the five men. Their petition had been moderate and respectful; Defoe's response, *Legion's Memorial* (1701), was not. He addressed it to the speaker of the House of Commons, Robert Harley, and "commanded" him to deliver it to the House. In it, he insisted upon "the unquestion'd Right of the People of *England*" to "Require" and even "Compel" Parliament to protect the country's interests. He included seven demands, including the recognition of the French threat and the immediate release of "all Persons *illegally imprison'd*." He signed it "*Legion, and we are Many.*"

Throughout his career, Defoe explained and defended "revolution principles." At the time when others were declaring Queen Anne's right to the throne hereditary, Defoe wrote in the *Review* (May 1709):

The present government stands upon the foot of the Revolution; every act of government her Maj-

esty exerts, every step the present ministry takes
. . . everything done in the state, whether it be Parliament, Council or Convocation, all recognise the Revolution; all set their seal . . . to this principle established by the Revolution, that the people of Britain have an original right to limit the succession of the crown.

As Edmund Burke would do later, Defoe was quick to recognize that the Sacheverell trial came about because a group of men hoped "by a judicial sentence of the highest authority to confirm and fix whig principles as they had operated both in the resistance to King James and in the subsequent settlement." The Reverend Henry Sacheverell had preached and immediately published an inflammatory sermon in which he attacked the bishops, the Dissenters, religious toleration, and, by implication, the legality of the Act of Settlement. At first, almost everyone hoped that the sermon would soon be forgotten, but sixty thousand copies of it sold within two months. The House of Commons voted to impeach Sacheverell. During this trial, Defoe ridiculed Sacheverell, often by allying him with the Pope, in pamphlets like *Instructions from Rome* (1710) and continued to argue the legality and benefits of the revolution. In *A Speech without Doors* (1710), for instance, he ridiculed the principle of nonresistance just as he had in *Jure Divino* (1706) and other earlier works. Throughout this trial and its aftermath and again upon George I's accession, Defoe affirmed what he believed to be the intention of the Revolution Settlement and the primacy of people's "birthright."

It was during Anne's reign that Defoe came to be known as England's premier controversialist and as a "mercenary hack." His contemporaries paid tribute to his ability and effectiveness even as they heaped the most rancorous abuse on him. Because he was a Whig writing for what had become a Tory ministry and a Dissenter supporting the government at a time when High Churchmen dominated Parliament, he found himself insisting fruitlessly that his own principles had not changed and he was a moderate, not a party, man. Political parties in his time were associated with factions, special interests, and competition for appointed offices. Even one of the most partisan politicians of his time, Henry St. John, Viscount Bolingbroke, said, "Faction hath no Regard to national interests," and Robert Harley had attempted to maintain power without strong party alliance. In the charged and polarized England that existed after the Sacheverell trial, Defoe could not avoid the party label.

A major issue during this period was the continuation of the War of Spanish Succession. England and her allies had been attempting to prevent the accession of Louis XIV's grandson Philip to the Spanish throne. War broke out in 1702 when Louis recognized the Pretender (James Francis Edward Stuart) as the legitimate heir to the British throne. Brief hopes for peace in 1709 came to nothing, and neither side seemed close to victory. By 1711 the ministry's—and Defoe's—position was complex. The situation had changed drastically with the death of Joseph I, Emperor of the Holy Roman Empire, in April of that year; he had been the person the Allies hoped to put on the Spanish throne, because he would not unite Spain with France or the Empire (because of a treaty of renunciation). With his death his throne would go to Charles VI, who had already proclaimed himself king of Spain; that would unite Spain with the Empire, a coalition perhaps as much to be feared as a close alliance between the weakened France and Spain. England's reason for fighting and the most-frequent battle cry in Parliament, "No Peace without Spain," had become a travesty. Moreover, England was experiencing serious economic problems, and the people were definitely war weary.

Defoe's writing reflects the subtle, nearly contradictory line the ministry had to take. The country had to support the war and its commanding general, Charles Churchill, Duke of Marlborough, vigorously enough to make the French believe they would continue to fight until they got the peace they wanted. Yet the ministry had to appear eager enough to make peace to satisfy the voters. Marlborough, adamantly against making any peace without the full participation of the allies, had to be discredited in order for the queen to replace him with a man willing to cooperate if the Dutch and the German states continued to hinder negotiations.

In this, one of his most prolific periods, Defoe continued to use the *Review* and wrote dozens of pamphlets. *Reasons Why This Nation Ought to Put a Speedy End to this Expensive War* (1711), *Reasons Why a Party among Us, and also among the Confederates, are Obstinately Bent against a Treaty of Peace* (1711), *An Essay at a Plain Exposition of that Difficult Phrase a Good Peace* (1711), *No Queen; Or, No General* (1712), *Peace, or Poverty* (1712)—tracts with titles like these—poured from his pen, and he worked to appeal to all segments of the Brit-

Annotations by Defoe in his copy of a 1605 edition of Francis Bacon's Advancement of Learning *(Robert H. Taylor Collection at Princeton University; by permission of the Princeton University Library). Defoe probably made these marginal notes when he was past the age of fifty-five.*

ish population. He reminded the merchants that peace would make sea trade safe, he sympathized with the landowners paying heavy taxes to finance the war, he summarized the small gains in "barrier" towns along the Dutch-French border—gains purchased at such loss of British life—and he reviewed England's ancient rivalry with the Dutch and the advantages of trade with France.

When the "separate peace" became public knowledge, Defoe defended England's right to negotiate without her allies, drew upon Parliamentary documents demonstrating that the allies had consistently failed to meet their quotas of men, ships, and supplies, and defended the clauses in the treaty, including the notorious Treaty of Commerce and Navigation that Parliament would ultimately reject. In truth England had reason to be disappointed. After years of successful campaigns, they gained little, and France emerged as a trading partner with most-favored-nation status. Modern scholars have established that Defoe remained loyal to several basic principles but have found contradictions and significant silences.

Apparent contradictions can be found in Defoe's work. He could call the Dutch "the best Friends that *England* had" and General Marlborough a "glorious," unequaled leader in one pam-

Frontispiece for A System of Magick *(courtesy of Special Collections, Thomas Cooper Library, University of South Carolina)*

phlet and accuse the Dutch of "cunning" and Marlborough of ambition and shortsightedness in another. Close reading usually reveals an artistic use of point of view rather than substantive differences in his basic positions. That he could argue, for instance, that Queen Anne had the right to negotiate with France separately even as he said she ought and would not made him vulnerable to misunderstandings. Like so many of his contemporaries, he believed that events in Europe and the economic situation of England made some of the initial reasons for the war irrelevant and peace an urgent concern. That his position in 1712 differed in some ways from his opinions in 1708 was not apostasy but largely response to change.

As a master propagandist, Defoe had to reach a number of different audiences, and, to do so, he needed to adopt different perspectives.

In the last few years before Anne's death, he learned to write from points of view ranging from opposition Whig to moderate Tory. He brought diction, tone, anecdotes, and metaphors into harmony for each type of narrator. Carefully appealing to the interests and prejudices of each group, he would, for example, describe the advantages peace would have for trade in pamphlets such as *An Enquiry into the Danger and Consequences of a War with the Dutch* (1712), which was directed to the Whigs, or he could rehearse the ways the Dutch had gained at British expense in order to justify separate negotiations to the Tories in tracts like *Peace, or Poverty* (1712). He could portray Marlborough as a victim of the Junto struggle for power and his relatives' greed, or he could remind the nation of the enormous casualties at Malplaquet, site of one of the last battles where Marlborough was in command, and of the nature of Marlborough's personal demands.

A typical pamphlet of this period would begin with a statement of the issue to be discussed, definitions, and an anecdote or, at least, a witty saying. He would insist that his motive was to open the eyes of his countrymen, to undeceive the misguided. Defoe liked to use history to explain how the problem or disagreement arose or to offer instructive parallels, and he often included statistics, quotations from treaties, or references to recent, familiar events to make his case seem irrefutable. His conclusions tended to be exhortations; were they to accept his point of view and follow his advice, they and the entire country would prosper. *The Present State of the Parties in Great Britain* (1712), for instance, begins with one of Defoe's favorite metaphors: "Satyr, like Incision, becomes necessary when the Humour rankles, and the Wound threatens Mortification: When Advice ceases to work. . . ." He explains that this book will give the "present state of the Nation," describe the "divisions" parties have caused, provide a history of parties, and end with special attention to the Dissenters. He carries out this plan and concludes in the manner of a sermon—they will be tested and must be prudent and steadfast.

Although he never gave up political pamphlet writing entirely, after the death of Queen Anne, Defoe wrote far fewer. Realizing that periodicals and more fictional forms reached a broader audience, he chose to address the English people in other ways. The diminution of political-party strife reduced the payment and market for the kind of ephemeral pamphlets that Parliamentary debates, elections, and diplomatic developments had called forth. To compare the subjects and numbers of pamphlets written before and after 1714 shows a more selective Defoe. His opposition to the Jacobites motivated pamphlets that praised King George and his policies (such as *An Account of the Proceedings of the Government against the Rebels, compared with the Persecutions of the Late Reigns*, 1716). His desire for the continuation of moderate Whig power and government stability led to pamphlets in support of the Triennial Act, and his hopes for an end to the legal restrictions on the Dissenters produced a group of pamphlets including the optimistic *The Question Fairly Stated, Whether Now is not the Time to do Justice to the Friends of the Government* (1717). Somewhat later, he wrote pamphlets to support the domestic wool trade (*A Brief State of*

the Question, between the Printed and Painted Callicoes and the Woollen and Silk Manufacture, 1719) and to encourage international trade (*An Humble Proposal to the People of England, For the Encrease of their Trade*, 1729). At age sixty-seven he could be aroused to argue the advantages of a war with Spain, and he traced the origins and implications of the conflict as cogently as he had that with France when he was forty-five.

Since boyhood Defoe had read history avidly. He once said that he had read "all the Histories of Europe, that are Extant in our Language, and some in other Languages." The methods and purposes of historiography attracted him early. *The Storm* (1704) is a combination of what Francis Bacon would call the history of an event and a collection of "remarkable provinces," God's actions in the world or proofs of God's presence in the world. He called the *Review* "history writing by inches" and initially designed it as the explanation of how the War of Spanish Succession began and an exploration of the characteristics, strengths, and weaknesses of the participating nations. In 1709 he published *The History of the Union of Great Britain*, an account of the event he considered the greatest achievement of Queen Anne's reign. About the same time he began the *Memoirs of the Church of Scotland*, which he did not publish until 1717. A book of more than four hundred pages, it came out in April to support the Parliamentary presentation of a delegation from the Commission of the General Assembly of the Church of Scotland who hoped for the repeal of the imposition of the Oath of Abjuration, the oath that required them to aid in barring all members of their own Church from the throne of Great Britain. His earlier histories were written from the point of view of an objective eyewitness; in this one, he characterized himself as "an officious Stranger" and called the Church's history a revelation to him, a "*Terra incognita*, a vast Continent of hidden, undiscovered Novelties." Defoe began with the Reformation and characterized the Church of Scotland's history as one of dedicated resistance to Roman Catholicism. He hoped that with a sympathetic understanding of the Church of Scotland, M.P.'s might heed the arguments that the Oath of Abjuration should not be required of Scots or should even be revised in their favor.

Late in his life, he began an ambitious universal history, *A General History of Discoveries and Improvements* (1725-1726), and wrote three historical accounts of the preternatural: *The Political History*

Frontispiece for The Political History of the Devil *(courtesy of Special Collections, Thomas Cooper Library, University of South Carolina)*

of the Devil (1726), *An Essay on the History and Reality of Apparitions* (1727), and *A System of Magick* (1727). *A General History of Discoveries and Improvements*, like other universal histories, began in biblical times and encompassed the entire earth. Promising to absorb all useful knowledge, the histories collected whatever the writer believed worth knowing and preserved it for the benefit of new generations. Defoe's history was part of his elaborate campaign to persuade his countrymen of the benefits of exploration and colonial expansion, and he explained that he intended to give a "view of what may yet be undertaken." The history was originally published in four installments, and, by the second, Defoe had established a parallel between the British and the Phoenicians, the great "Improvers of what others invented" who had been great merchants and traders. He surveyed the great discoveries (like the Americas) and inventions (like the uses of the lodestone in navigation) and suggested ways that the British could increase their wealth.

In *The Political History of the Devil*, Defoe collects stories and legends about Satan including those from the Bible and Milton's *Paradise Lost* (1667). He concludes that the Devil exists but that many representations of him are ridiculous. Defoe promises that *A System of Magick* will provide a profitable and diverting history of magic beginning with the Chaldeans. He describes the

Chaldeans as mathematicians and, like all of the earliest magicians, men of learning and observation. As they were made to serve governments and turned to more and more arcane studies, their reputations suffered, he concludes, and magicians came to take dishonest advantage of the superstitions and curiosities of people. *An Essay on the History and Reality of Apparitions* is intended to support religion by giving what evidence he can for good spirits, angels, and other divine manifestations and to discourage superstition by ridiculing delusions and naive credulity. In this book, too, he collects many examples of apparitions, including material from such sources as the Bible and John Aubrey's *Miscellanies* (1696).

Historical examples and anecdotes are everywhere in his writing. He offers biblical and secular examples as proof of the principles and general truths in almost everything he wrote. *Jure Divino* (1706), a twelve-book verse essay, includes books of summaries of the actions and miserable ends of tyrants, and he can refer to Second Samuel, Hugo Grotius, and Abraham Cowley with equal ease and familiarity. In ordinary pamphlets such as *An Essay on the Treaty of Commerce with France* (1713), he habitually draws upon history as he does here when he summarizes the history of trade agreements, quotes them, and then insists that the Treaty of Commerce is more to Britain's advantage than France's. He is capable of including such detailed information as the reasons for the trade restrictions imposed after the Treaty of Ryswick. One of his earliest manuscripts, the *Historical Collections*, brings together anecdotes from sources as diverse as Richard Knolles's *Generall Historie of the Turkes* (1603), Plutarch's *Lives*, and Bede's *History of the English Church and People* (completed in 1731). *A Tour thro' the Whole Island of Great Britain* (1724, 1725, 1727) uses historical anecdotes to bring English towns and places to life and to characterize the British people. For instance, Defoe describes the chapel built on the stone bridge over the Calder in Yorkshire. It was built, he says, by Edward IV in memory of the Battle of Wakefield, where his father, Richard, Duke of York, died in 1460. He finds this memorial no less remarkable than a small fenced square of ground between two nearby towns where the common people had erected a stone cross on the spot where the Duke of York actually fell. In another place, he records the way the Hadley residents maintain a stone to mark the spot where the Protestant martyr Rowland Taylor died at the stake.

A Tour thro' the Whole Island of Great Britain, a twelve-hundred-page travel book, is the only one of Defoe's books that has been accorded the status of belles lettres without change from its publication to our own day. It appeared serially; the first volume (May 1724) described eastern and southern England, the second (June 1725) the West Country, Midlands, Wales, and London, and volume three (August 1726 but dated 1727) Scotland and the northern counties. For almost every county, Defoe would describe the topography, towns, rivers, harbors, population, occupations, notable families, major buildings, and evaluate the agriculture, manufacture, and transportation. He would include accounts of important historical events that took place there and of interesting facts about the place, such as the fact that all the ships that go to sea from London depart from Gravesend. He would also include amusing personal memories and sights; in a village in Sussex, for instance, he had seen a woman go to church in an ox-drawn carriage.

Defoe said in 1711 that he had been in every county in England except one, and, in 1724, he told his readers: "As . . . I made myself Master of the History, and *ancient State* of *England*, I resolv'd in the next Place, to make my self Master of its *Present State* also; and to this Purpose, I travell'd in three or four several Tours, over the whole Island, critically observing, and carefully informing myself of every thing worth observing in all the Towns and Countries through which I pass'd." Above all, *A Tour thro' the Whole Island of Great Britain* reflects Defoe's love for travel and his insatiable curiosity about the economy and how all manner of people live. So valuable has this book been to economic and social historians that Defoe as its author has been called "a special correspondent for posterity." In his classic introduction to it, G. D. H. Cole wrote that *A Tour thro' the Whole Island of Great Britain* "is by far the most graphic contemporary account of the state of the economic and social affairs near the beginning of the eighteenth century." A recent critic called the book "a vision of nationhood."

Also concerned with the state of the British economy are *The Royal Progress* (1724), *The Complete English Tradesman* (1726, 1727), *A General History of Discoveries and Improvements* (1725-1726), *A Plan of the English Commerce* (1728), *Atlas Maritimus & Commercialis* (1728), and several shorter works such as *An Humble Proposal to the People of England, For the Encrease of their Trade, and En-*

couragement of their Manufactures (1729). In these books, Defoe characterizes the English people, identifies their strengths and advantages, and charts their course to greatness. Typically, he begins with surveys—of the present state of England (*A Tour thro' the Whole Island of Great Britain*) and of their place in worldwide commercial history (*A General History of Discoveries and Improvements*)—and with guides for the most basic cogs in the machine (*The Great Law of Subordination Consider'd* [1724] and *The Complete English Tradesman*).

Defoe's plan for his country is nothing less than world domination. Trade, not military might, would make this conquest. In *A Plan of the English Commerce*, he writes, "Trade is the Foundation of Wealth, and Wealth of Power," and, in *The Advantages of Peace and Commerce* (1729), he says, "if any one Nation could govern Trade, that Nation would govern the World." In book after book he catalogues what England had to sell and enumerates the luxuries she bought. In contrast to her substantial exports of wool, corn, minerals, and manufactured goods, he lists imports of wine, brandy, raisins, currants, oranges, coffee, tea, chocolate, olives, nutmeg, cinnamon, and pepper.

Books such as *A Plan of the English Commerce* and *Atlas Maritimus* target countries and products and challenge Englishmen to develop trade with them. In them, Defoe surveys the globe and determines what each part of the world has to offer. Besides improving territory already held, he urges the establishment of new settlements and colonies. In the aftermath of the disappointing Treaty of Utrecht, Defoe's countrymen can hardly disagree. He returns to the arguments of his 1712 pamphlets and reminds people how necessary peace is for a flourishing trade and that the longest purse, not the longest sword, wins wars. Conquest, he reminds them, is a "Thing attended with Difficulty, Hazard, Expence, and a Possibility of Miscarriage."

Defoe had once said that a conduct book could be written for each stage of life, and *The Complete English Tradesman*, published in 1726 and 1727 is part of the economic series written late in his life but also related to a group of his books that rivaled his novels in popularity. As early as 1715, Defoe had published *The Family Instructor*, and he followed this book, which outsold everything else he wrote except *Robinson Crusoe* for the next century, with a second *Family Instructor* (1718), *Religious Courtship* (1722), *Conjugal Lewd-*

ness (1727), *A New Family Instructor* (1727), and the posthumously published *Compleat English Gentleman* (1890). Defoe's readers would have instantly recognized these books as additions to a widely popular kind of literature. The domestic-conduct book had grown up beside the courtesy book and, by the early eighteenth century, held a secure place in the personal libraries of all social classes. Courtesy books were largely directed at the upper classes and chapters included "Of Friendship," "Of Temperance," and "Of Diversions," while those in conduct books more often read "Of the Duty of Parents in Educating their Children" and "Of Duty to Parents; Magistrates, Pastors." Conduct books, or works of "practical divinity," addressed a broader audience, emphasized moral relationships, and concentrated upon marriage and household governance.

Defoe divides *The Family Instructor*, his first conduct book, into three parts: "I: Relating to Fathers and Children. II. To Masters and Servants. III. To Husbands and Wives." These categories are standard, but his book is unusual in that it is highly narrative, made up of realistic dialogues, and addressed to the parents of older children. Parts one and three describe the efforts of parents who had been shamed by their youngest child to recall the family to sober piety. Part two concerns two apprentices, and their contrasting situations. The second *Family Instructor* has two parts. The first portrays two couples who argue and nearly destroy their marriages over religious differences. The rancor between the couples that grows almost to the point of violence prefigures material in his novel *Col. Jack*. Always ready to draw the broadest conclusions possible, Defoe has one character say that their quarrels "put me in mind of the Divisions among the People of this Nation about Religion; methinks the Church and the Dissenters act a little as you and I did, one goes this way and another that . . . , but all meet, I hope in Heaven at last. . . ." The second part illustrates the correct discipline of children. In a series of dialogues, Defoe tells the story of a good but hot-tempered London tradesman, of two other fathers (one too lenient and the other brutal), and of a sea captain who marries a religious servant named Margy.

Religious Courtship, the most narrative and unified conduct book yet, follows the lives of three daughters commanded by their dying mother to marry pious men. The youngest, exemplary in her obedience to her mother, brings her

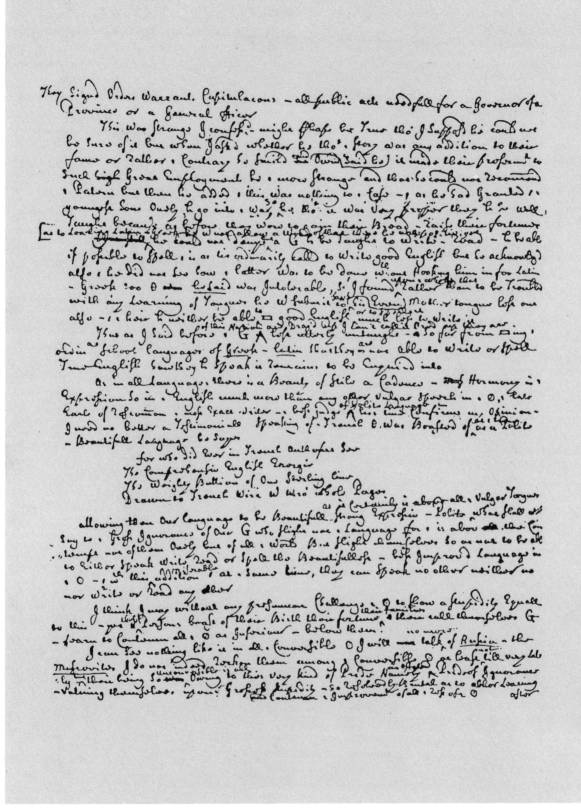

Pages from the manuscript for The Compleat English Gentleman *(by permission of the Trustees of the British Library)*

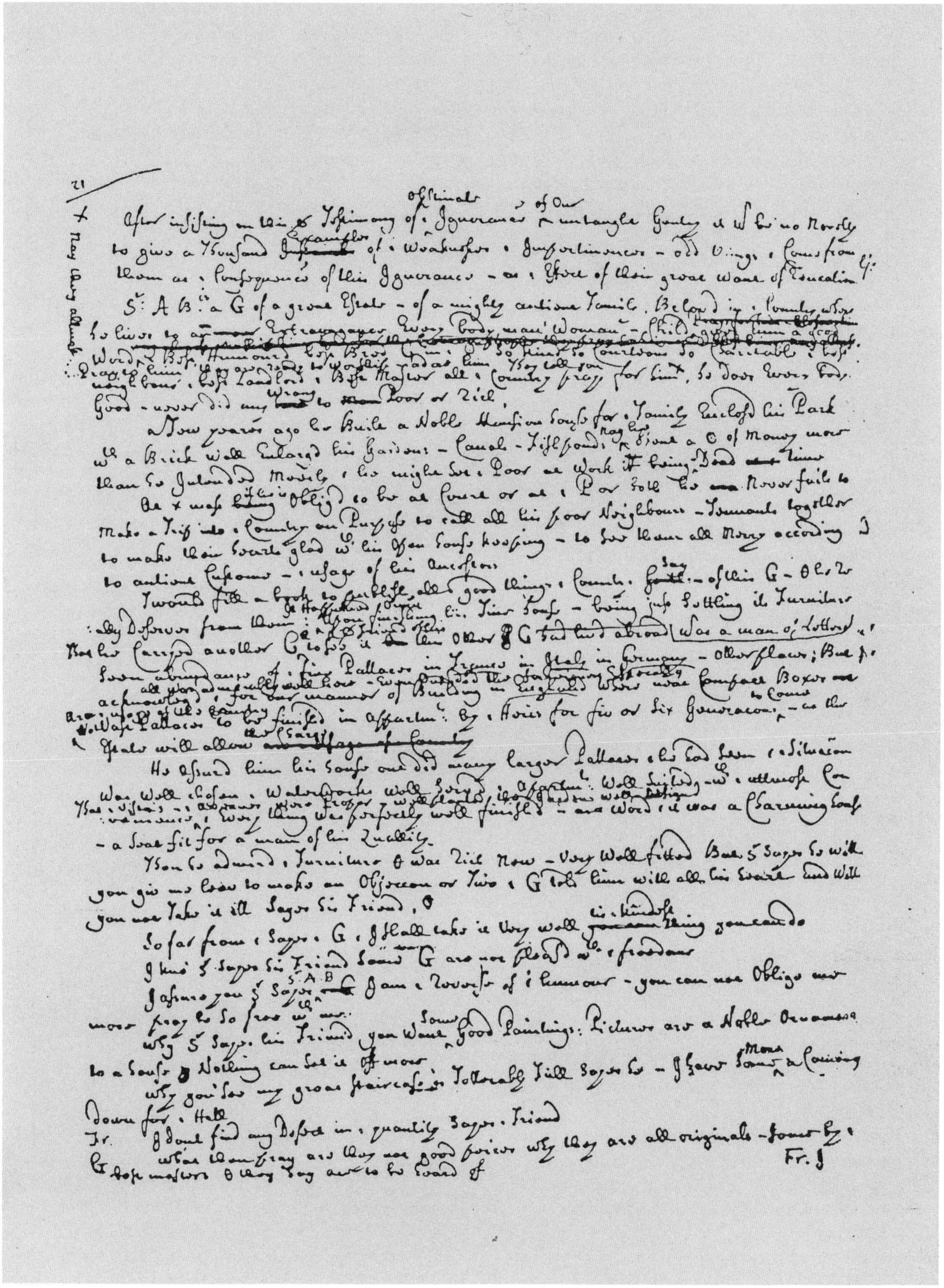

suitor to religion, but the second marries for money and is horrified to discover that she has married a Catholic. This book, too, has lengthy sections on the obligations of masters to servants and on the wisdom of choosing religious servants. In *Conjugal Lewdness* Defoe analyzes the reasons for unhappiness in marriage and illustrates the mutual respect he believes necessary. He discusses many intimate aspects of marriage such as having intercourse during pregnancy. Here he combines essays with lively dialogues. *A New Family Instructor* offers an exemplary family with a father who has made his chief business to instruct his children in "the most Essential Points of the Christian Religion." He explains how to instruct children, how to adapt material appropriately for each age group, and what the result will be. As part of its strongly anti-Catholic theme, the book shows one of the brothers becoming Catholic and the object of pity from his family, who often laugh at his "ignorance" and mistaken opinions. *A New Family Instructor* includes one of Defoe's longest discussions of reading fiction and of the most effective means of education. Written after the publication of his last novel, *Roxana*, his statements, even though made to a conservative audience, have considerable interest. He says,

> the End and Use of every Fable was in the Moral. . . .
>
> . . . .where the Moral of the Tale is duly annex'd, and the End directed right . . . making just and solid Impressions on the Mind; recommending great and good Actions, raising Sentiments of Virtue in the Soul . . . in such Cases, Fables, feigned Histories, invented Tales, and even such as we call *Romances*, have always been allow'd as the most pungent Way of writing or speaking; the most apt to make Impressions upon the Mind. . . .for some Ages, it was the most usual, if not the only Way of Teaching in the World. . . .

Somewhat related to the conduct books are others like *The Great Law of Subordination Consider'd*. As he had in the conduct books, he discusses the proper duties and obligations of masters to servants and servants to masters. He gives instructive illustrations and didactic admonitions, but he also offers "projects." In the eighteenth century "projects" meant plans or schemes designed to improve something and often to attract investors or patrons. People often satirized projectors as impractical, officious dreamers or even busybodies. Defoe's first full-length book had been *An Essay upon Projects* (1697), and the last work

published in his lifetime was *An Effectual Scheme for the Immediate Preventing of Street Robberies* (1731). *An Essay upon Projects* includes plans for improving roads, teaching military arts, building an academy for women, and establishing a Merchant Court similar to the Admiralty Court. He continued to suggest such schemes in his periodicals and novels and returned openly to projecting in the last six years of his life. He said that he hoped to produce a "useful kind" of writing, and at one point he described such books as "Testimony of my good Will to my Fellow Creatures." *Every-body's Business, Is No-body's Business* (1725), *The Protestant Monastery* (1727), *Parochial Tyranny* (1727), *Augusta Triumphans* (1728), and *Second Thoughts are Best* (1729) belong in this category. These books, with *The Great Law of Subordination Consider'd*, return to some of his 1697 concerns—gambling, education, the treatment of seamen—and all show a keen awareness of injustice.

> Every Man ought . . . to contribute in his Station, to the publick Welfare, and not be afraid or ashamed of doing or at least, meaning well.
>
> I hope therefore the Reader will excuse the Vanity of an over officious *Old Man*, if like *Cato*, I enquire whether or no before I go hence and be no more, I can yet do anything for the Service of my Country.

Tempered by a hint of self-deprecating humor, these works cast in gentler form the Defoe of *An Essay upon Projects* and even of the Queen Anne propaganda, but here individual and domestic concerns take precedence. In *Augusta Triumphans*, for instance, he rails against the treatment of foundling children and the use of private madhouses to confine unwanted wives. In *Parochial Tyranny*, he condemns the results of the policy that the parish in which an indigent child is born must care for it and asks, "How many poor Women in Labour have been lost, while two Parishes are contending to throw her on each other. . . ?" Here, too, he proposes a home for old people where they can live healthful, dignified lives.

Yet another group of substantial works are part of the crime literature of the period. Defoe wrote them during the 1720s, the time when the popularity of such works was at its height. Readers could choose broadsides, ballads, chapbooks, newspapers, pamphlets, "anatomies," *Old Bailey Sessions Papers, Accounts* by the Ordinary of Newgate, and collections such as *A Compleat Collection of Remarkable Tryals*. *Moll Flanders* is, of course, Defoe's best-known book about crime. Moll's mul-

The manner of
John Shepherd's Efcape
out of the Condemn'd Hole in Newgate.

Frontispiece for A Narrative of all the Robberies, Escapes &c. of John Sheppard

titude of adventures and resilient, lively personality, even as the book addresses serious moral, economic, and social issues, assure its well-deserved, lasting appeal. Before he wrote *Moll Flanders*, however, Defoe had written about the Scottish rebels imprisoned after the 1715 rebellion and may have written about the famous Scottish outlaw Rob Roy, highwaymen, and housebreakings for periodicals such as Mist's *Weekly Journal* and *Applebee's Journal*. Some of these reports have been interpreted as sources or sketches for *Moll Flanders*. An *Applebee's* for 16 July 1720 is a "letter" from a woman who went from pickpocket to shop thief, was caught, tried, transported, and has returned to England just as Moll did. The

writer, "Moll" of Rag-Fair, mentions that her adventures are too long for the letter.

In 1724, Defoe wrote two entertaining pamphlets on John Sheppard, the thief who achieved his greatest fame from his astonishing escapes from prison. His *History of the Remarkable Life of John Sheppard* and *A Narrative of all the Robberies, Escapes, &c. of John Sheppard* portray Sheppard as a clever jester who exchanges jokes, "[I] made the door my humble servant." It was Sheppard's violent attack on one of the most famous criminals in English history as he was led to prison that helped bring about Jonathan Wild's downfall. Wild had come to the public's attention first as the proprietor of his "Office for the Recovery of

Lost and Stolen Property" and then as the thief taker chiefly responsible for the destruction of London's four largest gangs. Two years later, Wild was exposed as the man who received thieves' plunder and sold it back to their victims. In 1724 Defoe wrote at least one life of Wild, and Wild was the model for John Gay's Peachum in *The Beggar's Opera* (1728). Defoe's *A Brief Historical Account of the Lives of the Six Notorious Street-Robbers, Executed at Kingston* was published in 1726. From then until his death, Defoe published proposals for reducing crime, especially in London. He wrote *Some Considerations upon Street-Walkers* (1726), *Second Thoughts are Best* (1729), *An Effectual Scheme for the Immediate Preventing of Street-Robberies* (1731), and periodical essays on subjects such as the current opinion that soldiers and sailors were brutal men who turned criminal in peacetime. Defoe's sense of justice and respect for humankind shows in lines such as these from a 5 March 1726 *Applebee's*:

> Though there is a kind of Poverty and Distress necessary to bring a poor Man to take Arms . . . and run the risk of Life and Limb, for so mean a Consideration as a red Coat and 3s. a Week. Yet those poorest of Men may have principles of Honour and Justice in them, at least it should be supposed they have, till something appears to the Contrary. . . .

Some of Defoe's nonfiction can still be read with pleasure. Some—*A Tour thro' the Whole Island of Great Britain*, *The History of the Union of Great Britain*, groups of his pamphlets—are essential sources for political and economic historians. Others, such as *A History of Apparitions*, offer the folklorist unmined treasures. All have some interest for those who would understand Defoe and his time. In a 1731 proposal to reprint the best pamphlets of the last century, William Oldys called them "the liveliest Pictures of their Times" and "The truest Images of their Authors" because they are written hastily and, therefore, show the mind "in the most natural Form and Symmetry." He continues to say that in them we can "discover the genuine Abilities of an Author." Oldys intended to reprint several of Defoe's works, and the modern reader of Defoe's nonfiction can certainly recognize the truth of Oldys's statement.

Defoe's greatest legacy, however, is surely his contribution to journalism. During his lifetime the power of the press as we know it was established, and Defoe deserves a considerable share of the credit. When he began his *Review*, nothing like the modern newspaper existed. Newspapers printed a sentence or two, or at most a few paragraphs, on even the most important events. These items came from the official *London Gazette* or the best French or Dutch newspapers. A few special-interest periodicals like John Dunton's question-answer paper *The Athenian Gazette* existed. The *Review*, published first as a kind of serial history intended to explain the causes and implications of the War of Spanish Succession and to evaluate the strengths and weaknesses of both sides, quickly became an essay periodical with timely comment on current events, controversies, and topics of discussion. Although it began and remained primarily political, it included some poetry, letters from readers, and articles on bankrupts, education, and city happenings. Especially in *The Little Review, Miscellanea*, and the Scandal Club, the *Review* resembled the later *Tatler* and *Spectator*. Here Defoe satirized rival journalists, foolish young men, and bickering married couples.

The *Review* became increasingly political, and Defoe demonstrated the potential papers had to interpret events and shape opinion. He wrote the *Review* almost alone for nine years and, during that time, covered nearly every political and religious issue that arose, was a tireless champion of England's emerging credit economy, served as apologist for most of Robert Harley's policies and positions, and intelligently explained foreign events as remote from the ordinary Englishman's knowledge as the Great Northern War, the changes made in Russia by Peter the Great, and the African trade.

Defoe well understood the power of the press; at one time he owned every newspaper in Edinburgh and, during the reign of George I, infiltrated Tory periodicals in order to diminish their effectiveness. One of these, Mist's *Weekly Journal*, he transformed by filling the paper with entertaining, nonpolitical material. The *Weekly Journal* became a magazine filled with lively anecdotes and letters on every subject under the sun. The novel, even bizarre, nature of reported incidents, the variety of strong personalities displayed in the letters, and the "letters introductory" invented by Defoe became the paper's most distinctive features. It soon had a circulation of eleven thousand copies a week, remained the most popular journal in England for years, and set the standard for this increasingly popular kind of periodical.

He wrote several papers, including the *Mercator* (26 June 1713 - 20 July 1714) and the *Manufacturer* (30 October 1719 - 17 February 1720), to support individual causes (the Treaty of Commerce and the weavers' campaign for protective legislature in these cases). Among his other papers were *The White-Hall Evening Post* (18 September 1718 - circa 14 October 1720), a good, standard newspaper; *The Daily Post* (3 October 1719 - circa 27 April 1725), one of the rare early eighteenth-century dailies and a lucrative paper because of its large number of advertisements; and *The Commentator* (1 January - 16 September 1720), an amusing and informative essay periodical that he wrote "to pry into the Faults and Follies of Mankind." Articles on superstition, freak shows, medicine, education, human foibles break up an important, lively eyewitness account of the South Sea mania.

Perhaps no writer in human history has written so knowledgeably and sympathetically on so many subjects. Whatever kind of writing he took up, he transformed. He combined genres, he invented new arts of persuasion, and he brought his country and his time to life. He felt his audience to be the English people in the broadest sense, and his sturdy, confident prose cajoled, admonished, teased, exhorted, prophesied, explained and—occasionally—ridiculed. He told them stories endlessly and, above all, caught them up in his enthusiasm, his wonder, his vision for the future, and his imaginative vigor. Defoe will always be remembered for *Robinson Crusoe*, but the broad knowledge, strong opinions, and amazingly diverse interests found in the nonfiction stand behind the great novel.

Letters:
Letters of Daniel Defoe, edited by George Healey (Oxford: Clarendon Press, 1955);
Paula R. Backscheider, "John Russell to Daniel Defoe: Fifteen Unpublished Letters," *Philological Quarterly*, 61 (Spring 1982): 161-177;
Backscheider, "Robert Harley to Daniel Defoe: A New Letter," *Modern Language Review*, 83 (October 1988): 817-819.

Bibliographies:
John Robert Moore, *A Checklist of the Writings of Daniel Defoe* (Bloomington: Indiana University Press, 1960);
John A. Stoler, *Daniel Defoe: An Annotated Bibliography of Modern Criticism, 1900-1980* (New York: Garland, 1984);

Spiro Peterson, *Daniel Defoe: A Reference Guide 1731-1924* (Boston: G. K. Hall, 1987).

Biographies:
James Sutherland, *Defoe* (London: Methuen, 1937; revised, 1950);
John Robert Moore, *Daniel Defoe: Citizen of the Modern World* (Bloomington: Indiana University Press, 1958);
Frank Bastian, *The Early Life of Daniel Defoe* (London: Macmillan, 1981);
Paula R. Backscheider, *Daniel Defoe: His Life* (Baltimore: Johns Hopkins University Press, 1989).

References:
Paul Alkon, *Defoe and Fictional Time* (Athens: University of Georgia Press, 1979);
Hans Anderson, "The Paradox of Trade and Morality in Defoe," *Modern Philology*, 39 (August 1941): 23-46;
Paula R. Backscheider, "Cross-Purposes: Defoe's *History of the Union*," *CLIO*, 11 (Winter 1982): 165-186;
Backscheider, *Daniel Defoe: Ambition and Innovation* (Lexington: University Press of Kentucky, 1986);
Backscheider, "Defoe's Prodigal Sons," *Studies in the Literary Imagination*, 15 (Fall 1982): 3-18;
Rodney Baine, *Daniel Defoe and the Supernatural* (Athens: University of Georgia Press, 1979);
G. D. H. Cole, Introduction to *A Tour thro' the Whole Island of Great Britain*, 2 volumes (New York: Kelley, 1968);
J. Alan Downie, *Robert Harley and the Press* (Cambridge: Cambridge University Press, 1979);
Alistair Duckworth, " 'Whig' Landscapes in Defoe's *Tour*," *Philological Quarterly*, 61 (Fall 1982): 453-465;
Peter Earle, *The World of Defoe* (New York: Atheneum, 1977);
John Forster, *Daniel De Foe and Charles Churchill* (London, 1855);
Maximillian E. Novak, *Defoe and the Nature of Man* (Oxford: Clarendon Press, 1963);
Novak, *Economics and the Fiction of Daniel Defoe* (Berkeley: University of California Press, 1983);
Novak, *Realism, Myth, and History in Defoe's Fiction* (Lincoln: Nebraska University Press, 1983);
William Payne, *Mr. Review: Daniel Defoe as the Author of the Review* (New York: King's Crown Press, 1961);

John Richetti, *Defoe's Narratives* (Oxford: Clarendon Press, 1975);

Pat Rogers, "Defoe at Work: The Making of *A Tour thro' Great Britain*, Volume I," *Bulletin of the New York Public Library*, 78 (Summer 1975): 431-450;

Rogers, *Eighteenth-Century Encounters* (Sussex: Harvester, 1985);

Rogers, ed., *Defoe: The Critical Heritage* (London: Routledge, 1972);

Lois Schwoerer, *No Standing Armies!* (Baltimore: Johns Hopkins University Press, 1974);

Arthur Secord, *Studies in the Narrative Method of Defoe* (Urbana: University of Illinois Press, 1968);

Secord, ed., *Defoe's Review, Reproduced from the Original Editions*, 22 volumes (New York: Published by the Facsimile Text Society for Columbia University Press, 1933);

Geoffrey Sill, *Defoe and the Idea of Fiction* (Newark: University of Delaware Press, 1983);

G. A. Starr, *Defoe and Spiritual Autobiography* (Princeton: Princeton University Press, 1965).

Papers:

Manuscripts: *The Compleat English Gentleman* and *Of Royal Education* are in the British Library; the "Meditations" are at the Huntington Library, San Marino, California; the *Historical Collections* and "Humanum est Errare" are at the William Andrews Clark Library, Los Angeles. Locations of letters written by Defoe (most are in the British Library) are given in Healey's edition of the letters.

John Dennis

(16 September 1658 - 6 January 1734)

David Wheeler
University of Southern Mississippi

SELECTED BOOKS: *Poems in Burlesque* (London: For the booksellers of London & Westminster, 1692);

The Impartial Critick, or Some Observations upon a late book entitul'd A short view of tragedy, written by Mr Rymer (London: Printed for R. Taylor, 1693);

Miscellanies in Verse and Prose (London: Printed for James Knapton, 1693);

The Court of Death; a Pindarick Poem, dedicated to the Memory of Her most Sacred Majesty, Queen Mary (London: Printed for James Knapton, 1695);

Remarks on a Book Entitul'd Prince Arthur, an Heroick Poem, with some General Critical Observations, and Several New Remarks upon Virgil (London: Printed for S. Heyrick & R. Sare, 1696);

The Nuptials of Britain's Genius and Fame: A Pindarick Poem on the Peace (London: Printed for R. Parker & Sam. Briscoe, sold by R. Baldwin, 1697);

A Plot and No Plot; a Comedy, as it is Acted at the Theatre-Royal in Drury Lane (London: Printed for R. Parker, P. Buck & R. Wellington, 1697);

The Usefulness of the Stage to the Happiness of Mankind, to Government and to Religion. Occasion'd by a Late Book Written by Jeremy Collier, M.A. (London: Printed for Richard Parker, 1698);

Rinaldo and Armida, a Tragedy, as it is Acted at the Theatre in Little-Lincoln's-Inn-Fields (London: Printed for Jacob Tonson, 1699 [i.e., 1698]);

Iphigenia, a Tragedy, acted at the Theatre in Little Lincoln's-Inn-Fields (London: Printed for Richard Parker, 1700 [i.e., 1699]);

The Advancement and Reformation of Modern Poetry. A Critical Discourse in Two Parts (London: Printed for R. Parker, 1701);

The Comical Gallant; or the Amours of Sir John Falstaffe. A Comedy as it is Acted at the Theatre-Royal in Drury Lane by His Majesty's Servants. . . . To which is added A Large Account of the Taste in Poetry and the Causes of the Degeneracy of it (London: Sold by A. Baldwin, 1702);

The Danger of Priestcraft to Religion and Government: with Some Politick Reasons for Toleration (London, 1702);

The Monument: A Poem Sacred to the Immortal Memory of the Best and Greatest of Kings, William the Third, King of Great Britain &c. (London: Printed for D. Brown & A. Bell, 1702);

An Essay on the Navy, or England's Advantage and Safety, Prov'd Dependant on a Formidable and Well-disciplined Navy (London: Printed for the author & sold by John Nutt, 1702);

A Proposal for Putting a Speedy End to the War, by Ruining the Commerce of the French and Spaniards, and Securing Our Own (London: Printed for Daniel Brown & Andrew Bell, 1703);

Liberty Asserted. A Tragedy as it is Acted at the New Theatre in Little Lincoln's-Inn-Fields (London: Printed for G. Strahan, 1704);

The Grounds of Criticism in Poetry, contain'd in some New Discoveries never made before, requisite for the Writing and Judging of Poems surely (London: Printed for Geo. Strahan & Bernard Lintott, 1704);

Britannia Triumphans: or the Empire Sav'd, and Europe Deliver'd, by the Success of her Majesty's Forces under the Wise and Heroick Conduct of his Grace the Duke of Marlborough. A Poem (London: Printed for J. Nutt, 1704);

Gibraltar: or the Spanish Adventure. A Comedy as it was Acted at the Theatre in Drury Lane (London: Printed for W. Turner & sold by J. Nutt, 1705);

An Essay on the Opera's after the Italian Manner, which are about to be establish'd on the English Stage: With some Reflections on the Damage which they may bring to the Publick (London: Printed for J. Nutt, 1706);

The Battle of Ramillia: or the Power of Union. A Poem in Five Books (London: Printed for Ben Bragg, 1706);

John Dennis (engraving after a portrait attributed to William Hogarth)

Appius and Virginia, a Tragedy as it is Acted at the Theatre-Royal in Drury-Lane by Her Majesty's Sworn Servants (London: Printed for B. Lintott, 1709);

Reflections Critical and Satyrical upon a late Rhapsody called An Essay upon Criticism (London: Printed for Bernard Lintott, 1711);

An Essay upon Publick Spirit; Being a Satyr in Prose upon the Manners and Luxury of the Times, The Chief Sources of Our Present Parties and Divisions (London: Printed for Bernard Lintott, 1711);

An Essay on the Genius and Writings of Shakespear: with Some Letters of Criticism to the Spectator (London: Printed for B. Lintott, 1712);

Remarks upon Cato, A Tragedy (London: Printed for B. Lintott, 1713);

A Poem upon the Death of Her Late Sacred Majesty Queen Anne, and the Most Happy and Most Auspicious Accession of his Sacred Majesty King George, To the Imperial Crowns of Great Britain, France and Ireland. With an Exhortation to all True Britons to Unity (London: Printed by H. Meere & sold by J. Baker, 1714);

Priestcraft distinguish'd from Christianity (London: Printed for J. Roberts, 1715);

A True Character of Mr. Pope (London: Printed for Sarah Popping, 1716);

Remarks upon Mr. Pope's Translation of Homer; with Two Letters concerning Windsor Forest and the

Temple of Fame (London: Printed for E. Curll, 1717);

Select Works, 2 volumes (London: Printed by J. Darby, 1718; enlarged edition, London: Printed for J. D., 1721);

The Invader of His Country: or The Fatal Resentment. A Tragedy As it is Acted at the Theatre-Royal in Drury-Lane, By His Majesty's Servants (London: Printed for J. Pemberton, 1720);

The Characters and Conduct of Sir John Edgar (London: Printed for M. Smith, 1720);

The Characters and Conduct of Sir John Edgar, in a Third and Fourth Letter (London: Printed & sold by J. Roberts, 1720);

A Defence of Sir Fopling Flutter, A Comedy written by Sir George Etheridge (London: Printed for T. Warner, 1722);

Julius Cæsar Acquitted, and His Murderers Condemned (London: Printed for J. Mack-Euen & sold by J. Roberts, 1722);

Remarks on a Play, call'd The Conscious Lovers, a Comedy (London: Printed for T. Warner, 1723);

Vice and Luxury Public Mischiefs; or Remarks on a Book Intitul'd, The Fable of the Bees; or, Private Vices Public Benefits (London: Printed for W. Mears, 1724);

The Stage Defended from Scripture, Reason and the Common Sense of Mankind for Two Thousand Years. Occasion'd by Mr. Law's late Pamphlet against Stage Entertainments (London: Printed for N. Blandford, 1726);

Miscellaneous Tracts, volume 1 [no more printed] (London: Printed for the author, 1727);

Remarks on Mr. Pope's Rape of the Lock. In Several Letters to a Friend. With a Preface, Occasion'd by the late Treatise on the Profound and The Dunciad (London: Printed for J. Roberts, 1728);

Remarks upon Several Passages in the Preliminaries to the Dunciad. . . . And upon Several Passages in Pope's Preface to his Translation of Homer's Iliad (London: Printed for H. Whitridge, 1729).

Editions: *The Critical Works of John Dennis*, 2 volumes, edited by Edward Niles Hooker (Baltimore: Johns Hopkins University Press, 1939, 1943);

The Plays of John Dennis, edited by J. W. Johnson (New York: Garland, 1980).

PLAY PRODUCTIONS: *A Plot and No Plot*, London, Theatre Royal, Drury Lane, 8 May 1697;

Rinaldo and Armida, London, Lincoln's Inn Fields, November 1698;

Iphigenia, London, Lincoln's Inn Fields, December 1699;

The Comical Gallant, London, Theatre Royal, Drury Lane, April 1702;

Liberty Asserted, London, Lincoln's Inn Fields, 24 February 1704;

Gibraltar, London, Theatre Royal, Drury Lane, 16 February 1705;

Appius and Virginia, London, Theatre Royal, Drury Lane, 5 February 1709;

The Invader of His Country, London, Theatre Royal, Drury Lane, 11 November 1719.

John Dennis is known best, perhaps, as an example in Alexander Pope's *Essay on Criticism* (1711) of what a critic ought not to be and as one of the diving contestants in *The Dunciad* (1728, 1743). But he was not always a joke. During the last decade of the seventeenth century and the first decade of the eighteenth, Dennis was the foremost literary critic of his day, a force to be reckoned with, and an opponent well worthy of combat with Pope, or Richard Steele, or Joseph Addison. As a poet, playwright, critic, and political pamphleteer, Dennis pursued the kind of career that any Augustan man of letters might envy. Though his poetry and drama no doubt deserve the neglect they have suffered during the intervening centuries, his literary criticism does not, and, appropriately, Dennis, as a critic, is once again appreciated in his own right and not just laughed at as one of Pope's dunces. As a historical figure, his involvement in the Thomas Rymer and Jeremy Collier controversies, his participation in the literary warfare over the relative merits of the ancients and moderns, and his seemingly constant feuding with his more renowned contemporaries make Dennis a convenient window through which to view his era. More important, Dennis's theories on the role of the sublime in literature, on the necessity of emotion, on the relationship between literature and its cultural and geopolitical contexts, and his early championing of John Milton as the great English poet chart an unexpected direction in eighteenth-century literary theory and accordingly merit attention.

The only child of saddler Francis Dennis and his wife, Sarah, John Dennis was born in London on 16 September 1658. Dennis received rigorous training in the classics at Harrow under the direction of Dr. William Horne, who had previously been at Eton. On 13 January 1675 Dennis en-

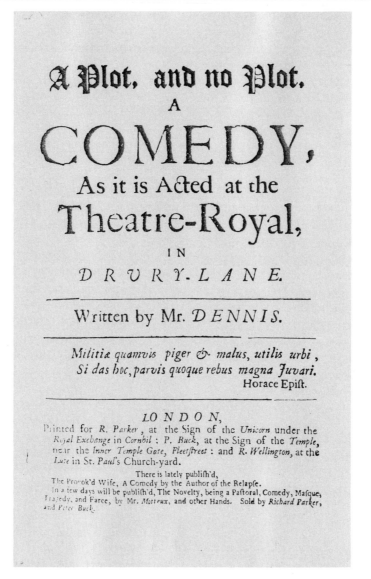

Title page for Dennis's first play, which Jeremy Collier, author of A Short View of the Immorality and Profaneness of the English Stage *(1698), called "scandalously Smutty and Profane."*

tered Caius College, Cambridge, as a common scholar. Dennis's reputation for sparking controversy apparently began at an early age as he was expelled from Caius for wounding fellow student Charles Glenham with a sword. After his expulsion Dennis remained at Cambridge, enrolling in Trinity Hall, where he received his M.A. in 1683.

Inheritances from his stepfather, Thomas Sanderson, and from a wealthy uncle, Simon Eve, made possible a tour of the Continent, which Dennis undertook with former Harrow classmate Lord Francis Seymour. Dennis's journey over the Alps from France to Italy in 1688 evoked responses that bear upon the theories of the sublime and the role of passion in literature

he was to develop in essays published a decade and a half later. "We walked upon the very brink, in a litteral sense of Destruction," Dennis wrote in a letter. "The sense of all this produc'd different emotions in me, *viz.* a delightful Horrour, a terrible Joy, and at the same time, that I was infinitely, pleas'd I trembled. . . . Transporting Pleasures follow'd the sight of the *Alpes*." In such passages Dennis seems to anticipate midcentury poets, such as Thomas Gray and the Wartons, for whom the craggy cliff signals the sublime.

Returning to London, Dennis set about actively to associate himself with the group of Restoration wits who congregated at Will's Coffeehouse, where legend has it that "a pinch from Dryden's snuff box was equal to taking a degree in the academy of wit." Though Dennis sometimes differed with Dryden's critical pronouncements—especially with Dryden's lack of appreciation for Milton—he saw himself allied with the great poet during his lifetime and as carrying his torch after his death: "I am he of all his Acquaintances," Dennis wrote in a letter published long after Dryden's death, "who, tho' I flatter'd him least while living, having been content to do him justice behind his back and before his Enemies Face, am now the foremost to assert his Merit and vindicate his Glory." Consequently, Dennis's first two full-length critical pieces, *The Impartial Critick* (1693) and *Remarks on a Book Entitul'd Prince Arthur* (1696), were both directed at Dryden's enemies—Thomas Rymer and Richard Blackmore—and were no doubt motivated, at least in part, by a desire to please England's reigning man of letters. Indeed, the similarities between Dennis's *Impartial Critick* and Dryden's unpublished "Heads of an Answer to Rymer" led one noted Dryden scholar, George Saintsbury, to conjecture that Dennis had been permitted to see Dryden's work.

Dennis's painful history of financial troubles began early. By the early 1690s the inheritance was gone, and he was forced to apply to the leading literary patrons for support of his work. Financial difficulty probably led him also to try his hand at profitable kinds of writing: political poetry and pamphlets and drama. In 1695 Dennis published *The Court of Death*, a Pindaric ode on the death of Queen Mary, and in 1697 he published *The Nuptials of Britain's Genius and Fame*, another Pindaric, celebrating the Peace of Ryswick. Both poems are written in the high style appropriate to the form, but a few lines from the latter poem will indicate why they are now forgotten:

> What divine Rapture shakes my Soul?
> What Fury rages in my Blood,
> And drives about the stormy Flood?
> What makes my sparkling Eye-balls rowl?

Despite this bombast, Dennis earned for himself through these efforts some reputation as a poet and some financial reward.

As a playwright, Dennis enjoyed only modest success. Of his eight plays, three were produced during the late 1690s. The sole comedy of this group, *A Plot and No Plot* (1697), is an anti-Jacobite love intrigue, described by Jeremy Collier as a play which "swears at length and is scandalously Smutty and Profane." *Rinaldo and Armida*, a peculiar combination of pastoral, opera, and tragedy, modeled after Tasso's *Jerusalem Delivered*, received some notoriety the following year. Dennis's *Iphigenia* (1699), an adaptation of Euripides, produced from the playwright the following optimistic account of its reception: "When *Orestes* discovered his passion for *Iphigenia* in the fourth act there ran a general murmur through the Pit, which is what I had never seen before." Though these plays would provide in succeeding decades endless (and often appropriate) ammunition for Dennis's literary enemies, they also provided for Dennis direct experience in the theater, which served him well in his drama criticism.

Dennis's career as a critic may be divided into three categories—his role as defender of modern drama and the function of the theater in society; his contributions to a general theory of poetry; and his remarks upon specific literary works, often prompted by personal attacks from their authors.

The first major piece of drama criticism by Dennis is *The Impartial Critick* (1693), which consists of a prefatory letter and five imaginary dialogues between two witty men-about-town. As an answer to Thomas Rymer's strictures against modern English drama and against Shakespeare specifically, *The Impartial Critick* establishes Dennis's positions as a staunch proponent of the moderns in the ancients-versus-moderns controversy and as adamantly anti-French, positions advocated earlier by Dryden in the *Essay on Dramatic Poesy* (1668). The opening letter emphasizes the importance of considering a nation's particular religion, geography, culture, and politics to determine appropriate methods of tragic representation. This relativistic argument allows Dennis to oppose Rymer's strict application of classical "rules" to modern English tragedy. Dennis finds absurd, for example, Rymer's insistence upon the presence of a chorus in English drama because such singing and dancing, while intrinsic to ancient Greek religion, is inconsistent with English religious practice.

In the second dialogue Dennis defines a proper tragic hero as a figure both virtuous and flawed because only such a character could evoke in the audience an identification necessary in producing the requisite pity and terror. These notions of the significance of the prevailing religion and of the evocation of emotional response in an

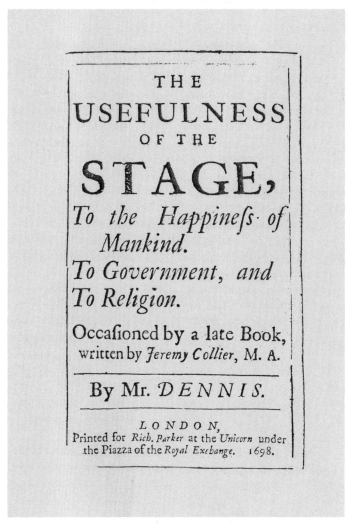

THE USEFULNESS OF THE STAGE,

To the Happiness· of Mankind.
To Government, and
To Religion.

Occasioned by a late Book,
written by *Jeremy Collier*, M. A.

By Mr. *DENNIS*.

LONDON,
Printed for *Rich. Parker* at the *Unicorn* under
the Piazza of the *Royal Exchange*. 1698.

*Title page for Dennis's reply to Collier's attack on playwrights such as John Dryden, William Wycherley,
and William Congreve, as well as Dennis himself*

audience (or reader) are important tenets of Dennis's poetic, and ones he would return to in later, more comprehensive, theoretical statements. The critical procedure employed in this early essay—syllogistic logic supported by quotations from literary texts and from critical authorities—is also characteristic of Dennis's later work. *The Impartial Critick* seems unfinished, however, as the promised response to Rymer's Shakespeare criticism is undelivered, appearing only in *An Essay on the Genius and Writings of Shakespear*, which, prompted by Nicholas Rowe's edition of Shakespeare, did not appear until 1712.

Dennis's next major work on the drama was *The Usefulness of the Stage*, published in 1698 as a reply to Jeremy Collier's *A Short View of the Immorality and Profaneness of the English Stage*, published earlier that year. In a work that is at once logical,

systematic, and learned, Dennis does a thorough job of refuting the clergyman. Dennis begins by asserting that human action is dictated by a drive for happiness, which, for Dennis, is equivalent with pleasure. Pleasure is a result of passion, not reason, but must work in consort with reason and not against it. Siding with Aristotle against Plato, Dennis argues that tragedy purges passions rather than exciting them and that the passions are most pleasing in tragedy. In addition to providing individual pleasure, tragedy is useful to the state (to both the governor and the governed) in depicting examples of pride leading to falls and examples of misguided rebellions. Comedy, by providing negative examples, is also morally instructive, and Dennis disagrees with Collier's observations that modern comedies ridicule the clergy by arguing that they expose not clergy or religion in general but hypocrisy, which has always been a comic target. Additionally, profaneness, as with any other vice, must be shown onstage in order to give the audience a proper aversion to it. Dennis observes that historically the greatest periods of philosophical inquiry, scientific discovery, and military conquest have coincided with a nation's greatest dramatic periods and that the theater has always been opposed "by those, who, by their Writings and by their Examples, have strenuously endeavor'd to ruin both Church and State." Thus, Dennis's defense is similar in its critical content to others, such as William Congreve's, though his religious and political emphases are more marked. Insisting on pleasure and emotion, Dennis remains at once moral and patriotic.

To understand Dennis's attitude toward Shakespeare, one must appreciate the general view during the early eighteenth century of England's greatest dramatist, for Dennis was, by and large, in the mainstream. The Restoration and early eighteenth century is notorious for its critical blindspots regarding Shakespeare and for its nearly complete rewriting of his canon. Though no one (not even Rymer) denied Shakespeare's genius, his texts (such as they were in that time) were not sacred; the early editors from Rowe through William Warburton (1747) conjectured freely about "printer's errors" and "intention," amending the text as they saw fit. Additionally, during the century all of Shakespeare's plays were revised, and it was the revised versions (or adaptations) that were performed onstage. While Nahum Tate's happy-ending *King Lear* is perhaps the best known of these adaptations, many of the leading playwrights from Dryden to David Garrick adapted Shakespearean plays for reasons ranging from the theoretical to the personal. Consequently, Dennis's views on Shakespeare present themselves not only in critical works such as *An Essay on the Genius and Writings of Shakespear* (1712) but also in his own two adaptations, *The Comical Gallant* (1702), an adaptation of *The Merry Wives of Windsor*, and *The Invader of His Country* (written 1710-1711, performed 1719), a reworking of *Coriolanus*.

The Comical Gallant is an attempt to correct what Dennis perceived as plot irregularities in the original. Dennis observes in *A Large Account of the Taste in Poetry*, the critical preface attached to the play, that "Humour is the business of Comedy, and not Wit. The business of a Comick Poet is to show his Characters and not himself, to make ev'ry one of them speak and act, as such a

person in such circumstances would probably act and speak. Comedy is an Image of common Life, and in Life, a Man, who has discerning Eyes, may find something ridiculous in most People, but something that is witty in very few." As a result of this notion, Dennis transforms a comedy of language into a comedy of humors, a form that provides ample opportunity to ridicule human folly and that is thus conducive to his view of the instructive function of comedy.

Dennis's alterations of *Coriolanus* also derive from his dramatic theory. The changes that Dennis justifies at length in *An Essay on the Genius and Writings of Shakespear* concern his desire to make the play illustrative of moral truth, both public and private. Consequently, Dennis alters the work in adherence to his favorite theory of poetic justice in order to provide moral instruction on an individual level, and he politicizes the work in accommodation to the current British scene in order to provide public instruction. In adapting Shakespeare's play to fit the current political situation, Dennis uses the material the same way that Pope uses the Horatian material or Samuel Johnson uses the Juvenalian—to afford political commentary. As observed above, Dennis believed that tragedies should demonstrate by example the general principles of good government; consequently, Dennis's version points out the divisive dangers of party politics and of strongman rule, suggesting always a middle course between anarchy and tyranny.

Dennis had pleaded succinctly his case for the necessity of poetic justice in a series of letters and pamphlets directed against Addison, who had argued against strict adherence to the principle. With regard to *Coriolanus*, Dennis is equally clear: "The Good must never fail to prosper, and the Bad must be always punish'd: Otherwise the Incidents, and particularly the Catastrophe which is the grand Incident, are liable to be imputed rather to Chance, than to Almighty Conduct and to Sovereign Justice. The Want of this impartial Distribution of Justice makes the *Coriolanus* of Shakespeare to be without Moral." Dennis, through his use of distributive (poetic) justice, corrects this fault (which for Dennis, as for Samuel Johnson half a century later, is inexcusable) and, with a glance at the recent Jacobite Rebellion, closes *The Invader of His Country* with the following overt moral lesson:

But they who thro' Ambition, or Revenge,
Or impious Int'rest, join with foreign Foes,

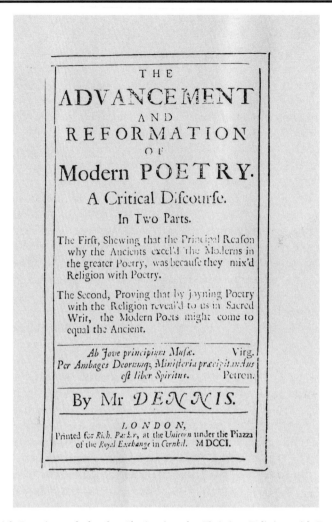

THE

ADVANCEMENT
AND

REFORMATION
OF

Modern POETRY.

A Critical Difcourfe.

In Two Parts.

The Firft, Shewing that the Principal Reafon why the Ancients excel'd the Moderns in the greater Poetry, was becaufe they mix'd Religion with Poetry.

The Second, Proving that by joyning Poetry with the Religion reveal'd to us in Sacred Writ, the Modern Poets might come to equal the Ancient.

Ab Jove principium Mufæ.   Virg.
Per Ambages Deorumq; Minifteria præcipitandus
eft liber Spiritus.   Petron.

By Mr *DENNIS.*

LONDON,
Printed for *Rich. Parker,* at the *Unicorn* under the *Piazza* of the *Royal Exchange* in *Cornhil.* M DCCI.

Title page for the work in which Dennis concludes that "by joyning the Christian Religion with Poetry" his contemporaries might, as Protestants, "have the assistance of a Religion that is more agreeable to the design of Poetry than the Grecian Religion"

T' invade or to betray their Native country,
Shall find, like Coriolanus, soon or late,
From their perfidious Foreign Friends their Fate.

Thus, Dennis's efforts at improving Shakespeare involve combining Shakespeare's obvious raw power with the refinements of the stage incorporated since the Restoration.

Dennis's major contributions to the history of English literary criticism and theory are two long essays, *The Advancement and Reformation of Modern Poetry* (1701) and *The Grounds of Criticism in Poetry* (1704). His reputation established by his early poetry and his work on the drama, Dennis at the turn of the century was one of London's leading men of letters, and these essays, best viewed as companion pieces, represent the hallmark of his career. Jonathan Swift's *Battle of the Books* (1704) is no doubt the best-known English work that concerns itself with the controversy

over the relative merits of the ancients and the moderns. *The Advancement and Reformation of Modern Poetry* is also part of this controversy, but, whereas Swift had preferred the ancients, Dennis acknowledges their superiority only in the higher poetic forms—the epic, the tragedy, and the great ode—arguing that the moderns excel in lesser forms, especially comedy and satire. The bulk of Dennis's essay, however, is devoted to remedying perceived deficiencies in modern English poetry as a means of surpassing the accomplishments of the ancients in the higher forms.

"Poetry," claims Dennis, "is an Imitation of Nature, by a pathetick and numerous Speech." By "numerous," he means no more than that poetry must be metrical, but the insistence upon the ability of poetry to evoke an emotional response from the reader is a somewhat radical departure from customary definitions of poetry at this time. For Dennis, the superiority of the ancients results from their selection of subjects that are intrinsically more capable of producing emotion. Dennis distinguishes between ordinary passion "whose Cause is clearly comprehended by him who feels it, whether it be Admiration, Terror, or Joy" and poetic enthusiasm, which is "a Passion guided by Judgment, whose Cause is not comprehended by us." Dennis continues to assert that "no Subject is so capable of supplying us with Thoughts that necessarily produce these great and strong Enthusiasms, as a Religious Subject: For all which is great in Religion, is most exalted and amazing; all that is joyful, is transporting; all that is sad, is dismal; and all that is terrible, is astonishing." Since ancient poetry in the higher forms is largely religious, it is superior, and the remedy for modern poets is to write about religious subjects. In this endeavor the moderns have the advantage over the ancients because they possess the true Protestant religion.

Interesting in Dennis's essay is his discussion of the relationship between passion and reason (or judgment). He believes that human misery is a result of continual conflict between these two human qualities, a rupture that resulted from the Fall. Just as Christianity produces human happiness by restoring harmony of the faculties, so too does poetry "better than any other Human Invention whatever." Thus, for Dennis, even the moral function of literature is derivative of passion, an odd position in what is still sometimes referred to as the "Age of Reason."

The later *Grounds of Criticism in Poetry* extends the ideas set forth in the earlier essay. Here Dennis defines poetry as "an Art, by which a Poet excites Passion . . . in order to satisfy and improve, to delight and reform the Mind, and so to make Mankind happier and better: from which it appears that Poetry has two Ends, a subordinate, and a final one; the subordinate one is Pleasure and the final one is Instruction." Such statements recall more traditional assertions regarding the purpose of poetry that pleasure is the means to the poetic end of instruction, but Dennis's emphasis on the emotional/psychological process rather than the rational constitutes an important development and anticipates later thinkers on the subject. "Poetry attains its final End, which is reforming the Minds of Men," Dennis claims, "by exciting of Passion. And here I dare be bold to affirm, that all Instruction whatever depends upon Passion."

Dennis also elaborates on the distinction between ordinary passion (which he renames "vulgar passion" in this essay) and enthusiastic passion: vulgar passion is moved by physical objects themselves or by ideas of them in the ordinary course of life; enthusiasm, on the other hand, is moved by ideas in contemplation of things not common to life. "As for example, the Sun mention'd in ordinary Conversation, gives the Idea of a round flat shining Body, of about two foot diameter. But the Sun occurring to us in Meditation, gives the Idea of a vast and glorious Body, and the top of all the visible Creation, and the brightest material Image of the Divinity." Such contemplation produces for Dennis emotional response similar to that discussed by William Wordsworth a century later, but for Dennis the ultimate reflection is almost always of God. Consequently, when he produces a list of those objects capable of producing such enthusiasm (a list of the potentially sublime, like those found in the aesthetic work of Addison or Edmund Burke), the resulting admiration or terror or joy is religious in nature.

When Dennis comes to provide poetic examples to illustrate such effects, he turns to *Paradise Lost* (1667) and quotes extensively. Dennis, then, represents one of the earliest admirers of the emotional power in Milton. The critical methodology Dennis employs in *The Grounds of Criticism in Poetry* is essentially the Longinian one of critical principle followed by quoted example, a far different procedure from the customary Augustan one of discussing sequentially a poem's constituent parts and of relating parts to whole, which is the Aristotelian method. Dennis's work was foundational in developing the theory of the sublime that was to prove so important to midcentury English poets and to aesthetic theorists from Addison to Burke to Immanuel Kant.

Dennis's enthusiasm for poetic enthusiasm provoked often satiric responses from his contemporaries. In a well-known passage in his *Essay on Criticism* Pope refers to Dennis as one who "reddens at each Word you speak, /And *stares, Tremendous!* with a *threatning Eye.*" And Pope, John Gay, and John Arbuthnot, in their play *Three Hours after Marriage* (1717), allude to Dennis in their character "Sir Tremendous Longinus." Nevertheless, Dennis's contribution to significant developments in both critical theory and poetry should not be underestimated, nor should his literary stature in the first decade of the eighteenth century. And "had he died in 1710," according to his biog-

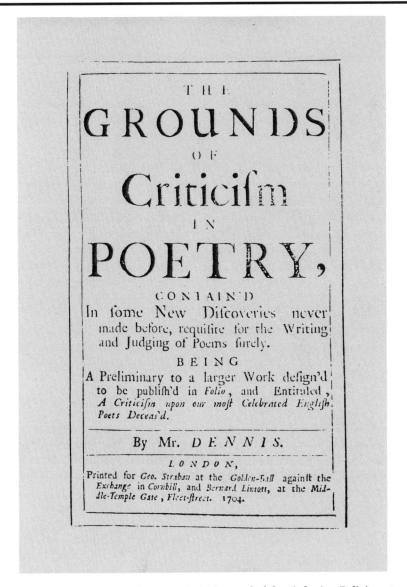

Title page for the work in which Dennis asserts that poetry is the best method for "inforcing Religion upon the Minds of Men"

rapher H. G. Paul, "Dennis would now be remembered as a small dramatist and pamphleteer and as a much better critic—a man who, for the most part, was esteemed and respected by his contemporaries; and he would have been spared a petulant old age filled with quarrels with some of his celebrated contemporaries—Swift and Steele, Addison and Pope, brawls which for two centuries have been used to stigmatize him in literary history."

During the first decade of the century Dennis continued to write occasional verse, including his longest, most ambitious poem, *The Battle of Ramillia: or the Power of Union* (1706). A loyal, but independent Whig, Dennis was no hack party writer. His 1704 play *Liberty Asserted* is a Whig-

gish attempt at keeping national sentiment firmly against the French, but it also represents Dennis's own attitude toward that nation and its people. Many years earlier Dennis had termed the French "affected and impudent, which are but the necessary effects of that National Vice, their Vanity." Dennis was appointed in 1705 with an annual stipend as one of the royal waiters in the London Custom House, a position he held until January 1715 when he, of necessity, sold it to Benjamin Hudson. But Dennis was continually in financial distress, and records indicate that he was occasionally confined in the Fleet Prison for debt, a fact alluded to by Pope in *The Dunciad*.

As the circle of wits with whom Dennis associated in the 1690s died, yielding their place to a new generation of literati, Dennis was disturbed by both the party nature of much of the writing and what he regarded as the unmerited success of some of his contemporaries. Particularly discomforting to Dennis was the publicity surrounding Addison's *Cato* (1713). The remarks Dennis published on this immensely popular play immediately cast him as a critic out of touch with prevailing taste and as an appropriate target for any writer wanting to make a name for himself. Later, Dennis speculated upon Pope's role in the matter: "At the height of his [Pope's] profession of friendship for Mr. Addison, he could not bear the success of Cato, but prevails upon B. L. [the publisher Bernard Lintot] to engage me to write and publish Remarks on that Tragedy, which after I had done, A. P--E, the better to conceal himself from Mr. Addison and his friends, writes and publishes a scandalous Pamphlet [*Narrative of Dr. Norris*] equally foolish and villainous, in which he pretends that I am in the hands of a quack who cures madmen."

The relationship between Dennis and Pope is a fascinating, yet complicated one. To whom the title of aggressor falls depends upon who is conferring the title: Pope scholars point the finger at Dennis; Dennis scholars blame Pope. Pope's lines in the *Essay on Criticism*, perhaps motivated by a desire to please Addison, who was currently debating several critical issues such as poetic justice with Dennis, are the first sally and evoked surprise from Dennis: "The Recommendation of Mr. [Henry] Cromwell induced me to be about thrice in his [Pope's] Company, after which I went into the Country and never saw or thought of him, till I found myself attacked by him in the very superficial Essay on Criticism." Whatever their origin, attacks continued in Pope's *Narrative of Dr. Norris* (1713), *Three Years After Marriage*, *Peri Bathous* (1727), and *The Dunciad*, as well as in pieces by Pope's allies, Swift and Gay, in particular. Dennis responded in *Reflections Critical and Satyrical upon a late Rhapsody called An Essay upon Criticism* (1711), *Remarks on Mr. Pope's Rape of the Lock* (1728), *Remarks upon Mr. Pope's Translation of Homer* (1717), *Remarks upon Several Passages in the Preliminaries to the Dunciad* (1729), and *A True Character of Mr. Pope* (1716). Dennis's commentary in these works is often mean-spirited and vengeful and sometimes on the mark, such as his perception of the inconsistency of Pope's use of key terms like *wit* in the *Essay on Criticism*. Pope, in reply to Joseph Spence's query, "Did you never mind what your angry critics published against you?" answered "Never much:—only one or two things, at first—when I heard, for the first time, that Dennis had written against me, it gave me some pain: but it was quite over as soon as I came to look into his book, and found he was in such a passion." The fact remains, however, that Pope is better known than Dennis, and his portrait of Dennis as a Dunce is better known than Dennis's depiction of him as a superficial critic.

The disagreements Dennis had with Sir Richard Steele center on Steele's delay in staging *The Invader of His Country* at Drury Lane. Dennis was hurt not only financially but personally as well. Referring to his long championing of the theater, Dennis lamented, "Thus did they [the Drury Lane managers] take occasion to exercise a real Barbarity upon an old Acquaintance to whom they and their stage are more oblig'd than to any Writer in England." Dennis, at this stage in his career not one to check his pen, retaliated to his perception of managerial conspiracy with the two parts of *The Characters and Conduct of Sir John Edgar* (1720) and *Remarks on a Play, call'd The Conscious Lovers* (1723). The most famous (though perhaps apocryphal) of Dennis's remarks about his victimization at the hands of theater managers is one occasioned by his viewing a production of *Macbeth*, where the means of artificially producing thunder was apparently the same as the one he had devised for his own *Appius and Virginia*. Dennis is reported to have jumped from his seat and shouted that the managers had "stolen his thunder": "That is my thunder, by God! the villains will play my thunder but not my plays," thus coining the phrase "to steal one's thunder."

Of his later life Dennis says, "I was till five and forty plung'd in the Conversation of the Great World, and was every Day in Company with Gentlemen, who are universally known to be Men of no ordinary Merit.... For these last fifteen years I have retir'd from the World, and confin'd my Conversation to three or four of my old Acquaintance." Dennis's poverty and ill health (he became nearly totally blind) evoked sympathy from even his old enemy Pope, who attempted shortly before the old critic's death to generate money for him by a benefit performance of *The Provoked Husband* in the Haymarket on 18 December 1733. Dennis died shortly thereafter, on 6 January 1734. An indication, perhaps, of how far Dennis's reputation had sunk might be found in the sale catalogue of Brindley's library (1818), which records that Dennis's works, in twelve volumes, went for only one pound, thirteen shillings.

As recent literary histories of the period continue to revise the old assumptions of a monolithic neoclassical criticism that passed from Dryden to Pope to Johnson and of a neoclassical poetry that passed from Edmund Waller and Sir John Denham to Dryden and Pope, Dennis assumes increasing importance. It is now undeniable that his work on the sublime, on the roles of emotion and religion in poetry, and on the poetic values to be found in Milton influenced many later critics and poets. Not only the midcentury neo-Miltonic, "graveyard" poets—Edward Young, William Collins, Thomas and Joseph Warton, and Thomas Gray—but also William Wordsworth and Samuel Taylor Coleridge owe debts to his theoretical assessments about the emotional and pyschological response to literary texts.

Letters:

Letters upon Several Occasions: Written by and between Mr. Dryden, Mr. Wycherley, Mr.-----------, Mr. Congreve, and Mr. Dennis. Publish'd by Mr. Dennis (London: Printed for Sam. Briscoe, 1696);

Original Letters, Familiar, Moral and Critical, 2 volumes (London: W. Mears, 1721).

Biographies:

Charles Gildon, *Lives and Characters of the English Dramatic Poets* (London, 1699);

Giles Jacob, *The Poetical Register*, volume 2 (London: Printed for E. Curll, 1719-1720);

Life of Mr. John Dennis, the Renown'd Critick (London: Printed for J. Roberts, 1734);

H. G. Paul, *John Dennis: His Life and Criticism* (New York: Columbia University Press, 1911).

References:

W. P. Albrecht, *The Sublime Pleasures of Tragedy: A Study of Critical Theory from Dennis to Kant* (Lawrence: University Press of Kansas, 1975), pp. 13-24;

Jeffrey Barnouw, "The Morality of the Sublime: To John Dennis," *Comparative Literature*, 35 (Winter 1983): 21-42;

Joan C. Grace, *Tragic Theory in the Critical Works of Thomas Rymer, John Dennis, and John Dryden* (Rutherford, N.J.: Fairleigh Dickinson University Press, 1975), pp. 61-88;

James A. W. Heffernan, "Wordsworth and Dennis: The Discrimination of Feelings," *PMLA*, 82 (October 1967): 430-436;

Edward Niles Hooker, "Pope and Dennis," *ELH*, 7 (September 1940): 188-198;

Samuel Holt Monk, *The Sublime: A Study of Critical Theories in XVIII-Century England* (New York: Modern Language Association of America, 1935);

David B. Morris, *The Religious Sublime: Christian Poetry and Critical Tradition in 18th-Century England* (Lexington: University Press of Kentucky, 1972);

Avon Jack Murphy, *John Dennis* (Boston: Twayne, 1984);

John T. Shawcross, "John Dennis," in *A Milton Encyclopedia*, 8 volumes, edited by William B. Hunter and others (Lewisburg, Pa.: Bucknell University Press, 1978-1980), II: 141-143;

Clarence DeWitt Thorpe, *The Aesthetic Theory of Thomas Hobbes* (Ann Arbor: University of Michigan / London: Oxford University Press, 1940);

Thorpe, "Two Augustans Cross the Alps: Dennis and Addison on Mountain Scenery," *Studies in Philology*, 32 (July 1935): 463-482;

David Wheeler, "Eighteenth-Century Adaptations of Shakespeare and the Example of John Dennis," *Shakespeare Quarterly*, 36 (Winter 1985): 438-449.

Papers:

Only a few Dennis manuscripts survive, and they are to be found in the British Library and in the Folger Shakespeare Library, Washington, D.C.

John Dryden

(9 August 1631 - 1 May 1700)

Cedric D. Reverand II
University of Wyoming

See also the Dryden entry in *DLB 80: Restoration and Eighteenth-Century Dramatists, First Series.*

SELECTED BOOKS: *Astraea Redux. A Poem On the Happy Restoration and Return Of His Sacred Majesty Charles the Second* (London: Printed by J. M. for Henry Herringman, 1660);

To His Sacred Majesty, A Panegyrick On His Coronation (London: Printed for Henry Herringman, 1661);

To My Lord Chancellor, Presented on New-years-day (London: Printed for Henry Herringman, 1662);

The Rival Ladies (London: Printed by W. W. for Henry Herringman, 1664);

The Indian Emperour, or The Conquest of Mexico by the Spaniards (London: Printed by J. M. for H. Herringman, 1667); second edition republished with "A Defence of An Essay of Dramatique Poesie" in some copies (London: Printed for H. Herringman, 1668);

Annus Mirabilis: The Year of Wonders, 1666 (London: Printed for Henry Herringman, 1667);

Of Dramatick Poesie: An Essay (London: Printed for Henry Herringman, 1668 [i.e., 1667]);

Secret-Love, or The Maiden-Queen (London: Printed for Henry Herringman, 1668);

Sr Martin Mar-All, or The Feigned Innocence (London: Printed for H. Herringman, 1668);

The Wild Gallant (London: Printed by Tho. Newcomb for H. Herringman, 1669);

The Tempest, or The Enchanted Island, by Dryden and William Davenant (London: Printed for Henry Herringman, 1670);

Tyrannick Love, or The Royal Martyr (London: Printed for H. Herringman, 1670);

An Evening's Love, or The Mock Astrologer (London: Printed by T. N. for Henry Herringman, 1671);

The Conquest of Granada by the Spaniards: In Two Parts (London: Printed by T. N. for Henry Herringman, 1672);

Marriage A-La-Mode (London: Printed by T. N. for Henry Herringman & sold by Joseph Knight & Francis Saunders, 1673);

The Assignation: or, Love in a Nunnery (London: Printed by T. N. for Henry Herringman, 1673);

Amboyna (London: Printed by T. N. for Henry Herringman, 1673);

Notes and Observations on the Empress of Morocco, by Dryden, John Crowne, and Thomas Shadwell (London, 1674);

Aureng-Zebe (London: Printed by T. N. for Henry Herringman, 1676);

The State of Innocence and Fall of Man (London: Printed by T. N. for Henry Herringman, 1677);

All for Love: or, The World Well Lost (London: Printed by Tho. Newcomb for Henry Herringman, 1678);

Oedipus, by Dryden and Nathaniel Lee (London: Printed for R. Bentley and M. Magnes, 1679);

Troilus and Cressida, or, Truth Found too Late (London: Printed for Jacob Tonson and Abel Swall, 1679);

The Kind Keeper; or, Mr. Limberham (London: Printed for R. Bentley and M. Magnes, 1680);

His Majesties Declaration Defended (London: Printed for T. Davies, 1681);

Absalom and Achitophel (London: Printed for J. T. & sold by W. Davis, 1681);

The Spanish Fryar, or The Double Discovery (London: Printed for Richard Tonson & Jacob Tonson, 1681);

The Medall. A Satyre against Sedition (London: Printed for Jacob Tonson, 1682);

Mac Flecknoe, or a Satyr Upon the True-Blew Protestant Poet, T.S. [unauthorized edition] (London: Printed for D. Green, 1682);

Religio Laici or a Laymans Faith (London: Printed for Jacob Tonson, 1682);

John Dryden, 1693 (portrait by Sir Godfrey Kneller; by permission of the National Portrait Gallery, London)

The Duke of Guise, by Dryden and Lee (London: Printed by T. H. for R. Bentley and J. Tonson, 1683);

The Vindication [of the Duke of Guise]: or The Parallel of the French Holy-League, and The English League and Covenant (London: Printed for Jacob Tonson, 1683);

Threnodia Augustalis: A Funeral-Pindarique Poem Sacred to the Happy Memory of King Charles II (London: Printed for Jacob Tonson, 1685);

Albion and Albanius, by Dryden, with music by Lewis Grabu (London: Printed for Jacob Tonson, 1685);

A Defence of the Papers Written by the Late King of Blessed Memory and Duchess of York (London: Printed for H. Hills, 1686);

The Hind and the Panther (London: Printed for Jacob Tonson, 1687);

A Song for St Cecilia's Day, 1687, by Dryden, with music by Giovanni Baptista Draghi (London: Printed for T. Dring, 1687);

Britannia Rediviva: A Poem on the Birth of the Prince (London: Printed for J. Tonson, 1688);

Don Sebastian, King of Portugal (London: Printed for Jo. Hindmarsh, 1690);

Amphitryon; or The Two Socia's, by Dryden, with music by Henry Purcell (London: Printed for J. Tonson & M. Tonson, 1690);

King Arthur: or The British Worthy, by Dryden, with music by Purcell (London: Printed for Jacob Tonson, 1691);

Eleonora: A Panegyrical Poem Dedicated to the Memory of the Late Countess of Abingdon (London: Printed for Jacob Tonson, 1692);

Cleomenes, The Spartan Heroe (London: Printed for Jacob Tonson, 1692);

Love Triumphant; or, Nature Will Prevail (London: Printed for Jacob Tonson, 1694);

An Ode, on the Death of Mr. Henry Purcell; Late Servant of his Majesty, and Organist of the Chapel Royal, and of St. Peter's Westminster (London: Printed by J. Heptinstall for Henry Playford, 1696);

Alexander's Feast; Or The Power of Musique. An Ode, In Honour of St. Cecilia's Day (London: Printed for Jacob Tonson, 1697).

Editions: *The Works of John Dryden,* 18 volumes, edited by Walter Scott (London: William Miller, 1808); revised by George Saintsbury (Edinburgh: William Paterson, 1882-1893);

The Dramatic Works of John Dryden, 6 volumes, edited by Montague Summers (London: Nonesuch Press, 1931);

The Works of John Dryden [The California Dryden], 20 volumes, edited by Edward Niles Hooker, H. T. Swedenberg, and others (Berkeley: University of California Press, 1955-);

The Poems of John Dryden, 4 volumes, edited by James Kinsley (Oxford: Clarendon Press, 1958);

John Dryden: Of Dramatic Poesy and Other Critical Essays, 2 volumes, edited by George Watson (London: J. M. Dent / New York: E. P. Dutton, 1962).

PLAY PRODUCTIONS: *The Wild Gallant,* revised from an older play, possibly by Richard Brome, London, Vere Street Theatre, 5 February 1663;

The Rival Ladies, London, Theatre Royal, Bridges Street, possibly autumn of 1663;

The Indian-Queen, by Dryden and Sir Robert Howard, London, Theatre Royal, Bridges Street, January 1664;

The Indian Emperour, London, Theatre Royal, Bridges Street, early months of 1665;

Secret Love, London, Theatre Royal, Bridges Street, final days of January 1667;

Sir Martin Mar-All, by Dryden and William Cavendish, Duke of Newcastle, London, Lincoln's Inn Fields, 15 August 1667;

The Tempest, revised from William Shakespeare's play by Dryden and William Davenant, London, Lincoln's Inn Fields, 7 November 1667;

An Evening's Love; or, The Mock Astrologer, London, Theatre Royal, Bridges Street, 12 June 1668;

Tyrannic Love, London, Theatre Royal, Bridges Street, 24 June 1669;

The Conquest of Granada, part 1, London, Theatre Royal, Bridges Street, December 1670; part 2, January 1671;

Marriage A-la-Mode, London, Theatre Royal, Bridges Street, probably late November or early December 1671;

The Assignation; or, Love in a Nunnery, London, Lincoln's Inn Fields, not later than early autumn of 1672;

Amboyna, London, Lincoln's Inn Fields, possibly February 1673;

Aureng-Zebe, London, Theatre Royal, Drury Lane, 17 November 1675;

All for Love, London, Theatre Royal, Drury Lane, probably 12 December 1677;

The Kind Keeper; or, Mr. Limberham, London, Dorset Garden Theatre, 11 March 1678;

Oedipus, by Dryden and Nathaniel Lee, London, Dorset Garden Theatre, autumn 1678;

Troilus and Cressida, revised from Shakespeare's play, London, Dorset Garden Theatre, not later than April 1679;

The Spanish Fryar, London, Dorset Garden Theatre, 1 November 1680;

The Duke of Guise, by Dryden and Lee, London, Theatre Royal, Drury Lane, 30 November 1682;

Albion and Albanius, opera with text by Dryden and music by Louis Grabu, London, Dorset Garden Theatre, 3 June 1685;

Don Sebastian, London, Theatre Royal, Drury Lane, 4 December 1689;

Amphitryon, London, Theatre Royal, Drury Lane, probably early October 1690;

King Arthur, opera with text by Dryden and music by Henry Purcell, London, Dorset Garden Theatre, early June 1691;

Cleomenes, by Dryden and Thomas Southerne, London, Theatre Royal, Drury Lane, on or before 16 April 1692;

Love Triumphant, London, Theatre Royal, Drury Lane, probably late January 1694;

"The Secular Masque," inserted into *The Pilgrim,* revised from John Fletcher's play by John Vanbrugh, London, Theatre Royal, Drury Lane, late April or early May 1700.

OTHER: "Upon the Death of the Lord Hastings," in *Lachrymae Musarum: The Tears of the Muses: Exprest in Elegies; Written By divers persons of Nobility and Worth, Upon the death of the most hopefull, Henry Lord Hastings* (London: Printed by Thomas Newcomb, 1649);

"To his friend the Authour on his divine Epigrams," in *Sion and Parnassus*, by John Hoddesdon (London: Printed by R. Daniel for G. Eversden, 1650);

"Heroique Stanzas, Consecrated to the Glorious Memory of his most Serene and renowned Highnesse Oliver Late Lord Protector of this Common-Wealth, &c.," in *Three poems Upon the Death of his late Highnesse Oliver Lord Protector of England, Scotland & Ireland* (London: Printed by William Wilson, 1659);

"To My Honored Friend, Sr Robert Howard, On his Excellent Poems," in *Poems*, by Sir Robert Howard (London: Printed for Henry Herringman, 1660);

"To My Honour'd Friend, Dr Charleton," in *Chorea Gigantum, or The most Famous Antiquity of Great-Britain, Vulgarly called Stone-Heng, Standing on Salisbury Plain, Restored to the Danes*, by Walter Charleton (London: Printed for Henry Herringman, 1663 [i.e., 1662]);

The Indian-Queen, by Dryden and Howard, in *Four New Plays*, by Howard (London: Printed for H. Herringman, 1665);

Ovid's Epistles, Translated by Several Hands, includes a preface, and translations of three epistles by Dryden (London: Printed for Jacob Tonson, 1680);

Nahum Tate, *The Second Part of Absalom and Achitophel*, includes contributions by Dryden (London: Printed for Jacob Tonson, 1682);

"The Life of Plutarch," in volume 1 of *Plutarchs Lives, Translated from the Greek by Several Hands*, 5 volumes (London: Printed for Jacob Tonson, 1683-1686);

Miscellany Poems, includes the authorized version of *Mac Flecknoe* and twenty-five other contributions by Dryden (London: Printed for Jacob Tonson, 1684);

Louis Maimbourg, *The History of the League*, translated by Dryden (London: Printed by M. Flesher for Jacob Tonson, 1684);

"To the Memory of Mr. Oldham," in *The Remains of Mr. John Oldham in Verse and Prose* (London: Printed for Jo. Hindmarsh, 1684);

Sylvae; or, the Second Part of Poetical Miscellanies, includes a preface and seventeen contributions by Dryden (London: Printed for Jacob Tonson, 1685);

"To the Pious Memory Of the Accomplisht Young Lady Mrs Anne Killigrew, Excellent in the two Sister-Arts of Poësie, and Painting. An Ode," in *Poems By Mrs. Anne Killigrew* (London: Printed for Samuel Lowndes, 1686 [i.e., 1685]);

Dominique Bouhours, *The Life of St. Francis Xavier, of the Society of Jesus*, translated by Dryden (London: Printed for Jacob Tonson, 1688);

The Satires of Decimus Junius Juvenalis Translated into English Verse. By Mr. Dryden, and Several other Eminent Hands. Together with the Satires of Aulus Persius Flaccus Made English by Mr. Dryden . . . To which is Prefix'd a Discourse concerning the Original and Progress of Satire (London: Printed for Jacob Tonson, 1693 [i.e., 1692]);

Examen Poeticum: Being the Third Part of Miscellany Poems, includes fifteen contributions by Dryden (London: Printed by R. E. for Jacob Tonson, 1693);

"A Character of Polybius and His Writings," in *The History of Polybius the Megalopolitan*, translated by Sir Henry Sheeres (London: Printed for S. Briscoe, 1693);

"To my Dear Friend Mr. Congreve, On His Comedy, call'd, The Double-Dealer," in *The Double-Dealer*, by William Congreve (London: Printed for J. Tonson, 1694);

"To Sir Godfrey Kneller," in *The Annual Miscellany: for the Year 1694. Being the Fourth Part of Miscellany Poems* (London: Printed by R. E. for Jacob Tonson, 1694);

Charles Alphonse du Fresnoy, *De Arte Graphica*, Latin text, with prose translation and "A Parallel of Poetry and Painting" by Dryden (London: Printed by J. Heptinstall for W. Rogers, 1695);

The Works of Virgil: Containing His Pastorals, Georgics, and Æneis, translated by Dryden (London: Printed for Jacob Tonson, 1697);

Fables Ancient and Modern; Translated into Verse, from Homer, Ovid, Boccace, & Chaucer; with Original Poems, translated by Dryden (London: Printed for Jacob Tonson, 1700);

"A Dialogue and Secular Masque," in *The Pilgrim*, by John Fletcher, revised by John Vanbrugh (London: Printed for Benjamin Tooke, 1700);

"The Life of Lucian," in volume 1 of *The Works of Lucian, Translated from the Greek by Several Emi-*

nent Hands, 4 volumes (London: Printed for
S. Briscoe, 1711);

[Heads of an Answer to Rymer], in volume 1 of
*The Works of Mr Francis Beaumont and Mr
John Fletcher*, 7 volumes (London: Printed
for J. Tonson, 1711).

John Dryden was not only the leading
writer of the Restoration period, but also one of
those rare major authors equally adept and accomplished in several literary genres. He began as a
playwright, creating comedies, tragedies, operas,
and adaptations so free as to qualify as original
plays—for instance, *All for Love* (performed in
1677), Dryden's version of *Antony and Cleopatra*,
was so highly regarded that it displaced the Shakespearean original from the English stage for a century. After establishing himself as a dramatist,
and helping reestablish the English theater,
which had been thoroughly stifled by the Puritans during the Interregnum, Dryden turned increasingly toward poetry, producing an impressively wide range of verse—dedicatory poems,
panegyrics, elegies, songs, sharp verse satires on
politics and on literature, straight, exploratory
poems (usually with a touch of satire) on science,
religion, philosophy, music, painting. If that were
not range enough, he gradually expanded into
translation, part of his effort to pay tribute to the
classics and to locate the English poetic tradition
within a broader context. His most sustained effort in this mode, an achievement he regarded
with particular pride, was his translation of the
Aeneis (1697), whereby he not only made Virgil
alive and relevant to a seventeenth-century English audience, but also appropriated the authority and stature of the great epic author to his
own person, which is what Alexander Pope was
subsequently to do with his own highly successful
translation of Homer.

In all his literary productions, Dryden is
both the conservative, ever concerned with the
past, and the innovator, looking ahead to the future of English literature. In drama, he paid his respects to his forebears with adaptations of Shakespeare (both *All for Love* and *Troilus and Cressida*),
and Milton (*The State of Innocence*, Dryden's 1677
closet-drama version of *Paradise Lost*, undertaken
with Milton's approval). But Dryden also ushered
in the new Restoration comedies and reached beyond the tradition of the previous age by developing a new genre, the exalted heroic play (to
twentieth-century tastes, this would appear to be
overreaching). In poetry he produced high-flown

Pindarics (the ode to Anne Killigrew, *Alexander's
Feast*) in the mode of the Metaphysical poet Abraham Cowley, whom Dryden once called "the Darling of my youth," but he also developed the
verse satire, the medium that was to flourish in
the next generation, thanks in large part to Pope,
who idolized Dryden. In his memorial poem to
fellow-satirist John Oldham (1684), Dryden, not
one to be humble about his achievements, lays
claim to the distinction of being England's first
verse satirist. He might have claimed much
more; what he could not have known at the time
was that the verse form chosen for his satires, the
heroic couplet, was to dominate English poetry
for the next century. Dryden's Janus-like stance,
looking to the past and future simultaneously, is
not as two-faced as it might appear. Rather, both
views combine to serve a coherent purpose: in recovering the English literary heritage, in tracing
its classical precedents, Dryden could be said to
be reinventing the English tradition for the express purposes of justifying his own contributions, and shaping the immediate future of English literature to his own tastes.

Dryden was no less distinguished in writing
critical prose, although his accomplishments in
this area tend to be overshadowed by his more obvious achievements in drama and poetry. His criticism also presents special problems for twentieth-
century readers, for any number of reasons. For
one thing, nearly all of it is occasional, scattered
among prefaces, dedications, defenses, apologies,
which are then attached to poems, plays, and translations. Since it is attached to something else, the
criticism seems to be of secondary importance,
and since it is occasional, it is far from systematic. We encounter another difficulty because Dryden's tone oftentimes does not sound like the
poised, reasonable voice we prefer to associate
with criticism. At times, he can sound huffy, intem-
perate, and unnecessarily severe, as in his "Defence of An Essay of Dramatique Poesie" (1668),
where he spends twenty pages responding forcefully to a mild, and mostly favorable, three pages
of commentary by Sir Robert Howard. It is difficult to appreciate that this sort of behavior was
normal, not aberrant. One must remember that
Dryden lived in an age when fierce critical warfare, parry, thrust, counterthrust, and crude personal abuse were normal parts of the literary
scene. Like Pope in the next generation, Dryden
was sufficiently prominent and successful to be
a conspicuous target throughout his career:
George Villiers, Duke of Buckingham, parodied

Richard Busby, the headmaster of the Westminster School, London, where Dryden was enrolled circa 1644 (portrait by John Riley, circa 1690; by permission of the Curator of Pictures, Christ Church College, Oxford)

him, Thomas Rymer lampooned him, Jeremy Collier took him to task for writing blasphemous and bawdy plays, Thomas Shadwell conspired against him, Tom Brown published abusive, and not terribly funny, anti-Dryden pamphlets. Once, in 1679, Dryden was ambushed in Rose Alley, near Covent Garden, by hired thugs who knocked him senseless; his assailants, careless in matters of detail, were punishing him for writing a poem that was actually written by John Sheffield, Earl of Mulgrave. We expect literary debate to be a bit more refined, genteel, or at least more accurate than this. But in Dryden's time, which after all was an age of satire, the game was oftentimes rude and ugly, though refreshingly lively as well. If anything, Dryden restrained himself

more often than not, allowing many of the attacks and lampoons to remain unanswered, shrugging others off with a joke. Although he sometimes seems to overreact, it is only sometimes, and it would not have seemed excessive behavior on the literary battlefield of the late seventeenth century.

As a participant in this literary warfare, Dryden was ever defending himself, and that brings us to another potential obstacle standing between us and his criticism. Almost all of his critical prose, even that which seems to be mainly theoretical, is an act of self-justification. His theories on rhyme in drama arose because he wished to promote or had to defend his own rhymed plays. His discussion of kinds of translation occurred not because of a disinterested curiosity about the subject, but because he was about to publish his own translations and needed to soften up the audience. To some extent any kind of criticism can be considered self-justifying, but in the case of a critic who is also a practicing author adding explanations to most of his publications, the self-interest is overt and may offend those who prefer the modest pose. But why should Dryden be modest? Samuel Johnson observed Dryden's penchant for mentioning himself too frequently, but reminded us, in his scrupulously judgmental way, that while Dryden "forces himself upon our esteem, we cannot refuse him to stand high in his own." Though he was often driven into self-defense and counterattack, he had the good fortune to be bearing arms on behalf of a major author worth the battle, himself.

John Dryden was born 9 August 1631 at Aldwincle in Northamptonshire and grew up in nearby Titchmarsh. He was the firstborn son of Erasmus Dryden and Mary Pickering, country gentry who raised their son in the Puritan traditions of their families. Theirs was not a radical Puritanism (of a kind that would lead to the deposition of the king), but rather a deeply conservative version, and one suspects that Dryden's Puritan childhood helped shape his conservative character and instill his lifelong penchant for endorsing hierarchical order. Dryden may have attended school in Oundle; his regular, formal education, however, began somewhere around 1644, when he was sent to Westminster School in London to study under the fervent Royalist headmaster, Richard Busby, later to become one of the many footnoted victims of Pope's *Dunciad*, a schoolmaster known for his rigor, who loaded chain upon chain of classical learning on his young charges. The curriculum Busby enforced, the standard mix of classical translations, exercises, and recitations, not only guaranteed a shared level of cultural literacy among Westminster's students, but also gave Dryden an intimate knowledge of the ancient authors he would later promote and translate professionally. Since he was at Westminster School in the days when the Puritans surged to power—Charles I was executed not a half mile from where Dryden was studying, and Parliament was just across the street—we can surmise that Dryden's lifelong concern for political stability may have owed something to his being educated amidst unsettling and bloody political upheaval, most of it just around the corner.

From Westminster School, where he was a King's Scholar, Dryden was admitted to Trinity College, Cambridge, in 1650. Our knowledge of his undergraduate years is rather thin; one record survives to indicate that he was once restricted to quarters for insubordination, but whether this was the result of an academic infraction or, as one might prefer, some witty satirical prank, we simply do not know. Dryden took a B.A. in 1654 and remained one further year at Trinity. Then, rather than pursue an academic career, he moved to London in 1655, where, thanks to his well-connected Puritan relatives, he served in a minor capacity as clerk and translator under Cromwell's Protectorate. This brought Dryden into contact with both Marvell and Milton (all three poets were to participate in Cromwell's funeral procession), but we know nothing of their interaction. That their paths should have crossed is intriguing, but we should note that there is little reason to expect much in the way of an interchange, since there was a sizable gap between the well-known Milton (born in 1608) and the up-and-coming Marvell (born in 1621) on the one hand, and the young, untested, unaccomplished Dryden (born in 1631) fresh out of university on the other.

Except for Dryden's first published poem, "Upon the Death of the Lord Hastings" (1649), with its excruciating, Metaphysical conceits (as tasteless as Richard Crashaw's), a short and feeble poem to John Hoddesdon (1650), and some lines in a letter to his cousin Honor (1653), we have no extant verse from Dryden's Cambridge years. Nor do we have much hint in this meager early verse of the poet to come. His first important poem is "Heroique Stanzas to the Glorious Memory of Cromwell" (1659), written in a stanzaic form borrowed from William Davenant's *Gondibert* (1651); this was followed by a prefatory poem, "To My Honored Friend, Sr Robert Howard" (1660), and two poems celebrating the Restoration of Charles II, *Astraea Redux* (1660) and *To His Sacred Majesty* (1661). Dryden was later criticized for this quick about-turn, ennobling Cromwell one day, exalting Charles II the next, but since all of England turned enthusiastically in the same direction, Dryden's behavior does not seem unusual. Again, a Samuel Johnson comment—"if Dryden changed, he changed with the nation"—seems pertinent. Dryden's first extensive poem was *Annus Mirabilis* (1667) and his first significant satire *Mac Flecknoe* (probably written in 1676, but first published in 1682). It is difficult to believe

*An anonymous portrait of Dryden, dated 1657 but probably painted circa 1662 (by permission of the
Curators of the Bodleian Library, Oxford)*

that Dryden suddenly happened upon his vocation only when he was in his thirties, that he wrote only a handful of lines between 1649 and 1660; it may well be that he destroyed his juvenilia out of embarrassment once he achieved some status as a poet.

When Charles returned, and the theaters reopened, Dryden began his career as playwright in earnest; in 1663, the same year that he married Lady Elizabeth Howard, Dryden's first play, *The Wild Gallant*, was acted, followed by *The Rival Ladies* (perhaps acted in 1663), and by *The Indian-Queen* (performed in 1664), a collaboration with his brother-in-law, Sir Robert Howard. Then came Dryden's first important piece of criticism, *An Essay of Dramatick Poesie*, published in 1667, but probably written in 1665-1666, when he removed himself to the country to avoid the plague. Dryden's essay, a rich, speculative work that summarizes current theatrical notions, examines and challenges them, and looks forward to his future work as a dramatist, remains the best-known example of his prose, primarily because it is his only freestanding, nonoccasional essay. It consists of six set speeches by characters who are

sitting in a boat, wiling away the time in airy discourse while the English navy is busy defeating the invading Dutch. As they drift along the Thames, the four speakers—Crites, Eugenius, Lisideius, and Neander (Dryden's spokesman)—couch their arguments in three separate dialogues: first, Crites versus Eugenius; then, Lisideius versus Neander; and finally, Crites versus Neander.

The debate form itself, with one lengthy speech followed by another, is just as significant as the issues addressed, for it reveals a habit of mind typical of Dryden. He does not merely take a position and advocate it; instead, he seems to be on all sides of each issue, arguing for the superiority of the ancients (Crites), then for the moderns (Eugenius); preferring the French to the English (Lisideius), then praising the English at the expense of the French (Neander); advocating blank verse in plays (Crites), and then endorsing rhyme (Neander). This is not a matter of indecisiveness, but rather a normal procedure for somebody with a skeptical frame of mind. Dryden liked to debate all sides of an issue; his training at Westminster and Trinity in rhetoric and contro-

Thomas Howard, first Earl of Berkshire, father of Lady Elizabeth Howard, whom Dryden married on 1 December 1663 (an eighteenth-century miniature by Athow, after a lost miniature by Apthorpe; by permission of the Ashmolean Museum, Oxford)

versy, a training that took place when large conflicting forces were shaping England, prepared him for this way of thinking. And he was to use the same strategy in his poetry. *Absalom and Achitophel* (1681), written in support of Charles II's position during the Exclusion Crisis, does not argue the king's side of the case until after giving free play to the opposing arguments in speeches by Achitophel (Anthony Ashley, Earl of Shaftesbury) and Absalom (James Scott, Duke of Monmouth). There is seldom any doubt as to what side Dryden stands on, but his procedure of arguing different sides of an issue has misled some readers into thinking him ambivalent.

In *An Essay of Dramatick Poesie*, Dryden makes a case, finally, for the advantages of English "variety and copiousness" over classical (and French) regularity and tidiness, for the superiority of the English theater to the French, and for the suitability of rhyme in plays where heightened imitation is the key. That is his position, but

it emerges only after he subjects his material to vigorous dialectical tugging. Were we to stop after the first major speech in the essay, where Crites defines and defends the unities, we might consider Dryden a rigorous classicist, and a pedantic one at that. (Crites' stuffy and bullheaded tone owes something to the fact that Dryden is summarizing Sir Robert Howard's position and, ever the satirist, is also parodying Howard's peremptory manner.) Yet no sooner does Dryden establish this classic piece of classicism—significantly, this is the first use of the phrase "The Three Unities" in English criticism—than other speakers enter to chip away at the neoclassical edifice. Eugenius argues that the unities impose a narrow compass, discusses classical plays that defy the unities, and demonstrates that, far from being Aristotelian, the unities are instead impositions "in our own age" by "the *French* Poets." Nor is the argument over once the topic changes. By associating constricting classical rules with French authors, Eugenius sets up Lisideius's speech in praise of the regular French, regular because they best have incorporated classical verities into their theater. This speech in turn sets up Neander's response, which praises English drama and at the same time questions once again the value of the unities; Neander argues that English plays are superior to the French, partially because they demonstrate what can be achieved when one is *not* constrained by the unities, as the French are.

That Dryden's spokesman, Neander, should turn to English plays as his touchstone is also significant, because it reveals another Dryden instinct. Whatever the issue, however persuasive the theory or weighty the authority behind a point of view, Dryden tends to decide the case ultimately on a pragmatic basis. Plays should not have subplots, should not mingle tragedy with mirth, and should not cram thirty or forty years together in five acts. These prohibitions all make perfect classical sense to Lisideius, who has the unities and classical precedent in front of him. Neander, turning to "the experience of our own Stage," discovers that Shakespeare abounds with subplots, frequently mingles tragedy with mirth, and extends his history plays over decades; theoretically, this should confuse the audience, but apparently the English audience is not well versed in theory. Shakespeare's imperfections, which render him "ridiculous" in Lisideius's eyes, do not diminish him in Neander's view. On the contrary, the bard's cavalier violations of classical precepts provide variety and are especially pleasing. At one point Neander agrees with Lisideius in principle: large, violent actions should be barred from the stage, since they cannot be carried off convincingly (we all know that those deadly swords are blunt), yet Neander readily changes his mind when he looks at this practically, and admits that combats and the like are expected on the English stage. It may be incorrect to retain them, and it may be a want of taste on the part of the crude English audience that encourages their inclusion, but, if something works on stage, then it must be admitted as appropriate to drama. Besides, the alternative—expressing passion by speeches—works dismally; "long Harangues" do not so much raise the passions as bore audiences, which Dryden, as a practicing playwright, would have learned rather swiftly.

Neander's examination of specific plays serves a larger purpose than just proving a point about what is "practicable." He is also engaged in a standard Drydenian enterprise, assembling an English literary heritage by naming, linking, and evaluating authors—in this case Shakespeare, Francis Beaumont, John Fletcher, and Ben Jonson. Even in the satirical *Mac Flecknoe* (written in 1676), Dryden engages in something of this sort; the victim of the poem, playwright Thomas Shadwell, is associated with hack authors, such as Richard Flecknoe, Thomas Heywood, James Shirley, and John Ogilby, who constitute a kind of antitradition, a lineage of dullness, but at the same time, that lineage is distinguished from the line of worthy playwrights, Fletcher, Jonson, and George Etherege. In a nonsatirical poem, such as Dryden's "To my Dear Friend Mr. Congreve" (1694), we see a similar procedure, and we hear some of the same names: William Congreve is not merely good, but is also the embodiment of the best qualities of two generations of English playwrights, Fletcher and Jonson from the past, Etherege, Thomas Southerne, and William Wycherley from the current generation. With hindsight, we are likely to admire Dryden's taste. He generally names the figures we still include in anthologies, and condemns those we now regard as negligible (it would be difficult, to say the least, to find anybody who admires Flecknoe or Ogilby). Dryden consistently rates Shakespeare as the greatest of English dramatists, and does this at a time when Beaumont and Fletcher were more frequently acted. We also should recognize, however, that Dryden's canon formation is self-serving. He is not objectively assessing a tradition, but rather shaping it to justify his own endeavors, invoking the past as a precedent, and hoping to gain favor by the implicit claim of being of the same company as the great playwrights he discusses.

It is all too easy, over the stretch of three centuries, to forget that Dryden had immediate professional concerns, and to get lost in a fruitless quest for discovering how to square his theories with one another. For example, it might seem puzzling that Dryden finds the unities potentially constraining, but in the same essay argues in favor of rhyme over blank verse—surely, rhyme is also constraining. However, this is not just a matter of abstract theory; rather, it is a matter of practice, and in particular, Dryden's practice. Charles II had a preference for rhymed plays; the English stage was moving toward rhymed heroic plays, and Dryden was one of the movers, beginning with *The Indian-Queen* (performed in 1664), followed by a sequel, *The Indian Emperour* (performed in 1665), Dryden's first real theatrical suc-

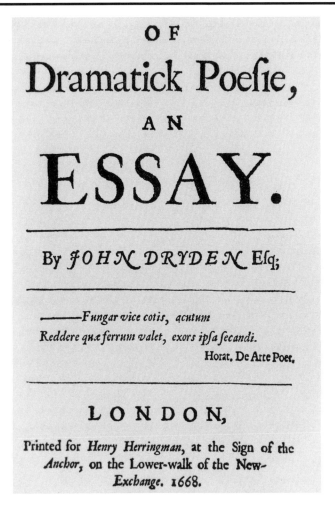

OF

Dramatick Poesie,

AN

ESSAY.

By *JOHN DRYDEN* Esq;

———*Fungar vice cotis, acutum*
Reddere quæ ferrum valet, exors ipsa secandi.

Horat. De Arte Poet.

LONDON,

Printed for *Henry Herringman*, at the Sign of the
Anchor, on the Lower-walk of the New-
Exchange. 1668.

Title page for Dryden's first important work of literary criticism, commonly known as An Essay of Dramatick Poesie,
a title it was given on the running heads in this first edition

cess (both plays precede the publication of *An Essay of Dramatick Poesie*, although the essay had been written, in preliminary form at least, two years earlier). As an index to Dryden's strategic purposes, one might note that he has Neander allude specifically to the popular taste for such plays: "no serious Playes written since the Kings return have been more kindly receiv'd . . . then the *Siege of Rhodes* [by William Davenant], the *Mustapha* [by Roger Boyle, Earl of Orrery), *The Indian-Queen*, and *Indian Emperour*." There is something wry about Dryden having a character nonchalantly invoke Dryden's own plays in support of an argument. The point to stress is that the argument on behalf of rhyme and on behalf of "Nature wrought up to an higher pitch" is a blatant piece of self-promotion, a pragmatic justification for what Dryden himself has been doing, and an attempt to clear the way for what he is about to do: in 1669 Dryden's rhymed religious drama

Tyrannick Love was to appear on stage, and that would be followed by Dryden's most accomplished effort in the rhymed heroic play, *The Conquest of Granada*, ten acts played in two parts (the first half in December 1670, the second in January 1671).

Two subsequent Dryden critical essays could be considered extensions of *An Essay of Dramatick Poesie*, both because they develop ideas that had first appeared here, and because they even more pointedly serve as self-promotion, more ammunition in the battle to defend Dryden's elevated, rhymed heroic plays: first, Dryden's "A Defence of An Essay of Dramatique Poesie" (1668), and second, his "Of Heroique Playes" (1672). Dryden's "Defence" is not the sort of work by which a critic would like to be remembered, which perhaps explains why, after it appeared in the second edition of *The Indian Emperour* (1668), he dropped it from further reprintings of the play.

As already mentioned, this essay is not so much a defense as it is an all-out attack on Sir Robert Howard, who, in the preface to his play *The Duke of Lerma* (1668), had taken issue with "the Author of an Essay of Drammatick Poesie." Dryden's double-barreled response is startling, especially when we discover that Howard's criticisms are relatively mild; although he indulges in a few snide, condescending remarks, they are not rapier thrusts, and he actually, albeit begrudgingly, acknowledges Dryden to be the superior playwright. Even the areas of disagreement are slight. Howard argues against the unities because they bind playwrights; he thinks taste, not mathematical rules, should govern the artist; and he dislikes rhyme in serious plays because it is not natural for people to converse in rhyme. Except on the issue of rhyme, these ideas are not very different from Dryden's. Howard rejects the efficacy of the unities, but Dryden does not adhere to them religiously; rather he admits them, but remains wary of their constraining effect and regards them as useful for "rais[ing] perfection higher where it is," but "not sufficient to give it where it is not," as Neander puts it in *An Essay of Dramatick Poesie.*

Nonetheless, despite the small apparent differences of opinion, Dryden's answer to Howard is downright nasty. The "Defence" includes fussy corrections of Howard's Latin translations, point-by-point dissections of his garbled syntax, interspersed with sarcastic cuts and contemptuous insults. One wonders how issues such as rhyme and the three unities could induce such anger. As is sometimes the case, however, the apparent occasion is not really the occasion. Dryden had other reasons for being furious with Howard, one of them political: the former chancellor, Edward Hyde, first Earl of Clarendon, who had been Dryden's patron, was now in public disgrace, and while Dryden was probably lamenting Clarendon's sorry state, Howard was attacking him (*The Duke of Lerma* was part of the attack), piling it on even after Clarendon had already suffered defeat and had gone into exile. And there were no doubt personal frictions between the two brothers-in-law, perhaps unavoidable given that the pompous Howard, Dryden's superior in rank, was now watching a former collaborator, a junior clerk whom Howard had helped get started on the stage, outstrip him as an author. No doubt there would have been fewer sparks flying if only Howard had had the same high opinion of Dryden's talent as Dryden had.

If we look behind Dryden's wrath, we find some familiar issues. In urging the case for rhyme, Dryden explains his reasons more fully than he had in *An Essay of Dramatick Poesie.* Certainly, blank verse (which is closer to prose than rhyme) is more natural than heroic couplets, but why should "bare imitation" of nature be a goal? Dryden has a different conception of what serious drama should accomplish. Rather than hold the mirror up to nature, plays should present characters who serve as models for emulation. It follows that plays are enhanced by unnatural rhetorical artifices, such as enriched metaphors and rhyme, because such devices heighten the intensity and the theatrical effect. Heroes should speak in rhyme because they are heroes, not ordinary mortals; to put it another way, rhyme, by being elevated, is natural for heroes. Besides, modern plays written in rhyme have pleased audiences (whatever the theory or the history, Dryden clinches his argument by pointing to the actual experience of the stage).

Dryden also adds something else. He says that should rhyme cease to please, "I will be the first who shall lay it down. For I confess my chief endeavours are to delight the Age in which I live. If the humour of this be for low Comedy, small Accidents, and Raillery, I will force my Genius to obey it, though with more reputation I could write in Verse. I know I am not so fitted by Nature to write Comedy." We not only hear Dryden readily complying to what the market will bear, but we also learn that his inclination is in another direction. Furthermore, Dryden's statement about what would happen should theatrical tastes change actually happened, because tastes changed: rhyme ceased to be popular, and Dryden *did* lay it down. This shift, from eagerly embracing rhyme to casting aside his "long-lov'd Mistris" (prologue to *Aureng-Zebe*, 1676), is one of the changes that has led some to accuse Dryden of inconsistency. He certainly changed his mind, but in adjusting his productions to the demands of the "Age in which I live," Dryden has remained consistent, consistent in suiting his practice to the tastes of his audience; he changed as did the age, and if one writes for a living, this is a sound procedure.

Dryden continues his case for serious drama in "Of Heroique Playes," a short prefatory essay appearing in the published version of *The Conquest of Granada* (1672), which, as one might expect, provides a rationale for the play to follow. Dryden does not bother to take up the issue of

OF HEROIQUE PLAYES.

An Essay.

Hether Heroique verse ought to be admitted into serious Playes, is not now to be disputed: 'tis already in possession of the Stage: and I dare confidently affirm, that very few Tragedies, in this Age, shall be received without it. All the arguments, which are form'd against it, can amount to no more than this, that it is not so near conversation as Prose; and therefore not so natural. But it is very clear to all, who understand Poetry, that serious Playes ought not to imitate Conversation too nearly. If nothing were to be rais'd above that level, the foundation of Poetry would be destroy'd. and, if you once admit of a Latitude, that thoughts may be exalted, and that Images and Actions may be rais'd above the life, and describ'd in measure without Rhyme, that leads you insensibly, from your own Principles to mine: You are already so far onward of your way, that you have forsaken the imitation of ordinary converse. You are gone beyond it; and, to continue where you are, is to lodge in the open field, betwixt two Inns. You have lost that which you call natural, and have not acquir'd the last perfection of Art. But it was onely custome which cozen'd

a 2　　　　　　　　　　　　　　　　　　　us

First page of the preface to The Conquest of Granada *(1672), in which Dryden continues the defense of his own dramatic practice that he began in* An Essay of Dramatick Poesie

rhyme again, deftly skirting it by declaring that since rhyme is "already in possession of the Stage," the argument is as good as settled. He expands somewhat on heightened imitation, working in a quotation from Petronius distinguishing between the historian who records real events, and the heroic author, a free spirit who strives after something more exalted. Dryden also takes pains to defend the play's hero, Almanzor, a problematic character; Almanzor is an uncompromising, noble soul who scorns the petty world beneath him, but he also looks like a posturing, egotistical, adolescent bully who keeps changing his allegiances at a whim. When he asserts that "I alone am King of me," he may be expressing su-

preme independence, but he is also likely to earn a few snickers for his blustering self-importance. In *The Rehearsal* (1671), Buckingham lampooned Almanzor (as the character Drawcansir) and the entire heroic mode, scoring some palpable hits upon Dryden, who appears as the playwright Bayes. Now that *The Conquest of Granada* was in print, Dryden found himself in the middle of another literary debate, only this time, rather than stooping to vitriolic counterattack, Dryden took the high road (he would get Buckingham later, in *Absalom and Achitophel*, 1681). In "Of Heroique Playes" Dryden justifies his ranting hero by linking him to Homer's Achilles and Tasso's Rinaldo (another arrogant, heroic bully, "who was a

151

copy" of Achilles), thereby invoking great authors of the past to imply that such as Homer is shall Dryden be. He elevates the genre by suggesting that Homer's central epic principle—union preserves a commonwealth, and discord destroys it—is also the central principle of *The Conquest of Granada*, and to make the connection tighter, he asserts that "an Heroick Play ought to be an imitation, in little, of an Heroick Poem."

Such an assertion is suggestive. Dryden had admitted in "A Defence of An Essay of Dramatique Poesie" (1668) that comedy and raillery, though popular on stage, were not his natural mode. Here, he is in a way hinting at the corollary, suggesting what his natural mode really is: the epic. As early as 1670, in his dedication to *Tyrannick Love*, Dryden had expressed an interest in writing an original epic, a subject he returned to repeatedly throughout his career. In his "Discourse concerning the Original and Progress of Satire" (1692), Dryden even sketches out the possibilities of building an English epic around the exploits of King Arthur. And Dryden would eventually get some satisfaction from producing a well-received translation of Virgil's *Aeneis* (1697), a partial fulfillment of his lifelong dream. But in 1672, as a busy playwright preoccupied with earning a reputation, Dryden was unable to turn his attention toward such a grand project. In advocating heroic drama and imposing upon it the requirements of the epic, however, Dryden is in effect accommodating his own inclinations to the tastes of the age: he has adopted a popular genre that is the closest he can get, as a playwright, to the epic he really wants to write.

In reaching back to Homer for a central epic principle applicable to *The Conquest of Granada*, Dryden is repeating the familiar operation of constructing a tradition, and he is fiddling with the facts in order to justify his own cause. He names Homer, Virgil, Statius, Ariosto, Tasso, and even Spenser, but he also pays particular attention to Davenant and his *Siege of Rhodes* (1656). Dryden conveniently minimizes his own debt to foreign sources, and to English plays from the Elizabethan and Jacobean eras—for instance, he nowhere mentions Christopher Marlowe, whose overreaching heroes are strikingly similar to Dryden's Almanzor. This is a clever ploy; by emphasizing the classics, Dryden invokes the authority of the noble and ancient past, but by tracing the line from Davenant to himself, Dryden also makes the ancient tradition seem new, fresh, and English. In Dryden's hands, the modern heroic play comes into its own with the return of the monarch, by which Dryden can hope to elicit support from the patriotic, who would probably be less impressed with the Englishness of all this if they recognized Dryden's debts to Pierre Corneille and French romances.

At the end of *The Conquest of Granada* Dryden included another essay, "Defence of the Epilogue. Or, An Essay on the Dramatique Poetry of the last Age," ostensibly an attempt to explain his criticisms of Ben Jonson that appear in the epilogue. Dryden argues that his own age, by being more civilized than the last, has improved the English stage. He maintains that Shakespeare, for all his greatness, keeps slipping into "some Solecism of Speech, or some notorious flaw in Sence," and he analyzes passages from Ben Jonson, finding numerous barbarities. Neither author is to be blamed. The fault is in the age: "the times were ignorant in which they liv'd." And in ignorant times, language itself was primitive, while in Dryden's gallant age, we witness "*An improvement of our Wit, Language, and Conversation; or, an alteration in them for the better.*"

When Dryden discussed playwrights of the previous age in *An Essay of Dramatick Poesie* (1667), he took a different position. There, he praised Shakespeare as "the largest and most comprehensive soul," faults notwithstanding; declared that Fletcher and Beaumont, "with the advantage of *Shakespeare*'s wit, which was their precedent," built upon that precedent and polished the language; and argued that "the most learned and judicious" Ben Jonson added regularity and correctness. One gets the sense that Dryden considers the accomplishments of that generation as supreme, difficult to match; Neander admits that Jonson, Fletcher, and Shakespeare "are honour'd, and almost ador'd by us, as they deserve; neither do I know any so presumptuous of themselves as to contend with them." In the "Defence of the Epilogue," however, Dryden dares to be presumptuous. If in one essay Shakespeare and his contemporaries seem to contain all there is, from richness, to polished wit, to correctness, in the later essay the present age of wit will obscure the past. Taken together, these opposing viewpoints suggest Dryden's difficulty in coming to grips with his predecessors. What remains constant is his admiration for the previous age; even when he claims that his own age is superior, he treats the grand old playwrights with respect, and he makes a revelatory comment: "let us render to our Predecessors what is their due, without confining our selves to a servile imitation of all they writ." This may explain why Dryden now seems eager to separate his age from the old days—so as to avoid "servile imitation." It may also provide us with an insight as to why Dryden takes such pains to promote heightened imitation. His heroic plays are a new mode, based presumably on classics and on epic rather than on English plays of the last generation; they are also Dryden's attempt to do something radically different, an attempt to match Elizabethan grandeur, but do it under new rules, since the Elizabethans and Jacobeans could not be beaten at their own game.

In 1668, after the death of William Davenant, Dryden became poet laureate. Although he had yet to write any of the poems for which he is chiefly remembered today, he had done all the right things, in all the right ways, to make himself the logical choice for the post. By 1668 he was England's leading playwright—in 1667 alone, five of his plays were in production on the London stage. He had shown himself to be a loyal defender of the court in *Annus Mirabilis* (1667). He had also written numerous smaller poems in praise of the right people. He even lent the king five hundred pounds (not repaid until 1673), a princely sum, considering that the stipend for laureate was one hundred pounds per annum (plus the traditional butt of wine), which Dryden seldom received on time. In 1670, after the death of James Howell, Dryden was appointed historiographer royal, which increased his total stipend to two hundred pounds per annum (also seldom paid on time). Little wonder that the essays attached to *The Conquest of Granada* sound assertive, judgmental, and confident. He had succeeded on stage, and as laureate, he had the official stamp of approval and the comforting promise of an annual pension. He could indulge in authoritative judgments of other dramatists, because he was now no longer Neander, the new man, but rather the established, successful, official poet.

In the years following *The Conquest of Granada*, however, Dryden's newfound sense of security began to unravel. The Theatre Royal in Bridges Street, where most of Dryden's plays had been performed, burned to the ground in 1672, plunging the King's Company, in which Dryden was a shareholder, into a financial crisis from which it would never recover. Furthermore, Dryden's patron, Thomas Clifford, who had helped secure overdue payments of the laureate's stipend, was pressured to resign his position as lord

treasurer because of his resistance to the Test Act; two months later (in 1673), Clifford hanged himself, which brought Dryden grief as well as further uncertainty. How was the laureate to obtain his pension, and what was he to do for a patron? Younger authors were competing against him in heroic drama, and more important, were winning potential patrons away from him. Younger authors, including his rival Thomas Shadwell, were also competing against Dryden in comedy, and one of Dryden's comedies, *The Assignation: or, Love in a Nunnery* (performed in 1672), proved to be an embarrassing flop. If at the time of *The Conquest of Granada* he could confidently declare that his plays were "already in possession of the Stage" ("Of Heroique Playes"), that was no longer true in the years to follow, and Dryden found himself struggling in an effort to retain his position as a prominent playwright, and to make money. He even wrote a potboiler, *Amboyna, or the Cruelties of the Dutch to the English Merchants* (probably performed in 1673), a propaganda piece aimed to coincide with England's entry into the Third Dutch War (1672-1674).

Dryden found himself reconsidering his former positions, especially his earlier advocacy of rhymed heroic drama. Undoubtedly, this was hastened by the gradual decline in the popularity of heroic plays, but Dryden had other reasons as well for moving in a different direction. He may have felt that he had exhausted the genre in *The Conquest of Granada* and that to write further heroic plays would be to risk becoming a servile imitator of himself. Also, he may have become sensitive to the limitations of the genre, and we get some hint of this from an anonymous pamphlet, *Notes and Observations on the Empress of Morocco* (1674), parts of which are probably by Dryden. The pamphlet attacks Elkanah Settle, one of those younger playwrights of minimal talent who had followed Dryden's lead into the heroic play. If Dryden did indeed contribute to the pamphlet, he was in essence satirizing some of the views he himself had previously endorsed. In ridiculing Settle, whose heroic drama was ludicrously bombastic, Dryden may have realized how close his own rhymed drama could have been to unintentional comedy, which would have been a difficult thing to admit openly, since this is precisely the charge that Buckingham leveled at Dryden; much of the humor in *The Rehearsal* arises from the laughable, chest-thumping behavior of its Drydenian characters.

Dryden circa 1683 (portrait by John Riley; from David Piper, The Development of the British
Literary Portrait up to Samuel Johnson, *1968)*

Dryden's last rhymed drama, *Aureng-Zebe*, was performed at the end of 1675. By the time the play was published, in 1676, Dryden was ready to acknowledge his change of heart. In the prologue, as already noted, he confesses that he is weary of rhyme; in the dedication, he refers to the "unsettl'dness of my condition" and explains some of the reasons why he has become dissatisfied with his own plays: "I never thought my self very fit for an Employment, where many of my Predecessors have excell'd me in all kinds; and some of my Contemporaries, even in my own partial Judgment, have out-done me in *Comedy*. Some little hopes I have yet remaining, and those too, considering my abilities, may be vain, that I may make the world some part of amends, for many ill Playes, by an Heroique Poem." The self-deprecating tone is part of Dryden's strategy, an attempt to win over the potentially sympathetic reader. Characteristically, Dryden ends on a posi-

tive note, emerging from his unsettled state with optimistic hopes of what he might yet accomplish, an epic of his own; he is not so much abandoning a genre out of frustration or disappointment as he is restlessly seeking to do something different. Although he did not produce an original epic, Dryden during the years after *The Conquest of Granada* began trying his hand at different kinds of poetry, including: a rhymed, opera-drama version of *Paradise Lost*, the satire *Mac Flecknoe* (written in 1676), a blank-verse adaptation of *Antony and Cleopatra*, the biblically resonant, heroic satire *Absalom and Achitophel* (1681). In a sense, one can regard all of these as experimental efforts at achieving some kind of grandeur, or in the case of *Mac Flecknoe*, mock grandeur, now that rhymed heroic drama no longer seemed an effective vehicle.

We get a sense of Dryden's unsettled condition not only from his experimentation with various genres, but also from a rambling essay, misleadingly entitled "The Author's Apology for Heroique Poetry, and Poetique License," that appears as the preface to *The State of Innocence* (published in 1677), Dryden's stage adaptation of *Paradise Lost*. The essay does deal with the heroic, but most of it is devoted to defending figurative language. Dryden no longer talks in terms of "Nature wrought up to an higher pitch"; instead, he refers to just plain "imitation of Nature," and he even wonders whether in some cases "the flights of Heroique Poetry" could be "concluded bombast, unnatural, and mere madness." This is certainly a new direction for Dryden, and yet he is not quite ready to abandon his former position. While he acknowledges the difficulties inherent in the genre, he still insists on the supremacy of heroic poetry, which he calls "the greatest work of humane Nature." He faces the problem of reconciling his belief in the nobility of the idiom with his growing awareness that "*Homer, Virgil, Tasso,* or *Milton's Paradice*" can seem "too far strained" and "all fustian and meer nonsense." What Dryden seems to want is exalted expression and naturalism at the same time. He tries to argue for both, leaning on Longinus and defending "boldness of expression," and then contending that there is nothing unnatural about this, especially if one is dealing with passions, which are both heightened and natural.

Dryden's blank-verse tragedy, *All for Love* (performed in 1677), confirms his shift away from the rhymed heroic and toward something new. In his preface (1678), which spends most of its energy attacking aristocrats who dare set up for poets and who may have recently satirized him (by which Dryden means John Wilmot, Earl of Rochester), Dryden proclaims that he has "disincumber'd" himself from rhyme in order to imitate Shakespeare more freely. Although Dryden earlier had advocated superhuman heroes as models for emulation, he now prefers his central characters to be fallible human beings, imperfect, but not wicked, who would be capable of evoking pity, an idea lifted straight from Aristotle. Dryden also explains that he has regularized the "Divine *Shakespeare*" by observing the unities "more exactly . . . than, perhaps, the *English* Theater requires," and more exactly, one might add, than Dryden has previously required. While these ideas all reflect changes, they also reflect Dryden's continued interest in achieving grandeur, which is also apparent in his attempt to rewrite Milton, and then imitate Shakespeare. One

can also detect in Dryden an increased confidence in his own poetic powers, even while he is reexamining premises and reconsidering what drama should be and how it should operate. Instead of trying to outreach the immortal Shakespeare in some new, exalted genre, Dryden now has the confidence to take on Shakespeare directly and attempt to refine him. For us, tampering with Shakespeare seems sacrilegious, but for Dryden, it represented an opportunity to synthesize two apparently contrary attitudes: he placed the Shakespeare on a pedestal, but he also claimed that the present age was more civilized than the past. By adjusting Shakespeare's *Antony and Cleopatra* to the more refined present, which meant reducing the number of characters, excluding large actions from the stage, and reorganizing the plot so as to conform to the three unities, Dryden could satisfy both claims.

Sometime between the production and the publication of *All for Love*, Dryden had read Thomas Rymer's *Tragedies of the Last Age* (published in 1677, but dated 1678), which may explain Dryden's renewed interest in discussing Aristotle and the unities. Rymer, a rigid neoclassicist who felt that English drama had gone astray and who tried to correct it by enforcing classical precedent, had in effect challenged Dryden, whose criticism, even when it faulted previous authors, was consistently patriotic in advancing the claims of English drama, in building a lineage, and in arguing for a progress. Dryden's considered response to Rymer's challenge came in a long essay that appears in *Troilus and Cressida* (published in 1679); it is actually two essays joined, the first a brief preface, largely concerned with explaining how Dryden has "new modelled" Shakespeare's play, the second "The Grounds of Criticism in Tragedy," wherein Dryden answers Rymer. However, before this, probably sometime in 1677, Dryden scribbled some notes to himself in the endpapers of his own copy of Rymer's *Tragedies of the Last Age*, notes that were later published (in 1711) as "Heads of an Answer to Rymer." This is a rough, exploratory piece, with Dryden attempting to defeat Rymer's inflexible classicism in order to restore the English tradition Rymer had attacked. But Dryden finds himself in a quandary. Try as he might, he cannot overthrow the rules derived from the ancients; he ventures out with different arguments, proposes possible approaches, but each trail leads to a dead end.

When we turn from "Heads of an Answer to Rymer" to "The Grounds of Criticism in Tragedy," however, we find Dryden emerging from his quandary with a different line of attack. Unable to dismiss Rymer's classicism, Dryden instead appropriates it and uses Rymer's own weapon to defend the English tradition. "The Grounds of Criticism in Tragedy" begins with an approving summary of Aristotle, and then expands into a discussion that employs a shrewd, double-edged rhetorical strategy. First, Dryden discusses Sophocles, Euripides, Fletcher, and Shakespeare all at the same time, moving back and forth, approving and criticizing each of them, which of course puts the English playwrights on the same plane as the classical authors. Second, Dryden demonstrates how often Sophocles and Euripides fall short of adhering to Aristotelian rules, while Fletcher and Shakespeare at times display classical features. Such an argument entails considerable strain, since the English dramatic tradition is indigenous, not classical, its plays relying upon complex interactions of multiple characters in multiple plots, quite unlike the more focused, unitary drama of the Greek stage. Dryden is imposing a progression on a discontinuity, but this is understandable, given his interest in both shaping and elevating his native theatrical tradition. He may be stretching his argument, but he does so with a larger purpose, and that in itself distinguishes him from Rymer. Like many a lesser critic, Rymer's main talent lies in ridiculing mistakes, in "finding out a poets blind sides," as Dryden explains in a letter to his patron, Charles Sackville, Earl of Dorset; Dryden, by contrast, is not so much a faultfinder as a tradition builder.

In "The Grounds of Criticism in Tragedy" (1679), we also discover Dryden backing further away from some of his previous positions. As noted before, he had begun to question the idea of "Nature wrought up to an higher pitch" in "The Author's Apology for Heroique Poetry, and Poetique License" (1677); now, using the same metaphor, he suggests that tuning the passions to a higher pitch can be ruinous, "for what melody can be made on that Instrument, all whose strings are screw'd up at first to their utmost stretch." And although in "The Author's Apology" he had argued for boldness of expression, he now discards highly wrought figurative language as unnatural, taking as a bad example his own metaphoric excesses in *The Indian Emperour* (1665). With the publication of his tragicomedy, *The Spanish Fryar* (1681), Dryden's public rejection of his earlier accomplishments becomes

more overt and uncompromising. In his prefatory letter, he confesses that as he reads *Tyrannick Love* (1670) and *The Conquest of Granada* (1672), his own verses "cry, Vengeance upon me for their Extravagance." To his self-criticism, he adds some petulant remarks about the medium of the theater. "In a Playhouse," he asserts, "every thing contributes to impose upon the judgment; the Lights, the Scenes, the Habits, and, above all, the Grace of Action . . . But these false Beauties of the Stage are no more lasting than a Rainbow." It is because of the delusive, spectacle-filled stage that many, including Dryden, have willingly produced "abominable fustian," which is "bad enough to please"; Dryden resolves that he henceforth "will settle my self no reputation by the applause of fools. 'Tis not that I am mortified to all ambition, but I scorn as much to take it from half-witted Judges." This contempt for his audience is in part snobbery, gentleman Dryden attempting to separate himself from the vulgar rabble; it is also in part the normal frustration of any professional author who wishes to write one way, has to write another to meet public demand, and finds himself resentful and eager to please at the same time. His shift away from extravagance and toward naturalism, evident in both "The Grounds of Criticism in Tragedy" and the introductory letter to *The Spanish Fryar*, is little more than the final step in Dryden's gradual abandonment of exalted heroic drama and overwrought language. And his disarming self-criticism is his way of announcing that he has grown, has moved away from the genres of his early years, and is ready for new genres and new challenges.

As fate would have it, the political crises of the 1680s allowed Dryden to leave drama and turn toward the published poetry for which he is now primarily remembered. The heating up of political battles, involving Shaftesbury's attempts to exclude the duke of York (James II) from the throne and get Charles II to acknowledge as his heir his illegitimate son, the duke of Monmouth, induced the laureate to come to the service of his king, which Dryden did by writing the grand, Miltonic *Absalom and Achitophel* (1681) and the grandly vituperative *The Medall* (1682). The great public success of the former no doubt helped Dryden rise above his earlier unsettled position, although it also made him the target for attacks in print. Following the success of *Absalom and Achitophel*, Dryden was able to raise his fees for prologues and epilogues, which he began to pro-

PLUTARCH

Illustration from volume 1 (1683) of the translation of Plutarch's Lives *that includes Dryden's life of the Greek biographer*

duce in abundance. A pirated edition of his earlier satire, *Mac Flecknoe* (written in 1676), was published in 1682, the same year that saw the publication of his *Religio Laici*. By 1684 Dryden was no longer only the playwright laureate, but also England's leading living poet, which was confirmed when Jacob Tonson's *Miscellany Poems* (1684) appeared, a volume containing twenty-six Dryden poems, including reprints of *Absalom and Achitophel*, *The Medall*, and *Mac Flecknoe*, as well as new translations of Virgil, Theocritus, and Ovid. During the same period, Dryden paid less attention to the stage, producing only *The Spanish Fryar* (performed in 1680, published in 1681), and collaborating with Nathaniel Lee on *The Duke of Guise* (acted in 1682, published in 1683), a highly charged political play that attacks Mon-

mouth (represented by Guise) and the Protestant Association.

The decade of the 1680s, although filled with some of Dryden's greatest accomplishments as a poet, contained little in the way of criticism. When he turned to prose, the issues that occupied his attention were not so much literary as political. In 1681 he wrote a pamphlet titled *His Majesties Declaration Defended*, which amounts to more Tory propaganda on behalf of Charles, defending the king's recent dismissal of two parliaments (although the evidence for authorship is inconclusive, recent scholarship suggests that the pamphlet is probably by Dryden). Dryden's *The Vindication [of the Duke of Guise]* (1683), like his earlier "Defence of An Essay of Dramatique Poesie" (1668), is an embarrassing piece of self-jus-

Frontispiece for the translation of Louis Maimbourg's The History of the League *that Dryden undertook in 1684, probably by command of Charles II*

tification, a point-by-point rebuttal of his critics, a work that does not engage large issues, but instead squirms its way through the specious argument that Dryden and Lee's play does not contain the political parallels it obviously does contain. In 1684 Dryden translated Louis Maimbourg's *The History of the League*, another piece of political propaganda, a chore apparently assigned to the historiographer royal by the king himself. The only significant critical work from this period is Dryden's preface to an edition of *Ovid's Epistles* (1680), and his preface to another Tonson miscellany, *Sylvae* (1685). Between these two interesting essays, he wrote a "Life of Plutarch" (1683), his first venture into literary biography, occasionally cited as a pioneering experiment in this as yet unestablished English genre.

(It is in this essay that Dryden coins the word *biography*.) There is less here than meets the eye: Dryden's "Life of Plutarch" is a piece of hackwork, mostly derivative, an example of Dryden in a hurry, patching together summaries from various sources, rather than Dryden at his reflective and exploratory best.

While engaged in these political projects, Dryden, intellectually restless as ever, was examining issues of faith, which is apparent in his *Religio Laici* (1682), a poem that defends the Anglican church, with Dryden, as usual, arguing different religious positions before settling on the Anglican solution. Dryden's soul-searching would ultimately lead to his conversion to Catholicism sometime late in 1685 (the first hard evidence we have of his conversion is John Evelyn's account of Dryden attending mass in January of 1686). The death of his king in 1685, and the rumors of Charles's deathbed conversion to the Catholic faith, in all likelihood influenced Dryden powerfully, as did his extensive reading in theological tracts and disputes (which has only recently been documented). Once he converted, the man who had argued for the Anglican cause in *Religio Laici* daringly published a poem arguing for the Catholic cause, *The Hind and the Panther* (1687). As he might have expected, his enemies gleefully noticed the conflicting positions taken in these poems, and, although *Religio Laici* on its publication was greeted by public indifference, after 1687 it was resurrected and used as a club by those eager to batter the newly converted laureate. Like his changed attitude toward rhyme in drama, and his change of mind about heightened imitation, his religious conversion is no sudden or unexpected defection, but merely the next step in a process of self-scrutiny; Dryden proves to be a man not content to rest on unexamined principles, or to lead an unexamined life.

The occasional poems from this period include two fine elegies, one the restrained "To the Memory of Mr. Oldham" (1684), the other an exalted Pindaric ode, "To the Pious Memory Of the Accomplisht Young Lady Mrs Anne Killigrew" (1685). The death of two young poets, John Oldham, a vigorous though "rugged" fellow satirist, and Anne Killigrew, a minor talent who wrote conventional pastoral verse as well as Pindarics, gave Dryden the opportunity to reexamine his role as a poet. In the Oldham poem, Dryden speaks with low-keyed pride about his own preeminence as a satirist. In the Killigrew ode, on the other hand, he speaks self-critically, praising Anne as a pure poet who might serve as a recompense for those who, like Dryden, have been "hurry'd down / This lubrique and adult'rate age" of obscene playwrighting. Coming near the time of his conversion, and just before *The Hind and the Panther*, this is Dryden's confession that he has wasted his time on what he unflatteringly calls "the steaming Ordures of the Stage." As before, he discredits drama, although in this case it is not the puffed heroic but the racy plays he once willingly wrote for an audience eager for that kind of fare. (One should observe that compared to the rest of Restoration drama Dryden's plays are not particularly filthy.) Dryden's self-examination, in these poems and in the self-critical essays of the last few years, suggests his growing awareness of his greater responsibilities—he should

not and cannot stoop to the low tastes of an audience, as he once did. He may have accepted greater responsibilities, may have demanded more of himself, after realizing that he was now a greater poet from whom more was expected.

These two entirely new genres for Dryden—the confessional *Religio Laici* and the beast fable, *The Hind and the Panther*—reveal the poet moving outward in new directions. We also see this movement in his contributions to *Sylvae*, which contains interesting experiments in versification, including anapestic meter, tetrameter couplets, and stanzaically irregular Pindarics (the Killigrew ode is also a Pindaric). That he allows himself to listen to youthful poets, such as Oldham and Anne Killigrew, suggests that Dryden is in a retrospective mode, admiring youthful promise now that he himself is middle-aged, and seeking from younger talents guidance for the rest of his career, looking backward with both pride and disappointment, while also looking forward with hope. Retrospective Dryden also looks further back, seeking guidance from a deeper source; his contributions to *Ovid's Epistles* (1680) and *Sylvae* (1685) mark his rediscovery of the ancient authors he had long admired. These anthologies also mark the beginning of a new phase of Dryden's career; the playwright who developed into a poet had just begun to turn toward translation, an enterprise that would increasingly occupy his attention for the rest of his life.

Dryden's prefatory essays to the Ovid collection and to *Sylvae* are companion pieces in that they both analyze the qualities of good translations, and defend the necessity of artistry on the part of the translator, a point that in all probability became more obvious to Dryden as he ploughed through the stultifying translations by John Ogilby and by Thomas Hobbes, both of whom Dryden mentions. In his preface to *Ovid's Epistles*, Dryden makes his famous distinction between three kinds of translation, ranging from the doggedly literal "Metaphrase," to the extremely free "Imitation," with "Paraphrase," that is, translation with latitude, standing in the middle. Given the differences in language and idiom, literal translation fails to capture the essential spirit of the author, while free translation, such as Abraham Cowley's Pindarics, captures instead the spirit of the translator. Not too surprisingly, Dryden, who was in the habit of arguing one side of the case, then the other, and setting up an apparent via media position, does the same thing here. The man who in *Religio Laici* began heading toward an apparent mean with the words "What then remains, but, waving each Extreme, / The Tides of Ignorance, and Pride to stem," here adopts a similar strategy. Having discussed the limitations of literal metaphrase and the excesses of unbridled imitation, Dryden insists that "the two Extreams . . . ought to be avoided; and therefore . . . I have propos'd the mean betwixt them."

This habit of arguing two extremes and settling in the center has led some critics to regard Dryden as a moderate, someone who perpetually searches for the middle of the road, but one should reflect that this is a rhetorical strategy designed to make Dryden *appear* moderate. In *Religio Laici* he does not quite waive both extremes—individual interpretation of the scriptures versus reliance on age-old tradition—but rather leans toward tradition, leaning all the way by converting to Catholicism within a few years. And in his translations, he is not halfway between literal and free, as he implies, although this is difficult to recognize in our own age, when Latin and Italian originals are Greek to most modern readers, who are thus unlikely to recognize Dryden's substantial alterations. While he comes nowhere near the flights of a Cowley, who tends to use the original as a musical subject on which he composes high-flown variations, Dryden's own changes, subtractions, and additions to his versions to Homer, Virgil, or fellow Englishman Chaucer, entail considerable latitude—what we read is Homer, Virgil, or Chaucer with a heavy Dryden accent.

Dryden's preface to *Sylvae* (1685) continues the argument for liberal translation, paying homage to the ideas expressed by Wentworth Dillon, Earl of Roscommon, in his *Essay on translated Verse* (1684); Dryden then expands into a comparative stylistic account of Virgil, Theocritus, Horace, and Lucretius, with sidelong attention to Ovid and Claudian. Virgil outshines the rest, but because he is both majestic and succinct, traits that are difficult to combine in English, he is a "plague to Translatours," and a supreme challenge to Dryden. Although Virgil may have priority, what Dryden seems to appreciate is the variety of style and tone available, from brisk, good-humored Horace, to rough Lucretius, to simple, pastoral Theocritus, to witty, but sometimes overly witty, Ovid. Dryden is doing what he did with the lineage of Elizabethan playwrights, sorting, comparing, criticizing, even establishing a progress (the rough Lucretius came before the re-

finement in language and custom that made Virgil possible). And as he nostalgically tours the classics, to "renew" his "old acquaintance" with the authors he admires, Dryden still acts as a tradition builder. Behind his interest in translating ancient authors without losing their individual personalities and idiosyncratic beauties, in rendering each of the past masters as "if he were living, and an *Englishman*," lies Dryden's goal of planting the classical tradition in English soil.

As the 1680s came to a close, Dryden entered the last phase of his career. He paid his final tribute to Charles II with a funeral Pindaric, *Threnodia Augustalis* (1685), which hopefully stresses the links between the passing regime and the one to come, with sufficient efficacy to get Dryden's laureateship renewed by James II. Dryden served his new monarch with loyalty, in 1688 celebrating the birth of a male heir to the throne with *Britannia Rediviva*, a poem that endorses the official order, but with a sense of apprehensive urgency rather than with confidence. Knowing the warlike character of his king, Dryden admonishes him to act with justice and moderation, traits alien to the stubborn, authoritative James, whose heavy-handed attempts to impose Catholicism on England would soon bring about his own downfall. James was in flight within a few weeks of the publication of *Britannia Rediviva*, and William of Orange on his way from Holland to accept the English throne. As the so-called Glorious Revolution of 1688 unfolded, bringing in a new Protestant order, Dryden, who had long served as spokesman for the Stuart dynasty, found himself entering the most troublesome and frustrating period of his life. Unwilling to forswear his Catholicism, he lost his post as laureate and now faced the prospect of writing not as the spokesman of the established order, but as an outsider confronting a hostile regime that regarded him with suspicion. As a professed Catholic, and a prominent one at that, he had to struggle to survive during a period when Catholics were doubly taxed, perpetually harassed, and occasionally imprisoned. The man who had steadfastly endorsed the lineal succession of the monarchy in *Absalom and Achitophel* and *The Medall* now had to accommodate himself to a usurping, foreign king he could not endure, and while Dryden at first harbored hopes for a return of James, these were soon to be dashed by William's decisive defeat of the Jacobite forces at the Battle of Boyne in July of 1690.

Dryden, now moving into his sixties, had to endure everything from small nuisances, such as watching his nemesis Shadwell succeed him as laureate, to large difficulties, such as having to scramble to secure a reliable income now that his pension was gone. He also began to suffer from frequent bouts of gout which, aside from causing him physical pain, also periodically forced him to put aside some of the writing on which he depended for survival. Nonetheless, he produced some of his richest poetry during the troublesome final years of his life; the outcast laureate managed to write four plays, an opera, contributions to two further miscellanies of verse translations (*Satires of Juvenal and Persius* in 1692, and *Examen Poeticum* in 1693), a steady flow of occasional poems, prologues, epilogues, not to mention his translation of Virgil (1697) and his last anthology, *Fables Ancient and Modern* (1700). Much of his writing in his last decade is filled with allusions to his unfortunate plight and with scathing criticisms of the Williamite government. At times, Dryden whines, as in his prefatory letter to *Examen Poeticum*, which begins with an unattractive display of self-pity coupled with self-righteousness. At other times, he treats his "bad circumstances" with engaging self-mockery, as in the prologue to *Don Sebastian* (performed in 1689, published in 1690), where he jokes about the double tax rates imposed upon Catholics, and about the prohibition against their owning a horse worth more than five pounds.

Most often, however, Dryden accommodates himself to the regime he despised by relying upon satire and innuendo, a natural instinct, both because humor is the one recourse available to artists who feel themselves trapped in a politically repressive environment, and because satire was as basic to Dryden as breathing. As he accurately put it in his poem "To Sir Godfrey Kneller" (1694), "Satire will have room where e'er I write." His plays *Don Sebastian* (performed in 1689), *Amphitryon* (performed in 1690), *Cleomenes* (finished in 1689, performed in 1692), and his opera *King Arthur* (written in 1684, revised and performed in 1691) all bristle with political innuendo; indeed, *Cleomenes* was temporarily banned from performance because of suspected Jacobite sympathies, with Dryden having to demonstrate that any resemblance between an exiled monarch in *Cleomenes* and a recently deposed James II was purely coincidental. Faced with continued inconveniences because of his political allegiances and his unfashionable religion, Dryden

nonetheless seemed to take every opportunity to castigate warlike William and the inauspicious times, so much so, that one often wonders how he could get away with his pointed remarks. But that is one of the beauties of satire. When in the Kneller poem Dryden attacks an invading, "rude Northern Race" and the "stupid Military State" that together repress the arts, he clearly means to indict the monarch recently arrived from Holland, who had just plunged England into what historians still call "King William's War" (1686-1697), but ostensibly the passage refers to the Goths and Vandals of the Dark Ages who destroyed the ancient splendors of Greece and Rome; thus, Dryden could make his criticism clear without making it clear that he was criticizing.

Dryden's prose work during the 1690s includes some rapidly churned out pieces, including the derivative "Character of Polybius and His Writings" (1693), and a "Life of Lucian," written in 1696, perhaps suppressed, and published posthumously in 1711. Dryden also translated Charles Alphonse du Fresnoy's *De Arte Graphica*, to which he affixed an essay entitled "A Parallel of Poetry and Painting" (1695), sometimes cited approvingly as the first study in English of the relationship between the sister arts, an essay that Pope, who was to explore the subject more thoroughly, admired. "A Parallel of Poetry and Painting" may be another "first" in critical history, but it is sheer hackwork, written in twelve days by a man who knew little about painting. Dryden's sympathy for painting is at best limited, as his poem to Godfrey Kneller implies. In addressing Kneller, who was the official painter of his monarchs as Dryden had been their official poet, Dryden dutifully acknowledges painting as a sister art, but at crucial points, he makes her a weak sister; back in the days of innocence, Eve sang hymns, demonstrating that poetry came first, "Before she fell with Pride, and learn'd to paint."

Dryden also produced more substantial essays, most notably his "Discourse concerning the Original and Progress of Satire" which is prefixed to *Satires of Juvenal and Persius* (1692), and his dedication to his translation of the *Aeneis* (1697). Both essays are distinguished by being detailed, lengthy studies of a literary genre, although arguably the "Discourse concerning the Original and Progress of Satire" is the more interesting of the two. It is his one essay perhaps closest to modern literary history, with Dryden going back to the very origin of a genre, "from its first

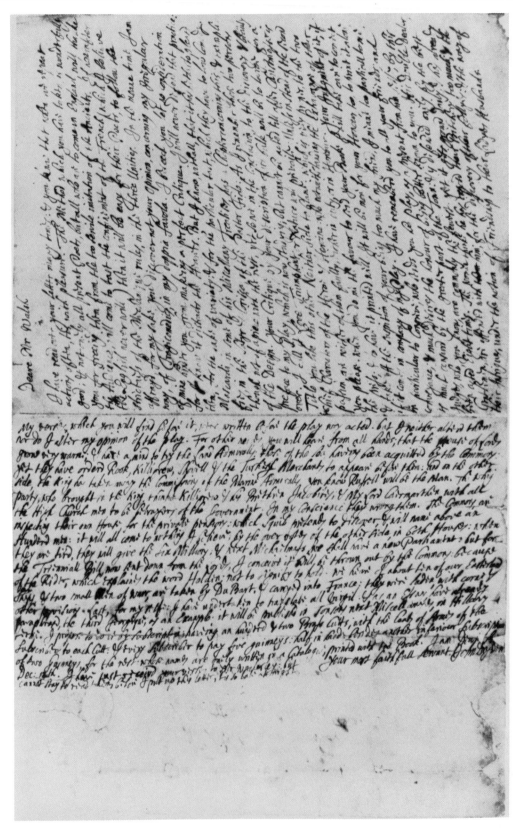

Letter to poet and critic William Walsh (12 December 1693), in which Dryden discusses his soon-to-be-acted play, Love
Triumphant, *and William Congreve's* The Double Dealer, *for which Dryden provided prefatory verses
(MA 130; by permission of the Pierpont Morgan Library)*

Rudiments of Barbarity, to its last Polishing and Perfection," summarizing and debating scholarly commentators. This may be Dryden's most conspicuously learned piece, although most readers will find his leisurely and redundant critical summaries of Casaubon, Scaliger, and Dacier far less interesting than those places where Dryden leaves the critics behind and instead ventures his own personal opinions. This occurs in his extended comparative account of Horace and Juvenal, which, like his comparisons between Shakespeare and Jonson, is Dryden at his best, discriminating, persuasive, practical minded, and neatly balanced. Having described the purpose of literature as teaching and delighting, and the function of satire as exposing folly and excoriating vice, Dryden sees Horace as the more profitable instructor, Juvenal the more delightful poet, Horace as the master in exposing folly, Juvenal as the supreme scourger of vices. Like Dryden's other balancing acts, he may seem to totter back and forth, but the scale does, eventually, come down firmly at one end. Dryden prefers Juvenal to Horace (he prefers both to Persius), largely, one suspects, because the direct attack on great vices from an indignant satirist living in "an Age that deserv'd a more severe Chastisement" seemed more personally relevant to a disgruntled former laureate who felt honor bound to continue to lash out at William III and his "stupid Military State."

Far from being a disinterested survey of a literary form, Dryden's study of satire also serves the important purpose of dignifying his own genre by fleshing out its heritage and assigning it noble motives. And although he says little about English satire explicitly, he does offhandedly mention his own *Absalom and Achitophel* and *Mac Flecknoe* with humble but well-considered approval. He also manages to praise fellow satirists in passing, often while criticizing them—he had done the same thing in his poem to John Oldham (1684), whom he praised for sharp satire, but criticized for being somewhat harsh and uneven. In "Discourse concerning the Original and Progress of Satire," Dryden mentions Samuel Butler's *Hudibras* (1663-1678) with affection, but argues, as only a working poet would, about the disadvantages of tetrameter in English verse, and the advantages of the heroic couplet. He also praises John Donne's talent as a satirist, but laments his imperfect versification and his annoying habit of perplexing "the Minds of the Fair Sex with nice Speculations of Philosophy." Casual

as Dryden's remarks on Donne are, they have had an important bearing on literary history; in commenting that Donne "affects the Metaphysicks," Dryden coins the term, reinforced later by Samuel Johnson in his *Life of Cowley*, that we still use to describe the unusual, intellectualized poetry of Donne and his contemporaries.

Dryden's account of the noble motives behind satire, and his insistence on the difference between virtuous satire and libelous lampoon, establish the more or less standard defense of the genre. When we read Pope's urbane discussion of satire in his Horatian imitations of the 1730s, for instance, we are in many ways reading an elegant expansion and versification of Dryden's arguments (which are also Horace's arguments). Similarly, Dryden's definition of satire as "fine Raillery," and his remark that "there is still a vast difference betwixt the slovenly Butchering of a Man, and the fineness of a stroak that separates the Head from the Body, and leaves it standing in its place," have become frequently quoted descriptions of satire's sly methods. However, here Dryden is pushing things, defending his satirical bent by going on the offensive and claiming the field for virtue. While it is true that Dryden used the deft slash, it is also true that he could bludgeon his victims to a pulp. Calling Shaftesbury a "formidable Cripple" and his Whig followers "Frogs and Toads, and all the Tadpole Train" in *The Medall* is not exactly a fine stroke, and when Dryden disparages scurrilous lampoons because "We have no Moral right on the Reputation of other Men," it is difficult to keep a straight face. One wonders what Shadwell would have thought of such a claim.

More convincing, perhaps, is Dryden's account of his unfulfilled plans to write an original epic. After proposing a model for an English epic, arguing that it would be possible to write an epic with a Christian hero, using Christian machinery in place of the colorful but preposterous classical gods, Dryden wistfully admits that he has been unable to attempt the task. In the most confessional passage in "Discourse concerning the Original and Progress of Satire," he again alludes to his plight: "now Age has overtaken me; and Want, a more insufferable Evil, through the Change of the Times, has wholly disenabl'd me." He mentions that he has served two kings "more Faithfully than Profitably to my self," but he agrees to suffer patiently under the third king. Dryden does not so much lash out or grumble as accept his fate; instead of self-righteous indigna-

The portrait of Dryden painted for bookseller Jacob Tonson by James Maubert in about 1695 (by permission of the National Portrait Gallery, London)

tion, he expresses disappointment, directed not just at the hostile age, but also at himself. He seems to hope that, if he has not written his epic, he has "at least chalk'd out a way, for others to amend my Errors in a like Design." Looking to the future, and to future hopefuls, may take the edge off his bitterness, as it does, for example, in his poem "To my Dear Friend Mr. Congreve" (1694). Here, Dryden stabs at the bad times, as usual, making direct hits on the nonlineal king, and on Shadwell and Rymer (who had succeeded to the post of historiographer royal after Shadwell's death in 1692). But if English kingship has gone the way of William and English poetry has gone the way of that prince of dullness,

Shadwell, still Dryden can hope to keep the values of the true laurel intact and pass them on to a worthy successor. By anointing young William Congreve, and asking him to "shade those Lawrels which descend to You," Dryden can appease his indignation and find a modicum of compensation for his own sense of disappointment and displacement.

By the time Dryden finished his translation of the *Aeneis* (1697), a difficult labor of three years, there was no need to seek psychological compensation. His translation was a popular success, with the advance subscriptions providing enough revenues to make Dryden feel more secure. That the subscribers included men of every political stripe, Catholics and Protestants, Jacobite sympathizers as well as staunch Whigs, gave Dryden reason to feel that his art had transcended partisan politics. When the stewards for the St. Cecilia's Day Feast visited Dryden to ask him to write the ode for the 1697 celebration, their request must have confirmed the success of his *Aeneis* and marked a moment of personal triumph, especially since Dryden had last written the official ode in 1687, and the intervening years saw that assignment fall into the hands of such lackluster luminaries as Thomas Durfey, Theophilus Parsons, Nicholas Brady, and Thomas Shadwell. The Pindaric ode Dryden supplied for 1697, *Alexander's Feast*, is a celebration of his moment of triumph, a remarkably ebullient poem from a poet who only recently had been complaining about his own sad circumstances.

Behind the ode's purpose of demonstrating the power of music, and providing composer Jeremiah Clarke the opportunity of displaying a host of different musical effects (in a score long since lost), lies a recurrent Drydenian concern. As we watch the poem's hero, the bard Timotheus, create a song that exerts control over the moods and actions of the supposedly great Alexander, we recognize Dryden making a statement about the awesome power of the artist, in this case, the power of the artist to manage monarchs, as Dryden liked to think he was doing when he was laureate, as he liked to think he was doing now, when even as an outsider he was addressing comments to his king. In the dedication to the *Aeneis*, Dryden continued to develop the theme of the artist's power, emphasizing the parallels between himself and Virgil, both writing in an age when "the Old Form of Government was subverted," and between his monarch and Augustus, both usurping kings who came to rule "by force of Arms, but seemingly by the Consent of the . . . People." In praising Virgil because he "dext'rously . . . mannag'd both the Prince and People," Dryden expresses his own hope to accomplish similarly constructive goals. If he could not write his own English epic, he could take some satisfaction in acting as England's Virgil, in advising his king, whether or not the king approved, and in achieving a great translation "for the honour of my Country."

Most of Dryden's dedication to the *Aeneis* is devoted to an account of the epic, an enterprise roughly comparable to his survey of satire in "Discourse concerning the Original and Progress of Satire." However, Dryden does not so much cover the history of the epic as defend Virgil, arguing that anachronisms are acceptable, that weeping heroes can be effective (more so than Homer's raging heroes), that epic similes enrich the poem rather than impede the action. This section of the dedication is largely an adaptation of Jean Regnauld de Segrais's preface to his own *Enéid* (1668), as Dryden readily admits, and although it occupies the bulk of the essay, it is not terribly interesting, because Dryden is summarizing rather than criticizing. The more interesting portions are the plentiful digressions and asides, where Dryden, writing "in a loose, Epistolary way," offers his own opinions. In some cases we hear him rehearsing previous positions, and even referring back to his earlier treatments of certain topics, in effect building a convenient anthology of his own favorite Dryden critical opinions. He once again summarizes the unities, this time declaring that Aristotle drew his "Rules of imitating Nature" from Homer and "fitted" them to the drama; he then advocates flexible application of the rules, because it is "better a Mechanick Rule were stretch'd or broken, than a great Beauty were omitted." This seems to be Dryden's final opinion on the subject, both favoring the unities and resisting their restrictive force, but of course this is also what Dryden had advocated as early as *An Essay of Dramatick Poesie* (1667). Echoing his commentary in the preface to *The Spanish Fryar* (1681), Dryden makes the case for the superiority of written literature to drama, arguing again that "many things" that "are real Beauties in the reading, wou'd appear absurd upon the Stage," a position he may have felt more comfortable with now that he had re-created the heroic Aeneas, "a Character of perfect Virtue," without risking the danger of producing an Almanzor who would be laughed at and parodied for his arrogant bullying. Dryden also continues his defense of liberal translation, begun in the prefaces to *Ovid's Epistles* (1680) and *Sylvae* (1685), maintaining that his own version of Virgil lies "betwixt the two Extreams, of Paraphrase, and literal Translation," and affirming that as translator his purpose is "to make *Virgil* speak such *English*, as he wou'd himself have spoken, if he had been born in *England*, and in this present Age"—and one might add, if he had been Dryden.

If in parts of the dedication we encounter summaries of old arguments, in other parts, we see Dryden stepping into new territory, particularly when he begins to talk about the capacities of individual languages, a topic that is naturally

Dryden circa 1698 (portrait by Sir Godfrey Kneller; by permission of the Master and Fellows of Trinity College, Cambridge)

fresh in the mind of a man who has just spent three years laboring on a major translation. His specific comments on the distinctions between Latin and English are pragmatic explanations of the difficulties he encountered in moving from a concise language, sweet sounding because of its balanced distribution of vowels and consonants, to a wordier language, harsher sounding because of its abundance of consonants and frequent use of monosyllables. Along the way, Dryden drops the tantalizing hint that he has been working on a treatise, an "*English Prosodia*, containing all the Mechanical Rules of Versification," another project that, like the original English epic, apparently never got past the dreaming stage. His interest in refining his language can be traced back to his ear-

lier years; in his dedicatory letter to *Troilus and Cressida* (1679), he had lamented that French grammars and dictionaries were well in advance of comparable English ventures, and in the 1680s he apparently joined the earl of Roscommon in planning a society for fixing the standards of English, an enterprise about which we know next to nothing.

Dryden's attitude toward the English language in the dedication to the *Aeneis* is an interesting combination of self-consciousness and pride, depending on whether he looks back through history, or just across the channel. On the one hand, he finds English "much inferiour to *Latin*," and confesses that he has had to coin Latinisms in order to increase the native linguistic treasury with "sounding Words" suitable for achieving Virgilian richness. On the other hand, when Dryden turns to French, a language he finds purer than English, he proudly makes a case for the superiority of his own imperfect, irregular tongue. French "is not strung with Sinews like our *English*. It has the nimbleness of a Greyhound, but not the bulk and body of a Mastiff. . . . Like their Tongue is the Genius of their Poets, light and trifling in comparison of the *English*." Thus, French is "more proper for Sonnets, Madrigals, and Elegies," while English, because of its "Masculine Vigour," is suitable for the noblest of all literary genres, heroic poetry.

Dryden's balancing of the virtues of French against those of English—this time the scale descends on one side with a swift thud—serves a twofold purpose. First, it provides a justification for the superiority of Dryden's English translation of Virgil to all the presumably lightweight French competitors. If Dryden's argument holds, then it is impossible for anybody writing in French to do justice to a majestic epic. Second, Dryden's comparative discussion of languages enables him once again to pay an honor to his own country, this time by thumbing his nose at a favorite target, the French. Lisideius had argued for the superiority of the French stage, and Neander had responded by taking the side of the less constrained and richer English theatrical tradition, a typical example of Dryden mixing his admiration for French accomplishments with an unshakable belief in the superiority of his native heritage. Moving away from the theater and to the more basic issue of the languages themselves, Dryden takes his case a step further: now, he makes French literary deficiencies a result of their intrinsic rococo triviality, a national trait embedded in their very language.

Dryden's final work, published two months before his death, is *Fables Ancient and Modern* (1700), an anthology of four original poems and seventeen translated tales that was the one work by which Dryden was best known in the eighteenth and nineteenth centuries. *Fables Ancient and Modern* includes virtually all of Dryden's familiar concerns and issues, reviewed, reconsidered, reasserted, qualified—love and war, power and kingship, the heroic code, the Christian ideal, the role of the poet—all assembled in a masterful collection that includes eulogy, panegyric, satire, epic fragment, beast fable, philosophical disquisition, romance. Now in his late sixties, Dryden was ending his career not by fading, but by shining out brilliantly in what Pope warmly describes as Dryden's "most glorious season," when his "fire, like the Sun's, shin'd clearest toward its setting." In his preface to *Fables Ancient and Modern* Dryden remarks that despite sickness, age, and slightly decaying memory, he finds himself overwhelmed with ideas: "Thoughts, such as they are, come crowding in so fast upon me, that my only Difficulty is to chuse or to reject." If anything, he sounds joyfully bewildered at his own fertile imagination, seeing "such a Variety of Game springing up before me, that I am distracted in my Choice, and know not which to follow."

The intentionally loose arrangement of the tales within *Fables Ancient and Modern*, patterned after the famous collections by Ovid, Boccaccio, and Chaucer, makes Dryden's anthology not so much a synthesis or summary of Dryden as a spacious, leisurely retrospective. His previous efforts in inventing a native literary tradition, his later attempts to strengthen it by importing the seeds of classical literature and planting them in English soil, his lifelong concern to establish a lasting reputation of his own, all meet in *Fables Ancient and Modern*. By including himself alongside Homer, Ovid, Boccaccio, and Chaucer, Dryden creates a lineage, one that begins with classical literature, moves to Chaucer, who was the match of Homer and Virgil, and, significantly, descends to Dryden himself. If in the poem to Congreve (1694), Dryden sought to gain some comfort for his disappointment by assigning his laurel to a young contemporary, in *Fables Ancient and Modern* there is no feeling of resignation and no need to defer hopes to the future. Rather than concern himself with who will follow him, Dryden concerns himself with himself; it is not Congreve who will shade the laurels that descend from Dryden, but Dryden who shades his own laurels.

Dryden also justifies his endeavors in his final critical essay, the preface to *Fables Ancient and Modern*, first by launching a vigorous counterattack on his detractors, and second by the more indirect method of associating himself with the authors he translates and stressing the idea of lineal descent. Even though he had enjoyed warm public recognition in his final years, Dryden was still the victim of attacks, and he could not resist responding incisively. Toward the end of the preface, we hear the voice of the experienced disputant, this time wittily defending himself from three irritating assailants, Jeremy Collier, Luke Milbourne, and Richard Blackmore. Collier, in his *Short View of the Immorality and Pro-*

Madam

Even your Expostulations are pleasing to me: for though they shew you angry, yet they are not without many expressions of your kindness: & therefore I am proud to be so chidden. Yet I cannot so far abandon my own defence, as to confess any idleness or forgetfulness on my part. what has hindred me from writing to you, was neither ill health nor a worse thing ingratitude: but a flood of little businesses, which yet are necessary to my subsistance. & of which I hope to have given you a good account before this time; but the Court rather speaks kindly of me, than does any thing for mee though they promise largely: & perhaps they think I will advance, & they go backward: in which they will be much deceiv'd: for I can never go an Inch beyond my conscience & my Honour. If they will consider me as a Man who have done my best to improve the Language; & especially the Poetry, & will be content with my acquiescence under the present Government, & forbearing satire on it, that I can promise, because I can perform it: but I can neither take the Oaths, nor forsake my Religion, because I know not what Church to go to. if I leave the Catholique; they are all so divided amongst them selves in matters of faith, necessary to Salvation: & yet all assuming the name of Protestants. May God be pleas'd to open your Eyes, as he has open'd mine: Truth is but one; & they who have once heard of it, can plead no Excuse, if they do not embrace it. But these are things too serious, for a trifling Letter. — If you desire to know any thing more of my Affairs, The Earl of Dorsett, & your Cousin Montague, have both seen the two Poems, to the Dutchess of Ormond, & my worthy Cousin Driden: And are of opinion that I

Page from Dryden's 7 November 1699 letter to a young cousin, Mrs. Elizabeth Steward, in which he expresses his hope to be remembered "as a Man, who have done my best to improve the Language" and proclaims his unwillingness to leave the Catholic church for reasons of political expediency (MA 130; by permission of the Pierpont Morgan Library)

faneness of the English Stage (1698), had charged Dryden with "Blasphemy and Baudry"; Dryden admits that in the past he has been guilty of immorality in some of his poetry, but he also counters Collier's charge by explaining that much of the apparent obscenity is not in his works until Collier perverts Dryden's meaning and essentially injects the obscenity himself. The pedantic Milbourne, author of *Notes on Dryden's Virgil* (1698), had accused Dryden of sloppy translation, which Dryden is able to dismiss by alluding to Milbourne's bathetic attempts to translate Virgil, commenting that "while [Milbourne] and I live together, I shall not be thought the worst Poet of the Age." And last, as well as least, Sir Richard Blackmore, the Cheapside Knight, had made a satirical reference to Dryden, sufficient to annoy him, perhaps, but also insufficiently potent to evoke a stinging answer. However, Blackmore had committed a more serious crime; he had the temerity to borrow Dryden's plan for an epic on King Arthur and crank out his own rumbling, rhyme-forced, hack-verse version, thereby ruining a promising idea. Listening to Dryden debate authors long since forgotten makes us wonder why he bothered, but it also serves to remind us of the lively, contentious atmosphere in his literary world, not so much a community devoted to common artistic pursuits as a loose assortment of armed irregulars shooting perpetual volleys at one another. Dryden's response is a flurry of fine satirical strokes rather than a reasoned argument, a satirical dismissal of his enemies rather than a deliberate rebuttal.

Dryden's more expansive efforts at self-justification in the preface to *Fables Ancient and Modern* occur in his accounts of the specific authors and tales he has chosen to translate. He pauses in his survey to make evaluative commentary, typically by balancing one author against another—Homer versus Virgil, Ovid versus Chaucer, Boccaccio versus Chaucer (his contrast of fiery and copious Homer to sedate and confined Virgil is an expansion of a similar comparison begun in the preface to *Examen Poeticum* in 1693). One cannot help but notice that in comparing Chaucer to both Ovid and Boccaccio, patriotic Dryden gradually decides, after an apparently impartial balancing of their virtues, that in the final analysis, "our Countryman" Chaucer is the superior author. Dryden goes even further, departing from his comparative approach to dwell on an extended defense of the medieval poet whom Dryden considers a "rough Diamond" that "must

first be polish'd e'er he shines." Dryden's analysis of Chaucer is an important piece of criticism, even though much of it is mistaken. Uninformed about medieval pronunciation, Dryden gives a misguided, inaccurate account of Chaucer's verse as rugged, lame, imperfect, irregular. Unaware of many of the sources from which Chaucer borrowed his material, Dryden mistakenly singles out Chaucer from other ancient authors for being more original.

Given the crude state of medieval scholarship in the seventeenth century, Dryden's lack of knowledge is typical of the times (it was not until Thomas Tyrwhitt published his edition of *Canterbury Tales* in 1775-1778 that anybody had worked out the principles of Chaucerian meter so as to scan the poetry properly). Yet despite his erroneous conclusions about Chaucer, and despite his condescending attitude toward an author he presumed to be writing in the primitive days of English versification, Dryden sees and warmly appreciates the virtues of Chaucer. Dryden calls him "the Father of *English* Poetry" and praises him for his "wonderful comprehensive Nature," high praise indeed, especially if we recall that Neander had praised Shakespeare similarly for having "the largest and most comprehensive soul." Dryden earns a place of honor in literary history for acknowledging the greatness of Chaucer, but one should remember that by promoting Chaucer, whom he calls his "Predecessor in the Laurel," Dryden is also promoting Dryden, not merely shading the laurel, but burnishing it before assuming it himself. By arguing for the necessity of rendering Chaucer's obscure language so that he becomes a living writer, accessible to a contemporary audience, Dryden hopes "to promote the Honour of my Native Country," and simultaneously, to promote his own honor, since he is the translator who hopes to recover that legacy for all of us, as well as the self-proclaimed successor to that legacy.

Dryden died 1 May 1700 of complications arising from a swollen leg that had become gangrenous, the result of St. Anthony's fire (now known as ergotism). After a brief interment in St. Anne's, Soho, which lay within a quarter mile of his home in Gerrard Street, his body was exhumed and carried to Westminster Abbey in a ceremony filled with pomp. He would probably have been amused at the public funeral procession had he known that the nation that usually paid his pension late, sometimes forgot it altogether, and later doubled his taxes, spared no expense when it came to sending him off eternally. Having professed that he had always been "studious to promote the Honour of my Native Country," he might also have been pleased to see his country ultimately acknowledge the honor. His body was reinterred, fittingly, in the same grave as Chaucer's, next to the graves of Cowley, whom Dryden had called the "Darling of my youth," and Spenser, whom Dryden had acknowledged as his master in framing the English language. Appropriately, the poet-critic who had done so much to assemble the English literary legacy lies alongside many of his heroes, poets he had helped establish as heroes, buried in the section of Westminster Abbey that has since become known as Poets' Corner. As a master of several genres, Dryden was the prototype of other great English poet-critics, such as Samuel Taylor Coleridge, Matthew Arnold (who despised Dryden's poetry), and T. S. Eliot (who praised Dryden repeatedly). And as a critic, even though his works were occasional and self-promotional, he had a lasting influence, in part because of Samuel Johnson, who admired Dryden, who followed many of his leads in his own literary criticism, and who justly awarded Dryden the distinction of being "the father of English criticism." For the author who relied upon the idea of lineal descent in poetry and who helped shape the English literary tradition as we still know it, such a tribute from a great successor makes a fitting epitaph.

Letters:
The Letters of John Dryden: With Letters Addressed to Him, edited by Charles E. Ward (Durham: Duke University Press, 1942).

Bibliographies:
Hugh Macdonald, *John Dryden: A Bibliography of Early Editions and of Drydeniana* (Oxford: Oxford University Press, 1939);

John A. Zamonski, *An Annotated Bibliography of John Dryden: Texts and Studies, 1949-1973* (New York: Garland, 1975);

David J. Latt and Samuel Holt Monk, *John Dryden: A Survey and Bibliography of Critical Studies, 1895-1974* (Minneapolis: University of Minnesota Press, 1976);

James M. Hall, *John Dryden: A Reference Guide* (Boston: G. K. Hall, 1984).

Biographies:
Samuel Johnson, "John Dryden, " in *The Works of the English Poets, With Prefaces, Biographical*

and Critical, 68 volumes (London: Printed by H. Hughes for C. Bathurst and others, 1779-1781); in volume 1 of the standard edition, *Lives of the English Poets*, 3 volumes, edited by George Birkbeck Hill (Oxford: Clarendon Press, 1905);

Walter Scott, *The Life of John Dryden*, volume 1 of Scott's edition of *The Works of John Dryden* (London: William Miller, 1808); published separately in 1826;

Charles E. Ward, *The Life of John Dryden* (Chapel Hill: University of North Carolina Press, 1961);

George McFadden, *Dryden: The Public Writer, 1660-1685* (Princeton: Princeton University Press, 1978);

James Anderson Winn, *John Dryden and His World* (New Haven & London: Yale University Press, 1987).

References:
John Aden, "Dryden and the Imagination: The First Phase," *PMLA*, 74 (March 1959): 28-40;

Elias J. Chiasson, "Dryden's Apparent Scepticism in *Religio Laici*," *Harvard Theological Review*, 54 (July 1961): 207-221;

Lillian Feder, "John Dryden's Use of Classical Rhetoric," *PMLA*, 69 (December 1954): 1258-1278;

William Frost, *Dryden and the Art of Translation* (New Haven, Conn.: Yale University Press, 1955);

Thomas H. Fujimura, " 'Autobiography' in Dryden's Later Work," *Restoration*, 8 (Spring 1984): 17-29;

Fujimura, "The Personal Element in Dryden's Poetry," *PMLA*, 89 (October 1974): 1007-1023;

Achsah Guibbory, "Dryden's Views of History," *Philological Quarterly*, 52 (April 1973): 187-204;

Philip Harth, *Contexts of Dryden's Thought* (Chicago: University of Chicago Press, 1968);

Harth, "Dryden's Public Voices," in *New Homage to John Dryden* (Los Angeles: Clark Library, 1983), pp. 3-27;

Robert Hume, "Dryden on Creation: 'Imagination' in the Later Criticism," *Review of English Studies*, new series 21 (August 1970): 295-314;

Hume, *Dryden's Criticism* (Ithaca: Cornell University Press, 1970);

Arthur C. Kirsch, Introduction to *Literary Criticism of John Dryden*, edited by Kirsch (Lincoln: University of Nebraska Press, 1966), pp. ix-xvii;

Harold Love, "Dryden's Rationale of Paradox," *ELH*, 51 (Summer 1984): 297-313;

Dean T. Mace, "Dryden's Dialogue on Drama," *Journal of the Warburg and Courtauld Institutes*, 25 (January-June 1962): 87-112;

Earl Miner, *Dryden's Poetry* (Bloomington: Indiana University Press, 1967);

Miner, "Renaissance Contexts of Dryden's Criticism," *Michigan Quarterly Review*, 12 (Spring 1973): 97-115;

Miner, *The Restoration Mode from Milton to Dryden* (Princeton: Princeton University Press, 1974);

Miner, ed., *John Dryden*, Writers and their Background Series (Athens: Ohio University Press, 1972);

Samuel Holt Monk, "Dryden and the Beginnings of Shakespeare Criticism in the Augustan Age," in *The Persistence of Shakespeare Idolatry: Essays in Honor of Robert W. Babcock*, edited by Herbert M. Schueller (Detroit: Wayne State University Press, 1964), pp. 47-75;

Edward Pechter, *Dryden's Classical Theory of Literature* (London: Cambridge University Press, 1975);

Cedric D. Reverand II, "Dryden's 'Essay of Dramatick Poesie': The Poet and the World of Affairs," *Studies in English Literature*, 22 (Summer 1982): 375-393;

Alan Roper, "Characteristics of Dryden's Prose," *ELH*, 41 (Winter 1974): 668-692;

Roper, *Dryden's Poetic Kingdoms* (London: Routledge & Kegan Paul, 1965);

Eric Rothstein, "English Tragic Theory in the Late Seventeenth Century," *ELH*, 29 (September 1962): 306-323;

H. T. Swedenberg, *The Theory of the Epic in England 1650-1800*, University of California Publications in English, 15 (Berkeley: University of California Press, 1944);

Mary Thale, "Dryden's Critical Vocabulary: The Imitation of Nature," *Papers on Language and Literature*, 2 (Fall 1966): 315-326;

Thale, "Dryden's Dramatic Criticism: Polestar of the Ancients," *Comparative Literature*, 18 (Winter 1966): 36-54;

Hoyt Trowbridge, "The Place of Rules in Dryden's Criticism," *Modern Philology*, 44 (November 1946): 84-96;

George Watson, "John Dryden," in *The Literary Critics: A Study of English Descriptive Criticism*, second edition (Harmondsworth, U.K.: Penguin, 1973), pp. 24-52.

Papers:

The major collection of Dryden materials is at the William Andrews Clark Memorial Library, University of California at Los Angeles, home of the definitive, California Edition of Dryden, although there is little in the way of actual Dryden manuscripts anywhere. There remain fewer than eighty letters, several of which are in the Clark Library, the others being scattered in the British Library, the Bodleian, and other collections. There is but one extant holograph of any Dryden poem, a fair copy of the Cromwell elegy in the British Library.

Henry Fielding

(22 April 1707 - 8 October 1754)

Brian McCrea
University of Florida

See also the Fielding entries in *DLB 39: British Novelists, 1660-1800* and *DLB 84: Restoration and Eighteenth-Century Dramatists, Second Series.*

SELECTED BOOKS: *The Masquerade, A Poem. Inscribed to C---t H--d--g--r. . . . By Lemuel Gulliver, Poet Laureat to the King of Lilliput* (London: Printed & sold by J. Roberts & A. Dodd, 1728);

Love in Several Masques. A Comedy, as it is acted at the Theatre-Royal, by His Majesty's Servants (London: Printed for John Watts, 1728);

The Temple Beau. A Comedy. As it is Acted at the Theatre in Goodman's-Fields (London: Printed for J. Watts, 1730);

The Author's Farce; and The Pleasures of the Town. As Acted at the theatre in the Hay-Market, as Scriblerus Secundus (London: Printed for J. Roberts, 1730; revised edition, London: Printed for Watts, 1750);

Tom Thumb. A Tragedy. As it is Acted at the theatre in the theatre in Hay-Market (London: Printed & sold by J. Roberts, 1730);

Rape upon Rape; or, The Justice Caught in his own Trap. A Comedy. As it is Acted at the Theatre in the Hay-Market (London: Printed for J. Watts, 1730); republished as *The Coffee-House Politician; or, The Justice Caught in his own Trap. A Comedy. As it is Acted at the Theatre Royal in Lincoln's Inn-Fields* (London: Printed for J. Watts, 1730);

The Letter-Writers; Or, a New Way to Keep a Wife at Home. A Farce, in Three Acts. As it is Acted at the Theatre in the Hay-Market, as Scriblerus Secundus (London: Printed & sold by J. Roberts, 1731);

The Tragedy of Tragedies; or The Life and Death of Tom Thumb the Great. As it is Acted at the Theatre in the Hay-Market. With the Annotations of H. Scriblerus Secundus (London: Printed & sold by J. Roberts, 1731);

The Welsh Opera: or, The Grey Mare the better Horse As it is Acted at the New Theatre in the Hay-Market, as Scriblerus Secundus (London: Printed for E. Rayner & sold by H. Cook, 1731); republished as *The Genuine Grub-Street Opera* (London: Printed & sold for the benefit of the Haymarket Comedians, 1731); republished as *The Grub-Street Opera* (London: Printed & sold by Roberts, 1731 [most likely printed by Andrew Millar in 1755]);

The Lottery: A Farce (London: Printed for J. Watts, 1732);

The Modern Husband. A Comedy. As it is Acted at the Theatre-Royal in Drury-Lane. By His Majesty's Servants (London: Printed for J. Watts, 1732);

The Old Debauchees. A Comedy. As it is Acted at the Theatre-Royal in Drury-Lane. By His Majesty's Servants. By the Author of The Modern Husband (London: Printed for J. W. & sold by J. Roberts, 1732);

The Covent-Garden Tragedy. As it is Acted at the Theatre-Royal in Drury-Lane. By His Majesty's Servants (London: Printed for J. Watts & sold by J. Roberts, 1732);

The Mock Doctor. or The Dumb Lady Cur'd. A Comedy. Done from Molière. As it is Acted at the Theatre-Royal in Drury-Lane, By His Majesty's Servants. With the Musick prefix'd to each Song (London: Printed for J. Watts, 1732);

The Miser. A Comedy. Taken from Platus and Molière. As it is Acted at the Theatre Royal in Drury-Lane, by His Majesty's Servants (London: Printed for J. Watts, 1733);

The Intriguing Chambermaid. A Comedy of Two Acts. As it is Acted at the Theatre-Royal in Drury-Lane, By His Majesty's Servants. Taken from the French of Regnard (London: Printed for J. Watts, 1734);

Don Quixote in England. A Comedy. As it is Acted at the New Theatre in the Hay-Market (London: Printed for J. Watts, 1734);

*An Old Man taught Wisdom; or, The Virgin Unmask'd. A Farce. As it is Perform'd By His Majesty's Company of Comedians at the Theatre-Royal in Drury-Lane. With the musick prefix'd to

Henry Fielding (engraving by James Basire, after a drawing by William Hogarth). This portrait, done from memory nearly eight years after Fielding's death, served as the frontispiece to the 1762 edition of Fielding's works.

each song (London: Printed for John Watts, 1735);

The Universal Gallant: or, The Different Husbands: A Comedy. As it is acted at the Theatre-Royal in Drury-Lane. By His Majesty's Servants (London: Printed for John Watts, 1735);

Pasquin. A Dramatick Satire on the Times: Being the Rehearsal of Two Plays, viz. a Comedy call'd, The Election; And a Tragedy call'd The Life and Death of Common-Sense. As it is Acted at the Theatre in the Hay-Market (London: Printed for J. Watts, 1736);

Tumble-Down Dick: or, Phaeton in the Suds. A Dramatick Entertainment of Walking, in Serious and Foolish Characters: Interlarded with Bur-

lesque, Grotesque, Comick Interludes Call'd, Harlequin a Pick-Pocket. As it is Perform'd at the New Theatre in the Hay-Market. Being ('tis hop'd) the last Entertainment that will ever be exhibited on any Stage. Invented by the Ingenious Monsieur Sans Espirit. The Musick compos'd by the Harmonious Signior Warblerini. And the Scenes painted by the Prodigious Mynheer Van Bottom-Flat* (London: Printed for J. Watts, 1736);

The Historical Register for the Year 1736. As it is Acted at the New Theatre in the Hay-Market. To which is added a very merry Tragedy, called Eurydice Hiss'd, or, A Word to the Wise (London: Printed & sold by J. Roberts, 1737);

Fielding's birthplace, Sharpham House, near Glastonbury

The Champion: or, British Mercury, by Capt. Hercules Vinegar, nos. 1-158 by Fielding and James Ralph (London, 15 November 1739 - December [?] 1740); essays of nos. 1-94 (15 November 1739 - 19 June 1740); republished as *The Champion: Containing a Series of Papers, Humourous, Moral, Political, and Critical,* 2 volumes (London: Printed for J. Huggonson, 1741);

The Military History of Charles XII. King of Sweden, Written by the express Order of His Majesty, By M. Gustavus Adlerfeld. . . . Translated into English, translated by Fielding, 3 volumes (London: Printed for J. & P. Knapton, J. Hodges, A. Millar & J. Nourse, 1740);

Of True Greatness. An Epistle to the Right Honourable George Dodington Esq. (London: Printed for C. Corbett, 1741);

The Vernon-iad. Done into English, From the Original Greek of Homer. Lately found at Constantinople. With Notes in usum, &c. Book the first (London: Printed for Charles Corbett, 1741);

An Apology for the Life of Mrs. Shamela Andrews. In which, the many notorious Falshoods and Misrepresentations of a Book called Pamela, are exposed and refuted; . . . By Mr. Conny Keyber (London: Printed for A. Dodd, 1741);

The Crisis: A Sermon, on Revel. XIV. 9, 10, 11. Necessary to be preached in all the Churches in England, Wales, and Berwick upon Tweed, at or before the next General Election. Humbly inscribed to the Right Reverend the Bench of Bishops. By a Lover of his Country (London: Printed for A. Dodd, E. Nutt & H. Chappelle, 1741)—probably by Fielding;

The History of Our Own Times, by a Society of Gentlemen, nos. 1-4 (15 January - 5 March 1741)—probably by Fielding;

The Opposition. A Vision (London: Printed for T. Cooper, 1742 [i.e. 1741]);

The History of the Adventures of Joseph Andrews, and of his Friend Mr. Abraham Adams. Written in Imitation of The Manner of Cervantes, Author of Don Quixote, 2 volumes (London: Printed for A. Millar, 1742);

A Full Vindication of the Dutchess Dowager of Marlborough: Both With regard to the Account Lately Published by Her Grace, and to Her Character in general; against The base and malicious Invectives contained in a late scurrilous Pamphlet, entitled Remarks on the Account, &c. . . . (London: Printed for J. Roberts, 1742);

Miss Lucy in Town. A Sequel to The Virgin Unmasqued. A Farce; With Songs. As it is Acted at the Theatre-Royal in Drury-Lane, by His Majesty's Servants (London: Printed for A. Millar, 1742);

Plutus, the God of Riches. A Comedy. Translated from the Original Greek of Aristophanes: With Large Notes Explanatory and Critical, translated by Fielding and William Young (London: Printed for T. Waller, 1742);

Some Papers to Be Read before the R---l Society Concerning the Terrestrial Chysipus, Golden-Foot or Guinea; an insect or vegetable, resembling the polypus, which has this surprising property, that being cut into several pieces, each piece becomes a perfect animal, or vegetable, as complete as that of which it was originally only a part. Collected by Petrus Gualterus, but Not Published till After His Death (London: Printed for A. Millar, 1743);

The Wedding-Day. A Comedy, As it is Acted at the Theatre-Royal in Drury-Lane. By His Majesty's Servants (London: Printed for A. Millar, 1743);

Miscellanies, 3 volumes (London: Printed for the author & sold by A. Millar, 1743)—includes first printings of *A Journey from This World to the Next* (in volume 2) and *The Life of Mr. Jonathan Wild* (volume 3);

An Attempt towards a Natural History of the Hanover Rat (London: Printed for M. Cooper, 1744)—probably by Fielding;

The Charge to the Jury: or, The Sum of the Evidence on the Trial of A.B.C.D. and E.F. All M.D. for the Death of One Robert at Orfud, at the special commission of oyer and terminer . . . before Sir Asculapius Dosem, Dr. Timberhead, and others . . . (London: Printed for M. Cooper, 1745);

A Serious Address to the People of Great Britain. In which the Certain Consequences of the Present Rebellion, Are fully demonstrated (London: Printed for M. Cooper, 1745);

The History of the Present Rebellion in Scotland. . . . Taken from the Relation of Mr. James Macpherson, Who Was an Eyewitness of the Whole (London: Printed for M. Cooper, 1745);

A Dialogue between the Devil, the Pope, and the Pretender (London: Printed for M. Cooper, 1745);

The True Patriot; and The History of Our Own Times, nos. 1-33 (London: Printed for M. Cooper, 5 November 1745 - 17 June 1746);

The Female Husband: or, The Surprising History of Mrs. Mary, Alias Mr. George Hamilton, who was convicted of having married a young woman of Wells and lived with her as her husband. Taken from Her Own Mouth since Her Confinement (London: Printed for M. Cooper, 1746);

Ovid's Art of Love Paraphrased, and Adapted to the Present Time. With Notes. And a most correct Edition of the Original. Book I (London: Printed for M. Cooper, A. Dodd & G. Woodfall, 1747);

A Dialogue between a Gentleman of London, Agent for Two Court Candidates, and an Honest Alderman Of the Country Party. Wherein the Grievances under which the Nation at present groans are fairly and impartially laid open and considered. Earnestly address'd to the Electors of Great-Britain (London: Printed for M. Cooper, 1747);

A Proper Answer To a Late Scurrilous Libel, Entitled, An Apology for the Conduct of a late celebrated Second-rate Minister. By the Author of the Jacobites' Journal (London: Printed for M. Cooper, 1747);

The Jacobite's Journal, by John Trott-Plaid, Esq., nos. 1-49 (London, 5 December 1747 - 5 November 1748);

The History of Tom Jones, a Foundling, 6 volumes (London: Printed for A. Millar, 1749);

A Charge Delivered to the Grand Jury, at the Sessions of the Peace Held for the City and Liberty of Westminster, &c. On Thursday the 29th of June, 1749 (London: Printed for A. Millar, 1749);

A True State of the Case of Bosavern Penlez, Who Suffered on Account of the late Riot in the Strand. In which The Law regarding these Offences, and the Statute of George the First, commonly called the Riot Act, are fully considered (London: Printed for A. Millar, 1749);

An Enquiry Into the Causes for the late Increase of Robbers, &c. with Some Proposals for Remedying this Growing Evil (London: Printed for A. Millar, 1751);

A Plan of the Universal Register Office (London, 1751);

Amelia, 4 volumes (London: Printed for A. Millar, 1751);

The Covent-Garden Journal. By Sir Alexander Draw-cansir, Knt. Censor of Great Britain, nos. 1-72 (London, 4 January 1752 - 25 November 1752);

Examples of the Interposition of Providence in the Detection and Punishment of Murder . . . With an introduction and conclusion, both written by Henry Fielding, Esq. (London: Printed for A. Millar, 1752);

A Proposal for Making an Effectual Provision for the Poor, for Amending their Morals and for Rendering them useful Members of the Society (London: Printed for A. Millar, 1753);

A Clear State of the Case of Elizabeth Canning, who hath sworn that she was robbed and almost starved to Death by a Gang of Gipsies and other Villains in January last, for which One Mary Squires now lies under Sentence of Death (London: Printed for A. Millar, 1753);

The Life of Mr. Jonathan Wild the Great. A New Edition with considerable Corrections and Additions (London: Printed for A. Millar, 1754);

The Journal of a Voyage to Lisbon (London: Printed for A. Millar, 1755);

The Fathers; or, The Good-Natur'd Man. A Comedy. As it is Acted at the Theatre-Royal, in Drury-Lane (London: Printed for T. Cadell, 1778).

Editions: *The Works of Henry Fielding, Esq.: with the Life of the Author*, 4 volumes, edited by Arthur Murphy (London: Printed by A. Millar, 1762);

The Works of Henry Fielding, 12 volumes, edited by Edmund Gosse (Westminster: Constable / New York: Scribners, 1899);

The Complete Works of Henry Fielding, Esq., 16 volumes, edited by W. E. Henley (London: Heineman, 1903);

The Covent-Garden Journal, 2 volumes, edited by Gerard Edward Jensen (New Haven: Yale University Press / London: Oxford University Press, 1915);

Journal of a Voyage to Lisbon, edited by Harold Pagliaro (New York: Nardon, 1963);

The Wesleyan Edition of the Works of Henry Fielding, 16 volumes to date, edited by W. B. Coley and others (Oxford: Clarendon Press / Middletown, Conn.: Wesleyan University Press, 1967-   );

Jonathan Wild and The Journal of a Voyage to Lisbon, introduction by A. R. Humphreys, notes by Douglas Brooks (London: Dent / New York: Dutton, 1973);

The Jacobite's Journal and Related Writings, edited by Coley (Oxford: Clarendon Press / Middle-

town, Conn.: Wesleyan University Press, 1975);

The True Patriot and Related Writings, edited by Coley (Middletown, Conn.: Wesleyan University Press, 1987);

An Enquiry into the Causes of the Late Increase of Robbers and Related Writings, edited by Malvin R. Zirker (Middletown, Conn.: Wesleyan University Press, 1988);

New Essays by Henry Fielding: His Contributions to The Craftsman and Other Early Journalism, edited by Martin C. Battestin (Charlottesville: University Press of Virginia, 1989).

PLAY PRODUCTIONS: *Love in Several Masques*, London, Theatre Royal, Drury Lane, 16 February 1728;

The Temple Beau, or The Intriguing Sisters, London, Odell's Theatre in Ayliffe St., Goodman's Fields, 26 January 1730;

The Author's Farce, London, Little Theatre in the Hay-Market, 30 March 1730;

The Pleasures of the Town, London, Little Theatre in the Hay-Market, 30 March 1730;

Tom Thumb, London, Little Theatre in the Hay-Market, 24 April 1730;

Rape upon Rape, or The Justice Caught in his own Trap, London, Little Theatre in the Hay-Market, 23 June 1730; revived as *The Coffee-House Politician*, London, Lincoln's Inn Fields, 4 December 1730;

The Letter-Writers, or A New Way to Keep a Wife at Home, London, Little Theatre in the Hay-Market, 24 March 1731;

The Tragedy of Tragedies; or, The Life and Death of Tom Thumb the Great, London, Little Theatre in the Hay-Market, 24 March 1731;

The Welsh Opera, or the Grey Mare the Better Horse, London, Little Theatre in the Hay-Market, 22 April 1731; revised as *The Genuine Grub-Street Opera*; later revised as *The Grub-Street Opera* (neither version staged in Fielding's lifetime);

The Lottery, London, Theatre Royal, Drury Lane, 1 January 1732;

The Modern Husband, London, Theatre Royal, Drury Lane, 14 February 1732;

The Covent Garden Tragedy (Honours of Covent Garden), London, Theatre Royal, Drury Lane, 1 June 1732;

The Old Debauchees (also known as *The Debauchees, or The Jesuit Caught in his own Trap*), London, Theatre Royal, Drury Lane, 1 June 1732;

The house at East Stour, Dorset, where Fielding spent his childhood

The Mock Doctor, or the Dumb Lady Cured, London, Theatre Royal, Drury Lane, 23 June 1732;

The Miser, London, Theatre Royal, Drury Lane, 17 February 1733;

Deborah, or A Wife for You All, London, Theatre Royal, Drury Lane, 6 April 1733;

The Intriguing Chambermaid, London, Theatre Royal, Drury Lane, 15 January 1734;

Don Quixote in England, London, Little Theatre in the Hay-Market, 5 April 1734;

An Old Man Taught Wisdom, or The Virgin Unmask'd, London, Theatre Royal, Drury Lane, 6 January 1735;

The Universal Gallant, or The Different Husbands, London, Theatre Royal, Drury Lane, 10 February 1735;

Pasquin, London, Little Theatre in the Hay-Market, 5 March 1736;

Tumble-Down Dick: or, Phaeton in the Suds, London, Little Theatre in the Hay-Market, 29 April 1736;

Eurydice, or The Devil Henpecked, London, Theatre Royal, Drury Lane, 19 February 1737;

The Historical Register for the Year 1736, London, Little Theatre in the Hay-Market, 21 March 1737;

Eurydice Hiss'd, or A Word to the Wise, London, Lit-tle Theatre in the Hay-Market, 13 April 1737;

Miss Lucy in Town, a Sequel to The Virgin Unmasked, revised by Garrick and perhaps others, London, Theatre Royal, Drury Lane, 6 May 1742;

The Wedding-Day, London, Theatre Royal, Drury Lane, 17 February 1743;

The Fathers; or, The Good Natured Man, reworked by David Garrick and Richard Sheridan, London, Theatre Royal, Drury Lane, 30 November 1778.

Many critics, Martin C. Battestin and C. J. Rawson perhaps most prominent among them, have described Henry Fielding both as the last and one of the greatest representatives of the Augustan Age in English literature. In their rather different accounts of Fielding's achievement, Battestin and Rawson share an implicit sense that the Augustan spirit in literature is characterized by concern for significant literary form. Rawson argues that in Fielding's novels the allegiance to "formal ordering" of earlier Augustan writers such as Alexander Pope and Jonathan Swift comes under "stress." Rawson is fascinated by Serjeant Atkinson's physical awkwardness in *Amelia* (1751), fascinated by tokens of Fielding's sympathies with the disorderly and unruly. Battestin is fascinated by the careful artifice of *Tom Jones* (1749)—the counterpointing of characters, the richly orchestrated plotting, the recurrent suggestion of an emblematic dimension in the characterization. He sees in all this an echoing by Fielding of Pope's famous lines in *An Essay on Man* (part 1, 1732):

> All Nature is but Art, unknown to thee;
> All Chance, Direction, which thou canst not see;
> All Discord, Harmony, not understood;
> All partial Evil universal Good[.]

Battestin goes beyond the term Augustan and finds in Fielding's novels a design "as artificial as the pure geometrical shapes of a building by Palladio, in which the principles of symmetry and balance, the harmonious relationship of part to part, are strictly observed." In finding a "Palladian" structure in Fielding's work, Battestin extends and enriches an insight that goes back at least as far as Samuel Taylor Coleridge's oft-cited remark: "What a master of composition Fielding was! Upon my word, I think the *Oedipus Tyrannous*, *The Alchemist*, and *Tom Jones*, the three most perfect plots ever planned."

The form of Fielding's novels is important because it embodies the faith of Fielding and his age in Order. Rawson sees that faith threatened; Battestin sees it receiving a triumphant final expression. But the Augustan Ideal, both in the classical period and in the Age of John Dryden and Alexander Pope, involved more than the formal ordering of literary parts. Like Virgil and Horace, Dryden, Swift, and Pope all assumed that the writer had an important public role to play. The *Aeneid*, whatever its striking formal qualities, was a national epic; the poem, at least in part, existed to promote good citizenship, to inculcate patriotism. If Augustus did save the manuscript from being burned, his action was politically astute as well as literarily crucial. As Augustus and Maecenas patronized Virgil and Horace—associated with them and learned from them—they provided a model for the political influence that Dryden, Swift, and Pope hoped to have but never achieved. While twentieth-century critics, led by Maynard Mack, have tended to analyze the satires of the English Augustans in terms of their formal features, focusing in particular upon the rhetorical function of the persona (the

speaker), we can add that one reason for both the power and the bitterness of works such as *Mac Flecknoe* (1682), *Gulliver's Travels* (1726), and *The Dunciad* (1728, 1742) is that Dryden, Swift, and Pope all hoped, in the words of Swift, to "wonderfully mend the World." In his *Epilogue to the Satires* (1738), at the end of his career, Pope bitterly complains that the world has not reformed, has not listened: "Not twice a twelvemonth you [Pope] appear in print, / and when it comes, the Court see nothing in it." But what Thomas R. Edwards has described as the "darkness" of Pope's final vision should not obscure the public role that Pope earlier assumed to be his. The court has not listened, but Pope clearly implies that it should have, that, in the Age of Augustus, it would have.

All the great writers of the English Augustan period—Joseph Addison, Richard Steele, and Swift in particular—had important political connections and held important political positions. In a series of lectures titled *The English Humourists of the Eighteenth Century* (1853), William Thackeray lists admiringly, perhaps enviously, the state offices that major writers (Swift, Addison, Steele) and minor writers (Thomas Tickell, Matthew Prior, John Gay) held. Addison rose to the position of secretary of state; Swift, as chief propagandist for the ministry of Robert Harley, Earl of Oxford (1710-1714), spent much time in 1714 trying to reconcile the split between Harley and his onetime political partner, Henry St. John, Viscount Bolingbroke, which contributed to the ministry's demise. Dryden and Pope were more narrowly literary, and their Roman Catholicism excluded them from direct political action. But even in their cases, political involvement was persistent and important. Pope agonized over his testimony in the trial for treason of Bishop Francis Atterbury, but he finally gave it; Dryden's support of the Stuart succession was consistent and, finally, costly.

If Fielding's commitment to Augustan notions of form and order appears most clearly in his three great novels—*Joseph Andrews* (1742), *Tom Jones* (1749), *Amelia* (1751)—his commitment to a public role, to wonderfully mending the world, appears most clearly in the nonfiction prose he published from 1739 to 1754. In his essays and pamphlets, he addresses the major social and political issues of his day. While Fielding's reputation as a writer depends, and will always depend, upon the great novels, his nonfiction prose provides perhaps the most reliable guide to his Weltanschauung. In his nonfiction prose, particularly the social pamphlets of the 1750s, Fielding reveals a sensibility that is profoundly conservative—a conservatism sometimes obscured by the genial good nature of *Joseph Andrews* and *Tom Jones*. Brian McCrea recently has pointed out that Fielding's portrayal of the social elite in *Joseph Andrews* and *Tom Jones* and his use of birth-mystery plots in those novels both serve to rescue the elite from his sharp satire upon their weaknesses and corruptions. Fielding's tone, of course, is rich and ambiguous, and the interpretations of individual readers will differ. But when Joseph Andrews and Tom Jones are revealed to be gentlemen after all, when Squire Booby becomes the source of financial reward and social placement in the finale of *Joseph Andrews*, wealth and class are vindicated, even as Fielding's early portrayals of upper-class venality and stupidity will remain, to varying degrees, in readers' memories. Similarly when Fielding pauses in the conclusion of *Joseph Andrews* to rehabilitate the justice of the peace who behaved so incompetently in his earlier interrogation of Adams and Fanny—when the justice reappears to inform Adams that "he had found the Fellow who had attempted to swear against him and the young woman . . . and had committed him to Salisbury Gaol, where he was charged with many Robberies"—no formal feature of the plot requires his presence. Rather, Fielding brings him back in order to vindicate precisely that system of law and order with which he earlier had so much fun.

The social and political conservatism expressed in Fielding's nonfiction prose points to his complicated family background as well as to important changes in eighteenth-century English life. Fielding had ties to one of England's great aristocratic families; his father, Edmund, was first cousin to Basil Fielding, Fourth Earl of Denbigh. But those ties paid no bills, secured no place for him. Edmund Fielding achieved success and some fame as a soldier, rising to the rank of lieutenant general. He also was improvident and chronically in debt. Henry's maternal grandfather, Sir Henry Gould, was a judge of the Queen's Bench, and it was at his family seat, Sharpham Park, that Henry was born. The Gould family was wealthy and landed, but except for the gift of a sizable farm to Henry and his brothers and sisters—a farm that eventually had to be sold off—the Gould wealth was not Henry's to inherit. When Henry's mother, Sarah Gould Fielding, died in April 1718, an ongoing custody

battle over the Fielding children (Henry had five sisters and one brother) ensued. Edmund, who quickly remarried and was in need of money, wanted control of his children's property; Lady Gould, their maternal grandmother, sought and eventually won custody of the children and their farm. By the time the custody battle was decided in 1722, Henry was at Eton with classmates including William Pitt the Elder and George Lyttelton. Again, however, Fielding's connection with the social elite would be tenuous. While his classmates went on to Oxford, Fielding in 1728 and 1729 briefly and intermittently attended the University of Leyden until his father's funds ran out. He then returned to London, a gentleman born and bred, but with no fortune to inherit. He is reported to have told his cousin Lady Mary Wortley Montagu that he had the choice of becoming a hackney writer or a hackney coachman.

Even a brief sketch of his family background reveals the different, sometimes contradictory social attitudes Fielding would try to reconcile. He tended to idealize rural life, its traditions and constancy; Martin Battestin has shown how Paradise Hall in *Tom Jones* is "an imaginative synthesis of details associated primarily with Sharpham Park . . . and secondarily with Hagley Park and Prior Park, the estates, respectively, of Fielding's patrons, George Lyttelton and Ralph Allen." But Fielding chose to make his living in London. He was classically educated, but, in the career as a playwright he began upon his return from Leyden, he appealed to popular taste—seeking patronage from theater managers rather than Roman emperors. Perhaps most important about his somewhat equivocal patrimony is the likely political effect that his father's military career had upon him. Edmund Fielding, whatever his failings as a manager of money and family, served John Churchill, Duke of Marlborough, bravely and gallantly during the duke's finest hour, the Battle of Blenheim. His son Henry never failed to express admiration for the duke and thus to support, at least implicitly, the economic and social revolution in which the duke's war played a major part. While in some of his early literary satires Fielding referred to himself as "H. Scriblerus Secundus" and in the 1730s he perhaps wrote as many as forty-one essays for the great opposition journal, *The Craftsman*, Fielding's loyalty to Marlborough ultimately separated him from Swift and Pope, both of whom saw the duke as a venal and power-hungry man. Swift hated Marlborough intensely because he, fol-

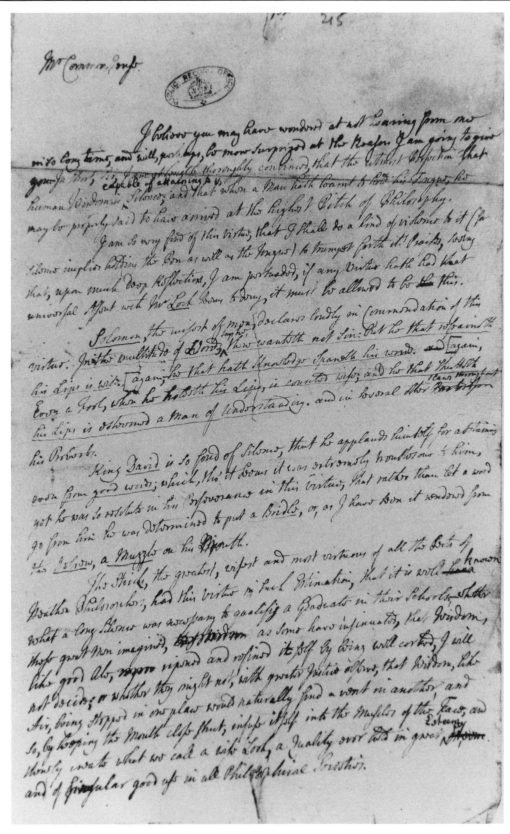

Page from the manuscript for Fielding's essay on the wisdom of silence, first published in the 1 April 1738 issue
of Common Sense *(S.P.9.35; Public Record Office, London)*

lowing Bolingbroke, believed that Marlborough's expensive campaigns on the European continent during the War of the Spanish Succession had changed the English social, economic, and, ultimately, political status quo.

To finance first the War of the League of Augsburg, then the War of the Spanish Succession, the English had to fund a rapidly growing national debt. The financial innovations of Charles Montagu (later Earl of Halifax) in the early 1690s—the establishment of a national debt (1692) and the foundation of the Bank of England (1694)—became vital parts of British life as the War of the Spanish Succession dragged on through the first decade of the eighteenth century. Marlborough's war intensified the tendency of English life to become more urban, more commercial. Wealth came to be based upon paper, not land, and people made and lost fortunes speculating in joint-stock companies, such as the South Sea and East India, which were founded on trade monopolies granted by the government in exchange for a promise by the company to pay part of the national debt. Fielding lived within and was loyal to this new economic order—an order Swift futilely devoted his political career to defeating. The national debt, the London stock exchange, and paper money had become parts of English life by Fielding's time. In his "Epistle to Bathurst" (1733) Pope wrote of "Blest paper Credit, last and best Supply / That leads corruption lighter Wings to fly." He thus summarized the Tory argument against the new economic order. But Fielding lived on credit and valued the financial opportunities that London offered. Thus his social conservatism, while powerful and basic, was of a different order from that of Swift, Pope, and the other Scriblerians. His economic values were much closer to those of the Whig writers, Joseph Addison and Richard Steele.

The nonfiction prose of Fielding includes four major periodicals—*The Champion* (1739-1740), *The True Patriot* (1745-1746), *The Jacobite's Journal* (1747-1748), and *The Covent-Garden Journal* (1752)—separately published political pamphlets written in the early 1740s, and series of influential pamphlets on the relationship between crime, poverty, and the law published in the late 1740s and early 1750s. In addition, it now appears that from 1734 to 1738 Fielding contributed essays to *The Craftsman*, although his ties to that journal were clandestine. The central figure of controversy in Fielding's early career is Sir Robert Walpole, first lord of the treasury from 1722

to 1742, often designated the first "prime minister" of England, and described, by his biographer J. H. Plumb, as a crucial agent in bringing political stability to England. Walpole's achievements were problematic for Fielding, however, because they were accompanied by a venality, not to say corruption, that departed from the standard set by Augustus. As Bertrand A. Goldgar has shown, Walpole's main test of artistic achievement was the loyalty to himself expressed in the work. John B. Owen has studied in detail the ways Walpole used political patronage to establish an "Old Corps" of Parliamentary Whigs that enabled him to control Parliament for twenty years. E. P. Thompson and his students more recently have traced how Walpole changed centuries-old customs in the Royal Forests in order to eliminate poaching, thus pleasing his king as well as promoting better hunting for himself and his friends.

In short, Walpole, known as the "Great Man," was a controversial and unavoidable figure—one who seemed, in his own life-style and in his political methods, to discredit the Whig principles whose triumph he assured. The system of public credit—the stock market, the national debt, the Bank of England—all became well established during Walpole's tenure. He rescued the new political and economic order from the discontent caused by the collapse of the South Sea Bubble in 1721, and went on, in the next twenty years, to accrue great power and great wealth. It was perhaps the ostentatiousness of his venality, the flamboyance of his political wheeling and dealing, that most enraged Swift and Pope. For them Walpole came to symbolize the decline of English letters and civilization. Aubrey Williams has described how skillfully and persistently Pope in his *Dunciad* gives this symbolic dimension to Walpole. Colley Cibber was Walpole's laureate, so, in *The Dunciad*, Walpole becomes Dullness's minister. In this late reference from that poem, Walpole is linked with both the decline of rural traditions and the destruction of traditional political liberties. Dullness foresees a time in England when

> The sturdy Squire to Gallic masters [will] stoop
> And drown his Lands and Manors in a Soupe.
> Others import yet nobler arts from France.
> Teach Kings to fiddle, and make Senates dance.
> Perhaps more high some daring son [Walpole] may
>   soar.
> Proud to my list to add one more Monarch more;
> And nobly conscious Princes are but things

Born for First Ministers, as Slaves for Kings,
Tyrant supreme! shall three Estates command,
And make one Mighty Dunciad of the Land!

Walpole had served as secretary of war during the War of the Spanish Succession—and been impeached and imprisoned by the Oxford ministry for his pains. Support for him was part of Fielding's political patrimony. But his venality would cloud Fielding's attitude toward him, and lead Fielding to treat him in ways that critics have found confusing, even equivocal.

When Fielding came to London in 1727 with his play *Love in Several Masques* (performed in 1728), the City was in a period of political uproar, if not upheaval. George I had died on 11 June, and with his death a Parliamentary election had to be called. For the first time since his rise to power in 1722, the electorate would have a chance to judge Walpole. The general election was held in July and August and led to extensive and vituperative pamphleteering on the part of Walpole's friends and foes. The leading opposition journal was *The Craftsman*, which, in 1727, was an organ for Bolingbroke and thus associated with the Tory cause. Fielding, at this time, was loyal to Walpole, perhaps because his play was produced with the patronage of his second cousin, Lady Mary Wortley Montagu, an ardent Walpole supporter. Satires upon Walpole, however, were popular and, most important, were written by some of the literary giants of the day—Swift, Pope, Gay. After Walpole emerged politically victorious in 1727, with a Parliamentary majority that would secure his rule for the next seven years, satire upon his abuses and excesses became increasingly tempting for Fielding. In the plays he wrote from 1728 to 1737 he alternated between sentimental comedies in the vein of Steele and Cibber, and satiric farces and ballad operas in the vein of the Scriblerians. His career as a playwright was, as Charles B. Woods has judged, "undistinguished," principally because he could not decide which type of play he wished to write. His sentimental comedies are disrupted by unmotivated satiric interludes; his satires are marred, their tone confused by sentimental scenes and characters. One of his comedies, *The Modern Husband* (performed in 1732), is dedicated to Walpole. His later satires, *Pasquin* (performed in 1736) and *The Historical Register for the Year 1736* (performed in 1737), satirize Walpole so sharply that he pushed through the Stage Licensing Act of 1737 to give the government more control over the plays produced on the London stage. During the 1730s Fielding also was contributing to *The Craftsman*, but the journal at this time was identified more with Whig opposition to Walpole than with Bolingbroke and the Tories. Fielding responded to the Stage Licensing Act not by a fomenting political protest, but by entering the Inner Temple to begin a career as an attorney—the career for which his maternal line would have seemed to predestine him.

Fielding's ambivalent response to Walpole was not entirely inconvenient for him. In his satires upon the Great Man, he could pretend that Walpole, whom he portrayed as a deceiver and a manipulator, was the cause of all that was wrong with English life, that Walpole alone was responsible for the political corruption and bad taste against which Swift and Pope railed so heartily. In effect, by focusing narrowly upon Walpole as the source of bad politics and bad taste, Fielding could avoid difficult questions about the "constitution" of English society as a whole. As he attacked Walpole, he narrowly avoided attacking the political and economic principles the Great Man served. In Fielding's political and social writing after Walpole's fall, corruption and evil become much more threatening and problematic. In those writings he expresses a darker and more pessimistic view of English life, particularly of the upper classes.

The pattern in which Fielding's political and social commentary proceeded, then, is approximately as follows. In the 1730s a young Fielding moved uncertainly among different political positions and even experimented with an opposition politics close to that of the Tories—Pope, Swift, and Bolingbroke; he wrote, albeit anonymously, for *The Craftsman*, and in *The Champion* associated himself with sharp attacks on Walpole. In the 1740s, disappointed by the quality of the opposition to the Great Man, he began to reconcile himself to Walpole and to reestablish his allegiance to the economic, social, and political interests Walpole served. In the mid 1740s, Fielding committed himself to defending the Hanoverian Succession during the Jacobite Rebellion of 1745, and to serving the "Broad-Bottomed" ministry of Henry Pelham, the Whig politician who succeeded Walpole, but governed without Walpole's excesses. Having redefined his Whig principles and achieved political certainty in the mid 1740s, Fielding, through the rest of his life, was troubled with the problem of illegal and immoral behavior within his society. He had direct contact

Night Walkers before a Justice (or A Frenchman at Bow Street*); the justice (seated at left) may be Fielding (drawing by Marcellus Laroon, 1740?; Windsor Castle, Royal Library; copyright 1990 Her Majesty Queen Elizabeth II)*

with the society's criminal element and lower orders in his work as justice of the peace for the City of Westminster and County of Middlesex (1748-1754). He was left to wonder why in a society that was properly constituted and now properly administered (by Pelham's Broad-Bottomed ministry) corruption still flourished. His analysis of that question motivates his social pamphlets of the 1750s and his last, posthumously published work, *The Journal of a Voyage to Lisbon* (1755).

　　Throughout the years 1729-1754, as Fielding adopted different political allegiances, so he also changed literary models. Swift and Pope, of course, provided the great examples of satire for him, and at those points when he dissented most sharply from Whig orthodoxy—when he was most angered by Walpole's venality—he wrote as a second-generation Scriblerian. But his most basic political and social allegiances were closer to the Whig views of Addison and Steele, and thus, as he moved toward political certainty in the mid 1740s, his work both alluded to and resembled theirs. In the end it was Fielding's genius for combining satire and sentiment, the influences of

both the Scriblerus and the Kit Kat clubs, that underlies the rich sagacity of his great novels, the famous narrative voice that is at once knowing and tolerant, calculating and affectionate.

　　When Fielding began work on *The Champion* in November 1739, his political indecisiveness manifested itself in several ways. The great models for the journal were *The Tatler* and *The Spectator* of Addison and Steele. Yet the content of the journal included attacks on the prime minister and his arts. Fielding's coadjutor on *The Champion*, James Ralph (1705-1762), was much more political than Fielding, and it is to Ralph that Fielding left the journal's most strident, most vociferous political commentary. A typical issue of *The Champion* would open with a moral essay by Fielding followed by the "Index of the Times," a section written by Ralph in which specific political issues—the Place Bill, the standing army, royal visits to Hanover (which left Walpole in charge)—would be aired. Fielding's own sense of his role in the journal perhaps is best indicated by his farewell to the reader in no. 91 (12 June 1740): "Lastly, as to politics, our Readers are to regard

The Political Libertines: or, Motion upon Motion *(1741); Fielding is depicted at left, in a barrister's wig and gown, as a supporter of the opposition party (engraving by an unknown artist)*

them as their Physic, not their Food; and they may be assured Dr. *Lilbourne* [Ralph's pseudonym] will dose them as often as is requisite."

The advertisement to the 1741 collected edition of *The Champion* carefully indicated "that all Papers distinguished with a C. or an L. [Fielding adopted Addison's initials for his contributions to *The Spectator*] are the Work of one Hand; those marked thus * * or signed Lilbourne, of another, to whose Account, likewise, except a few Paragraphs, the *Index of the Times*, is to be plac'd." Fielding at a meeting of the partners in *The Champion* 29 June 1741 voted against the sale of the collected edition, principally because, we can guess, he was moving toward a reconciliation with Walpole and wanted to separate himself from the anti-Walpole commentary of the journal. Outvoted by the partners, Fielding used the advertisement to separate himself from Ralph, to absolve himself, as it were, from responsibility for Ralph's political opinions.

Whatever the attitudes expressed about Walpole, *The Champion* is consistent in its praise for the new economic order and for the opportunities offered by London. Hercules Vinegar, the persona of the paper, is a former wrestler and cudgelplayer—a participant in the Smithfield entertainments of which Pope was so contemptuous. He expresses views that tend to be egalitarian rather than aristocratic, that celebrate innovation rather than tradition. In no. 2 (17 No-

vember 1739), after a positive reference to Steele's satire upon concern for genealogy in *The Conscious Lovers* (1722), Vinegar speaks for Fielding: "I have often wondered how such Words as *Upstart, First of his Family*, etc. crept into a Nation, whose Strength and Support is Trade, and whose personal Wealth (excepting a very few immense Fortunes) is almost entirely in the Hands of a Set of sturdy Scrubs, whose chief Honour is to be descended from Adam and Eve." Because Fielding's attitudes toward trade and class more closely approximate those of Addison and Steele than those of Swift and Pope, in those instances when he attacks Walpole, he tries to separate the Great Man from the society he dominated. Typically, Fielding will compare Walpole and his ministerial power to foreign political leaders—the Turkish "first minister," the "Vizier"—to distance Walpole from British political traditions. Or he will compare Walpole to the Harlequin, John Rich. For Fielding, the great virtue of this analogy was that Rich's theater depended upon illusion and disguise. By equating Walpole with Rich, Fielding implied that the electors of Britain had been gulled rather than corrupted—that, undeceived, they could make the political system function properly.

No. 25 (10 January 1740) offers one of the better examples of Fielding's politics in *The Champion* and of his rhetorical method as well. The paper opens with Vinegar claiming that "I con-

In this 1741 engraving by an unknown artist, The Funeral of Faction, *Fielding carries the banner of* The Champion *in the procession mourning the defeat of an attempt to impeach Sir Robert Walpole on 13 February 1741. By the end of the year Fielding had changed his mind about Walpole.*

sider my Paper as a Sort of Stage Coach, a Vehicle in which every one has a right to take a Place." This simile recurs in both *Joseph Andrews* and *Tom Jones* and indicates the artistry Fielding brings to the journal. His lead essays tend to be witty, learned, and figurative rather than directly political. The paper then goes on to print what is supposedly a letter from a critic of Vinegar's. The rhetorical premise of the paper becomes quite complicated. As the correspondent attacks Vinegar for taking too much power unto himself, the letter actually becomes an ironic attack upon Walpole, repeating the standard Opposition Line that the Great Man, by controlling both Parliament and the king, has accrued so much personal power that he has become the tyrant against which the English constitution was established. The correspondent defends the political opposition and, perhaps most significantly, refers to Addison and Steele as both political and literary models:

> It is not Friend [Vinegar], as you would Insinuate ... out of any private Spleen or Pique against you that you are opposed; nor are your Opposition such as desire themselves to establish

the Characters of Authors, or set up a Paper. No, Friend, it is that you should not debauch nor corrupt the Taste and Manners of the People, nor expose the Character of the *English* Genius (hitherto famous) by your vile Works. It is from a Contempt of your Parts, from knowing you to be utterly disqualified for the Office you have taken upon you. An Office too great for any one Man to execute, and which hath formerly employed the best Heads in the Nation, such as *Addison* and *Steele*, and many others. How ridiculous must it seem then, to see a Fellow of low Capacity and a mean Behaviour, investing himself with this Office, placing his Family over all the Professions, and shaking a Club at the whole Nation.

The correspondent then goes on to criticize Vinegar's "Foreign Affairs" and to claim, "Domestic Matters are what you most shine, or, rather, are deficient in. Yet here it is notorious, that you are the greatest Plunderer who ever dealt in them." These are the standard opposition complaints about Walpole: he took too much power unto himself; he gave places to his family; he tainted the Whig politics of the previous generation as he ostentatiously sought his own financial betterment;

his foreign policy was weak and pacific. But the attack is indirect, if obvious. It still addresses Vinegar-Walpole as "Friend" and holds up Addison and Steele, early associates of Walpole, as models. (In several *Champion* papers—nos. 13, 50, and 80—Fielding is critical of Pope.) Fielding leaves it to Ralph, in the "Index of the Times" that follows the letter, to cinch the political point: "tho' the Darts contain'd in this letter, are feather'd with my name, they are levell'd at a much *larger Mark*."

Fielding takes as his great theme in *The Champion* the Scriblerian fight against the tendency to "debauch . . . Taste and Manners"; Vinegar is the defender of the English "Genius." The paper tries to make Walpole the source of all that is wrong, even though Fielding's most natural political loyalty was to Walpole. Thus Fielding creates complicated rhetorical strategies that permit him to criticize the Great Man but to protect the commercial and financial interests the Great Man served. He shares a target with the Scriblerians but not a worldview. When the opposition disappointed Fielding by revealing a desire for political power and profit every bit as strong as Walpole's—when William Pulteney and John Carteret revealed that they actually did want to "set up a paper"—Fielding began the rapprochement with Walpole that his rhetorical indirectness always had left open to him. As early as *The Champion* no. 26 (12 January 1740), Vinegar had alluded to this possibility, arguing that the word "*Turn-coat*" frequently is misapplied and that "no Man is so good as Judge of the true Merits of a Cause, as he who hath been on both Sides of it."

Fielding's change was heralded by a pamphlet published in December 1741, *The Opposition. A Vision.* In this piece the opposition is figured as a wagon that is drawn by ill-favored mules and stuck in dirt. Its "Trunk of Grievances" contains "little more" than a few newspapers, one titled *The Champion*, one "onsense, the letter N being, I supposed, folded down." The wagon cannot move until it receives fresh recruits from the North (Parliamentary seats Walpole lost in the 1741 election), and its leaders (the wagonmasters) have no plan or vision, but only a desire to pass a coach and six in their way. That coach belongs to "a fat gentleman who . . . appeared to have one of the pleasantest, best-natured Countenances I had ever beheld." When the wagon drivers can offer no motive for their trip, other than hatred for the fat man, passengers leave the wagon, and the man (apparently

Walpole) finally turns the mules loose in a pleasant pasture. Fielding implies that he has rejoined Walpole's cause, received again his financial support. This probably accounts for his unwillingness to authorize the collected edition of *The Champion* as well as for Walpole's name on the list of subscribers to Fielding's *Miscellanies* (1743). Martin C. Battestin has suggested that Fielding sometime in 1741 or earlier had finished *Jonathan Wild* (1743) and withheld it from publication until he could mute its anti-Walpole satire.

Walpole, contra Fielding's prediction in *The Opposition*, would fall from power in early 1742, but Fielding's return to his Whig patrimony would continue in a pamphlet written to offer *A Full Vindication of the Dutchess Dowager of Marlborough* as well as in satire upon the opposition in *Joseph Andrews*, book 2, chapter 10. As he responded to the Jacobite Rebellion of 1745, Fielding completed his return to the Whig establishment. The rebellion provided a convenient threat for Fielding because the success of the Stuarts depended upon the apathy of the English people, who did not find George II a particularly attractive or compelling king. In both *The True Patriot* and *The Jacobite's Journal* as well as in three political pamphlets contemporary with them—*The History of the Present Rebellion in Scotland, A Serious Address to the People of Great Britain,* and *A Dialogue between the Devil, the Pope, and the Pretender*—Fielding reminds the English of their political traditions and attempts to define their political interests. In reminding the public at large, he rediscovers his political faith—the Whiggism with which he had arrived in London in 1727 and which his complicated relationship with Walpole had obscured. These journals and pamphlets are less rhetorically complex than *The Champion*, more narrowly dedicated to achieving their political task.

Fielding calls for support of the Hanoverian succession and of the Broad-Bottomed Ministry—Pelham succeeded Pulteney and Carteret in 1743; Walpole died early in 1745—for reasons religious and economic. He claims that the Pretender will attempt to restore Roman Catholicism as the state religion; thus he always surrounds Charles Edward with Italian-speaking priests. And he claims that the Pretender will disown the national debt and thus ruin the system of public credit. Both *The True Patriot* and *The Jacobite's Journal* include sections that adumbrate the business section in today's newspaper. They quote stock market prices and give interest rates. In *The True*

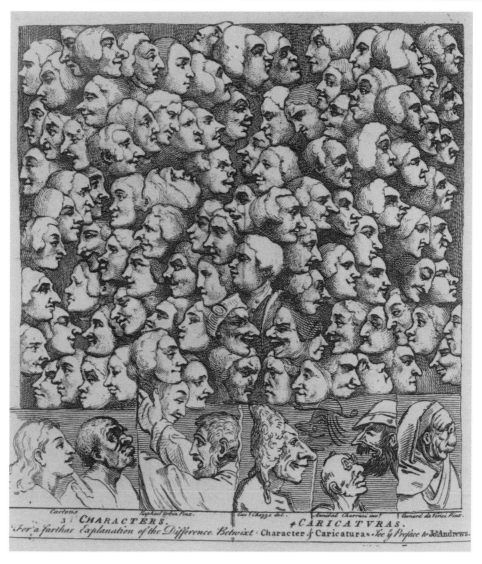

In this 1743 print William Hogarth caricatured himself and Fielding. Fielding is the second head directly above the w *in "Betwixt." Hogarth is facing him.*

Patriot no. 2 (12 November 1745), Fielding published a letter from "An Old Gentlewoman" addressed to those who "have their whole Fortunes in the Public Funds." She urges people not to panic and sell out. Fielding then speaks as the True Patriot, and asserts directly and unequivocally: "It is impossible to make your Money more secure than it is: If this Rebellion should be unsuccessless [*sic*], your Property is not only safe, but will be more valuable than at present; if on the contrary, the Rebellion should have an Issue which there is now (God be praised) no great reason to apprehend, your Money will be as insecure in your own Chests as in those of the Public." Fielding appeals directly to the financial interest of his audience, showing Jacobitism to be

an absurd political faith because of the threat it poses to established financial institutions. Nowhere do we see more clearly his distance from Swift and Pope than in his comments upon the "Funds." Fielding accepts paper as property, while Swift, Pope, and Bolingbroke all hoped to end the War of the Spanish Succession, pay off the debt incurred during the war, and return social, economic, and political power to the "Landed-Men."

The True Patriot no. 3 (19 November 1745) envisions the consequences of a Jacobite victory. In the narrator's nightmare, he finds himself imprisoned for his support of the Hanoverian side. One of his fellow prisoners bemoans the fact that "my whole Estate was in the Funds, by the wiping out of which I was at once reduced to the Condition in which you now see me.... I found a Royal Decree had reduced me to downright Beggary." The prison guards speak with Italian accents. Fielding predicts a scene of universal desolation following a Jacobite triumph, and concludes the paper with a relevant allusion: "Of such a Scene my learned Reader may see a fine Picture drawn by *Silius Italicus*, in his second Book, where he describes the sacking of the City of Saguntum by a less savage army." The direct political appeal of the paper is enriched by Fielding's erudition. No. 4 (26 November 1745) opens by explicitly restating the great theme of the previous paper: "every good and worthy Protestant in this Nation, who is attached to his Religion and Liberties, or who hath any Estate or Property, either in Church-lands or in the Funds, (which includes almost every Man who hath either Estate or Property in the Kingdom) is concerned, in the highest Degree, to oppose the present Rebellion."

This direct appeal is very different from the complex rhetoric of *The Champion*, principally because Fielding's political attitude has passed from ambivalence to certainty. The final issues of *The True Patriot*, particularly no. 30, offer explicit and extended defenses of Pelham and his men and, since Pelham was Walpole's protégé, conclude Fielding's rapprochement with the Great Man. Political certainty was difficult for Fielding, however, because it meant that he no longer could blame one bad man, one foreign harlequin, for the ills of the society. Fielding's satiric sensitivity to corrupt and venal behavior remained sharp, but from 1746 until his death he had to consider that "the Character of the English Genius (hitherto so famous)" might be flawed. *The True Patriot* nos. 7 and 13 include letters from Abraham Adams, but his character has an effect very different from that in *Joseph Andrews*. In the novel Adams is an innocent; he encounters and reveals evil, but he does not understand or recognize it. In *The True Patriot* he has been to London, the city he never reaches in *Joseph Andrews*, and he now sees the success of the rebels as a judgment upon the evil ways of the English people, particularly of the elite. Adams makes his first appearance just as Fielding announces in the "Present History" section of the paper (the news section) that the rebels have begun their retreat. With the convenient Jacobite threat on the wane, Fielding begins to consider more directly the moral nature of the British state. In his prose writings of 1747-1748, Fielding tries to use the outdated Jaco-

bite threat to build national unity. In *A Dialogue between a Gentleman of London, Agent for Two Court Candidates, and an Honest Alderman Of the Country Party* (23 June 1747) and *A Proper Answer To a Late Scurrilous Libel* (24 December 1747), as well as in *The Jacobite's Journal* (5 December 1747 - 5 November 1748), Fielding defends the memory of Walpole and praises the Pelham ministry as one "composed really of all the great Men, whose Abilities of any Kind make them worthy of any Place in it." *The Jacobite's Journal* no. 30 (25 June 1748) includes a reference to "your great Patterns, *Addison* and *Steele*," thus indicating Fielding's alignment with the Whig establishment in both politics and literature.

Fielding attempts to establish a persona somewhat like Hercules Vinegar in *The Jacobite's Journal*. The first sixteen issues are spoken by one John Trott-plaid, a Jacobite who continually describes Jacobitism as a "Mystery." Trott-plaid functions principally to admit that Jacobitism is absurd and illogical and then to embrace the absurdity. In no. 17 (26 March 1748), Fielding drops the persona, claiming that "I am weary of personating a Character for which I have so solemn a Contempt." He goes on to say, "it is high time to speak in a plainer Language than that of Irony, and to endeavour to raise something more than Mirth in the Mind of the Reader." Fielding here seeks to be direct and unequivocal; political certainty, we might say, leads to rhetorical simplicity. The rest of *The Jacobite's Journal* is devoted principally to defense of the Pelham ministry, particularly Fielding's Eton classmate George Lyttelton, and of "the present Royal Establishment," particularly George II's son William, Duke of Cumberland, who had taken a leading role in defeating and then destroying the Highland Clans.

Fielding's prose writing after *The Jacobite Journal* is profoundly affected by his experience as a magistrate; his appointments as justice of the peace for Westminster and for Middlesex clearly were rewards for the political service he had given the Pelham ministry from 1745 onward. Of course, it is something of a critical commonplace that Fielding's vision grew darker in the late 1740s because of the criminals with whom he had to deal. But the nature of his nonfiction prose points to perhaps an even more basic problem that darkened his view of life. The prose divides into two types: Fielding returns to Scriblerian satire in *The Covent-Garden Journal* and, in a special sense, *The Journal of a Voyage to Lisbon*; he also offers grudging vindication of the political and social status quo in a series of social pamphlets written in the late 1740s and early 1750s. In these pamphlets he justifies his actions in famous criminal cases and anatomizes the causes of crime and corruption in English society. The pamphlets reveal most clearly how convenient a scapegoat Walpole had been for Fielding and how much Fielding's reconciliation with the Great Man and his political legacy complicated Fielding's treatment of the English "Genius."

In these pamphlets Fielding repeatedly finds himself in the position of defending legal and social practices that he seems to feel are unjust or corrupt. In *A True State of the Case of Bosavern Penlez* (1749) and *A Clear State of the Case of Elizabeth Canning* (1753), Fielding defends actions he took as a magistrate in cases in which he had been publicly criticized for his cruelty. The Canning pamphlet defends a judicial system which moves slowly in capital cases. Elizabeth Canning claimed she was robbed, kidnapped, and held hostage for almost a month (1 January - 29 January 1753); Fielding must explain the improbability of Canning's testimony, but also admit the power of her grievance. He finds himself trying to make sense of a case so complicated and difficult that it seems to elude adjudication. He concludes the pamphlet by admitting his own fallibility and indicating his willingness to be proven wrong. The Penlez case offers clearer facts but a more difficult moral problem. Penlez was arrested with goods he took from a bawdy house during a night of rioting by sailors and others in which several such houses were burned and destroyed. Fielding finds himself in the position of defending the Riot Act, which he had invoked, and of asserting the importance of property. Fielding argues that the rioters' claims against the bawdy houses were only "pretence" and that "Property" must be protected. Penlez had to be hanged because he stole, no matter from where.

In his classic essay "Fielding's Social Thought" (1956) George Sherburn argues convincingly that "Fielding's social philosophy is founded upon the concept of a stratified society, such as might constitute a small section of the great scale of being. He believes that all government is based on a principle of subordination and that the duty of all classes of men is to contribute to the good of the whole." This basic social conservatism manifests itself in the Penlez and Canning essays as well as in *An Enquiry Into the Causes for the late Increase of Robbers* (1751) and *A Proposal for Making an Effectual Provision for the Poor*

(1753). Whatever his sympathy for poor postilions in his fiction, Fielding here asserts that the poor must be controlled; he envisions a kind of super workhouse for them. The poor lack property—the means by which Fielding, following John Locke, domesticates self-interest in his political writing—and thus they must be controlled by force. Fielding had invoked the Riot Act to control the mob of which Penlez was a member.

When Fielding traces the cause of illegal and immoral behavior by the poor in his *Enquiry Into the Causes for the late Increase of Robbers* as well as in his *Charge Delivered to the Grand Jury* (1749), he is clear-sighted and honest enough to see that the poor merely imitate their betters. It is immorality among the social elite that leads to crime among the poor. But this insight, given Fielding's basic social conservatism, is problematic for him.

When Fielding in *The Covent-Garden Journal* (1752) returns to periodical writing, he attacks the elite, but only after he opens the paper by announcing, "I disclaim any Dealing in Politics." *The Covent-Garden Journal*, which includes some of Fielding's wittiest, most subtle writing outside of the great novels, puts him one last time in the mode of Scriblerian satire; in no. 5 (18 January 1752) he makes positive reference to a conversation with Alexander Pope. Taking the persona of "Sir Alexander Drawcansir, Knight Censor of Great Britain," Fielding writes in a Hercules Vinegar-like character, and as he comments upon the "Taste" of his age, his tone frequently is complex, difficult to assess. No. 2 (7 January 1752), for example, opens with Drawcansir attempting "to prove, that we live in the best . . . one of the most virtuous Ages that hath ever appeared in the world." As he goes on to describe the age's virtues—most notably, liberty and charity—Fielding quite clearly is ironic; the age does not measure up to the Augustan standard. But that irony does not totally qualify Drawcansir's opening warning that it is too easy to dismiss one's age as the worst.

In *Tom Jones* Fielding attempts to enrich our sense of what true prudence is. In *Joseph Andrews*, charity. In *The True Patriot*, patriotism. So *The Covent-Garden Journal* exposes us to widely different definitions and applications of "Taste." Pervasive in the journal is the sense that the taste of the social elite—the old English "Genius"—is flawed. But that satiric sense of social decadence cannot operate politically because Fielding continues loyal to the Pelham ministry, to the Whig so-

Fielding circa 1753 (drawing attributed to Sir Joshua Reynolds; by permission of the Trustees of the British Museum)

cial, political, and economic establishment. He attenuates his political role in order to offer his satiric rebukes. Attempting to reform the elite, Fielding compares himself to Hercules cleansing the stables of Augeus (no. 5, 18 January 1752). But in his case, the filth mounts because he is unwilling to change those social institutions and hierarchies that produce it. His satiric sense still is sharp, but he lacks the target, the focus Walpole provided in the 1730s.

The image of Fielding as a despairing Hercules in an endlessly filthy Augean stable recurs in his posthumously published *Journal of a Voyage to Lisbon.* In summer 1754 Fielding journeyed to Lisbon in a futile attempt to save his life, and he wrote the journal to provide income for his family. Fielding had married his first wife, Charlotte,

the model for both Sophia Western and Amelia Booth, on 28 November 1734, and she died in early November 1744. The couple had five children, but all of them, save a daughter, Harriet, predeceased Fielding. With his second wife, Mary, to whom he was married on 27 November 1747, Fielding had four children, three of whom—a daughter, Sophia, and sons William and Allen—survived him. Besides recounting the last days of one individual, the journal gives a political dimension to Fielding's plight. He opens it by comparing his physical state to the state of the British body politic upon the death of Henry Pelham in 1753. He makes full amends to Robert Walpole, describing him as "one of the best of men and ministers." He continues, as in the social pamphlets, to trouble with the problem of lower-class immorality and violence—with the problem of the mob. In the powerful opening scene of the *The Journal of a Voyage to Lisbon*, a debilitated Fielding requires aid to board the ship that will carry him to Lisbon. As he is lifted on board, dockworkers and watermen jeer at him and threaten him. He must rely on a tyrannical "Captain Bashaw" to protect him. Similarly, a grim irony is present in the very situation of the journal. The lifelong Whig Fielding is journeying to Portugal—a country Roman Catholic in religion and ruled by an absolute monarch—to save his health. The journal brings into sharp relief all the doubts about the English social constitution to which Fielding's political faith in Pelham led.

If Fielding's last years were characterized by increasing darkness in his view of British society, two of his late prose works reveal the persistence of views he held throughout his life. In *Examples of the Interposition of Providence in the Detection and Punishment of Murder* (1752) he gives brief histories of famous capital cases in which murderers either reveal themselves because of the horrible guilt they feel or are revealed by unlikely circumstances and events. The pamphlet reveals Fielding's faith in providential order to be strong, even in the midst of the dark world of criminal behavior to which his magistracy had exposed him. Perhaps even more revealing of Fielding's worldview is his almost unknown *A Plan of the Universal Register Office* (1751). The Universal Register Office, which he set up with his half brother John in 1751, was one of several money-making schemes in which the chronically cash-short Fielding involved himself. The office was to include an employment agency, a marriage bureau, and a real-estate brokerage. *A Plan of the Universal Register Office* expresses Fielding's faith that man is a social animal (not a Hobbesian individual) and that great cities are the clearest, most powerful testimonies to that sociability. "In large and populous Cities, and wide extended Communities, it is most probable that every human Talent is dispersed somewhere or other among the Members; and consequently every Person who stands in Need of that Talent, might supply his Want if he knew where to find it; but to know this is the Difficulty, and this Difficulty still increases with the Largeness of the Society." While George Sherburn surely is right to emphasize Fielding's social conservatism, *A Plan of the Universal Register Office* and the other social and political writings reveal the context of that conservatism to be profoundly different from the con-

text of the conservatism of the Scriblerians. Fictional portraits of rural life aside, Fielding is a city man. He is his father's son insofar as he is loyal to those economic innovations—the bank, the stock exchange, paper credit—that Marlborough 's battles led to, and Walpole's ministry firmly entrenched. For Pope and Swift London symbolizes all that is wrong with the new England, and they call for a return to a classical past. Fielding is sensitive to the crime and corruption occurring in London, but he hopes that better administration, better communication can minimize them. His literary satires of London life never try for the symbolic dimension found in Pope's *Dunciad*. He, instead, tries to portray abuses as specific rather than cultural, although, late in his career, he begins to trouble with the notion that the English constitution or "Genius" may be flawed.

Fielding's nonfiction prose, then, is important because it provides a source for and helps to chart the most outstanding feature of his fiction—the feature that gives the fiction its richness and complexity, its enduring greatness. Fielding, through his marvelous narrative skill, combines a tolerant, almost democratic good nature with a classical, almost elitist commitment to narrative design, to literary and social hierarchy. As he describes Betty the amorous chambermaid or notes that the poor postilion who gives his coat to Joseph Andrews later was transported for robbing a hen roost, Fielding appears most egalitarian in his social attitudes. But when he gives the new form of prose fiction—what we will call the novel—a classical patrimony, he reveals his literary conservatism. Just as when he rehabilitates Squire Booby or reveals Tom Jones to be a gentleman, he indicates his social conservatism. Fielding's political career is best understood as one instance in the transition of Whiggism from a revolutionary political philosophy to a conservative, property-defending political cliché. Fielding's social views reflect a similar adaptation of the hierarchical notions of Swift and Pope, with their emphasis upon class and subordination, to the new world of trade and commerce, of urban life. Fielding's nonfiction prose reveals him continually struggling to combine a genial, tolerant modern view of man with a classical, satiric, and conservative view. The combination Fielding so triumphantly achieves in the narrative voice of his great comic fiction is adumbrated in the political and social accommodations made in the nonfiction prose.

Fielding's monument in the English cemetery, Lisbon

Bibliographies:

H. George Hahn, *Henry Fielding: An Annotated Bibliography* (Metuchen, N.J.: Scarecrow Press, 1979);

John A. Stoler and Richard D. Fulton, *Henry Fielding: An Annotated Bibliography of Twentieth-Century Criticism, 1900-1977* (New York: Garland, 1980).

Biographies:

Wilbur L. Cross, *The History of Henry Fielding*, 3 volumes (New Haven: Yale University Press, 1918);

Pat Rogers, *Henry Fielding: A Biography* (New York: Scribners, 1979);

Martin C. Battestin with Ruthe R. Battestin, *Henry Fielding: A Life* (London & New York: Routledge, 1989).

References:

Martin C. Battestin, "Fielding and 'Master Punch' in Panton Street," *Philological Quarterly*, 45 (January 1966): 191-208;

Battestin, "Four New Fielding Attributions: His Earliest Satires of Walpole," *Studies in Bibliography*, 36 (1983): 69-109;

Battestin, "Henry Fielding, Sarah Fielding, and 'the dreadful Sin of Incest,' " *Novel: A Forum on Fiction*, 13 (Fall 1979): 6-18;

Battestin, *The Moral Basis of Fielding's Art: A Study of Joseph Andrews* (Middletown, Conn.: Wesleyan University Press, 1959);

Battestin, "Pictures of Fielding," *Eighteenth-Century Studies*, 17 (Fall 1983): 1-13;

Battestin, *The Providence of Wit: Aspects of Form in Augustan Literature and the Arts* (Oxford: Clarendon Press, 1974);

Battestin, ed., *Twentieth-Century Interpretations of Tom Jones* (Englewood Cliffs, N.J.: Prentice-Hall, 1968);

Battestin, with R. R. Battestin, "Fielding, Bedford, and the Westminster Election of 1749," *Eighteenth-Century Studies*, 11 (Winter 1977/1978): 143-185;

Frederic T. Blanchard, *Fielding the Novelist: A Study in Historical Criticism* (New Haven: Yale University Press, 1926);

Leo Braudy, *Narrative Form in History and Fiction: Hume, Fielding, and Gibbon* (Princeton, N.J.: Princeton University Press, 1970);

John Butt, *Fielding* (London: Longmans, Green, 1954);

Thomas R. Cleary, *Henry Fielding: Political Writer* (Waterloo, Ont.: Wilfrid Laurier University Press, 1984);

William B. Coley, "Fielding's Two Appointments to the Magistracy," *Modern Philology*, 63 (November 1965): 144-149;

Coley, "Henry Fielding's 'Lost' Law Book," *Modern Language Notes*, 76 (May 1961): 408-413;

R. S. Crane, "The Concept of Plot and the Plot of *Tom Jones*," in *Critics and Criticism: Ancient and Modern*, edited by Crane (Chicago: University of Chicago Press, 1952);

Peter Jan De Voogd, *Henry Fielding and William Hogarth: The Correspondences of the Arts* (Amsterdam: Rodopi, 1981);

Irvin Ehrenpreis, *Fielding: Tom Jones* (London: Arnold, 1964);

Morris Golden, *Fielding's Moral Psychology* (Amherst: University of Massachusetts Press, 1966);

Bertrand A. Goldgar, *The Curse of Party: Swift's Relations with Addison and Steele* (Lincoln: University of Nebraska Press, 1961);

Goldgar, *Walpole and the Wits: The Relation of Politics to Literature: 1722-1742* (Lincoln: University of Nebraska Press, 1976);

Bernard Harrison, *Henry Fielding's Tom Jones: The Novelist as Moral Philosopher* (London: Sussex University Press, 1975);

Glenn W. Hatfield, *Henry Fielding and the Language of Irony* (Chicago: University of Chicago Press, 1968);

William Hazlitt, *Lectures on the English Comic Writers* (London, 1819);

Eleanor Newman Hutchens, *Irony in Tom Jones* (University: University of Alabama Press, 1965);

Michael Irwin, *Henry Fielding: The Tentative Realist* (Oxford: Clarendon Press, 1967);

Robert William Irwin, *The Making of Jonathan Wild* (New York: Columbia University Press, 1941);

Wolfgang Iser, *The Implied Reader: Patterns of Communication in Prose Fiction from Bunyan to Beckett* (Baltimore: Johns Hopkins University Press, 1974);

Benjamin Maelor Jones, *Henry Fielding: Novelist and Magistrate* (London: Allen & Unwin, 1933);

Donald Kay, ed., *A Provision of Human Nature: Essays on Fielding and Others in Honor of Miriam Austin Locke* (University: University of Alabama Press, 1977);

George R. Levine, *Henry Fielding and the Dry Mock: A Study of the Techniques of Irony in His Early Works* (The Hague: Mouton, 1967);

John Loftis, *Comedy and Society from Congreve to Fielding* (Stanford: Stanford University Press, 1959);

Thomas E. Maresca, *Epic to Novel* (Columbus: Ohio State University Press, 1974);

Brian McCrea, " 'Had Not Joseph Withheld Him': The Portrayal of the Social Elite in *Joseph Andrews*," in *Man, God, and Nature in the Enlightenment*, edited by Donald C. Mell, Jr., Theodore E. D. Braun, and Lucia M. Palmer (East Lansing: Colleagues Press, 1988), pp. 123-128;

McCrea, *Henry Fielding and the Politics of Mid-Eighteenth-Century England* (Athens: University of Georgia Press, 1981);

McCrea, "Rewriting *Pamela*: Social Change and Religious Faith in *Joseph Andrews*," *Studies in the Novel*, 16 (Summer 1984): 137-149;

Alan D. McKillop, *The Early Masters of English Fiction* (Lawrence: University of Kansas Press, 1956);

Henry Knight Miller, *Essays on Fielding's Miscellanies: A Commentary on Volume One* (Princeton, N.J.: Princeton University Press, 1961);

Miller, *Fielding's Tom Jones and the Romance Tradition* (Victoria, B.C.: University of Victoria, 1976);

Robert Etheridge Moore, *Hogarth's Literary Relationships* (Minneapolis: University of Minnesota Press, 1948);

John B. Owen, *The Rise of the Pelhams* (London: Methuen, 1957);

Ronald Paulson, *Satire and the Novel in Eighteenth-Century England* (New Haven: Yale University Press, 1967);

Paulson, ed., *Fielding: A Collection of Critical Essays* (Englewood Cliffs, N.J.: Prentice-Hall, 1962);

Paulson and Thomas Lockwood, *Henry Fielding: The Critical Heritage* (London: Routledge & Kegan Paul / New York: Barnes & Noble, 1969);

J. H. Plumb, *Sir Robert Walpole: The King's Minister* (Boston: Houghton Mifflin, 1961);

Martin Price, *To the Palace of Wisdom: Studies in Order and Energy from Dryden to Blake* (Garden City, N.Y.: Doubleday, 1964);

C. J. Rawson, *Henry Fielding* (London: Routledge & Kegan Paul / New York: Humanities Press, 1968);

Rawson, *Henry Fielding and the Augustan Ideal under Stress* (London: Routledge & Kegan Paul, 1972);

Rawson, ed., *Henry Fielding: A Critical Anthology* (Harmondsworth, U.K.: Penguin, 1973);

Eric Rothstein, *Systems of Order and Inquiry in Later Eighteenth-Century Fiction* (Berkeley & Los Angeles: University of California Press, 1975);

Archibald Bolling Shepperson, "Fielding on Liberty and Democracy," in *English Studies in Honor of James Sothall Wilson*, University of Virginia Studies (Charlottesville, Va., 1951), pp. 264-276;

Arthur Sherbo, *Studies in the Eighteenth-Century English Novel* (East Lansing: Michigan State University Press, 1969);

George Sherburn, "Fielding's Social Thought," *Philological Quarterly*, 35 (January 1956): 1-23;

Sean Shesgreen, *Literary Portraits in the Novels of Henry Fielding* (DeKalb: Northern Illinois University Press, 1972);

William Makepeace Thackeray, *The English Humourists of the Eighteenth Century* (London: Smith, Elder, 1853);

E. P. Thompson, *Whigs and Hunters: The Origins of the Black Act* (New York: Pantheon, 1975);

Ethel M. Thornbury, *Henry Fielding's Theory of the Comic Prose Epic* (Madison: University of Wisconsin Press, 1931);

Ian Watt, *The Rise of the Novel: Studies in Defoe, Richardson, and Fielding* (Berkeley & Los Angeles: University of California Press, 1957; London: Chatto & Windus, 1957);

Ioan Williams, ed., *The Criticism of Henry Fielding* (London: Routledge & Kegan Paul, 1970; New York: Barnes & Noble, 1970);

Murial Brittain Williams, *Marriage: Fielding's Mirror of Morality* (University: University of Alabama Press, 1973);

Andrew Wright, *Henry Fielding: Mask and Feast* (Berkeley & Los Angeles: University of California Press, 1965; London: Chatto & Windus, 1965);

Marvin R. Zirker, Jr., *Fielding's Social Pamphlets* (Berkeley & Los Angeles: University of California Press, 1966).

Papers:
The only extant literary manuscripts by Fielding are the poems (ca. 1729 to 1733) in the collection of the Harrowby MSS Trust, Sandon Hall, Stafford; and the printer's copy for an essay he contributed to the periodical *Common Sense* (1738) at the Public Record Office, Chancery Lane, London. The largest collection of his letters available to the public is the correspondence addressed to the duke of Bedford and his agent on deposit at the Bedford Office, London. Miscellaneous documents and letters listed by Cross and Dudden in appendices to their biographies are dispersed among several private and institutional collections, including the British Museum, Harvard University, the Huntington Library, the Hyde Collection, the Morgan Library, Princeton University, and the Victoria and Albert Museum.

John, Lord Hervey

(16 October 1696 - 5 August 1743)

Isobel Grundy
University of Alberta

BOOKS: *Monimia to Philocles* (Dublin [*sic*], 1726);

An Answer to the Occasional Writer. No. II (London: Printed for A. Moor, 1727);

The Occasional Writer. No. IV. To His Imperial Majesty (London: Printed for A. Moore, 1727);

A Summary Account of the State of Dunkirk, and the Negociations relating thereto (London: Printed for J. Roberts, 1730);

Observations on the Writings of the Craftsman (London: Printed for J. Roberts, 1730);

Sequel of a Pamphlet intitled Observations on the Writings of the Craftsman (London: Printed for J. Roberts, 1730);

Farther Observations On the Writings of the Craftsman. Or Short Remarks upon a Late Pamphlet, entituled, An Answer to the Observations on the Writings of the Craftsman (London: Printed for J. Roberts, 1730);

A Satyr. In the Manner of Persius. In a Dialogue between the Poet and His Friend (London [Dublin?], 1730);

A Letter to Caleb D'Anvers Esq, doubtfully attributed to Hervey (London: Sold by J. Roberts, 1731);

The Modish Couple. A Comedy, doubtfully attributed to Hervey and Frederick, Prince of Wales (London: Printed for J. Watts, 1732);

Some Remarks on the Minute Philosopher. In a Letter from a Country Clergyman to his Friend in London (London: Printed for J. Roberts, 1732);

The Reply of a Member of Parliament to the Mayor of his Corporation (London: Printed by J. Roberts, 1733);

A Letter to the Craftsman, on the Game of Chess (London: Printed for J. Peele, 1733);

Verses Address'd to the Imitator of the First Satire of the Second Book of Horace, by Hervey and Lady Mary Wortley Montagu (London: Printed for A. Dodd, 1733); also published as *To the Imitator of the Satire of the Second Book of Horace* (London: Printed for J. Roberts, 1733);

An Epistle from a Nobleman to a Doctor of Divinity (London: Printed for J. Roberts, 1733);

The Conduct of the Opposition, and the Tendency of Modern Patriotism (More particularly in a Late Scheme to Establish a Military Government in this Country) Review'd and Examin'd (London: Printed for J. Peele, 1734);

Ancient and Modern Liberty Stated and Compar'd (London: Printed for J. Roberts, 1734); facsimile, edited by H. T. Dickinson, Augustan Reprint Society, nos. 255-256 (Los Angeles: William Andrews Clark Memorial Library, 1989);

The Quaker's Reply to the Country Parson's Plea (London: Printed for T. Cooper, 1736);

A Letter to the Author of Common-Sense or The Englishman's Journal, of Saturday, April 16 (London: Printed for T. Cooper, 1737);

An Examination of the Facts and Reasonings Contain'd in a Pamphlet intitled a Letter from a Member of Parliament (London: Sold by J. Roberts, 1739);

A Letter to Mr. C--b-r, On his Letter to Mr. P--- (London: Printed for J. Roberts, 1742);

The Difference between Verbal and Practical Virtue (London: Printed for J. Roberts, 1742);

The Patriots are Come, or a New Doctor for a Crazy Constitution (London: Printed for W. Webb, 1742);

Miscellaneous Thoughts On the present Posture both of our Foreign and Domestic Affairs (London: Printed for J. Roberts, 1742);

The Question Stated, with Regard to Our Army in Flanders (London: Printed for J. Roberts, 1743);

Memoirs of the Reign of George II, 2 volumes, edited by John Wilson Croker (London: John Murray, 1848; Philadelphia: Lea & Blanchard, 1848);

Some Materials Towards Memoirs of the Reign of George II, 3 volumes, edited by Romney Sedgwick (London: Eyre & Spottiswoode, 1931).

John Hervey was born in London, eldest child of John Hervey of Ickworth, Suffolk, and his second wife, Elizabeth Felton Hervey; he had

John, Lord Hervey, Vice-Chamberlain to the King's Household (portrait by John Fayram; at Ickworth, by permission of the National Trust)

sixteen full and three half siblings. His father became Baron Hervey of Ickworth in 1703 and earl of Bristol in 1714; his half brother's death in 1723 gave John the courtesy title of Lord Hervey. His parents were both courtiers, though his father's roots and taste lay in country life; he was early introduced to the company of the powerful, as well as to riding in horse races at Newmarket. He attended Westminster School (from the late age of sixteen) and Clare Hall, Cambridge (1713-1715). After his Grand Tour (1716-1717 extending only to Paris and Hannover, since "Mama's tears & fears" forbade him to proceed to Italy) he began to frequent the court in earnest. In April 1720 he married Mary Lepell,

maid of honor to the Princess of Wales and friend of Alexander Pope. Hervey's bride was rich in beauty and charm but not in money: they kept the marriage secret for six months, presumably to postpone her losing her job and salary. The first of their eight children was born the next year; others rapidly followed. Hervey became M.P. for Bury St. Edmunds in 1725.

A writer of amusing letters and occasional verses from his youth, Hervey made his first English appearance in print involuntarily. (He had contributed Latin verse to a Cambridge volume welcoming George I in 1714.) In 1726 a printer pirated his Ovidian verse epistle *Monimia to Philocles*, which—based on an actual seduced and

...rest, we will all go to bed, for staying here we do the poor Q. no good, & our selves hurt, & so dismissing Ld H. they all retired.

I will relate no farther Particulars how the two following Days pass'd, as such a narration would be only recapitulating a Diary of the two former, without any material Variation. The Q. grew so perceptibly weaker every Hour that every one she lived was more than was expected; she ask'd Pesier on Sunday in the Evening with no seeming Impatience under any Article of her present Circumstances but their duration; how long he thought it was possible for all this to last? to wch he answer'd; je crois que votre majté sera bien tôt soulagée & she calmly reply'd — tant mieux. about 10 a clock on Sunday night the K. being in bed & asleep on the floor at the Feet of the Q.s Bed, & the Ps Emely in a couch-bed in a corner of ye Room, the Q. began to rattle in ye Throat, & Mrs Purcel giving the allarm that she was expiring, all in the Room started up, Ps Caroline was sent for & Ld H. but before the last arrived the Q. was just dead; all she say'd before she dy'd was — I have now got an asthma — open ye Window — then she say'd — pray — upon wch the Ps Emely began to read some prayers which she scarce repeated

Page from Hervey's manuscript for his Memoirs of the Reign of George II *(by permission of the West Suffolk Record Office, Bury St. Edmunds)*

abandoned maid of honor, here called by a name borrowed from Thomas Otway—is genuinely moving though florid and long-winded. Among the many poetic genres which Hervey attempted, his favorites seem to have been dramatic monologues on love topics, often from a female viewpoint (Lady Mary Wortley Montagu kept copies of several, including a lesbian proposition alluding to actual people); polemics (his notable political pamphlets include verse as well as prose); verse attacks on Pope (of the three he wrote, Lady Mary collaborated on the strongest, *Verses Address'd to the Imitator of the First Satire of the Second Book of Horace*, 1733); occasional verse (in 1736, when he was in trouble over an epigram, Queen Caroline advised him to give up writing, and he replied at length in verse: "But how shall I this flippant pen restrain . . . I should go mad were I to stop the drain"); and poems of friendship and personal feeling (Voltaire begged a copy of a 1729 epistle to Lady Hervey from Paris and Dodsley's 1748 *Collection* printed "To Mr Fox, written at Florence," 1728).

Hervey's first political pamphlet, *An Answer to the Occasional Writer. No. II* (1727), is a response to Henry St. John, Viscount Bolingbroke, leading pamphlet opponent of Sir Robert Walpole. The genre—the form in which Hervey wrote his best work after his *Memoirs of the Reign of George II* (posthumously published in 1848)—ran naturally to capping the arguments of others, at which he excelled. A second intervention in the same controversy quickly brought him a government pension; in 1728 he was chosen to move the address of thanks to George II for opening his first session of Parliament. He seemed to have found his métier.

But this virtuoso of court dealings was always ambivalent about court life. Later that year he set out for Italy with a recently met friend, Stephen Fox, who was already the object of his passionate devotion. One reason given for their journey was Hervey's always wretched health. Each of the friends was severely ill in Italy, and Hervey also underwent surgery for a benign tumor under his chin. His friendship with Stephen Fox (and with Stephen's brother Henry) was to endure throughout his life, but its fervor had cooled by 1736, when Fox married (chiefly for money) and Hervey succumbed to the charms of a young adventurer with literary talent, Francesco Algarotti.

After returning to England and his wife in late 1729, Hervey kept his relationship with Fox

warm in intimate, humorous, revelatory letters. He was appointed vice-chamberlain to the royal household in 1730, resumed his political writing, and won popularity by fighting a duel in 1731 with William Pulteney, who had smeared him with sexual innuendo in a pamphlet lampoon. Hervey's polemical works included the nonpolitical; here too he confined himself usually to answering the initiatives of others. He became philosophical in *Some Remarks on the Minute Philosopher* (1732), a pamphlet about George Berkeley, for which he assumed the persona of a country parson. He became literary in challenging Pope. Of all Hervey's battles this was the least equally matched: Pope set Hervey's carapace immovably in amber in the Sporus portrait of the *Epistle to Dr. Arbuthnot* (1735).

Hervey's *Memoirs of the Reign of George II* bear some relation to history. He sets out "to inform rather than to please," though later he espouses the aim of pleasing; he includes the texts of letters, documents, and speeches when he can. They also have some relation to autobiography, though after confident use of an authorial "I" in his opening paragraphs, Hervey says that when he appears as a figure in his own story he will "have recourse to the old refuge of speaking always of myself in the third person," to avoid "disagreeable egotisms."

They also resemble a powerful novel combining acute psychological insight with mythic heightening. Believing that history is swayed by "the fortuitous influence of chance" working itself out through the quirks of individuals, Hervey opens (at a point just before George I's death) with detailed sketches of his "chief actors." He keeps his analyses of the new king and queen back until a little later, so that they emerge for readers as they do for the waiting politicians, as the reign gets under way.

At the heart of the *Memoirs of the Reign of George II* stands a tightly related group of forces held in tension against each other. Walpole, who controls the Commons, needs Hervey to control the Lords and a chain of influence passing through Hervey and the queen to control the mulish and headstrong king. The royal couple both chafe under the necessity of exercising constitutional rather than autocratic power and of keeping within bounds their hatred of their eldest son. Walpole and Hervey, as the forces of reason among rampaging passions and ignorant self-interest, repeatedly restore equilibrium to the processes of government, until the queen's death,

A Full and True
ACCOUNT
OF A
Sharp and Bloody DUEL,

Which was fought in St. James's-Park, *on* Tuesday *the* 26th. *of* January, 1730. *Between* William Poltney Esq; *and the Lord* Harvey. *Mr. Fox, and Mr. Russet were the two Seconds.*

ON Tuesday the 26th of *January,* 1730. In *St. James's Park,* their happen'd a Sharp and bloody Duel between Esq; P————y, and the Lord H————y, being a Man a true Lover of his Country, and has always Good him for the welfare of his Fell-w Subj-cts, which perhaps did make him not so well Respected as could be wish'd for by all true Englishmen, who when they have a friend ought to make much of him, for in those miserable times, who find but few many there is anded that would plunder and Pilledge this our flourishing Nation, nay and i think if the Eyes of Menkind were open they would see who strives to Ruin and undoe teem.

And because that brave and generous Temper'd Man would not put a Bridle upon his Temper, but boldly Speak his Countries Wooes, and the base Transactions of a Great M—- of S—, must he be Challeng'd to answer'd the Threat, because he is not a Bird of the Feather, which makes the Rooks and Crows peck d at him, because it is impossible that the impossible that the Innocent Dove's Feathers should be like those of Robins, who has deck'd himself in Plumes of Gold; which the Generous P————y scorns to obtain by a vicious or covetous Temper, which he oft nti res publickly declar'd; which caused many of Robins Nest to make Reflections on this Innocent Gentleman, which caused a Challenge, there being a Heart burning between the Lord H————y and Esq; P————y.

Which was a Sharp and Bloody Duel, each exerting themselves in the greatest Passions that ever Men were in. The Lord H————y receiv'd three slight Wounds, and the Valiant P————y receiv'd a slight Wound on his Wrist.

Sir Wm. R————el who was chose to be Second to P————y, upon some ill usage he drew his Sword, and Challeng'd Mr. F--x, Second to the Lord H————y to answer at the Point of Sword, but being afraid to draw his Sword, it put Sr Wm. R————t into a great Agony. But several of the Nobily happen'd to come by and parted them; but it is hop'd such Feuds and Distractions will end among Noblemen, till Robin is brought to Justice, which is the Hearty desire of all true Englishmen, that all Things may be brought to a True Light.

LONDON; Printed for Messieurs FIGG and SUTTON.

A broadside account of Hervey's duel with William Pulteney (courtesy of the Henry E. Huntington Library and Art Gallery)

Lord Hervey (pointing to an architectural drawing) and his friends: (from left) Reverend P. L. Wilman, Stephen Fox, Henry Fox, T. Winnington, and John Churchill, Duke of Marlborough (painting by William Hogarth, circa 1738-1739; at Ickworth, by permission of the National Trust)

when equilibrium and Hervey's text each come to an abrupt end.

Several of Hervey's opening sketches are devastating in the candor of their contempt. His measured style, full of ingenious antitheses and triplets, suggests a smooth and skillful ordering of chaotic materials by the superior intelligence of the narrator. The first high point in the story, Walpole's weathering the dangerous passage from George I to George II, is achieved not by skill but by the ineptitude of his opponent.

Every crisis fuses the personal and the political: Anne, Princess Royal's stoic acceptance (after misgivings, with backslidings of purpose) of marriage to the deformed, dwarfish William, Prince of Orange; Frederick, Prince of Wales's rushing his wife from Hampton Court to St. James's in labor, so that his child should be born in the opti-

mum strategic location; Hervey's own triangular sexual relationship with the prince and the Honorable Anne Vane. This last episode is incomplete: Hervey's grandson, Frederick William Hervey, first Marquess of Bristol, destroyed the section of manuscript containing it. Hervey asserts no claim to pass moral judgment on his characters, only judgment as to intelligence and enlightened self-interest. If there is one quality he admires, it is the capacity to look unpleasant truth in the face without shrinking.

Writing, a habit of continuous, sardonic assessment and commentary, was second nature to Hervey. In 1731 he wrote for his children an account of his medical regimen, hoping thereby to compensate for leaving them hereditary health problems. He writes with cool detachment of his sufferings and with modest self-congratulation of stabilizing the "tottering and . . . crazy . . . building . . . I had to prop." He may have written, jointly with the Prince of Wales, *The Modish Couple*, a short-lived comedy of 1732, on the corruptions of modern marriage. He amused the queen in 1736 with "The Death of Lord Hervey, or, A Morning at Court, A Drama," in which he supposes himself attracting several throwaway epitaphs: "to be sure there was a vivacity, and a great many words, and all that." News of his death plays a very minor part in the poem, shouldered aside (far more thoroughly than in Swift's poem on a parallel subject, "Verses on the Death of Dr. Swift") in everybody's thoughts by breakfast, tittle-tattle, irrelevant backbiting, and routine. The author retains the last laugh, since the news is revealed to be a trick played in order to find out what people would say.

On Queen Caroline's death in November 1737, Hervey suffered personal desolation and professional setback: he would no longer be so indispensable to Walpole. He imagined replacing the prime minister, but wrote him a long, formal letter complaining of inadequate reward for his services. He became lord privy seal in 1740; when Walpole fell in February 1742 Hervey clung to office for five more months—until the last possible moment. He published his last pamphlet in January 1743. In June, six weeks before his death, he sent Lady Mary Wortley Montagu a last letter, which reclaims the stoic dignity his recent political maneuverings had forfeited, and re-

asserts his firmness in face of the unacceptable.

Letters:

Letters Between Lord Hervey and Dr. Middleton concerning the Roman Senate, edited by Thomas Knowles (London: Printed for W. Strahan & T. Cadell, 1778);

Lord Hervey and His Friends, 1726-38; based on Letters from Holland House, Melbury, and Ickworth, edited by Lord Ilchester (London: John Murray, 1950).

Biography:

Robert Halsband, *Lord Hervey, Eighteenth-Century Courtier* (Oxford: Clarendon Press, 1973).

References:

J. J. Peereboom, "Hervey and the Facts as He Saw Them," *Dutch Quarterly Review of Anglo-American Letters*, 16 (1986): 326-340;

Charles B. Woods, "Captain B----'s Play," *Harvard Studies and Notes in Philology and Literature*, 15 (1933): 243-255.

Papers:

The West Suffolk Record Office, Bury St. Edmunds, holds the bulk of Hervey's family and other papers including his own manuscript (mutilated by his grandson) of the *Memoirs of the Reign of George II*. A copy made by his son Gen. William Hervey, which shares the one major omission, though not others, is in the royal archives at Windsor Castle. General Hervey's copy is the basis for restored text in Sedgwick's edition.

John Locke

(29 August 1632 - 28 October 1704)

G. A. J. Rogers
University of Keele

See also "Eighteenth-Century Background: John Locke," in *DLB 31: American Colonial Writers, 1735-1781.*

BOOKS: *Epistola de Tolerantia ad Clarrissimum Virum T.A.R.T.O.L.A. Scripta a P.A.P.O.I.L.A.* (Gouda: Apud J. ab Hoeva, 1689); translated by William Popple as *A Letter Concerning Toleration. Humbly Submitted, &c. Licensed Octob. 3, 1689* (London: Printed for A. Churchill, 1689);

Two Treatises of Government: In the Former, The False Principles and Foundation of Sir Robert Filmer, and His Followers, Are Detected and Overthrown. The Latter Is an Essay Concerning the True Original, Extent, and End of Civil-Government (London: Printed for A. & J. Churchill, 1690);

An Essay concerning Humane Understanding. In Four Books (London: Printed by Eliz. Holt for T. Basset, 1690; second edition, with large additions, London: Printed for T. Dring & S. Manship, 1694; fourth edition, with large additions, London: Printed for A. & J. Churchill and S. Manship, 1700; fifth edition, with many large additions, London: Printed for A. & J. Churchill and S. Manship, 1706):

A Second Letter concerning Toleration. Licensed, June 24, 1690 (London: Printed for A. & J. Churchill, 1690);

Some Considerations of the Consequences of the Lowering of Interest and Raising the Value of Money. In a Letter to a Member of Parliament (London: Printed for A. & J. Churchill, 1692);

A Third Letter for Toleration to the Author [J. Proast] *of the Third Letter concerning Toleration* (London: Printed for A. & J. Churchill, 1692);

Some Thoughts concerning Education (London: Printed for A. & J. Churchill, 1693);

Short Observations on a Printed Paper, Intituled, For Encouraging the Coining Silver Money in England, and After for Keeping it Here (London: Printed for A. & J. Churchill, 1695);

The Reasonableness of Christianity, as Delivered in the Scriptures (London: Printed for A. & J. Churchill, 1695);

A Vindication of the Reasonableness of Christianity, &c. from Mr. Edwards's Reflections (London: Printed for A. & J. Churchill, 1695);

Further Considerations concerning Raising the Value of Money, Wherein Mr. Lowndes's Arguments for It in His Late Report, concerning 'An Essay for the Amendment of the Silver Coins' Are Particularly Examined, anonymous (London: Printed for A. & J. Churchill, 1695);

A Second Vindication of the Reasonableness of Christianity, &c. By the Author of the Reasonableness of Christianity, &c (London: Printed for A. & J. Churchill, and E. Castle, 1697);

A Letter to the Right Reverand Edward Ld. Bishop of Worcester, concerning Some Passages Relating to Mr. Locke's Essay of Humane Understanding; in a Late Discourse of His Lordship's, in Vindication of the Trinity (London: Printed for A. & J. Churchill, 1697);

Mr. Locke's Reply to the Right Reverand the Bishop of Worcester's Answer to His Letter, concerning Some Passages Relating to Mr. Locke's Essay of Humane Understanding; in a Late Discourse of His Lordships in Vindication of the Trinity (London: Printed by H. Clark for A. & J. Churchill and E. Castle, 1697);

Mr. Locke's Reply to the Right Reverand the Bishop of Worcester's Answer to his Second Letter (London: Printed by H. C. for A. & J. Churchill and E. Castle, 1699);

A Paraphrase and Notes on the Epistles of St. Paul to the Galatians, I & II Corinthians, Romans, and Ephesians. To Which Is Prefix'd 'An Essay for the Understanding of St. Paul's Epistles, by Consulting St. Paul Himself,' published in parts (London: Printed for A. & J. Churchill, 1705-1707);

Posthumous Works of Mr. John Locke: Viz. I. Of the Conduct of the Understanding. II. An Examination of P. Malebranche's Opinion of Seeing All Things in God. III. A Discourse on Miracles.

John Locke, 1672 (portrait by John Greenhill; by permission of the National Portrait Gallery, London)

IV. Part of a Fourth Letter on Toleration. V. Memoirs relating to the Life of Anthony First Earl of Shaftesbury. To which is Added, VI. His New Method of a Common-Place-Book. Written Originally in French, and Now Translated into English (London: Printed by W. B. for A. & J. Churchill, 1706);

A Collection of Several Pieces of Mr. John Locke, Never Before Printed or Not Extant in His Works, edited by Pierre Des Maizeaux (London: Printed by J. Bettenham for R. Francklin, 1720).

Editions: *The Works of John Locke,* 3 volumes (London: Printed for J. Churchill & S. Manship,

1714); eighth edition, 4 volumes, edited by Edmund Law (London: Printed for W. Strahan, 1777); new edition, corrected, 10 volumes (London: Printed for T. Tegg, 1823);

An Essay Concerning the Understanding, Knowledge, Opinion, and Assent, edited by Benjamin Rand (Cambridge, Mass.: Harvard University Press, 1931)—Locke's longer and later draft of the *Essay Concerning Human Understanding,* known as Draft B;

An Early Draft of Locke's Essay, edited by R. I. Aaron and Jocelyn Gibb (Oxford: Clarendon Press, 1936)—Locke's earlier and shorter 1671 draft of the *Essay Concerning Human Understanding*, known as Draft A;

Locke's Travels in France As related in his Journals, Correspondence and Other Papers, edited by John Lough (Cambridge: Cambridge University Press, 1953);

Essays on the Law of Nature, The Latin Text with a Translation, Introduction and Notes, Together with Transcripts of Locke's Shorthand in his Journals for 1676, edited by W. Von Leyden (Oxford: Clarendon Press, 1954);

Two Treatises of Government: A Critical Edition, edited by Peter Laslett (Cambridge: Cambridge University Press, 1960; second edition, revised, 1967);

Two Tracts on Government, edited by Philip Abrams (London: Cambridge University Press, 1967);

The Clarendon Edition of the Works of John Locke, 30 volumes (Oxford: Clarendon Press, 1975-)—includes *An Essay Concerning Human Understanding*, 1 volume, edited by Peter H. Nidditch (1975); *A Paraphrase and Notes on the Epistles of St. Paul*, 2 volumes, edited by Arthur W. Wainwright (1987); *Some Thoughts Concerning Education*, 1 volume, edited by John Yolton and Jean Yolton (1989); *Drafts of 'An Essay Concerning Human Understanding' and Other Philosophical Writings*, 3 volumes, edited by Nidditch and G. A. J. Rogers (1990-   ).

OTHER: *Aesop's Fables in English & Latin, Interlineary; for the Benefit of Those Who Not having a Master Would Learn Either of These Tongues*, edited by Locke (London: Printed for A. & J. Churchill, 1703).

John Locke is probably the most important, and certainly the most influential, of all English philosophers. Although he published his first work, typically anonymously, when he was fifty-seven, by the end of his life, barely fifteen years later, he was, with Isaac Newton, regarded as the leading English thinker of his day. In the eighteenth century Locke's reputation spread through Europe and North America so that he came to occupy a place of dominance not only in the English-speaking world but also in France and other major European countries. His philosophy may be seen at the heart of the Enlightenment, influencing almost all the major thinkers even if they were not always persuaded by him. It was from his claims that virtually all the innova-

tions in epistemology and metaphysics began, and it was from his conception of man and the state that moral and social theory, not to mention education, psychology, and theology, began their inquiries. He achieved this prominent position not simply through the power of his argument and because his philosophy meshed with the major advances in the natural sciences, of which he was much more than a merely passive spectator, but perhaps even more because his views on man, religion, and the nature and limits of political authority anticipated positions that achieved widespread popularity in the century following his death. Central to his philosophy was the belief that the ultimate source of all knowledge is experience and that, as human experience is necessarily limited by our nature, there is much beyond our comprehension. However, our faculties are appropriate to our purpose, which is to live a just, useful, and Godly life on this earth and thereby achieve the reward of eternal salvation in the next. This commonplace of Christian theology, together with what were to become the commonplaces of modern science—themselves only just then being formulated, often by Locke's friends and colleagues—provides the context within which his philosophical argument is deployed.

Locke was born in the village of Wrington, in Somerset, some few miles from the important city of Bristol. When he was still a baby the family moved to Pensford, another village in the same part of Somerset, and close to the stone circle at Stanton Drew, which captured Locke's imagination as a boy and about which he corresponded with John Aubrey in later life.

Locke's father, also named John, was a lawyer, clerk to the justices of the peace, and a small landowner. Like his wife, Agnes Keene Locke, his family was Puritan, and his father had been a clothier. He apparently talked little, and to Locke as a boy he seemed remote, but in later years the philosopher always expressed great respect and affection for him. In *Some Thoughts concerning Education* (1693) the philosopher saw it as highly desirable that a father should be distant and formal with his children while they are young, so that there would be no indulgence, but that this relationship should gradually relax as the child grows to maturity.

A leading justice of the peace with whom Locke senior worked was Alexander Popham, who also served as Member of Parliament for Bath. At the outbreak of the Civil War in 1642 he was created a colonel in the Parliamentary Army and appointed Locke senior as a captain. After defeat at the hands of the Royalists in July 1643 neither Popham nor Locke engaged further in military matters. Instead, Locke became county clerk for sewers. What the impact of the Civil War was on the young Locke we may only guess. But the caution which he was to exhibit in later life may in part be attributed to his childhood experience of being a member of a Puritan family in an area controlled by Royalists.

At the close of the war Popham was able to obtain for his friend's son a place at Westminster School. It was an event that was decisive for his education and all that followed, for Westminster was at the time the leading school in the country. Its master was the remarkable Richard Busby, himself a Royalist, and among his pupils were numbered many of the great names of English life in the later seventeenth century, including John Dryden and Christopher Wren.

Busby established for himself a reputation as a great teacher. He also had an appetite for inflicting severe physical punishment on his charges. Such experiences at Westminster no doubt contributed to Locke's strong opposition in later life to corporal punishment, except as a last resort.

In Locke's second year at Westminster there occurred close by the execution of Charles I (30 January 1649), but Locke did not witness it. Instead Busby kept the boys in, at prayer for the king about to be condemned. For Locke, the young man from the Puritan home, the experience of a Royalist master at a school across the way from Parliament, controlled by the Puritans, must only have reinforced his no doubt already strong awareness of the major political and religious forces in the country.

Despite dislike for aspects of the regime Locke made good academic progress at Westminster, and with his election as a King's Scholar at Christ Church, Oxford, in May 1652, his application to his Latin, Greek, and Hebrew was rewarded.

He went up to Christ Church in the following November, accompanied by Colonel Popham, who remained in Oxford a few days to see his protégé settled in what was Oxford's largest and most important college. The university, which had been staunchly Royalist, was just recovering from the effects of the Civil War. Oliver Cromwell had purged the king's supporters and placed Puritans in the key positions of influence.

Probably the most important of these was John Owen, who became dean of Christ Church, and thus head of the college, and Cromwell also appointed him vice-chancellor of the university. Owen was not only a distinguished theologian, but he had had a fine record as a soldier in the Civil War. He was also a man of moderation, determined to return the university to proper academic function and to minimize friction. He remained the most powerful man in Oxford throughout Locke's undergraduate days. Owen was not Locke's tutor, but the spirit of the man pervaded the college and the university and contributed much to an environment of serious academic study. Nor did he thrust a Puritan theology upon his charges, allowing Anglicans toleration as long as their worship was conducted discreetly. It was in this atmosphere that Locke pursued his studies, but he was apparently not much taken with what it was that he was expected to master. His friend James Tyrrell reported that although Locke had been regarded as one of the clever young men of the college, Locke himself had found his early years of study in Oxford far from satisfying, encouraging him to think of other careers than that of the scholar. He also found the method of debate, "the trade of disputing," contrary to the pursuit of truth but rather "invented for wrangling or ostentation." Instead of studying, he said that he spent his time in the company of pleasant and witty men.

Despite such distractions he graduated B.A. in February 1656, and he found the life at Oxford attractive enough to look forward to the three further years residence required for the M.A. The attractions were not of the traditional academic kind but those new interests that Locke was beginning to acquire in the natural sciences. They were to hold Locke's attention for the rest of his life.

To understand Locke's new studies we must remember that the standard curriculum in the universities was still dominated by scholasticism through the study of the philosophy of Aristotle via his many commentators. It was not Aristotle himself to whom Locke objected, for he had the highest regard for the great Greek philosopher. Rather it was the caricature, or worse, of his philosophy by his commentators to which Locke took exception, and he took exception, too, to what was required of him, the rote learning of the commentators without serious examination of their claims. In this gloomy shade of academe Locke was delighted to discover that new light was

Beginning of a scribal copy of Locke's fifth lecture on natural law, with a revision of the opening passage, in Locke's hand, on the facing page (MS. Locke ff. 61ᵛ and 62ʳ; by permission of the Curators of the Bodleian Library, Oxford University). Written in 1664, these Latin lectures were first published, with English translations, as Essays on the Law of Nature *in 1954.*

being thrown by the natural philosophers who, under Cromwell's patronage and under their own inclination, had come to Oxford. These included such leading luminaries of the new science as John Wilkins, Warden of Wadham College, Thomas Willis, William Petty, and, above all, Robert Boyle. Before Locke became deeply involved in the new science, however, there was the work of one man that he studied which particularly turned his attention toward philosophy in all its aspects, and that was the French philosopher René Descartes (1596-1650). It was, Locke said much later, the study of Descartes that first gave him an interest in philosophical things, not because he immediately agreed with Descartes's claims, but because Descartes expressed his new vision of the world so clearly and forcefully. Much of Locke's later philosophy may be seen as though Locke were conducting a debate with the great Frenchman.

By that time, Locke was becoming deeply involved in the study of medicine. Through his interest in the natural sciences, he came into contact with Robert Boyle and attended chemistry classes, central to iatrochemistry, that Boyle organized. From there it was not long before Locke was actually engaged in medical research with Boyle, specifically on problems generated by William Harvey's discovery of the circulation of the blood, which brought into sharp focus the whole question of the nature and function of respiration. Recognition of Locke's work in this area has come late, even though Boyle paid tribute to it in the dedication of his work on human blood to "the very Ingenious and Learned Doctor J. L." Thus, although Locke did not himself make anything of his achievement as an experimental scientist, research in his manuscripts has revealed his work to be of high quality.

Locke graduated M.A. on 29 June 1658 and was immediately elected to a senior studentship, the equivalent of a fellowship at other Oxford colleges. At about the same time we find Locke commenting on the issue of toleration, which was to be the subject of his first published book. But at this stage his approach was one of caution, undoubtedly at least partly reflecting his experiences with Quakers and other dissenters. These, Locke found, too often had what to him was a major flaw. Their religion exhibited too much of what in the seventeenth century was called "Enthusiasm," in which strength of emotional conviction was taken as evidence of direct knowledge of God and his purposes. Suspicion of such sentiments was to remain with Locke all his life and led in later years to his adding a chapter on the subject to the fourth edition (1700) of *An Essay Concerning Human Understanding*.

Locke's correspondence at this time is marked by several exchanges with ladies with whom Locke had, or had ambitions to have, romantic attachments. How serious they were and why they came to naught is not possible to tell, but it must be remembered that as a member of an Oxford college Locke was not allowed to marry, and an alternative career in the church may have been unattractive to him for theological reasons. He was in the meantime deeply engaged in medical studies and acting as tutor to undergraduates.

It was in this period that Locke engaged in his first sustained pieces of academic writing. The first of these is now known as *Two Tracts on Government*, written in 1660 and 1661-1662, and published only in 1967. The second is now known as the *Essays on the Law of Nature*, though prepared as lectures in 1664. (They were not translated from their original Latin or published until 1954.)

For those familiar with only Locke's later views on toleration the *Two Tracts on Government* present a surprising view of Locke. In this early work, written at a time of the great political crisis of the Restoration, Locke argues the conservative, Hobbesian position with regard to the authority of the sovereign: that the formation of the state requires each citizen to abandon his liberty of the state of nature and to obey the commands of the sovereign, even in matters not required by the Law of Nature. The move from this highly authoritarian position to that of his later writings is one of the few major changes in intellectual position that may be detected in Locke's thought.

In the *Essays on the Law of Nature* Locke argues that there is a Rule of Morals or Law of Nature given to us and that it can be known by the light of nature. But this does not imply that the Law is inscribed innately in the minds of men. Nor can we come to it from the general consent of mankind. Rather, through a combination of reason and sense experience, men may discover a Law which is perpetual and universal. The lectures finish with a repudiation of ethical egoism.

In 1665 Locke accepted a post as secretary to the diplomatic mission of Sir Walter Vane to Brandenburg, where Charles II hoped to find another ally against the Dutch, with whom Britain was then at war. The mission was unsuccessful, but Locke found the trip interesting, and he was impressed by the religious toleration enjoyed by Calvinists, Lutherans, and Catholics alike.

On his return Locke found Oxford thrown into disorder and worse by the removal of the court there from London because of the plague, but he continued with his medical researches. Through his friendship with the physician David Thomas, with whom he opened a laboratory, Locke came to meet a man who was to give a completely new direction to his life. That man was Anthony Ashley Cooper, later the first earl of Shaftesbury.

Shaftesbury, already a major political figure, and destined for high office as lord chancellor, is remembered for his activities in favor of a Protestant succession to the throne and his commitment to religious toleration, as well as for his skills as an administrator and politician. Although his ambition made him many enemies, there can be no doubting his abilities, and through him Locke entered a world he might otherwise have scarcely touched.

The two men met when Shaftesbury came to Oxford for medicinal reasons. Locke was asked by David Thomas to see to the visitor's needs, and Shaftesbury was clearly impressed. In the following year Shaftesbury asked Locke to join his household in London as his personal physician, and Locke accepted. He moved to Exeter House in the Strand in the spring of 1667.

Locke was soon active as Shaftesbury's physician. In May of 1668 he supervised an operation on his patient for a suppurating hydatid cyst of the liver, and inserted a tube into the wound from which Shaftesbury was able to drain the abscess for the rest of his days. Shaftesbury was convinced that Locke had saved his life.

An Essay concerning toleration
1667

In the Question of liberty of conscience, which has for
some years beene soe much bandied among us. One thing
that hath cheifly perplexed the question, kept up the
dispute, & increased the animosity, hath been (I conceive) this,
that both Partys haue with equall zeale, & mistake too
much enlargd their pretensions, whilst one side preach up
absolute obedience, & the other claime universall liberty in
matters of conscience, without assigneing what those things
are wch haue a title to liberty or shewing the boundarys of
imposition & obedience.

To cleare the way to this I shall lay downe this
for a foundation, wch I thinke will
not be questiond or denied viz ~~I shall assert~~

That the whole trust power & authority of the magistrate
is vested in him for noe other purpose but to be made use of
for the good, preservation, & peace of men in that society over wch
he is set. & therfor that this alone & ought to be the
standard & measure acording to wch he ought to square &
proportion his laws: model & frame his governmt. ffor if
men could liue peaceably & quietly, togeather without growing
whiteing under certaine laws &
into a common=wealth, there would be noe need at all of
magistrates or politos, wch were only made to preserve
men in this world from the fraud & violence of one an
other. soe yt what was the end of erecting of governmt
ought

Pages from a manuscript, presumed to be in Locke's hand, for an essay that grew out of Locke's early discussions with Shaftesbury and that lies behind Locke's 1689 Epistola de Tolerantia *(HM 584; by permission of the Henry E. Huntington Library and Art Gallery)*

10

safely, without the inforceing of those duty, by
the injunctions & penalty of laws, It is certaine the
law maker ought not to proscribe any rules about them.
~~or endeavour to reclaime out of vice with the good~~
~~together~~ but leave the practife of them intirely
to the discretion & confiences of his people. ffor
could ever thofe morall virtues & vices be separated
from the ~~weale~~ relation they have to the weale of the
publike, & ceafe to be a means to settle or disturbe mens
peace & propriety, they would then ~~only~~ become only
the private & super-politicall concernmt. betweene god
& a mans soule, wherein the magistrats authority is
not to interpose. God hath appointed the magistrat
his vice gerent in this world, with power to command;
but is but like other deputys, to command only
in the affairs of that place where he is vice gerent

~~goods & & & &u begarhs with interction of wper~~
~~hath caufe under priviledge of the third thing~~. The
magistrat hath nothing to doe with the good of
mens soules or their concernmt in an other life
but is ordeind & intrusted with his power, only for
the quiet & comfortable liveing of men in society
one with an other, as hath bene already sufficiently proved
And it is yet farther evident, that yr magistrat
commands not the practice of virtues, because
they are virtues & obleige the confience, or are

(3)
who ever medle in
the affairs concernmt
of the other world, have
noe other power, but
to intreate, & perswade

C

Shaftesbury found that Locke had other talents for which he had use. Clearly the men discussed politics, religion, and philosophy as well as medicine, and Locke was soon drafting papers on toleration which expressed the views of both men. By this time Locke was speaking in the liberal voice with which his philosophy has become associated. However, his scientific and medical interests were not neglected. Soon he was collaborating with the leading physician of his day, Thomas Sydenham, accompanying him on his rounds and writing papers on medical practice.

Locke was elected a fellow of the Royal Society on 23 November 1668. Many of the leading members were familiar to him from Oxford and even from Westminster, and although he was not very active, preferring a smaller group with whom to discuss and carry out research, it kept him in contact with scientific developments.

One of the groups that Locke attended met in his chamber in Exeter House, and it was at one of its gatherings that the long gestation began of the work for which Locke is most famous, *An Essay Concerning Human Understanding*. That was in the winter of 1671, and in that year Locke completed two drafts of his work, which are still extant. They show that he had already formulated the main lines of his philosophy, and in the remaining years of his life he honed and refined them, testified by the five succeeding editions from 1690 to 1706.

While living at Exeter House, Locke held several positions. The first of these was as secretary to the Lords Proprietors of Carolina, and in this capacity he was a party to drafting *The Fundamental Constitutions for the Government of Carolina*, principles which were, however, never put into effect.

Another position arose for Locke in 1672-1673 while Shaftesbury was lord chancellor, the highest ministerial office in the land. He made Locke secretary of presentations, with responsibility for supervising ecclesiastical matters that came under the chancellor's control. When Shaftesbury was removed from the chancellorship in November 1673, Locke lost his position, but he gained another, the much more interesting one of secretary to the Council of Trade and Plantations, a post he held until March 1675.

In February 1675 Locke was awarded the M.B. from Oxford, which enabled him to practice as a physician, and he was at the same time elected to one of two medical studentships at Christ Church. In the following autumn he set out for France, possibly as an agent for Shaftes-

bury and the Whig opposition, who were currently in secret negotiations with the French. Whatever the reason for the visit, which lasted until the spring of 1679, Locke was happily placed for the entire period of the negotiations.

Locke made good use of his time in France. He studied medicine in Montpellier, read widely in current French science, medicine, philosophy, travel, education, and theology, and became acquainted with many of France's leading intellectual figures.

He returned to a country in which the political debate was approaching yet a further crisis. Shaftesbury had himself spent a year in prison in Locke's absence, but he was now free again and had been replaced in the Tower of London by his rival Sir Thomas Osborne, Earl of Danby. Shaftesbury led the anti-Catholic movement with enormous energy and enlisted great popular support for his cause. He made as much as he could of the alleged Popish Plot and campaigned in Parliament for the exclusion of the Catholic duke of York (later James II) from the succession. What part Locke played, if any, is impossible to say, but it was probably more than the surface evidence suggests.

Meanwhile the political argument continued, and before the end of the decade Locke was formulating his text for the *Two Treatises of Government* (1690). Like *An Essay Concerning Human Understanding*, it would not appear in print until after Locke's return from Holland in 1689. That Locke had substantially completed the text of the *Two Treatises of Government* by the early 1680s is of some importance because the work was long regarded as having been written to justify the Revolution of 1688.

Two Treatises of Government, as its name implies, consists of two works. Together they first refute the claim of Sir Robert Filmer that the monarch's authority to rule descends from Adam, and then offer instead an account of political authority based on natural rights and a social contract. Filmer's *Patriarcha, or the Natural Power of Kings* had argued, from the assumption of the absolute truth of the Bible, that the right to rule had been given by God to Adam and descended from him to the monarch. In 1680, when the work was posthumously published, it was used to support the king's position against Shaftesbury and the Exclusionists. Locke wrote his first treatise to meet this argument. His case is that Filmer's analogy between fatherhood (Filmer, Locke notes, conveniently ignores the biblical au-

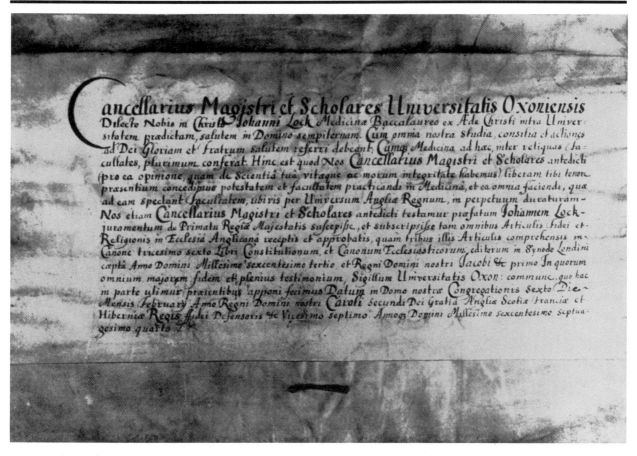

Locke's medical license, granted on 6 February 1675 (by permission of the Curators of the Bodleian Library, Oxford)

thority of motherhood) and citizenship breaks down at almost every point. Further, there is no basis to the claim for absolute parental authority either in scripture or in reason if there were, all children and citizens would forever be slaves. Nor can any monarch claim inheritance from Adam, for the records to establish Adam's eldest line do not exist.

Locke's first treatise was composed within a very specific political context but one which Locke rightly saw as extending into the post-1688 period; yet its perennial appeal might be less apparent today. The argument of the second treatise is much more obviously enduring, and, because its claims are very positive, it provided a political justification for reform and a program for those who see sovereign power infringing the rights of citizens. Granted that Filmer's account of political authority was flawed, Locke set out to answer the question as to the nature and origin of the sovereign's right to rule.

Locke begins his analysis from a consideration of the state of man before he enters civil society. Man, he says, is in a perfect state of freedom within the bounds of the law of nature. He means that men are entitled by nature to do what they wish so long as their action does not infringe on the moral law. Each is also in a state of equality with his fellowmen so that no one is naturally master of another. The natural condition of liberty and equality applies to all adults; children have liberty in proportion to their rationality and ability to fend for themselves, which normally increase as they approach adulthood. On the other side, parents have obligations to their offspring which arise naturally from the condition of parenthood. Individuals may in this state enter into contracts with others that place obligations on them in addition to those which flow naturally from the state of nature. They may, for example, agree to live together as man and wife, or to enter into other relations such as that of master and servant. And persons may acquire property rights in land and products by work, of which the most typical instance is "mixing one's labour with the soil." Thus although the earth, Locke agrees, was given by God to all men in common, we may acquire private possession in some part of it by cultivation, which changes what was comparatively useless into something very useful. The state of nature is, then, one in which men live peaceably with one another according to the law of nature, recognizing each other's rights and fulfilling their duties. Unfortunately it is a condition rarely, if ever, found. For although all are free and equal in the state of nature, not all are prepared to grant or recognize the natural rights of others. To resist such threats, men may forego the liberty of the natural condition and enter into a civil society which is formed when any number of men agree to make one community or government. Provided that there is no infringement of the natural rights of individuals—a provision of the utmost importance—other matters relating to the community should follow the will of the majority.

Men have a natural right to as much of the product of their labor as they can use without it spoiling—for example, crops rotting. Beyond that, others may make a call on their produce if they themselves would otherwise go without and risk starvation. In such a state there are very real limitations on the amount that may legitimately accrue to any one person, though Locke accepted exchange of goods as natural and legitimate. The introduction of money, however, changes the situation dramatically. The acceptance of money—which has a merely conventional value since it has no natural use—is a voluntary act, but it allows a man to change what will spoil—crops—into something which will not—gold. Society thus provides a framework in which great differences of wealth may arise but which in themselves do not infringe on the natural rights of anybody.

For Locke the end of government is to provide conditions in which each individual may fully enjoy his natural rights, of which the most important are his rights to life, liberty, and property, rights in which all human beings have an interest. He saw this interest as being best served if no one person or body, no matter how benevolent, was to exercise uncontrolled power. He therefore argued for a constitution that distinguished between legislative and executive functions.

At least as important, and in the political context of 1688, perhaps even more important, Locke sanctioned the removal of governments which themselves infringed on the natural rights of the citizens. For those which exercise arbitrary power over the people place themselves in a state of war with them and may be removed by whatever means are necessary. Locke believed it was

just such a condition which existed in England under James II in 1688. He thus saw the settlement of the crown on William and Mary as entirely justified.

This last event was still several years in the future as Shaftesbury struggled desperately to prevent James coming to the throne, no doubt with the discreet support of his "secretary," as Locke was increasingly described. But Locke was not wholly engaged in politics, for in 1682 he met Damaris Cudworth, daughter of Ralph Cudworth the Cambridge Platonist, and with whom Locke was to have the closest personal friendship of his life. In early 1683 a romantic attachment developed between them, which lasted into Locke's exile in Holland in the autumn of that year. But in the years that he was away Damaris at length accepted the proposal of another man, Sir Francis Masham, whom she married in 1685. This event was not, however, to be the end of her relationship with Locke.

Meanwhile Shaftesbury had had to flee the country, and in January 1683 he died in Amsterdam. It was undoubtedly a major blow to Locke in every sense. Without his patron his place in the world was far from clear. He was merely a comparatively obscure Oxford don who spent most of his time in London, apparently writing nothing, and barely engaged in the practice of medicine. His well-hidden political activities were, however, to continue. When, in the summer of 1683, news broke of the Protestant Rye House plot to kidnap the king—a kidnapping which never occurred but which brought the arrest of leading Whigs—Locke felt himself threatened. He left London for Oxford and the West Country, and by September he was in Holland. He was to remain there until February 1689.

Locke claimed that he went to Holland for his health. Allowing the ambiguity in that remark, it was no doubt true. He also claimed that he spent most of his time either writing *An Essay Concerning Human Understanding* or in innocent company with friends. It is certainly true that he wrote much of the final draft of the essay in Holland, and certainly Locke soon established a circle of new friends. But the innocence of his activities must be seriously doubted. The evidence of journals, letters, and account books, and the pattern of his movements, strongly suggest that he was deeply involved with the powerful group of English dissidents plotting first James Scott, Duke of Monmouth's unsuccessful rebellion of 1685 and then William's invasion of 1688.

Locke found much to his liking in Holland. He found physicians who already practiced the new style of medicine that he and Sydenham had advocated in London. He found an atmosphere of liberal toleration in matters of worship which exemplified the principles that he and Shaftesbury had worked out in Exeter House. And, despite his involvement in the plotting of the defeat of the Catholic succession in England, he did have time to write and to return to the text of his beloved *De Intellectu,* as he often called the manuscript of *An Essay Concerning Human Understanding.*

Before its completion, however, there was further bad news. In November 1684 he was expelled from Christ Church by order of the king. As Locke said, it was the only home he had. His expulsion for political reasons clearly hurt him, though we cannot now accept his protestations of innocence as sincere. This was followed in February by the death of Charles II, and reports of the new king's Catholic advisers obtaining a strong hold on the monarch were soon reaching Holland. The following July the invasion of England by Monmouth floundered in the mud of Sedgemoor, and Monmouth himself suffered the terrible death of those found guilty of treason. In October Louis XIV revoked the Edict of Nantes, and persecuted Protestants came pouring into Holland with tales of iniquity at the hands of a Catholic ruler. No doubt Locke found writing on toleration a way of responding to these setbacks, and writing *An Essay Concerning Human Understanding* a pleasant diversion.

Religious toleration was an issue that had long exercised Locke. We have already noted his earlier views and his shift, in the company of Shaftesbury, to the more liberal position for which he is remembered. In Holland he set these down for his first printed book, published in Latin in 1689 under the supervision of his Dutch friend Philip van Limborch.

In the *Epistola de Tolerantia* Locke argues that there should be freedom of worship so long as the method of worship does not infringe the civil rights of others. He attacks the persecution of sects as being contrary to scripture, and urges all men to seek salvation through complying with the law of God rather than spending their time attacking others. A man has no higher duty than to seek salvation, and persecution as such will not cause him to change his mind as to how it may be achieved. Only the atheist should be opposed because he is not bound by the oaths and prom-

ises which form the bonds of civil society. Furthermore, assemblies of worshipers do not in themselves threaten civil peace, and if they do nothing other than practice their religion according to their own lights, they will not be of concern to the magistrate. Above all, we should recognize that every man should enjoy the same rights that are granted to others.

By the end of 1686 Locke was able to inform Edward Clarke that he had completed the fourth and last book of *An Essay Concerning Human Understanding.* The task Locke had set himself in writing it was essentially a preliminary one to other investigations. He likened it to that of an underlaborer, clearing the ground a little. The task of expanding our knowledge he left to such "masterbuilders" as Boyle, Sydenham, Huygens, and the "incomparable Mr. Newton."

We have already noted that it was reading Descartes that first interested Locke in philosophy and the natural sciences. It is not therefore surprising to find that, while rejecting much of Descartes, *An Essay Concerning Human Understanding* also includes many signs of his influence. Locke begins his inquiry into the understanding with an attack on the doctrine of innate ideas. These have been invoked by, among others, Descartes and by the contemporary school of Cambridge Platonists, of whom Henry More and Ralph Cudworth were the best known, to explain why it is that we can be said to have certain kinds of knowledge. The doctrine was supposed to account for such things as our ability to recognize logical principles, such as "whatever is, is," and "a thing cannot both be and not be," and certain moral and religious truths, such as that men should keep their compacts or that God exists. Locke totally rejected the doctrine, which he saw as potentially and actually a threat to free inquiry. For if it were once allowed that there is innate knowledge, then anybody in authority who could claim to identify what that knowledge is would be in a strong position to enforce acceptance of the claim. It was, in short, a doctrine which threatened to undermine the liberal toleration of different opinions in areas where Locke believed the truth is hard to establish, and which should not be settled by a short and potentially authoritarian appeal to innate notions.

But if innate ideas were not allowed, how comes the mind to be furnished with the many ideas which are undoubtedly to be found there? Locke answers with one word, *experience.* And it is to explaining the source of our ideas in experi-

An Essay concerning
Humane Understanding
Lib. 1. Cap. 1
Since it is y⁹ understanding y⁴ sets man above
...

Pages from the third extant draft (1685) for Locke's best-known work, possibly in the hand of a scribe (by permission of the Pierpont Morgan Library). Locke finished the first complete draft for this essay in December 1686 and continued to revise it for the next two and a half years.

l. 2   L. 2. C. 1

Of the Original of our Ideas

1   Every man being conscious to himselfe yt he thinks
& wch his minde is imployd about whilst thein being
being ye Ideas yt are there ty patt doubt yt men have
in their mindes sevrall Ideas such as are those
Expressed by ye words whitenesse, hardnesse, sweet-
nesse, thinking motion, man, Elephant, army
drunkennesse, & others, it is in ye first place then
to be enquird how he comes by them. I know it
is a received doctrine yt men have native Ideas
& originall characters stamped upon their mindes
in their very first being. This opinion I have
at large Examined already & I suppose wf I have
above sd will be much more easily admitted when
I have shewd (wch I thinke every ones Experience will when he weighs it make out to him)
how all ye Ideas he has come into his minde
by degree & upon occasion.

2   Let us then suppose ye minde to be as we say
white paper void of all characters all Ideas how
comes it to be furnished? whence comes it by yt
vast store wch ye busy & boundlesse phansy of men
comes to dress it selfe up in wth an almost endlesse
variety wch furnish hee imploy an imployment
to ye reason & knowledge of mankind. And
to this I answer in one word Experience In

ence that book two of *An Essay Concerning Human Understanding* is devoted. Ideas come into the mind either by sensation, through the five senses, or by reflection, by which he understands such intellectual powers as those exemplified by the imagination and memory. The ideas themselves may be divided into simple and complex. Simple ideas are the atoms of our experience and cannot be divided further. Examples are the hardness and coldness of a piece of ice, the whiteness of a lily, thinking, and willing. Complex ideas, such as that of a chair or a dog, are combinations of simple ideas.

One idea which we have is that of physical objects, and Locke devotes a chapter which has had a lasting impact on philosophy to explaining its nature and origin. In it he makes use of a distinction which had become widely accepted in contemporary scientific accounts of matter, that between the primary and secondary qualities of objects. The distinction is an inheritance from ancient atomic theories of matter, which in modern dress were advocated by Galileo, Descartes, Pierre Gassendi, and, in most detail, and with considerable experimental support, by Robert Boyle. Locke's version of it is philosophically the most sophisticated, and a part of his philosophy which was widely accepted, though few readers appreciated all his subtleties. Locke draws an important distinction between the *qualities* of objects as they are in bodies and our *ideas* of those qualities as they are in our mind. He argues that the essential qualities of objects, such as extension, shape, size, and solidity, resemble the ideas which these qualities produce in our minds, and these he calls the primary qualities. The secondary qualities are powers in the object to produce in us ideas such as color, taste, and smell, where our ideas do not resemble their causes, which are a function of the texture, size, and other primary qualities of the particles of which the object is composed. Although Locke's distinction was to be the subject of attack, particularly by George Berkeley, it has remained widely accepted by philosophers who both want to accept modern science as showing that we live in a world of material objects with complex microcosmic structures and that those structures cause us to have the experiences that we do. This account of the world has become so widely accepted since Locke's day that it is now widely regarded as common sense, which is some measure of Locke's penetration of our culture. His account is, however, not without difficulty. One on which his philosophy has often

been claimed to founder is this: if all that we are aware of consists of ideas, how then may we ever know that there is a material world, for any evidence we might wish to offer could only take the form of further ideas.

Another influential chapter in *An Essay Concerning Human Understanding* is Locke's account of personal identity, a topic on which he was the first important writer, and an issue which remains in the forefront of philosophy. Locke argues that the crucial criterion for personal identity is not bodily continuity, as it would be for material objects, or "participation in the same life," as it would be for the oak tree or the horse, but memory, or, as Locke puts it, the continuity of consciousness. Although Locke's claim was to be strongly attacked in the following century, his discussion of the issues still remains the essential starting point for debate.

In the third book of *An Essay Concerning Human Understanding* Locke offers the first sustained account of language and meaning by a modern philosopher. His thesis is that words in their primary signification stand for ideas in the mind of him who uses them, and secondly, that they often also "stand for the reality of things" in the world around us. Locke goes on to consider how different kinds of words come about, such as general terms and the names we give to particular kinds of natural things, which Locke calls "substances."

In the fourth book he turns to the issue of knowledge, its nature and extent. His position is that true knowledge is remarkably limited, confined to intuitively obvious truths, demonstrations, as in deduction, or to the knowledge of the existence of particular objects directly before us. Within demonstrative knowledge he allows mathematics and holds out the theoretical possibility of a demonstrative system of ethics. But he is less sanguine about the natural sciences, which he sees as requiring a knowledge of general truths that is not, nor perhaps can ever be, forthcoming. However, this is not important for the human condition. We can have probable belief for many areas of human inquiry, and, as he said at the beginning of *An Essay Concerning Human Understanding*, our business is not to know all things, but only those which concern our conduct. His doubts about the natural sciences did not detract from his commitment to them, but he discouraged overoptimistic claims about their results.

While he was in Holland Locke had advised his friend Edward Clarke by letter about the edu-

Locke in 1704 (portrait by Sir Godfrey Kneller; by permission of The President and Council of the Royal Society of London)

cation of his son. On his return to England he was encouraged to publish the correspondence in revised form, and it duly appeared in 1693. It was a book that became popular and one of his most influential. Locke was in a strong position to write such a work. In Oxford he had been an outstanding tutor of boys between the ages of fourteen and eighteen, and in Exeter House he had taken on the education of Shaftesbury's sole heir, who later became the third earl and a philosopher of influence in his own right. It was a task at which he had evidently excelled.

Locke held firmly to the view that happiness depends on a sound mind in a sound body.

It is not then surprising that *Some Thoughts concerning Education*, written as a guide for the sons of gentlemen, begins from considerations of health. His recommendations include warm clothes, plenty of exercise, and a plain diet. Turning to matters of discipline, Locke cautions against spoiling children by overindulgence and holds that proper instruction in behavior should begin early. Children must, for example, learn as soon as possible that not all their desires may be satisfied. The parents' authority must be established early, but not by severe punishment, which is generally harmful, and he emphasizes the value of praise and other rewards. The most important thing is to establish in the child good habits of behavior by supervised practice. Locke was far from confident that schools, because of the bad company of other boys, were an advantage, and he recommends tutoring children at home.

Locke lays special emphasis on the development of moral qualities in the child, and only in the later sections of the work does he turn to book learning. He deplores the amount of time spent on learning Latin and Greek. The child should be taught to read, of course, but this instruction should be made enjoyable, and he should then be given books that are easy and amusing but that also instruct. Locke recommends *Aesop's Fables* as the best, a work which he later edited himself. Some things should be learned by heart—such as the Lord's Prayer, the Creeds, and the Ten Commandments—and some parts of the Bible should be read. The child should also be taught to write, and even taught shorthand. He should then learn French, and, when he can speak that well, Latin. Little time should be spent on composing verse in any language, but time would not be wasted in reading the great Latin poets. Other important subjects are geography, arithmetic, geometry, chronology, and Roman history.

Although the knowledge of virtue is best taught by practice, the young man should also read the Bible for moral instruction, and also Tully's *Offices*, Samuel, Baron von Pufendorf, and Hugo Grotius. But Locke has no time for formal disputation, which only encourages wrangling, rather than the search for truth. In the sciences, although there is no agreed system, Descartes's is most in fashion, and corpuscular philosophies seem better than that of the Peripatetics. Other skills that should be mastered include dancing, music, fencing, and riding, and there should be opportunity for play as a relaxation. Finally, in the education of their children Locke encourages his readers to consult their reason, rather than relying merely on custom.

On Locke's return from Holland he was offered at least one major diplomatic post, which he turned down, and he was appointed a commissioner of appeals and then given an important post at the Board of Trade. It was a position he discharged very effectively despite poor health. Partly for this last reason he left London, where the smoke was bad for his chest, and made his home with Sir Francis and Lady Damaris Masham at their country house named Oates, in the parish of High Laver in Essex. Here he was able to settle down to his writing once more, and he not only revised *An Essay Concerning Human Understanding* and other works, but he also wrote on economic policy and engaged in his long controversy with Edward Stillingfleet, Bishop of Worcester, in works of considerable philosophical interest.

He also wrote *The Reasonableness of Christianity* (1695), in which he argues that the evidence of Christ's life, through his fulfilling the prophecies and the testimony of his miracles, gives reasonable evidence to support the Christian faith, whose fundamental article is that Christ is the Messiah. Other theological writing also engaged him, including long defenses of *The Reasonableness of Christianity* and *A Paraphrase and Notes on the Epistles of St. Paul* (1705-1707).

By this time Locke was a famous man, and many distinguished visitors came to Oates to see him, including his friend Isaac Newton, with whom Locke talked theology and with whom he probably shared secret Unitarian beliefs.

In the autumn of 1704, Locke fell ill for the last time, and on 28 October, as Damaris Masham was reading the Gospel to him, he died. He was buried in High Laver Church, and his Latin epitaph, which he had written, reminds us that he was always a servant of truth and that if we should wish to know what he stood for we should read his works.

Letters:

The Correspondence of John Locke, 9 volumes, edited by E. S. de Beer, The Clarendon Edition of the Works of John Locke (Oxford: Clarendon Press, 1976-).

Bibliographies:

H. O. Christophersen, *A Bibliographical Introduction to the Study of John Locke* (Oslo: I Kommisjon Hos Jacob Dybwad, 1930);

Jean S. Yolton and John W. Yolton, *John Locke: A Reference Guide* (Boston: G. K. Hall, 1985).

Biographies:

Peter, Seventh Baron King, *The Life of John Locke, with Extracts from His Correspondence, Journals, and Common-Place Books* (London: Henry Colburn, 1829);

H. R. Fox Bourne, *The Life of John Locke*, 2 volumes (New York: Harper, 1876; London: H. S. Knight, 1876);

Maurice Cranston, *John Locke: A Biography* (New York: Macmillan, 1957; London & New York: Longmans, Green, 1957);

Kenneth Dewhurst, *John Locke. Physician and Philosopher. A Medical Biography* (London: Wellcome Historical Medical Library, 1963).

References:

Richard I. Aaron, *John Locke* (Oxford: Clarendon Press, 1937; third edition, 1971);

Peter Alexander, *Ideas, Qualities, and Corpuscles. Locke and Boyle on the External World* (Cambridge: Cambridge University Press, 1985);

Richard Ashcraft, *Revolutionary Politics and Locke's 'Two Treatises of Government'* (Princeton: Princeton University Press, 1986);

John Dunn, *The Political Thought of John Locke* (Cambridge: Cambridge University Press, 1969);

James Gibson, *Locke's Theory of Knowledge and Its Historical Relations* (Cambridge: Cambridge University Press, 1917);

John Harrison and Peter Laslett, *The Library of John Locke* (Oxford: Oxford University Press, 1965);

Sterling P. Lamprecht, *The Moral and Political Philosophy of John Locke* (New York: Columbia University Press, 1918);

Kenneth MacLean, *John Locke and English Literature of the Eighteenth Century* (New Haven: Yale University Press / London: Oxford University Press, 1936);

W. M. Spellman, *John Locke and the Problem of Depravity* (Oxford: Clarendon Press, 1988);

James Tully, *A Discourse on Property: John Locke and His Adversaries* (Cambridge: Cambridge University Press, 1980);

John W. Yolton, *John Locke and the Compass of Human Understanding* (Cambridge: Cambridge University Press, 1970);

Yolton, *John Locke and the Way of Ideas* (Oxford: Clarendon Press, 1956).

Papers:

The Bodleian Library, Oxford, has the major collection of Locke's papers, which includes most of his extant manuscripts (with some important exceptions) and much of his original library. It also has microfilm of other manuscript material.

Bernard Mandeville

(circa 13 November 1670 - 21 January 1733)

Irwin Primer
Rutgers University

BOOKS: *Bernardi à Mandeville de Medicina Oratoria Scholastica* (Rotterdam: Typis Regneri Leers, 1685);

Disputatio Philosophica de Brutorum Operationibus.... Publice defendendam assumit Bernardus de Mandeville (Leyden: Apud Abrahamum Elzevier, Academiae Typograph, 1689);

Disputatio Medica Inauguralis de Chylosi Vitiata.... Publico examini subjicit Bernardus de Mandeville (Leyden: Apud Abrahamum Elzevier, Academiae Typograph, 1691);

The Pamphleteers: A Satyr (London, 1703);

Some Fables after the Easie and Familiar Method of Monsieur de la Fontaine (London, 1703);

Æsop Dress'd; or a Collection of Fables Writ in Familiar Verse. By B. Mandeville, M.D. (London: Printed for Richard Wellington, 1704; London: Sold at Lock's Head, 1704?);

Typhon: or The Wars Between the Gods and Giants; A Burlesque Poem in Imitation of the Comical Mons. Scarron (London: Printed for J. Pero & S. Illidge, and sold by J. Nutt, 1704);

The Grumbling Hive: or, Knaves Turn'd Honest (London: Printed for Sam. Ballard and sold by A. Baldwin, 1705);

The Virgin Unmask'd: or, Female Dialogues Betwixt an Elderly Maiden Lady, and Her Niece, On several Diverting Discourses on Love, Marriage, Memoirs, and Morals, &c. of the Times (London: Sold by J. Morphew & J. Woodward, 1709); republished as *The Mysteries of Virginity* (London: Sold by J. Morphew, 1714);

A Treatise of the Hypochondriack and Hysterick Passions, Vulgarly call'd the Hypo in Men and Vapours in Women; In which the Symptoms, Causes, and Cure of those Diseases are set forth after a Method intirely new.... By B. de Mandeville, M.D. (London: Printed for the author, D. Leach, W. Taylor & J. Woodward, 1711); "third" edition published as *A Treatise of the Hypochondriack and Hysterick Diseases.... By B. Mandeville, M.D.* (London: Printed for J. Tonson, 1730);

Wishes to a Godson, with Other Miscellany Poems. By B. M. (London: Printed for J. Baker, 1712);

The Fable of the Bees: or, Private Vices, Publick Benefits (London: Printed for J. Roberts, 1714); republished as *The Fable of the Bees: or, Private Vices Publick Benefits. Containing, Several Discourses, to demonstrate, That Human Frailties during the degeneracy of Mankind, may be turn'd to the Advantage of the Civil Society, and made to supply the Place of Moral Virtues* [the added subtitle was excluded from all later editions] (London: Printed for J. Roberts, 1714; second edition, enlarged, London: Printed for Edmund Parker, 1723; third edition, enlarged, London: Printed for J. Tonson, 1724);

The Mischiefs that Ought Justly to be Apprehended from a Whig-Government (London: Printed for J. Roberts, 1714);

Free Thoughts on Religion, the Church, and National Happiness. By B. M. (London: Sold by T. Jauncy & J. Roberts, 1720);

A Modest Defence of Publick Stews: or, an Essay upon Whoring, As it is now practis'd in these Kingdoms ... Written by a Layman (London: Printed by A. Moore, 1724);

An Enquiry into the Causes of the Frequent Executions at Tyburn: and a Proposal for some Regulations concerning Felons in Prison, and the Good Effects to be Expected from them.... By B. Mandeville, M.D. (London: Sold by J. Roberts, 1725);

The Fable of the Bees. Part II. By the Author of the First (London: Sold by J. Roberts, 1729);

An Enquiry into the Origin of Honour, and the Usefulness of Christianity in War. By the Author of the Fable of the Bees (London: Printed for J. Brotherton, 1732);

A Letter to Dion, Occasion'd by his Book call'd Alciphron, or The Minute Philosopher. By the Author of the Fable of the Bees (London: Sold by J. Roberts, 1732).

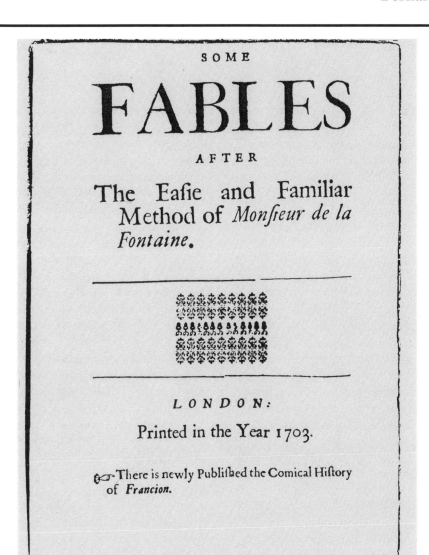

SOME

FABLES

AFTER

The Eafie and Familiar
Method of *Monfieur de la
Fontaine.*

LONDON:

Printed in the Year 1703.

☞ There is newly Publifhed the Comical Hiftory
of *Francion.*

Title page for the first English version of fables by La Fontaine, translated by Mandeville and including two fables of his own invention

Edition: *The Fable of the Bees*, 2 volumes, edited by F. B. Kaye (Oxford: Clarendon Press, 1924).

OTHER: "In authorem de usu interno cantharidum scribentem," in *De Tuto Cantharidum in Medicina Usu Interno*, by Joanne Groenevelt, M.D. (London: Typis J. H., prostant venales apud Johannem Taylor, 1698); translated by John Marten as "Upon the author, treating of the internal use of *Cantharides*," in *A Treatise of the Safe, Internal Use of Cantharides in the Practice of Physick*, by John Greenfield (London: Printed for Jeffery Wale & John Isted, 1706);

A Sermon Preach'd at Colchester, to the Dutch Congregation. On February 1, 1707/8. By the Reverend
C. Schrevelius; being his first or Introduction Sermon, after his being Elected, And Translated into English, by B.M., M.D., translation attributed to Mandeville (London, 1708);

"A Society of Ladies," 32 papers signed Lucinda or Artesia, in *The Female Tatler*, nos. 52-111 (London, 2 November 1709 - 29 March 1710);

Letters to *St. James's Journal*, 20 April 1723, p. 311; 11 May 1723, p. 329;

Letter signed Philantropos, *British Journal* (24 April and 1 May 1725)—related to letters collected in *An Enquiry into the Causes of the Frequent Executions at Tyburn* (1725) but not included in that pamphlet.

One of the most outspoken and provocative authors of his century, Bernard Mandeville influenced many later writers including Jean-Jacques Rousseau, Voltaire, Claude Adrien Helvétius, David Hume, and Adam Smith. He is remembered by historians of economic theory for his ideas on luxury, wealth and poverty, and government regulation of commerce, and he is also recognized as a significant forerunner of modern sociology. When we ponder his wide cultural impact, the paucity of facts about his life seems most regrettable.

The son of Michael and Judith (Verhaar) de Mandeville, he was born in Dort or Rotterdam in 1670, attended the Erasmian School in Rotterdam, and later studied philosophy and medicine at the University of Leyden, receiving the M.D. in 1691 and thereby continuing a family tradition with a career in medicine. A few passages in his published work suggest that he may have visited Paris and Rome. In 1693 he traveled to England, probably returned to Holland in 1694, and later immigrated to England, possibly in flight from a scandal in which his father (also a physician) was involved. In 1693 he was summoned before the officials of the Royal College of Physicians for practicing medicine without their license. Though he did not apply for a license, he was apparently able to continue his practice without it. In 1698 he took the liberty of disparaging the College of Physicians in a Latin commendatory poem prefixed to a book on the internal use of cantharides, by a friend, countryman and fellow physician Dr. John Groenevelt (anglicized: Greenfield).

For a Dutchman England would then have seemed a desirable place to visit or reside in, because William of Orange, the Dutch husband of England's Queen Mary, had ascended the British throne after the Glorious Revolution of 1689. Mandeville acquired an excellent command of English, and at some point decided to settle there for life. On 1 February 1699 he married an Englishwoman, Ruth Elizabeth Laurence, who gave birth to their son, Michael, one month later. They later had at least one other child, Penelope; these are named in his surviving will. About a year after he married he served—as a translator, apparently—in the divorce trial of Henry Howard, seventh Duke of Norfolk.

Only three short documents in Mandeville's own hand have come to light: his will (1729), a professional letter to the eminent physician Sir Hans Sloane, and a letter about his own son's illness to his patron, the first Lord Macclesfield. We do not know when he first met Sir Thomas Parker, later Earl of Macclesfield, or when Macclesfield became his patron. Macclesfield, who was lord chancellor from 12 May 1718 to 4 June 1725, was tried for corruption and convicted, but not a word on that event appears in any of Mandeville's literary remains. Two years before Macclesfield's trial, Mandeville himself had achieved public notoriety when the Middlesex Grand Jury "presented" his *Fable of the Bees* to the judges of the King's Bench as a public nuisance. Less than a year after Macclesfield died (23 April 1732), Mandeville's death on 21 January 1733 was reported in various newspapers.

Apart from records relating to his ancestry (published in F. B. Kaye's edition of *The Fable of the Bees*), his immediate family, his friends, and his professional acquaintances, we have no documentary evidence on his character or person beyond a celebrated passage in Franklin's *Autobiography*. Benjamin Franklin, who in the 1720s had seen and possibly met Mandeville in London, later described him as "a most facetious, entertaining companion," and the "soul" of a club that met at an alehouse in Cheapside. As for other acquaintances, it seems likely that Mandeville was known to those booksellers whose names turn up on his title pages—John Brotherton, A. Baldwin, Jacob Tonson, J. Morphew, James Woodward, G. Strahan, Dryden Leach, Edmund Parker, T. Jauncy, T. Warner, and especially James Roberts—but how well did they know him?

Had Mandeville ever met Joseph Addison or Richard Steele—fellow Whigs? It was in Macclesfield's company that he reportedly characterized Addison as "a parson in a tye-wig." Steele's *Tatler* in particular had been a target of Mandeville and others who wrote for *The Female Tatler* in 1709-1710, and in his *Fable of the Bees* he pointedly ridiculed what he called Steele's "Elegant Flatteries of his Species" as a grossly misleading doctrine. On the positive side, Mandeville championed John Gay's *Beggar's Opera* (1728) against those "Wrongheads . . . [who] . . . fancy Vices to be encouraged, when they see them expos'd." Had he met Gay, or had he at least seen Gay's masterpiece performed? No portrait or even a rough sketch survives that might enable us to guess at Mandeville's physical stature or physiognomy. Unless significant biographical evidence turns up, most of what we regard as Mandeville's "life" will continue to be whatever life of his mind survives in his publications.

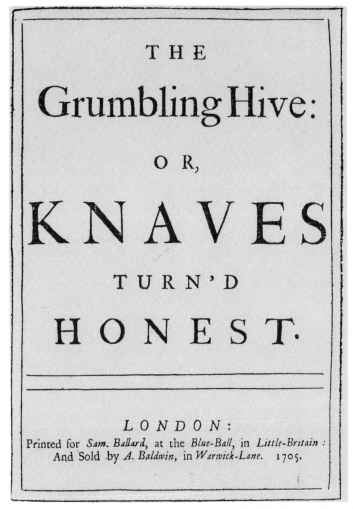

THE

Grumbling Hive:

OR,

KNAVES

TURN'D

HONEST.

LONDON:
Printed for *Sam. Ballard*, at the *Blue-Ball*, in *Little-Britain* :
And Sold by *A. Baldwin*, in *Warwick-Lane*. 1705.

Title page for the poem that serves as the foundation for The Fable of the Bees

Before immigrating to England, Mandeville had had three academic works printed, all in Latin. The first (1685) is a school oration announcing his interest in medicine, before entering the university. In the next, a thesis in philosophy presented at Leyden University in 1689, he supports René Descartes's argument that, since animals are automatons without feeling, they therefore lack souls. His third and most important academic work, *Disputatio Medica Inauguralis de Chylosi Vitiata* (concerning a "depraved Chylification") appeared in 1691, when he was awarded the M.D. at Leyden. In Mandeville's later medical treatise (1711), the author's spokesman reports that in his study of digestive disorders he found "the Cause of the Hysterick and Hypochondriack Passions."

His earliest publications in English are now thought to be two anonymous works, *The Pamphleteers: A Satyr* and *Some Fables after the Easie and Famil-*

iar Method of Monsieur de la Fontaine, both dated 1703. In the first poem Mandeville inveighs against those "pamphleteers" who depreciate the Glorious Revolution and the recently deceased King William III, yet wish to honor the incumbent monarch, Queen Anne. *Some Fables*, a loose translation or "imitation" of selected fables by Jean de la Fontaine, has the distinction of being the first group of La Fontaine's *Fables* to be rendered in English. A somewhat expanded second edition appeared in 1704 as *Æsop Dress'd; or a Collection of Fables Writ in Familiar Verse. By B. Mandeville, M.D.* Choosing not to emulate the polish of La Fontaine, he freely translated some of his fables in bumptious octosyllabic couplets inspired by the author of *Hudibras* (1663-1680), "the incomparable Butler," as Mandeville later called him. Within his translations Mandeville also sandwiched two verse fables of his own, inviting his readers to identify them. These two, "The Carp" and "The Nightingale and Owl," foreshadow not only Mandeville's later comic verse (most notably, *The Grumbling Hive*, 1705) but also his prose on political themes.

In his next poem, *Typhon: or The Wars Between the Gods and Giants; A Burlesque Poem in Imitation of the Comical Mons. Scarron* (1704), Mandeville continued to indulge his taste for "low" poetry by turning upside down the epic gods and heroes of Homer and Virgil. Clearly designed as a lark, this piece is at the outset dedicated to the "Numerous Society of F[oo]ls"—a bit of homage to one of his most revered Dutch models, Desiderius Erasmus's *The Praise of Folly* (1511). (The title page of *Typhon* names no author, but the dedication is signed B. M.) We soon see what Mandeville is up to when, in his mock invocation, he refers to Aeneas as "the burnt-out pious Lad, / So fam'd for carrying of his Dad."

The Grumbling Hive: or, Knaves Turn'd Honest (1705), an original verse fable in Mandeville's favorite Hudibrastic meter and "low" style, is by far the best known of his early English writings and serves as the foundation of his masterpiece, *The Fable of the Bees*.

Mandeville's last volume of verse, *Wishes to a Godson, with Other Miscellany Poems* (1712), is not more significant than any of his earlier verse, but it invites our attention for at least two reasons. First, it reveals that Mandeville also tried his hand at erotic poetry—an aspect of his literary creativity not hitherto offered to the public. In "On CELIA's Bosom" the pleasure of sight is far exceeded by that of touch: "But when I touch'd th' inviting Skin, / What Furnaces I found within." The other significant feature of this collection is the presence of a revised version of his poem "On Honour," which he had previously included in one of his *Female Tatler* papers. Honour, "an Inchantress of Renown" who lured Aeneas away from Dido, and Ulysses from Circe, sits "gay" in bloody fields, and for her, "wild Sparks . . . / Are cutting one another's Throats." Mandeville continued to satirize false honor, almost obsessively, to the end of his career.

Mandeville's first major effort in prose was *The Virgin Unmask'd: or, Female Dialogues Betwixt an Elderly Maiden Lady, and her Niece, On several Diverting Discourses on Love, Marriage, Memoirs, and Morals, &c. of the Times* (1709). Although his title seems to promise erotic delights, any reader who purchased the book for such ends was bound to be disappointed. Its erotic dimension is interesting, but more important is the book's total out-

look on the temptations and possible misfortunes facing any young lady who begins to yearn for male attention. What advice does the maiden aunt, Lucinda, give to her inexperienced, nubile niece, Antonia? The answer is found throughout their ten dialogues, and the gist of that advice is this: proceed with caution, because men are dangerous, especially suitors who appear polite and well bred; furthermore, do not judge the felicity of married persons merely on the basis of rumor or common knowledge; and most important—know thyself. At the outset Lucinda berates her niece for exposing too much of her bosom; Antonia responds that she is merely following fashion and custom. With blunt realism Lucinda soon reviews the stages of Antonia's sexual awakening, which she did not encourage for fear of losing her the sooner.

Their discussions cover different aspects of the battle of the sexes and the marriage debate. Lucinda, who remained single by choice, defends all women who choose to stay unwed rather than make unsatisfactory marriages. Antonia, believing that happy marriage does exist, points to their acquaintance Aurelia as an example of such bliss, but Lucinda undeceives her by narrating a longish tale of Aurelia's previous marriage, founded on impulsive passion, contrary to the wishes of her wealthy father. When her father disinherits and disowns the couple, the husband, Dorante, gradually comes to abuse and degrade his wife, even insisting that she prostitute herself to increase their income. More miseries follow, including the death of their son. Eventually Dorante dies in a duel, and providentially a wealthy kinsman offers Aurelia marriage, which she accepts. Continuing her case against marriage, Lucinda asserts that married mothers suffer more than childless spinsters. She rejected marriage in order to avoid its many dangers, including madness.

Lucinda turns out to be a strong-minded feminist pursuing her rational self-interest, and she bluntly criticizes the evils of male dominance: "They have Enslaved our Sex." She has the leisure and inclination, like Mandeville himself, to follow ancient and modern politics and history. Like Mandeville, again, it pleases her to uncover the secret springs of motivation in the world's leaders—in this case, King Louis XIV. Recognizing his magnificent achievements, she concludes that he is nevertheless a culpable tyrant. Certain of her remarks on courage reflect Mandeville's lifelong interest in that passion. But she is not exclusively his mouthpiece; in her pronounced mis-

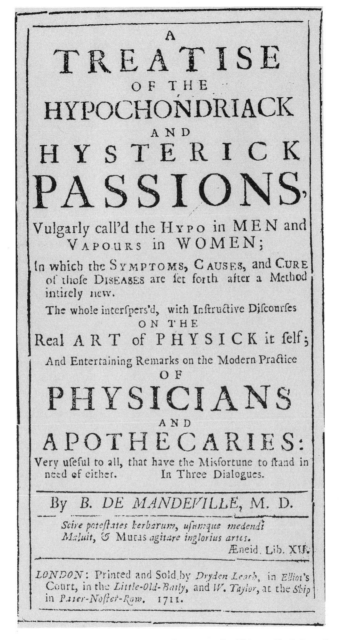

Title page for the main source of information about Mandeville's medical thought and practice

anthropy she is also a butt of his irony and satire.

The work ends with a second cautionary tale recited by Lucinda for Antonia's edification—the tale of Leonora who, separated by accident from her favored suitor, avoids being seduced by a duke, and, after marrying the duchess's jeweler, finally faces the agonizing choice of surrendering her wifely virtue to the lust of unscrupulous Mincio (who skillfully pretends to be *dying* for love of her person), or retaining her virtue and thereby hastening his death. At this point the tale—and the book!—abruptly end. If Mande-

ville had hoped that his readers would clamor for a continuation volume to resolve the issue, then he was temporarily a disappointed author. In his essay in *Mandeville Studies* (1975) G. S. Vichert has identified a possible source for this work in earlier female dialogues between an older courtesan and a novice, and he also sees it as an anticipation of the new genre of the novel emerging in European literature. Other models include the popular seventeenth-century genre of advice to a daughter, and the feminist tracts of writers such as Mary Astell. Feminist themes also appear in scattered numbers of the periodical to which Mandeville was contributing about this time.

Modern scholars have attributed at least thirty-two numbers of *The Female Tatler* (2 November 1709 - 29 March 1710) to Mandeville. Using the fiction of a "Society of Ladies" who meet for discussions at either Lucinda's or Artesia's dwelling, Mandeville assigns authorship of these numbers to both ladies, in alternation. Occasional visitors include two males, Colonel Worthy, who recently returned from military duty in Flanders, and an "Oxford Gentleman," whose views coincide remarkably with those of Mandeville himself.

Joining a discussion on human nature and the bases of society, the Oxford Gentleman asserts that it is not the virtues such as "Humility, Temperance [or] Frugality" that enable modern nations to flourish, but the vices, because they entail consumption, spending, and therefore the circulation of wealth without which society would stagnate. The interrelated vices of avarice and prodigality contribute to this process, as when the young freely spend the fortunes that their elders painfully amassed in their own lifetimes; therefore both of these vices are necessary to society (as in *The Grumbling Hive*). In no. 64 the Oxford Gentleman defends luxury, stressing the absurdity of anyone's desiring both "a flourishing Trade, and the decrease of [the vices of] Pride and Luxury," a position that virtually restates the moral of Mandeville's *Grumbling Hive*. He also subscribes to the Mandevillean view that it is the task of "skilful politicians" to extract social benefits from all human activity ranging from the best to the very worst. Mandeville's perennial attraction to the subject of honor is again visible (nos. 78, 80, 84, and elsewhere); the Oxford Gentleman argues that honor is not the virtue that it is popularly thought to be, but another disguise of the vice of pride.

While all of these topics significantly anticipate major portions of *The Fable of the Bees* and other works, one must recall that *The Female Tatler* was a somewhat parasitical journal called into being by the success of Steele's *Tatler* (1709-1711). Hence some of Mandeville's contributions are written in calculated opposition to the views of Isaac Bickerstaff, Steele's persona in *The Tatler*. Bickerstaff accepted the platitudes that human nature has an innate dignity and that the moral virtues make society possible and enable it to survive. In 1723 Mandeville would continue to attack essentially these same views, focusing not on Steele but on the moral "system" of Anthony Ashley, third Earl of Shaftesbury.

At this point in his career he was still virtually unknown to the reading public. He had put his name to *Æsop Dress'd*, and only his initials to prefatory prose in *Typhon* and *The Virgin Unmask'd*. Getting into print would already have yielded him the initial gratifications of authorship, but with no substantial emolument. We must assume that he was supporting his family through his medical practice, an assumption validated by the general tenor of his next book.

What we know about Mandeville's medical thought and practice derives almost entirely from *A Treatise of the Hypochondriack and Hysterick Passions, Vulgarly call'd the Hypo in Men and Vapours in Women* (1711). In this set of dialogues Mandeville becomes the physician Philopirio ("lover of experience"), who converses with his new patient Misomedon ("hater of doctors") and speaks briefly with Misomedon's wife. The husband, who rather pedantically displays his learning with Latin quotations, suffers from the disease of the learned, hypochondria; the wife and their (offstage) daughter both suffer from the fashionable woman's disease, the vapors, or the "hysterick passion." Philopirio explains to Misomedon that he is very distrustful not only of the medicines prescribed by other doctors but also of the greedy apothecaries who fill those prescriptions, and for these reasons he personally "cooks" (prepares) his own simple prescriptions for his patients. For the hysteric passion he especially recommends physical exercise such as swinging and riding, together with modifications of diet. He skillfully plays up to Misomedon's passion (to be admired as erudite) by citing Latin passages from Cicero, Terence, Ovid, Horace, and others.

One purpose of this book is to show his contemporaries how concerned and unpretentious a doctor Philopirio-Mandeville really is, with instructions on how to get in touch with him if anyone so desires! Unlike his wealthier competitors, Philopirio is unable to treat many patients because his method requires close observation for extended periods of time. He criticizes physicians (Thomas Willis, for instance) who are excessively speculative and rationalistic in dealing with the multitude of symptoms to be found in almost any illness. The importance that Mandeville places upon the patient-doctor relationship has frequently been regarded in our time as an anticipa-

THE
FABLE
OF THE
BEES:
OR,
Private Vices,
Publick Benefits.

LONDON:
Printed for J. RORERTS, near the *Ox-*
ford Arms in *Warwick Lane,* 1714.

Title page for the first edition of Mandeville's best-known work, in which he republished his poem The Grumbling Hive *with a preface, an explanatory essay, and "Remarks." He published enlarged editions in 1723 and 1724 and a second part in 1729.*

tion of current methods in psychiatry and Freudian psychoanalysis.

One facet of this work that may particularly have pleased Mandeville is its learned citations and allusions, for in the second edition (1730) he added more of them to the discourse of both main speakers; and to make that go down more easily with the less literate public, he also included translations of all of the Latin citations. The final impression is that of a very human and caring physician, not willingly pedantic, and detesting obscurantism. The word *treatise* in the title seems to promise a work of musty scholarship, but that turns out to be the book's first irony because it is far removed from the laboriously systematic "treatises" and "institutes" that were staples in the medical literature of that era.

Following his medical treatise Mandeville's next major publication was the first edition of the book that eventually would make him internationally famous, *The Fable of the Bees: or, Private Vices, Publick Benefits.* This title first appeared in 1714, but the entire book evolved over a span of twenty-four years, beginning with the poem that became its permanent nucleus, *The Grumbling Hive* (1705). In this 433-line poem Mandeville continued to exploit the tradition of the fable from Æsop to La Fontaine. Because of the notoriety that he earned two decades later, it is quite likely that this versified fable about bees can be regarded as the single most influential fable to emerge following the revival of that genre by La Fontaine. Like the human beings that they obviously represent, Mandeville's bees enjoy a thriving society full of life-enhancing advantages and even luxuries, but their hive is also full of vices. When many bees petition Jove to replace their vices with virtues, Jove accedes to their request by eliminating all of the hive's vice—but with disastrous results unforeseen by the "virtuous" faction of the bees. With the triumph of honesty, prices fall, many professions and trades (lawyers, judges, jailors, purveyors of luxury goods and services) wither away; many bees become unemployed; and the entire hive is attacked by enemies grown more powerful, so that the bees are eventually forced to abandon their hive and retreat into a hollow tree.

The moral of this fable is that any attempt to secure a completely virtuous society is "a vain / Eutopia seated in the brain" and is doomed to fail: "Fools only strive / To make a Great an Honest Hive." Though a wealthy, flourishing society must necessarily discourage crime by appropriately punishing its criminals, that society should nevertheless make ample allowance for numerous common vices. A corollary not stated yet implied in the poem is that human beings are governed more by their passions than by reason, and all of their passions refer ultimately to their self-love and self-interest. Thus Mandeville's psychology—his Hobbesian "selfish system"—which he developed in *The Fable of the Bees* in great detail, was already implicit in his *Grumbling Hive*, as were some of his economic and political ideas. The poem's highly developed mercantile society will almost certainly be "warlike," because opportunistic enemies will always threaten its trade, wealth, and power. The poem nowhere refers directly to any external context that would account for its creation, but it seems likely that it was a critical reaction to the propaganda of the then-popular Societies for the Reformation of Manners—self-appointed morals squads whom Mandeville ridiculed later in his *Modest Defence of Publick Stews*.

As the work grew between 1705 and 1729, Mandeville amplified its arguments and targets of satire, using a mixture of genres and a wide variety of prose styles. Though often ironic and playfully paradoxical, his prose supplements reveal a new seriousness not easily deducible from their foundational poem alone. In 1714 he transformed his poem into a small book by adding (all in prose) a preface, "An Enquiry into the Origin of Moral Virtue," and twenty "Remarks," all under a new title, *The Fable of the Bees: or, Private Vices, Publick Benefits*. The "Remarks," ranging from a paragraph to a full essay, expand upon se-

lected passages from the poem, but with an important shift in emphasis. His thesis that a complete moral reformation (or "eutopia") would entail disastrous consequences for advanced nations continues to be developed, but Mandeville now pays more attention to two separate but related inquiries:

(A) He elucidates minutely the "seeming paradox" in his subtitle, that society actually "benefits" from the evils that befall it, whether from the vices and crimes of its members, or from their physical weaknesses and ills, or from disasters caused by Nature. Most of his "character" essays, anecdotes, fables, and vignettes show how private vices *in some instances* are or may become socially beneficial. For instance, the trade of the locksmith increases where thieves are active, and the Great Fire of London created new employment for many workers.

(B) As a reader of disguised human motives, he also places greater emphasis upon analyzing the operations of our passions (irrational drives and desires) in their endless permutations. In this second agenda Mandeville attempts to outdistance all previous "treatises of the passions" (a medical/psychological genre that mushroomed in the preceding century), and he claims to have succeeded in that effort. At the center of his theory of the passions is the postulate that persons in nature (that is, those who are not transformed by supernatural grace) are driven by their self-regarding passions and always feed their own passions (private vices), even when they seem to be acting contrary to their self-interest. Each person is ruled by successive passions such as avarice, love, public esteem or honor, ambition, fear of death, and shame. Reason is incapable of triumphing over any passion; the only way to dislodge a passion is to install another passion in its place. When Mandeville turns to such other subjects as ethics, manners, politics (or government), economic theory, or religion and church, his fundamental theory of human nature always intrudes.

In the sphere of morals and conduct (as F. B. Kaye pointed out) Mandeville maintains a double standard. By insisting that there can be no virtue without self-denial, Mandeville erects a strict standard of Christian morality that very few have either the power or the inclination to adopt. What Kaye called Mandeville's "rigorism" entails a severe narrowing of the kinds of conduct that may be called virtuous. By this means Mandeville enlarges the sphere of vice and posits a rival

Sir

Mr. Duberick persists in ye use of ye medicines prescrib'd, all but ye white decoction pro potu ordinario, instead of which I have order'd ye diet drink & ye Emulsion alternatly, for he has but one stool a day & that not loose. Besides his Hectic he has every night an assault of a fever that lasts for seven or eight hours: he has not those colliquative Sweats, after ye Heat at least they are not so copious as before, yet he visibly looses flesh & has now a perfect facies Hippocratica. I am altogether of ye opinion of St. Hans, that ye country would do him more good than we can The patient chuses Camberwell, because he has receiv'd benefit from that air before. Porters might easily carry him down stairs and a horse litter is not very fatiguing for an hour. This fine weather I bid 'em open ye windows in ye middle of ye day, & ye air seems to refresh him: he is weak but not more, than when you saw him last, & to my thinking ye Stamina vitæ are yet more firm, than that he should dye by ye way: but as I entirely submit to your Sagacity I shall do nothing without your assent: his cough is considerably less than it was and, what I wonder at, without any encrease of ye Dyspnœa. A fortnight ago I pronounc'd him dying; I have often thought of it since & am not yet certain, whether I ought to accuse Artis vanitatem, an meam; however I shall make no more Prognosticks but continue to be diligent in observing & pray God for more knowledge, remaining with all imaginable respect

Sir

your most obedient humble
servant B Mandeville

Tuesday night

Letter to Sir Hans Sloane, written at some time after 3 April 1716 (Sloane MS. 4076, f. 110; by permission of the Trustees of the British Library)

ethic which emphasizes not the (virtuous or vicious) motives of human actions, but the results of those actions for society in general; this ethic Kaye identified as "utilitarian." Mandeville uses the "rigorous" standard of strict virtue to show that many actions normally considered virtuous are in fact motivated by self-regarding passions and are therefore vicious.

He especially satirizes the complacent self-esteem of the polite and the well-bred who sincerely imagine that their fine manners are synonymous with virtuous conduct. Their polite behavior, he argues, is not at all virtuous because there can be no true virtue without palpable self-denial. Polite conduct presupposes an education into hypocrisy: "The well-bred Gentleman places greatest Pride in the skill he has of covering it with dexterity" ("Remark M"). These gentlemen are also taught early to defend their honor, but Mandeville finds their "honour" far removed from the dictates of Christian morality. (He later extended his attack on the system of honor in his *Enquiry into the Origin of Honour*, 1732.)

Both the culpable behavior of the fashionable elite and Mandeville's egoistic psychology, taken together, bear directly upon a central tenet of his economic theory: the defense of luxury spending and luxury consumption. Anything that causes money to circulate, he believes, is advantageous to society. Sumptuary laws (limiting consumption of luxuries) are harmful, and "Frugality is like Honesty, a mean starving Virtue." Thus imports of foreign luxuries are beneficial, but it is also necessary to observe the balance of trade: imports should never exceed the value of the nation's exports. With all of his obvious enthusiasm for the busy, thriving "hive," he also includes some devastating satire on the greed, hypocrisy, and sharp practices of businessmen everywhere. Thus the trade in luxury goods thrives on the vices of tradesmen, whose goods and services feed the quenchless desires (other vices) of the affluent and the prodigal. The greatness of the nation arises from these countless transactions in which individuals and groups pursue their self-interests. Mandeville seems to be trumpeting the advantages of capitalistic free trade, but it is patently incorrect to regard him as an advocate of unfettered laissez-faire policy, because he frequently insists that government must maintain civil order and military power, and regulate commerce as needed.

Between 1714 and 1723, which marks the next amplification of *The Fable of the Bees*, Man-

deville published two somewhat propagandistic works on politics and religion. The first of these, attributed to him recently, is *The Mischiefs that Ought Justly to be Apprehended from a Whig-Government* (1714), a dialogue between a Whig, Loveright, and a Tory, Tantivy. Reflecting Mandeville's political values, Loveright triumphs in debate with Tantivy over the goals and relative merits of both parties at a critical time in English history—the accession of the new line of Hanoverian kings beginning with George I. For Loveright this means a Protestant succession, and he is thankful that the nation has been providentially "snatch'd from the Jaws of Popery and Perdition"—an allusion to the threatening activities of the Jacobites, supporters of exiled James II. Protestants and Whigs generally opposed the return of James's line, the Stuarts, because they feared another civil war might erupt. Many of the topics broached in this debate reappeared at greater length six years later, after the Jacobite invasion of 1715 had been smashed, and just following Bishop Benjamin Hoadly's attacks on those High-Church Anglicans who desired to strengthen the temporal powers of priests and church.

Mandeville's *Free Thoughts on Religion, the Church, and National Happiness* appeared in 1720, the fateful year in which Britain was preoccupied with the financial crash called the South Sea Bubble. But no sign of the event appears anywhere in this book. Once again he only hints at his authorship on the title page: not even "B. M., M. D.," but merely "B. M."—initials that applied to at least one other contemporary author. The book was reviewed in journals of the learned, but it attracted no unusual attention. Of course, the phrase "free thoughts" was probably a lure of the sort that he had earlier used in his unlascivious *Virgin Unmask'd*, for freethinking in that era was a phrase dear to the religious radicals (see, for example, Anthony Collins's *A Discourse of Free-Thinking*, 1713) and abhorrent to the pillars of Church and State.

Though he makes no case for deism but writes as a loyal supporter of the Church of England, Mandeville surveys various excesses belonging to church history in a manner that contemporary deists might well have approved. Fundamentally the book purveys establishment Whig propaganda; its intent is anti-inflammatory or irenic. He speaks as an independent voice urging (as John Locke did) reasonableness in religion and limited religious toleration. He supports the legitimacy of the current monarch and the virtues of mixed government—England's balance of political powers in king, lords, and commons. He inveighs against the acts of lawless violence committed so often in the past by religious forces that seized political and punitive powers for their own aggrandizement. Quoting Lord Shaftesbury with approval, he reminds his readers of the ruinous bloodshed that religious "enthusiasm" had caused in the preceding century.

An early chapter contains a few fictional "character" portraits illustrating the hypocrisy of some who regard themselves as upright and pious, but in most of the book he surveys well-known *topoi* in Christianity such as: the Church's gradual accumulation of rites, images, and vestments in order to please the multitude; the early controversies on the trinity; skepticism and knowledge; reason, faith, belief, and the Christian mysteries; the origin of evil; and more, all with copious examples lifted mainly from Pierre Bayle's *Historical and Critical Dictionary* (1695, 1697; 1702). In his chapter on free will and predestination Mandeville remarks that the will is not as free as most men imagine it to be—which is what we might expect from a thinker who emphasizes that human conduct is often motivated by "irrational" passions unperceived by the agent. His main targets in this work are usually the errors of the Catholic church, overzealous divines of any sect, any person's or church's claims to exclusive truth or authoritative divine inspiration; religious hypocrisy in any guise, and any disturbers of the peace for ostensibly religious reasons. Because of the numerous anticlerical passages in this work, Mandeville may have been expecting angry denunciations from that quarter, but that did not happen. The anticipated outburst, partly inspired by his *Free Thoughts*, occurred three years later soon after the second edition of his *Fable of the Bees* appeared.

The first edition of *The Fable of the Bees* in 1714 evoked almost no critical notice, but the second (1723)—in particular its new "Essay on Charity and Charity-Schools"—produced a torrent of indignant responses from both the pulpit and the press. In this essay Mandeville argues that the entire charity-school movement was far less pure than its managers and supporters claimed; that those who began and operated the charity schools used them for personal advancement and prestige; that the education provided to charity-school children might spoil them for the lives of drudgery—to which they were socially pre-

destined—by instilling desires for advancement; and that the Anglican church was involved in the political as well as religious indoctrination of these children of poverty. Mandeville satirizes the hypocrisy of officious "do-good" institutions as well as of ostentatiously charitable individuals; he opposes the growing popular sentimental benevolence of his age with the unpleasant "realities" of the radical baseness of human nature. Distrusting the "advantages" bestowed upon the charity-school children, he brazenly asserts that advanced societies absolutely require the existence of a large uneducated working class to perform all of their hard labor and menial drudgery.

By the summer of 1723 the Grand Jury of Middlesex "presented" the book as a public nuisance for its blasphemy and immorality. Because Mandeville had always withheld his authorship of *The Fable of the Bees*, only his publisher was named in the presentment. After the presentment appeared in a few newspapers, he had it published—together with "an abusive letter" and his own defense—as *A Vindication of the Book, from the Aspersions contain'd in a Presentment of the Grand-Jury of Middlesex, and an abusive Letter to Lord C.* in a six-penny pamphlet (1723, nonextant) and at the end of the 1724 edition of *The Fable of the Bees*. By then he had become truly famous as well as notorious. Among his better-known detractors in the eighteenth century were John Dennis, William Law, George Berkeley, Francis Hutcheson, Alexander Pope, David Hume, Samuel Richardson, Henry Fielding, and Adam Smith. In some accounts his name became "Man-devil," and the Mandeville Controversy remained active long beyond the year of his death. His *Vindication* gave rise to an entertaining hoax a few years later, but in the meantime he wrote two pamphlets in which he assumed the well-known mask of the benevolent "projector."

While printed attacks on him were increasing, he taunted his antagonists by publishing *A Modest Defence of Publick Stews* (1724), a seventy-eight-page pamphlet that was no less provocative and irreverent than anything already complained of in the Grand Jury's presentment. The germ of this work had already appeared in "Remark H" of *The Fable of the Bees* (1714), where he observes that "Chastity may be supported by Incontinence." Behind that maxim is the centuries-old argument for tolerating prostitution—namely, that if prostitution were outlawed, virgins and wives would be in far greater danger of sexual assault.

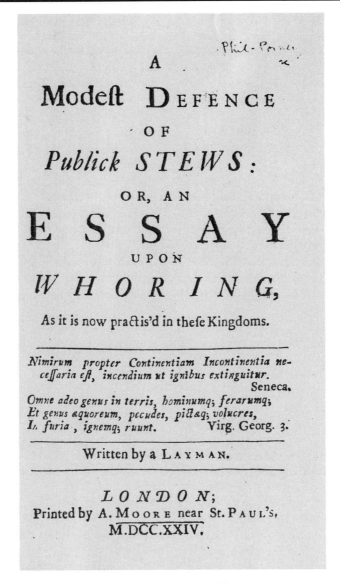

Title page for the pamphlet in which Mandeville argues that "Chastity may be supported by Incontinence"

Building his argument on this proposition, he makes it serve his central pragmatic purpose: to palliate the evils of prostitution and render it socially useful.

In the course of his argument he assures his readers that marriage is an absolutely vital social institution, valuable for (among other things) maintaining important differences in social rank. He is concerned to preserve that institution without making it an instrument of oppression, which too often happens when persons marry hastily in order to satisfy their lust. His solution ultimately requires the availability of prostitution, because the best husbands, he claims, are those who have had a sufficient quantity of "safe" premarital sex-

ual experience; the inexperienced "chaste" bridegroom may soon realize that his expectations of ideal bliss cannot be fulfilled and may therefore come to despise his wife.

After arguing that prostitution has significant social utility, he devotes most of his pamphlet to the challenges presented by the evils of that profession. To that end he divides whoring into "public" and "private" varieties. Both subject the customer to theft, high risk of infection from venereal diseases, and even violence, but "private whoring" can more easily induce him to indulge his passion excessively, thus leading to serious complications, including impotence. His solution is to promote "public whoring" (that is, state-

429

My Lord

My Son is extreamly ill. Last tuesday he was
Seiz'd with a terrible cold fit that lasted above
three hours & was Succeeded by a hot, which continued
with great Violence till friday morning, when he had
an intermifsion of about three hours: then another
cold fit came upon him; three hours after ye heat
returned, which he labours under still. I never heard
or read of any agues with fair intermifsions,
where ye first fit was of that continuance. The
mullberrys, which he has tried Several times, this year
have had no Effect upon him & once he thought they
made him loose, contrary to what they did ever before.
He was with me, ye day he was taken all ye morning &
went home without feeling ye least difsordre till two in
ye afternoon & I knew nothing of it before wednesday
night. The Pain in his head & back are So raging, that
they overcome his great patience, ye Sight of which is
very afflicting to me. next monday I Shall take ye liberty
of writing again. I hope your Lordship & all your family
are well. Pray, my humble Duty to Lady Macclesfield
& Service to Mr Heathcote & Lady Betty. I am
      my Lord
            your Lordships most faithful &
             most obedient servant B Mandeville

London
oct: 8. 1720

Letter to Lord Macclesfield in which Mandeville reports the illness of his son (Stowe MS. 750, f. 429; by permission of the Trustees of the British Library)

controlled brothels), for that would be much healthier for both courtesans and their customers than the dangerous practice of "private whoring." Under "public whoring" prostitutes would be periodically inspected for disease, and the entire transaction would be safe, orderly, convenient, and decent.

Though his pamphlet might shock any supporter of repressive middle-class morality, he dedicates it especially to those "Gentlemen of the Societies [for the Reformation of Manners]" who, in their crusade against all manner of profaneness and immorality, drove prostitutes into hiding, had them flogged when apprehended, and shut down bordellos whenever they could. Mandeville argues that such treatment, besides being unnecessarily cruel, fails of its purpose because it can never stamp out the evil that it punishes. To support his corrective proposal, he also informs us that state-controlled prostitution has been known and practiced for centuries; for recent examples he points to Holland, Germany, and Italy.

This sounds serious enough, but the speaker's seriousness is frequently punctuated by "low" comparisons, sexual puns, and bawdy allusions; throughout we sense the joco-serious mode inherited from Erasmus, François Rabelais, Miguel de Cervantes, and their tradition. On the title page the author calls himself a "Layman," and he signs his dedication "Philporney," a lover of prostitutes. Is the entire proposal merely a jeu d'esprit? For most modern interpreters, the final impression is that behind a veneer of naughtiness and "X-rated" subject matter, the author's seriousness of purpose reflects a physician's concern for the health of his society. "For tho' the Laws can't prevent Whoring, they may yet regulate it." This passage exemplifies and echoes the concluding maxim of his *Fable of the Bees* in 1723: "Private Vices by the dextrous Management of a skilful Politician may be turn'd into Publick Benefits."

It was no doubt for the public benefit also that Mandeville produced his next pamphlet, *An Enquiry into the Causes of the Frequent Executions at Tyburn* (1725), a revised version of two letters signed "Philantropos" and published serially in nos. 128-133 of the *British Journal* (27 February; 6, 13, 20, and 27 March; 3 April 1725). This work marks a deliberate departure from the bawdy innuendos of his previous pamphlet. He fearlessly subscribed his name on the title page of *An Enquiry into the Causes of the Frequent Executions at Tyburn*: "B. Mandeville, M.D." Appropriating once again the role of projector/reformer, he depicts glaring evils arising from his society's system of crime and punishment. To improve that system he recommends that the public be more protective of private property and that they also cease to cooperate with thieves and their accomplices by refusing to pay for the return of stolen goods. Moreover, he would improve the penal system by preventing the criminal from freely associating with other imprisoned felons; prisons must no longer be permitted to serve as schools for crime.

Mandeville was appalled by the carnival atmosphere at executions, where huge crowds encouraged the drunkenness and blasphemy of the felon about to be hanged. Hence he would also reform the execution ritual, the true purpose of which is not simply to terminate the felon's life but rather to instill fear among the living. He would eliminate the carnival by having the criminals executed only in a completely sober and spiritually prepared condition. Interestingly, his concern as a physician appears where he discusses the aftermath of the hangings: "the next Entertainment is a Squabble between the Surgeons and the Mob, about the dead Bodies of the Malefactors that are not to be hanged in Chains." Mandeville backs the surgeons by arguing on utilitarian grounds that it is vital for all practitioners of medicine to understand human anatomy, and to that end corpses are needed for dissection.

We have no reason to think that he was not perfectly sincere in urging these reforms, but the context of this uncharacteristic pamphlet suggests a more complex agenda. In the year following the presentment of the Grand Jury, John Law, Francis Hutcheson, John Dennis, and Richard Fiddes in separate books castigated his *Fable of the Bees* as a work of immorality and irreligion. From this perspective the two versions of the *Tyburn* piece in 1725 can perhaps be read as an indirect response to Mandeville's accusers. This time he not only stands forth as a promoter of respectable reforms, but he even shows compassion for condemned criminals. Thus he may have wanted to demonstrate that while he enjoyed taunting officious do-gooders, he was also seriously committed to meaningful social reforms.

In the preface to his next work, a book-length continuation of his *Fable of the Bees*, Mandeville creates continuity by reminding his readers of the *Vindication* that he had added to part 1 of his book in 1724. In the *Vindication* he informs his adversaries that, "if in the whole Book there is to be found the least Tittle of Blasphemy or

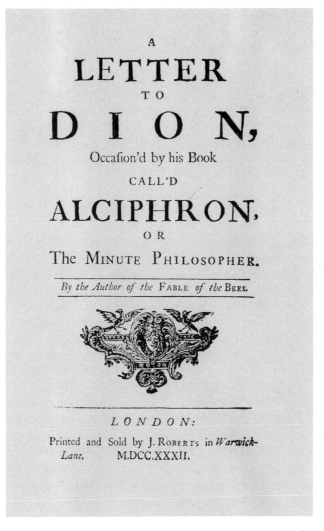

A
LETTER
TO
DION,
Occaſion'd by his Book
CALL'D
ALCIPHRON,
OR
The Minute Philosopher.

By the Author of the FABLE *of the* BEES.

LONDON:
Printed and Sold by J. ROBERTS in *Warwick-Lane,* M.DCC.XXXII.

Title page for Mandeville's response to George Berkeley's criticism of The Fable of the Bees

Prophaneness, or anything tending to Immorality or the Corruption of Manners," he will publicly recant, ask for pardon, and burn his book "at any reasonable Time and Place" his adversaries will name. At least one adversary, the Reverend Alexander Innes (now remembered for fraudulent literary practices), took Mandeville at his word and designated 1 March 1728 "before St. *James*'s Gate" for the recantation and book burning. On 9 March the *London Evening Post* reported that "A Gentleman, well dress'd, appeared at the Bonfire before St. *James*'s-Gate," declared himself to be the author of *The Fable of the Bees* and then committed his book to the flames. This "news" item immediately preceded an advertisement for a book against Mandeville, supposedly written by Innes. Seizing upon this fib and exposing it as a hoax, Mandeville with much satisfaction republished the item with ironic commentary in the preface

to his *Fable of the Bees, Part II. By the Author of the First* (1729).

In this preface he also discusses his attraction to dialogue as a medium for expressing controversial matters, explains why he is retaining the same title (because his subject matter is essentially the same), and presents extended "characters" of the two male interlocutors in the announced dialogues. The general "plot" of these six dialogues reveals how Cleomenes (an accomplished gentleman who admires *The Fable of the Bees* and is most often Mandeville's spokesman) finally convinces Horatio (his genteel friend and a professed admirer of Lord Shaftesbury's "social system") that the social system is a very defective representation of the realities of human nature and of the origins of civil society. At the outset of their dialogue it becomes clear that part 2 was intended as, among other things, an extension of Mandeville's *Vindication*.

Apart from elevating Mandeville's "selfish system" (the "scheme of deformity," as Horatio calls it) above the ruins of the "social system," another aim of part 2 was to fire a broadside at the complacent self-esteem of the wealthy and privileged upper classes. The function of their education into genteel refinement is to instruct them in enhancing their lives of pleasure and comfort. Mandeville delights in pointing out that while religious observance is part of that code of gentility, decency (or the rules of fashionable intercourse) forbids any inquiry into one's personal morality or religious affections. The fashionable genteel imagine they are virtuous, but the truth of the matter is that their education conflicts radically with the teachings of Christianity. Using his "severe" standard of virtue (no true virtue without self-denial), Mandeville pursues at greater length his earlier attack on the hypocrisy of the fashionable well bred who delude themselves into imagining that they are truly virtuous, moral, charitable, kind, benevolent, and sufficiently religious. He uses Shaftesbury as an exemplar and symbol of that class's moral hypocrisy, and argues that Shaftesbury's view of virtue as natural or innate in man is a great invitation to self-deception. (His attack on Shaftesbury is not new; Mandeville began to rebut Shaftesbury in "A Search into the Nature of Society" in *The Fable of the Bees*, 1723.) Not satisfied merely to explode his lordship's system, Mandeville also attacks Shaftesbury's personal conduct by describing his retirement from public service as a sign of reprehensible selfishness. At the very end Cleomenes concludes that Shaftesbury "favour'd Deism, and, under Pretence of lashing Priestcraft and Superstition, attack'd the Bible it self . . . with Design of establishing Heathen Virtue on the Ruins of Christianity."

Yet another significant "revision" in part 2 is Mandeville's attempt to explain the origins of civil society not—as he had done earlier—by means of a myth of skillful politicians who flattered the untamed multitude into obedience and subordination, but by describing (in accordance with empirical probability) how civilization gradually emerged from savagery. He posits three decisive causes in this conjectural progression: the banding together of savages for their mutual defense against animals, the stimulation of men's innate pride and courage through threats and attacks by other men, and the invention of letters, by which means laws would remain stable and trustworthy instead of being subject to the errors of oral tradition. Though at the end he accuses Shaftesbury of having attempted to subvert Christianity, it is a part of his deliberate irony to ignore the biblical version of the rise of civil society, in favor of a naturalistic and secular approach.

In his last major book, *An Enquiry into the Origin of Honour, and the Usefulness of Christianity in War* (1732), Mandeville produced a second continuation of his *Fable of the Bees*, for in this philosophical dialogue he again uses Cleomenes and Horatio as interlocutors, and revives subjects that had interested him well before his *Fable of the Bees* first appeared. Because he was dealing once again with sensitive matters, Mandeville's only admission of authorship is the inscription "*By the Author of the* Fable *of the* Bees."

The double purpose of this work is not only to present a redefinition of "honour" by subdividing its meanings and kinds, but also (in the latter half) to probe deliberately into "the usefulness of Christianity in war." Early in this book Cleomenes defines two senses of honor, not only clarifying their different meanings but also explaining how they emerged in different historical eras. *Honor* (1) "in its first literal Sense [is] a Means which Men by Conversing together have found out to please and gratify one another"; it is "as Ancient as the oldest Language." *Honor* (2), only some hundreds of years old, "signifies . . . a Principle of Courage, Virtue and Fidelity." Moreover, "it is an Invention of Politicians, to keep Men Close to their Promises and Engagements, when all other Ties prov'd ineffectual; and the Christian Religion itself was often found insufficient for that Purpose."

It is *honor* (2) that belongs to the "Man of Honour," who not only must fight courageously in his country's defense but "must likewise be ready to engage in private Quarrels, tho' the Laws of God and his Country forbid it." He must defend his honor with his life by challenging anyone who "insults" him, and he must also pay debts incurred among his peers. If he maintains his honor in these particulars, then "the world" allows him to whore as often as he desires and to be negligent in heeding the duns of the shopkeepers. One might reasonably conclude that Mandeville, after thus exposing the hypocrisy of the so-called man of honor, would surely recommend the complete extirpation of this false system of honor and the vices that it encourages. As a realist, however, and since at least as far back as the appearance of his Colonel Worthy in 1709, Mande-

London April 2d. 1729.

J. Bernard Mandeville M.D. declare this
to be my last Will & Testament:

To Penelope my Daughter J bequeath
twenty Shillings for a Ring.

To Elizabeth my Wife one hundred
Pounds Sterl. to be paid out of ye five hun
dred Pounds I. Lea Annuitys J have in hands
of Messrs. Cornelius & John Backer.

The Remainder of ye said Annuitys, & what
ever else J shall be possest'd of at ye hour
of my death, J leave to Michael Mande
ville my Son, whom J constitute. & appoint
to be my sole Executor; desiring of him
to bury me as near by and in as private
a manner as shall be consistent with ye
Cheapest Decency, B Mandeville.

Mandeville's will (Somerset House, London)

ville seems to have argued that while duelists must be apprehended and punished, it is nevertheless essential for the survival of politeness and civility that the custom of dueling not be entirely eradicated. Once again he finds that there is some social benefit to be extracted from even the worst kinds of individual behavior.

It is much easier to comprehend the message of the second half of this work, because for Mandeville there is absolutely no use for Christianity—the teachings of Jesus—in war. He is well aware that for centuries the clergy had accompanied armies to the battlefield in order to lead soldiers in prayer, to inspire them with courage and religious conviction of the rightness of their cause, and to minister to the needs of the dying. But for Mandeville such clerical participation means a departure from the very essence of Jesus' message in the New Testament, and soldiers who slaughter in order to install a theocracy or to replace one kind of church government with another are either dupes or opportunists and hypocrites. If the Puritan Revolution succeeded (though only temporarily), that was owing to the manipulative and hypocritical role-playing of Oliver Cromwell and other "saints." Mandeville admits that while there may have been some pious Christians in the Puritan army, the motives of most of their soldiers were less than pure. As for the soldiers in later wars under John Churchill, Duke of Marlborough, they were not militantly engaged in behalf of a particular church; their loyalty and zeal were founded instead upon the notion of personal honor, that is, honor in the second of the two senses previously elucidated.

Though noticed in the journals of the learned, this last book by Mandeville made no unusual splash. It was too new to have been used by his most distinguished recent antagonist, the Reverend George Berkeley, and Mandeville's contemporaries would not have been surprised by the drift of his latest arguments.

Having resisted the temptation to reply publicly to individual adversaries, Mandeville finally was goaded into responding by Berkeley's *Alciphron; or, The Minute Philosopher* (1732), a clergyman's blast against various freethinkers, including Shaftesbury as well as Mandeville. It is widely agreed that in the second dialogue Berkeley's freethinker Lysicles deplorably distorts Mandeville's message. In *A Letter to Dion* (Berkeley), Mandeville calls this interlocutor a lawless libertine. Shocked by Berkeley's misrepresentations

of his views, Mandeville begins by asserting that an honest man such as Berkeley could not possibly have read *The Fable of the Bees* with any close attention—if indeed he had read it at all—and still have produced such a travesty of its content. He then reminds Berkeley, by copious self-quotation, that he has always "preferred the road that leads to virtue." He insists that crimes such as murder, robbery, and the like, should be vigorously prosecuted and all criminals punished in accordance with the gravity of their crimes; and he denies that his book in any way praises public houses of prostitution (a charge popularized by the presentment of the Grand Jury of Middlesex). And far from encouraging a libertine disrespect for the rules of society, he had frequently emphasized that government and laws are absolutely necessary for the very existence of modern society. He also argues that if Berkeley had troubled to read his frequently reprinted *Vindication* he would not have penned the gross distortions that appear in *Alciphron*.

Though Mandeville ably discredits Berkeley's assault on *The Fable of the Bees*, an equally valuable feature of *A Letter to Dion* is his own distillation of the central arguments in his masterpiece. Insisting upon a strict interpretation of Christian conduct (that is, requiring self-denial and the sacrifice of the heart), Mandeville implies that Berkeley, like many other divines, compromises his Christianity. The vices Mandeville exposes are those of the fashionable and the prosperous, and he makes it clear to Berkeley that he is intent upon exposing hypocrisy—false pretension to piety, virtue, charity, or benevolence—wherever it occurs. Toward the end he reviews the economic aspects of his social thought, citing his paradox that "the Invention of Hoop'd and Quilted Petticoats" has contributed to the worldly greatness of advanced nations almost as much as the Reformation did to those nations that adopted it. He concludes by extensively quoting a celebrated passage from his *Fable of the Bees*, in which he defends international trade and luxury consumption—a reminder, perhaps, of Berkeley's attack on luxury a decade earlier, in the wake of the South Sea Bubble.

No record survives of any intention or attempt by Berkeley to respond to Mandeville's charges. Soon afterward Mandeville died, leaving Berkeley in the unenviable position of having received a powerful counterattack. For Berkeley personally, Mandeville's death may have seemed providential—a fortunate release from a controversy that might well have become more embarrassing to him.

Twentieth-century readers of Mandeville always face the central Mandeville Problem: were his professions of religious faith sincere? He repeatedly professed that he always preferred the path to virtue, but according to Kaye, his best editor, Mandeville's rigorism was insincere, and his deepest identification was with the industry, commerce, conveniences, and pleasures of his society. Some interpreters of Mandeville in the twentieth century do regard his ethical rigorism and Christian faith as sincere, viewing it either as a somewhat unusual survival of Calvinist/Augustinian doctrine (in which the spheres of grace and sin are sharply separated), or as representative of the mainstream of humanistic Christianity since the Renaissance. Most readers seem to accept some version of Kaye's view, seeing Mandeville as an apologist for worldly wealth, "real pleasures," trade, luxury, and all of the refinements of advanced civilization. It is at least possible that he lived in "divided and distinguished worlds" as a Christian libertine; he loved paradox.

Bibliography:

F. B. Kaye, "The Writings of Bernard Mandeville: A Bibliographical Survey," *Journal of English and Germanic Philology*, 20 (1921): 419-467.

References:

Elias J. Chiasson, "Bernard Mandeville: A Reappraisal," *Philological Quarterly*, 49 (1970): 489-519;

Richard I. Cook, *Bernard Mandeville* (New York: Twayne, 1974);

H. T. Dickinson, "Bernard Mandeville: an independent Whig," *Studies on Voltaire and the Eighteenth Century*, 151-155 (1976): 559-570;

Thomas R. Edwards, Jr., "Mandeville's Moral Prose," *ELH*, 31 (1964): 195-212;

M. M. Goldsmith, *Private Vices, Public Benefits: Bernard Mandeville's Social and Political Thought* (Cambridge: Cambridge University Press, 1985);

Goldsmith, " 'The Treacherous Arts of Mankind': Bernard Mandeville and Female Virtue," *History of Political Thought*, 7 (1986): 93-114;

Phillip Harth, "The Satiric Purpose of the *Fable of the Bees*," *Eighteenth-Century Studies*, 2 (1969): 321-340;

F. A. Hayek, "Dr. Bernard Mandeville," *Proceedings of the British Academy*, 52 (1966): 125-141;

George Hind, "Mandeville's *Fable of the Bees* as Menippean Satire," *Genre*, 1 (1968): 307-315;

Albert O. Hirschman, *The Passions and the Interests: Political Arguments for Capitalism before its Triumph* (Princeton: Princeton University Press, 1977);

Thomas A. Horne, *The Social Thought of Bernard Mandeville: Virtue and Commerce in Early Eighteenth-Century England* (New York: Columbia University Press, 1978);

Terence Hutchison, *Before Adam Smith: The Emergence of Political Economy, 1662-1776* (Oxford: Blackwell, 1988);

Malcolm Jack, "Progress and Corruption in the Eighteenth Century: Mandeville's 'Private Vices, Public Benefits,' " *Journal of the History of Ideas*, 37 (1976): 369-376;

F. B. Kaye, Commentary in *The Fable of the Bees*, 2 volumes, edited by Kaye (Oxford: Clarendon Press, 1924);

Kaye, "The Influence of Bernard Mandeville," *Studies in Philology*, 19 (1922): 83-108;

A. O. Lovejoy, *Reflections on Human Nature* (Baltimore: Johns Hopkins University Press, 1961);

J. C. Maxwell, "Ethics and Politics in Mandeville," *Philosophy*, 26 (1951): 242-252;

Hector Monro, *The Ambivalence of Bernard Mandeville* (Oxford: Clarendon Press, 1975);

Martin Price, *To the Palace of Wisdom: Studies in Order and Energy from Dryden to Blake* (Garden City, N.Y.: Doubleday, 1964);

Irwin Primer, ed., *Mandeville Studies: New Explorations in the Art and Thought of Dr. Bernard Mandeville (1670-1733)* (The Hague: Nijhoff, 1975);

Nathan Rosenberg, "Mandeville and Laissez-Faire," *Journal of the History of Ideas*, 24 (1963): 183-196;

Louis Schneider, *Paradox and Society: The Work of Bernard Mandeville* (New Brunswick, N.J.: Transaction Books, 1987).

Papers:

Mandeville's letters to Sir Hans Sloane and Lord Macclesfield are in the British Library. His will is at Somerset House.

Lady Mary Wortley Montagu

(26 May 1689 - 21 August 1762)

Isobel Grundy
University of Alberta

BOOKS: *Court Poems* (London: Printed for J. Roberts, 1706 [i.e., 1716]);

The Genuine Copy of a Letter Written From Constantinople . . . (London: Printed for J. Roberts & A. Dodd, 1719);

Verses Address'd to the Imitator of the First Satire of the Second Book of Horace, by Montagu and John, Lord Hervey (London: Printed for A. Dodd, 1733); also published as *To the Imitator of the Satire of the Second Book of Horace* (London: Printed for J. Roberts, 1733);

The Dean's Provocation For Writing the Lady's Dressing-Room (London: Printed for T. Cooper, 1734);

The Nonsense of Common-Sense, nos. 1-9 (London: Printed for J. Roberts, 16 December 1737 - 21 February 1738);

Six Town Eclogues. With some other Poems (London: Printed for M. Cooper, 1747);

Letters Of the Right Honourable Lady M--y W--y M--e: Written, during her Travels in Europe, Asia and Africa, To Persons of Distinction, Men of Letters, &c. in different Parts of Europe, 3 volumes (London: Printed for T. Becket & P. A. De Hondt, 1763);

An Additional Volume To The Letters Of the Right Honourable Lady M--y W--y M--e, mostly spurious (London: Printed for T. Becket & P. A. De Hondt, 1767; Philadelphia: Printed by Robert Bell?, 1768 [i.e., 1769]);

The Poetical Works Of the Right Honourable Lady M--y W--y M--e (London: Printed for J. Williams, 1768);

The Works of The Right Honourable Lady Mary Wortley Montagu. Including her Correspondence, Poems and Essays, 5 volumes, edited by James Dallaway (London: Richard Phillips, 1803);

Original Letters . . . to Sir James & Lady Frances Steuart (Greenock, 1818);

The Letters and Works of Lady Mary Wortley Montagu, Edited by Her Great Grandson Lord Wharncliffe (3 volumes, London: Richard Bentley, 1837 [i.e., 1836]; 2 volumes, Philadelphia: Carey, Lea & Blanchard, 1837);

The Letters and Works of Lady Mary Wortley Montagu, third edition, 2 volumes, edited by W. Moy Thomas (London: Bohn, 1861);

The Nonsense of Common-Sense, 1737-1738, edited by Robert Halsband, Northwestern University Studies in the Humanities, no. 17 (Evanston, Ill.: Northwestern University Press, 1947);

The Complete Letters of Lady Mary Wortley Montagu, 3 volumes, edited by Halsband (Oxford: Clarendon Press, 1965-1967);

The Selected Letters of Lady Mary Wortley Montagu, edited by Halsband (London: Longman, 1970; New York: St. Martin's Press, 1971);

Essays and Poems, with Simplicity, *A Comedy*, edited by Halsband and Isobel Grundy (Oxford: Clarendon Press, 1977);

Court Eclogs Written in the Year, 1716: Alexander Pope's Autograph Manuscript of Poems by Lady Mary Wortley Montagu, edited by Halsband (New York: New York Public Library and Readex Books, 1977).

Lady Mary Wortley Montagu, known in her lifetime as a wit and poet, has since been most admired for her letters: for their brilliant observation of life and customs in London, Turkey, and Europe; for their social satire, bons mots, acute and original opinions, and sinewy style. She fully exploited the potential of the epistolary genre, building a distinctive relationship with each of her correspondents within which to realize some aspects of the authorial self. The development of feminist positions and retrieval of women's writing are revealing her to be—in the letters and in a range of poetry and short prose pieces (many left unpublished and therefore hard to date)—an important figure in the female literary tradition.

Mary Pierrepont was born in fashionable Covent Garden, London. Her mother, Lady Mary Fielding, was the daughter of the third earl of Denbigh; her father, Evelyn Pierrepont, a youngest son who outlived his brothers to become earl (1690) and then duke (1715) of Kings-

Lady Mary Wortley Montagu (portrait attributed to Charles Jervas; location unknown, from Maynard Mack, Alexander Pope: A Life, *1985)*

ton. The earldom made Mary into Lady Mary, but as a girl, although the eldest child, she stood to inherit little. Her mother died young; her father (a rake, she said) "did not think himselfe oblig'd to be very attentive to his children's Education," though he did give her her first taste of glory at seven, by introducing her in person as a toast of the Kit-Kat Club. In his splendid library she "stole" the Latin language and introduced herself to a wide range of English and French books, including many by women.

In her teens she experimented with many voices and styles in verse, with epistolary fiction, translation (from Epictetus, like Elizabeth Carter later), and inventive letters to female friends. With one of them she invented a private language for discussing their marital prospects: going to heaven, hell, or limbo meant marrying a man one loved, detested, or merely tolerated. These letters cloak their confidences in flippancy, their anxiety about desire and compulsion in a libertine air of religious terms put to worldly use.

Two years of a very different correspon-

Edward Wortley Montagu

dence, sober in tone, emotionally probing and parrying on both sides, and on hers at least suggesting a sustained effort at precise and serious self-analysis, preceded Lady Mary's runaway marriage, in August 1712, to Edward Wortley Montagu, made under the threat of imminent consignment to "Hell." Wortley plainly feared that those qualities which led her to transgress by forming her own opinions and corresponding with him, might lead her to further transgressions in which as her suitor or husband he would be implicated. Her self-defense—resting on a claim to reason and dispassionateness—was compromised by the very fact of the correspondence. Simple assertions of moral worth were not available to a

woman addressing a man, as they might be for a romance hero or didactic author. Equivocation was necessary.

Her first letter to him (written on 28 March 1710, after the death of his sister, who had been serving as her nominal addressee) goes to the heart of the matter: "You distrust me. I can neither be easy nor lov'd where I am distrusted . . . ." For two more years she deployed the arts of rhetoric to secure his trust, to counter demands and accusations with straightforward self-justifications, varying shades of humble and mock-humble acceptance of blame, logical chains of reasoning, and sometimes verbal gestures of despair or submission. Need to differentiate herself from other young ladies leads her to construct both a self and a context: to interrogate female failings and female constraints, and to explore the feasibility of a married model of rural retirement. Her handling of two favorite topics, women's role and the search for the good life, is already complex.

Wavering between protest and submission, she achieves piercing insights into her dilemma: "I had rather passe all my Life as I do, than with one who thinks entirely ill of me" (? circa 26 October 1710); "I begin to be tird of my Humillity" (circa 19 November 1710). She calls herself "very far from thinking a Woman the most important busynesse of a Man's life" (circa 27 November 1710). As the moment for action approaches, her breath seems to come shorter: "I tremble for what we are doing. Are you sure you will love me for ever? Shall we never repent? I fear, and I hope" (15 August 1710). Next day, "I am fainting with Fear.—Forgive my Instabillity.—If I do it, Love me; if I dare not, do not hate me.—" After a few more days, and several bungled attempts at elopement, she concludes, "Adeiu. I am entirely yours if you please" (circa 20 August 1710).

These letters approach the condition of dramatic speech. Lady Mary later rehandled this material in the style of romance fiction, whose rapid narrative excludes most of the social and emotional detail which makes the letters so enthralling. Here the heroine's unusual intellectual attainments cause no unease to her suitor or herself; on the contrary, they first secure his regard.

She bore a son, Edward Wortley Montagu, Jr., on 16 May 1713. In cheap country lodgings, her husband in London, she occupied her time in writing. Her "proper matrimonial stile" in letters soon shifted from oblique expression of rapture to increasingly direct reproaches for neglect. Her letters to Wortley Montagu became dull; the play of her mind probably went into the diary which she kept from her marriage onward; her daughter, Mary, Countess of Bute, admired its trenchancy, but reluctantly burned it just before her own death, fearing that nonfamily readers would condemn its author as uncharitable.

At this time Lady Mary also wrote pieces angled toward her husband's literary friends: a rather formal analysis of Joseph Addison's *Cato* (1713), "Wrote at the Desire of Mr. Wortley, suppress'd at the desire of Mr. Adison" (unpublished until 1803), and a sparkling *Spectator* (no. 573, 28 July 1714): a letter from the president of a widows' club, who has been wife to a dotard, a rake, a miser, and others but never a passive victim even as a child bride, when "I resented his Contempt as I ought to do, and as most poor passive blinded Wives do, till it pleased Heaven to take away my Tyrant." Mrs. President has chosen most of her husbands herself, out of ambition, whimsy, or even spite or desire; the suitor still unchosen, estimable but pompous and self-interested, is "the Honourable *Edward Waitfort*"—surely a personal gibe. This essay makes highly original use of stock satirical butts: its lively sketches of husbands are outshone by its overall picture of marriage as a stalking ground for predators; its authorial persona, heartlessly good-humored and resilient, is one of the few complex female characters in the *Spectator*. Its publication marks Lady Mary's emergence as a fully mature writer.

Early in 1715 she went to London and formed exciting new alliances. Literary friends, Alexander Pope and John Gay, provided the stimulus for her mock-pastoral eclogues, and court attendance for an undated, untitled fragment first published in 1837 as "Account of the Court of George I." Its portraits recall those which open her friend John, Lord Hervey's *Memoirs of the Reign of George II*, rendering character through epigram and antithesis. George I "would have grown rich by saveing, but was incapable of laying schemes for getting." The future George II "look'd on all the Men and Women he saw as Creatures he might kick or kiss for his diversion." But any interaction between these characters is lost.

Wortley's appointment in 1716 as ambassador to Constantinople, and her unusual decision to accompany him, changed Lady Mary's life. Her friends, who could not foresee his recall after only two years, must have expected a much longer absence. In Turkey she investigated Persian poetry, translating it both literally and according to English poetic convention, and wrote a fine verse epistle while pregnant with her daughter, Mary Wortley Montagu, born in February 1718. She also kept two albums headed "Copys of Letters"; comparison with her "Heads" of letters actually sent (a manuscript summary of letters dispatched between 1 April 1717 and 1 March 1718) and the single one known to be extant in manuscript after going through the post, shows that her "Copys of Letters" preserved the informative and virtuoso but ignored the gossipy, personal, or repetitious elements in actual letters.

here, they generally shape their 228
Eyebrows, & ye Greeks & Turks have
a custom of putting round their Eyes
on ye inside a black Tincture, yt at a distance,
or by Candle-light adds very
much to ye Blackness of ym. I fancy
many of our Ladys would be overjoy'd
to know ye secret, but 'tis too visible
by day. they dye their Nails rose
colour, I own I cannot enough
accustom my selfe to ys fashion, to
find any Beauty in it. as to their
Morality or good conduct, I can
say like Arlequin, 'tis just as 'tis
wth you, & the Turkish Ladys
don't commit one Sin the less for
not being Christians. now I am a

A page from a 1 April 1717 letter to Lady Mar, as Montagu transcribed it in one of her "Copys of Letters" albums during her stay in Turkey (Harrowby MSS, vol. 253, p. 228; by permission of the Earl of Harrowby)

Her Turkish embassy letters, unlike all her others, were shaped not by the demands and norms of personal relationship but by those of the travel book. This remains true even though the "Copys of Letters" bear traces of their origins (in matching, for instance, of subject matter to recipient), and even if Lady Mary never seriously intended, while she lived, to publish them, although urged by Mary Astell, who added a manuscript preface "To the Reader" in 1724. Lady Mary's class thought of printing one's writings as indecorous, especially for a woman, though handing manuscript work round, among one's personal friends, was acceptable.

The prospect of death enlarged the bounds of the permissible: as Lady Mary was "dragging my ragged remnant of life to England," she left her "Copys of Letters" with the Reverend Benjamin Sowden, an English clergyman at Rotterdam, "to be dispos'd of as he thinks proper. This is the will and design of M. Wortley Montagu, Dec. 11, 1761." By then she intended this manuscript for the hands of a publisher, not her family.

It quickly won her posthumous renown. Astell had some grounds for claiming that it shows "to how much better purpose the LADYS Travel than their LORDS." While most travel books stuck to enumerating "sights," wonders, and the inferiority of foreign cultures to their own, Lady Mary firmly resolved not to imitate their "common stile" either in list making, in retailing imaginary or exaggerated marvels, or in narrow-mindedness.

Her first qualification was zest for travel: neither storms at sea, nor sleeping in a hovel in her clothes, nor vertiginous mountain tracks at night with postilions dropping asleep on their horses, nor wolf-infested forests, nor a recent battlefield "strew'd with the Skulls and Carcases of unbury'd Men, Horses and Camels," could deter her (to Alexander Pope, 12 February 1717). She did not blink at the horrific, such as the oppressions of janissaries (who freely threatened death on her behalf in response to minor inconvenience) and killings of politicians or of an unidentified young woman found still warm and bleeding near her house. No moralizing or consoling comment distances herself, or her readers, from these events, which she allows to strike home in all their rawness.

Rambling unnoticed on foot through successive cities, she also seized on less headline-catching detail: merchandise in shops, the common people's dress and living standard, the circumstances and habits of women especially. She anticipates Samuel Johnson in making human life the great object of remark. Repeatedly she describes herself as affected by the spirit of the place: penny-pinching in Holland, pleasure-loving in Turkey, "infected by the Poetical air" of the classics-haunted Mediterranean (to the Abbé Conti, 31 July 1718).

Her taste for the various and the exotic rests on an Augustan belief in the essential uniformity of human things: "the manners of Mankind do not differ so widely as our voyage Writers would make us believe" (to her sister Frances, Lady Mar, 1 April 1717). She enjoys confounding expectations of nation or class with unexpected comparison: the imperial court dress of Vienna reminds her of May Day peasant finery in England; Turkish ladies naked at their public baths accept a strangely clad foreigner more civilly than would those of any European court. She often remarks the outlandishness that others must find in her. She maintains that both Christianity and Islam cover a spectrum from the sanest and most rational (equally in each to be recognized and respected) to the superstitious fringes (equally in each to be laughed at).

At first hearing the claim that Islamic women are just as free as Christians, she vigorously disputes it. Arrived at Adrianople, she soon accepts that they are *more* free, having not only the sexual license given by a dress that conceals their identity, but also the right to retain their own fortunes in case of divorce. Lady Mary is eager to reshape her views, happy to abandon consistency for paradox, polemic, and the undermining of Western complacency.

She is quick, too, to discover likeness between apparently fictional literature and the actual conditions of the Near East. Theocritus and Homer, she finds, were unsuspected realists; the sublime but unpolished imagery of the epic and the Bible lives on in present-day Oriental poetry; even the material splendors of the *Arabian Nights* are a transcription of life. She finds learning experiences everywhere; yet, as a final paradox, she concludes with a passage of anti-Enlightenment skepticism as to the value of learning: knowledge of the Mediterranean, she now fears, will only make her discontented with England.

Within four years after her return to England in the autumn of 1718 she settled near Pope at Twickenham, outside but within easy reach of fashionable London, whose goings-on

An engraving by one of Montagu's contemporaries

she reported to her sister Lady Mar (an exile in Paris because of her husband's Jacobitism). These scathing, scintillating letters blend hilarity, cynicism, and an astonishment more frequent than in her letters from the East. It seems a strange recipe for cheering a depressive like Lady Mar, but the message seems to be that alienation from society is normal for the sensitive and the intelligent.

In a rare mention of politics Lady Mary links social pleasures with the effects of arbitrary power: "no body pretends to wince or Kick under their Burdens, but we go on cheerfully with our Bells at our Ears, ornamented with Ribands and highly contented with our present condition" (to Lady Mar, June 1726). Marriages, infidelities, and quarrels provide much farcical en-

tertainment. Her own relation to this frenetic world is unstable: the first scandal threatened is her own, over the resentment of an admirer whom she has caused to lose money in the South Sea affair. Her self-presentation varies from the staid ("We wild Girls allways make your prudent Wives and mothers," to Lady Mar, September 1725) to the outrageous: "There is but three pretty Men in England and they are all in love with me at this present writing" (to Lady Mar, circa 15 July 1726).

She keeps personal feeling (over the deaths, for instance, of her father and younger sister) on a tight rein. She admits being "vex'd to the blood by my young Rogue of a Son" when he runs away to sea (to Lady Mar, August 1727), but soon reestablishes her prevailing mood: "I run about thô I have 5,000 pins and needles running into my Heart. I try to console with a small Damsel who is at present every thing that I like, but alas, she is yet in a white Frock. At 14 she may run away with the Butler" (to Lady Mar, September 1727). Lady Mary will not exempt herself from the tone in which she has chosen, for this correspondent, to report on human travail.

The letters virtually ignore several of her modes of activity, most notably her battle to introduce inoculation against smallpox. Having lost her only brother and a close childhood friend to the disease, and herself been partly disfigured by it in 1716, she brought an open mind to the prophylactic system practiced in Turkey. (The embassy physician shared her interest.) She had both her children inoculated. Her daughter, Lady Bute, later recalled the hostility that her mother faced when making house visits during her campaign, which was such that she dared not let her little girl (a valuable piece of evidence) out of sight for fear of harm being done her. The medical profession and the clergy uttered authoritative, public condemnation; the experience must have been a radicalizing one. Lady Mary's one identified writing on the subject, "A Plain Account of the Innoculating of the Small Pox by a Turkey Merchant," a newspaper letter published in *The Flying-Post; or, Post-Master* (11-13 September 1722), has a savagery which the editor dared not print uncensored. It calls two deaths following inoculation "Murders," and attributes them to the wrong methods—*not* the ignorance—of English doctors; it satirically hopes that "this terrible design against the Revenue of the College may be entirely defeated," and wretched smallpox victims pay medical fees as before.

Lady Mary mentions various quarrels of her own to Lady Mar, but not the one with Pope which was to bulk so large in his poetry and her reputation. She may have disliked the superficially flattering, flirtatious, but essentially patronizing tone of his letters to her during the embassy; she declined to produce sentimental tears at his bidding. Likely sore points included attribution of anonymous writings (especially lampoons), opposed political views, and Lady Mary's friendship with Lord Hervey. (Unfortunately her letters to Hervey do not survive.) The unlikely tale of her mockingly rejecting advances from Pope was not recorded until a century later.

Lady Mary's poetry during these years includes incisive comment on gender relations, counterattacks (some written jointly with Henry Fielding or Hervey) escalating in step with Pope's attacks, and some plangent expressions of personal feeling. Her one known play is *Simplicity* (unpublished until 1977), a free adaptation of Pierre de Marivaux's *Le Jeu de l'amour et du hasard* (1730). Its original was staged in London in 1734. It returns to the topic of courtship and perceptively relates issues of gender and class. A young lady adopts (with her father's approval) a stoop-to-conquer strategy for her unknown suitor, not knowing that just as she is wearing her maid's clothes he is wearing those of his valet: his disguise gives her an unsuspected safety net, but Lady Mary brilliantly depicts the disturbance the young lady feels when she thinks she is falling in love with a servant. In prose, and on less explosively personal topics, Lady Mary showed her versatility in *The Nonsense of Common-Sense* (16 December 1737 - 21 February 1738, titled after the Opposition newspaper *Common Sense*), which embraces economic analysis, social comment (on the education and status of women), and science fiction (proposing robots to replace costly foreign opera singers). It seems that her authorship remained unguessed.

She left England for the Continent in 1739, following the will-o'-the-wisp of a passion for Francesco Algarotti (a talented, flighty, literary careerist of about her son's age), probably impelled also by the Pope affair and her consequent notoriety, by political "Noise, croud, Division," and perhaps by marital dissatisfaction and general restlessness. Her letters to Algarotti (mostly in French, with some trace of the gallant epistolary models that language offered) expose her feelings with less caution than any others she left, though never without a conscious elegance of style and a sardonic grain of self-scrutiny. Writing to him, she says, she can hardly "restrain my pen from falling into the extravagancys of Poetry, which indeed are only fit to attempt the expressing my thoughts of you or to you" (21 October 1736). Several surviving texts besides letters bear witness to the accuracy of this remark. She notes in herself an all-too-human tendency to self-congratulation on the "uncommon" strength of her passion: even in its grip she retains her habit of self-evaluation.

Lady Mary lived a year in Venice (without Algarotti, who never appeared), enjoying the informal and uncensorious Venetian manners. She then explored other Italian cities, deeply impressing several young Englishmen on the Grand

THE
Numb. I.

Nonfenfe of Common-Senfe.

To be Continued as long as the Author thinks fit, and the Publick likes it.

FRIDAY, DECEMBER 16, 1737. *all these wrote by me M.W.M. to serve an unhappy worthy Man*

PROVERBS i, 4.

To give Suttlety to the Simple, to the young Man Knowledge and Difcretion.

THE Title of this Paper would appear very abfurd, if thefe Words, *Common-Senfe,* were to be now underftood in the fame Manner they were laft *Chriftmas,* when they were fuppofed to mean that low Degree of Underftanding, which directed a reafonable Man in the Courfe of his ordinary Affairs; for as to all Projectors and Refiners in Politicks, under whatever Shape they appeared, they were never believed to be under the Guidance of *Common-Senfe.* But thefe poor Words have fince been applied very differently; they now mean a certain Paper with many Flights and fmall Reafon, that is handed about at Coffee-Houfes and Tea-Tables, for the Amufement of the Idle, the Entertainment of the Malicious, and the Aftonifhment of the Ignorant, who are very numerous in this Part of the World.

Out of a real Compaffion for thefe People, and being as fenfible as the Author himfelf,

June, and is fure to end in *September.* ---- The other *nine* Months I would have them appear in a Habit that does Honour to their own Country, and would be an univerfal Benefit to the Nation. ---- The Gentry would feel it in the Payment of their Rents, and the Tenants in the Sale of their Wool. ---- And, what fhould touch our pretty female Hearts, I can affure them it would be highly advantageous to their Complexions.---- Many cold Faces I have feen at an Opera, *deckt* in flight *Tabbies* and *Peaudefoys,* and *disfigured* with Red Tips of Nofes, would have had an agreeable Glow of natural Heat, if their Bodies had been covered with the warm Produce of our native Sheep.

I do not doubt but the Encouragement of the Woollen Trade had fome Share in his Majefty's Confideration, together with the Refpect juftly due to the Memory of his beloved Confort.---- The Covering of the Coaches with Black Cloth will be a fenfible Benefit to the Clothiers, and the Expence only fall on thofe who can afford it. ---- No Man is compelled to keep an Equipage; and if there be any *Peer* that cannot *honeftly* afford to pay for it, I think he may

it dropp'd, and the Sheriffs were left to do as they pleas'd.

On Thurfday the 8th Inftant both Houfes of Parliament met at Weftminfter, purfuant to their laft Prorogation, and were (by Virtue of a Commiffion fign'd by his Majefty, directed to the Rt. Hon. the Lord Chancellor, the Right Hon. the Earl of Wilmington, Prefident of his Majefty's Council; his Grace the Duke of Dorfet, Lord Steward of his Majefty's Houfhold, and others) further prorogued to Tuefday the 24th. of January next.

The fame Day two Writs pafs'd the Great Seal for the further Prorogation of the Convocations of Canterbury and York, which ftood prorogu'd to the 9th Inftant, to the 10th of February next.

The next Day in the Evening was iffued his Majefty's Royal Proclamation, for calling the Parliament to meet on Tuefday the 24th Day of January next at Weftminfter, then and there to fit for the Difpatch of divers weighty and important Affairs.

The Right Hon. the Earl of Ila, one of the Sixteen Peers of Scotland, is appointed Lord

The first issue of Montagu's anonymous periodical response to attacks on Sir Robert Walpole in the Opposition-party paper Common Sense

Tour, settled for four years at Avignon (1742-1746), and then traversed war-torn northern Italy to the province of Brescia. The circumstances of her sojourn there remain mysterious. A memoir which she later drew up in Italian, for use in a projected lawsuit, details her awkward involvement with Count Ugolino Palazzi, who escorted her from Avignon, afforded her refuge when she fell seriously ill, and then rented her a dilapidated though charming "little house" or "castle" at Gottolengo. He also found her an easy touch for sums of much-needed cash: traveling expenses, gambling debts, extravagantly estimated repairs and improvements. She gradually embellished a retreat, which in certain moods she felt to be almost ideal, and varied her life with summers at the lakeside resort of Lovere, where in 1754 she bought a second dwelling. But Palazzi was a constant annoyance. In 1756 she moved to Padua and Venice, where at last she shook him off.

This move put her in touch again with English and Italian notables, including the now decorously friendly Algarotti. Her letters to the Jacobite exiles Lady Frances and Sir James Steuart reflect her pleasure in a true meeting of minds; they also reflect a new trouble, a feud between herself and the British consul in Venice (Joseph Smith, a well-known book collector) and his circle. Its origin was political, but the form it took was social baiting of Lady Mary both as old woman and as learned lady. Harassed in Venice, she returned to London in 1761, following her husband's death, in a new, undignified, not easily explicable panic. In the cramped little West End house which her daughter found for her, already dying of breast cancer, she longed in vain to return to Venice.

Her letters home from 1739 onward make little or no mention of her various difficulties. Before leaving she had already found in her old friend Henrietta Louisa, Lady Pomfret (who was living in continental Europe for reasons of econ-

Lady Mary Wortley Montagu, 1739 (painting by Carolus de Rusca; Wharncliffe Collection)

omy), a recipient for musings on life, less fluent and personal than her best manner, but spiced with sardonic gossip which is a faint echo of that to Lady Mar. She sent her husband detailed accounts of the English abroad, of her more touristic activities, of the civilities she met with, and, perhaps most interesting, of classical relics and scientific curiosities. As time passed, the dutiful element and the space given to matters of health increased. A similar but more courtly tedium infects her letters to Henrietta, Lady Oxford; courtliness is leavened with straight talking and wit in letters (in French) to Mme Chiara Michieli.

Lady Mary's earliest surviving letters to her daughter (one from 1746 and one from 1747) are brief and formal, bearing the marks of emotional as well as geographical separation. But those extant increase steadily in warmth, freedom of expression, and an intimacy constructed entirely through this epistolary dialogue. Their richness and variety of texture capture the flow of her inner life. She finds both contentment and melancholy in a "solitude not unlike that of Robinson Crusoe" (3 June 1753); again, she describes its picturesque invasion by various categories of visitors unimaginable in England. As years pass she turns increasingly from the present to the past, but whether writing of her present neighbors or of people long dead, of gardening or books, of her own intellectual pursuits or the education of granddaughters, she makes each topic illustrate personal philosophy: eager for everything that is to be enjoyed, stoical for everything that is to be endured; deeply invested in comprehending her world, with little hope of any good result from doing so.

The nonepistolary writing that survives from the years of exile is mostly in French and Italian, but this is no index of her actual productivity. On 1 October 1752 she told Lady Bute that she was writing a history of her own times, although "I regularly burn every Quire as soon as it is finish'd." Extant fragments on Queen Anne's death and on George I may be part of this foray into the popular court-memoir genre. She judges herself to be well qualified as a historian by close personal knowledge and nonpartisanship, but to have cogent reasons for suppressing her work: the truth cannot win applause. "Or were it otherwise, Applause to me is as insignificant as Garlands on the Dead." Although death is her common metaphor for her exile or absence, she undoubtedly connected her voluntary self-suppression with her sex. This letter goes on to juxtapose a female and a male silence: "[I] have no concern beyond my own Family. [But] your Father's silence gives me great pain." Many readers can be glad that Lady Mary's self-imposed silence was so sporadic.

Biographies:

George Paston (Emily Morse Symons), *Lady Mary Wortley Montagu and Her Times* (London: Methuen, 1907);

Lewis Melville (Lewis S. Benjamin), *Lady Mary Wortley Montagu: Her Life and Letters, 1689-1762* (London: Hutchinson, 1925);

Robert Halsband, *The Life of Lady Mary Wortley Montagu* (Oxford: Clarendon Press, 1956).

References:

Isobel Grundy, " 'The Entire Works of Clarinda': Unpublished Juvenile Verse by Lady Mary Wortley Montagu," *Yearbook of English Studies*, 7 (1977): 91-107;

Grundy, "Lady Mary Wortley Montagu's 'Rambling Destiny' Ends in Mayfair," in *Godly Mayfair*, edited by Ann Callendar (London: Grosvenor Chapel, 1980), pp. 13-17;

Grundy, "New Verse by Henry Fielding," *PMLA*, 87 (March 1972): 213-245;

Grundy, " 'New' Verse by Lady Mary Wortley Montagu," *Bodleian Library Record*, 10 (February 1981): 237-249;

Grundy, "Ovid and Eighteenth-Century Divorce: An Unpublished Poem by Lady Mary Wortley Montagu," *Review of English Studies*, 23 (November 1972): 417-428;

Grundy, "The Politics of Female Authorship: Lady Mary Wortley Montagu's Reaction to the Printing of her Poems," *Book Collector*, 31 (Spring 1982): 19-37;

Grundy, "A 'Spurious' Poem by Lady Mary Wortley Montagu," *Notes and Queries*, 225 (October 1980): 407-410;

Grundy, "*Verses Address'd to the Imitator of Horace*: A Skirmish between Pope and Some Persons of Rank and Fortune," *Studies in Bibliography*, 30 (1977): 96-119;

Robert Halsband, "Addison's *Cato* and Lady Mary Wortley Montagu," *PMLA*, 65 (December 1950): 1122-1129;

Halsband, " 'Condemned to Petticoats': Lady Mary Wortley Montagu as Feminist and Writer," in *The Dress of Words: Essays on Restoration and Eighteenth Century Literature in Honor of Richmond P. Bond* (Lawrence: University of Kansas Press, 1978), pp. 35-52;

Halsband, "An Imitation of Perrault in England: Lady Mary Wortley Montagu's 'Carabosse,' " *Comparative Literature*, 3 (Spring 1951): 174-177;

Halsband, "Lady Mary Wortley Montagu As Letter-Writer," in *The Familiar Letter in the Eighteenth Century*, edited by Howard Anderson, Philip B. Daghlian, and Irvin Ehrenpreis (Lawrence: University of Kansas Press, 1966), pp. 43-70;

Halsband, " 'The Lady's Dressing-Room' Explicated by a Contemporary," in *The Augustan Milieu, Essays Presented to Louis A. Landa*, edited by H. K. Miller, E. Rothstein, and G. S. Rousseau (Oxford: Clarendon Press, 1970), pp. 225-231;

Halsband, "New Light on Lady Mary Wortley Montagu's Contribution to Inoculation," *Journal of the History of Medicine*, 8 (October 1953): 390-405;

Halsband, "Pope, Lady Mary, and the *Court Poems* (1716)," *PMLA*, 68 (March 1953): 237-250;

Halsband, "Virtue in Danger, The Case of Griselda Murray," *History Today* (October 1967): 692-700;

Halsband, "Walpole *versus* Lady Mary," in *Horace Walpole: Writer, Politician, and Connoisseur*, edited by Warren Hunting Smith (New Haven: Yale University Press, 1967);

Ann Messenger, "Town Eclogues: Lady Mary Wortley Montagu and John Gay," in her *His and Hers: Essays in Restoration and Eighteenth-Century Literature* (Lexington: University of Kentucky Press, 1986), pp. 84-107;

Genevieve Miller, *The Adoption of Inoculation for Smallpox in England and France* (Philadelphia: University of Pennsylvania Press, 1957), pp. 70-80;

Bruce Redford, *The Converse of the Pen: Acts of Intimacy in the Eighteenth Century Familiar Letter* (Chicago: University of Chicago Press, 1987);

Jill Rubenstein, "Women's Biography as a Family Affair: Lady Louisa Stuart's 'Biographical Anecdotes' of Lady Mary Wortley Montagu," *Prose Studies*, 9 (May 1986): 3-21;

Patricia Mayer Spacks, "Imaginations Warm and Tender, Alexander Pope and Lady Mary Wortley Montagu," *South Atlantic Quarterly*, 83 (Spring 1984): 207-215;

Geoffrey Tillotson, "Lady Mary Wortley Montague and Pope's *Elegy to the Memory of an Unfortunate Lady*," *Review of English Studies*, 12 (October 1936): 401-412.

Papers:
Most of Lady Mary's papers (letters, other prose, poetry, and annotations in books) belong to the Harrowby Manuscripts Trust, Sandon Hall, Stafford. Other letters are held by the Lincoln Record Office, the National Library of Scotland (Bute Manuscripts; also volumes of plays with Lady Mary's annotations), Sheffield City Library (Wharncliffe Manuscripts; also Lady Mary's "Italian Memoir"); and the Biblioteca Civica, Treviso, Italy; others again are scattered, many in private collections. Her commonplace book is in the Fisher Library University of Sydney, Australia. Poems transcribed by others are in the Portland Papers (owned by the Marquess of Bath), at Yale University (the Osborn Collection), Cornell University (copied by Joseph Spence), the British Library (several collections), the Pierpont Morgan Library and the New York Public Library (copied by Pope), and the Huntington Library.

Samuel Pepys

(23 February 1633 - 26 May 1703)

E. Pearlman
University of Colorado at Denver

BOOKS: *Memoirs Relating to the State of the Royal Navy in England, for Ten Years, determin'd December 1688* (London: Printed for R. Griffin, 1690); facsimile, edited by J. R. Tanner as *Pepys' Memoires of the Royal Navy, 1679-1688* (Oxford: Clarendon Press, 1906);

An Account of the Preservation of King Charles after the Battle of Worcester, edited by Sir David Dalrymple (London: Printed for William Sandby, 1766);

Memoirs of Samuel Pepys, Esq., F. R. S., Secretary to the Admiralty in the Reigns of Charles II. and James II., Comprising His Diary from 1659 to 1669, Deciphered by the Rev. John Smith, 2 volumes, edited by Richard, Lord Braybrooke (London: Colburn, 1825);

Diary and Correspondence of Samuel Pepys, F. R. S., Secretary to the Admiralty in the Reigns of Charles II. and James II. . . . 3rd Edition, Considerably Enlarged, 5 volumes, edited by Braybrooke (London: Colburn, 1848, 1849);

Diary and Correspondence of Samuel Pepys, Esq., F. R. S., from His Manuscript Cypher in the Pepysian Library, 6 volumes, deciphered and edited by Rev. Mynors Bright (London: Bickers, 1875-1879);

The Diary of Samuel Pepys, 10 volumes, edited by Henry B. Wheatley (London & New York: Bell, 1893-1899);

Samuel Pepys's Naval Minutes, edited by J. R. Tanner (London: Printed for the Navy Records, 1926);

The Tangier Papers of Samuel Pepys, edited by Edwin Chappell (London: Printed for the Navy Records Society, 1935);

Mr. Pepys upon the State of Christ-Hospital, edited by Rudolf Kirk (Philadelphia: University of Pennsylvania Press / London; Oxford University Press, 1935);

Charles II's Escape from Worcester: A Collection of Narratives Assembled by Samuel Pepys, edited by William Matthews (Berkeley & Los Angeles: University of California Press, 1966);

The Diary of Samuel Pepys: A new and complete transcription, 11 volumes, edited by Robert Latham and William Matthews (Berkeley & Los Angeles: University of California Press, 1970-1983).

Samuel Pepys, author of the finest and best-known diary in English, was born in Salisbury Court near Fleet Street in London on 23 February 1633. He was the fifth of eleven children, of whom only three (Pepys the eldest) survived to adulthood. His father, John Pepys, was a tailor, his mother, Margaret Kite Pepys, the sister of a butcher. Pepys attended Huntingdon Grammar School, whose best-known graduate was Oliver Cromwell. From about 1646 Pepys studied at St. Paul's School, at that time adjacent to the great London cathedral. The curriculum was weak in mathematics, strong enough in classical languages and Hebrew to have well served John Milton, who had preceded Pepys by a generation. In his diary Pepys confessed to being "a great roundhead when . . . a boy." After 1660, when royalty had been restored, Pepys repented of his youthful radicalism. He met an old classmate and was "much afeared that he would have remembered the words that I said the day that the King was beheaded (that were I to preach upon him, my text should be: 'The memory of the wicked shall rot')." From St. Paul's Pepys proceeded in 1650 to Magdelene College, Cambridge. Among his fellow students at Magdalene was John Dryden (a remote relation), with whom he maintained a lifelong acquaintanceship. At Cambridge Pepys composed a romance called "Love a Cheat," which he destroyed ten years later: "I wondered a little at myself at my vein at the time when I wrote it, doubting that I cannot do so well now if I would try." From about the age of twenty, Pepys suffered from kidney stones. On 26 March 1658, with "the pain growing insupportable," Pepys underwent major surgery and was relieved of a stone about the size of a tennis ball. He hon-

Samuel Pepys (portrait by Sir Godfrey Kneller; auctioned by Sotheby and Co., 1 April 1931)

ored the date of his delivery with an annual feast.

Pepys was distantly connected to the powerful and wealthy Mountagu family. During the late 1650s, some time after he took his bachelor's degree in March 1654, while employed as a clerk to George Downing in the Exchequer, Pepys also served as secretary and man of business to Edward Mountagu (later first earl of Sandwich). On 1 December 1655 Pepys married Elizabeth St. Michel, who was fifteen years old, unconnected, and penniless. He later recalled that he had been "really sick" for love of her and compared his emotions to the feeling of being "ravished" by music.

Despite the youthful passion, the couple lived apart for a short period during 1657—a separation caused, Pepys says cryptically, by "differences" (possibly an attack of his recurrent jealousy). The separation was a harbinger of a generally stormy marriage. On the first day of 1660, Pepys began the shorthand diary which he kept so assiduously until the last day of May 1669:

> Blessed be God, at the end of the last year I was in very good health, without any sense of my old pain but upon taking of cold.
> I lived in Axe-yard, having my wife and servant Jane, and no more in family then us three.

Elizabeth Pepys (engraving by James Thomson, after a portrait by John Hayls)

My wife, after the absence of her terms for seven weeks, gave me hopes of her being with child, but on the last day of the year she hath them again.

Pepys's patron Mountagu, once a strong parliamentarian, had become, with George Monck, one of the architects of Charles II's return from exile. In May 1660 Mountagu arranged for Pepys to accompany his fleet to Holland for the purpose of bringing Charles back to England, and it was Mountagu who in June procured Pepys's appointment as Clerk of the Acts to the Navy Board. Although Pepys was honest enough to admit that "chance without merit brought me in," he made the most of his opportunity. Public

service became his life's work and earned him a niche in administrative as well as naval history. As clerk he was one of the four senior officers on the Navy Board. Pepys was appointed to a navy that was totally chaotic by today's standards: ships might or might not be owned by the state; seamen were not regularly employed, and as a result there was no clear distinction between civilian and military; no regular systems were in place for supplying the ships or paying the men; officers were likely to be courtiers appointed without experience at sea; many administrators seem regularly to have jumbled their public and private accounts; the taking of gifts—bribes in modern terminology—was a standard procedure and considered one of the perquisites of office. Pepys pioneered thousands of small changes that would eventually transform this chaos into an orderly and professional navy.

Pepys established his reputation as a knowledgeable and skilled public servant during the disastrous Second Dutch War (1665-1667). The failures of the navy, which were especially evident in Michel Adriaanszoon de Ruyter's courageous and daring Medway raid, were under investigation by angry committees of the Commons. Pepys took the lead in defending the management of the war, following the advice of his mentor Sir William Coventry "to be as short as I can, and obscure, saving in things fully plain," and he conducted himself so that "all the world that was within hearing, did congratulate me, and cry up my speech as the best thing they ever heard."

Pepys's marriage was under strain in 1668 and 1669 after Elizabeth discovered him with his "main" in his pubescent maid Deb Willet's "cunny." On 31 May 1669, troubled by severe pain in his eyes and convinced that he was going blind, he drew his diary to a poignant close: "and therefore resolve from this time forward to have it kept by my people in longhand, and must therefore be contented to set down no more then is fit for them and all the world to know.... And so I betake myself to the course, which is almost as much as to see myself go into my grave—for which, and all the discomforts that will accompany my being blind, the good God prepare me."

A few months later, on a holiday in the Low Countries and France, Elizabeth Pepys contracted a fever. She died on 10 November shortly after returning to England. Pepys never remarried; his intimate relationship with Mary Skinner began shortly after 1669 and continued to his death in 1703.

In June of 1673 Pepys left his clerkship for the Admiralty (to which the Navy Board reported). The admiral was King Charles's Roman Catholic brother James, whose exclusion from office at that time under the terms of the Test Act gave Pepys scope for administrative initiative. Pepys was able to prosecute a series of important reforms in shipbuilding, pensions, and what would now be called personnel practices. Pepys's seat in the House of Commons in 1673-1678, 1679, and 1685-1687 gave him a forum to speak on behalf of the navy. In 1678-1679, during the anti-Catholic hysteria associated with the Popish Plot, Pepys was accused of being a secret Papist.

He was imprisoned for six weeks under suspicion of espionage; the charges were ultimately dropped but not until he had spent an enormous amount of time and effort developing an elaborate defense. Pepys was out of office until 1683-1684, when he served as secretary to an expedition to supervise the abandonment of the Tangier Mole, a massive and expensive breakwater built to create an artificial harbor, which was perhaps the century's greatest military folly. His so-called second diary covers these events. In 1683 Pepys was suddenly returned to the Admiralty with a great deal more authority than he had previously enjoyed, but with the revolution of 1688, he left office never to return. He devoted his retirement years to expanding and cataloguing his collections and corresponding with some of the great men of his time. (He had served as President of the Royal Society in the 1680s.) On 26 May 1703 his great friend John Evelyn wrote in his own diary: "This day dyed Mr. Sam: Pepys, a very worthy, Industrious & curious person, none in England exceeding him in the Knowledge of the Navy.... [He] was universally beloved, Hospitable, Generous, Learned in many things, skill'd in Musick, a very great Cherisher of Learned men." It is difficult to discover the raffish young man of Pepys's diary in so respectable an epitaph.

The diary itself is an acute record not only of Pepys's life but of the public events of the first decade of the Restoration. It was kept with admirable diligence: in the 113 months from the beginning of January 1660 to the end of May 1669, there are only a handful of days for which Pepys made no entry. Altogether the diary is a massive work of about one and a quarter million words. Some years are more extensively chronicled than others: eighty-four thousand words in 1661, more than two hundred thousand in 1667. The diary was kept in a shorthand code based on Thomas Shelton's well-known *Short Writing* (1626, twenty-one subsequent editions before 1710). The system provided Pepys with the security which allowed him to write frankly and without fear of discovery. Pepys did not advertise the existence of his diary. He records mentioning it only to "the lieutenant of the *Swiftsure*" and to Coventry, and there is no reason to believe that during his lifetime it was ever glimpsed by any eyes other than his own. Erotic passages were kept in a macaronic cryptograph which, although not especially difficult to decipher, provided further protection from intrusion. But Pepys seems to

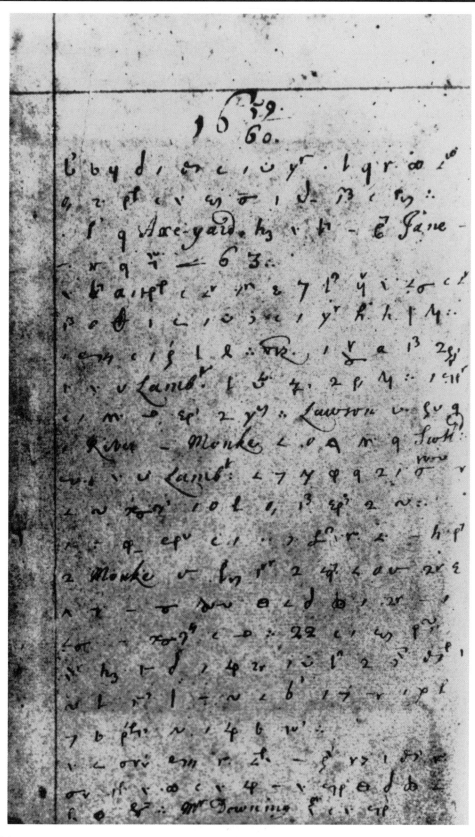

First and last pages from Pepys's shorthand diary (by permission of the Master and Fellows, Magdalene College, Cambridge)

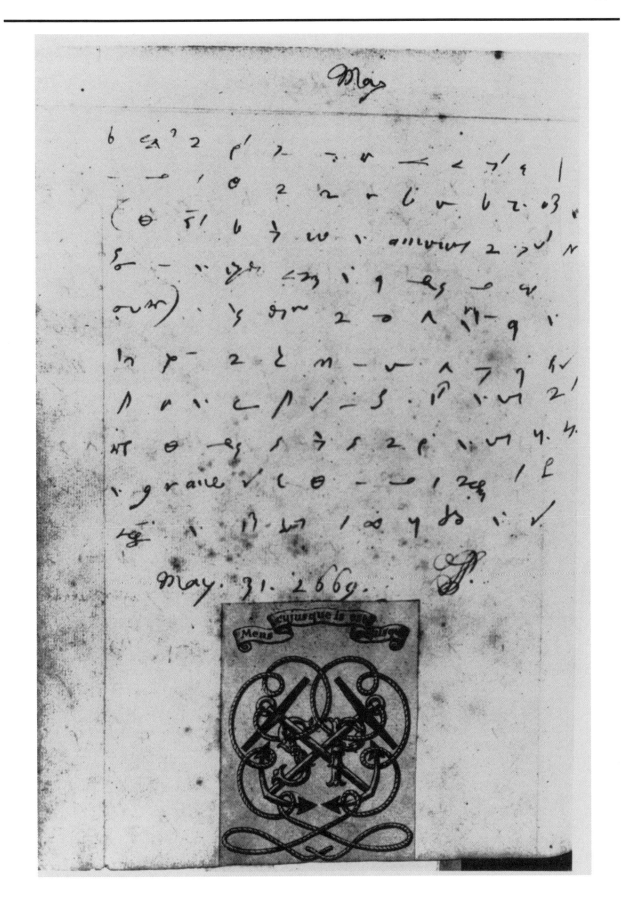

May. 31. 1669.

have intended to bequeath the diary to posterity. It was carefully bound in six volumes, each labeled "IOVRNAL," and displayed publicly among the collections he willed to Magdalen College. The diary was decoded and printed, but only in part, in 1825. Successive editions added more material, but the whole—including the passages which Leslie Stephen announced in his *Dictionary of National Biography* entry "could not possibly be printed"—did not appear until the monumental and scrupulous edition of Robert Latham and William Matthews (1970-1983), which is an invaluable repository of information not only about Pepys but of almost everything and everyone he encountered or mentioned during the diary years. It is the principal resource for students of the diary or the diarist.

The diary is engaging both for content and style. It is best known and admired for two great anthology pieces—the accounts of the plague and fire of 1666. Now that it is available in unexpurgated form, Pepys's tormented affair with Deb Willet will become equally notorious. But the diary can be best appreciated by wide reading, especially of the later volumes, when the texture of experience deepens and Pepys reveals more and more about himself.

A reader of the diary becomes acquainted with a man of great verve and wide interests. Pepys was a virtuoso—a "learned and ingenious person"—curious about whatever was new and exciting, whether it was shipbuilding, the new sciences, music, languages, prints, ballads, mathematics, or the theater. He was also a Baconian who seemed never to be without his copy of Sir Francis Bacon's *Faber Fortunae*. He was enthusiastic about beauty, especially the beauty of music and women; yet he labored constantly to resist the temptations of drink, of the theater, and of the numerous "Mrs. Bagwells" whom he pawed in closet, kitchen, or coach. He remained the tailor's son who admired clothes, both his own and others. He was extravagant about his own pleasures but kept his wife on a short financial leash. Pepys was a connoisseur of the ephemeral who preferred Sir Samuel Tuke's *Adventure of the Five Hours* to *Othello*, and *Sir Martin Mar-all* to *A Midsummer Night's Dream*. He was an eminently clubbable man and counted among his friends such distinguished individuals as Robert Hooke, Robert Boyle, John Wilkins, William Petty, and of course John Evelyn. He was an extraordinarily acquisitive and patient collector of ship models, scientific instruments, portraits, ballads, money, and

women. Pepys's diary may well be thought of as the most sophisticated expression of his instinct to collect and possess.

Pepys's prose style is worthy of the closest inspection. Here are two representative sentences drawn from his account of the days when the great fire was finally burning itself out: "At home did go with Sir W. Batten and our neighbor Knightly (who, with one more, was the only man of any fashion left in all the neighborhood hereabouts, they all removing their goods and leaving their houses to the mercy of the fire) to Sir R. Ford's and there dined, in an earthen platter a fried breast of mutton, a great many of us. But very merry; and endeed as good a meal, though as ugly a one, as ever I had in my life." Even so small a sample reveals a great deal about Pepys, including the fact that he was resilient enough to make sure that the disaster to the city would not compromise the pleasure of the table. The buoyant and heightened emotion that marks the diary is present in the superlatives which come so easily to his pen—"a great many," "very merry," "as ever I had in my life." Pepys has the eye for detail of a great novelist. Whenever possible, the general is supplanted by the particular: "an *earthen* platter"; "a *fried* breast of mutton." Pepys's world is specific, material, diverse, and a mingled yarn of the superlatively ugly and extraordinarily good.

The illusion of realism is created by the heaping of details, while the diary's immediacy is contrived by unobtrusive but effective tricks of style. The most obvious of these is ellipsis: "At home did go" omits the subject "I"; "But very merry" leaves out "we were." The elisions create the appearance of haste, spontaneity, even breathlessness. Spontaneity is also generated by Pepys's fluid grammar. In the first sentence above, for example, there are four successive grammatical subjects: first the elided "I"; next the first person plural which joins Pepys to his companions; third, the men "of fashion" of the neighborhood who are mentioned in the parenthetical insertion; and finally, the principal grammatical subject of the sentence—"a great many of us"—which makes its appearance as an enclitic tacked on to the end of the sentence, almost as afterthought. The suspended subject mimics the rhythms of informal conversation and generates the intimacy which make Pepys as much a companion as a figure out of the past. Added to these qualities is the wonderful appearance of verisimilitude. Neighbor Knightly, Pepys affirms, is the only "man of any fashion" who has not abandoned the blighted area. But the attentive reader must be subtly influenced by unemphatic modifiers ("with one more"; "hereabouts"). Pepys is content to allow a little vagueness; either he knows or thinks he may remember some other gentleman who also stayed on, or perhaps he waffles on the definition of "neighborhood." The modifiers reassure us that Pepys strives for exactness and accuracy, and they help to establish confidence and trust between diarist and reader.

In these two representative sentences, in fact, there is only one flaccid phrase: the gesture toward piety in the formulaic "*to the mercy* of the fire." On the whole Pepys artistically creates that sense of spontaneity, immediacy, trust, and verisimilitude which makes sustained reading of the Diary so easy and pleasurable. The passage sounds as if it were written "to the moment." But it is an illusion. Further reading in the diary tells us that Pepys did not compose this entry until 18 January 1667, or about three months after the events took place; rather, he kept notes on "loose papers," as seems to have been his general practice, and wrote in the diary when time permitted. Pepys is not a naive genius but an artist.

It is frequently asserted that Pepys is a modern person, recognizable as a member of our own civilization rather than of the late medieval world that we have lost. Pepys has been described as an individualist in an age of emerging individualism and a protocapitalist in a period marked by burgeoning entrepreneurship. Certainly, Pepys was a member of the first cohort of Englishmen for whom experience was organized not primarily around theology or faith, but around secular experience. Pepys was Christian in ceremonial terms, but indifferent to ideology. When Daniel Mills, the rector of St. Olave's, delivered "an unnecessary sermon upon Originall Sin, neither understood by himself nor the people," Pepys dismissed him as a "lazy fat priest." But on another occasion the same Mills distinguished himself, in Pepys's eyes at least, with "a very excellent and persuasive, good and moral sermon. Shewed like a wise man, that righteousness is a surer moral way of being rich, than sin and villainy." Mills's welcome and reassuring sermon was clearly part of the mysterious process by which Calvinist introspection was transformed into the Protestant ethic and became the servant rather than the antagonist of capitalism. Pepys's religion was tepid (though he was secretly attracted to the forms of Catholic worship), and his religious exclamations

unselfconsciously comic; casting his accounts, "I did find myself really worth 1900 1., for which the Great God of Heaven and Earth be praised." Church attendance too had its consolations: "I did entertain myself with my perspective glass up and down the church, by which I had the great pleasure of seeing and gazing a great many very fine women. . . ."

The genuine modernity of Pepys is implicit in his attitude toward religion and can best be illustrated by comparing him with another diarist of his generation. Pepys's exact contemporary, Philip Henry, also recorded his reaction to the fire of London, but in very different terms. Henry confined his description of the event itself to a few general sentences, and then turned immediately to find a "use" for this "sad providence." Henry drew a series of lessons: that he should "get [his] heart deeply affected with . . . sin the cause of it, the nations sin . . ."; that he should distrust worldly success "seeing in one moment it makes to itself wings and flies away"; that the fire is a warning of that "terrible day . . . when all the world shall be of fire." Henry's diary entry is ingenious, allegorical, exotic, and stakes a claim to universality; Pepys's entry is richly detailed, concrete, and while indifferent to transcendent truth, is nevertheless convincing and human. A second example: when Philip Henry's son died, his diary entry paid only the scantest attention to the child and explored instead Henry's spiritual relationships: "Lord wherefore is it that thou contendest, show mee, show mee. Have I overboasted, over-loved, over-prized?" Pepys's response to the death of his brother Tom is egocentric in the modern sense. Its appeal is not to the supernatural but to the self, and Pepys is frank about his amusement with both human frailty and his own nature: "But Lord, to see how the world makes nothing of the memory of a man an hour after he is dead. And indeed, I must blame myself; for though at the sight of him, dead and dying, I had real grief for a while, while he was in my sight, yet presently after and ever since, I have had very little grief indeed for him." It is in these forthright sentences rather than in Philip Henry's allegorizing that we recognize ourselves.

The changes in his own personality that Pepys records also contribute to the sense of the modernity of his own person. Learning self-discipline and learning how to keep to business are the principal themes of the diary. In the beginning, Pepys regularly suffered the chagrin of the chronically dissolute: "at night to Sir W. Battens

Pepys's library in York Buildings, King Street, where he went to live in 1679. The book presses are now in the Pepys Library at Magdalene College, Cambridge (drawing by Nichols, circa 1693; by permission of the Master and Fellows, Magdalene College, Cambridge)

and there very merry with a good barrell of oysters; and this is the present life I lead." The conflict between the desire for pleasure and the need for industry constitutes the comic backdrop of the diary: "But Lord, to consider how my natural desire is to pleasure, which God be praised that he hath given me the power by my late oaths to curb so well as I have done, and will do again after two or three plays more." Indeed, the diary records in full the contention between industry and idleness: "Against my nature and will (yet such is the power of the Devil over me I could not refuse it) to the Theatre and saw *The Merry Wives of Windsor*, ill done. . . . And after supper to prayers." Pepys struggled mightily to gain control of his hedonistic impulses, even to devising an elaborate scheme of oaths and monetary penalties to keep himself out of harm's way: "So I . . . to the office, where I did with great content faire a vow to mind my business and laisser aller les femmes for a month." Though the battle remained unresolved, there is ample evidence that Pepys had become productive and efficient.

In sum, several qualities combine to make Pepys's diary so wonderful. Pepys was curious about all things and at the center of important events. He was both passionate and honest. His prose style is uniquely suited to its purpose. In addition, the diary reveals almost novelistic themes—the secularization of theology, the struggle between idleness and diligence, the pleasures and pains of marriage and infidelity. One final set of traits also contributes mightily to the success of the diary. The same Pepys who was so frank about the achievement of discipline was also very vain of his orderliness. Even Edward Hyde, Earl of Clarendon congratulated him saying, according to Pepys, that "no man in England was of more method. . . than myself." Pepys was sometimes amazed at his own passion for order: "my delight is in the neatness of everything, and so cannot be pleased with anything unless it be very neat, which is a strange folly." He was also a fanatic about secrecy, and once attacked his brother John, calling him "Asse and Coxcomb, for which I am sorry" for leaving a door unlocked. "One thing that I hate in others and more in myself, to be careless of keys." Verve alone would have resulted in a marvelous life, but verve allied to secrecy and orderliness produced the marvelous diary.

Letters:

Private Correspondence and miscellaneous papers of Samuel Pepys, 1679-1703, 2 volumes, edited by J. R. Tanner (London: Bell, 1926; New York: Harcourt, Brace, 1926);

Further Correspondence of Samuel Pepys, 1662-1679, edited by Tanner (London: Bell, 1929; New York: Harcourt, Brace, 1929);

Letters and the Second Diary of Samuel Pepys, edited by E. G. Howarth (London: J. M. Dent / New York: Dutton, 1932);

Shorthand Letters of Samuel Pepys, edited by Edwin Chappell (Cambridge: Cambridge University Press, 1933);

Letters of Samuel Pepys and His Family Circle, edited by Helen Truesdell Heath (Oxford: Clarendon Press, 1955).

Bibliography:

Dennis G. Donovan, *Elizabethan Bibliographies Supplements XVIII John Evelyn (1920-1968) Samuel Pepys, 1933-1968* (London: Nether Press, 1970).

Biographies:

Arthur Bryant, *Samuel Pepys*, 3 volumes (Cambridge: Cambridge University Press / New York: Macmillan, 1933);

John Harold Wilson, *The Private Life of Mr. Pepys* (New York: Farrar, Straus & Cudahy, 1959);

Richard Ollard, *Pepys: A Biography* (London: Hodder & Stoughton, 1974).

References:

Marjorie Hope Nicolson, *Pepys' Diary and the New Science* (Charlottesville: University Press of Virginia, 1965);

E. Pearlman, "Pepys and Lady Castlemaine," *Restoration*, 7 (Fall 1983): 43-53;

Ivan E. Taylor, *Samuel Pepys* (New York: Twayne, 1967).

Papers:

Pepys's books and papers, including the manuscript for his diary, are in the Pepys Library at Magdalene College, Cambridge.

Alexander Pope

(21 May 1688 - 30 May 1744)

Edward Tomarken
Miami University

See also the Pope entry in *DLB 95: Eighteenth-Century British Poets, First Series.*

SELECTED BOOKS: *An Essay On Criticism* (London: Printed for W. Lewis & sold by W. Taylor, T. Osborn & J. Graves, 1711);

The Critical Specimen (London, 1711);

Windsor-Forest. To the Right Honourable George Lord Lansdown (London: Printed for Bernard Lintott, 1713);

The Narrative of Dr. Robert Norris, Concerning the strange and deplorable Frenzy of Mr. John Denn-- (London: Printed for J. Morphew, 1713);

The Rape of the Lock. An Heroi-Comical Poem. In Five Canto's (London: Printed for Bernard Lintott, 1714; revised, 1718);

The Temple of Fame: A Vision (London: Printed for Bernard Lintott, 1715);

A Key to the Lock. Or, A Treatise proving, beyond all Contradiction, the dangerous Tendency of a late Poem, entituled, The Rape of the Lock, to Government and Religion. By Esdras Barnivelt, Apoth. (London: Printed for J. Roberts, 1715);

The Dignity, Use and Abuse of Glass-Bottles. Set forth in A Sermon Preach'd to an Illustrious Assembly, And now Publish'd for the Use of the Inferiour Clergy, sometimes attributed to Pope (London: Printed & sold by the Booksellers of London & Westminster, 1715);

The Iliad of Homer, Translated by Mr. Pope, 6 volumes (London: Printed by W. Bowyer for Bernard Lintott, 1715-1720);

A Full and True Account of a Horrid and Barbarous Revenge by Poison, On the Body of Mr. Edmund Curll, Bookseller (London: Sold by J. Roberts, J. Morphew, R. Burleigh, J. Baker & S. Popping, 1716);

God's Revenge Against Punning [single sheet] (London: Printed for J. Roberts, 1716);

A Further Account of the most Deplorable Condition of Mr. Edmund Curll, Bookseller (London: Printed & sold by all the Publishers, Mercuries, and Hawkers within the Bills of Mortality, 1716);

The Works of Mr. Alexander Pope (London: Printed by W. Bowyer for Bernard Lintot, 1717; enlarged edition, Dublin: Printed by & for George Grierson, 1727);

A Clue To the Comedy of the Non-Juror. With some Hints of Consequence Relating to that Play. In a Letter to N. Rowe, Esq; Poet Laureat to His Majesty (London: Printed for E. Curll, 1718);

The Odyssey of Homer, 5 volumes, translated by Pope (London: Printed for Bernard Lintot, 1725-1726);

Miscellanea. In Two Volumes.—Never before Published. —Viz. I. Familiar Letters Written to Henry Cromwell Esq. by Mr. Pope. II. Occasional Poems by Mr. Pope, Mr. Cromwell, Dean Swift, &c. III. Letters from Mr. Dryden to a Lady (London, 1727 [i.e., 1726]);

The Dunciad. An Heroic Poem. In Three Books (Dublin, Printed, London Reprinted for A. Dodd [i.e., London: Printed for A. Dodd], 1728);

The Dunciad, Variorum. With the Prolegmena of Scriblerus (London: Printed for A. Dod, 1729);

An Epistle To The Right Honourable Richard Earl of Burlington. Occasion'd by his Publishing Palladio's Designs of the Baths, Arches, Theatres, &c. of Ancient Rome (London: Printed for L. Gilliver, 1731); enlarged as *Of False Taste . . .* (London: Printed for L. Gilliver, 1731 [i.e., 1732]);

Of The Use of Riches, An Epistle To the Right Honorable Allen Lord Bathurst (London: Printed by J. Wright for Lawton Gilliver, 1732);

The First Satire Of The Second Book of Horace, Imitated in a Dialogue between Alexander Pope of Twickenham in Comm. Midd. Esq.; on the one Part, and his Learned Council on the other (London: Printed by L. G. & sold by A. Dodd, E. Nutt & the Booksellers of London & Westminster, 1733);

Alexander Pope, circa 1737 (portrait attributed to Jonathan Richardson; by permission of the National Portrait Gallery, London)

An Essay On Man. Address'd to a Friend.—Part I (London: Printed for J. Wilford, 1733);

An Essay On Man. In Epistles to a Friend.—Epistle II (London: Printed for J. Wilford, 1733);

An Essay On Man. In Epistles to a Friend.—Epistle III (London: Printed for J. Wilford, 1733);

The Impertinent, Or A Visit to the Court. A Satyr (London: Printed for John Wileord [Wilford], 1733);

An Epistle To The Right Honourable Richard Lord Visct. Cobham (London: Printed for Lawton Gilliver, 1733 [i.e., 1734]);

An Essay On Man. In Epistles to a Friend.—Epistle IV (London: Printed for J. Wilford, 1734);

An Essay on Man, Being the First Book of Ethic Epistles. To Henry St. John, L. Bolingbroke [Epistles I-IV] (London: Printed by John Wright for Lawton Gilliver, 1734; Philadelphia: Printed by William Bradford, 1747);

A Most Proper Reply to the Nobleman's Epistle to a Doctor of Divinity (London: Printed & sold by J. Huggonson, 1734);

The First Satire Of The Second Book of Horace, Imitated in Dialogue Between Alexander Pope of Twickenham in Com' Mid' Esq; and his Learned Council.—To which is added, The Second Satire of the same Book (London: Printed for L. G., 1734);

Sober Advice From Horace, To The Young Gentlemen about Town. As deliver'd in his Second Sermon (London: Printed for T. Boreman, 1734); republished as *A Sermon against Adultery* (London: Printed for T. Cooper, 1738);

An Epistle From Mr. Pope, To Dr. Arbuthnot (London: Printed for Lawton Gilliver, 1735);

The Works of Mr. Alexander Pope, Volume II (London: Printed for L. Gilliver, 1735);

Of The Characters of Women: An Epistle To A Lady (London: Printed for Lawton Gilliver, 1735);

Letters of Mr. Pope, and Several Eminent Persons (London: Printed & sold by the Booksellers of London & Westminster, 1735);

A Narrative of the Method by which Mr. Pope's Private Letters were procured and published by Edmund Curll, Bookseller (London, 1735);

The Second Epistle Of The Second Book of Horace, Imitated (London: Printed for R. Dodsley, 1737);

The First Epistle Of The Second Book of Horace, Imitated (London: Printed for T. Cooper, 1737);

Letters of Mr. Alexander Pope, and Several of his Friends (London: Printed by J. Wright for J. Knapton, L. Gilliver, J. Brindley & R. Dodsley, 1737);

The Sixth Epistle Of The First Book of Horace Imitated (London: Printed for L. Gilliver, 1737 [i.e., 1738]);

The First Epistle Of The First Book Of Horace Imitated (London: Printed for R. Dodsley, 1738);

One Thousand Seven Hundred and Thirty Eight. A Dialogue Something like Horace (London: Printed for T. Cooper, 1738);

One Thousand Seven Hundred and Thirty Eight. Dialogue II (London: Printed for R. Dodsley, 1738);

Letters between Dr. Swift, Mr. Pope, &c. (London: Printed for T. Cooper, 1741);

The Works of Mr. Alexander Pope, In Prose. Vol. II (London: Printed for J. & P. Knapton, C. Bathurst & R. Dodsley, 1741);

The New Dunciad: As it was Found In the Year 1741 (London: Printed for T. Cooper, 1742);

The Dunciad, in Four Books. Printed according to the complete Copy found in the Year 1742 (London: Printed for M. Cooper, 1743);

The Last Will and Testament of Alexander Pope, of Twickenham, Esq. (London: Printed for A. Dodd, 1744);

The Works of Alexander Pope Esq. In Nine Volumes Complete. With His Last Corrections, Additions, And Improvements; As they were delivered to the Editor a little before his Death; Together With the Commentaries and Notes of Mr. Warburton (London: Printed for J. & P. Knapton, 1751).

Editions: *The Prose Works of Alexander Pope,* volume 1 edited by Norman Ault (Oxford:

Blackwell, 1936); volume 2 edited by Rosemary Cowler (Hamden, Conn: Archon Books, 1986);

Memoirs of the Extraordinary Life, Works, and Discoveries of Martinus Scriblerus, by Pope, Jonathan Swift, John Arbuthnot, John Gay, Thomas Parnell, and Robert Harley, Earl of Oxford; edited by Charles Kerby-Miller (New Haven: Yale University Press, 1950);

Literary Criticism of Alexander Pope, edited by Bertrand A. Goldgar (Lincoln: University of Nebraska Press, 1965);

Selected Prose of Alexander Pope, edited by Paul Hammond (Cambridge: Cambridge University Press, 1987).

OTHER: *The Works of Shakespear,* 6 volumes, edited, with a preface, by Pope (London: Printed for Jacob Tonson, 1725);

Preface to *Miscellanies in Prose and Verse. The First Volume,* edited by Pope and Jonathan Swift (London: Printed for Benjamin Motte, 1727);

"Memoirs of P. P. Clerk of This Parish," "Stradling versus Stiles," and "Thoughts on Various Subjects," in *Miscellanies. The Second Volume,* edited by Pope and Swift (London: Printed for Benjamin Motte, 1727);

Peri Bathous: or, Martinus Scriblerus. His Treatise of the Art of Sinking in Poetry, in *Miscellanies. The Last Volume,* edited by Pope and Swift (London: Printed for B. Motte, 1727);

"To The Reader" and letters, in *The Posthumous Works of William Wycherley, Esq; In Prose and Verse. The Second Volume,* edited by Pope (London: Printed for J. Roberts, 1729);

"A Strange but True Relation How Edmund Curll of Fleetstreet, Stationer, Out of an extraordinary Desire of Lucre, went into Change-Alley, and was converted from the Christian Religion by certain Eminent Jews: And how he was circumcis'd and initia-ted into their Mysteries" and "An Essay Of the Learned Martinus Scriblerus, Concerning the Origine of Science," in *Miscellanies. The Third Volume,* edited by Pope and Swift (London: Printed for Benj. Motte, 1732).

SELECTED PERIODICAL PUBLICATIONS:
["On the Desire of Distinction"], sometimes attributed to Pope, *The Spectator,* no. 224, 16 November 1711;

THE

NARRATIVE

OF

Dr. *Robert Norris,*

Concerning the ftrange and deplorable

FRENZY

OF

Mr. JOHN DENN---

An Officer of the *Cuftom-houfe* :

Being an exact Account of all that paft
betwixt the faid Patient and the Doctor till this prefent Day ; and a full
Vindication of himfelf and his Proceedings from the extravagant Reports of the faid Mr. *John Denn—*

———*excludit fanos Helicone Poetas*
Democritus——— ——— Hor.

London: Printed for *J. Morphew* near *Stationers-Hall,* 1713. Price 3 *d.*

Title page for Pope's second response to John Dennis, characterizing his responses to An Essay On Criticism
and Joseph Addison's Cato *as the irrational acts of a madman*

["The Additional Graces"], sometimes attributed to Pope, *The Spectator,* no. 292, 4 February 1712;

["On Idleness"], sometimes attributed to Pope, *The Spectator,* no. 316, 3 March 1712;

["On Affectation"], *The Spectator,* no. 404, 13 June 1712;

["On a City and Country Life"], *The Spectator,* no. 406, 16 June 1712;

["On Reason and Passion"], *The Spectator,* no. 408, 18 June 1712;

["A Dream of the Seasons"], *The Spectator,* no. 425, 8 July 1712;

["Proposals of News Papers"], *The Spectator,* no. 452, 8 August 1712;

["Proposals for News Papers II"], *The Spectator,* no. 457, 14 August 1712;

["On the Love of Praise"], sometimes attributed to Pope, *The Spectator,* no. 467, 26 August 1712;

["On a Fan"], *The Spectator,* no. 527, 4 November 1712;

["On the Last Words of Adrian"], *The Spectator,* no. 532, 10 November 1712;

["On Dedications"], *The Guardian,* no. 4, 16 March 1713;

["The Grand Elixir"], *The Guardian,* no. 11, 24 March 1713;

["On False C48" — "On False Cricks"], sometimes attributed to Pope, *The Guardian,* no. 12, 25 March 1713;

["On Easy Writing"], sometimes attributed to Pope, *The Guardian,* no. 15, 28 March 1713;

["On Pastorals"], *The Guardian,* no. 40, 27 April 1713;

["Against Barbarity to Animals"], *The Guardian,* no. 61, 21 May 1713;

["A Receit to make an Epick Poem"], *The Guardian,* no. 78, 10 June 1713;

["The Club of Little Men I"], *The Guardian,* no. 91, 25 June 1713;

["The Club of Little Men II"], *The Guardian*, no. 92, 26 June 1713;

["On a Dream of a Window in his Mistress's Breast"], sometimes attributed to Pope, *The Guardian*, no. 106, 13 July 1713;

["On Sickness"], *The Guardian*, no. 132, 12 August 1713;

["On Nature and Death"], sometimes attributed to Pope, *The Guardian*, no. 169, 24 September 1713;

["On the Origin of Letters"], sometimes attributed to Pope, *The Guardian*, no. 172, 28 September 1713;

["On Gardens"], *The Guardian*, no. 173, 29 September 1713.

Alexander Pope's prose, even when most intimate, bears directly or indirectly upon his poetry. Accordingly, his essays range from short pieces such as the defense of his pastoral poetry to the extended critical discussions that appear in his translations of Homer and his edition of Shakespeare. And the narratives vary from brief tales, as in the reply to John Dennis's attack on the *Essay on Criticism*, to longer pieces, as in the *Memoirs of Martinus Scriblerus* and the lengthy critical discourse *The Art of Sinking in Poetry*. Even those prose writings which do not bear directly upon the poetry, such as the essay "On Gardens" or "The Club of Little Men," pertain to Pope's public presentation of himself as a poet. In a larger sense, the prose writings illuminate not only Pope's poetry and personal life but also the general situation of the satirist in the early eighteenth century. But Pope's skillful interweaving of his life and his work makes it at times almost impossible to separate fact and fiction. For instance, most of the prose works listed above were published anonymously and never acknowledged by Pope, who sought thereby to protect himself from personal attack and his poetry from biased critical judgment. As a result, decisions about the canon must often be highly speculative.

In the year of Alexander Pope's birth, 1688, a Protestant, William of Orange, was invited to the throne, replacing James II, a Roman Catholic. As a Catholic, Pope—who was born in London to Alexander Pope, a merchant, and his second wife, Edith Turner—was prevented throughout his life from assuming any public office. In addition to religious difficulties, Pope was continually afflicted by serious physical problems that Samuel Johnson describes in his *Lives of the English Poets* as follows:

The person of Pope is well known not to have been formed by the nicest model. He has, in his account of the "Little Club," compared himself to a spider, and by another is described as protuberant behind and before. He is said to have been beautiful in his infancy; but he was of a constitution originally feeble and weak; and as bodies of a tender frame are easily distorted, his deformity was probably in part the effect of his application. His stature was so low, that, to bring him to a level with common tables, it was necessary to raise his seat. But his face was not displeasing, and his eyes were animated and vivid.

By natural deformity, or accidental distortion, his vital functions were so much disordered, that his life was a "long disease." His most frequent assailant was the headache, which he used to relieve by inhaling the steam of coffee, which he very frequently required.

One of the results of religious discrimination and of his physical disability was that after the age of twelve Pope was educated at home, often without a tutor. He was therefore open to attack from his enemies on three counts, his religion, his physical appearance, and his lack of formal education. As his fame increased, the attacks became more frequent and virulent.

Pope's dilemma is dramatically illustrated by his first published prose work. Responding to John Dennis, who in criticizing *An Essay on Criticism* (1711) had characterized its author as a "downright monkey," Pope replied first in *The Critical Specimen* (1711) and then in *The Narrative of Dr. Robert Norris* (1713). The former describes Dennis as a critic who "took a *Hobby-Horse* for *Pegasus*," assuming that his own personal and eccentric recipe for sublimity was the only means of creating great poetry. The latter tells the story of Dennis's madness, commencing with his sudden irrational aversion to Joseph Addison's *Cato* (1713) and to Pope's *Essay on Criticism* and ending with his actual physical attack upon the books, tearing pages out of the offending texts. Here Pope suggests that the madman's inability to separate the physical from the intellectual content of the book is analogous to Dennis's refusal to remove personal animosity from his criticism. These early prose works show Pope working toward a technique he perfected in his great poems, the controlled presentation of personal invective in a literary form that transformed local disputation into general satire.

During this same period (1711-1713), Pope befriended Addison and Richard Steele and contributed various essays to *The Spectator* and *The*

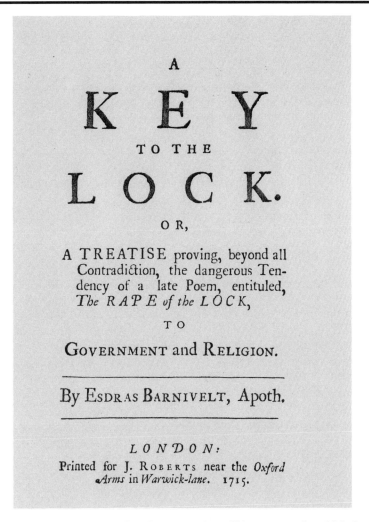

A

KEY

TO THE

LOCK.

OR,

A TREATISE proving, beyond all
Contradiction, the dangerous Ten-
dency of a late Poem, entituled,
The RAPE of the LOCK,

TO

GOVERNMENT and RELIGION.

By ESDRAS BARNIVELT, Apoth.

LONDON:
Printed for J. ROBERTS near the *Oxford
Arms* in *Warwick-lane.* 1715.

Title page for Pope's satiric political interpretation of his own recently published poem

Guardian. As a whole (and it should be kept in mind that some of the attributions here are by no means certain), these essays constitute early formulations of the central themes to be found throughout Pope's work: the use and abuse of ambition, country life versus city life, the passions in relation to reason, the vanity of affectation, the function of rural nature in both its wild and cultivated state. A brief summary of a few of these essays will suggest the extraordinary ability of Pope, who wrote most of them before he was twenty-five. *The Guardian* no. 4 (16 March 1713) considers the excesses of dedications, showing how inflated praise is self-defeating. Adopting the light, genial tone of Mr. Spectator, Pope writes that he accidentally discovered a typical dedication in the lining of a lady's hatbox and concludes by offering a dedication which "may serve for about any Book." Pope thus brings this art to perfection, demonstrating that a tribute to any-

one is a tribute to no one. In *The Guardian,* the dedication becomes the lining of a hatbox; by the time of *The Dunciad,* it would be assigned to the jakes. The essay on the pastoral (*The Guardian,* no. 40, 27 April 1713) is probably Pope's earliest work of literary criticism. By way of an ironic comparison between his pastorals and those of Ambrose Philips, the anonymous narrator deftly suggests that the pastoralist must mediate between the present and the past, adapting the ancient conventions of the genre to the needs of the eighteenth-century poet. Strategic examples show how Philips either slavishly imitates the ancients or needlessly violates the conventions of the genre. The implication is that Pope's pastorals are to be distinguished from those of Philips in their appropriation of classical conventions to the concerns of his day. Although a successful self-defense, this essay seems to have begun the deterioration of Pope's friendship with both Addison and Steele. Addison had been a defender of Philips's pastorals; Steele published Pope's essay before comprehending its ironical intent. Perhaps the most original of Pope's *Spectator* essays is that on idleness (no. 316, 3 March 1712). Samuel Slack writes of his desperate need of a cure for this dire disease; so grave is his infection, he suggests, that after his death his bones should be ground up for use as an antidote for "too exorbitant a Degree of Fire." Slack is locked into the dilemma of one who treats a psychological problem in physical terms. Pope uses his deft touch to highlight the social ramification of idleness; later in the century, Samuel Johnson attends to the spiritual dimension, declaring that "to be idle is to be vicious."

After the dedication to Miss Arabella Fermor, a member of a prominent Roman Catholic family, was appended to the first separate edition of *The Rape of the Lock* (1714), Pope published *A Key to the Lock* (1715). Because of his religion and friendship with Henry St. John, Viscount Bolingbroke, who was thought to be in league with the government of France, Pope had been accused of Jacobitism, which at this time was a very real threat to the British sovereign; descendants of James II continued to press their claim to the throne until 1745. Anticipating this approach to his work, in *A Key to the Lock* Pope treats the poem as an allegorical document of the events and personalities involved in the breach of the Barrier Treaty, an agreement opposed by France. This satire is probably the first of Pope's works written in the manner of the Scriblerus papers. In 1713 Pope met Jonathan Swift, and by later that same year Swift accepted the idea for the Scriblerus project. Pope wrote in a letter to John Gay (23 October 1713), "Dr. Swift much approves what I proposed, even to the very title, which I design shall be, The Works of the Unlearned." The final fruits of this project were *Memoirs of the Extraordinary Life, Works, and Discoveries of Martinus Scriblerus*, first published in *The Works of Mr. Alexander Pope, In Prose. Vol. II* (1741). The Scriblerian Club grew out of Swift's wish to form a Tory literary group in opposition to Addison's "little senate," which met at Button's coffeehouse, and out of Pope's ambition to form a journal to satirize pedantry and false criticism. "What emerged," according to Rosemary Cowler, "was something different from both, yet appropriate to each—a small social group of kindred spirits [comprised of Pope, Swift, Gay, Dr. John Arbuthnot, Thomas Parnell, and Robert Harley, Earl of

Oxford] whose collaboration, at three stages over a fifteen-year period (1714, when the Club was formally organized with scheduled dinner meetings; 1716-1718; and 1726-1729, the occasion of Swift's visits to England and the publication of *The Dunciad*), resulted in an outline for a broad satire of human folly, organized around a hero-pedant, who was to function as the author of such satires as they would themselves write or to whom they could ascribe the works of contemporaries whom they wished to ridicule." Esdras Barnivelt, the narrator of *A Key to the Lock*, is a prototype of Martinus Scriblerus. Barnivelt's argument is a perfect tautology. Setting out to demonstrate that *The Rape of the Lock* is a satire of the Barrier Treaty, he asks only one concession: "that by the *Lock* is meant *The* Barrier Treaty." Here in parodic form is a major abuse of criticism: an interpretation can be consistently applied without considering whether it is appropriate to the poem. Of course, Pope had political motives for protecting himself from this particular abuse, but it is typical of him to transform his own personal inconvenience into a literary work of general and intrinsic importance.

The first of Pope's writings employing the Scriblerian technique suggests that by "learning" the Scriblerians meant criticism, if the term is taken in the broad sense of scholarship and explication of all kinds of discourse. One of the most delightful of the writings in this vein is *The Dignity, Use and Abuse of Glass-Bottles* (1715), whose attribution to Pope has been suggested by Norman Ault. The work would suggest the influence of Swift even if the title page did not assert "By the Authour of the Tale of a Tub." Ault believes that Pope used the ploy of presenting Swift as the author to protect himself from attack. The question of authorship of any of the material related to the Scriblerus project is hopelessly tangled, since it involved at various stages conversation and the exchange of letters, collaboration among different members of the group at different times, and revisions by still others. Aside from the Scriblerian pieces acknowledged by Pope, it seems safe to assume that he had at least a hand in the others, if only in his capacity as the final reviser who presented the finished text to the publisher.

This moment in Pope's career represents a turning point in financial terms. In 1715 he published the first part of his translation of Homer's *Iliad*, which was not completed until 1720. This project was one of the earliest, and certainly the most

Pope, circa 1717 (painting by Charles Jervas; by permission of the National Portrait Gallery, London). The young woman has sometimes been identified as Pope's friend Martha Blount, but this portrait does not resemble other likenesses of her.

successful, of the subscription texts, a means of publication whereby the author asked for money in advance of publication and promised in return that each subscriber would receive a particularly luxurious edition with his name imprinted on the title page. This venture was so successful that Pope followed it with a translation of *The Odyssey* and an edition of Shakespeare. Although it is often pointed out with some justice that Johnson announced the end of the age of patronage in his 1755 letter to Philip Stanhope, Earl of Chesterfield, Pope must be seen to have begun the process of literary independence, being possibly the first British writer who by his early thirties no longer had to write for money. But the process was by no means easy. A rival translation of *The Iliad* by Thomas Tickell was "puffed" by the "Buttonians," one of whom, Bishop Gilbert Bur-

net, attacked Pope personally. Since the bishop was well known for indulging himself in drink, Pope devised the sermon on *The Dignity, Use and Abuse of Glass-Bottles* in reply. Typical of Pope, the sermon intertwines the personal animosity against Burnet with the literary problem, the rival translation of Homer. The hilarious tone of the sermon can be illustrated by the opening sentence: "My Beloved, yea, most dearly Beloved Vessels of Election! I call not upon you to open your Ears, since for the most part Ears you have none, or only such as the Prophet speaketh of, *Ears which do not hear*; but I rejoice to behold you with open Mouths, gaping as it were, and thirsting for the Word of the Lord." The prefatory remarks make clear how a sermon *on* bottles comes to be preached *to* bottles because, as the narrator admits, most of us prefer to hear about ourselves:

Alexander Pope, circa 1718 (portrait attributed to Jonathan Richardson; by permission of Viscount Cobham)

Who ever heard of a Sermon without a Text? *And pray before that Custom begun, who ever heard of One with a Text? Had the Art commenc'd without it, it had been as prepost'rous now to have us'd it; and what is all this but* Custom? Custom, *which has involv'd us in fifty Errours for every single Truth it has produc'd....*

The custom of reproducing the text and attending to it is, of course, the task of the translator, and those who refuse to respect the classical texts are like bottles which are filled by the past but incapable of hearing the message from it. In the preface to *The Iliad*, Pope makes clear that for him the great epic is like nature itself and that Homer's most distinguishing characteristic, his *"invention,"* entails the art of listening or selecting from

and recombining elements of nature, rather than attempting to drink it all in. *The Iliad* is an intensified form of nature. Pope's labor on this text should be seen, then, not as a "neoclassical" worship of the past, but as an expression of his belief that Homer isolates those elements of life common to past, present, and future. Specifically, Homer's insight into nature can be seen in his skill at "fable," which takes the form either of human stories or allegories of philosophical import. Pope also has high praise for Homer's variety and consistency of character, a further means of humanizing nature, which is embellished by images, "supernumerary Pictures of the Persons or Things they are join'd to." Concerning the content, *The Iliad* is compared to the scriptures, particularly in its sublime aspects. For Pope, the great epic, like the Bible, functions spiritually to carry us beyond ourselves, beyond the solipsism of the bottles addressed in the sermon.

After completing *The Iliad* in 1720, Pope turned for the next six years to his edition of Shakespeare (1725) and his translation of *The Odyssey* (1725-1726), both of which boosted his financial state and his poetic reputation but involved him in critical difficulties. The former work was attacked by Lewis Theobald, who was awarded the throne of dullness in the first version of *The Dunciad* (1728). The latter involved Pope in explaining how *The Odyssey* could be as great as *The Iliad* when it lacked the sublime language of the earlier epic. In the "Postscript to The Odyssey" (published in volume 5, 1726), Pope explains that since the story is a domestic one, sublime terminology of the sort found in *The Iliad* would be inappropriate. Indeed, he goes one step further:

> it will be found a just observation, that the *low actions of life* cannot be put into a figurative style without being ridiculous, but *things natural* can. Metaphors raise the latter into Dignity, as we see in the *Georgicks*; but throw the former into Ridicule, as in the *Lutrin*. . . .

The human world for Pope is marked by an absolute hierarchy not present in nature. He confronted a similar problem the previous year in the preface to *The Works of Shakespear*: how can Shakespeare's language be learned and philosophical when he had little formal education and often uses "low" and literal vocabulary for sublime subjects? In explanation, Pope develops John Dryden's view that Shakespeare was a natural, unschooled genius:

> If ever any Author deserved the name of an *Original*, it was *Shakespear*. *Homer* himself drew not his art so immediately from the fountains of Nature, it proceeded thro' *Aegyptian* strainers and channels, and came to him not without some tincture of the learning, or some cast of the models, of those before him. . . .

Concerning the inappropriately low diction of Shakespeare, Pope explains that being himself an actor and writing for the theater, Shakespeare naturally responded to the desires of the audience. Here we see Pope's hierarchy of genres: the implication being that had Shakespeare turned his genius to the epic, he would have employed a more consistently sublime vocabulary. Pope concludes

with a bibliographic consideration of the texts of the plays. However one judges Pope's own editorial practices, he provides in this discussion the first clear understanding of the complex relationship between the folios and the quartos and recognizes the need for a detailed collation of both to render the most authoritative text.

In 1727-1728 Pope published the first three volumes of the Pope-Swift *Miscellanies*. As Cowler points out, the best explanation for this project comes from Pope's 16 February 1733 letter to Swift.

> There is nothing of late which I think of more than mortality, and what you mention of collecting the best monuments we can of our friends, their own images in their writings: (for those are the best, when their minds are such as Mr. Gay's was, and as your is.) I am preparing also for my own, and have nothing so much at heart, as to shew the silly world that men of Wit, or even Poets, may be the most moral of mankind. A few loose things sometimes fall from them, by which censorious fools judge as ill of them, as possibly they can, for their own comfort: and indeed, when such unguarded and trifling *Jeux d'Esprit* have once got abroad, all that prudence or repentance can do, since they cannot be deny'd, is to put 'em fairly upon that foot; and teach the publick (as we have done in the preface to the four volumes of miscellanies) to distinguish betwixt our studies and our idlenesses, our works and our weakness. . . .

The most important work of Pope's to appear at this time in the *Miscellanies* is *Peri Bathous: or, Martinus Scriblerus. His Treatise of the Art of Sinking in Poetry* (1727), Pope's longest critical essay and one which establishes an important link between Dryden's *Mac Flecknoe* (1682) and *The Dunciad*. This treatise considers satirically the subject of the material on Homer and the preface to *The Works of Shakespear*, appropriate poetic imagery and diction. It is carefully modeled after Longinus's *On the Sublime*: even the title is a parody of Longinus's *Peri Hypsos*. Pope begins by placing his narrator in the tradition of Dryden's Shadwell, one who understands the nature of the decline of taste in his time and plans to profit from it:

> it is with great pleasure I have observ'd of late the gradual decay of Delicacy and Refinement among mankind, who are become too reasonable to require that we should labour with infinite pains to come up to the taste of the Mountain-

Pope's villa at Twickenham, circa 1750 (watercolor attributed to Charles Knapton; by permission of the Libraries Department, London Borough of Richmond upon Thames). Pope settled there and began renovating the house and grounds in 1719.

eers, when they without any, may condescend to ours. But as we have now an unquestionable Majority on our side, I doubt not but we shall shortly be able to level the Highlanders, and procure a farther vent for our own product, which is already so much relish'd, encourag'd, and rewarded, by the Nobility and Gentry of Great Britain.

The profits to be made from demotic writing have increased since Dryden's day.

While the Restoration satirist could concentrate on single individuals, Pope must face groups of dunces. Moreover, a clear distinction between good and bad writers is no longer possible, since, as the narrator notes, "our greatest Adversaries" sometimes descend to the "Bathos itself." The result of this interfusion is that the texts must be cited in detail. Accordingly, the dissertation consists in large part of illustrative passages which are the richest part of the work, the raw material from which Pope built his later versions of *The Dunciad*. A few examples will suffice to show Pope's "inventive" genius, a notion which itself has altered since the work on Homer because al-

though most of the examples are "found in nature" some are created by Pope. Most of the chapters begin with a brief description of an abuse of poetry followed by examples. For instance, chapter seven focuses on "low thoughts": "The Physician, by the study and inspection of urine and ordure, approves himself in the science; and in like sort should our author accustom and exercise his imagination upon the dregs of nature." Explaining that only in this way can our writers fathom deeper than mere mediocrity, Martinus Scriblerus numbers among his examples the following on a lady taking the water at Bath:

> She drinks! She drinks! Behold the matchless dame!
> To her 'tis water, but to us 'tis flame:
> Thus fire is water, water fire by turns,
> And the same stream at once both cools and burns.

The prose only begins to describe the nature of the poetry, a product of Pope's bathetic genius. Consider the following passage Pope cites from Sir Richard Blackmore's *Prince Arthur* (1695), exemplary of "The Vulgar . . . a Species of the *Diminishing*: By this a spear flying into the air is com-

Pope in 1722 (portrait by Sir Godfrey Kneller; by permission of Viscount Harcourt)

pared to a boy whistling as he goes on an errand.

> *The mighty* Stuffa *threw a massy spear,*
> *Which, with its* Errand *pleas'd, sung thro' the air."*

The texture of the poetic examples in *The Art of Sinking in Poetry* goes beyond the scope of the axioms they exemplify; in this sense, they initiate a project to be completed in *The Dunciad Variorum* (1729) and *The Memoirs of Martinus Scriblerus*, both endeavors on which Pope was assisted by the Scriblerians, who were meeting during the period 1726-1729. The conclusion of *The Art of Sinking in Poetry* prepares the way for these later works. Promoting a mechanical contrivance which will permit writing without genius, Martinus describes a "Rhetorical Chest of Drawers," each of which is divided into "Cells, resembling those of Cabinets for Rarities," containing different figures, the "Hyperbole," "Periphrasis," "Apologue," and others which have been produced by specialists. The result would be mechanically pro-

duced literature without the least attention to context and overall design. Here we start to see why Pope begins to turn to texts combining literature and criticism, such as *The Dunciad Variorum*, in order to show how the two forms of writing when abused work at cross-purposes with one another.

During this period Pope's letters first began to appear. In 1726 Edmund Curll published the correspondence of Pope and Henry Cromwell without the permission of either. Pope satirized Curll on several occasions and actually had physical revenge by serving him a strong emetic disguised as a drink of reconciliation. In 1729 the correspondence with William Wycherley appeared in volume 2 of *The Posthumous Works of William Wycherley*. In 1735 Pope devised an elaborate plot whereby Curll was to receive "unauthorized" Pope letters from an anonymous source and publish them surreptitiously, forcing Pope to publish an authorized version. The plan misfired to some

Pope in or before 1736 (portrait by Jonathan Richardson; by permission of the Museum of Fine Arts, Boston, James T. Fields Collection)

extent, although it did enable Pope to present his correspondence to the world in 1737. It has been said in defense of this ruse that in the eighteenth century it was not acceptable to publish one's own letters and that Pope had intended to bring Curll's unscrupulous publishing practices to public attention at a time when the Booksellers Bill was being considered by Parliament. The letters are a large (more than two thousand pages) and important body of material, touching upon most of the literary, and many political, matters of the early eighteenth century. It should be kept in mind that, as Swift wrote to Pope, "I find you have been a writer of Letters almost from your infancy, and by your confession had Schemes even then of Epistolary fame." Swift is here referring to the fact that Pope altered much of his corre-

spondence to make it presentable in his terms to the public. Victorian scholars regarded this practice as unscrupulous; modern commentators have sought to explain it as an understandable part of the social strategy of an adept but vulnerable satirist. In any case, the modern reader needs to be warned that Pope's letters often appear in two forms. In his edition, George Sherburn has endeavored to present some of the correspondence as it was first written before being revised by Pope for publication. For a recent sample of the letters as Pope intended them to appear as well as a selection of Pope's other prose writings, see Paul Hammond's edition of Pope's prose.

Pope's letters were intended to range from intimacy to formality. To his friend and fellow Catholic John Caryll, he admits the justness of John

Milton, Spenser, and Chaucer attending the dying Pope, the title-page vignette from William Mason's Musaeus: A Monody to the Memory of Mr. Pope, In Imitation of Milton's Lycidas *(1747)*

Dennis's criticism of the *Essay on Criticism*, even while continuing to attack Dennis in his writing: "What he observes . . . was objected by ourself at Ladyholt, and had been mended but for the haste of the press." By contrast, consider this beginning of a letter Pope published in 1737 as a 30 July 1713 letter to Addison. (Pope had, in fact, created it by using parts of a 19 November 1712 letter to Caryll.) "I am more joy'd at your return than I should be at that of the Sun, so much as I wish for him this melancholy season; but 'tis his fate too, like yours, to be displeasing to Owls and obscene animals, who cannot bear his lustre." The letters are particularly revealing concerning Pope's relationship with women, his attraction to, followed by bitterness toward, Lady Mary Wortley Montagu and continued teasing devotion to Martha Blount, to whom he left the bulk of his estate. As we would expect, the most important literary-critical material is found in the correspondence with Swift, and one will also discover here a genuine intellectual rapport, a meeting of the minds that helps one understand how this friendship formed the basis of the Scriblerian project.

In 1735, after the death of Arbuthnot, Pope received the Scriblerus papers, being now the only one of the Scriblerians left in England. Why he delayed publication for six years is not altogether clear. Having been attacked by Lady Mary, Lord Hervey, and others during the 1730s, he may have felt unable to withstand the onslaught on his own. At any event, in 1741 he published the *Memoirs of the Extraordinary Life, Works, and Discoveries of Martinus Scriblerus* in *The Works of Mr. Alexander Pope, In Prose. Vol. II*, a companion volume to his correspondence with Swift. The *Memoirs of Martinus Scriblerus* are seminal to an understanding of early-eighteenth-century satire; the Scriblerian materials make plain that Swift, Gay, and Pope saw *Gulliver's Travels* (1726), *The Beggar's Opera* (1728), *The Rape of the Lock*, and *The Dunciad* as related to the project. In fact, it would not be an exaggeration to say that Martinus Scriblerus is a recognized relative of Gulliver, the beggar, and the dunces. Combining literature and criticism, the *Memoirs of Martinus Scriblerus* suggest how the great satirists of the age wanted their satires to be read.

Modeled after *Don Quixote* (1605), the memoirs use the ploy of the found manuscript, containing the adventures of Martinus. In this way both the subject of the tale and the manner of telling it can become targets of the satire. Moreover, the introduction makes clear that these are but some of the papers of the illustrious Martinus Scriblerus and that others will be forthcoming, in particular "his Strictures on *The Dunciad.*" The slender work (eighty pages in the Kerby-Miller edition) is comprised of seventeen chapters loosely connected and of varying styles and quality. The early chapters establish the pedantry and humorlessness of the Scriblerus household. On the night before Martinus's birth Mrs. Scriblerus dreamed of an "Ink-horn," a "Crab-tree," Wasps, and Mushrooms. Cornelius Scriblerus, the father, explains that these signs mean that the child will be a voluminous writer, a wit whose satire will have the sting of the wasp. As for the mushroom, it is seen to imply "great fertility of fancy, but no long duration of his works," but "the Father was of another opinion." Chapters two through eight concern Cornelius's falsely learned conceptions of how to educate his child, strikingly anticipating the similar eccentricities of Walter Shandy. By chapter nine, Martinus, with the aid of his servant Crambe, an inveterate punster, has decided to become a critic. His project is by way of "assembling parallel sounds" to emend and correct ancient authors. Not content to limit himself to the realm of the mind, Martinus turns to "Physic" in order to relate matters of body and soul. In chapter twelve, on the "Seat of the Soul," we find a typical example of humor in the memoirs. Having tried to locate the soul in the brains, stomach, and heart and having rejected the hypothesis that it shifts from one to the other depending upon the sex, age, and profession of the individual, Scriblerus "grew fond of the *Glandula Pinealis.*" Discovery that this gland is similar in slaves and philosophers, tigers and statesmen, foxes and sharpers, peacocks and fops, he expects to find a similar resemblance in highwaymen and conquerors. These experiments excite such interest that he receives a letter from the society of freethinkers, who suggest that he has not been able to find the seat of the soul because Man does not have one. In order to demonstrate their point, these ingenious people have erected an hydraulic engine containing chemical blood

flowing in elastic channels, like arteries and veins, generated by artificial lungs which are regulated by ropes and pulleys, similar to nerves, tendons, and muscles: "And we are persuaded that this our artificial Man will not only walk, and speak, and perform most of the outward actions of the animal life, but (being wound up once a week) will perhaps reason as well as most of your Country Parsons." Here the Scriblerians show how the obtuse intellectual's search for the soul can end by ignoring the entire spiritual realm. The genius which Martinus sought to exclude from literature in *The Art of Sinking* has here become the soul of criticism. The most famous and amusing of the chapters in the *Memoirs of Martinus Scriblerus* demonstrates that, in having lost touch with his own soul, Martinus is also unable to express his passion. Here our hero has the misfortune to fall hopelessly in love with one half of a "double mistress," Siamese twins attached at the back and thought to share a reproductive organ. One mistress despises poor Martinus as much as the other adores him; even when, after great struggles, the marriage is consummated, one charges him with rape. Here we see demonstrated how the passions of the pedant, the idle curiosity of the virtuoso—he first found the double mistress in a sort of raree-show—lead to entanglement in self-defeating projects. In spite of its loose organization and inconsistent style, the *Memoirs of Martinus Scriblerus* does contain some of the subtlest suggestions about how to approach Pope's poetry.

As a prose writer, Pope shows great range and ability in different genres, moving with ease from the formal letter addressed to a respected elder to the tender epistle of affection, if not love, from the scurrilously familiar pamphlet to the scholarly preface. But since his prose, like most other elements of his existence, centered on his poetry, it is only natural to compare Pope's abilities in these two domains. One of the last of the works found in the collected prose volumes is "A Letter to a Noble Lord," a reply to Lord Hervey's attack on him; its poetic equivalent is the famous portrait of Sporus in the *Epistle to Dr. Arbuthnot* (1735). Written in 1733 and first published in the 1751 edition of Pope's *Works*, this letter shows Pope's prose to its best advantage: with admirable control, it articulates matters that were very personal and deeply hurtful. Although negligible as poetry, Lord Hervey's satire was extremely insulting in its vivid, physical detail. In his letter Pope adopts a posture above such degrading behavior, complimenting Hervey on his handsome appearance. Our sympathies are brilliantly commanded by Pope, but his means of doing so is to reveal his wounds. The historical dilemma of Pope is prominent, that of a deformed, marginalized satirist bound to be treated by the establishment like any other entertainer, one moment in favor, the next out. In the portrait of Sporus, however, Pope transforms all the personal bile into irony of general import beyond the biographical material pertaining to Lord Hervey or Alexander Pope. But it should be remembered that Pope chose not to publish this letter in his lifetime. Did he perhaps recognize what Martinus Scriblerus is unable even to consider as a possibility, that his prose might be properly seen as ancillary to his great poetry?

Letters:

The Correspondence of Alexander Pope, 5 volumes, edited by George Sherburn (Oxford: Clarendon Press, 1956).

Bibliography:

Reginald Harvey Griffith, *Alexander Pope: A Bibliography*, 1 volume in two parts (Austin: University of Texas Press, 1922, 1927);

J. V. Guerinot, *Pamphlet Attacks on Alexander Pope: 1711-1744 A Descriptive Bibliography* (London: Methuen, 1969).

Biographies:

Samuel Johnson, *Lives of the English Poets*, edited by George Birkbeck Hill (Oxford: Clarendon Press, 1905), volume 3;

George Sherburn, *The Early Career of Alexander Pope* (Oxford: Clarendon Press, 1934);

Maynard Mack, *Alexander Pope: A Life* (New Haven: Yale University Press, 1985).

References:

Howard Erskine-Hill, *The Social Milieu of Alexander Pope: Lives, Example and the Poetic Response* (New Haven: Yale University Press, 1975);

Brean S. Hammond, *Pope and Bolingbroke: A Study of Friendship and Influence* (Columbia: University of Missouri Press, 1984);

Maynard Mack, *Collected in Himself* (Newark: University of Delaware Press, 1982);

James McLaverty, "The First Printing and Publication of Pope's Letters," *Library*, sixth series 2 (September 1980): 264-280;

Pat Rogers, *An Introduction to Pope* (London: Methuen, 1975);

Austin Warren, *Alexander Pope as Critic and Humanist* (Princeton: Princeton University Press, 1929);

James Anderson Winn, *A Window in the Bosom* (Hamden, Conn.: Archon Books, 1977).

Papers:

The British Library has the largest number of Pope's papers, but a valuable collection is also to be found at the Houghton Library, Harvard University.

Thomas Rymer

(1643? - 13 December 1713)

David Wheeler
University of Southern Mississippi

BOOKS: *The Tragedies of the last Age Consider'd and Examin'd by the Practice of the Ancients, and by the Common sense of all Ages. In a letter to Fleetwood Shepheard, Esq.* (London: Printed for Richard Tonson, 1678);

Edgar; or The English Monarch; an Heroick Tragedy (London: Printed for Richard Tonson, 1678);

A General Draught and Prospect of Government in Europe, and Civil Policy. Shewing the Antiquity, Power, Decay of Parliaments. With other Historical and Political Observations relating thereunto. In a Letter (London: Printed for Tho. Benskin, 1681);

A Poem on the Prince of Orange his Expedition and Success in England (London: Printed for Awnsham Churchill, 1688);

A Poem on the Arrival of Queen Mary. February the 12th. 1689 (London: Printed for Awnsham Churchill, 1689);

A Short View of Tragedy; It's Original, Excellency, and Corruption. With Some Reflections on Shakespear, and other Practitioners for the Stage (London: Printed & are to be sold by Richard Baldwin, 1693);

Letters to the Right Reverend the Ld. Bishop of Carlisle. Occasioned by some Passages in his Late Book of the Scotch Library ... Letter I (London: Printed for James Knapton, 1702); *Letter II* (London: Printed for Tho. Hodgson, n.d.); *Letter III* (London, 1706).

Editions: *A Short View of Tragedy*, in volume 2 of *Critical Essays of the Seventeenth Century*, 3 volumes, edited by J. E. Springarn (Oxford: Oxford University Press, 1908-1909);

The Critical Works of Thomas Rymer, edited by Curt A. Zimansky (New Haven: Yale University Press, 1956).

OTHER: *Epithalamia Cantabrigiensia In Nuptias Auspicatissimas Serenissimi Regis Caroli II, Britanniarum Monarchæ, et Illustrissimæ Principis Catherinæ, Potentissimi Regis Lusitaniæ*

Sororis Unicæ, includes a Latin poem by Rymer (Cambridge: John Field, 1662);

Reflections on Aristotle's Treatise of Poesie, Containing the Necessary, Rational, and Universal Rules for Epick, Dramatick, and the other Sorts of Poetry ... By R. Rapin, translated, with a critical preface, by Rymer (London: T.N. for H. Herringman, 1674);

Ovid's Epistles, Translated by Several Hands, includes translations by Rymer (London: Printed by Jacob Tonson, 1680);

Historica Ecclesiastica Carmine Elegiaco Concinnata. Authore Thoma Hobbio Malmesburiensi, preface in Latin by Rymer (London, 1688);

Poems, &c. on Several Occasions: with Valentinian, A Tragedy. Written by the Right Honourable John late Earl of Rochester, preface by Rymer (London: Jacob Tonson, 1691);

Foedera, Conventiones, Literae, et Cujuscunque Generis Acta Publica, inter Reges Angliae, et alios quosvis Imperatores, Reges, Pontifices, Principes ... ; Rymer edited the first 15 of the 20 volumes and assembled the material for volume 16 (London: A. & J. Churchill, 1704-1735).

Curious Amusements: Fitted for the Entertainment of the Ingenious of Both Sexes ... To which is added, Some Translations from Greek, Latin, and Italian Poets; with other Verses and Songs on Several Occasions, not before printed. By T. Rymer, Esq; late Historiographer-Royal, includes poems by Rymer on pp. 133-192 (London: D. Browne, W. Mears & J. Browne, 1714).

Because Thomas Rymer is best known for his scurrilous critique of William Shakespeare's *Othello*, still frequently (and usually condescendingly) quoted, it is easy to forget how important he is to the history of English literary criticism. From his translation of René Rapin to his discussions of tragedy, Rymer was at the forefront in transferring French neo-Aristotelian formalism across the Channel. Central in the Restoration de-

THOMAS RYMER.

Engraving by an unknown artist; courtesy of the Henry E. Huntington Library and Art Gallery

bates about the relative merits of the ancients and moderns and about the relationship between art and nature, Rymer wrote the first English history of a literary genre (the epic), performed the first systematic analysis of a Shakespearean play, and coined the crucial critical term "poetical justice." If Samuel Johnson was correct in asserting that John Dryden was the "father of English criticism," then surely Rymer was a wealthy uncle who contributed greatly to its upbringing. His influences, both positive and negative, may be seen not only in his contemporaries—Dryden, John Dennis, and Jeremy Collier, for instance—but also in the hordes of Shakespeare's defenders and early editors from Nicholas Rowe to Johnson and in the very definitions of literary bat-

tlegrounds—the distinction between poetry and history, the necessity of morality, the role of decorum, the test of probability.

Rymer was born probably in 1643 in Yafforth, Yorkshire, the son of Ralph Rymer, a man of considerable substance with a strong interest and participation in the turbulent politics of the day. Consequently, Rymer's early years were dominated by the Civil War. As early as 1645, according to Rymer's modern editor Curt Zimansky, Ralph Rymer "was concerned with provisioning Fairfax' troops and from 1650 his name is associated with Yorkshire financial matters," as he was appointed justice of the peace and county treasurer by the Commonwealth government. At Thomas Smelt's school in nearby Northallerton, where he studied for eight years, Rymer received a political education that contrasted sharply with the parliamentary politics of his father. George Hickes, a classmate of Rymer, records that "when we came to read Homer, he [Smelt] would take occasion from the many passages in that poet which the learned know are written for the honour of Kings, to read us a lecture against rebels and regicides, whom he compared to the giants that fought against the gods."

In 1659 Rymer left the Northallerton school to enroll at Sidney Sussex College, Cambridge, where he published his first verse (in Latin) and left apparently without taking his degree. Zimansky conjectures that "family troubles intervened" with Rymer's education. Indeed, Rymer's father suffered financially upon the Restoration; he lost his office and much of his property. Ralph Rymer, though not actually present at the armed assembly, was one of the leaders of the "Presbyterian Rising" on 12 October 1663. As a result of his participation in the event, Rymer's father was hanged, drawn, and quartered, and his head was among those displayed at York, Doncaster, and Northallerton. Rymer's brother Ralph was sentenced to life imprisonment and held in York castle until he was released for reasons of health on 16 July 1666. Though the immediate effect on Rymer of these events was financial, it is interesting to speculate psychologically about their influence on his later insistent differentiation between the accidents of history and the ideal constructs of the literary artist.

Rymer entered Gray's Inn on 2 May 1666 and was called to the bar on 16 June 1673. During these years in London Rymer became acquainted with Sir Fleetwood Sheppard (to whom *The Tragedies of the Last Age* is addressed), who most likely introduced him to leading literary figures such as Sir Charles Sedley; John Wilmot, Earl of Rochester; Charles Sackville, Earl of Dorset; and Dryden. Like most young authors in Restoration London, Rymer tried his hand at a play, the tragedy *Edgar*, written in heroic couplets, and published in late 1677 or early 1678. As indication that Rymer was beginning to be known, we have the evidence of William Wycherley's letter to John Sheffield, Earl of Mulgrave of 20 August 1677: "This last piece [*The Tragedies of the Last Age*] is written after the Epistolary Way of Politick Fops, directed to Mr. Shepheard, I suppose from one Room to another at the George and Vulture Tavern, when the Wine was dead, and the Spirits of the Brandy

too much wasted by Burning."

As Gerard Reedy has noted, "Rymer's life of writing splits in half." From the translation of René Rapin (1674) to the publication of *A Short View of Tragedy* (1693) Rymer was a literary critic; when Thomas Shadwell died on 19 November 1692, the two royal posts he held—poet laureate and historiographer royal—were split between Nahum Tate and Rymer, respectively, and from this time Rymer devoted his writings to antiquarian and historical studies, the most notable of which is the monumental *Foedera* (1704-1735).

Rymer's first critical effort was the preface to his anonymously published translation of Rapin's *Reflections on Aristotle's Treatise of Poesie*, a work that helped to make Rapin the most influential of the French formalists in England during this period and also helped the career of the translator. In the preface to a 1706 English edition of Rapin's works, the author declares that Rymer's "Judicious Preface, with which he adorned his Translation, gave him almost as eminent a Name among the *English* Critics, as his Author held among the French." Several features of Rymer's short preface are typical of his later criticism. Most noticeable, perhaps, are his interest in literary history and the demonstration of his considerable learning: the historical sketch of the epic shows Rymer's ability to quote and comment upon poetry in several languages. This critical method of quoting passages and then comparing and analyzing them is one that Rymer will employ in his later, more important works and one that Zimansky asserts "is here applied to English poetry practically for the first time." Rymer's later reputation as a "common sense" critic perhaps begins in this preface with remarks such as the following (which sounds much like Alexander Pope in the *Essay on Criticism*, 1711): "What *Aristotle* writes on this Subject, are not the dictates of his own magisterial Will, or the dry deductions of his Metaphysicks: But the Poets were his Masters, and what was their practice, he reduced to principles."

Most important, perhaps, is his notion of history and probability. After chastising Lucan for writing poetry on a historical subject, Rymer charts the different path from history that poetry must take: "*Aristotle* tells us, *That Poetry is something more excellent, and more philosophical, than History*, and does not inform us what has been done; but teaches us what may, and what ought to be done." Rymer claims of Edmund Spenser that "blindly rambling on *marvellous* Adventures, he

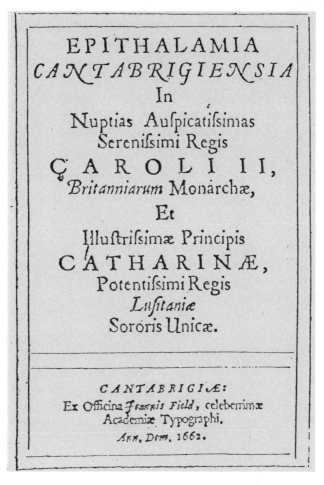

EPITHALAMIA
CANTABRIGIENSIA
In
Nuptias Auſpicatiſsimas
Sereniſsimi Regis
ÇAROLI II,
Britanniarum Monàrchæ,
Et
Illuſtriſsimæ Principis
CATHARINÆ,
Potentiſsimi Regis
Luſitaniæ
Soróris Unicæ.

CANTABRIGIÆ:
Ex Officina *Joannis Field*, celeberrimæ
Academiæ Typographi.
Ann. Dom. 1662.

Title page for the book that includes Rymer's first published work, an untitled Latin poem

makes no Conscience of *Probability*. All is fanciful and chimerical, without any uniformity, without any foundation in truth; his Poem is perfect *Fairyland*." For poetry Rymer insists on a middle ground between fact and fancy, a subject matter neither historically true nor completely fictional but one that is true to the laws of probability, true to universal truths, and capable of providing instruction to readers. On these principles Rymer would construct much of his criticism, including his commentary on *Othello*.

Unlike Rymer's often rambling and digressive criticism, *Edgar* is composed along strict formalist rules; Wycherley condemned it as a "Pattern for Exact Tragedies." Probably written in London several years before its publication, *Edgar* apparently was never performed. In an advertisement, Rymer, sounding much as he does in the Rapin preface, proclaims, "This I call an Heroick Tragedy, having in it chiefly sought occasions to extoll in that verse which, with Cowley, Denham, and Waller, I taken to be the most

proper for epic poetry." Though it received little attention upon publication, *Edgar*, with its lead-heavy couplets, sank to the level of a joke by the end of the century, no doubt helped by the notoriety Rymer attained with his attacks on Shakespeare. Dryden and Charles Gildon take swipes at the play, and in *Spectator* 592 Addison reports Shakespeare's revenge on his detractor as shredded copies of *Edgar* were to be used to provide a snow scene in a production of *King Lear*.

The publication of *The Tragedies of the Last Age*, however, marked Rymer's arrival as a critic. In this work, written as a letter to his friend Fleetwood Sheppard, Rymer claims no systematized method to his argument. Rymer seeks to explain why the English, who "want neither genius nor language for so great a work," fall so short of the ancients in the field of tragedy. Rymer declares early that he has "chiefly consider'd the *Fable* or *Plot*, which all conclude to be the *Soul* of a *Tragedy*; which with the *Ancients*, is always found to be a *reasonable Soul*; but *with us*, for the most part, a *brutish* and often worse than *brutish*." After a brief history of tragedy, Rymer offers critical analyses of three plays in the Beaumont-Fletcher canon: *Rollo, Duke of Normandy* (usually known as *The Bloody Brother*); *A King and No King*; and *The Maid's Tragedy*. If it seems strange that Rymer comments at such length on plays not now generally known, it must be pointed out that the reputation of Francis Beaumont and John Fletcher was perhaps at its zenith and that all three plays were extremely popular during the Restoration. Indeed, *Rollo*, one of the few plays actually staged during the Commonwealth period, had been singled out by Dryden in the *Essay on Dramatic Poesy* (1668) as one that "has that uniformity and unity of design in it, which I have commended in the French." As with his later assault on *Othello*, Rymer had selected his targets carefully, choosing formidable works rather than easy marks.

Interspersed with his commentary (often sarcastic and acerbic) on specific passages from the plays, Rymer lays down several of his guiding principles of criticism: poetic justice, decorum, and probability. All three critical principles arise from Rymer's analyses of plot; thus, all three are involved in Rymer's notion of poetic representation, or imitation. Rymer seems quite neoclassical in his insistence that poets—as opposed to historians, who relate particular truths—are to imitate the "ideal" or "universal" in nature. Rymer believes that the ancients well understood this distinction but that modern dramatists apparently do not: with regard to the representation of kings, Rymer claims that if we "examin the Kings of their [Greeks'] *Tragedies*, they appear all *Heroes*, and ours but *Dogs*, in comparison of them." Speaking of *Rollo*, in particular, Rymer admits " 'Tis possible that a Prince may abandon himself to be rul'd by some busie creature of no consideration. The *Annals of Normandy* may mention such Dukes. *History* may have known the like. But *Aristotle* cries shame. *Poetry* will allow of nothing so unbecoming, nor dares any Poet imagine that God Almighty would trust his Annointed with such a Guardian Devil." Rymer's sense of tragic decorum requires that kings behave as ideal kings, that women, servants, and subjects behave as their ideal types: "In Poetry no woman is to kill a man, except her quality gives her the advantage above him, nor is a Servant to kill the Master, nor a Private Man, much less a Subject to kill a King."

Decorum is linked to poetic justice by the necessity of the poet to provide moral instruction, another principle understood by the ancients, who, "finding in History, the same *end* happen to the *righteous* and to the *unjust* . . . saw these particular *yesterday-truths* were imperfect and unproper to illustrate the *universal* and *eternal truths* by them intended." The ancients "concluded, that a *Poet* must of necessity see *justice* exactly administered, if he intended to please." Armed with these principles, Rymer lays waste to the plots of Beaumont and Fletcher.

As Zimansky has observed, "none of these ideas of drama was original with Rymer, though his application of them was individual and fresh to English criticism." Though heavily indebted to French formalism, Rymer, Zimansky notes, may be distinguished from his French sources in two important areas: in his conviction that the end of poetry is pleasure and in the emphasis Rymer places on literary history. Though Rymer had always displayed an interest in history, he owes, as Earl Miner has observed, at least some of his historical emphasis to Dryden: "Rymer took from Dryden two historical insights that remain so fundamental to our own historical thought about literature that we presume that they had always existed." The first is what Miner calls a "conception of a literary period or age," and the second is Dryden's use of "*present* history to illuminate the *literary* historical past and present." Both of these insights seem essential to the construction of rudimentary literary histories (particularly of individual genres) made in the Restoration by Rymer and others.

The relationship between Rymer and Dryden, however, was one of mutual influence. The impact of *The Tragedies of the Last Age* may best be seen in Dryden's "Heads of an Answer to Rymer" (the title first given to this work by Malone in his 1800 edition of Dryden's works) and in the preface to Dryden's *Troilus and Cressida* (1679). The "Heads," though probably composed in 1677, immediately after the appearance of *The Tragedies of the Last Age*, was not published until Jacob Tonson included it in the preface to his 1711 edition of the works of Beaumont and Fletcher; Samuel Johnson then included it (in a radically different arrangement of the paragraphs) in his 1779 *Life of Dryden*. Dryden's composite assessment of Rymer's work is positive: "My judgment on this piece is this, that it is extremely learned; but that the author of it is better read in the Greek than in the English poets;

that all writers ought to study this critique as the best account I have ever seen of the Ancients." But Dryden continues to hope "that we may be taught here justly to admire and imitate the Ancients, without giving them the preference, with this author, in prejudice to our own country." Indeed, Dryden's points of disagreement with Rymer afford the "Heads" its importance.

"The cardinal importance of the 'Heads of an Answer to Rymer,'" according to George Watson, "can be simply stated: it is the one critical document in English between the Restoration and Johnson's Shakespeare in which the *Poetics* of Aristotle are attacked frontally and without qualification." While Watson may be overstating his case, Dryden takes Aristotle's work for what it is: a critical analysis of Greek tragedy, particularly that of Sophocles. Accordingly, we find in the "Heads" Dryden's well-known refutation of Rymer: " 'Tis not enough that Aristotle has said so, for Aristotle drew his models of tragedy from Sophocles and Euripides; and if he had seen ours, might have changed his mind." Dryden brings to his criticism two important qualities lacking in Rymer. First, he has vast practical experience in the theater; he knows how drama works to effect proper audience response, and he knows that, despite irregularities in plot and decorum, the plays of Beaumont and Fletcher (and those of Shakespeare) succeed on stage. Secondly, Dryden understands the notion of historical relativism: though human nature may be universal, audiences, languages, and literary tastes are not.

This knowledge and understanding forces Dryden to challenge the supremacy of plot in tragedy (one of Rymer's basic premises) and to advance other dramatic qualities that he perceives are inferior in the Greek playwrights. Foremost among these is variety, a crucial element to stage effectiveness. To achieve the desired variety, Dryden recommends emotions other than pity and fear—particularly love. He also, in what may be the most important critical contribution of the "Heads," argues for the quality of poetry in the English dramatists: "If the plays of the Ancients are more correctly plotted, ours are more beautifully written." If Rymer displays critical blindspots, it is here: he often simply ignores (or is insensitive to) the poetic quality of Shakespeare and his contemporaries, and he often fails to consider the emotional impact such language has on its audience. In the preface to *Troilus and Cressida*, Dryden offers his own theory of tragedy. In it, Dryden combines Aristotelian formalism with

Longinian emotion and discusses specifically Shakespeare's faults and beauties, striving, in his own play, to present an amalgam of Elizabethan power and Restoration refinement. Nevertheless, the "Heads" (though disorganized and seemingly fragmentary) remains Dryden's immediate response to Rymer.

After the publication of *The Tragedies of the Last Age* evidence about Rymer's life becomes sporadic. In 1680 Rymer contributed to Jacob Tonson's edition of Ovid's *Epistles*, and throughout the decade provided Tonson with materials for several others of his collections. In 1681 Rymer published, again in letter form, his *A General Draught and Prospect of Government in Europe*. Zimansky describes this piece as arguing "chiefly from medieval chronicles the rights of parliaments against royal prerogative." Appearing, as it does, at the height of the monarchy's troubles with the Whigs over the succession, *A General Draught and Prospect of Government in Europe* must be seen to place Rymer's political sympathies with the Whigs at this point in his career. His political views are also evident in the poems he wrote during this period, which were published posthumously in the *Curious Amusements* (1714). Among these poems are complimentary and amorous verses written to members of extreme Whig families, especially the family of Thomas Grey, Second Earl of Stamford, who was imprisoned for his part in the Rye House plot of 1685, regaining his prominence only after the 1688 Revolution. Rymer apparently spent considerable time on the Grey estates in Leicestershire during the late 1670s and early 1680s. Rymer's celebratory poems on the arrival of William of Orange in 1688 and of Mary in 1689 further define his politics and perhaps help to explain his appointment several years later as historiographer royal.

Rymer's last and best-known critical work, *A Short View of Tragedy* was published in 1693. Despite its notoriety, Zimansky notes that "the entire volume, with its disproportion of parts, misnumbered chapters, and numerous printing errors, gives the impression of having been thrown together with materials at hand rather than written to a plan." *A Short View of Tragedy* consists essentially of three parts: a short chapter on the role of the chorus in tragedy, a history of tragedy, and the critique of *Othello* for which Rymer would be remembered and damned.

Rymer's appreciation of the chorus betrays the bias for the ancients that Dryden had castigated, and it prompted a successful rebuttal by

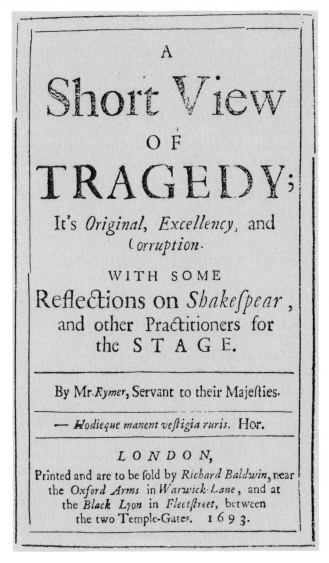

A

Short View

OF

TRAGEDY;

It's *Original, Excellency,* and
Corruption.

WITH SOME

Reflections on *Shakespear*,
and other Practitioners for
the S T A G E.

By Mr. *Rymer,* Servant to their Majesties.

— *Hodieque manent vestigia ruris.* Hor.

LONDON,
Printed and are to be sold by *Richard Baldwin,* near
the *Oxford Arms* in *Warwick-Lane,* and at
the *Black Lyon* in *Fleetstreet,* between
the two Temple-Gates. 1693.

Title page for the book that includes Rymer's well-known attack on Othello

John Dennis. Briefly, Rymer considers the chorus as successfully combining action and speech (as French opera, an "empty show," does not) and proclaims it "always the most necessary part of tragedy."

The interesting part of the historical section is Rymer's high esteem for the drama. Noting that plays were sacred to the Greeks, Rymer states "in the days of Aristophanes, it was on all hands agreed, that the best *Poet* was he who had done the most to make men vertuous and serviceable to the Publick." No doubt this belief in the reformative function of drama contributes to Rymer's concern with poetic justice and decorum as proper means to the end. For various literary periods, Rymer defends the drama against assaults by detractors (such as early Christians), justi-

fying the art on the grounds of instructive fables and allegory. He includes an original assessment of the "Provencial" poets and concludes with fairly standard Restoration hyperbole about Edmund Waller, proclaiming him the best poet since Virgil. Rymer also demonstrates considerable knowledge of sixteenth-century English drama, praising *Gorbuduc,* which "might have been a better direction to *Shakespear* and *Ben. Johnson* than any guide they had the luck to follow."

At this point in his chronicle he turns his attention to *Othello,* chosen because "from all the Tragedies acted on our English Stage, *Othello* is said to bear the Bell away." His objections to the play, like his objections to Beaumont and Fletcher, center upon notions of probability and decorum. "Nothing is more odious in Nature,"

Rymer maintains, "than an improbable lye; And, certainly, never was any Play frought, like this of *Othello* with improbabilities." Rymer's obvious racism precludes his accepting the love and marriage between Desdemona and Othello or even Othello's appointment as general by the Venetians. Rymer objects vociferously to the time scheme in the play—the hasty marriage, instantaneous sea travel, honeymoon jealousy, and the like. But he returns repeatedly to decorum: "What is most intolerable is *Iago*. He is no Black-amoor Souldier, so we may be sure he should be like other Souldiers of our acquaintance; yet never in Tragedy, nor in Comedy, nor in Nature was a Souldier with his Character." For Rymer, just as kings are not rascals, neither are soldiers deceitful, especially to their commanders. Rymer objects to the play's vulgar language, the language of Roderigo and Iago when speaking to Brabantio, the language of Othello when chastising Desdemona.

Though Rymer's tone is acerbic and sarcastic, his point is always the same: the lack of decorum prohibits the morally instructive capacity of the play. Perhaps most quoted of all Rymer's works is his recital of *Othello*'s "instructive" fables: "First, This may be a caution to all Maidens of Quality how, without their Parents consent, they run away with Blackamoors.... Secondly, This may be a warning to all good Wives, that they look well to their Linnen. Thirdly, This may be a lesson to Husbands, that before their Jealousie be Tragical, the proofs may be Mathematical." Pointed and witty, Rymer's criticisms are sometimes silly and sometimes hit their mark. T. S. Eliot remarked in his 1919 essay on *Hamlet* that he had "never, by the way, seen a cogent refutation of Thomas Rymer's objections to *Othello*." In just such a refutation, Nigel Alexander acknowledges that Rymer's "criticism is directed at the three vital questions of the play": the nature and validity of the marriage, the source and direction of Iago's terrifying power, and the trifle of the handkerchief. Nevertheless, Alexander believes that the "tragic action develops and becomes possible when Othello comes to share this vulgar view of his own marriage—the view which is also held by Thomas Rymer." "The tragedy is made possible," Alexander continues, "because all of the characters on stage believe Iago to be the pattern of the honest soldier described by Horace," and, we might add, longed for by Rymer.

Burdened by the excess baggage of his dogmatism regarding race, the military, the class struc-

ture, and the formal requirements of tragedy, Rymer misses again the emotional impact of the play on its audience. His is the voice of the theoretical critic rather than of the practicing playwright. His comment on Shakespeare's sources is crucial to an understanding of his critical vantage point: "the ground of all this Bedlam-Buffoonry," Rymer asserts, "were Carpenters, Coblers, and illiterate fellows [who acted the English Cycle plays]; who found that the Drolls, and Fooleries interlarded by them, brought in the rabble.... Our *Shakespear*, doubtless, was a great Master in this craft. These Carpenters and Coblers were the guides he followed. And it is then no wonder that we find so much farce and *Apochryphal Matter* in his Tragedies. Thereby un-hallowing the Theatre, profaning the name of Tragedy; And instead of representing Men and Manners, turning all Morality, good sence, and humanity into mockery and derision." Shakespeare wrote for his audience, and, if he did not write Greek tragedies, it must be remembered that his audience was not Greek.

It is unfortunate that perhaps the most direct influence of *A Short View of Tragedy* is on the famous detractor of the stage, Jeremy Collier, the title of whose major work, *A Short View of the Immorality, and Profaneness of the English Stage* (1698), recalls Rymer's. Like Rymer, Collier emphasizes fable and its instructive capability and applies the theories of poetic justice and decorum. Often, even the tone seems similar. Collier's moral assault on the licentiousness of Restoration comedy helped bring about profound changes in eighteenth-century drama, changes for the worse, perhaps, but not changes that can be laid upon Rymer.

When Thomas Shadwell died in 1692, Rymer was appointed his successor as historiographer royal at two-hundred pounds per year. Rymer was probably assisted in this appointment by Charles Sackville, Earl of Dorset, to whom *A Short View of Tragedy* was dedicated. Rymer's career changed drastically at this point, as one of his first assignments in the new post was the compilation of the monumental *Foedera*. On 26 August 1693, under the seal of Queen Mary, a royal order directed Rymer to "transcribe and publish all the leagues, treaties, alliances, capitulations, and confederacies, which have at any time been made between the Crown of England and any other kingdoms, princes, and states." The *Foedera* was prompted by and modeled after similar undertakings in Europe, including Gottfried Wilhelm Leibnitz's *Codex Juris Gentium Diplomaticus*, published at Hanover in March 1693. Though Rymer's biographer Thomas Duffus Hardy finds that "a political play, party pamphlets, and absurd dramatic criticisms do not seem to be a very fitting preparation for so important a task," historians have marveled at the comprehensiveness and diligence with which Rymer carried out his work.

Rymer edited the first fifteen of the twenty volumes and compiled the materials for the sixteenth before his death in 1713. His life during this period was marked by hard work and hardship. Records indicate that he frequently had to petition in order to be paid what he was promised for the work, and, in a letter to Leibnitz, Rymer complains, "I am kept at hard work in the Royal Archives, hidden from the eyes of men, and where I grub and dig daily among decaying parchments covered with dirt and mildew." Perhaps his knowledge of and great interest in history bolstered his spirits against the poverty and neglect he suffered while performing this historical service, but there is little actual record of his life at this time. Rymer died on 13 December 1713 at his lodgings in Arundel Street and was buried four days later in an unmarked grave at St. Clement Danes.

Ever since his pronouncements on *Othello* Thomas Rymer has been a critic to whom one responds rather than a critic whom one endorses, and a study of his reputation reveals a history (at least until recently) of steady decline. Consequently, it is easy to forget that in his own time Rymer was second only to Dryden as a critic. In the next generation Pope said of Rymer, "he is generally right, though rather too severe in his opinion of the particular plays he speaks of; and is, on the whole, one of the best critics we ever had." In his *Life of Dryden* Johnson compares the two critics, concluding that if we find truth in Dryden, she is "drest in the graces of elegance"; with Rymer "Truth, if we meet her, appears repulsive by her mien and ungraceful by her habit. Dryden's criticism has the majesty of a queen; Rymer's has the ferocity of a tyrant." In the nineteenth century, a literary period so confident of its own judgments, Sir Walter Scott asserted that "nothing can be more disgusting than the remarks of Rymer, who creeps over the most beautiful passages of the drama with eyes open only to defects, or their departure from scholarly precept." Finally, there is Thomas Babington

Macaulay's quip that Rymer was "the worst critic that ever lived."

With J. E. Spingarn's *Critical Essays of the Seventeenth Century* (1908-1909), Eliot's work to revive the seventeenth century, and, most important, the 1956 publication of Zimansky's edition of Rymer's criticism, a new wave of attention to Rymer has helped to display his historical role in a proper light. Thomas Rymer helps our understanding of the interrelationship between seventeenth-century French and English criticism and demonstrates how early English drama criticism grappled with the genius of Shakespeare.

Biography:

Thomas Duffus Hardy, *Syllabus (in English) of the Documents Relating to England and Other Kingdoms contained in the Collection Known as "Rymer's Foedera,"* 3 volumes (London: Longmans, Green, 1869-1885);

Curt A. Zimansky, Introduction to *The Critical Works of Thomas Rymer*, edited by Zimansky (New Haven: Yale University Press, 1956);

References:

Nigel Alexander, "Thomas Rymer and *Othello*," *Shakespeare Studies*, 21 (1968): 67-77;

Joan C. Grace, *Tragic Theory in the Critical Works of Thomas Rymer, John Dennis, and John Dryden* (Rutherford, N.J.: Fairleigh Dickinson University Press, 1975);

Arthur C. Kirsch, ed., *Literary Criticism of John Dryden* (Lincoln: University of Nebraska Press, 1966);

Earl Miner, "Mr. Dryden and Mr. Rymer," *Philological Quarterly*, 54 (Winter 1975): 137-151;

James Osborne, "Thomas Rymer as Rhymer," *Philological Quarterly*, 54 (Winter 1975): 152-177;

Gerard Reedy, "Rymer and History," *CLIO*, 7 (Spring 1978): 409-422;

F. G. Walcott, "John Dryden's Answer to Rymer's *The Tragedies of The Last Age*," *Philological Quarterly*, 15 (April 1936): 194-214;

George Watson, "Dryden's First Answer to Rymer," *Review of English Studies*, new series 14 (1963): 17-23.

Papers:

Several of Rymer's poems exist in manuscript; they have been deposited in the Yale University Library.

Anthony Ashley Cooper, Third Earl of Shaftesbury

(26 February 1671 - 15 February 1713)

Robert Voitle

University of North Carolina, Chapel Hill

BOOKS: *The Danger of Mercenary Parliaments*, by Shaftesbury and John Toland (London, 1698);

An Inquiry Concerning Virtue, in Two Discourses (London: Printed for A. Bell & S. Buckley, 1699);

Paradoxes of State, Relating to the Present Juncture of Affairs in England and the rest of Europe, by Shaftesbury and Toland (London: Printed for Bernard Lintott & sold by John Nut, 1702);

The Sociable Enthusiast. A Philosophical Adventure written to Palemon (N.p., 1704?);

A Letter Concerning Enthusiasm, To My Lord****** (London: Printed for John Morphew, 1708);

The Moralists, a Philosophical Rhapsody. Being a recital of certain conversations upon natural and moral subjects (London: Printed for John Wyat, 1709);

Sensus Communis: An Essay on the Freedom of Wit and Humour. In a letter to a friend (London: Printed for E. Sanger, 1709);

Soliloquy: or, Advice to an Author (London: Printed for John Morphew, 1710);

Characteristicks of Men, Manners, Opinions, Times, 3 volumes (London: Printed for John Darby, 1711; revised, 1714)—some copies of the 1714 edition include *A Notion of the Historical Draught or Tablature of the Judgment of Hercules* (1713) and some also include *A Letter Concerning the Art or Science of Design, written from Italy (on the occasion of Some Designs in Painting), to my Lord****** (1714);

A Notion of the Historical Draught or Tablature of the Judgment of Hercules (London, 1713);

The Life, Unpublished Letters, and Philosophical Regimen of Anthony Earl of Shaftesbury, edited by Benjamin Rand (London: Swan Sonnenschein, 1900)—includes the first printing of *ΑΣΚΗΜΑΤΑ; Second Characters, or the Language of Forms*, edited by Rand (Cambridge: Cambridge University Press, 1914);

Anthony Ashley Cooper, Third Earl of Shaftesbury . . . Complete Works, selected Letters and posthumous Writings, edited and translated by Gerd Hemmerich and Wolfram Benda (Stuttgart-Bad Cannstatt: Frommann-Holzboog, 1981-).

OTHER: *Select Sermons of Dr. Whichcot[e]*, edited, with a preface, by Shaftesbury (London: Printed for Awnsham & J. Churchill, 1698).

The third earl of Shaftesbury was important in his own day for his stress on the ultimate importance of the emotions in moral behavior—indeed was assumed to have invented the concept of "moral sense," before this idea was recognized as but part of a broad shift in the basis of ethics from reason to emotion. He was also famous in his own times for his attacks on religious enthusiasm. Today, perhaps, we are more concerned with him as an innovator in aesthetics, though recognition of this aspect of his work was slow in coming. It was first seen in his works by German writers such as Schiller, and from their writings, a focus primarily on the role of the creator of a literary work, rather than on its structure or on its impact on the reader, became a central part of the aesthetics of English Romanticism.

The son of Anthony Ashley Cooper, later second earl of Shaftesbury, Lord Ashley was born at Wimborne St. Giles, Dorset, on 26 February 1671. His childhood was strange by any day's standard; at the age of four he was legally adopted and brought up by his grandfather, the first earl (1621-1683). For several years later he remained in the large house for the most part alone, as his grandfather was so very wrapped up in politics, to put it mildly. A remarkable tutor, Elizabeth Birch, well versed in both Latin and Greek, had been chosen for him by John Locke, and continued to supervise his training both in Dorset and later in Clapham for at least six years. Locke, who was secretary to the first earl, tends to dominate Lord Ashley's childhood no matter which way one looks at it. Ashley was

Anthony Ashley Cooper, third Earl of Shaftesbury (at left)

even convinced that Locke had chosen his mother, Lady Dorothy Manners, daughter of the earl of Rutland, to be his father's wife, and certainly he did make all arrangements for the wedding; as a physician he gave advice to the young mother, and saw that her son was brought up according to his own well-known humane principles for education of the young. Because in this period Locke was very busy with his work for the first earl, and was further plagued by illness, which forced him to travel to the Continent, most of his efforts for Lord Ashley were by indirection, through Mrs. Birch and others. Whatever its benefits and failings, this phase of Lord Ashley's life came to an abrupt end when his grandfather, late in November 1682, was forced

to flee to Holland, where he shortly died, and Ashley was sent by his father to Winchester College, where he stayed about two years. No one can tell what the impact of his earlier isolation was, but it must have been reinforced by his miserable years at the college. The first experience involved physical separateness; now he entered a larger world and found it intensely hostile toward him. The college was High Church and strongly Royalist, and there were very few friends indeed for a young man already too thoughtful, who sprang from a line connected with Dissent, populist in sentiments, and republican in its political thought.

Though he was too young to have completed his courses in public school, we find Lord

Anthony Ashley Cooper, first Earl of Shaftesbury, who adopted his grandson, the future third earl, when he was four (portrait after J. Greenhill; by permission of the National Portrait Gallery, London)

Ashley in London in 1686, studying with a remarkably intelligent and capable Scot, Daniel Denoune. This man was to serve as his mentor for more than three years, when he took over Anthony's youngest brother, Maurice, whose translation of Xenophon's *Cyropaedia* was to remain standard for nearly a century. Anthony could not have been studying long before his mind turned to the final phase of his education, a grand tour of the Continent. This must have turned out better than the average parents could have expected; for many of the young men of England the tour must have provided an opportunity for sowing some wild oats before settling down as head of a family. Anthony used it to broaden his

experience, and polish both his education and his manners. From every major city Anthony visited he made full reports of his progress. Taking with him a baronet, Sir John Cropley (1663-1713), who became his best friend for life, and instead of the usual tour leader, his tutor, Denoune, he set off in July of 1687 for Rotterdam to spend some time with his old friend John Locke, who had left England, just after the first earl, to await a more favorable political climate. From there Ashley left in the late autumn for Paris, where we have little record of his activities, beyond a couple of letters to Locke. He was introduced at Versailles, and certainly much of the polish and affability he gained while abroad must derive from his visit to Paris.

After spending about the normal amount of time in Paris, about eight months, he commenced his giro d'Italia. He must have come over the Mont Cenis pass, for we find him proceeding from Turin to Milan, and he fills many pages in a hand so fine it is hard to read with a detailed account of his journeys, the people, the views, the art, and architecture he saw and so forth. What is missing are the descriptions of some large cities. Apparently, he wrote to his parents from these, and with the details fresh in mind had no need for notes. The high point of the trip is the visit to Naples, where he got slightly singed climbing Mount Vesuvius and gloried in the Roman ruins on the north shore of the bay. Up to this point, he followed the conventional path of most early travelers, but the abdication of James II made it impossible for him to return via France as he had intended, and a trip through the Balkans to Vienna, then Prague and the German principalities was necessary—all of which was to provide him with much rich material for his account. He left in March for Vienna and arrived back in London early in May 1689.

One can hope that Lord Ashley looked back with pleasure upon the adventures of his trip and the glories—as when the Elector of Brandenburg let him know that a one-day visit to his court in Berlin was not enough, that he wished to have the young English nobleman at his table for three nights—because many of the experiences which awaited him in England ranged from the tedious to the positively unpleasant. At the age of eighteen, he might well in his day have expected to accept considerable responsibility, but Wimbourne St. Giles was a house of sickness, neither parent having been well for some time. Anthony had six brothers and sisters, and the only one mature enough to help, John, a year younger, had already become a thoroughly dissolute young man, probably the fruits of his being the oldest child of the house after Anthony was adopted by his grandfather. Yet Ashley had to do everything and accept all responsibility, but he had no real power because up until his dying day, a decade hence, the earl had enough wit to know what was going on and had an obsession that someone was trying to make away with his authority.

John was the first problem; he had secretly married a nursery maid at St. Giles's. Ashley had to have the marriage dissolved, and then, after seeing John go from bad to worse in London, arranged to have him sent aboard a naval ship to the West Indies, where he died of a fever. Anthony never mentions him again. Another brother, Maurice, who started out well at Winchester, also began to show the effects of the lack of discipline in the Shaftesbury family. Happily, Denoune was available, and he agreed to tutor him and take him abroad. Even the family itself was under attack; no one who knows much about politics or the litigiousness of the English, will wonder much about the timing of this situation, arising as it did under the new Whig government. Anthony was by will one of the Lords Proprietors of the Carolina Colony, his father having had no say in the matter. The weaknesses of this system, where it took more than a year to issue an order and find out whether it had been obeyed, ought to have been clear before; now these weaknesses became all too clear to Anthony and caused him to write the bitterest letters we have from his pen. There were innumerable lawsuits, too, but the worst that happened was that his mother decided to separate from her husband after twenty years of marriage, and only with some difficulty her brother, the earl of Rutland, was able to extricate her from St. Giles's House.

As early as the winter of 1689-1690, when new elections seemed imminent, Lord Ashley was under pressure to stand for Weymouth, one of the seats which his family had traditionally controlled, but he refused, pleading that he had too many problems at home to oversee. There is considerable evidence that he had been active politically in the succeeding years, and when in 1695 the seat for Poole fell vacant, he stood for it and was chosen. Ashley's political alignments were in a sense anachronistic and grew more so as time went on; he was associated with Old or Country Whigs, most particularly those who had an admiration for the Commonwealth and for its theorists, such as James Harrington (1611-1677). The trouble with Lord Ashley's being a Country Whig was that the character of the Whig party gradually changed from 1689 on. The Country Whigs found that the bulk of the Whig party, with the changes of the leadership brought about by the Glorious Revolution, were moving toward the Court, and the Tories seemed more and more to represent the Country. Much had changed since the times before: England now had a Protestant monarch; the press was relatively free; the party in power ruled in a less arbitrary fashion, and so forth. Once when the Whigs became heavily involved in corruption, he was said to be considering joining the Tories, but this possibility was ridiculous; his fear of Catholicism and his distrust of his old enemy, Louis XIV, would have prevented it. To say that he was advocating principles that may have seemed more and more naive, does not suggest that there was anything naive in his political behavior. No, he proved highly skilled and shrewd, but too many tense hours in committee meetings brought on a violent attack of asthma, and he was forced to refuse to stand in 1698.

During the years after his mother's departure from Wimbourne St. Giles, her anger and that of her family were directed away from her husband and toward Ashley himself. The reasons are complex, but they centered around his refusal to intervene in the dispute. In 1696 he became desperate about the situation and asked his uncle, the earl of Rutland, to beg his mother to see him. The earl did, and after a while his mother relented, and after a dishonest steward was fired, she returned to St. Giles's House but in poor health, dying the next year.

Not long after his mother was buried, Ashley was in Rotterdam visiting his old friend Benjamin Furly (1636-1714) and recuperating. Anthony's problem was not too little energy; as John Locke said of him, the sword was too sharp for the scabbard. During this period Ashley was continually pulled by three forces: his domestic concerns, his political activity, and his literary and philosophical career. A visit to Holland might seem to pull him from all three, but it was the wrong country, and Furly's house was the wrong place to visit. This was Holland's golden age, and it was in a sense Europe's intellectual center. It was the center of publishing; it had fine universities and schools, and most important was the Dutch spirit of toleration, and the foreigners who fled there to escape oppression elsewhere in Europe. So far as Rotterdam was concerned, Furly's house and its magnificent library were its intellectual center.

Ashley's exercise book for the period is full of the conflicts he met here between the power of the people and their ideas, on the one hand, and his need for seclusion and recuperation on the other. The most notable figure he met was Pierre Bayle (1647-1706), and there have been a fair number of comments on Bayle's influence on Ashley. There are surely many parallel notions held by the two men: the thesis that an atheistic society can be morally superior to a misdevoted one; the notion that ridicule is the best weapon against folly; and their joint opposition to certain phases of the religious orthodoxy. (In these last it

would be hard to imagine Ashley not being influenced by Bayle's prose, so toughly logical, so trenchant and erudite.) Granting this and granting that as highly principled moralists, they speak the common language of toleration, it must also be allowed that there are very fundamental differences between them. Bayle is resolutely pessimistic while Ashley is essentially optimistic, and growing more so. The crucial difference is between a Calvinistic assurance of depravity on one hand, and a blend of old idealism and new optimism on the other. Among the many others whose company Ashley enjoyed in Rotterdam were Jean Le Clerc (1657-1736), scholar and editor, and the great Remonstrant author, Philip Van Limborch (1633-1712).

Meanwhile, back in England things were going from bad to worse for Ashley's family; the earl was becoming less and less competent, and family problems were piling up, such as the complex and ultimately unsuccessful negotiations for the marriage of one of Ashley's sisters. Ashley had forbidden anyone to write him anything but purely financial letters, but an old friend of Anthony's, Sir John Cropley, finally did so, and after only a nine-month stay abroad Anthony returned home. Even while in Rotterdam he had been dreaming of a new home in London, where he would be free from what were to him poisonous smogs. After settling some of the family's difficulties, he chose an older house in Chelsea—then remote from the city—to remodel. While work was still progressing on the house, his father fell seriously ill and died on 2 November 1699, making Anthony the third earl of Shaftesbury.

Ashley's first philosophical publication had come out the previous year, when he edited and wrote an introduction to some sermons he owned of Dr. Benjamin Whichcote (1609-1683). This must seem a strange task for someone whose name has become so closely associated with the rise of Deism, but it does not appear so odd when it is examined more closely. Ashley looks at the world rather differently than one might expect a moralist to do. First, for him there is the great bulk of humanity for whom there is no hope of moral behavior unless they follow religious principles—all else is in vain for their minds beset with temptations. Second, there is a very much smaller group to whom Ashley addressed his later publications. He hopes to make these love virtue for her own sake. Finally there is an almost minuscule group who, like Ashley, try to follow the ancient disciplines of Stoicism.

When he thinks of morality broadly, then, there is little difference between Whichcote's audience and Ashley's. Again, Whichcote was a leader of the Cambridge Platonists and shared Ashley's belief in a beneficent deity; a belief in this principle also implies an optimistic view of man. "Follow nature," Whichcote pleads continuously, not the nature of Rousseau, but human nature, where one will find inscribed the principles all men should follow, the *consensus gentium*. In his preface praising the principles, few of Ashley's readers would have noted the arch irony attacking those preachers who were not of Whichcote's persuasion.

If Whichcote's sermons were published by Ashley in order to counter the effect of Hobbes, the publication of *An Inquiry Concerning Virtue, in Two Discourses* in 1699 was intended to undercut the far more serious result of Locke's writings. Although he was very careful not to say much about Locke while his old mentor was still alive, Ashley had no hesitation about attacking him after his death. He puts the matter most concisely in a letter to his protégé Michael Ainsworth on 3 June 1709: " 'twas Mr. Lock that struck the home Blow (for Mr. Hobb's Character, and base slavish Principles . . . took off the poyson of his Philosophy). 'Twas Mr. Lock that struck at all Fundamentals, threw all *Order* and *Virtue* out of the World, and made our Very Ideas of these . . . *unnatural* and without foundation in our Minds." Locke often claimed that moral ideas are capable of strict demonstration, but he never did this, always returning to the point that the Gospel provides us with adequate rules to govern our behavior.

How does Ashley respond to Locke's effective undermining of the notion of innate ideas? First, he demonstrates with some prolixity that typical religious ethics, whether they are based on Calvinistic foreordination or conventional reward and punishment, are dependent upon the worship of a God who is in some degree demonic, rather than the good God of Theism whom he reveres. He then demonstrates that it matters little whether ideas of right or wrong are innate. The real question is whether the affection toward society is not natural, whether some spark of it does not exist in the heart of every man, however faint it may appear. Ashley connects this impulse with the *consensus gentium*, the social instinct of the natural-law philosophers, and thus he connects it with universal morality. Especially in this early version of the *Inquiry* all the language dealing with it is very rigorously Lockean, which is

one reason why Ashley's later contemporaries understood so well what he meant, unlike present-day readers. Many such instincts had been suggested in his times, "boniform faculties" and the like; his impulse differs only in the fact that it is described precisely in the terms of what was to become a widely accepted psychology, instead of being left in vague terms, and it forms the basis of the whole ethic which he is describing. Having defined both true religion and true virtue, Ashley then proceeds to describe the relation of one to the other, but his conclusions are easily imagined.

Perhaps it would pay to consider for a moment the impulses behind the publication of the book, which is most frequently described as being published by John Toland, without its author's consent. It is true that Ashley made a valiant effort to buy up all copies that were available when he returned to London; it is also true that we find him encouraging a French translation not too long after. Many arguments can be made on either side, but essentially the question is not really answerable. This fits well with his ambiguous attitudes toward the publication of his own works.

Certainly it is clear that Ashley never intended his *ΑΣΚΗΜΑΤΑ*, or *Exercises* for publication. These were very personal stoic diaries which he kept, beginning with his second visit to Holland in 1698-1699, for the rest of his life largely when he was more or less at leisure, though the entries grow less frequent as time goes on. Rand called them a philosophical regimen, which is likely to be misinterpreted because it implies some sort of rule book such as the *Enchiridion* of Epictetus. Instead these are more informally structured like the *Meditations* of Marcus Aurelius, and are intended to be rehearsed and read over by the beginner in Stoicism, so that by castigating himself he can change into a true stoic, capable of appreciating such works as the *Discourses* of Epictetus. Because he did not understand their corrective purpose, Rand was much embarrassed by some of the things he found, and silently omitted them from the version which he printed.

There is space here to comment only on some aspects of the *ΑΣΚΗΜΑΤΑ*, so complex is its subject. Stoicism involves three essential subjects: physis, ataraxia, and koinonia; nature, apathy (in the stoic sense), and community. Nature may seem peripheral to a philosophical system so strongly ethical in nature, but it is, of course, central. Marcus, upon whom Ashley depends so strongly in this phase of his stoic thought, tells us we must strive to "think of the Universe as one living creature, embracing one being and one soul; how all is absorbed into the one consciousness of this living creature; how it compasses all things with a single purpose, and all things work together to cause all that comes to pass, and their wonderful web and texture." This sort of thinking was easier when the only complex structures available as models were organic rather than mechanical. The whole is an intelligent presence, then, and this cosmology is distinguished from other cosmologies of the times in that it is wholly materialistic, which is one reason that Ashley avoids any sort of dualism in his thought.

The stoic notion of apathy is easier to understand than the cosmology in which it exists, however difficult it may seem of achievement. Man is free only to the extent to which he has control of his own nature—specifically, his emotions—this is all that matters. One need only think of Epictetus arguing with his fictive Emperor. How can he be enslaved if his mind is free? How imprisoned? How even killed? This last question brings up one of the least palatable aspects of stoic thought, the ultimate indifference toward suicide.

The whole notion of stoic apathy involves the practitioner in such a constant inner struggle that he would seem to have little time for the practice of koinonia—love of man and mankind. Certainly while the stoic is in the early stages of his career, while he is stripping himself of the usual worldly concerns, he may have to consciously avoid contact with his fellow man. Once he has achieved some degree of apathy, however, the opportunity is open to him, and he must be a person of the world to successfully practice the virtue. The best way to see this quality is in the lives of those whom we associate with Roman Stoicism: Epictetus, a slave much of his life, was a great and active teacher; his disciple, Arrian, was a colonial governor and general; Seneca labored hard for his emperor, and when he sought relief from the tensions of office, communicated with his larger audience; Panaetius of Rhodes, one of the fathers of Roman Stoicism, was a wealthy man of the world, and of course there is one of the greatest of Roman emperors, Marcus Aurelius. Even in the heroes the Stoics hold up for emulation we can sense this combination of activity and virtue. Ashley's favorite was the greatest of Stoic heroes, Hercules.

In any event, the necessity for concealment of his true religion taught Ashley much about the need to wear masks. Very few of his contemporaries knew of his faith, though he lived most of his life as a Stoic and certainly died a Stoic.

The estate that Shaftesbury inherited is roughly triangular in shape, about ten miles to the side, and lies in a very lush section of Dorsetshire. The facade of St. Giles's House, which lies on the southeast face of the triangle, is made of pink stone—and attached to one corner of the square which lies behind the facade is a long, loose structure, much of it added since the third earl's day. Overall, the house must have been very impressive because even before all the improvements made by Shaftesbury his grandfather there entertained Charles II.

In a way it was good that the new earl had been gradually introduced to his responsibilities over a long period of time; otherwise, it would have been a burden. Instead he had determined to remake the estate, and he accomplished much of what he had intended in the very short time that was left to him. "Behold another *Age*! . . . another Face of things, another Scene," he exclaims in the *ΑΣΚΗΜΑΤΑ*. First he regularized the operations of St. Giles's House and compiled over a short period of time an elaborate set of directions covering every detail of household operations from the sorts of meals which were to be provided visitors to the operations of the wine cellar. Shortly he forbade any of his servants accepting vails—tips from guests—and augmented their pay to make up the difference. The manor had been without a real lord for some time, and in his diary we see him acting as a landlord, dispensing charity, arbitrating disputes, making judgments which have the force of law, without himself sensing any real difference. He is simply holding court. He held property by leasehold, by copyhold (where the tenant pays a specific sum for a fourteen-year period), or by rack rent—which did not then have the perjorative connotation it now has. Shaftesbury's tendency was to convert properties rented at an annual rack rent to copyhold. In this way he got less money, but he had the cash, the tenant had a sense of security, and he got a tenant committed to the property he rented. The properties were very rich, some of the copyholds amounting to two or three thousand pounds, and Shaftesbury sought to make them richer by following the newest methods of agriculture on the home farms so that the tenants had a chance to see the advantages. He also tried to put the finances of the household on a rational basis; for instance, anyone who withheld a bill for more than forty shillings for six months would lose the custom of the family. Of course, the success of the earl's reforms depended a great deal on the skill and probity of the stewards who administered the estate. It is good in a way that Shaftesbury's head steward was so competent, because the earl tended too frequently to give the understewards yet another chance.

Naturally, when he became an earl he could no longer show too much overt interest in the elections to the House of Commons. He still had the political framework that his grandfather had built up in the west, and this he used to good effect during the elections of 1701, as most people in his situation would have. Queen Anne's government was so angry with him for interfering in the elections that he could not even get a minor appointment made to an office, though King William had offered him the secretaryship of state. He had to wait until the Tories grew stronger before the small band of Country Whigs he led could have a decisive influence; until then he continued to play his part in the Commons elections, but even more quietly than before.

Early in 1703 it became evident that he could no longer keep up the pace he had begun, so that in August he received his pass to go to Rotterdam, where he settled in much more secrecy than on his last visit.

He lived more privately now, but there was no way of escaping the bad news that came by post: his beloved sister Gertrude died; he had spent so much money rebuilding that there was a real need for thrift; his sister Frances married without her brother's consent; and so forth. He did manage to keep to his resolution to live privately, and there is no record of him seeing anyone but Bayle and Benjamin Furly. By the summer of the following year the earl was feeling better, and pressed by all to return home, he took a place on a yacht in a large flotilla which was awaiting a proper wind to return to England. Alas, the wind came too late, and he fell victim to his respiratory disease, returning in worse shape than when he had left the year before.

We are unsure of the date of publication of the rarest of Shaftesbury's books, *The Sociable Enthusiast*, but we have a record of a copy appearing in Holland in 1704, so that it is likely a product of his second visit there. There are three participants in the discussion: Palemon, a young man who knows all about nature but has little fondness for mankind; Philocles, who knows nothing and believes all; and Theocles, a mild and unbigoted enthusiast, who delivers the earl's message. Books 1 and 2 are pretty largely a repetition of what we learned from the *Inquiry*, though Shaftesbury now accepts a future state and the doctrine of reward and punishment. A look at the earl's final days convinces one that he has little faith in either of these propositions, but it is a tribute to his moral pragmatism that he accepts their necessity. Palemon, when he admits that there is a universal system, needs to have natural evil explained as resulting from a conflict of systems, but still persists in his dislike of mankind until it is pointed out to him that the hatred is illogical because it is a greater act of love to embrace the imperfect, especially since he has admitted that he loves his friends none the less for their failings.

The rhapsodic utterances of Theocles in book 3 hold much that is new. One utterance indeed proved so novel that it had to be altered in later editions. Shaftesbury's deep affection for the past—and his relative dislike for the Christian present—were both made all too clear. At one point he seems to alter the moral sense which he had defined earlier in the *Inquiry*, to a form of instinct, but anyone who knows Locke well enough will recognize that in the 1711 edition the sense is still described in fundamentally the same terms. It becomes quite evident here that Shaftesbury is becoming less of the systematizer that he had been earlier and is adapting very consciously the pose of a casual miscellany writer. This is apparent enough in his handling of Platonic materials. Philocles is converted to the beliefs of Theocles by alternating rational and rhapsodic utterances. From the rhapsodic material he may learn no more than he has from rational discourse, but the inspired meditations fix in his mind permanently that the cosmos is unified and presided over by a benign spirit. Only then does he consent to be called "a new enthusiast." It is by enraptured fancy—creative imagination—that there is hope of the individual glimpsing the ideal.

Many ideas which appear later in Shaftesbury's works are adumbrated here, but only one is stated so clearly that it ought to be noted now: "Therefore the Beautifying, not the Beautify'd, is really Beautiful." The ultimate effect was to turn attention to the artist and thus supply a basis for Romantic critical theory.

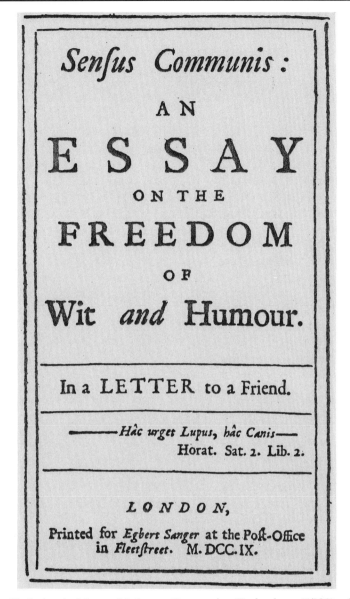

Title page for Shaftesbury's defense of A Letter Concerning Enthusiasm *(1708), which had been criticized for its suggestion that religious fanatics should be ridiculed rather than punished*

The period following his illness which he fell into on returning to England, up until 1708, might well be described as the years of retreat. Life went on to be sure, and we have the records of it, but he proceeded from health to illness and back again, and although we know he was writing, none of it appeared, so that for the general reader there is little to do but recite the principal events of the period. The first of these was the death of Locke on 28 October 1704. Despite the widening split in ideas, he and Ashley had maintained a lively intellectual discussion for some time in the early 1690s, but gradually the estrangement became clear after Locke got into an argu-

ment with the Countess Dowager over some funds which were due Locke, and Anthony inherited the disagreement. Locke was rather penurious, nor could he afford to be otherwise, and the correspondence dribbled off. Until the day of Shaftesbury's own death, his attitude toward Locke remained a classic example of real ambiguity: reverence for the man and all he had done for him; detestation of his ideas and their implications for society.

The nature of Shaftesbury's political activities become clear in 1705-1706, for which there survive some notes of Sir John Cropley addressed to Shaftesbury. They are so strange that if there were anything of the braggart in their author, one would be inclined to disbelieve him. Cropley is agent, secret agent, for Shaftesbury, managing the affairs of what he calls the "squadron," a small group of Country Whigs whose importance has grown with shifts of power in the Commons.

Indeed we can measure the strength of Shaftesbury's influence by the reaction of the Crown to him. At this stage, he was more or less an annoyance to the government, nothing much else. As more of his friends moved into posts of power, he expected to be heard, but he got little response until the winter of 1707-1708.

The years 1706 and 1707 were largely taken up with maintaining his health so that he could deal effectively with domestic affairs and his intellectual interests. We do not know today at any one time whether asthma or tuberculosis dominated—this despite elaborate analyses which have survived. It was possible for the severe asthmatic to survive then without falling into consumption, but only if he followed, as Locke did, a very strict personal regimen. In a sense this was impossible to a member of the nobility so politically motivated as Shaftesbury. Every October there arose the problem of when the wind would turn northeast, blowing the smoke of the city across Chelsea and perhaps making it impossible for him to attend even the opening of the House of Lords.

One of his intellectual interests is reflected in *A Letter Concerning Enthusiasm* (1708), which was occasioned by the uproar over a group of religious fanatics called the French Prophets. In his *Letter* he argues that the melancholy Prophets and other fanatics should be laughed at, not punished. Only ridicule will provide the test whether their gravity is true or false. False gravity is contagious, and if we rely on the magistrate to counter it, it may well grow worse. Indeed good religion requires good humor. Man, of course, has a natural inclination to enthusiasm, and it is our task to distinguish the ordinary species from divine enthusiasm or inspiration. The latter moves the right sort of heroes, statesmen, poets, orators, and so forth. What began as an attack on false enthusiasm ends up as a treatise on telling the false from the true species.

Reception of his *Letter Concerning Enthusiasm* was mixed, some of the pious attacking it in pamphlets, so that in 1709 he went to its defense in *Sensus Communis: An Essay on the Freedom of Wit and Humour*, in which he seeks to define more clearly what he meant by *ridicule*. There are solemn re-

provers of vice—more power to them—but he is not one of them; his function is to apply ridicule in a good-natured manner, and the mode of its application is the important part of the process. His conversationalists ridicule many aspects of life; yet they are unable to define common sense, to which they constantly appeal. This concept Shaftesbury finally defines as wholly dependent on the feeling for the common interest, which rises from a just sense of the common rights of mankind, and the natural equality there is among creatures of the same species.

As early as 1708, Shaftesbury gave up all hope that his younger brother, Maurice, would marry, and decided to get married himself and provide an heir to carry on the line. His rank and wealth were among his advantages in seeking a wife; against them must be balanced his very ill health, his necessarily reclusive pattern of life, and his very high expectations in a wife. The last of these disadvantages would count for little were he to marry Lady Anne Vaughan, daughter to one of the more evil creatures of the English nobility, John, second Earl of Carbery. Shaftesbury began to seek permission to court this paragon in the fall of 1708, and was still at it during the following summer. Carbery apparently used his daughter to taunt prospective suitors and never did give permission for her to marry anyone. When Shaftesbury finally realized what was going on he quickly decided to marry more or less secretly someone of good, solid background, whom he never even had seen until the negotiations were well under way, Jane, daughter of Thomas Ewer, of Bushy Hall, Hertfordshire. There is evidence that the choice was not altogether blind, because Shaftesbury must have known Jane's sister. In any case when he saw his intended bride, he was as charmed by her good looks as he had been by the reports of her character. They were married on 29 August 1709, and Shaftesbury sold his house in Chelsea and moved to more suitable quarters at Little Doods in Reigate, where he would be farther from London smoke and closer to his old friend Sir John Cropley.

This was a greatly productive period in his life, and his *Soliloquy: or, Advice to an Author* (1710) is in many ways Shaftesbury's most engaging work, for his miscellaneous and familiar style reaches its peak in it. He must have read the 1711 edition over and over, because there are changes on every page of the final edition. The sentences flow together readily yet can be pointed if he wishes them to be. Nowhere is his conviction of the superiority of the ancient over the modern writers more evident, but he is very careful to make a separation between secular and divine writings. Most of what he has to say on the matter is based on his cyclic but supple theory of history. He sees again a return to classical simplicity, now that the Glorious Revolution has assured for Britons freedom from political tyranny, but so long as Britons must fight against an absolute monarch there is a danger that their country may slip back. He praises the ancients for their reliance on colloquy, which needs to be carried on. Of course, for many years Shaftesbury had been conducting his own inward colloquy in his ΑΣΚΗΜΑΤΑ, which continually sharpened his thought, and it may have had to wait all these years to be mentioned because the third earl's own inward colloquy was so stoically bitter.

One is continually surprised when looking at how much Shaftesbury accomplished under such great difficulties. In part the answer is that he had so long been under attack by death, that he now feared it only as an interruption to his work. After a long bout with illness during the winter of 1710-1711, he must have been much cheered by the birth of the future fourth earl on 9 February 1711. This illness must also have convinced him that the only hope of completing his work was to journey to Italy, and in March 1711 he began a protracted series of letters to French authorities concerning his travels. He could no longer expect to survive a sea journey, nor a repetition of the journey through Eastern Europe that he had made on his first trip home from Italy, so that the only hope of getting there lay through France, now at war with England. He was surprised at how little difficulty French officials made for him. Indeed, they welcomed him wherever he went all the way from Calais to his last meeting with a French officer, a dinner on the frontier with Louis XIV's busy commander in the French Alps, the Duke of Berwick—son of James II and Arabella Churchill.

When his family—the son was too young to go along—arrived in Naples on 5 November 1711, three and one half wearying months of travel lay behind them. It was Lady Jane Shaftesbury, then, who first visited the Palazzo Mirelli in Chiaia, a western suburb, where they rented a portion of the house, and it was she who did most of the arduous work of getting them settled, buying everything from brooms to liveries and wall hangings, hiring servants, ordering calashes and all

sorts of animals, and arranging for windows to be glazed and fireplaces to be built.

But the earl was not idle long. In his preface to the collection of notes for a book entitled *Second Characters, or the Language of Forms*, published by Rand in 1914, he outlines the changes in his thought which had been taking place: the parallel effects of poetic and plastic art and the similar parallel in moral judgment; the identity of beauty and truth; and the notion of a perceivable wholeness in the universe. We have run into some of these ideas already, but now they are to be the central topics of an aesthetic rather than a moral thesis. In addition the later works stress the importance of colloquy in contrast to the dogmatism of the first version of the *Inquiry*; he becomes even less patient with the Deists who are the real dogmatists, he now feels, and the aesthetic impulses even affect his prose, making it more effective visually.

The *Second Characters* was to consist of four parts: the "Letter Concerning Design" makes a powerful statement of the dependence of art upon popular freedom; the second is an elaborate set of directions, which Shaftesbury originally wrote in French, so that his painter could follow them, *A Notion of the Historical Draught or Tablature of the Judgment of Hercules*; the third was not written; and the fourth is a complete set of notes for a very large book, "Plasticks, an Epistolary Excursion in the Original Progress and Power of Designatory Art," which amounts to a complete history of art and its techniques and theories up to the seventeenth century. Does all this mean that our moralist has turned aesthetician? Hardly. What has really happened is that his methods have changed. Given his early conviction of the immediate impact of art, and his final beliefs on how taste evolved, he was quite seriously attempting to construct a thoroughly moral aesthetic. If words alone cannot suffice to change man's behavior, perhaps art will.

Such convictions were enough to keep Shaftesbury busy, when neither his health nor the unexpectedly prolonged winter of 1711-1712 permitted him to go outside, but he had other interests that were also focused on art. For one thing, he decided that *Characteristicks* needed illustrations, and he must have been the ultimate designer of the highly emblematic plates that appeared in the second edition. He met Paolo de Matteis, judged to be first in rank among Neapolitan painters, bought a painting, and shortly thereafter had him at work on *The Judgment of Hercu-*

les. Intellectuals also began to visit him, and he especially delighted in the presence of the aging Don Giuseppe Valetta, who had the same sort of comprehensive genius represented by Benjamin Furly. In April he went forth and enjoyed showing Jane the scenes that had given him so much pleasure as a youth, and he was also able to repay in person the kindnesses of the viceroy, Count Borromeo, who extended to him protection in an area basically hostile to Englishmen. Toward the end of July, his periods of illness began to confine him more and more to the house, and he went into a gradual decline that convinced him that he would never see another spring. He faced death with fortitude, and even commissioned Paolo to paint him as a dying philosopher. He died at his house in Chiaia on 15 February 1713.

Letters:

Several Letters Written by a Noble Lord to a Young Man at the University (London: Printed for J. Roberts, 1716);

Letters from the Right Honorable the Late Earl of Shaftesbury, to Robert Molesworth, Esq. . . . with two letters written by the late Sir John Cropley, edited, with an introduction, by John Toland (London: Printed by W. Wilkins & sold by J. Peele, 1721);

Letters of the Earl of Shaftesbury collected into one volume (London, 1750).

Biography:

Thomas Fowler, *Shaftesbury and Hutcheson* (London: Sampson Low, Marston, Searle, & Rivington, 1882).

References:

Alfred Owen Aldridge, "Shaftesbury and the Deist Manifesto," *Transactions of the American Philosophical Society,* new series 41 (Philadelphia, 1951): 297-385;

R. L. Brett, *The Third Earl of Shaftesbury: A Study in Eighteenth-Century Literary Theory* (London: Hutchinson's University Library, 1951);

Ernst Cassirer, *The Platonic Renaissance in England,* translated by James P. Pettegrove (Austin: University of Texas Press, 1953);

Benedetto Croce, *Shaftesbury in Italy: The Presidential Address for 1923-4,* Publications of the Modern Humanities Research Association, no. 7 (Cambridge: Bowes & Bowes, 1924);

Esmond S. de Beer, ed., *The Correspondence of John Locke,* 9 volumes (Oxford: Oxford University Press, 1976-   );

Stanley Grean, *Shaftesbury's Philosophy of Religion and Ethics: A Study in Enthusiasm* (Athens: Ohio University Press, 1967);

Robert Marsh, *Four Dialectical Theories of Poetry: An Aspect of English Neoclassical Criticism* (Chicago: University of Chicago Press, 1965);

Felix Paknadel, "Shaftesbury's Illustrations of *Characteristics,*" *Journal of the Warburg and Courtauld Institute,* 37 (1974): 290-312;

Martin Price, *To the Palace of Wisdom: Studies in Order and Energy from Dryden to Blake* (Garden City, N.Y.: Doubleday, 1964);

Jerome Stolnitz, "On the Significance of Lord Shaftesbury in Modern Aesthetic Theory," *Philosophical Quarterly,* 11 (April 1961): 97-113;

J. E. Sweetman, "Shaftesbury's Last Commission," *Journal of the Warburg and Courtauld Institute,* 19 (1956): 110-116;

Esther M. Tiffany, "Shaftesbury as Stoic," *PMLA,* 38 (September 1923): 642-684;

Ernest L. Tuveson, *The Imagination as a Means of Grace: Locke and the Aesthetics of Romanticism* (Berkeley: University of California Press, 1960);

Robert Voitle, *The Third Earl of Shaftesbury* (Baton Rouge: University of Louisiana Press, 1984).

Papers:

The major collection of papers is in the Public Record Office, London, most of them designated PRO 30/24/19. Works derived from them, such as Rand's volumes, should be checked against the originals. Among other collections, the MSS. Locke in the Bodleian Library are the most valuable.

Richard Steele
(March 1672 - 1 September 1729)

Calhoun Winton
University of Maryland, College Park

See also the Steele entry in *DLB 84: Restoration and Eighteenth-Century Dramatists, Second Series.*

BOOKS: *The Procession. A Poem on Her Majesties Funeral. By a Gentleman of the Army* (London: Printed for Thomas Bennet, 1695);

The Christian Hero: An Argument Proving that no Principles but Those of Religion Are Sufficient to make a Great Man (London: Printed for J. Tonson, 1701);

The Funeral: or, Grief a-la-Mode. A Comedy. As it is Acted at The Theatre Royal in Drury-Lane, By His Majesty's Servants (London: Printed for Jacob Tonson, 1702);

The Lying Lover, or, The Ladies Friendship. A Comedy. As it is acted at the Theatre Royal *By Her Majesty's Servants* (London: Printed for Bernard Lintott, 1704);

The Tender Husband, or The Accomplish'd Fools. A Comedy. As it is Acted at the Theatre-Royal in Drury-Lane. By Her Majesty's Servants (London: Printed for Jacob Tonson, 1705);

Prologue to the University of Oxford. Written by Mr. Steel, and spoken by Mr. Wilks [broadside] (London: Printed for B. Lintott, 1706);

The Tatler. By Isaac Bickerstaff, Esq., nos. 1-271 (London: Printed by John Nutt for John Morphew, 12 April 1709 - 2 January 1711);

The Spectator, nos. 1-555, by Steele and Joseph Addison (London: Printed for Samuel Buckley & J. Tonson, 1 March 1711 - 6 December 1712);

The Englishman's Thanks to the Duke of Marlborough (London: Printed for A. Baldwin, 1712);

The Guardian, by Steele, Addison, and others, nos. 1-175 (London: Printed for J. Tonson, 12 March - 1 October 1713);

The Englishman: Being the Sequel of the Guardian, first series nos. 1-56 (London: Printed for Sam. Buckley, 6 October 1713 - 11 February 1714);

The Importance of Dunkirk Consider'd: In Defence of the Guardian of August the 7th. In a Letter to the Bailiff of Stockbridge (London: Printed for A. Baldwin, 1713);

The Crisis: Or, A Discourse Representing, from the most Authentick Records, the just Causes of the late Happy Revolution: and the several Settlements of the Crowns of England and Scotland on Her Majesty; and on the Demise of Her Majesty without Issue, upon the Most Illustrious Princess Sophia, Electress and Dutchess Dowager of Hanover, and The Heirs of Her Body Being Protestants . . . With Some Seasonable Remarks on the Danger of a Popish Successor (London: Printed by S. Buckley & sold by F. Burleigh, 1714);

The Englishman: Being the Close of the Paper so called, no. 57 (London: Printed for Ferd. Burleigh, 15 February 1714);

A Letter to a Member of Parliament Concerning the Bill for Preventing the Growth of Schism (London: Printed & sold by Ferd. Burleigh, 1714);

The French Faith Represented in the Present State of Dunkirk. A Letter to the Examiner, In Defense of Mr. S——le (London: Printed & sold by Ferd. Burleigh, 1714);

The Lover. Written in Imitation of the Tatler. By Marmaduke Myrtle, Gent., nos. 1-40 (London: Printed & sold by Ferd. Burleigh, 25 February - 27 March 1714);

The Reader, nos. 1-9 (London: Printed by Sam. Buckley, 22 April - 10 May 1714);

The Romish Ecclesiastical History of Late Years (London: Printed for J. Roberts, 1714);

Mr. Steele's Apology for Himself and His Writings; Occasioned by his Expulsion from the House of Commons (London: Printed & sold by R. Burleigh, 1714);

The Englishman, second series nos. 1-38 (London: Printed & sold by R. Burleigh, 11 July 1715 - 21 November 1715);

A Letter from the Earl of Mar to the King, Before His Majesty's Arrival in England. With some Remarks on my Lord's subsequent Conduct (London: Printed for Jacob Tonson, 1715);

Richard Steele, 1711 (portrait by Sir Godfrey Kneller; by permission of the National Portrait Gallery, London)

Town-Talk. In a Letter to a Lady in the Country, nos. 1-9 (London: Printed by R. Burleigh & sold by Burleigh, Anne Dodd, James Roberts & J. Graves, 17 December 1715 - 15 February 1716);

A Letter to a Member, &c. concerning the Condemn'd Lords, in Vindication of Gentlemen Calumniated in the St. James's Post *of Friday* March *the 2d* (London: Printed & sold by J. Roberts, J. Graves & A. Dodd, 1716);

Chit-Chat. In a Letter to a Lady in the Country. By Humphrey Philroye, nos. 1-3 (London: Printed & sold by R. Burleigh, March 1716);

An Account of the Fish-Pool, by Steele and Joseph Gillmore (London: Printed & sold by H. Meere, J. Pemberton & J. Roberts, 1718);

The Plebeian. . . . By a Member of the House of Com-

mons, nos. 1-4 (London, 14 March - 6 April 1719);

The Antidote, in a Letter to the Free-Thinker (London: Printed for J. Roberts, 1719);

The Antidote. Number II. In a Letter to the Free-Thinker (London: Printed for J. Roberts, 1719);

A Letter to the Earl of O——d, Concerning the Bill of Peerage (London: Printed for J. Roberts, 1719);

The Spinster: In Defence of the Woolen Manufactures (London: Printed for J. Roberts, 1719);

The Crisis of Property (London: Printed for W. Chetwood, J. Roberts, J. Brotherton & Charles Lillie, 1720);

A Nation a Family: Being the Sequel of the Crisis of Property (London: Printed for W. Chetwood,

J. Roberts, J. Brotherton & Charles Lillie, 1720);

The State of the Case Between the Lord-Chamberlain of His Majesty's Household, and the Governor of the Royal Company of Comedians. With the Opinions of Pemberton, Northey, and Parker, concerning the Theatre (London: Printed for W. Chetwood, J. Roberts, J. Graves & Charles Lillie, 1720);

The Theatre. By Sir John Edgar (London: Printed for W. Chetwood, J. Roberts & C. Lillie, 2 January - 5 April 1720);

A Prologue to the Town, as it was spoken at the theatre in Little Lincoln's Inn Fields. Written by Mr. Welstead. With an Epilogue on the same occasion, by Sir Richard Steele (London: Printed & sold by J. Brotherton & W. Meadows, J. Roberts, A. Dodd, W. Lewis & J. Graves, 1721);

The Conscious Lovers. A Comedy. As it is Acted at the Theatre Royal in Drury-Lane, By His Majesty's Servants (London: Printed for Jacob Tonson, 1723 [i.e., 1722]);

Pasquin, nos. 46 and 51 (London: Sold by J. Peele, 9 and 26 July 1723).

Editions: *Richard Steele*, edited, with an introduction and notes, by G. A. Aitken, Mermaid Series (London: Unwin / New York: Scribners, 1894)—includes notes and fragments of "The School of Action" from the Blenheim manuscripts, apparently since lost;

Tracts and Pamphlets by Richard Steele, edited by Rae Blanchard (Baltimore: Johns Hopkins Press, 1944);

Steele's The Englishman, edited by Blanchard (Oxford: Clarendon Press, 1955);

Steele's Political Journalism, 1714-16, edited by Blanchard (Oxford: Clarendon Press, 1959);

The Theatre, edited by John Loftis (Oxford: Clarendon Press, 1962);

The Spectator, 5 volumes, edited by Donald F. Bond (London: Oxford University Press, 1965);

The Plays of Richard Steele, edited by Shirley Strum Kenny (Oxford: Clarendon Press, 1971);

The Guardian, edited by John Calhoun Stephens (Lexington: University Press of Kentucky, 1982);

The Tatler, 2 volumes, edited by Bond (London: Oxford University Press, 1987).

PLAY PRODUCTIONS: *The Funeral*, London, Theatre Royal, Drury Lane, between 9 October and 11 December 1701;

The Lying Lover, Theatre Royal, Drury Lane, 2 December 1703;

The Tender Husband, Theatre Royal, Drury Lane, 23 April 1705;

The Conscious Lovers, Theatre Royal, Drury Lane, 7 November 1722.

Richard Steele was recognized, was indeed famous, in his own time as an innovative essayist, editor, and pamphleteer. No doubt the principal reasons for his being remembered today have to do with his activities as a writer of prose. His entry into the world of writing and publishing coincided exactly with the great explosion of printing after the Licensing Act expired in 1695, when government control over printing in the English-speaking world came to an abrupt end.

Steele was one of the first, it might be argued *the* first, to appreciate fully the consequences of this explosion, to understand the positive possibilities of the coming of print culture, when some of his most perceptive contemporaries saw only the dangers. Mass audiences for the first time in human history became theoretically available, and Richard Steele set about devising means of communicating with those audiences.

He was also a dramatist; he achieved his earliest recognition in London as a writer of popular comedies, and this should be remembered in assessing him as a prose writer. Dramatic concerns made their way into his prose writings. He was, for example, the virtual inventor of theater reviewing, which he introduced into the first issue of his *Tatler*, and his essay periodicals are a rich primary source of information about theatrical literature, personnel, and practices, as well as the locus of dramalike fictional scenes.

Richard Steele was born in Dublin in 1672, probably sometime in late February or early March because he was christened in St. Bride's parish church on 12 March of that year. His father, Richard Steele, an attorney, was a member of the Church of Ireland; he was, that is, a Protestant. Steele's mother was born Elinor Sheyles Symes; she was therefore a member of the ancient Irish family of O'Sheills; no doubt she was born a Roman Catholic. Steele came from divided ways; that may be one of the reasons the print medium, that great leveler of class and condition, appealed to him.

He did not spend his entire boyhood in Ireland, as did his contemporary Jonathan Swift; the elder Richard Steele died young and Richard his son was adopted, formally or informally, by his father's aunt Katherine and her second husband, Henry Gascoigne. As private secretary to James Butler, Duke of Ormonde, who was lord lieutenant of Ireland, Gascoigne was in a position to know that severe times were ahead for Ireland, and some time in the early 1680s he moved his household to London. Richard Steele was enrolled in the Charterhouse in November 1684, through Ormonde's influence. This was the beginning of his formal education as far as anyone knows. Charterhouse was, and still is, a demanding school, and Steele was forced into a curriculum rich with Latin and Greek, a late educational heritage of Renaissance humanism. In 1686 Joseph Addison, son of an Anglican priest, enrolled at the Charterhouse. London was an interesting and instructive place to be in the late 1680s, as the Catholic King James II attempted to recast British institutions in the old mold. London, by and large, resisted; so did the family circle in which Steele lived, a circle dominated by the presence of the duke of Ormonde; so of course did Addison's family connections. In 1688, with the coming of King William and Queen Mary in the revolution of that year, prospects looked better for Richard Steele than they ever had before.

On its social side the Charterhouse school was one of those winnowing institutions that English society has maintained for centuries, designed to educate to a passable extent the children of the aristocracy but also designed with places reserved for young men of unusual ability and not much in the way of financial resources who could be singled out and put on the road to education, leadership, and success. If one had inherited wealth and position, of course, one did not have to go to school at all and thus avoided the tiresome process of learning to translate Catullus and Horace. But for boys of intelligence and little money, boys such as Addison and Steele—or John Dryden, or Matthew Prior, or Samuel Johnson—schools such as the Charterhouse were steps up the social ladder. Influence helped, too. When Steele was ready for university in 1689, his foster father, Henry Gascoigne, was ready to help him: Gascoigne now had a place in King William's household, and he saw to it that young Richard was admitted to Christ Church, Oxford, the duke of Ormonde's old college. Aunt Katherine, who knew something about the value of appearances if not much about spelling, wrote Gascoigne, "[P]ray give him a pare of gloves, and Send him a Sord and Show him how to put it

one, That he may be like The young Lads nex doer."

Oxford, unlike London, provided little food for Steele's aesthetic imagination. Years later he looked back to his university days with an alumnus's fondness, but he never settled into the academic track. His friend Addison, who had preceded him there by two years, was already recognized as being on the way to a brilliant career. Lack of money probably made Steele restless, especially in a fashionable college such as Christ Church. In 1691 he migrated to Merton College as a portionista or postmaster, the name Merton has used over the centuries for its endowed scholarships. Legend has it that Steele wrote a comedy while he was at Merton but destroyed it on the advice of one of his fellow postmasters; nothing is known of what other writing, if any, he did at Oxford.

In the spring of 1692 King William was recruiting a larger army to pursue his campaign on the Continent against the French; in May of that year Steele went down from Merton, not to return as a student. At some time, presumably that spring, he enlisted as a trooper in the second troop of Life Guards, the royal bodyguard, then commanded by the young second duke of Ormonde, who had in 1688 succeeded his grandfather, Gascoigne's patron. Like their successors at Buckingham Palace today, the Life Guards were both a ceremonial and a fighting outfit. The second troop was on active service in Flanders for the campaigns of 1692 and 1693. Though the muster rolls do not exist to prove it, there seems no reason to doubt Steele's statement that he was there with them, as he reminisced years later, with a "broad Sword, Jack-Boots, and Shoulder-Belt, under the Command of the unfortunate Duke of *Ormond*."

Back in London, on guard duty in Whitehall and at St. James's Palace, Steele had plenty of time to pursue the advancement of his career, whatever that might turn out to be. Troopers of the Life Guards were officially referred to as "private gentlemen" and addressed as "Mister." With the Gascoignes living in London, providing a convenient address, Steele could see and be seen. In 1695 he left the Life Guards and joined the Coldstreamers, the second foot guards, commanded by John Baron Cutts, to whom Steele, not coincidentally, dedicated *The Procession*, a poem published in April. In April 1697 he was commissioned ensign in Lord Cutts's own company, with the brevet rank of captain. Hence, hereafter, Captain Steele.

Just at this time London was experiencing, more or less without recognizing it, the liberating effect brought about by the failure of King William to renew the Licensing Act in 1695. This act had severely limited the number of presses in the British Isles. When William had come ashore from Holland, in Exeter in 1688, he had been unable to find a printing press in the west of England on which to print his manifesto. None existed. Whatever the motives for William's action—whether he recognized the value of print for a sovereign or whether he sought some other means than the Licensing Act to control press and printing—the practical effect was to encourage the spread of printing throughout the English-speaking world.

The expansion of printing came in good time for Richard Steele. By 1700 his life and career seemed to have stalled: the Treaty of Ryswick had brought peace to Europe and unemployment to soldiers, though not to Steele himself. Much of what little money he had had literally gone up in smoke in alchemical experiments. He had fathered an illegitimate daughter and was financing her support; he had fought and won a duel in Hyde Park. Everything was in the past tense; at twenty-eight he had no prospects.

Then, suddenly, matters turned around. Like his fellow officers John Vanbrugh and George Farquhar, Steele turned to writing, producing in April 1701 his first major published work, a religious self-help book entitled *The Christian Hero*, and in December of that year his first play, *The Funeral*. Both were successes.

It was typical of Steele that he tried more than one road to fulfillment; for the rest of his active life, until his retirement to Wales, he would be mixing modes: writing poetry, prose, drama; living the soldier's life, the politician's life, the writer's life. This variety of experience contributed substantially to the success of what he wrote; several years later when he began his first, and in some ways his best, periodical, *The Tatler*, he took for it this motto from Juvenal's First Satire: "*Quicquid agunt homines . . . nostri farrago libelli*" (Whatever mankind does is grist for our mill).

Certainly the contrast in mode and manner between *The Christian Hero* and *The Funeral* is striking. *The Funeral* is a good-natured comedy about family relationships, with satiric touches and effective farcical episodes; *The Christian Hero* is a serious, even solemn work of popularized piety,

which, as Richard Dammers has shown, represents a response to the recent Stoic revival and an affirmation of ethical Christianity. The Christian heroes include Christ himself, Saint Paul, and, most significantly, King William III. From the point of view of his later career, perhaps the most interesting aspect of *The Christian Hero* is his inclusion of women and women's concerns. *The Christian Hero* was no masterpiece of prose: an early critic complained that he must have written it "on the Butt-end of a Musquet," but readers seem not to have minded: the book ran to some eight editions in his lifetime and was reprinted for many years. It is not farfetched to see *The Christian Hero* as part of William's effort to establish his presence in British, especially English, society, though Steele of course was sincere in his praise of the dour soldier-king.

Steele was given a commission as captain in the Thirty-Fourth Foot in 1702, probably partly because his book had attracted the right kind of attention, from the court's point of view. William's death in 1702, however, precluded any more royal favor, and Steele spent the next several years assigned to Landguard Fort in Suffolk, looking at the ships coming into and out of Harwich, and working on stage comedies in his spare time, which was plentiful. Two were actually produced: *The Lying Lover* in 1703, with indifferent success, and *The Tender Husband*, perhaps his best play, in 1705. *The Tender Husband* became a staple of the repertory theater, was revived every season except three for the next forty years, and was acted in the provinces and the American colonies for decades. With it Steele became an established figure in the London theater world.

He was feeling secure enough to sell his commission, probably in the spring of 1705, and to marry a widow, Margaret Stretch, who possessed a considerable estate in Barbados. By the end of 1706 she had died, but Steele, whether through charm, influence, or a combination of these, had received his first civil preferment—which was worth one hundred pounds a year, tax free—as gentleman waiter to Queen Anne's husband, Prince George of Denmark. At Margaret's funeral Steele met a young woman from Wales, Mary Scurlock—possibly a family friend—and on 9 September 1707 they were married, after a waiting period just within the bounds of social decorum. During the courtship Steele commenced a correspondence which continued until the death of Mary, or "Dear Prue" as Steele addressed her, in pregnancy in 1718. Preserved with meticulous

The first issue of Steele's first periodical, in which he promised to tell male readers "what to think" while also providing "Entertainment to the Fair Sex"

care by Mary, who evidently had a keener sense of literary merit than she has been given credit for, these hundreds of notes and letters written at all hours of the day and night and in every variety of emotional state constitute one of the great archives of the personal letter. Produced in an era when letter writing evolved from mere communication to an art form, Steele's letters to Dear Prue are comparable in quality with those of Swift or Horace Walpole or Fanny Burney, but entirely different in their character.

About the time he got married, in 1707, Steele received more preferment, this time a post in which, he fondly imagined, he could use his literary talents. He was appointed writer of the *London Gazette*, the official government news medium. His friends in the circle of Whig leaders known as the Junto recognized that theirs was becoming an age of political pamphleteering and that party leaders needed writers to help them get into office and to defend them when they were there. Steele received the appointment for political reasons, though the post was ostensibly nonpartisan, and lost it for the same reasons a few years later when the tide of politics turned against the Whigs, but the experience he gained in putting a newspaper out twice a week was invaluable. He was forced to learn about printer's deadlines, about distribution networks, about readership, even if he did not use those terms which were yet to be coined. This was beginning journalism when journalism itself was in the course of being invented. It paid well, too: three hundred pounds a year, which together with the hundred from his position as gentleman waiter totaled four hundred, a sum sufficient to keep a couple of modest tastes in considerable comfort.

But Steele's tastes were never modest. By 1708 he was involved in a lawsuit having to do with the estate of his first wife, and about that time he must have been meditating on ways to increase the family income. As it happened, that year Jonathan Swift was in London, casting his keen eye about for satiric targets. One target of opportunity was John Partridge, a former shoe repairman, now a quack doctor and astrologer, who was making a fortune by publishing an annual almanac full of vague predictions. Swift published his own *Predictions for the Year 1708*, writing under the name of one Isaac Bickerstaff, in which Bickerstaff, also an astrologer, predicted precisely the death of Partridge. In his next almanac Partridge, incredibly, denied that he was dead. London wits joined the chase; Swift himself produced an anonymous, richly ironic *Vindication of Isaac Bickerstaff, Esq.* (1709). A year after the publication of Swift's *Predictions for the Year 1708* everyone in literary London knew about John Partridge and his rival, Isaac Bickerstaff.

Steele and Swift were still enjoying amicable relations—political differences would soon change that—and, when Steele decided to publish a periodical paper on his own time (he was also editing the *Gazette*), he chose "Isaac Bickerstaff " as the name of the putative editor for *The Tatler*. On 12 April 1709 Bickerstaff produced the first number of his new paper, "By *Isaac Bickerstaff*, Esq.," a folio half sheet printed on both sides and resembling to twentieth-century eyes an oversized handbill, about eight inches by thirteen and a half. In the first issue Bickerstaff announced that he would tell his male readers "what to think," and that he would provide something of "Entertainment to the Fair Sex." Steele gave away the first four issues, then charged a penny each. The paper was to be published three times a week, to coincide with the mails posted to provincial towns. *The Tatler* proved to be a runaway success, without question the most

successful periodical in any language to that time.

This was not solely, or even principally, because of the Partridge-Bickerstaff controversy. Success was a result of Steele's own experience, judgment, and acumen. Even with the Licensing Act serving as a rein on press activity before 1695, many newspapers and periodicals of various kinds had been published earlier than 1709—public newspapers such as the *Gazette* and privately owned papers such as the *Daily Courant*. Some periodicals, such as the *Athenian Mercury*, were devoted entirely to questions and answers. Defoe was in the fifth year of his *Review*, which carried both news and editorial opinion. Steele identified and combined the appeals of various periodicals into one. The question-and-answer and the hoax letter appeared, for example—sometimes separate, sometimes combined—transfigured as the letter to the editor; shrewd editors have exploited the same device ever since. News was included at first to attract readers; Steele felt that as gazetteer he would have access to the freshest foreign news in the form of diplomatic reports. For various reasons this stratagem did not work out, and news as such gradually disappeared from *The Tatler*, though matters of topical interest continued to appear in differing forms.

The principal appeals, however, were just those Bickerstaff had announced in the first issue: variety, entertainment for the women and information for the men, and actually both for both. This is Horace's *prodesse aut delectare*, instruction and entertainment, in a new format attractive to the widest possible audience. Horace he had read at Charterhouse and Oxford; the possibility of a mass audience was a product of his observing the oncoming print culture. Ostensibly the audience addressed was the inner circle of wit and learning, those who knew of and laughed at the Partridge-Bickerstaff hoax. But Steele was speaking over the heads of these to the vastly larger circle of readers in London and the provinces and even the colonies who wanted to be told how to act, what to read, what—as Bickerstaff had put it in the first issue—to think; who wanted to learn these things outside of church or chapel and yet who were suspicious of the libertinism associated with the literary life since Charles II's reign. From our perspective in the twentieth century we see Steele's activities as an early aspect of the British Enlightenment.

On the practical side Steele had to contend with the triweekly demand for copy, with the re-

Frontispiece to The Lucubrations of Isaac Bickerstaff Esq. *(1710-1711), the first collected edition of* The Tatler

strictions of space which the half-sheet format imposed on him, and with the expenses of running a periodical. He had to fill his paper three times a week; it was a small paper but every copy cost money. How to balance these demands he had to learn on the job. No one had ever run a paper like this one, and so there was no one to tell him. In the first number he set up various departments: one for news, one for "poetry" (that is, literary and theatrical matters), another for "accounts of learning," and a fourth for "gallantry, pleasure, and entertainment." This gave him enough scope for variety, but since the maximum number of words that could be set on both sides of the half sheet was about three thousand, using all four departments each issue would make for short entries. In addition advertisements had to be accommodated. Advertisements, which were placed at the end of the editorial matter, meant income, but they also absorbed precious space. Furthermore, as the popularity of the paper increased so did the demand for advertising space. Editorial and business decisions had to be made by Steele, three times a week, every week. Modern journalism was born.

His decisions had consequences, but readers of *The Tatler* did not, it goes without saying, concern themselves with consequences; their response was simply to read or not read the paper. Steele developed a spectrum of strategies to keep them reading, introducing, for example, theatrical criticism in *Tatler* number 1 and continuing it regularly thereafter. This was an important development: for the first time actors and dramatic authors could look forward to seeing in print regular comment on the plays they had appeared in or written. Within a few weeks Bickerstaff was beginning to receive letters to the editor, and in *Tatler* number 9 he reported that he had received a communication from his "ingenious Kinsman" Humphrey Wagstaff, a poem written "in a Way perfectly new." Wagstaff was Jonathan Swift, and the poem was his "Description of the Morning," printed for the first time. From this point on Steele would be soliciting contributions from his friends and acquaintances for *The Tatler* and for its successors. These were always printed anonymously; when he wound up the papers Steele would sometimes identify the authors, and sometimes he would not, presumably according to the desires of the writers themselves. As far as one knows, there was no direct compensation for the contributions at first, but the prestige and wide readership of the papers made them good places in which to be published. Over the next three years Steele would publish more of Swift's work and contributions from, among many others, John Gay, Alexander Pope, and most important, Joseph Addison. In 1713 he printed several essays by the young philosopher George Berkeley in *The Guardian*. A legend has it that Berkeley was rewarded with a dinner at Steele's elegant new house and a guinea gold coin for each essay; if so, this would be perhaps the earliest example of direct payment for a journalistic contribution. Twenty-five years later Samuel Johnson would be making his living in London by this means.

In the early days of *The Tatler* Steele used the "departments" which he had set up in the first issue; this made for short entries of a few hundred words under each by- (or, more properly, from-) line. Fairly soon the paper evolved toward the single essay of some fifteen hundred or two thousand words that would take up both sides of the half sheet, less the advertising. This was the informal essay, derived ultimately from Montaigne, which became in *Tatler* form the periodical essay and gave the name to its vehicle, the essay periodical. Use of the essay form in periodicals was not new: Defoe had been writing them in his *Review* since 1704. It never became the exclusive form in *The Tatler* partly because the narrative persona, Isaac Bickerstaff, was inflexible. Defoe could write his essays more or less in his own voice, whereas Steele was constrained by the narrative mediation of Bickerstaff the astrologer, who was at the same time both an impediment and a benefit.

The persona of Isaac Bickerstaff had provided a starting point for the paper and an apparently convenient mask behind which Richard Steele could exercise his editorial authority. As the paper continued Bickerstaff took on a life of his own, attracted other kinspeople, including Humphrey Wagstaff and Jenny Distaff, who wrote him letters, and eventually achieved celebrity status by having his "portrait" drawn, from which prints were made and sold to the public. Bickerstaff was invited to a performance at the Drury Lane theater and someone—Steele in disguise?—attended and was applauded. By this time he had adopted the mock-heroic but half-serious title "Censor of Great Britain," bestowed on him by a correspondent in number 140.

Mock-heroic because Isaac Bickerstaff was no Marcus Porcius Cato, the stern Censor of the Roman republic; but also half-serious because one of the principal themes of *The Tatler*, and *The Spectator*, was the reform of manners. This subject is difficult to treat without appearing either pedantic or obvious. The virtues Steele, and Addison after him, advocated in this reform are the ordinary, homely ones: good sense, decency, kindness, simple generosity. Their reform is in the direction of tolerance and accommodation rather than stiffer laws and regulated conduct. Steele, for example, opposed dueling, with its strict code of "honor." He knew about dueling's cruelty because in June 1700 he had wounded Captain Henry or Harry Kelly with his sword in Hyde Park, and watched the blood run out of his body. There must be better ways, he might have thought then, to settle these things; later, in his periodicals, he would suggest some.

In the summer of 1709 Steele was fully employed: he had a new member of his family, his daughter Elizabeth, born in March, and he was meeting five deadlines a week, two for the *Gazette* and three for *The Tatler*. "Don't be displeased that I do not come home till eleven o'clock," he wrote Prue. Still, he had reason for satisfaction; he received another sinecure, a commissionership of the Stamp Office, at three hundred pounds a year. Better yet, his new paper was succeeding. The *British Apollo*, a question-and-answer journal, complained that it had lost "near two thousand Subscribers" to Bickerstaff but then went on to "recommend him to the Reading of all our Subscribers." Here is journalistic generosity indeed! Imitators appeared: *The Tatling Harlot, Titt for*

Joseph Addison and Richard Steele at the time they were collaborating on The Tatler

Tatt, The Grouler, and the longest-lived and best, "Mrs. Crackenthorpe's" *Female Tatler.*

This imitation may have gratified Steele's sensibility; nevertheless, a deadline was a deadline, and he desperately needed help. In the autumn of 1709, he received some. In September his friend and schoolmate Joseph Addison returned from Ireland, where he had been serving as secretary to the lord lieutenant, Thomas, Lord Wharton. From time to time he began contributing a department or an entire essay to *The Tatler.* It was still very much Steele's paper, however—he probably wrote three-quarters of the total wordage—and he did not scruple to take it into political areas where the more cautious Addison would hesitate to venture. In the fourth number and again in number 130, he heaped praise on members of the government, who were mostly his patrons the Junto Whigs. The new Tory paper, *The Examiner,* which was secretly sup-

ported by Robert Harley in his bid for political power, advised Bickerstaff, "Give me leave to tell you, you mistake your talent, whenever you meddle with matters of state . . ." (31 August 1710).

By the summer of 1710 the political balance of power was shifting visibly. In June the queen, with Harley's approval, dismissed Steele's immediate supervisor, Charles Spencer, Earl of Sunderland, from his post as secretary of state. Steele chose to fly his colors by publishing a series of partisan political *Tatlers* in June and July; in August Henry St. John, a leader of the resurgent Tories, associated Bickerstaff with a "Factious Cabal" in *A Letter to the Examiner.* In the middle of October Steele resigned the editorship of the *London Gazette,* as Harley consolidated his position. Steele's principles would not let him support a ministry which would, he knew, be hostile to his hero, John Churchill, Duke of Marlborough. Toward the end of 1710 Steele decided to wind *The Tatler* up; possibly it was the price Harley exacted from him for keeping the commissionership of stamps. He and his paper had become identified with the Whigs.

It had been an exciting time for Steele: in a year and a half *The Tatler* had established itself as far and away the outstanding periodical in English. In that same period of time Steele's image had been transformed in the London mind from that of a minor playwright and Junto Whig follower to that of Isaac Bickerstaff, Censor of Great Britain, editor of the best-known paper in the land. When he published the last *Tatler* on 2 January 1711, and signed it with his own name rather than Bickerstaff's, Steele must have realized that he possessed handsome resources; he was not yet forty years old and full of plans.

Addison was back in London, permanently, and as a Whig out of office he had time on his hands. He and Steele were able to plan a new periodical with some care; it was probably Addison's prudential counsel that led them to adopt a nonpartisan stance for it. The immediate political future was rather clear: the now-dominant Tories would attempt to discredit the duke of Marlborough and displace him from his position as commander-in-chief of the allied armies battling France. If Steele wished to write Whig propaganda, he could do so over his own signature. Both editors now had general experience in journalism and particular experience in essay periodicals. Steele was especially familiar with the business side of publishing. He would be the general editorial supervisor, responsible for seeing the paper through the press. Because a six-day-a-week publishing schedule was envisioned, two printing shops were signed on to take care of the anticipated volume, to be assisted at various times in the distribution by at least a dozen other establishments. On 1 March 1711, two months after the final *Tatler* appeared, Addison and Steele brought out the first issue of their new periodical, *The Spectator*. Like *The Tatler*, it found a waiting reading public and prospered from the first, as Steele, at least, devoutly hoped because he was being sued for debt at the time. It appeared daily except Sunday until 6 December 1712, a total of five hundred and fifty-five issues. As regards style, content, method, *The Spectator* is Addison's as *The Tatler* was Steele's. In the first number, for example, the narrator, self-described as "a Spectator of Mankind," declares that he has "never espoused any Party with violence, and am resolved to observe an exact Neu-

trality between the Whigs and Tories, unless I shall be forced to declare my self by the Hostilities of either Side."

In the second number he describes the Club of which he is a member: Sir Roger de Coverley, the country squire; an unnamed attorney; Sir Andrew Freeport, the eminent merchant; Captain Sentry, the retired army officer; Will Honeycomb, the aging fop; and the anonymous philosophic clergyman. These are intended to replace in a sense the various departments of *The Tatler*, offering Addison and Steele the opportunity to move in various directions as far as subject matter is concerned and at the same time separating the authors from their materials.

Although the various departments of *The Tatler* are abandoned and *The Spectator* moves toward a single-essay format (always with advertisements, however), considerable variety could be achieved even within that more restrictive format. Steele's number 11, for example, begins with the satiric presentation of a male-chauvinist fop who is put down by Mr. Spectator's learned friend Arietta, first as she reapplies one of Aesop's fables to him and then as she recites the story of Inkle and Yarico. Inkle is an English merchant who is left ashore in America by his companions but rescued and sheltered by the Indian maiden Yarico. They fall in love, and when a ship appears several months later bound for Barbados, the couple board it. In Barbados Inkle sells the pregnant Yarico into slavery, making "use of that Information [that she is pregnant], to rise in his Demands upon the Purchaser." This single "essay" thus proceeds from casual fictional comedy, presented in dramatic terms, to a pointed satire on male hypocrisy, to a poignant narrative depicting man's—and mankind's—inhumanity to mankind. The exuberant variety of *The Spectator*, like that of *The Tatler*, is one of the ingredients of its popular appeal, but the variety also renders formal literary criticism difficult; in fact, Michael Ketcham's *Transparent Designs* (1985) is, perhaps surprisingly, the first book-length essay in criticism on it ever published.

On the other hand, some aspects of the paper contribute to unity rather than variety: among others, the Club motif itself, of course; the various essay series; and the editorial tone. The Club, as Ketcham has pointed out, has the inward, unifying quality of such an organization, but is also infinitely extensible, so as to include all the periodicals' readers in its membership. The series, such as the twelve essays on "The Plea-

Richard Steele, 1712 (portrait by Jonathan Richardson; by permission of the National Portrait Gallery, London)

sures of the Imagination" or the eighteen on *Paradise Lost*, are largely the work of Addison, but Steele's many essays on the theater and drama also have a unity of attitude if not of focus. Editorial tone is the great unifying principle—and the great triumph of the editors: learned, witty, affable, faintly pedantic, slightly patronizing, it spoke to readers who were in the midst of the Enlightenment without realizing it.

Although *The Spectator* steered clear for the most part of direct political involvement, Steele and Addison discreetly arranged the paper's presentation so that the Whigs and commercial interests would at least not be depreciated. Sir Roger de Coverley, the Tory squire, is depicted as lovable but ineffectual, in sharp contrast to Sir Andrew Freeport, the merchant of broad vision who "will tell you that it is a stupid and barbarous Way to extend Dominion by Arms; for true

Power is to be got by Arts and Industry." Still, it behooved the authors to tread cautiously: 1711 and 1712 were turbulent years in British politics, and Steele needed the money the paper was garnering, in large amounts. Swift meanwhile had taken over, anonymously, editorial direction of the Tory periodical *The Examiner*, and in November 1711 published his brilliant pamphlet *The Conduct of the Allies*, which sought to discredit not only the departed Whig government, Steele's friends and patrons, but also the series of campaigns on the Continent directed by the much-admired duke of Marlborough. Marlborough was dismissed from all offices in December, and in January 1712 Steele published in reply to Swift a short pamphlet over the pseudonym "Scoto-Britannus," *The Englishman's Thanks to the Duke of Marlborough*. Although undistinguished in itself, it represents the first of many political pamphlets written by Steele over the succeeding ten years. Swift's and Steele's differing opinions about the great duke would result in the end of their friendship. As 1712 progressed, the Tories tightened their control of the government and pursued the peace treaty their political strategy called for.

By the end of the year 1712 Addison and Steele were ready to close out their paper, perhaps because both wanted to move on to something new, to end the game while they were ahead. With number 555 of 6 December 1712 the original series ended, Steele acknowledging over his signature some of those who had helped. In number 550 Addison, as Mr. Spectator, had remarked on his taciturnity, adding that he has "Thoughts of being very loquacious in the Club which I now have under Consideration." It was to begin "on the twenty-fifth of March next."

By that time Addison was involved with completing his tragedy *Cato* and seeing about its production at Drury Lane. Steele, therefore, began the new paper, *The Guardian*, on 12 March 1713, precisely as Mr. Spectator had predicted. He continued to edit it except for a month's relief by Addison in August until he brought it to a close on 1 October of that year. A folio half sheet in format, *The Guardian* continued the demanding six-issues-a-week schedule of *The Spectator*. Obviously Steele could not write it all himself, and he sought assistance from his acquaintances. Addison's 53 *Guardians* represent almost a third of the final total of 175 numbers. Alexander Pope was an important—and controversial—contributor. Steele entertained the young philosopher George Berkeley, just in from Dublin, at his fine new house in Bloomsbury Square and, as noted above, eventually printed about a dozen of his essays in the paper.

The persona of *The Guardian* was one Nestor Ironside, whose name bespeaks elderly wisdom and toughness; in the first number he declares his resolve to "make the Pulpit, the Bar, and the Stage, all act in Concert in the Care of Piety, Justice, and Virtue." Reform and entertainment as usual; the mixture of enlightenment and chitchat which had been proven in *The Spectator* were to remain the staple of *The Guardian*. Ironside has friends, a numerous Northamptonshire family named Lizard, who reside at Lizard Hall. Steele evidently expected them to take over some of the functions of Mr. Spectator's Club; in the seventh *Guardian*, for example, Nestor visits Lady Lizard at her tea table and participates in a discussion about the proper age for marriage. Mary

Lizard writes in number 43 of her attendance at Addison's *Cato*, with her brother Tom. Steele appears to have wearied of the idea: the Lizards never achieve the reality of Sir Roger de Coverley and his crew.

In number 98 Nestor describes his intention to set up a lion's mouth at Button's Coffeehouse, like the legendary receptacle in Venice, where communications could be deposited for the paper. A "lion" he had earlier identified as a "great Man's Spy." Some of the amusing letters he received did come by way of Button's lion; many were perhaps commissioned, such as that on sacred poetry by Steele's friend Edward Young, fellow of All Souls, Oxford. Steele wrote letters to the editor, to himself, as he had been doing ever since the days of *The Tatler*. Steele was busy. He had four children at home now, and was still supporting his illegitimate daughter. Perhaps he was so busy that he did not take in Alexander Pope's ploy in number 40, when he received copy for the paper from Pope. Pope been irritated by the praise of Ambrose Philips's pastorals in number 22; he felt his own work in the genre had been overlooked. *Guardian* number 40 is a straightfaced demonstration that Philips's pastorals are after all very like the Grub Street ballads of Tom D'Urfey. Philips was furious—he is said to have kept a switch on the bar at Button's, for use if Pope happened by. Steele presumably was embarrassed—but the controversy sold papers. Theatrical criticism, which Steele had virtually invented in *The Tatler*, continued as a popular feature in the new paper. John Gay's new comedy, *The Wife of Bath*, is handsomely puffed by Nestor Ironside in number 50.

Politics kept Swift from contributing to Steele's paper: they were entirely on opposite sides of the political fence now, with Swift providing hints for the Tory *Examiner* in its attacks on Marlborough, and on Steele himself. During the summer of 1713 Steele decided to sever all remaining ties with the Tory Ministry and run for Parliament in the general elections which were approaching in the fall. He resigned his preferments, including his earliest, the pension as gentleman waiter to Queen Anne's late husband. In early August Steele published a fiery political paper, *Guardian* number 128, in which he arraigned the government's conduct in certain aspects of the recently concluded Treaty of Utrecht. Fortifications for the port of Dunkirk, which the treaty had specified for removal, were still there, Steele complained. Propagandists, on

Richard Steele circa 1713 (perhaps a copy of a portrait by Sir James Thornhill; from Willard Connely,
Sir Richard Steele, *1934)*

Robert Harley's payroll, including Daniel Defoe, chose to interpret this as an attack on the queen; *The Examiner* (21 August 1713) called Steele's paper a "scandalous libel." In spite of the government's opposition, Steele was elected a member of Parliament for the borough of Stockbridge in Hampshire.

Elated no doubt by his election, Steele turned *The Guardian* over to Addison in September and on 22 September published a pamphlet called *The Importance of Dunkirk Consider'd*, which marked his full-time entry into the propaganda wars. The pamphlet sold well, going to a third edition within a week, and the Tories determined to strike back at Steele, along two lines of attack. The first was to find ways of expelling him from his seat in Parliament; the second was by direct answers to his pamphlet. Defoe published an anonymous reply in September and Swift his masterly ad hominem attack on Steele, *The Importance of*

the Guardian Considered, also anonymous, in October.

By then, Steele had ended *The Guardian*, on 1 October, without notice or explanation. It had been a fine periodical, second in quality only to *The Tatler* and *The Spectator*, but its reputation has suffered because Steele was caught up in the political battle. Even contributors such as Addison felt constrained to distance themselves somewhat from Steele and thus from the paper he had started and seen through to the end. On 6 October Steele began still another periodical, this one styled *The Englishman*, the narrator of which related that he had "purchased the Lion, Desk, Pen, Ink, and Paper, and all other Goods of NESTOR IRONSIDE, Esq." This was going to be a political paper; in the first issue Steele addressed a letter to Harley over his own name in which he announced his independence as a member of Parliament: "I am accountable to no Man, but the greatest Man in *England* is accountable to me."

We'll see about that, said Harley and the Tories in effect: *The Examiner* began to track Steele's paper closely; behind the scenes, preparations continued for his expulsion from Parliament when the new session opened. At first Steele tried to make at least a gesture toward matters of general interest, including, for example, a discussion of the formation of literary taste in number 7, and, importantly, an account in number 26 of Alexander Selkirk's marooning on Juan Fernandez Island, a paper that has often been cited as a source for Daniel Defoe's *Robinson Crusoe* (1719). Sometime in late 1713 Steele had business in Oxford; after a sentimental tour of his old haunts he wrote a celebration of the university in number 34 for 22 December. It was a turning point; henceforth the pages of the journal were closed to everything but politics. He was at the same time preparing a pamphlet on the present situation, as the Whigs saw it, to be titled *The Crisis* (1714).

The crisis in question was that of royal succession: Queen Anne's health, never hearty, had worsened, and worries were widespread that the Catholic Pretender might be introduced on her death. The Tories took the position that there was no such thing as a crisis, and that Steele's allegations about a crisis constituted sedition. When Steele's pamphlet was published with his name on the title page as author, it had a sensational sale: a hostile writer estimated that forty thousand copies were sold by subscription. No masterpiece of prose, *The Crisis* nevertheless made its point as Whig propaganda. In retrospect, one can see its importance as a landmark of propaganda, the earliest use of mass printing, advertising, and distribution techniques in a political context. Steele lent his encyclopedic knowledge of printing and distribution to the Whig cause: the employment of coordinated multiple printing presses and distribution networks, which had been invented to manufacture and circulate his periodicals, both within London and to provincial towns, was here devoted to political rather than literary ends. What the twentieth century would term mass-media techniques had come to politics. The example of *The Crisis* was not lost on politicians.

It demanded an answer by the Tories. Jonathan Swift's reply, published anonymously as usual with Swift, is one of his best pieces of political rhetoric, *The Publick Spirit of the Whigs* (1714). Swift met Steele's arguments by blandly denying that the Hanoverian succession was in danger at all and proceeding against the Whig author himself, branding his doubts about the situation "seditious."

This was a key word: Harley's ministry intended to punish Steele by charging him with sedition. Unlike most political writers of the day, he had signed his name to his propaganda, giving a convenient handle to his enemies. The result was a foregone conclusion: the Tories had the votes in the House of Commons and could make the charge stick. Although ably defended by Robert Walpole, Steele was expelled on 18 March 1714, by a vote of 245 to 152. It was only a paper defeat, however; within the year the Tories were out, after Queen Anne's death, and Steele was back in Parliament. No one could foresee this outcome, of course, and Steele returned to journalism, to help pay his many creditors.

Perhaps anticipating his expulsion, he had started a new periodical in February: *The Lover*, edited by one "Marmaduke Myrtle, Gent." As its name implies, love was its theme, or, as Marmaduke describes it in the first number, its purpose was "to trace the Passion or Affection of Love, through all its Joys and Inquietudes. . . ." This was a topic on which Richard Steele could pronounce with some authority. He had occasional assistance for this three-a-week publication, but *The Lover* was essentially his own. That spring the Scriblerus Club was meeting: Pope, Gay, Swift, John Arbuthnot, and Harley, literary Tories. Steele was on the other side of the fence politically, but he used a quotation from the newly expanded *Rape of the Lock* in his paper. *The Rape of the Lock* clearly fit the paper's organizing motif, being concerned with love, but the quotation was also intended as a friendly gesture on Steele's part. On 27 May, with issue number 40, Steele wound the paper up. Although *The Lover* is almost forgotten now, it was highly regarded in Steele's day: five collected editions appeared in his lifetime and four more before the end of the century. It contains some of his most effective writing.

He started a new political paper in April, *The Reader*, but it lacked distinction and survived for only nine numbers, expiring without warning on 10 May. The political situation had seemingly been almost talked out. However, in that same month he published *The Romish Ecclesiastical History of Late Years*, ostensibly an account of the canonization of several saints by Pope Clement XI. Interspersed with descriptions of the ceremony are speeches by Cardinal Gualterio that present politi-

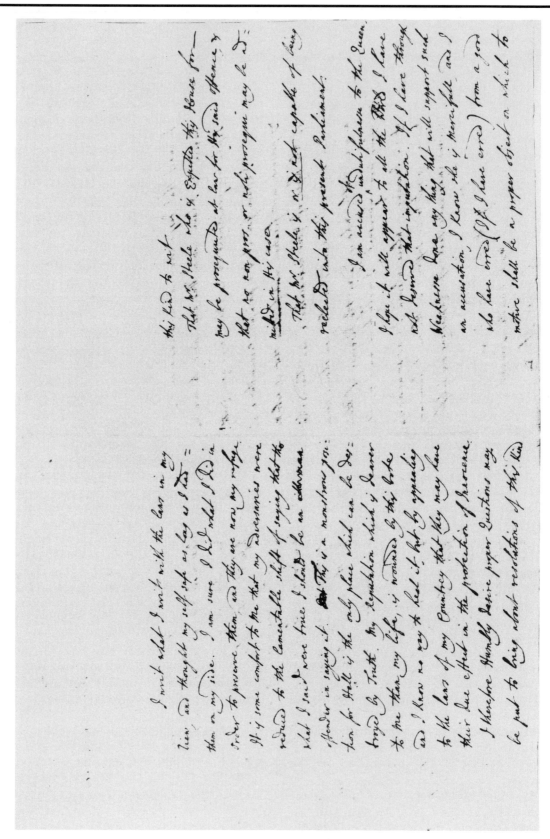

Pages from Steele's 19 March 1714 letter to Sir Thomas Hanmer, Speaker of the House of Commons, written the day after Steele was expelled from Parliament (by permission of the Pierpont Morgan Library)

cal conditions in England to the pope. These fictitious creations by Steele are intended to associate the English Jacobites, supporters of the Roman Catholic Pretender, with the Church of Rome, and of course, the Tories with the Jacobites. It was a propaganda line possessing special urgency in the spring of 1714, when the queen's health was deteriorating, but it proved to have enduring vitality even after the queen's death: if the English public could be persuaded that Tories were really Catholic Jacobites, or Jacobite sympathizers in disguise, the Tories could be (and were) kept out of office for decades. This turned out to be a potent argument, however specious in fact it might be—the English Catholics were a tiny, almost powerless, minority. Echoes appear more than thirty years later, in Henry Fielding's *Tom Jones* (1749), where Fielding portrays Tom's servant Partridge as a crypto-Jacobite. If Steele did not invent the line, he certainly implemented its circulation.

In the spring of 1714 the threat of the Pretender's return seemed real enough to Steele and his Whig associates, and in fact the Tory ministry was engaged in secret negotiations with the Pretender, looking toward his possible return. The queen, however, still possessed some power of her own; after dismissing Robert Harley, Earl of Oxford, on her deathbed she handed the treasurer's white staff of office to Charles Talbot, Duke of Shrewsbury, a Hanover Tory. Queen Anne's death on 1 August 1714 signaled a change of momentous consequence for most of the important writers of the time: Swift and his Tory associates would be in opposition for the rest of their lives—and would produce satire of enduring brilliance, from their point of view as outsiders. Addison, Steele, and their Whig colleagues now made up the government; their literary output dwindled. Politics came first—*had* to come first if one was in the governing majority as both Addison and Steele now were.

Paradoxically, and sadly, the literary partnership which had been so fruitful in the days of *The Tatler* and *The Spectator* was nearing an end. Addison revived *The Spectator*, but Steele did not contribute. In a few years the former partners found themselves on different sides of a political dispute, and at Addison's death, in 1719, they were estranged, perhaps not on speaking terms. Addison had achieved high political office, becoming a secretary of state in 1717, and was immensely rich, with an official income estimated at about ten thousand pounds a year. Steele's political rewards were more modest but they were considerable: a safe seat in Parliament was found for him, Boroughbridge in Yorkshire, to which he was duly elected in 1715. He leased a house with a fashionable address for his family, 26 St. James's Street, just up the hill from the palace. In October 1714 he was named governor of the theater in Drury Lane, where his comedies had been produced, with a stipend of seven hundred pounds a year, and on 9 April 1715 he was knighted by King George I. Sir Richard's knighthood, pleasing as it was to this Irish orphan, was of course a political reward, and he knew it. It was bestowed not on the essayist and dramatist but on the pamphleteer and member of Parliament. As such, he was expected by the governing Whig coalition to render support to their policies, in the House of Commons and in the press. Steele was willing to do so, but only up to a point, the point at which their policies conflicted with his beliefs. This was to cause him plenty of problems.

He was active in the management of Drury Lane, and very busy in Parliament, sitting on more than a dozen committees during his first year of service in the House. The government called on him to start a periodical that would be used to discredit the fallen Tories, a group which included the duke of Ormonde. In June 1715 the impeachment of Robert Harley, Earl of Oxford, was moved, and on 11 July Steele began his new paper, called *The Englishman* like his periodical of 1713-1714, but published anonymously. He was not especially happy in his assignment; he had, after all, ridden with Ormonde and had worked for and respected Harley. He dutifully ground out the twice-a-week propaganda sheet, which sold a few hundred copies an issue, a flyspeck compared to the circulation of *The Tatler* and *The Spectator*. Still, the paper made money. Steele and his printer, the veteran Samuel Buckley, now knew how to adjust their operations so that the theoretical break-even point was a mere 240 copies sold per issue. Low break-even points, Steele had discovered, were an important factor in the burgeoning popularity of essay periodicals.

When word reached London that the Pretender had invaded Scotland, Steele had a topic that he could treat with enthusiasm. Instead of harrying defeated politicians, his task was now that of sounding the alarm. This was civil war, and the theme Steele emphasized was James the Pretender's Catholicism. Many ordinary Englishmen thought highly of the House of Stuart and had no regard for the German Hanoverian kings, but nothing like a majority could possibly be assembled in favor of a Catholic sovereign. The defeat of a Jacobite army at Preston in early November 1715 signaled the beginning of the end for the rebels. With the prospect of another session of Parliament and a new season at Drury Lane before him, Steele ended the life of the second *Englishman* with number 38 on 21 November.

He was working about this time on a biography of his hero—and Swift's archvillain—the duke of Marlborough, apparently being supplied biographical materials by the duke and duchess, but it was a project he never finished. More to his style of the literary life was an essay periodical, and he started another one in December, *Town-Talk. In a Letter to a Lady in the Country.* Drury Lane was experiencing a disappointing season, and it may be that Steele's fellow actor-managers persuaded him to begin the new paper, which would supply that lady in the country and her counterparts in London with news of what was going on in the metropolis, especially at the theater. Steele writes about the importance of producing plays of merit, and Drury Lane was in fact mounting a total of eight plays by Shakespeare during the season. He discusses Addison's new comedy, *The Drummer* (but does not mention the author's name), as an example of the encouragement of good living writers. *Town-Talk*, as Steele conceived it, was essentially theatrical criticism, which he had virtually invented in *The Tatler*. This was the time to support the theater, for the patent was his major source of income, and he was desperately short of money. He was writing political pamphlets, which would sell in those troubled times, and in the ninth, and as it proved, the last *Town-Talk*, he quit theatrical matters to talk of the sentencing of the six noblemen who had pleaded guilty to participation in the Pretender's rebellion. A few months later, in June 1716, he was named to the commission which would administer and sell the estates of those noblemen forfeited to the Crown.

His stipend as commissioner was a handsome thousand pounds a year and with the income from Drury Lane should have made life on St. James's Street easy. But then, in the spring of 1716, his health gave way. He was stricken with a severe attack of what his physician, Dr. John Woodward, diagnosed as gout, a condition that left him helpless and immobile. Woodward adminis-

tered purgatives and clysters, in accordance with his theories of medicine, but Steele recovered anyway. Still, it was an ominous event. He was investing effort and money in a scheme, called the Fish Pool, which sought to deliver fish alive to the London market. His duties on the commission of course entailed his going to Scotland, and Drury Lane required at least token attention. Not much time and strength were left over for writing, though he did grind out what amounted to an advertising pamphlet for the Fish Pool.

In late 1718 his wife died, probably from complications in pregnancy, and in the following year he was involved in a bruising pamphlet war with his old collaborator and friend, Joseph Addison. The issue was a complicated one involving representation in the House of Lords, the so-called Peerage Bill. Steele was in opposition, while Addison represented the government's position in a periodical called *The Old Whig*. Steele, in his new periodical, *The Plebeian*, alleged that Addison was only masquerading as a Whig: "I am afraid he is so *old a Whig* that he has quite *forgot his Principles*." The famous friendship ended in this wretched political wrangle. Addison named James Craggs his literary executor—a pointed affront to Steele, of course—and died on 17 June 1719.

In retribution for his part in opposing them, the government, represented by Thomas Pelham-Holles, Duke of Newcastle, as lord chamberlain, moved to revoke Steele's license as manager of Drury Lane. Steele began what was to be the last of his periodicals, *The Theatre*, on 2 January 1720. He intended to, and did, plead his side of the case in his new paper, but he also called on the expertise derived from years in the editor's chair to produce a lively publication, mingling comment and anecdote in the manner he knew best, of all living men. The new paper succeeded beyond the printer's expectations; the first impression of several numbers sold out, and more had to be printed to meet the demand. His arguments did not prevail, however; he was effectively excluded from the Drury Lane enterprise. When he ended *The Theatre* with number 28 on 5 April 1720 and began preparing to go to Scotland for the commission meetings, it seemed that his career in the theater might be over. But then in 1721, in the aftermath of the South Sea scandal, Steele's friend Sir Robert Walpole took control of the government and called on Newcastle to restore Steele to his place in the management of Drury Lane. There he was able to see pro-

Sir Richard Steele in 1722 or 1723 (miniature on ivory, attributed to Christian Richter; by permission of the National Portrait Gallery, London)

duced his last play, *The Conscious Lovers*, in November 1722. It was his greatest success in the theater, though not his best play, and the last extended piece of writing which he was able to complete. His health was declining steadily; in 1724 he chose to retire to Wales, to preserve what money he had for his children's inheritance. He lived on an estate his late wife had left him, until his death on 1 September 1729. He was buried in St. Peter's Church, Carmarthen.

Steele's literary reputation, high in his own day and indeed throughout the next century as well, has declined drastically in the twentieth century. The New Criticism was unable to deal effectively with periodical journalism; under its terms Addison was judged, correctly, to be the more discriminating prose stylist, and Steele was scarcely judged at all. Recent interest in the concept of print culture, in rhetorical practice, and in the history of printing and journalism, however, has made Steele once more a subject of study. His

mark was set principally as a literary innovator. After having made all the necessary allowances for anticipation, influence, and assistance, one returns to the judgment that the essay periodical was effectively his idea. He invented *The Tatler* and the rest followed. Better than anyone else of his time, except perhaps Defoe, he understood the possibilities of using the medium of print to communicate with mass audiences. Later in the century the truly revolutionary implications of his discovery would be worked out in America and France.

Letters:

The Correspondence of Richard Steele, edited by Rae Blanchard (London: Oxford University Press, 1941).

Biographies:

George A. Aitken, *The Life of Richard Steele*, 2 volumes (London: Wm. Isbister, 1889);

Calhoun Winton, *Captain Steele* (Baltimore: Johns Hopkins Press, 1964);

Winton, *Sir Richard Steele, M.P.* (Baltimore & London: Johns Hopkins Press, 1970).

References:

Rae Blanchard, Introduction to *Steele's The Englishman*, edited by Blanchard (Oxford: Clarendon Press, 1955);

Blanchard, Introduction to *Steele's Periodical Journalism 1714-16*, edited by Blanchard (Oxford: Clarendon Press, 1959);

Donald F. Bond, Introduction to *The Spectator*, 5 volumes, edited by Bond (London: Oxford University Press, 1965);

Bond, Introduction to *The Tatler*, 2 volumes, edited by Bond (London: Oxford University Press, 1987);

Richmond P. Bond, *The Tatler: The Making of a Literary Journal* (Cambridge, Mass.: Harvard University Press, 1971);

Richard H. Dammers, *Richard Steele* (Boston: Twayne, 1982);

Michael G. Ketcham, *Transparent Designs* (Athens: University of Georgia Press, 1985);

Brian McCrea, *Addison and Steele Are Dead* (Newark: University of Delaware Press, 1989);

Louis T. Milic, "The Reputation of Richard Steele: What Happened?," *Eighteenth-Century Life*, 1 (June 1975): 81-87;

Fritz Rau, *Zur Verbreitung und Nachahmung des Tatler und Spectator* (Heidelberg: Carl Winter, 1980);

Peter Smithers, *The Life of Joseph Addison* (Oxford: Clarendon Press, 1954);

John Calhoun Stephens, Introduction to *The Guardian*, edited by Stephens (Lexington: University Press of Kentucky, 1982);

William B. Todd, "Early Editions of *The Tatler*," *Studies in Bibliography*, 15 (1962): 121-133;

Calhoun Winton, "Addison and Steele in the English Enlightenment," *Studies on Voltaire and the eighteenth century*, 27 (1963): 1901-1918;

Winton, "Richard Steele, Journalist—and Journalism," in *Newsletters to Newspapers: Eighteenth-Century Journalism*, edited by Donovan Bond and W. R. McLeod (Morgantown: West Virginia University School of Journalism, 1977), pp. 21-31.

Papers:

The British Library holds the most important collection of Steele's papers, mostly correspondence. The collection at Blenheim, seat of the dukes of Marlborough, which was consulted by Aitken and others earlier in this century, has apparently been dispersed in recent years, presumably by private sale. Yale has some of Steele's letters.

Jonathan Swift

(30 November 1667 - 19 October 1745)

Peter J. Schakel
Hope College

See also the Swift entries in *DLB 39: British Novelists, 1660-1800* and *DLB 95: Eighteenth-Century British Poets, First Series.*

SELECTED BOOKS: *An Answer to A Scurrilous Pamphlet, Lately Printed, Intituled, A Letter from Monsieur De Cros* (London: Printed for Randal Taylor, 1693);

A Discourse Of The Contests and Dissensions Between The Nobles and the Commons In Athens and Rome, With The Consequences they had upon both those States (London: Printed for John Nutt, 1701);

A Tale Of A Tub. Written for the Universal Improvement of Mankind. Diu multumque desideratum. To which is added, An Account of a Battel Between The Antient and Modern Books in St. James's Library (London: Printed for John Nutt, 1704); expanded as *A Tale of a Tub. The Fifth Edition: With the Author's Apology and Explanatory Notes By W. W-tt-n, B. D. and Others* (London: Printed for John Nutt, 1710);

Predictions For The Year 1708. Wherein the Month and Day of the Month are set down, the Persons named, and the great Actions and Events of next Year particularly related, as they will come to pass. Written to prevent the People of England from being further impos'd on by vulgar Almanack-makers. By Isaac Bickerstaff Esq. (London: Sold by John Morphew, 1708);

The Accomplishment Of the First of Mr. Bickerstaff's Predictions: Being an Account Of the Death of Mr. Partrige, The Almanack-Maker, upon the 29th Inst., in A Letter to a Person of Honour (London, 1708);

An Elegy on Mr. Patrige, the Almanack-maker, who Died on the 29th of this Instant March, 1708 [single sheet] (London, 1708);

A Vindication Of Isaac Bickerstaff Esq; Against What is Objected to Him by Mr. Partrige, in his Almanack for the present Year 1709. By the said Isaac Bickerstaff, Esq (London, 1709);

A Letter From A Member of the House of Commons In Ireland To A Member of the House of Commons In England, Concerning the Sacramental Test (London: Printed for John Morphew, 1709);

A Famous Prediction of Merlin, the British Wizard; written above a Thousand Years ago, and relating to this Present Year. With Explanatory Notes. By T. N. Philomath [single sheet] (London: Printed & sold by A. Baldwin, 1709);

A Project For The Advancement of Religion, And The Reformation of Manners. By a Person of Quality (London: Printed for Benj. Tooke, 1709);

A Meditation Upon A Broom-Stick, And Somewhat Beside; Of The Same Author's (London: Printed for E. Curll, 1710);

The Virtues of Sid Hamet the Magician's Rod [single sheet] (London: Printed for John Morphew, 1710);

The Examiner, nos. 13-45 (London: Printed for John Morphew, 2 November 1710 - 14 June 1711);

A Short Character Of His Ex. T. E. of W. L. L. of I------. With An Account of some smaller Facts, during His Government, which will not be put into the Articles of Impeachment (London: Printed for William Coryton, 1711);

Miscellanies in Prose and Verse (London: Printed for John Morphew, 1711)—includes "The Sentiments of a Church-of-England Man," "A Letter from a Member of the House of Commons in Ireland," "A Project for the Advancement of Religion," and "An Argument Against Abolishing Christianity";

Some Remarks Upon a Pamphlet, Entitl'd, A Letter to the Seven Lords of the Committee, appointed to Examine Gregg. By the Author of the Examiner (London: Printed for John Morphew, 1711);

The Conduct Of The Allies, And Of The Late Ministry, In Beginning and Carrying on The Present War (London: Printed for John Morphew, 1712 [i.e., 1711]);

Jonathan Swift, circa 1718 (portrait by Charles Jervas; by permission of the National Portrait Gallery, London)

An Excellent New Song: Being The Intended Speech of a famous Orator against Peace [single sheet] (N.p., [1711]);

The W--ds-r Prophecy [single sheet] (N.p., 1711);

Some Advice Humbly Offer'd to the Members Of The October Club, In A Letter From A Person of Honour (London: Printed for John Morphew, 1712);

The Fable of Midas [single sheet] (London: Printed for John Morphew, 1712);

Some Remarks On The Barrier Treaty, Between Her Majesty And The States-General. By the Author of The Conduct of the Allies (London: Printed for John Morphew, 1712);

A Proposal For Correcting, Improving and Ascertaining The English Tongue; In A Letter To the Most Honourable Robert Earl of Oxford and Mortimer, Lord High Treasurer Of Great Britain (London: Printed for Benj. Tooke, 1712);

Some Reasons To Prove, That no Person is obliged by his Principles, as a Whig, to Oppose Her Majesty Or Her Present Ministry. In a Letter to a Whig-Lord (London: Printed for John Morphew, 1712);

Peace and Dunkirk; Being An Excellent New Song upon the Surrender of Dunkirk to General Hill [single sheet] (London, 1712);

A Hue and cry after Dismal: Being a full and true Account, how a Whig L--d was taken at Dunkirk, in the Habit of a Chimney-sweeper, and carried before General Hill [single sheet] (London, 1712);

*A Letter Of Thanks From My Lord W****n To The Lord Bp of S. Asaph, In the Name of the Kit-Cat Club* (N.p., 1712);

Mr. C—ns's Discourse Of Free-Thinking, Put into plain English, by way of Abstract, For The Use of the Poor. By a Friend of the Author (London: Printed for John Morphew, 1713);

Part of the Seventh Epistle Of The First Book Of Horace Imitated: And Address'd to a Noble Peer (London: Printed for A. Dodd, 1713);

The Importance Of The Guardian Considered, in a Second Letter To The Bailiff of Stockbridge. By a Friend of Mr. St---le (London: Printed for John Morphew, 1713);

A Preface To The B----p of S--r--m's Introduction To the Third Volume of the History of the Reformation Of The Church of England. By Gregory Misosàrum (London: Printed for John Morphew, 1713);

The First Ode Of The Second Book Of Horace Paraphras'd: And Address'd to Richard St--le, Esq (London: Printed for A. Dodd, 1713);

The Publick Spirit Of The Whigs: Set Forth in their Generous Encouragement of the Author Of The Crisis: With Some Observations On The Seasonableness, Candor, Erudition, and Style of that Treatise (London: Printed for John Morphew, 1714);

A Letter From A Lay-Patron To A Gentleman, Designing for Holy Orders (Dublin: Printed by E. Waters, 1720); republished as *A Letter To A Young Gentleman, Lately enter'd into Holy Orders, By a Person of Quality* (London: Printed for J. Roberts, 1721);

A Proposal For the Universal Use Of Irish Manufacture, In Cloaths and Furniture of Houses &c., Uterly Rejecting and Renouncing Every Thing wearable that comes from England (Dublin: Printed & sold by E. Waters, 1720);

The Bubble: A Poem (London: Printed for Benj. Tooke, 1721);

Epilogue, To be spoke at the Theatre-Royal This present Saturday being April the 1st. In the Behalf of the Distressed Weavers [single sheet] (Dublin: Printed by J. W., [1721]);

The Bank thrown down. To an Excellent New Tune [single sheet] (Dublin: Printed by John Harding, [1721]);

The last speech and dying words of Ebenezor Elliston, who is to be executed this second day of May, 1722. Publish'd at his desire for the common good [single sheet] (Dublin: Printed by John Harding, [1722]);

Some Arguments Against enlarging the Power of Bishops, In letting of Leases. With Remarks on some Queries Lately published (Dublin: Printed for J. Hyde, 1723);

A Letter To The Shop-Keepers, Tradesmen, Farmers, and Common People of Ireland, Concerning the Brass Half-Pence Coined by Mr. Woods, with a Design to have them Pass in this Kingdom. By M. B. Drapier (Dublin: Printed by John Harding, 1723-4);

A Letter To Mr. Harding the Printer, Upon Occasion of a Paragraph In His News-Paper of Aug. 1st. Relating to Mr. Woods's Half-Pence. By M. B. Drapier (Dublin, [1724]);

Some Observations Upon a Paper, Call'd, The Report Of The Committee Of The Most Honourable the Privy-Council In England, Relating to Wood's Half-Pence. By M. B. Drapier (Dublin: Printed by John Harding, [1724]);

A Serious Poem Upon William Wood, Brasier, Tinker, Hard-Ware-Man, Coiner, Counterfeiter, Founder and Esquire [single sheet] (Dublin: Printed by John Harding, [1724]);

A Letter To The Whole People Of Ireland. By M. B. Drapier (Dublin: Printed by John Harding, [1724]);

To his Grace The Arch-Bishop of Dublin, A Poem [single sheet] (Dublin: Printed by John Harding, [1724]);

An Excellent New Song Upon His Grace Our good Lord Archbishop Of Dublin. By Honest JO, one of His Grace's Farmers in Fingel [single sheet] (Dublin: Printed by John Harding, 1724);

Prometheus, a Poem [single sheet] (Dublin, 1724);

Seasonable Advice. Since a Bill is preparing for the Grand Jury, to find against the Printer of the Drapier's last Letter, there are several things maturely to be considered by those Gentlemen, before whom this Bill is to come, before they determine upon it [single sheet] (N.p., 1724);

The Presentment Of The Grand-Jury Of The County of the City Of Dublin [single sheet] (Dublin: Printed by Pressick Rider & Thomas Harbin, 1724);

A Letter To the Right Honourable the Lord Viscount Molesworth. By M. B. Drapier, Author of the Letter to the Shop-keepers, &c. (Dublin: Printed by John Harding, [1724]);

Fraud Detected: Or, The Hibernian Patriot. Containing, All the Drapier's Letters to the People of Ireland (Dublin: Reprinted & sold by George Faulkner, 1725);

The Birth Of Manly Virtue, From Callimachus (Dublin: Printed by & for George Grierson, 1725);

Cadenus And Vanessa. A Poem (Dublin, 1726);

Travels Into Several Remote Nations Of The World. In Four Parts. By Lemuel Gulliver, First a Surgeon, and then a Captain of several Ships, 2 volumes (London: Printed for Benj. Motte, 1726);

A Short View Of The State Of Ireland (Dublin: Printed by S. Harding, 1727-8);

An Answer To A Paper, Called A Memorial Of the Poor Inhabitants, Tradesmen and Labourers of the Kingdom of Ireland. By the Author of the Short View of the State of Ireland (Dublin: Printed by S. Harding, 1728);

The Journal Of A Dublin Lady; In a Letter to a Person of Quality (Dublin: Printed by S. Harding, [1729]);

A Modest Proposal For preventing the Children Of Poor People From being a Burthen to their Parents, Or The Country, And For making them Beneficial to the Publick (Dublin: Printed by S. Harding, 1729);

An Epistle To His Excellency John Lord Carteret Lord Lieutenant of Ireland (Dublin, 1730);

A Vindication Of His Excellency The Lord C----T, From The Charge Of favouring none but Tories, High-Churchmen, and Jacobites. By the Reverend Dr. S-T (London: Printed for T. Warner, 1730);

Traulus. The first Part. In A Dialogue Betwen Tom and Robin (N.p., 1730);

Traulus The Second Part (N.p., 1730);

*Considerations Upon Two Bills Sent down from the R- H- the H-- of L-- To the H--ble H-- of C--- Relating to the Clergy of I*****d* (London: Printed for A. Moore, 1732);

An Examination Of Certain Abuses, Corruptions, and Enormities In The City of Dublin (Dublin, 1732);

The Lady's Dressing Room. To which is added, A Poem On Cutting down the Old Thorn at Market Hill. By the Rev. Dr. S—T (London: Printed for J. Roberts, 1732);

The Advantages Propos'd By Repealing The Sacramental Test, Impartially Considered (Dublin: Printed by George Faulkner, 1732);

The Life And Genuine Character Of Doctor Swift. Written by Himself (London: Printed for J. Roberts, 1733);

The Presbyterians Plea Of Merit; In Order to take off the Test, Impartially Examined (Dublin: Printed & sold by George Faulkner, 1733);

An Epistle To A Lady, Who desired the Author to make Verses on Her, In The Heroick Stile. Also A Poem, Occasion'd by Reading Dr. Young's Satires, Called, The Universal Passion, earliest extant edition (London: Reprinted for J. Wilford, 1734 [i.e., 1733]);

On Poetry: A Rapsody, earliest known edition (London: Reprinted & sold by J. Huggonson, 1733);

A Beautiful Young Nymph Going to Bed. Written for the Honour of the Fair Sex. Pars minima est ipsa Puella sui. Ovid Remed. Amoris. To which are added, Strephon and Chloe. And Cassinus and Peter (London: Reprinted for J. Roberts, 1734);

A Proposal For Giving Badges To The Beggars In All The Parishes of Dublin. By the Dean of St. Patrick's (Dublin: Printed by George Faulkner, 1737);

The Beasts Confession To The Priest, On Observing how most Men mistake their own Talents. Written in the Year 1732 (Dublin: Printed by George Faulkner, 1738);

A Complete Collection Of Genteel and Ingenious Conversation, According to the Most Polite Mode and Method Now Used At Court, and in the Best Companies of England. In Three Dialogues. By Simon Wagstaff, Esq (London: Printed for B. Motte & C. Bathurst, 1738);

Verses On The Death Of Doctor Swift. Written by Himself: Nov. 1731 (London: Printed for C. Bathurst, 1739);

Some Free Thoughts Upon The Present State Of Affairs. Written in the Year 1714 (Dublin: Printed by and for George Faulkner, 1741);

Directions To Servants. By the Revd. Dr. Swift, D. S. P. D. (Dublin: Printed by George Faulkner, 1745);

The Story Of The Injured Lady (London: Printed for M. Cooper, 1746);

A True Copy Of The Late Rev. Dr. Jonathan Swift's Will (Dublin: Printed by Edward Bate, 1746);

Brotherly Love. A Sermon, Preached In St. Patrick's Church; On December 1st, 1717. By Dr. Jonathan Swift, Dean of St. Patrick's, Dublin (Dublin: Printed by George Faulkner, 1754);

The History Of The Four Last Years Of The Queen. By the late Jonathan Swift, D. D. D. S. P. D. (London: Printed for A. Millar, 1758).

Editions: *The Works Of J. S., D. D., D. S. P. D. In Four Volumes* (Dublin: Printed by & for George Faulkner, 1735);

The Works Of Dr. Jonathan Swift, Dean of St. Patrick's, Dublin, 14 volumes (London: Printed for C. Bathurst, 1751);

The Works Of Jonathan Swift, D. D. Dean of St. Patrick's, Dublin, Accurately revised, . . . Adorned with Copper-Plates; With Some Account of the Author's Life, and Notes Historical and Explanatory, 17 volumes, edited by John Hawkesworth (London: Printed for C. Bathurst, C. Davis & others, 1754-1775)—

includes *Letters*, volumes 1-3, edited by
Hawkesworth (1766); volumes 4-6, edited by
Deane Swift (1768);

*The Works Of The Rev. Dr. Jonathan Swift, Dean Of
St. Patrick's, Dublin. Arranged, Revised, And Cor-
rected, with Notes*, 17 volumes, edited by
Thomas Sheridan (London: Printed for
Charles Bathurst, 1784); corrected and re-
vised by John Nichols, 24 volumes (New
York: Durrell, 1812);

*The Works Of Jonathan Swift, D.D. Dean Of St.
Patrick's, Dublin; Containing Additional Letters,
Tracts, and Poems, Not Hitherto Published; With
Notes, And A Life Of The Author*, 19 volumes,
edited by Sir Walter Scott (Edinburgh:
Printed for Archibald Constable, 1814);

*A Tale of a Tub, To which is added The Battle of the
Books and the Mechanical Operation of the
Spirit*, edited by A. C. Guthkelch and D.
Nichol Smith (Oxford: Clarendon Press,
1920);

*The Drapier's Letters to the People of Ireland against re-
ceiving Wood's Halfpence*, edited by Herbert
Davis (Oxford: Clarendon Press, 1935);

The Poems of Jonathan Swift, 3 volumes, edited by
Harold Williams (Oxford: Clarendon Press,
1937);

The Prose Works of Jonathan Swift, 14 volumes, edited by Herbert Davis and others (Oxford:
Basil Blackwell, 1939-1968);

Journal to Stella, 2 volumes, edited by Williams (Oxford: Clarendon Press, 1948).

For most general readers, the name Jona-
than Swift is associated only with his satiric masterpiece *Gulliver's Travels*. They are not aware that,
in addition to it and hundreds of poems, he
wrote a great deal of nonfictional prose, much of
it of considerable interest, significance, and excellence. This essay will focus on the "nonfiction," including *A Tale of a Tub, An Argument Against Abolishing Christianity*, the *Journal to Stella, The Examiner*
papers, *The Drapier's Letters*, and *A Modest Proposal*. These works show Swift as a complex, fascinating man, controversial in his own day and the
subject of critical controversy to the present.

Swift was born in Ireland of English parents. His father and three uncles were solicitors
who had immigrated to Ireland at, or just before, the Restoration of Charles II in 1660, seeking better fortunes than Herfordshire promised
them. His mother was born in Ireland, of parents who moved there probably around 1634.
Swift was tied emotionally to England but linked

by birth to Ireland, a land he considered backward and uncultured. He sought throughout his
life to obscure those links and encourage others
to think of him as an Englishman; at times he
even denied them entirely. His Anglo-Irish heritage left Swift an outsider, always seeking acceptance, recognition, and respect from those he considered to be "inside."

His father, Jonathan, married Abigail Er-
rick in 1664. A daughter, Jane, was born in April
1666; Jonathan was born in November 1667, several months after the unexpected death of his father. When he was a year old, according to an account Swift wrote late in his life, his nurse took
him with her secretly to England, where he
stayed for three years because his mother did not
want to risk the danger of recrossing the Irish
Sea. If this story is true, he spent little of his
youth with his mother and endured a series of sep-
arations: from his mother, from his nurse, from
his mother again when he went off to school,
after which she moved to England, leaving Swift
in the care of relatives in Ireland. It would help explain his hunger for emotional security and his distrust of lasting relations with others (especially
women) to supply it.

At age six he entered the excellent Kilkenny
School, about sixty miles southwest of Dublin,
and at fourteen he was admitted to Trinity College, the University of Dublin. His record there
was mixed: excellent in subjects such as Greek
and Latin, weak in logic and mathematics. He received the B.A. degree in 1686. He apparently
was supported at Trinity College by his uncles,
and he complains that their allowance was inadequate for his needs. That may be true; but more
probably Swift's complaint reflects the fierce independence he held to all his life—his love of liberty (personal and political), his unwillingness to
be beholden to anyone.

For Swift independence existed in tension
with his need to depend on others for positions
and advancement, illustrated well in the following decade. He continued his studies at Trinity
College toward the M.A. degree until 1689,
when he left Ireland, along with many other Protestants, to escape an uncertain political situation,
as William III and Mary replaced James II in England, and as Richard Talbot, Earl of Tyrconnel,
tried to advance the Catholic cause in Ireland.
He went to England and entered the household
of Sir William Temple, a well-known and respected diplomat and statesman, now retired to
his country estate, Moor Park, to engage in a gen-

teel life of reading, contemplation, and writing. Swift was to live for more than a decade with Temple, whom he seems to have been drawn to and repelled by as a father figure, except for two absences: in 1690-1691 he returned to Ireland seeking better health through change of climate and a permanent position—he found neither and returned to Temple's employ; and in 1694, having in 1692 received his Master of Arts degree from Oxford University, he sought a permanent situation by being ordained into the Church of Ireland and was assigned to the prebend of Kilroot in northern Ireland, a poor area inhabited mostly by Catholics and Presbyterians, from which he returned to Moor Park in 1696, where he stayed until Temple's death on 27 January 1699.

Swift's time at Moor Park involved secretarial, administrative, and editorial duties for Temple: writing letters, keeping records, and helping prepare Temple's writings for publication. Swift was also sent to London to convey messages and political advice from Temple to the king. Beyond his duties it offered him time for a great deal of intensive reading in Temple's excellent library: church history, political history, theology, philosophy, classical literature, the works of the church fathers. In such an environment it seems almost natural that Swift should aspire to be a writer himself. His first ambition was to be a poet. During his years at Moor Park he wrote a series of formal, inflated, eulogistic poems, mostly odes imitating the style of Abraham Cowley. They were not successful, and now are almost unreadable.

Swift's earliest prose works, written in defense of Temple, also came out of the Moor Park years. The first was *An Answer to A Scurrilous Pamphlet, Lately Printed, Intituled, A Letter from Monsieur De Cros* (1693), replying to attacks made on diplomatic activities Temple undertook for Charles II. It was thought by early readers to be by Temple, but circumstances and style point toward Swift. As J. A. Downie noted, "The *Answer* reveals a number of Swiftian traits: a digressive, story-telling style; a reductive argument; a lofty assumption of superiority; classical references. But most of all it is the sarcastic aside which suggests Swift's hand."

Swift's next prose works also began as defenses of Temple and have the same traits. *A Tale of a Tub*, *The Battle of the Books*, and *The Mechanical Operation of the Spirit* were almost certainly written during Swift's last years at Moor Park, though they were not published until 1704. Like most of Swift's works, the volume containing them appeared anonymously; Swift never avowed authorship, and there have been numerous attempts—most recently by Robert M. Adams—to attribute *A Tale of a Tub*, or parts of it, to someone else, usually to a cousin, Thomas Swift. Despite such attempts most scholars believe it was written by Swift and includes some of his most original and brilliant satire.

The links to Temple are most direct in *The Battle of the Books*. It grew out of a controversy sparked by Temple's assertion, in "An Essay upon Ancient and Modern Learning" (1690), that the learning and accomplishments of the ancients were superior to those of the moderns in all areas of the arts and sciences. This led to a laborious defense of the moderns in William Wotton's *Reflections upon Ancient and Modern Learning* (1694). The dispute continued when Charles Boyle published an edition of Phalaris in which he cited Temple's opinion that the letters of Phalaris and the fables of Aesop were "the two most ancient [books] that I know of in prose, among those we call profane authors." Richard Bentley subsequently attacked the judgment and methods of Temple and Boyle and demonstrated that the letters and fables were not ancient or authentic.

Swift was not deeply concerned with the philosophical issues involved in the dispute, but he was loyal to his patron and offended by the personal tone of the attack upon Temple and Boyle. It is characteristic of Swift to turn abstractions into physical things as part of his reductive ridicule of them; so, here he writes a defense of Temple couched in terms of a battle between various books in a library. The work is written as a historian's account of the causes of a recent occurrence ("the Battel Fought last Friday, Between the Antient and the Modern Books in St. James's Library").

It is in three parts, each with a different literary form. The first is a pseudo-academic discourse outlining the background of the recent battle: the quarrel began on the hill Parnassus, as the Moderns inhabiting the lower of its two peaks asked the Ancients on the higher peak to exchange places or to cut it down to their level. The Ancients refused, and the Moderns turned down their offer to help raise the lower peak; as a result, books of controversy began fighting to establish their relative places. The second and most famous part is the allegorical fable of the spider and the bee. The spider, like modern thinkers

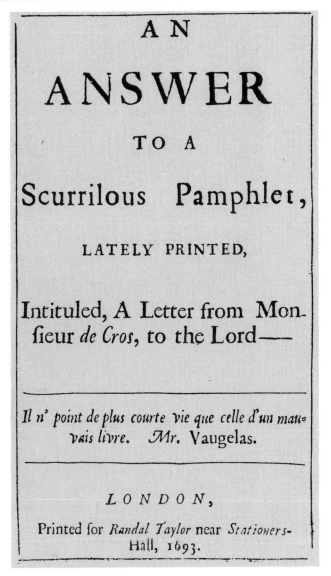

AN

ANSWER

TO A

Scurrilous Pamphlet,

LATELY PRINTED,

Intituled, A Letter from Monfieur *de Cros*, to the Lord——

Il n' point de plus courte vie que celle d'un mauvais livre. Mr. Vaugelas.

LONDON,

Printed for *Randal Taylor* near *Stationers-Hall*, 1693.

Title page for Swift's first pamphlet, a defense of William Temple's diplomatic activities in the service of Charles II

and authors, looks inward for his materials, or, as the fable puts it, draws dirt and poison from its own breast and *"turns all into Excrement and Venom; producing nothing at last, but Fly-bane and a Cobweb."* The bee, like the Ancients, looks outward to nature for materials and, *"by an universal Range, with long Search, much Study, true Judgment, and Distinction of Things, brings home Honey and Wax."* The third part is the battle itself, described in mock-epic terms rich with allusion to the *Iliad* and the *Aeneid*. Ancients such as Virgil and Aristotle encounter moderns such as John Dryden and Francis Bacon. Boyle defeats Wotton and Bentley, but the outcome of the entire battle is unclear because the final pages of the text are "missing."

Swift did not share Temple's naive belief that older thinkers are always superior to recent ones. His specific attack is on Wotton and Bentley as individuals, and this attack can be generalized to an attack on the pedantry and scientific approach to scholarship of the new generation, as opposed to the taste, decorum, and gentlemanly approach of an older generation. Beyond this, Swift redefined "Ancient" and "Modern" and used them as metaphors describing literary and intellectual attitudes and characteristics he endorsed and opposed. The "modern" mode of thinking is theoretical, rationalistic, speculative, and chaotic; "ancient" thought, whether in seventeenth-century England or classical Greece and Rome, is empirical, reasonable, concrete, and

Illustration for The Battle of the Books *in a 1769 edition of Swift's works*

orderly. Thus the moderns spin out airy edifices which, like cobwebs, may appear substantial and valuable, but lack *"Duration and matter."* The ancients, in contrast, *"by infinite Labor, and search, and ranging thro' every Corner of Nature"* produce *"Honey and Wax,"* thus *"furnishing Mankind with the two Noblest of Things, which are* Sweetness *and* Light."

The bee reflects the gentlemanly, English, Enlightenment values which Temple embodied and which Swift identified with consciously. The spider, as the "outsider," vulgar, explosive, and rebellious, carries the ideas and values Swift resisted. The bee, however, is fairly bland and uninteresting, even, in his smugness and superiority,

rather repelling; there is a mechanicalness about the list of his qualities, as if, though they were the right things to say, Swift had not really embraced them. Who was Swift, after all, to talk about "Sweetness and Light," John Traugott asks. Swift is remembered for his intensity, combativeness, and indecency, qualities which align him more closely with the spider than the bee. Perhaps Swift at a deeper level identified to some extent with the spider, and the freshness and energy in the passages describing it give vent to his resentment over his own subservient status and resistance to the orderly pretensions of the English aristocracy, as he admired—and perhaps hated—them in Temple.

A Tale of a Tub, though it includes attacks on Wotton and Bentley and implicit defense of Temple, seems to have been begun before the specific dispute pitting them against each other began. *A Tale of a Tub* is more complex and imaginative than *The Battle of the Books*. It is supposedly a work of modern literature, evincing the kind of disorganized, flighty, insubstantial writing Swift attributed to modernism. It involves two satiric thrusts, attacking (in words of the "Apology" he added to the fifth edition) *"the numerous and gross Corruptions in Religion and Learning."*

By "Corruptions in Religion" Swift meant what he regarded as deviations from pure ancient Christianity as set forth in the New Testament. Such deviations occur in the two directions he had become familiar with in his unhappy ministry to the parish of Kilroot: on the one hand, the deviations of Catholicism, consisting in what Swift regarded as additions to original Christianity, beliefs which for him lacked biblical basis, such as the papacy, purgatory, and transubstantiation. On the other hand are the deviations of Presbyterians and other "dissenters" from adherence to the Church of England, with their rejection of liturgy and music and their reliance on individual interpretation of scripture. Both extremes, for Swift, were examples of an unhealthy use of imagination or "inspiration"—thus of "modernism."

These corruptions are dealt with in the "Tale" proper: an allegory narrated in sections 2, 4, 6, 8, 10, and 11 of the *Tale*, each headed "A Tale of a Tub." The allegory tells the story of three brothers, Peter, Martin, and Jack, who, upon their father's death, are given new coats (the doctrine and faith of Christianity), a Will (the New Testament), and instructions to make no changes or additions to the coats. The story tells how Peter (who stands for the Catholic church) leads them in finding ways to add shoulder-knots and lace to their coats, and then turns tyrannical, insisting he was their father's sole heir and imposing various inventions and restrictions on his brothers. Eventually the brothers rebel against him (the Protestant Reformation). Jack (John Calvin and the more radical Protestants) rips off every ornament, leaving his coat torn and tattered, and ends up a frenzied madman. Between these extremes is the third brother, Martin, alluding to Martin Luther but standing especially for the Anglican church. Martin removes the worst of Peter's abuses, but with

caution and moderation. The "Tale," thus, is meant as a strong rejection of Catholicism and radical Protestantism, and a defense and endorsement of the Church of England (and Church of Ireland).

The attacks on "Corruptions in Learning" are handled in a profusion of prefatory materials and a series of digressions inserted between the chapters of the "Tale" proper (dedications, preface, introduction, sections 3, 5, 7, 9, conclusion). The satire here extends the attack on Wotton and Bentley, and thus, implicitly, the defense of Temple. The prefatory materials and digressions exemplify qualities Swift ascribed to modern learning and literary criticism: disunity, shallowness of thought, inadequacy of research and reading, carelessness and excesses in style, personal vindictiveness in approach. All "modern" ideas, in religion and in learning, are ridiculed as insanity in section 9, the brilliant "Digression on Madness." Here, then, is further attack on the spider, but conducted now from the inside, as Swift becomes the enemy and exemplifies the madness of thought and style he attributes to modernism.

As in *The Battle of the Books*, so here too is a tension between the relative lifelessness of the depiction of the professed ideals—Martin and the ancients—and the vividness with which Peter, Jack, and the moderns are presented. One reads with impatience the descriptions of Martin, but looks forward eagerly to the exploits of Peter and Jack; the implied endorsements of ancient excellencies are bland enough, while the imitation of modern faults has a compelling power.

Here is a crux of twentieth-century criticism of Swift. The revival of Swift's reputation in the 1930s, led by Ricardo Quintana and George Sherburn, proceeded on the assumption that Swift, contrary to the view of the previous century, embodies "the characteristic rationalism of the Enlightenment" with its emphases on reason, order, and uniformitarianism. Recent critics, including Claude Rawson, Edward Said, and Peter Steele, have challenged the tidiness of that assumption. They hold that in Swift are an underlying energy of mind and an anarchic impulse which subvert the professed desire for order and moderation. There is truth in Carole Fabricant's charge that several decades of critics turned Swift into what they could be comfortable with—a reasonable, middle-of-the-road, English-at-heart friend of Pope and Arbuthnot—and thus brushed aside what they did not want to see: an

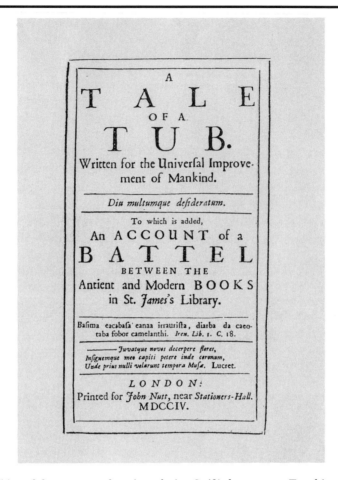

Title page for the first edition of three prose works written during Swift's last years as Temple's secretary. In addition to the writings listed on this title page, the volume also includes The Mechanical Operation of the Spirit.

alienated man driven by disruptive passions and deeply shaped by his Irish heritage.

Three issues in *A Tale of a Tub* illustrate the differences between the older, moderate view of Swift and the more recent, radicalized view. First is the issue of who speaks in the *Tale*. Midcentury critics of Swift sought to relieve Swift of responsibility for offensive materials by attributing them to a pseudo-author or "persona." Highly influential in that trend were an article on dramatic qualities in Swift by Quintana in 1948 and a study of Pope's satire by Maynard Mack in 1951. Building on their foundation, William Ewald in a book-length study of Swift's "masks" claims that *A Tale of a Tub* is narrated by "a 'modern' Grub Street literary hack" whose values and attitudes are directly opposite Swift's and become the target of Swift's ridicule. But the persona does not seem consistent throughout the *Tale*; so the idea emerged that there are two speakers, the "Modern Literary Hack" of the digressions and the "Modern Historian" of the allegory. Quintana,

who in 1936 had not mentioned any speakers, in 1955 found six, none of whom is "actually Swift."

When voices of speakers drown out Swift's voice, however, much of the power of the work is lost. Gardner Stout has argued persuasively the importance of remembering that Swift's voice creates the other "voices" through his mimicking and parodying of writers and forms he wants to ridicule. Although in the "Digression on Madness" Swift "personates" a mad modern thinker, his voice must be heard close behind. As Rawson has put it, the speaker of the *Tale* "needs to be distinguished from Swift, but hardly as a separate and autonomous being. He is an ebullient embodiment of many of Swift's dislikes, but the ebullience is Swift's."

Clearly there must be no return to taking the words of Swift's satires as expressing his literal beliefs; but neither must the idea of a "speaker" be used to shelter Swift from disturbing and unpleasant ideas or images. Denis Donoghue in one sense resolves the debate with his reminder that "the 'author' of the *Tale* is anonymous." Left as such he is and he is not Swift, and when he is not, he is whatever Swift wants him to be at the moment. That flexibility is lost, and the satire is diminished, if we insist on giving the speaker a character, a role, or a name. "We have to take [his] anonymity seriously." Or, in Frederik Smith's words, "The responsibility for distinguishing between sanity and insanity, truth and error, is in the *Tale* turned over to us," not resolved neatly by identifying the speaker.

A second, closely related issue is the structure of *A Tale of a Tub*. The *Tale*, as an imitation of "modern" literature, was deliberately given the appearance of lacking coherence and wholeness. Quintana in 1936 called the work "craftily constructed" and pointed to structural patterns in it, but accepted the divergent tendencies of the various parts. Subsequent critics, working from mid-century formalist axioms that literary works are self-sufficient organic wholes, tried in various ways to find order behind the apparent disorder of the *Tale*. Miriam Starkman in 1950 argued that each section of the allegory is linked by themes and techniques to the adjoining digressions to form a "carefully integrated pattern" attacking formlessness. Ronald Paulson in 1960 described the *Tale* as a "logically arranged encyclopedia of Gnostic sufficiency." And John Clark in 1970 called it "a single and complete work of mimetic art."

Recent critics have been less concerned with finding unity in the *Tale*, more concerned with appreciating its fluidity and complexity. "The *Tale*, for all we know, is shaped like a tub," says W. B. Carnochan. Adams treats it as an example of "open form," and Frank Palmeri adds, "Structurally [narrative satires] are chiastic, turning from one point of view once it has been elaborated to advocate its exact opposite, refusing to be bound by any one-eyed vision of the world." Leon Guilhamet observes that the flexibility a satirist needs "is achieved here by a manipulation of forms.... [The] narrator is as protean as the work itself." To seek for the tight unity of form and narrative approach prized by the New Criticism probably is futile: as Donoghue says, "only a bold reader would undertake to show that the *Tale* is as it is because it could not have been otherwise."

To grant that the *Tale* reflects more of mad discontinuity than reasonable continuity points toward a third critical issue, madness. Madness is a recurrent theme in Swift: in addition to its use in the *Tale*, Gulliver goes mad at the end of his *Travels*; madness is a theme in such poems as "Mad Mullinix and Timothy" and "Traulus"; and the Irish Parliament in "The Legion Club" is described as an insane asylum. Michael DePorte suggests that the Stoic paradox "every deviation from reason is a deviation into madness" enjoyed particular importance in eighteenth-century satire, partly because of the accessibility of observation of insanity afforded by Bethlehem Hospital to writers and their readers alike. Swift throughout his life was haunted by the fear of going mad: this was in large part due to his suffering from his Moor Park days on frequent and incapacitating bouts with giddiness, headache, and deafness. The effect was so devastating and its mysterious origin so unsettling (it has since been identified as labyrinthine vertigo, or Ménière's Syndrome, and controlled by pills used for seasickness) that Swift thought of it as an early symptom of insanity.

Swift's fear of the loss of his reason is closely related to his fear of the loss of reason's control over the imagination and over unconventional ideas, which he labels "madness" in the *Tale* and elsewhere. Swift was deeply conservative by nature and distrusted change; but he recognized in himself anarchic and skeptical tendencies which could overcome the orderly fabric of reason and order. Thus his endorsement of repressive social measures in part reflects the tight controls he exerted over his own inner impulses. "The violence which Swift deplores is mirrored by the violence with which he charges his own style," says Rawson. "His professed admiration for compromise, moderation and the common forms is balanced by moods or by contexts of suspicion or dislike for these very things." His conservative instincts led him to attack "modern" speakers; but his anarchic tendencies forced him to identify with them, creating a tension within him which is central to the effect of the *Tale* as well. To say with earlier critics that the *Tale* is a unified work attacking unreason and defending reason and tradition, separated from Swift by use of a "mad" speaker totally opposite from himself, is inadequate. The *Tale* is not just about the "moderns" without, but "modern" tendencies within Swift himself as well.

By the time *A Tale of a Tub* and *The Battle of the Books* were published with *The Mechanical Operation of the Spirit* in 1704, Swift's life had changed significantly. Several months after Temple's death in 1699, Swift returned to Ireland as chaplain to Charles, Earl of Berkeley, newly appointed as one of the lords justice of Ireland. In addition he became vicar of Laracor, and was given the prebend of Dunlavin in St. Patrick's Cathedral in Dublin. Although he would have preferred a position in England rather than one in Ireland, he at least had a footing in Dublin and a position which enabled him to return to England and become increasingly involved in religious and political affairs there. He did return, with Berkeley in 1701, and found political ferment which provoked him to write the first of what would become a long series of political pamphlets.

High Churchmen in Parliament were leading an attempt to impeach four Whig ministers on charges of arranging treaties without keeping Parliament informed. Swift was accustomed to think of himself as a Whig and rather automatically reacted on the side of the four ministers, without realizing that Whig interests no longer coincided with his own beliefs. Swift considered himself a Whig because he agreed with those who, in the 1670s, led by Anthony Ashley Cooper, first Earl of Shaftesbury, had favored exclusion of James, Duke of York, a Catholic, from the line of succession; the "Tories," on the contrary, had resisted any deviation from the natural line of succession. The political tensions of Swift's youth in the 1670s and 1680s and the influence of Temple's support of William III in the 1690s were the basis for Swift's acceptance of the Revolution Settlement and of a balance of power between the king, the House of Lords, and the House of Commons as the governmental ideal.

Seeking to influence current events and boost his own prospects for advancement, he wrote *A Discourse Of The Contests and Dissensions Between The Nobles and the Commons In Athens and Rome, With The Consequences they had upon both those States*, published in 1701. The pamphlet chastises the impeachment of the four Whig ministers by demonstrating the harms caused by dismissal of eminent statesmen by the public in parallel historical situations. It is not the typical attack on the Tories or defense of the Whigs; rather it is an affirmation of the division of powers in government, and a warning against upsetting the balance by any group (Whig, Tory, or other) claiming to represent the masses. In the end the discourse affirms "common Sense, and plain Reason" and, like *A Tale of a Tub*, condemns the madness of enthusiasm, innovation, and radical individuality.

From 1702 until 1707 he stayed in Ireland, tending to his own parish and becoming involved in the affairs of St. Patrick's Cathedral and the Irish clergy. He was awarded the Doctor of Divinity degree by Trinity College, Dublin, in 1702. He wrote little—most notably, drafts of a few personal poems and a feeble allegory, *The Story of the Injured Lady*, protesting England's union with Scotland while Ireland, the "injured lady," is rejected and taken advantage of.

When he next traveled to London, late in 1707, he went as a representative of the Church of Ireland, seeking to gain for the clergy of Ireland remission of some ancient fees paid by clergymen to the crown, the "First Fruits and Twentieth Parts"; such relief had been granted to the Church of England a few years earlier. Swift spent a year and a half waiting for instructions from Ireland and negotiating with Whig ministers, only to return to Ireland in June 1709 unsuccessful in his attempts to benefit the Church and to gain preferment for himself.

Those eighteen months were successful in a literary sense, however. He spent his time in the company of Whigs and gained recognition for brilliance as a writer and conversationalist. He wrote two of his best-known poems, "A Description of the Morning" and "A Description of a City Shower," both of which appeared in *The Tatler*, published by his new friends Joseph Addison and Richard Steele. He also wrote essays for *The Tatler*, though his contributions cannot be identified. His finest prose works in these years are the marvelously witty and amusing "Bickerstaff Papers." In them Swift's character Isaac Bickerstaff, in a series of almanaclike *Predictions for the Year 1708*, foretells the death of a dissenting almanac maker, John Partridge: "I have consulted the Star of his Nativity by my own Rules; and find he will infallibly die upon the 29th of *March* next, about eleven at Night, of a raging Fever." At the end of March appeared *The Accomplishment Of the First of Mr. Bickerstaff's Predictions*, announcing that Partridge had died at the time and in the manner foretold, which forced Partridge to issue announcements that such reports were false and he was indeed still alive.

The other pieces Swift wrote during these years grew out of events of the time and his growing awareness of his disagreements with modern Whigs. At the center of the problem was Whig alliance with and support of Protestant dissenters, while Swift was unequivocally loyal to the Church of England. As part of the Restoration settle-

First page from the fifth of Swift's "Bickerstaff Papers"

ment, political offices were restricted to members of the state church, a provision enforced by the Test Act, which required officeholders to take communion in an Anglican church at least once a year. This eliminated Roman Catholics, but unscrupulous Protestant dissenters got around the law by "occasional conformity"—that is, by receiving communion in the state church once annually, and attending dissenting meetinghouses the rest of the year. Swift strongly supported the Test Act and supported efforts to strengthen it by prohibiting occasional conformity; modern

Whigs opposed the Test Act and the need for conformity to it.

Three tracts he wrote around 1708 show the distance between his views and those of his political allies. The earliest (Swift said it was written in 1708 but it may have been earlier) is "The Sentiments of a Church-of-England Man, With Respect to Religion and Government," published in *Miscellanies in Prose and Verse* (1711). He presents what he calls a moderate, balanced position on religion, but what in fact expresses a fairly narrow point of view, endorsing the episcopal form of church government and the Test Act. The second, *A Letter From A Member of the House of Commons In Ireland To A Member of the House of Commons In England, Concerning the Sacramental Test* (1709), is a strong attack upon dissenters. They, according to Swift, pose the true danger to the state and church in Ireland, rather than the more numerous Roman Catholics, for the latter are bound with firm controls while current proposals would lift controls from dissenters.

The third, *A Project For The Advancement of Religion, And The Reformation of Manners* (1709), proposes, as a way to curb increasing vice and depravity, that the queen should promote to positions of power only men of virtuous lives and sound religious beliefs. She should oblige public officials "to a constant weekly Attendance on the Service of the Church; to a decent Behaviour in it; to receive the Sacrament four times a Year; to avoid Swearing and irreligious profane Discourses; and to the Appearance at least, of Temperance and Chastity." All of this would be enforced by such means as "strict Inspection of proper Officers," closer regulation of universities, censorship of the theater, and limiting of the press. Swift grants that an effect of such laws will be hypocrisy among some political leaders who will outwardly conform to such requirements without inwardly supporting them: but Swift accepts that since their actions—though not sincere—will give a better example to others than their present ones do, and since a few might "be brought over to true Piety" in the process.

Because hypocritical actions would be among the results of the proposal and because the word *Project* in Swift generally is pejorative (signifying a visionary, impractical scheme), Leland Peterson has argued that the pamphlet is satirical. That argument has been countered effectively by Phillip Harth and Jan R. Van Meter, among others. Swift's contemporaries took it as straightforward and significant. Swift's patron,

the earl of Berkeley, in a letter to Swift (22 April 1709), expressed the hope that it would be given to the queen, for "I am entirely of opinion, that Her Majestys reading of the book of the Project for the increase of Morality and Piety, may be of very great use to that end." Although it is not among his best works, it is valuable as an example of Swift as serious, moral-religious writer, advocating reform straightforwardly rather than indirectly, as in his satiric works.

Readers are perplexed and frustrated by *A Project For The Advancement of Religion* because of the contrast in tone and complexity between it and one of Swift's finest satirical essays, "An Argument Against Abolishing Christianity," written at about the same time and published in his 1711 *Miscellanies in Prose and Verse*. In it Swift imagines a situation—much like the ongoing controversy regarding the Test Act—in which freethinkers have proposed a bill in Parliament for the abolishment of Christianity and written pamphlets setting forth the advantages of their proposal. Swift's essay purports to be a reply to such pamphlets, questioning the advantages claimed for the proposal and setting forth disadvantages accompanying it which may not yet have been considered.

The essay is written in first person, but the "I" is a fictional voice mimicking a freethinking pamphleteer. Not enough detail is given to develop it into a character, only enough for Swift to attain the subtlety and complexity of attacking an ironically exaggerated proposal, not with his own sensible reasons, but with distorted reasons quite different from his own. The first hint that the "I" is not reliable comes at the end of the opening paragraph, when the essayist affirms that "in the present Posture of our Affairs at home or abroad, I do not yet see the absolute Necessity of extirpating the Christian Religion from among us." Until that point the "I" has said benignly sensible things that the reader—and presumably Swift—could agree with. But when he says he does not *yet* see the *absolute* necessity to eliminate Christianity, the qualifiers raise doubts about his understanding and commitment. Those doubts increase, three paragraphs later, when he refers to the Christian gospel as "antiquated" and "exploded," and claims the common people "are now grown as much ashamed of it as their Betters."

The basis of those statements becomes clear, a paragraph later, when the essayist notes that "every candid Reader will easily understand my Discourse to be intended only in Defence of *nomi-*

nal Christianity." When he defends Christianity, then, and claims there is no need for its extermination, he means the use of Christianity as a label, merely calling oneself a Christian, not the sort of faith and commitment that influences one's values and actions.

Those are not the sentiments of a Church of England man—such sentiments appear only briefly in "An Argument Against Abolishing Christianity" as the essayist dismisses "real Christianity" as outdated and impractical: "I hope, no Reader imagines me so weak to stand up in the Defence of *real* Christianity; such as used in primitive Times (if we may believe the Authors of those Ages) to have an Influence upon Mens Belief and Actions: To offer at the Restoring of that, would indeed be a wild Project." As "ancient" in *The Battle of the Books* was not limited to the Greeks and Romans, so "primitive" Christianity here does not refer just to the earliest centuries after Christ. It includes all times which accepted Christianity in its original sense of a deep commitment which shaped life and behavior— Christianity prior to its "modern" decline into tokenism and superficiality.

Much of the wit and humor comes from the reasons the essayist offers in rebuttal to advantages his opponents claim for abolishing Christianity. Nominal Christianity should be retained because it gives the Wits a trivial target to attack and diverts them from attacking important things like the government and political policies. When the opponents claim that abolishing Christianity would gain a day per week for business and pleasure, which now is wasted on worship, the essayist points out the benefits of having a day "for Traders to sum up the Accounts of the Week," for "Lawyers to prepare their Briefs," for business meetings, and for sleep. There is wit also in the wording of the absurd advantages themselves: "It is again objected, as a very absurd, ridiculous Custom, that a Set of Men should be suffered, much less employed, and hired to bawl one Day in Seven, against the Lawfulness of those Methods most in Use toward the Pursuit of Greatness, Riches, and Pleasure; which are the constant Practice of all Men alive on the other Six."

The exact target of Swift's satiric attack has been the subject of critical debate. In a 1937 book review Louis A. Landa suggested an idea developed in more detail in Ehrenpreis's biography, that "An Argument Against Abolishing Christianity" is directed against Whig efforts to eliminate the Test Act. In that reading, one simply substitutes "Test Act" for "Christianity" to get at what Swift intended. Thus the pamphlet's full title means "An Argument to Prove, That the Abolishing of the Test Act in England, May . . . Be Attended with Some Inconveniences, and Perhaps, Not Produce Those Many Good Effects Proposed Thereby," and other sentences can be amended similarly. Edward W. Rosenheim, Jr., replies that on this reading "An Argument Against Abolishing Christianity" is neither very startling nor effective, for it involves very little distortion of the actual. Rosenheim contends, instead, that the victim of the satire "can only be the nominal Christian himself, the lip service church member." Phillip Harth nicely resolves the dilemma by positing that Swift is satirizing both freethinkers and the nominal Christian: "Not one but two groups, in Swift's view, threaten Christianity, the first from outside, the second from within." The nominal Christian agrees with freethinkers that Christian doctrine is outdated and irrelevant and believes in freedom of thought and behavior, but "unlike them, he feels that the eviscerated Christianity which now obtains is the best social structure for the enjoyment of this freedom."

Swift returned to Ireland for just over a year, late June 1709 to late August 1710. During that time, the political world of London did a complete reversal. The Whigs, who had taken total control of the government in 1708, were ousted in 1710, when the public began to question the conduct of the war against France, the need for prolonging it, and the Whig policies in regard to the Church of England. They were replaced by an administration formed by Robert Harley. Swift, who had failed to gain concession of the First Fruits from the Whigs, was sent to London again to press the same cause with the new ministry. He achieved quick success with Harley, who not only granted the First Fruits for which Swift interceded, but also treated him with warmth and respect and recruited him to write on behalf of the government.

Although the Harley ministry from 1710-1713 became, and is known as, a Tory government, that was not Harley's intention, and it probably is not accurate to refer to Swift as having become a Tory. Harley was an "Old Whig," a 1680s Whig, a strong supporter of the Protestant succession and a balanced government, rather than a staunch Tory; his aim was to form a coalition government of Whigs and Tories with "Country" values, in opposition to the "New Whig," or

Numb. 17.

The EXAMINER.

From Thursday *November* 16, to Thursday *November* 23. 1710.

Qui sunt boni cives? qui belli, qui domi de patria bene merentur, nisi qui patriæ beneficia meminerunt?

I Will employ this present Paper upon a Subject, which of late hath very much affected me, which I have consider'd with a good deal of Application, and made several Enquiries about, among those Persons who I thought were best able to inform me; and if I deliver my Sentiments with some Freedom, I hope it will be forgiven, while I accompany it with that Tenderness which so nice a Point requires.

I said in a former Paper (Numb. 14.) that one specious Objection to the late removals at Court, was the fear of giving Uneasiness to a General, who has been long successful abroad: And accordingly, the common Clamour of Tongues and Pens for some Months past, has run against the Baseness, the Inconstancy and Ingratitude of the whole Kingdom to the Duke of M———, in return of the most eminent Services that ever were perform'd by a Subject to his Country; not to be equal'd in History. And then to be sure some bitter stroak of Detraction against *Alexander* and *Cæsar*, who never did us the least Injury. Besides, the People that read *Plutarch* come upon us with Parallels drawn from the *Greeks* and *Romans*, who ungratefully dealt with I know not how many of their most deserving Generals: While the profounder Politicians, have seen Pamphlets, where *Tacitus* and *Machiavel* have been quoted to shew the danger of too resplendent a Merit. Should a Stranger hear these furious Out-cries of Ingratitude against our General, without knowing the particulars, he would be apt to enquire where was his Tomb, or whether he were allow'd Christian Burial? Not doubting but we had put him to some ignominious Death. Or, has he been tried for his Life, and very narrowly escap'd? Has he been accus'd of High Crimes and Misdemeanors? Has the Prince seiz'd on his Estate, and left him to starve? Has he been hooted at as he passed the Streets, by an ungrateful Mob? Have neither Honours, Offices nor Grants, been conferr'd on Him or his Family? Have not he and they been barbarously stript of them all? Have not he and his Forces been ill pay'd abroad? And does not the Prince by a scanty, limited Commission, hinder him from pursuing his own Methods in the conduct of the War? Has he no Power at all of disposing Commissions as he pleases? Is he not severely us'd by the Ministry or Parliament, who yearly call him to a strict Account? Has the Senate ever thank'd him for good Success, and have they not always publickly censur'd him for the least Miscarriage? Will the Accusers of the Nation join issue upon any of these Particulars, or tell us in what Point, our damnable Sin of Ingratitude lies? Why, 'tis plain and clear; For while he is Commanding abroad, the Queen Dissolves her Parliament, and changes Her Ministry at home: In which *universal Calamity*, no less than *two Persons* allied by Marriage to the General, have lost their Places. Whence came this wonderful Simpathy between the Civil and Military Powers? Will the Troops in *Flanders* refuse to Fight, unless they can have *their own* Lord Keeper, *their own* Lord President of the Council, *their own* chief Governor of *Ireland*, and *their own* Parliament? In a Kingdom where the People are free, how came they to be so fond of having their Councils under the Influence of their Army, or those that lead it? who in all well-instituted States, had no Commerce with the Civil Power, further than to receive their Orders, and obey them without Reserve,

When a General is not so Popular, either in his Army or at Home, as one might expect from a long course of Success; It may perhaps be ascribed to his *Wisdom*, or perhaps to his Complexion. The possession of some one *Quality*, or a defect in some *other*, will extremely damp the Peoples Favour, as well as the Love of the Souldiers. Besides, this is not an Age to produce Favourites of the People, while we live under a Queen who engrosses all our Love, and all our Veneration; and where, the only way for a great General or Minister, to acquire any degree of subordinate Affection from the Publick, must be by all Marks of the most *entire Submission and Respect*, to Her Sacred Person and Commands; otherwise, no pretence of great Services, either in the Field or the Cabinet, will be able to skreen them from universal Hatred.

But the late Ministry was closely join'd to the General, by Friendship, Interest, Alliance, Inclination and Opinion, which cannot be affirm'd of the present; and the Ingratitude of the Nation, lies in the People's *joining as one Man*, to wish, that such a Ministry should be changed. Is it not at the same time notorious to the whole Kingdom, that nothing but a tender regard to the General, was able to preserve that Ministry so long, 'till neither God nor Man could suffer their continuance? Yet in the highest Ferment of Things, we heard few or no Reflections upon this great Commander, but all seem'd unanimous in wishing he might still be at the Head of the Confederate Forces; only at the same time, in case he were resolv'd to resign, they chose rather to turn their Thoughts somewhere else, than throw up all in Despair. And this I cannot but add, in defence of the People, with regard to the Person we are speaking of, that in the high Station he has been for many Years past, his *real Defects* (as nothing Human is without them) have in a detracting Age been very sparingly mention'd, either in Libels or Conversation, and all his *Successes* very freely and universally applauded.

There is an active and a passive Ingratitude; applying both to this Occasion, we may say, the first is, when a Prince or People returns good Services with Cruelty or Ill Usage: The other is, when good Services are not at all, or very meanly rewarded. We have already spoke of the former; let us therefore in the second place, examine how the Services of our General have been rewarded; and whether upon that Article, either Prince or People have been guilty of Ingratitude?

Those are the most valuable Rewards which are given to us from the certain Knowledge of the Doner, that they *fit our Temper best*: I shall therefore say nothing of the Title of *Duke*, or the *Garter*, which the Queen bestow'd the General in the beginning of her Reign; but I shall come to *more Substantial* Instances, and mention nothing which has not been given in the Face of the World. The Lands of *Woodstock*, may, I believe, be reckoned worth 40000 *l*. On the building of *Blenheim* Castle 200000 *l*. have been already expended, tho' it be not yet near finish'd. The Grant of 5000 *l*. per Annum on the Post-Office, is richly worth 100000 *l*. His Principality in *Germany* may be computed at 30000 *l*. Pictures, Jewels, and other Gifts from Foreign Princes, 60000 *l*. The Grant at the *Pall-mall*, the Rangership, &c. for want of more certain Knowledge, may be call'd 10000 *l*. His own, and his Dutchess's Employments

The fifth issue written by Swift of The Examiner

"Court," policies of the defeated ministry.

The name "Whig" in the 1690s came to refer to those who supported William III's policies of maintaining a standing army as an influence on the European situation, holding long Parliaments (which would be more susceptible to Court influence than shorter ones), and weakening the state church. Such policies were opposed, during the 1690s, the Harley period, and the 1720s and 1730s, by the "Country party," an alignment of Tories and disaffected Whigs which represented itself as a nonpartisan force protective of the nation's interests against the self-interested actions of those in power. Its adherents believed that the "Court party" was corrupting the nation by using patronage to buy support and was endangering liberty and the balance of authority in government by shifting power from the parliamentary branch to the executive. The coalition was held together by common support of policies which would put constraints on the Court: opposition to standing armies; advocacy of frequent, preferably annual, parliamentary elections; insistence that political power should follow landed rather than commercial wealth; and opposition to procedures which lead to corruption.

Downie has shown that such "Country" attitudes and policies characterized Swift's positions throughout his life. He did not consider himself a Tory, and never referred to himself as one; he always called himself an "Old Whig," though he admits in *Examiner* 33 that there is in fact little difference "between those who call themselves the *Old Whigs*, and a great Majority of the present *Tories*." Thus it was a natural step, not a radical switch or compromising of his ideals, for Swift to respond to Harley's attention and flattery and to agree to work for his "Old Whig" ministry. A deep bond of affection and perhaps hero worship linked Swift to Harley until the latter's death in 1724: as with Temple earlier, he was cultivating the friendship of an older man he liked and respected.

Harley invited Swift to assume responsibility for *The Examiner*, a weekly paper the ministry began publishing in August 1710 to defend its policies and positions to the nation. Harley was, for his time, unusually aware of the power of the press in shaping public opinion, and he realized that Swift had the abilities to develop that power. For Swift it was an opportunity to advocate unity and conciliation, in which he believed strongly, as opposed to what he saw as rampant party factionalism. Swift's first issue was number 13, 2 November 1710; he was in charge for almost eight months and wrote thirty-three issues, ending with number 45, 14 June 1711.

His authorship of *The Examiner* gave him access to the power centers of government and initiated three and a half exhilarating years which remained the high point of his life. He attended cabinet meetings and appears to have had some influence on policy decisions at them; he accompanied Harley and the court to Windsor; he dined with lords and ladies; he was plagued by people asking him to solicit favors from the great men he associated with. He surely had less influence and was less near the center of things than he thought; he definitely was not informed about everything going on in the ministry. Yet it was a heady affair, and he relished it thoroughly.

As a political essayist he was skillful in wielding the rhetoric of moderation. He cultivated a stance above parties, concerned only with upholding the constitution and exposing threats to it. From that lofty position, he defended the queen's change of ministries, advocated peace, answered essays in opposition papers, defended actions of the ministry, and lashed Thomas, Earl of Wharton, and John Churchill, Duke of Marlborough, as corrupt men and enemies of the nation.

Swift's *Examiners* were an adaptation to politics of the relatively new form of the periodical essay, developed by Richard Steele (with some help from Swift) in *The Tatler* (12 April 1709 - 2 January 1711) and perfected by Steele and Joseph Addison in *The Spectator* (1 March 1711 - 6 December 1712). Swift's pose as the "Examiner," a stable, impartial, public-spirited analyzer of the current political scene, resembles that of the "Spectator" similarly looking down on the state of society and values. Swift adapts Addison and Steele's devices of writing letters to the journal, which can speak for themselves or be answered, writing ironic answers to earlier issues, using fables and other narrative devices within essays, and invoking the coffeehouse world as a "location" of the essays and source of information. Swift also implies that his real concern is not merely political but moral; his emphasis on moral issues (falsehood, avarice, corruption) and his heavy use of allusions to the Bible imply that he is more concerned with the soul of the people and the nation than with day-to-day affairs of government.

Swift's prose style is clear, plain, straightforward—a little less easy and graceful than Addison's. He tends here toward long sentences in a rather cumulative style, seeming to add on thoughts and phrases as they come to him: "It is

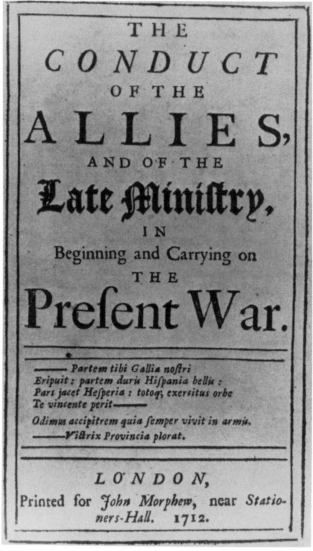

Title page for the pamphlet in which Swift argued that England should seek peace with France rather than continue in a war that was far less advantageous to England than to her allies

not sufficient to alledge, that a good and wise Prince may be allowed to change his Ministers without giving a Reason to his Subjects; because it is probable, that he will not make such a Change without very important Reasons; and a good Subject ought to suppose, that in such a Case there are such Reasons, although he be not apprised of them; otherwise, he must inwardly tax his Prince of Capriciousness, Inconstancy, or ill Design." The result is appropriate to the essay form, a sense not of a tightly organized and closely reasoned discourse, but the thoughts of a well-informed, commonsensical man reflecting on matters of importance. The use of similes, homespun analogies, lists, rhetorical questions, exaggeration, and sarcasm is typically Swiftian.

The most famous of the *Examiners*—on the art of political lying, the Examiner cross-examined, the letter to Crassus, and the Bill of Ingratitude—are among his early *Examiners*; after a few months the challenge seemed to be gone, and the quality of his essays becomes mixed. The most witty and imaginative is his answer in number 16 (23 November 1710) to those who claimed that England, and especially the new ministry, was ungrateful to Marlborough. The essay compares, in terms of money value, what England spent on Marlborough and what Rome customarily bestowed on one of her victorious generals. The "Bill of Roman Gratitude" consists of ten items, ranging in value from "A Triumphal Arch" costing £500 to "A crown of Laurel" costing tuppence, and totals exactly £994 lls. 10d. The "Bill of British Ingratitude" includes Blenheim Palace at £200,000 and five other expensive items, for a total of £540,000. The use of precise numbers and calculations to create an ironic attack anticipates the *Drapier's Letters* and *A Modest Proposal* in later years; the inventiveness and subtlety are typical of Swift's prose at its best.

Swift's editing of *The Examiner* ceased at the end of the Parliamentary session in June 1711—he had successfully justified the existence of the new ministry and was ready to move on to a new task. Secret conversations with the French about a peace treaty had progressed to open negotiations in the summer of 1711. Preliminary articles between France and England were signed in October and were to be brought to Parliament for approval in November. Swift wrote several pamphlets relating to these negotiations, the most important of which was *The Conduct Of The Allies, And Of The Late Ministry, In Beginning and Carrying on The Present War*, a summary of the ministry's point of view and of the arguments for peace. It was a great success: published near the end of November 1711, it went through six editions, eleven thousand copies, in two months.

Swift's thesis in the pamphlet is "that no Nation was ever so long or so scandalously abused" as England was by its domestic enemies and foreign allies. He lays out in clear, formal fashion three points he will treat: (1) that England foolishly carried a larger share of the cost of the war, in men and money, than the allies though they had more at stake; (2) that England unwisely committed herself to war on land (despite greater naval strength) because it was to Marlborough's advantage to do so; and (3) that the allies had not lived up to their commitments in the war, and had taken advantage of England whenever they could profit from it. The only reason to prolong the war, the pamphlet asserts, was self-interest—the self-interest of investors and military men at home, and of the allies abroad; but there were many reasons—especially the burden of war debt at home and the successful achievement of the war's aims abroad—to pursue peace.

The style here offers an interesting contrast to that of *The Examiner*. These are not the informal reflections of a dispassionate observer, but the terse, tightly organized arguments of a committed authority on the subject. The sentences are shorter and carefully thought out—honed to sharp, clear precision, without a word wasted or phrase out of place, in contrast to the leisurely, cu-

mulative style usual in *The Examiner*. There is, as Quintana puts it, a studied avoidance of anything having the appearance of rhetoric; the reader was to feel only the weight of facts. But this is itself a rhetorical device. By the way he marshals carefully selected facts, Swift supplies ostensible evidence—but no proof—of a conspiracy among the Whigs, the allies, the stockjobbers, and the Marlboroughs. As Downie explains it, "The target reader of Swift's pamphlet was not a truculent Whig but a sympathetic Tory. . . . He uses his knowledge of the fears of the target reader to outline a fictional political situation against which his audience will react violently, and he supplies unimpeachable facts to convince the country squire that this fictional situation is not fictional at all, but fact."

He succeeded very well in what he sought to do. When "No Peace without Spain" was debated in the House of Commons, Swift wrote to Stella, "Those who spoke, drew all their arguments from my book, and their votes confirm all I writ; the Court had a majority of a hundred and fifty." The measure was pushed through the House of Lords by having the queen create twelve new peerages—all Tories, of course; at the same time, the duke of Marlborough was dismissed from all his appointments.

At the beginning of 1712, then, the Tories seemed secure, and the Whigs defeated. But below the surface differences in personalities and policies were emerging which eventually were to tear the ministry apart. The tension between the slow, methodical, moderate Harley—made earl of Oxford in 1711—and the brilliant, impetuous, radically Tory Henry St. John—made viscount Bolingbroke in 1712—increased as Bolingbroke pressed for a unilateral treaty with France; Oxford insisted on including the Dutch, and won out in the Treaty of Utrecht in April 1713, but by then the feuding had become open and bitter. Swift throughout this period was in charge of government propaganda, hiring others to write pamphlets and newspapers defending government policies and editing and approving what they wrote. His role was broad and important enough in its scope to include "correcting" drafts of the queen's opening speeches to Parliament in 1713 and 1714.

He also assumed the function of official historian of the peace negotiations and worked furiously on an account which he hoped would be published before Parliament met to debate the treaty and would, like *The Conduct Of The Allies*, influ-

Esther Johnson, Swift's "Stella" (portrait by James Latham; by permission of the National Gallery of Ireland)

ence the course of that debate. The book traces the government's actions in search of peace from the crisis of December 1711 through the signing of the treaties at Utrecht. It seeks to establish the ministry's patriotic honesty, attach responsibility for delays and for the ministry's secrecy on "Dutch duplicity and Whig malice," and glorify Oxford and his role in the process. The ministry, however, delayed and eventually forbade its publication, understandably so, Ehrenpreis holds, in view of its inadequacies as history and as polemic. It was not published until 1758, as *The History Of The Four Last Years Of The Queen*.

Swift was disappointed, because of the effort he put into it and the high expectations he had for it, and because he hoped it, as culmination of his other services, would pave the way to

a church appointment in England. Swift's name had often been mentioned as a candidate for church vacancies in England, but each time he was disappointed. He blamed the ministers for not working hard enough on his behalf, and perhaps they could have been more concerned and energetic. But their options were limited: appointments of all English and Irish bishops and English deans had to be approved by the monarch, and Queen Anne—pious, conservative, of limited intellect—had declared that she would not endorse the author of *A Tale of a Tub* for any church position under her jurisdiction. The best the ministry could do for Swift was an appointment as a dean in Ireland, which did not need the queen's approval. Swift was made dean of St. Patrick's Cathedral in Dublin by the lord lieutenant, his friend James Butler, Duke of Ormonde, in April 1713, and installed at the cathedral on 13 June 1713.

He intended to remain in Ireland, but his friends persuaded him to return to London and attempt to heal the now open split between Oxford and Bolingbroke. There was, however, little that he, or anyone, could do. Oxford—drinking too much, more desultory than ever—was ineffective as leader, but managed to block Bolingbroke's efforts to replace him. The queen's health was declining rapidly. She died on 1 August 1714, ending the Tory ministry and the most exciting years of Swift's life. King George I would now ascend the throne, and Swift would have no place in the new Whig ministry that would soon be appointed. He quickly left England to take up his duties as dean, and spent the rest of his life, except for two brief visits to London, in what he called his "exile" in Ireland.

In addition to his political writings, Swift during the years of the Oxford ministry wrote at least twenty poems, a pamphlet parodying Anthony Collins's *Discourse of Free-Thinking* (1713), and *A Proposal For Correcting, Improving and Ascertaining The English Tongue* (1712), the only work he published under his own name. This pamphlet, written in the form of a letter to the earl of Oxford, advocates the establishment of an academy, comparable to the French Academy, with the goal of "*Ascertaining* and *Fixing* our Language for ever, after such Alterations are made in it as shall be thought requisite." Downie notes cogently that such a scheme is an extension of Swift's Old Whig attitudes in politics: "It retains the same nostalgic yearning for a bygone age and the same resistance to change. The language was to be ordered and regulated as ideally, in Swift's view, the state should be ordered and regulated."

Of Swift's prose works in this period the most entertaining is the *Journal to Stella*. At Moor Park Swift formed the deepest friendship of his life with Esther Johnson, whom he later came to call "Stella." When he first joined the Temple household she was eight years old, frail, and fatherless. Swift taught her penmanship, directed her reading, and "instruct [ed] her in the principles of honour and virtue." When he returned in 1696 she was fifteen, pretty, and an engaging companion. A lasting relationship grew between them—a love which was deeper than that of brother and sister, but which apparently never became that of husband and wife.

A year after Swift moved to Ireland in 1699, Esther Johnson and her companion Rebecca Dingley followed him and settled in Dublin, ostensibly because their meager incomes would go further in Ireland, but actually, it seems, to be closer to Swift. Feeling guilty about his absence and wanting to share what he was doing in London, he wrote them a series of letters between September 1710 and June 1713—his "journal" to Stella. Its interest stems in part from Swift's recounting of his daily activities and his references to people and events of the time; but it is also appealing for its evidences of his affection and concern for Esther, its intimate revelation of his own personality, and its literary characteristics (which Frederik Smith has analyzed closely and imaginatively).

On earlier trips to England, Swift had apparently written to Esther and Rebecca, referring to them as MD (My Dears), though those letters are lost. This time he wrote to inform them of his safe arrival first in England (from Chester, 2 September 1710) and a week later in London (9 September 1710). In the second letter he announced his intention to begin the journal: "Henceforth I will write something every day to MD, and make it a sort of journal; and when it is full, I will send it whether MD writes or no; and so that will be pretty." Beginning that day, Swift wrote daily or twice daily entries on large sheets of paper and sent them to Ireland at ten-to-twelve-day intervals, when the sheets were filled on both sides.

The entries soon fell into a regular pattern. He always told with whom he dined that day—an item of importance to him not just socially but financially, for he stretched his tight budget by rarely buying dinner for himself. He then summarized his activities—visits, conversations, business dealings. All of this allowed the letters to serve as a diary for himself as well as a journal for them: "I fancy I shall, some time or other, have the curiosity of seeing some particulars how I passed my life when I was absent from MD this time." He regularly mentioned current events, though not in detail (since the biweekly format meant the news would be old by the time the letters arrived), and he often recounted a sensational item—a husband killing his wife, her lover, and then himself, for example. And there was usually a personal section to the ladies—a long one on the days a letter from them arrived. Swift would urge Stella to care for her weak eyes and not read much, to go out riding often, and to keep up an active social life, visiting and playing cards. And he would

Jonathan Swift (portrait by Francis Bindon; by permission of the National Gallery of Ireland)

tease her about factual errors in her letters and about her poor spelling ("But who are those *Wiggs* that think I am turned Tory? Do you mean Whigs? Which *Wiggs* and *wat* do you mean?").

The intimacy and flavor of the *Journal* is created in part by Swift's use of "little language" and pet names. The "little language," a kind of baby talk (with *l*'s substituted for *r*'s and vice versa, for example), was edited away by Deane Swift when he published letters 2-40 in 1768 and then burned the manuscripts. Manuscripts of letters 1, 41, 53, and 55-65 (published by Hawkesworth in 1766) are extant, however, and modern editions attempt to reproduce the effect of the little language, as, for example, "Go play

Cards & be melly . . . & rove pdfr who roves Md bettle zan his Rife. Farewell deelest Md." Here and elsewhere Swift used combinations of letters as a form of personal address. "MD," My dear or My dears, usually meant both ladies but sometimes just Stella. Stella herself is "Ppt," Poppet, or Poor Pretty Thing. "D," or "d," is Dingley, or sometimes "Me," probably for Madame Elderly. Swift referred to himself as "Pdfr," pronounced "Podefar," standing for Poor Dear Foolish Rogue, or Poor Dear Fellow.

Such familiar language demanded a colloquial, conversational style, which is also part of the charm of the *Journal*. As Swift put it, by writing every day, sometimes morning and evening,

"I shall always be in conversation with MD, and MD with Presto." Much of the time the *Journal* is loose and chatty, as if Stella and Rebecca were present, and some parts even include both sides of conversations with them. Even the carelessness of the handwriting contributed to the intimacy and personalness of the effect: "Methinks when I write plain, I do not know how, but we are not alone, all the world can see us. A bad scrawl is so snug, it looks like a PMD."

The *Journal* frequently employs techniques characteristic of his other, "imaginative" works. There is his recognition that the "voice" in the written work is and is not his own voice. This is evident as he talks to and answers himself: "Well, but when shall we answer this letter N. 8. of MD's? Not till next year, faith. O Lord—bo—but that will be a Monday next. Cod's so, is it, and so it is: never saw the like," and even more so as he draws attention to differences between the Swift of the *Journal* and its little language, and the Swift of the political world: "But let me alone, sirrahs; for Presto is going to be very busy; not Presto, but t'other I."

There is also his typical tendency to dramatize what he describes. A measure of dramatic suspense is inherent in the journal form, since the writer does not know the outcome of events as he begins to write about them—as Swift was fully aware: "These letters of mine are a sort of journal, where matters open by degrees; and, as I tell true or false, you will find by the event whether my intelligence be good." Beyond the drama natural to the journal form, Swift also sets up little dramatic scenes within his entries. Thus he dramatizes his own acts of opening a letter from MD ("I . . . am now got into bed, and going to open your little letter: . . . Oh, I won't open it yet! yes I will! no I won't") and he makes a little scene out of a smell in his room: "What's this? faith I smell fire . . . faith I must rise, and look at my chimney, for the smell grows stronger, stay—I have been up, and in my room, and found all safe, only a mouse within the fender to warm himself, which I could not catch."

Also, there is a dynamic to the very activity of journal writing itself. As he writes he is fully aware of and a part of what goes on around him—of the watchman's call at midnight as he writes ("So, ladies, enough of business for one night. Paaaaast twelvvve o'clock"), of his servant moving about the room ("I write this while Patrick is folding up my scarf, and doing up the fire"), even of the physical appearance of the paper as he writes

(of a tobacco stain at the top of letter 6, or a crease in the sheet of letter 15). All of this unites to give a lively and detailed portrayal of the most exciting years of Swift's life. Nowhere else can one find such an unguarded, honest look into Swift's personality—his hopes, successes, frustrations, disappointments, failures, illnesses, pride, and above all, tenderness and affection. It reveals Swift's time, but most of all it reveals Swift himself.

Many readers have sensed a change in temper in the *Journal* from early 1712 on, a bit less playfulness, fewer expressions of affection, and fewer wishes to return to Ireland soon. Harold Williams in his edition points to several factors which can help explain the change: Swift was in poor health for more than a year; he was disheartened by the slowness of the peace negotiations, by the queen's uncertain health, and by the tensions within the ministry; and he was anxious over his failure to be given a worthy church appointment for his loyal services to the government. Others have held that an additional factor was his interest in another woman, Esther Vanhomrigh, or "Vanessa."

Swift may have known the Vanhomrighs in Dublin, where Esther's father, Bartholomew Vanhomrigh, was a prominent public figure before his death in 1703. If not, he met them at an inn in Dunstable when the family was moving to London in 1707. Swift renewed his acquaintance with them in 1709 and soon was seeing the family often—for a time Swift lived a few doors from them, on Bury Street. When that area became too expensive and he moved out to Chelsea (a two-mile walk which gave him good exercise), he left his "best gown and periwig" at their house and stopped by each morning to change into them and again each afternoon to change back to his older ones.

So there was convenience in the relationship, and countless free dinners, but the main attraction was Vanessa. She was young (twenty to his forty-one), vivacious, and ready to be impressed by a witty, good-looking man who moved in the highest circles of government and society. Swift was always attracted to fatherless younger women toward whom he could act as a tutor, adviser on manners and morals, and father figure. Swift surely intended that their relationship go no further than this, but go further it did. Dinners and evenings playing cards at the Vanhomrighs became more frequent; private times with Vanessa increased; letters passed between

Esther Vanhomrigh, Swift's "Vanessa" (portrait by Philip Hussey; by permission of the National Gallery of Ireland)

them; she visited him alone in Windsor. That most of this is not included in the *Journal* seems natural, to avoid giving concern to Stella; but it also indicates the embarrassment and uncertainty the relationship created for him.

His attentions to Vanessa and endearing statements in letters ("I will come as early on Monday as I can find Opportunity; and will take a little Grubstreet Lodging ... and dine with you thrice a week; and will tell You a thousand Secrets provided You will have no Quarrells to me") raised her expectations. As she, in person and in letters, became more passionate and possessive, Swift backed away: the long poem he wrote for her in 1713, *Cadenus And Vanessa* (1726), says he wanted only friendship, not romantic love, between them. He apparently regarded her as a London companion, and when he returned to Ireland, he intended to leave thoughts of her

behind: "I told you when I left England, I would endeavor to forget every thing there, and would write as seldom as I could."

She, however, could not forget and would not be left behind. She pursued him through letters and later, after her mother died, moved to Ireland with her sister. Swift visited her there, but obviously did not return the kind of affection she desired. An old legend holds that Vanessa heard Swift was married to Stella, that she wrote to Stella asking if it were true, that Stella gave the letter to Swift, who went to Vanessa, flung the letter in front of her, and left without uttering a word, and that this so crushed Vanessa that she died not long after. The truth is probably much more mundane, with Swift clumsily attempting to escape the entanglement without hurting Vanessa, and with Vanessa increasingly in poor health and alone, sadly living out her life unable to be content with the level of friendship and attention he was willing to give.

In seeking to leave Vanessa behind as he left London, Swift was returning to Stella as he returned to Ireland, though David Nokes suspects it was initially with somewhat mixed feelings. Swift enjoyed the passionateness, raillery, and irrepressible determination of Vanessa and perhaps turned from it with some reluctance; but his relation to Stella was older and deeper and demanded his loyalty. She was constant, and content with the kind of friendship he offered, and until her death in 1728, their relationship continued as it had been, with frequent visits (though never alone—a third person always was present), with Stella and Rebecca occupying the deanery during Swift's absences, and with Stella serving as Swift's hostess for social events and nursing him through illnesses. Swift began in 1719 the practice of sending birthday poems to Stella—graceful, tender tributes to her qualities and expressions of his deep affection for her. Legends about Swift and Stella began circulating from the time Swift returned to Ireland—chiefly that Swift and Stella were secretly married by St George Ashe in 1716 but continued to live apart as before. Of recent biographers, Ehrenpreis and Downie dismiss the story, while Nokes leaves it an open question. That they simply had an unconventional but deep commitment to each other without marriage seems most likely.

During his early years as dean of St. Patrick's Swift did very little writing. He was depressed at first about the Whig takeover and his own removal to Ireland: all the people he cared about except Stella were in England. He did compose two defenses of the fallen ministry— *Memoirs Relating To That Change which happened in the Queen's Ministry in the Year 1710* and, after Oxford was arrested and imprisoned on charges of treason, *An Enquiry into the Behaviour of the Queen's Last Ministry*, both of them first published in 1765 in Hawkesworth's edition of Swift's *Works*. But he was also busy with church matters, establishing himself as dean and solving problems within his chapter. Gradually he developed friendships and began to make extended visits in the country as a way of escaping the pressures of Dublin and his cathedral. And, despite his intention not to become involved, he was eventually drawn into Irish politics and came, in the 1720s, to wage a notable campaign against the exploitation and enslavement of Ireland.

The problem was that, as Oliver Ferguson explains, though in title a kingdom, eighteenth-century Ireland was in fact virtually an English colony. Most important positions in the government and church were held by Englishmen, and many other positions were filled by absentees who drew proceeds into England. Ireland had its own parliament, but it could not meet without consent of the king, and all measures passed by it had to be approved by the Privy Council in England.

A series of laws governing commerce were imposed to protect the English economy and to weaken Ireland and prevent her from becoming a threat to England. The export of livestock from Ireland to England was halted in the 1660s by prohibitory duties, thus eliminating the market which accounted for three-fourths of the trade of Ireland. In 1699 England prohibited Ireland from exporting woolen goods to any country; this virtually destroyed Ireland's most flourishing industry. Weavers emigrated from Ireland, or were left near starvation. Navigation acts required that goods imported into Ireland from the colonies pass through England, which greatly increased prices.

The Irish added to their own economic difficulties. Though they could not sell livestock to England, they could to other countries, and they continued to turn farmland into grazing land. Grazing land was less expensive to manage and required fewer tenants, but farmers thus were put out of work and off the land where they had been living and working. Wealthy Irish who lived in England drew a great deal of their income out of the country—Swift estimated that one-third of the annual rents were thus lost to the Irish economy. And the Irish who had money fostered tastes for foreign products, instead of buying Irish goods, which would have kept money in Ireland and given work to its people.

Those economic and political problems were compounded by the fact that Ireland was a divided nation. There was the division between the native Irish, the Anglo-Irish (the English who immigrated to Ireland and their descendants), and English politicians and bureaucrats temporarily living in Ireland. There was the division between Roman Catholics, Anglicans (Church of Ireland), and dissenters (Protestants outside the Church of Ireland). Animosities and suspicions between the groups were deep. As in England, non-Anglicans were excluded by the Test Act from civil and military positions: the Anglicans thus constituted a minority government. Catholics in addi-

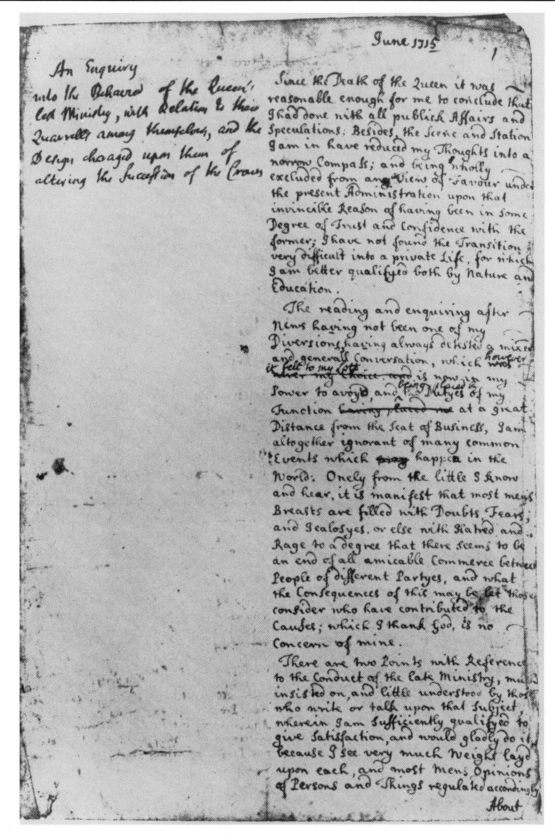

First page—in Stella's hand with corrections by Swift—from an early draft for one of Swift's defenses of the fallen ministry of Robert Harley, Earl of Oxford (by permission of the Master and Fellows of Trinity College, Cambridge)

tion could not purchase land or extended leases, could not possess or carry firearms, and could not own a horse valued at more than five pounds. Catholics who did own estates could not bequeath them to their eldest sons, but had to divide them among all their children; and any child who converted to Anglicanism could receive the entire estate. Catholics were required to educate their children in Protestant schools; priests were tightly regulated. Dissenters in Ireland were mostly Ulster Presbyterians, who migrated from Scotland and settled in tight-knit groups in the North. Their numerical dominance and economic means enabled them to evade some of the restrictions placed on Catholics and to function almost as the established church in parts of the North.

Swift approved of the restrictions on Catholics and dissenters, in England and Ireland, but he actively opposed the economic restrictions on Ireland and England's treatment of Ireland as a colony. The great period of his championing the Irish cause began in 1720, with the publication of *A Proposal For the Universal Use Of Irish Manufacture,... Uterly Rejecting and Renouncing Every Thing wearable that comes from England.* The pamphlet does put forward the proposal described in the title, but its broader purpose is to attack the English for their subjugation of Ireland, and to rail at the Irish for accepting such subjugation. In one sentence Swift sums up his overall challenge to the Irish: "The Scripture tells us, that *Oppression makes a wise Man mad*; therefore, consequently speaking, the Reason why some Men are not *mad*, is because they are not *wise*." Since the English can only be expected to take measures to benefit England, the Irish must help themselves. The tone is shaped by exaggeration, understatement, and the irony inherent in the situation, as the Irish pursue courses which hurt rather than help Ireland.

His greatest achievement on behalf of the Irish grew out of events beginning in England in 1722, when William Wood was awarded a patent authorizing him to coin and distribute a hundred thousand pounds worth of Irish copper farthings and halfpence. Ireland needed coins, but Irish leaders believed that the approved amount was at least five times the amount needed, which would reduce the value of money, and that the patent specified too little copper per coin, thus further reducing their value. Also, safeguards on quality and against overproduction were not provided in the patent. Beyond all these problems was the fact that Ireland was not permitted to have its own mint and make its own money and that authority to coin money for Ireland could be granted without even consulting the Irish. It was a blatant example of Ireland's dependent status.

Protests were raised by the commissioners of revenue in Dublin, by the Irish Parliament, by church leaders, and by other individuals, but Wood pressed on with his plans, and the English government gave no sign of backing down. Shipments of the coins began arriving in Ireland. The only solution was for the Irish to boycott the coins, since by law one was obligated to accept as legal tender only coins of silver or gold. This course was proposed by Archbishop William King and endorsed by political leaders, bankers, and businessmen. To be successful, however, it required the support of the lower classes; to reach them, Swift's assistance was sought.

Swift, preoccupied with personal problems (including the death of Vanessa) and busy writing *Gulliver's Travels*, had not become involved in the Wood affair in 1723. He was asked in February 1724 to join the campaign and immediately composed the first of his famous "Drapier's Letters," *A Letter To The Shop-Keepers, Tradesmen, Farmers, and Common People of Ireland.* In order to communicate with people in general, Swift posed as a draper, a dealer in cloth and dry goods, and used his typical stylistic and rhetorical devices (exaggeration, pushing to extremes, dramatized examples, and vivid comparisons—even, as Phyllis Guskin has shown, typography: italics and capitalization) to persuade people not to accept the new coins. Thus, in a supposedly straightforward summary of the situation, he greatly overstates the adulteration of Wood's coins: "Mr. WOODS made his HALF-PENCE of such *Base Metal*, and so much smaller than the *English* ones, that the *Brazier* would not give you above a *Penny* of good Money for a *Shilling* of his." If the coins are inferior in quality, they will not be worth their face value, and merchants accepting them will be cheated: "If a *Hatter* sells a Dozen of *Hatts* for *Five Shillings* a-piece, which amounts to *Three Pounds*, and receives the Payment in Mr. WOODS's Coin, he really receives only the Value of *Five Shillings*." As a result a merchant will be forced to "demand ten times the Price of his Goods, if it is to be paid in WOODS's Money." Soon a country squire coming to town to shop will need to "bring with him Five or Six Horses loaden with *Sacks* as the Farmers bring their Corn," and a landowner paying his annual rent will "require Twelve Hundred Horses to carry it." He mixes a biblical allusion (to the prohibition against touching anything "unclean"—see Leviticus 5:2) and the ever-present fear of the Black Death to set up powerful analogies: "*These HALF-PENCE are like the* accursed Thing, *which as the* Scripture *tells us, the* Children of Israel *were forbidden to touch, they will run about like the* Plague *and destroy every one who lays his Hands upon them.*" He then explains clearly and simply the stipulations in the law about legal tender, and urges readers to "stand to it One and All, refuse this *Filthy Trash*; It is no Treason to Rebel against Mr. WOODS."

Swift underwrote publication costs, so the pamphlet could be circulated widely. Other letters from the Drapier followed, to different audiences, as new developments took place. The second letter was designed to strengthen the will to resist after Wood made the concessions of cutting back the total number of coins and having their quality tested. It is an intense attack on Wood— and those who supported him—and a further vivid description of the effects that would follow if his coins were accepted. By now the country was united in its opposition to Wood, and various individuals and groups (including the butchers, the brewers, the bricklayers, and even the beggars) issued declarations—some possibly written by Swift—refusing to accept the new coins.

In the third letter, a new and larger theme, hinted at in the earlier letters, emerges: a protest that Ireland is an independent nation under the king and should not be subservient to English parliamentary control. "Were not the People of *Ireland* born as *Free* as those of *England?* . . . Are they not Subjects of the same King? . . . Am I a *Free-Man* in *England*, and do I become a *Slave* in six Hours by crossing the Channel?" That theme was intensified in the fourth letter, addressed "To the Whole People of Ireland" on the occasion of the arrival of the new lord lieutenant, Lord John Carteret, whose charge was to gain acceptance of the coins. In a daring, provocative paragraph, Swift wrote: "I *M. B. Drapier* . . . declare, next under God, I *depend* only on the King my Sovereign, and on the Laws of my own Country; and I am so far from *depending* upon the People of *England*, that if they should ever *Rebel* against my Sovereign (which God forbid) I would be ready at the first Command from his Majesty to take Arms against them." He moves on to a rousing affirmation of Irish rights: "By the Laws of GOD, of NATURE, of NATIONS, and of your own Country, you ARE and OUGHT to be as FREE a People as your Brethren in *England*."

To mention the topic of rebellion and taking arms, even in an unlikely hypothetical situation, was seditious. In context Swift's phrase "The Remedy is wholly in your own Hands" referred specifically to the Wood affair; but it could be applied to the Irish situation generally, with inflammatory effect. Swift, after provoking the government in earlier letters, finally forced it to act. The Irish Privy Council voted to arrest John Harding, the pamphlet's printer, condemned "several seditious and scandalous paragraphs" in the letter, and offered the huge reward of three hundred pounds (a family could live modestly on seventy-five pounds a year) for information leading to the discovery of the Drapier's identity. The reward was never claimed. That Swift had written the pamphlets was common knowledge, but by now he was regarded as a national hero, and the people united behind him personally as well as behind the cause. Flyers with the following verse from 1 Samuel 14 were posted throughout Dublin: "And the people said unto Saul, Shall Jonathan die, who hath wrought this great salvation in Israel? God forbid: as the Lord liveth, there shall not one hair of his head fall to the ground." Harding eventually was released after two grand juries refused to return a presentment against a later Drapier pamphlet. The Irish, united, gained victory: the English government had no choice but to withdraw Wood's patent, which it did in August 1725.

It was, however, only a symbolic victory: the fundamental attitudes and policies of England toward the Irish remained unchanged, and Ireland's situation worsened, aggravated by drought and famine. Swift now had enormous popularity within Ireland, especially among the common people, and to this day retains the status of "the Hibernian Patriot." He wrote other pamphlets seeking to improve the lives of the Irish people, such as *A Short View Of The State Of Ireland* (1728) and *A Letter to the Archbishop of Dublin, concerning the Weavers* (written in 1729; first published in 1765 in Hawkesworth's edition of the *Works*).

When such efforts produced no changes in policies, and conditions in Ireland continued to grow more severe, Swift responded in 1729 with one of his best-known pamphlets, *A Modest Proposal*. Faced with economic problems, Swift borrowed the form of an economic essay: it follows

Swift as M. B. Drapier, from the Faulkner edition of Swift's Works *(1735)*

the standard format for such a pamphlet, setting forth a problem, stating the proposed solution, outlining the advantages of the plan, and refuting possible objections to it (reinforced, as Charles A. Beaumont has shown, by the conventional structure of the classical oration).

The proposal is presented through Swift's typical use of a "voice," as he mimics the style and language of a serious proposer. The voice is developed slightly through a few discernible character traits: the "proposer" is Irish, perhaps Anglo-Irish since he opposes Catholicism; he is a public-spirited citizen deeply concerned about what is happening to his country; he is a practical man, careful and precise in his analyses, but a bit obtuse, failing to see the implications of and inconsistencies in what he advocates; he has a wife and children, the youngest about nine years old; he is objective and disinterested (trying to help others

who need help, not himself), but at the same time a visionary, a "projector"—that is, one who comes up with what others recognize as impossible, harebrained schemes.

The proposal is that children of the Irish poor, at about a year old, be sold to the rich for food. The horror of the suggestion comes out through the typically Swiftian use of abundant, concrete detail: there is imagery comparing the poor to cattle—the females are "Breeders," one male is sufficient to "serve" four females, the child is "dropt from its Dam"; there are slaughterhouse and butcher images—"Shambles may be appointed," "flay the Carcase" (to use the skin for fine gloves and boots); there is cooking imagery—children will be "a most delicious nourishing, and wholesome Food; whether *Stewed, Roasted, Baked,* or *Boiled,*" and there is imagery of mathematics and computation—"I calculate," "I have reckoned," "I have already computed." All of this is dehumanizing; it treats human beings as things to be used for someone else's benefit.

That is exactly the point about England's attitude toward the Irish: she dehumanizes them, uses them to her advantage without regard for their welfare. So too do the rich and landlords in Ireland. But not the Irish poor. True, they would sell their children, but not without regard for their welfare. They would do so knowing that this was preferable to the fate the Irish now endure. In a haunting paragraph, next to last in the pamphlet, Swift urges anyone who objects to this proposal to "ask the Parents of these Mortals, Whether they would not, at this Day, think it a great Happiness to have been sold for Food at a Year old . . . and thereby have avoided such a perpetual Scene of Misfortunes, as they have since gone through."

The proposal makes cannibals of the English and the rich landlords, but in effect they are cannibals already. The entire proposal grows out of a basic Swiftian literary technique, of literalizing metaphors—that is, treating a figure of speech, something nonphysical and nonliteral, as if it were literal and physical. Two such metaphors—"devoured" and "eat up"—are crucial to the pamphlet. The proposer notes, "I grant this Food will be somewhat dear [a splendidly effective pun], and therefore very *proper for Landlords*; who, as they have already devoured most of the Parents, seem to have the best Title to the Children." Later he says the food could, unfortunately, not be exported, "The Flesh being of too tender a Consistence, to admit a long Continuance in Salt; *although, perhaps, I could name a Country [England], which would be glad to eat up our whole Nation without it.*" At one level, then, *A Modest Proposal* merely shows in stark terms what the English and the rich Irish are already doing to Ireland, though the economic jargon of "protective duties" and "enclosures" is ordinarily used to cover up the grim truths of the case.

Behind the calm, analytical voice of the proposer is Swift's voice, expressing anger and bitterness in the lines on landlords and England quoted above and even addressing the reader directly in a paragraph listing sensible things the Irish could do to help themselves, all things Swift had urged in earlier pamphlets: "Let no man talk to me of other Expedients: *Of taxing our Absentees at five Shillings a Pound: Of using neither Cloaths, nor Houshold Furniture except what is of our own Growth and Manufacture: Of utterly rejecting the Mate-*

rials and Instruments that promote foreign Luxury." As Rawson has demonstrated, however, the division of the two voices usually is not that clearcut. A closer look prevents a neat, simple separation of the words and ideas of the proposer from those of Swift. Swift's compassion for the Irish is modified by a contempt of them expressed in other essays: hostility to beggars, abhorrence of the barbarian natives (including instances of cannibalism), nonironic references to them as animals. "The complicated interplay of compassion and contempt is . . . an explosive mixture, and Swift's feelings oscillate starkly among extreme positions." Here, at their clearest, are the complexity and paradoxicalness that make Swift fascinating: a man who seeks to prod and draw humans into being the better creatures he believes they will not become, a man who loves and longs for England but dwells mostly on her faults, a man who hated Ireland and regarded it as a prison yet devoted years to efforts to alleviate its misery and bring it freedom.

The decade of the 1720s was impressively productive for Swift: there were more essays on Ireland, carrying over into the early 1730s; he wrote a great deal of poetry, including most of his best verse; and he completed and published, anonymously as usual, his greatest work, *Gulliver's Travels*. He made two visits to London. The first was for about five months, in 1726, to visit old friends and arrange for the publication of *Gulliver's Travels*; his arrival back in Dublin was celebrated with ringing church bells, bonfires in the streets, and repeated acclamations of "Long live the Drapier." During the second, in 1727, he became involved in the opposition to the chief minister Robert Walpole, probably in the hope of yet securing a church position in England. Those hopes faded when George II ascended the throne in June and soon gave to Walpole at least as much confidence and power as he had enjoyed under George I.

From September 1727 on, Swift remained in Ireland. After 1732 he did little writing: "I have done with everything & of every kind that requires writing," he wrote in 1734, "except now & then a Letter." Stella, whose health was precarious during Swift's last visit to London, had died in 1728. His correspondence with friends in England and his contacts with friends in Ireland steadily lessened during the 1730s, as he became increasingly deaf and retreated into the deanery—though he remained a public hero to Dubliners, who rang bells and lit bonfires each year on his

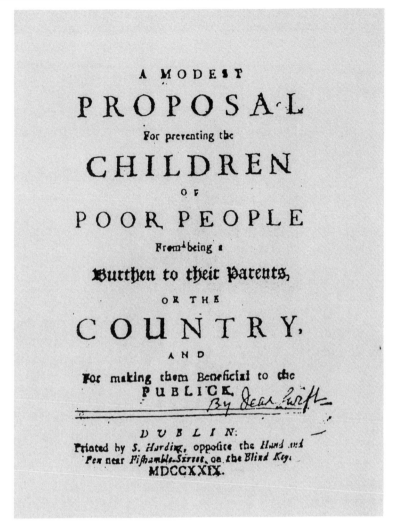

Title page for the pamphlet in which Swift satirizes England's dehumanization of the Irish by proposing that the children of the Irish poor be "sold for Food at a Year old" and thus avoid "a perpetual Scene of Misfortunes"

birthday for the rest of his life. In 1738 his memory began to fail, and in 1739 he put his authority as dean into the hands of a subdean, John Wynne. In 1742 he was found legally incapable of managing his own affairs, and a committee of guardians was appointed. Old legends assert that he went insane and lived his final years "a driv'ler and a show." Those legends are untrue: he suffered the effects of senility and various physical ailments, but he was never insane by modern definitions. He died in 1745, just short of the age of seventy-eight; for three days the people of Dublin crowded to view his body; he was, as he instructed, buried privately at midnight in the middle aisle of St. Patrick's Cathedral.

Letters:

The Correspondence of Jonathan Swift, 5 volumes, ed-

ited by Harold Williams (Oxford: Clarendon Press, 1963).

Bibliographies:

Herman Teerink, *A Bibliography of the Writings of Jonathan Swift* (The Hague: Nijhoff, 1937); second edition, revised and corrected, edited by Arthur H. Scouten (Philadelphia: University of Pennsylvania Press, 1963);

Louis A. Landa and J. E. Tobin, *Jonathan Swift: A List of Critical Studies Published from 1895-1945* (New York: Cosmopolitan Science & Art Service, 1945);

James J. Stathis, *A Bibliography of Swift Studies, 1946-1965* (Nashville, Tenn.: Vanderbilt University Press, 1967);

Richard H. Rodino, *Swift Studies, 1965-1980: An Annotated Bibliography* (New York: Garland, 1984).

Biographies:

John Boyle, Fifth Earl of Cork and Orrery, *Remarks on the Life and Writings of Dr. Jonathan Swift, Dean of St. Patrick's, Dublin, in a Series of Letters from John, Earl of Orrery, to His Son, the Honourable Hamilton Boyle* (London: A. Millar, 1752);

Thomas Sheridan, *The Life of the Rev. Dr. Jonathan Swift, Dean of St. Patrick's, Dublin* (London: Printed for C. Bathurst, W. Strahan, B. Collins, J. F. & C. Rivington, L. Davis, W. Owen, J. Dodsley, T. Longman, R. Baldwin, T. Cadell, J. Nichols, T. Egerton & W. Bent, 1784);

Irvin Ehrenpreis, *Swift: The Man, His Works, and the Age*, 3 volumes (Cambridge, Mass.: Harvard University Press, 1962-1983);

J. A. Downie, *Jonathan Swift: Political Writer* (London: Routledge & Kegan Paul, 1984);

David Nokes, *Jonathan Swift, A Hypocrite Reversed* (London: Oxford University Press, 1985).

References:

Robert M. Adams, "Jonathan Swift, Thomas Swift, and the Authorship of *A Tale of a Tub*," *Modern Philology*, 64 (February 1967): 198-232;

Adams, *Strains of Discord: Studies in Literary Openness* (Ithaca, N.Y.: Cornell University Press, 1958);

Charles A. Beaumont, *Swift's Classical Rhetoric* (Athens: University of Georgia Press, 1961);

Richmond P. Bond, "Isaac Bickerstaff, Esq.," in *Restoration and Eighteenth-Century Literature: Essays in Honor of Alan Dugald McKillop*, edited by Carroll Camden (Chicago: University of Chicago Press, 1963), pp. 103-124;

W. B. Carnochan, "Swift's *Tale*: On Satire, Negation, and the Uses of Irony," *Eighteenth-Century Studies*, 5 (Fall 1971): 122-144;

John R. Clark, *Form and Frenzy in Swift's "Tale of a Tub"* (Ithaca, N.Y.: Cornell University Press, 1970);

Richard I. Cook, *Jonathan Swift as a Tory Pamphleteer* (Seattle: University of Washington Press, 1967);

Herbert Davis, *Stella: A Gentlewoman of the Eighteenth Century* (New York: Macmillan, 1942);

Davis, "Swift's Use of Irony," in *The World of Jonathan Swift*, edited by Brian Vickers (Oxford: Blackwell, 1968), pp. 154-170;

Michael V. DePorte, *Nightmares and Hobbyhorses: Swift, Sterne, and Augustan Ideas of Madness* (San Marino: Huntington Library, 1974);

Denis Donoghue, *Jonathan Swift: A Critical Introduction* (Cambridge: Cambridge University Press, 1969);

Irvin Ehrenpreis, "Personae," in *Restoration and Eighteenth-Century Literature: Essays in Honor of Alan Dugald McKillop*, pp. 25-37;

A. C. Elias, Jr., *Swift at Moor Park: Problems in Biography and Criticism* (Philadelphia: University of Pennsylvania Press, 1982);

Frank H. Ellis, ed., *A Discourse of the Contests and Dissensions between the Nobles and the Commons in Athens and Rome* (Oxford: Clarendon Press, 1967);

A. B. England, "Private and Public Rhetoric in the *Journal to Stella*," *Essays in Criticism*, 22 (April 1972): 131-141;

William Bragg Ewald, Jr., *The Masks of Jonathan Swift* (Cambridge, Mass.: Harvard University Press, 1954);

Carole Fabricant, *Swift's Landscape* (Baltimore: Johns Hopkins University Press, 1982);

Oliver W. Ferguson, *Jonathan Swift and Ireland* (Urbana: University of Illinois Press, 1962);

Leon Guilhamet, *Satire and the Transformation of Genre* (Philadelphia: University of Pennsylvania Press, 1987);

Phyllis J. Guskin, "Intentional Accidentals: Typography and Audience in Swift's *Drapier's Letters*," *Eighteenth-Century Life*, 6 (October 1980): 80-101;

Phillip Harth, "Ehrenpreis's *Swift*: The Biographer as Critic," *Modern Philology*, 67 (1970): 273-278;

Harth, *Swift and Anglican Rationalism: The Religious Background of "A Tale of a Tub"* (Chicago: University of Chicago Press, 1961);

Harth, "Swift's *Project*: Tract or Travesty?," *PMLA*, 84 (March 1969): 336-338, 340-341;

Denis Johnston, *In Search of Swift* (Dublin: Hodges Figgis, 1959);

Louis A. Landa, Review of *The Mind and Art of Jonathan Swift* by Ricardo Quintana, *Modern Philology*, 35 (November 1937): 202-204;

Landa, *Swift and the Church of Ireland* (Oxford: Clarendon Press, 1954);

Joseph M. Levine, "Ancients and Moderns Reconsidered," *Eighteenth Century Studies*, 15 (Fall 1981): 72-89;

Levine, "Ancients, Moderns and History: The Continuity of English Historical Writing in the Later Seventeenth Century," in *Studies in Change and Revolution*, edited by Paul Korshin (Menston, England: Scolar Press, 1972), pp. 43-75;

Maynard Mack, "The Muse of Satire," *Yale Review*, 41 (September 1951): 80-92;

Frank A. Palmeri, " 'To write upon Nothing': Narrative Satire and Swift's *A Tale of a Tub*," *Genre*, 18 (1985): 151-172;

Ronald Paulson, *Theme and Structure in Swift's "Tale of a Tub"* (New Haven: Yale University Press, 1960);

Leland D. Peterson, "Swift's *Project*: A Religious and Political Satire," *PMLA*, 82 (March 1967): 54-63;

Martin Price, *Swift's Rhetorical Art: A Study in Structure and Meaning* (New Haven: Yale University Press, 1953);

Maurice J. Quinlan, "*Swift's Project for the Advancement of Religion and the Reformation of Manners*," *PMLA*, 71 (March 1956): 201-212;

Quinlan, "Swift's Use of Literalization as a Rhetorical Device," *PMLA*, 82 (1967): 516-521;

Ricardo Quintana, *The Mind and Art of Jonathan Swift* (London & New York: Oxford University Press, 1936);

Quintana, "Situational Satire: A Commentary on the Method of Swift," *University of Toronto Quarterly*, 17 (January 1948): 130-136;

Quintana, *Swift: An Introduction* (London: Oxford University Press, 1955);

Claude Rawson, "The Character of Swift's Satire: Reflections on Swift, Johnson, and Human Restlessness," in *The Character of Swift's Satire*, edited by Rawson (Newark: University of Delaware Press, 1983), pp. 21-82;

Rawson, *Gulliver and the Gentle Reader: Studies in Swift and Our Time* (London: Routledge & Kegan Paul, 1973);

Rawson, "A Reading of *A Modest Proposal*," in *Augustan Worlds*, edited by J. C. Hilson, M. M. B. Jones, and J. R. Watson (New York: Barnes & Noble, 1978), pp. 29-50;

Edward W. Rosenheim, Jr., *Swift and the Satirist's Art* (Chicago: University of Chicago Press, 1963);

Edward W. Said, "Swift's Tory Anarchy," *Eighteenth-Century Studies*, 3 (Fall 1969): 48-66;

George Sherburn, "Jonathan Swift," in *A Literary History of England*, edited by Albert C. Baugh (New York: Appleton-Century-Crofts, 1948), pp. 857-869;

Sherburn, "Methods in Books about Swift," *Studies in Philology*, 35 (October 1938): 635-656;

Donald T. Siebert, Jr., "Masks and Masquerades: The Animus of Swift's Satire," *South Atlantic Quarterly*, 74 (Autumn 1975): 435-445;

Frederik N. Smith, "Dramatic Elements in Swift's *Journal to Stella*," *Eighteenth-Century Studies*, 1 (June 1968): 332-352;

Smith, *Language and Reality in Swift's "A Tale of a Tub"* (Columbus: Ohio State University Press, 1979);

Miriam K. Starkman, *Swift's Satire on Learning in "A Tale of a Tub"* (Princeton: Princeton University Press, 1950);

Peter Steele, *Jonathan Swift: Preacher and Jester* (Oxford: Clarendon Press, 1978);

Gardner D. Stout, Jr., "Satire and Self-Expression in Swift's *Tale of a Tub*," in *Studies in the Eighteenth Century*, ii: *Papers presented at the Second David Nichol Smith Memorial Seminar, Canberra 1970*, edited by R. F. Brissenden (Canberra: Australian National University Press, 1973), pp. 323-339;

Stout, "Speaker and Satiric Vision in Swift's *Tale of a Tub*," *Eighteenth-Century Studies*, 3 (Winter 1969): 175-199;

John Traugott, "A Tale of a Tub," in *The Character of Swift's Satire*, pp. 83-126;

Jan R. Van Meter, "On Peterson on Swift [the *Project for the Advancement of Religion and the Reformation of Manners*]," *PMLA*, 86 (October 1971): 1017-1023;

David Wooley, "The Authorship of *An Answer to a Scurrilous Pamphlet* (1693)," in *Proceedings of the First Münster Symposium on Jonathan Swift*, edited by Hermann J. Real and Heinz J. Vienken (Münster: Wilhelm Fink, 1985), pp. 321-335.

Papers:

Swift manuscripts are widely distributed throughout Britain, Ireland, and the United States. Locations of most are identified in the standard editions of his works cited above. See also annotations to Ehrenpreis's *Swift: The Man, His Works, and the Age*; Herbert Davis's "Remarks on Some Swift Manuscripts in the United States," in Landa and Tobin's *A List of Critical Studies 1895-1945*, pp. 7-16; and George P. Mayhew's *Rage or Raillery: The Swift Manuscripts at the Huntington Library*.

Sir William Temple

(25 April 1628 - 27 January 1699)

Ann Cline Kelly
Howard University

BOOKS: *Observations upon the United Provinces of the Netherlands* (London: Printed by A. Maxwell for Sa. Gellibrand, 1673);

An Essay upon the Advancement of Trade in Ireland (Dublin, 1673);

Poems. By Sir W. T. (N.p.: Privately printed, 1679?);

Miscellanea [The First Part] (London: Printed by A. M. & R. R. for Edward Gellibrand, 1680); facsimile of "An Essay upon the Original and Nature of Government," introduction by Robert C. Steensma (Los Angeles: William Andrews Clark Memorial Library, 1964);

Miscellanea. The Second Part (London: Printed by T. M. for Richard & Ralph Simpson, 1690);

Memoirs of What Past in Christendom, from the War begun 1672 to the Peace concluded 1679 (London: Printed by R. R. for Ric. Chiswell, 1692);

An Introduction to the History of England (London: Printed for Richard & Ralph Simpson, 1695);

Miscellanea. The Third Part, published by Jonathan Swift (London: Printed for Benjamin Tooke, 1701);

Select Letters to the Prince of Orange (now King of England,) King Charles the IId and the Earl of Arlington upon important subjects. Volume III: To which is added an essay upon the state and settlement of Ireland, unauthorized edition (London: Printed for Tho. Bennet, 1701);

Memoirs. Part III. From the Peace concluded 1679. To the Time of the Author's Retirement from Publick Business. Published by Jonathan Swift (London: Printed for Benjamin Tooke, 1709);

The Early Essays and Romances of Sir William Temple, edited by G. C. Moore Smith (Oxford: Clarendon Press, 1930).

Editions: *The Works of Sir William Temple, Bart.*, 2 volumes (London: Printed for A. Churchill, T. Goodwin, and others, 1720);

Sir William Temple's Essay on Ancient and Modern Learning and On Poetry, edited by J. E. Spingarn (Oxford: Clarendon Press, 1909);

Observations upon the United Provinces of the Netherlands, edited by G. N. Clark (Cambridge: Cambridge University Press, 1932);

Five Miscellaneous Essays by Sir William Temple, edited by Samuel Holt Monk (Ann Arbor: University of Michigan Press, 1963).

Sir William Temple achieved success in a variety of prose genres: the familiar essay, for which he is best known; the political analysis, full of his reasoned responses to contemporary events; and the political memoir, a form he introduced into English literature. His style, which ranges from the conversational to the Ciceronian, won wide admiration during the eighteenth century. Samuel Johnson, for instance, praised Temple as the first to write English prose with cadence. Although Temple was not a profound or systematic thinker, his observations on issues as diverse as gout and government are fresh, often original, and always engaging because of his personal involvement, his sensible and balanced views, his cosmopolitan perspective, his open-mindedness, his seeming frankness, and his charming optimism about achieving that rarest of human amenities—happiness. Temple's writings were popular during his lifetime, and after his death, his collected works went through seven editions by the end of the eighteenth century (1720, 1731, 1740, 1750, 1754, 1757, 1770). Temple's reputation suffered in the nineteenth century when Thomas Babington Macaulay, in the *Edinburgh Review* (October 1838), depicted Temple as a shallow thinker and a moral coward, and William Makepeace Thackeray, in *The English Humourists* (1853), characterized him as the cranky, insensitive patriarch of Moor Park, who oppressed the genius of his secretary, Jonathan Swift. Temple's links to Swift have been a constant focus of attention, and from the late eighteenth century onward, rumors circulated that Temple fathered

Sir William Temple (portrait after Sir Peter Lely; by permission of the National Portrait Gallery, London)

Swift and Stella (Esther Johnson). Today, although he is still known largely because of his relationship with Swift and his part in the Ancients versus Moderns controversy that inspired *A Tale of a Tub* and *The Battle of the Books* (1704), Temple in his own right has attracted considerable interest, signaled by several monographs and new editions of some of his works.

The eldest son of Mary Hammond and Sir John Temple, William Temple was born into a prominent Anglo-Irish family with a tradition of public service. (His father was master of the Rolls in Ireland, and his grandfather was provost of Trinity College, Dublin.) Although he left Cambridge in 1648 without a degree, he spent the next four years, mostly on the Continent, continuing his education with the study of languages and political institutions. On his way to France,

he accidentally met the beautiful and vivacious Dorothy Osborne, who was traveling with her brother. He instantly fell in love with her, but neither family approved the match. The couple was separated for seven years, during which time Osborne sent Temple love letters that are some of the best in the language. (Extracts of her letters were first published by T. P. Courtenay in 1836, and several fuller editions followed. His letters to her are lost.) Finally married on 25 December 1654, the couple returned to the Temple estates in Ireland. After participating in the settlement of Ireland at the Restoration, Temple was elected to the Irish Parliament as a member from Carlow (1661). When the Parliament was prorogued in 1663, Temple moved to England and served the Crown on various diplomatic missions in Europe, for which he was rewarded with a baronetcy in

Miſcellanea.

I. A Survey of the Conſtitutions and Intereſts of the *Empire, Sueden, Denmark, Spain, Holland, France,* and *Flanders*; with their Relation to *England,* in the Year.1671.

II. An Eſſay upon the Original and· Nature of Government.

III. An Eſſay upon the Advancement of Trade in *IRELAND.*

IV. Upon the Conjuncture of Affairs in *Octob.* 1673.

V. Upon the Exceſſes of Grief.

VI. An Eſſay upon the Cure of the GOUT by *Moxa.*

By a Perſon of Honour.

LONDON:
Printed by *A. M.* and *R. R.* for *Edward Gellibrand,* at the *Golden-Ball* in St. *Pauls* Church-yard, 1680.

Title page for the first collection of Temple's essays

1666. Temple achieved fame by his remarkably expeditious negotiation of the Triple Alliance (1668) of England, Sweden, and the Netherlands against France. Soon after, when he realized that Charles and his ministers had no intention of adhering to the treaty, Temple retired to his estate at Sheen. He emerged from this retreat in 1674 to formalize a peace between England and Holland with the Treaty of Nimeguen, ratified in 1679. While abroad, Temple began a lifelong friendship with William of Orange and in 1677 helped to arrange the marriage of William to the Protestant heir to the English throne, Princess Mary.

Retiring permanently in 1680, Temple bought the estate at Moor Park with which his name is connected. At Moor Park, Temple wrote the essays that earned his literary reputation, the best known of which, besides the "Essay upon the Ancient and Modern Learning," is "Upon the Gardens of Epicurus; or, Of Gardening in the Year 1685," where he describes the transcendent enjoyment he derived from his horticultural projects, despite political reverses and personal loss. (Of nine children, only John and a daughter, Diana, survived childhood. Both of Temple's children and his wife predeceased him; Diana succumbed to smallpox in 1679, John committed suicide in

1689, and Dorothy Osborne Temple died in 1695.) When Temple died in 1699, he was famed as a polished writer and an incorruptible courtier. His will specified that Jonathan Swift should inherit his literary remains and that his heart be buried in a silver box beneath the sundial at Moor Park.

Many of William Temple's recurrent ideas appear in his first and longest single work, *Observations upon the United Provinces of the Netherlands*, based on his experiences abroad and published in 1673, when England and Holland were at war. Notwithstanding Temple's prefatory claim that the book is a detached political analysis written for amusement in an idle hour, *Observations upon the United Provinces of the Netherlands* argues strongly that the Dutch have created a utopia the English would do well to emulate. Without many natural resources, the Dutch nonetheless manage to be prosperous and peaceful. Toleration, which encourages religious refugees from other countries to settle in Holland and invest their capital and which eliminates the waste and disruption caused by internecine strife, is the key to their success. Being pragmatic rather than passionate, ingenious rather than imperious, the Dutch have created a rational, humane social order to promote their own happiness. In one of his rhythmic periods, Temple celebrates their salutary frugality: "For never any Countrey traded so much and consumed so little. . . . In short, they furnish infinite Luxury, which they never practise, and traffique in Pleasures which they never taste." Full of eyewitness detail, his discussion of the people, government, religion, and trade of the United Provinces is clear and lively. Within Temple's lifetime, the book went through six editions and was translated into Dutch and French. Because of continued demand, Cambridge University Press republished in 1972 Sir George Clark's 1932 edition of the book.

In 1680 Temple's *Miscellanea* [The First Part] first made public Temple's gifts as an essayist and political theorist. First in the volume is a "Survey of the Constitutions and Interests of the Empire, Sweden, Denmark, Holland, France, and Flanders, with their relation to England, in the year 1671," which subtly reiterates the importance of the Triple Alliance to contain the menace of France. With a characteristically cosmopolitan perspective, Temple stresses that English foreign policy should be constructed within a global framework. The second item, "An Essay upon the Original and Nature of Government,"

has attracted scholars because of its rejection of the idea of a social contract and its advocacy of a patriarchal model for government. With a typically vivid simile, Temple dismisses the antithetical views of mankind as either herdlike or predatory by asking how "if men are like sheep, why they need any Government: or if they are like Wolves, how can they suffer it."

The next essay, "The Advancement of Trade in Ireland," originally published separately in Dublin (1673), was addressed to Arthur Capel, Earl of Essex, then lord lieutenant of Ireland. Evoking parallels with Holland, it emphasizes the need to attract money and immigrants to Ireland by stabilizing the government and improving the balance of trade. Temple offers concrete proposals on everything from packing fish for export to organizing the privy council. In all cases, he would render the Irish interest subordinate to the English. Another political piece, "Upon the Conjuncture of Affairs in October, 1673" was, according to the heading, "Written to the Duke of Ormonde . . . upon his Grace's desiring me to give him my opinion" on what to do about the continuing war with Holland. Needless to say, given his unswerving admiration for the Dutch, Temple argues that the war can only hurt English interests, both at home and abroad.

In the last two pieces of *Miscellanea* [The First Part], Temple turns to the familiar essay. In a personal appeal "To the Countess of Essex, upon her grief occasioned by the loss of her only daughter" (dated in a headnote, Sheen, 19 January 1674), Temple argues that it is not natural, customary, or sensible to grieve immoderately for a child. He cites mourning customs from other cultures to support his thesis. At the heart of the essay is a general plea not to make life worse than it is and to try valiantly to seek happiness: "We bring into the world with us a poor needy uncertain life, short at the longest, and unquiet at the best; All the imaginations of the witty and the wise have been perpetually busied to find out the ways how to revive it with pleasures, or relieve it with diversions. . . ." Happiness can be achieved only through emotional moderation: "Better no passions at all, than have them too violent; or such alone, as instead of heightening our pleasures, afford us nothing but vexation and pain."

Written more in the chatty, digressive mode generally associated with some of the best of his essays, "The Cure of the Gout by Moxa" (dated in a headnote, Nimeguen, 18 June 1677) describes his grumpiness at having a condition that elicits little sympathy. Desperate to find some relief, Temple, donning the gown of a medical researcher, step-by-step investigates the healing properties of moxa, a moss from the East Indies. Reading about moxa's use and testing it on himself and others, Temple muses as he experiments. The moxa works, but the ultimate cure, he decides, is to eat like a poor man, without much meat or wine. Temple documents this conclusion with his own experience and with evidence from a wide geographical and historical range. Like much of Temple's other writing, the essay is developed with a charming combination of cosmopolitan knowledge and personal observation.

A second *Miscellanea*, dedicated to Cambridge University, was published in 1690. It contains four of Temple's most widely known and influential essays: "An Essay upon the Ancient and Modern Learning," "Upon the Gardens of Epicurus," "Of Heroick Virtue," and "Of Poetry." These were edited and republished with an excellent introduction by Samuel Holt Monk in 1963. In "An Essay upon the Ancient and Modern Learning," Temple entered the contemporary debate about the relative merits of classical and contemporary achievement, or otherwise stated, the idea of progress. The debate poses a false ultimatum to Temple, who accepts both the possibility of human improvement and the magnificent attainments of classical culture. Overstating his case and revealing his lack of academic training, Temple stresses the dangers of intellectual complacency, which he attributes to champions of the moderns. He emphasizes that one's perspective ought to be broad enough to include the distant past and other cultures. Only through a wide sampling of human experience can valid assumptions be inferred. In his survey of learning in the essay, Temple epitomizes the broad view by looking at the contributions not only of classical civilizations, but also those of the Incas, Chinese, and Brahmans. The essay, atypically polemical and thesis-ridden, is an attack on the pride that convinces man that he has no limitations, so that "when he has looked about him as far as he can, he concludes there is no more to be seen; when he is at the end of his line, he is at the bottom of the oceans; when he has shot his best, he is sure, none ever did or ever can shoot better or beyond it." Temple's unscholarly affection for ancient learning and the legacy of the past causes him to praise Aesop's *Fables* and the *Epistles of Phalaris* as examples of ancient writing without modern

peers and dismiss the value of modern writers. To him, Sir Philip Sidney, Francis Bacon, and John Selden were the only English writers who approached the caliber of the ancients. He also doubts the achievements of contemporary science, including the contributions of Copernicus and Harvey. Temple's assertions were attacked by William Wotton in his *Reflections upon Ancient and Modern Learning* (1694), and then more devastatingly by Richard Bentley, whose scholarly *Dissertation* (1697) conclusively showed the *Epistles of Phalaris* to be spurious. A pamphlet war ensued, with publications attacking and defending Temple, among them Swift's *The Battle of the Books*. Continued interest in the Ancients versus Moderns controversy has ensured the popularity of Temple's "Essay upon the Ancient and Modern Learning."

"Upon the Gardens of Epicurus; or, Of Gardening, in the Year 1685" dwells on more personal themes. Implicitly it offers reasons for Temple's decision to leave government service, where he felt frustrated and betrayed. Like Epicurus, Temple seeks the tranquillity of a garden, archetypally, as he shows with a global survey, the seat of ultimate pleasure. He explains that Epicurean pleasure is not sensual, but a relish of the essential calm that derives from "Human Wisdom, Innocence of Life, or Resignation to the Will of God." In this essay and others Temple expresses views that seem achristian or unchristian, causing critics, including Bishop Gilbert Burnet, to speculate about the nature of his religious belief. Moving from the abstraction of the garden as a metaphor for happiness, Temple discusses his own gardening practices with numerous personal anecdotes. He boasts about his apricots, and indeed Moor Park apricots still are offered in gardening catalogs. Although he thinks geometric gardens are best, he provides a description of irregular Chinese gardens that proved influential in English landscape design in the next century. Temple concludes by noting that "the measure of choosing well, is, Whether a Man likes what He has chosen, which I thank God has befallen me; and though, among the Follies of my Life, Building and Planting have not been the least, and have cost me more than I have the confidence to own, yet they have been fully recompensed by the sweetness and satisfaction of this Retreat," which he will never leave again to enter "any Publick Employments." Temple's decision to tend his own garden rather than further serve his country brought repeated criticism upon him.

The theme of happiness also dominates the third essay in the *Miscellanea. The Second Part*, "Of Heroic Virtue." In the essay Temple radically redefines heroism as a bureaucratic, rather than a martial, virtue, an idea he may have absorbed from Confucius, whom he praises. For Temple "the wise Institution of Laws and Government" that promotes human civilization and well-being is far more important than "great Conquests or Victories." To support his point Temple surveys four ancient kingdoms whose people have benefited by the promotion of good government by certain individuals: China, Peru, Scythia (or Tartary), and Arabia. The fascination with effective social engineering evident in Temple's *Observations upon the United Provinces of the Netherlands* is found here as well. No doubt it was his faith in the ability of government to make people's lives better that kept him in public service as long as he was.

The concluding essay, "Of Poetry," espouses several influential ideas, some of which are original. The best-known statement in the essay is Temple's assertion that, above all, poetry should give pleasure, since "when all is done, Humane Life is at the greatest and the best, but like a froward Child, that must be Play'd with, and Humor'd a little, to keep it quiet till it falls asleep, and then the Care is over." His survey of poetry in different cultures and times calls attention to Gothic runes and anticipates tastes prevalent later in the eighteenth century. In seeming contradiction to the thesis of "An Essay upon the Ancient and Modern Learning," Temple asserts that English comedy, particularly that of Shakespeare, is superior not only to all other modern comedy, but to ancient comedy as well because of its "humour." The freedom of English culture and the effect of English climate (the influence of climate on character is one of Temple's recurrent themes) foster the eccentricity that characterizes "humour."

Soon after he retired to the countryside, Temple began working on memoirs of his life as a public servant. As Swift points out in his preface to *Memoirs. Part III*, Temple is the first Englishman to employ this genre, heretofore dominated by the French. Temple composed the memoirs in reverse chronological order, writing about his most recent experience first in what came to be known as "Part III," which was not published until after his death. "Part II" of the memoirs, covering the period 1672 to the Treaty of Nimeguen, which Temple negotiated in 1679, appeared first in 1692, without Temple's name and seemingly without his authorization. "Part I" of

the memoirs, which describes the negotiation of the Triple Alliance, never appeared. According to Swift, Temple burned the history because it depicted questionable actions of Sir Henry Bennet, Lord Arlington. That thesis is undermined by Temple's permitting the publication of his letters written during the period covered by "Part I." Some scholars speculate that Temple may never have written the first part of the memoirs.

Homer Woodbridge, the most thorough student of Temple to date, ranks *Memoirs*, "Part II" (1692) "with the very best of Temple's work." Immediately popular, *Memoirs*, "Part II" prompted a second edition and a French translation in 1692. Other editions appeared in 1693, 1700, and 1709. Temple's seemingly verbatim account of conversations between himself and King Charles, as well as his talks with the principals who negotiated the Treaty of Nimeguen, takes the reader into the inner sanctums where the fates of nations are decided. The novelistic particularity and focus with which Temple develops the narrative and the characters who motivate it—himself included—make "Part II" of the *Memoirs* fascinating reading even today. An attractive image of Temple emerges from this work; he presents himself as rational, patient, honest, good-humored, loyal, and competent. But as Woodbridge points out, the real hero of the piece is William of Orange, whose fortunes Temple always supported. Conversations and anecdotes dramatize that prince's noble qualities. Distant, complex political events become clear and immediate in Temple's chatty narration. In the course of the memoirs, Temple remarks on the fraudulence of a Monsieur DeCros. DeCros retaliated by attacking Temple in print. Two anonymous defenses of Temple—*An Answer to a Scurrilous Pamphlet Lately printed, Intituled A Letter from M. de Cros* (1693), which Abel Boyer and others at the time thought was written by Temple himself (some have attributed it to Swift), and *Reflections upon Two Pamphlets Lately Published* (1693)—were volleyed back.

An Introduction to the History of England (1695) is the last work Temple published in his lifetime. In the preface Temple explains that he intends to create a general history of England in abridged form to encourage a more extended treatment by others, but his intention aside, Temple devotes the last two-thirds of the book to William the Conqueror and his reign. Abel Boyer, in his *Memoirs of the life and negotiations of Sir W. Temple* (1714), states that "it was the general Opinion, that Sir *William Temple*, who continued to the last

when He was in Italy, was called Wottoni,
therefore, He should be called so in England;
And I advise Him, that it should be Wottoni in
His next Edition.

But 'tis worth considering what kind of
Person our Reflector has thought proper for such
a Cavil: One brought up and long conversant
with Persons of the greatest Quality at home
and abroad; In Courts, in Parliaments, in privy
Councils, in Foreign Embassyes, in the Mediations
And the great Assemblyes not upon those Occasions
of generall Peace in Christendom; And yet perhaps
more ~~known~~ by his Writings than by the
great Employments He has had or refused; And
this is the Person, Mr Wotton pursues so
insolently with a pitifull Grammaticall Criticism
and a mistaken one too.

One would wonder who this great man
should be, that upon both Antients and Moderns
with such an Arrogance; Why, 'tis a young
Scholar that confesses He owes all the Comforts

of

Page from the manuscript for Temple's "Hints: written at the Desire of D^r. F. and of His Friend" (circa 1697), in the hand of Temple's secretary, Jonathan Swift, with one revision by Temple (Rothschild Collection, no. 2253; by permission of the Master and Fellows of Trinity College, Cambridge). Temple later expanded and reworked this essay as "Some Thoughts on Reviewing the Essay of Antient and Modern Learning."

a *true Friend* to the Prince of *Orange*.... publish'd ... his *Introduction to the History of* England ... to compliment that Prince, under the *Character* of the *Norman* Conqueror, which he draws and sets off to great Advantage...." Boyer's theory is more credible than Temple's statement that the Norman Conquest "fixed and established" all the important features of English government, and so the last six hundred years of history require no exegesis. Temple's sources were various. With the use of parallel passages, for instance, Homer Woodbridge illustrates Temple's unacknowledged debt to Samuel Daniel's *The Collection of the History of England* (1618). Other editions of Temple's *Introduction to the History of England* appeared in 1699 and 1708; it was translated into French shortly after it was first published (1695).

Two years after Temple's death in 1699, Swift published *Miscellanea. The Third Part*, including "Of Popular Discontents" and "Of Health and Long Life," both of which, according to Swift, Temple had specifically designated for the volume. In addition, Swift collected other writings Temple seemed not to have completed because of ill health, including "Some Thoughts on Reviewing the Essay of Antient and Modern Learning," and outlines of two essays on "Different Conditions of Life and Fortune" and "Conversation." Swift appended to the volume some of Temple's translations of Virgil, Horace, and Tibullus. "Of Popular Discontents" begins with a long speculation on the essential differences between man and the other animals, the most important of which, Temple believes, is that other animals are content with their situations whereas men are perpetually restless and discontent: "All are easily satisfied with themselves and their own Merit, though they are not so with their Fortune." Given the imperfect nature of man, how can government be constituted to guarantee some happiness and stability? Temple thinks that such government is possible if traditional forms are maintained, the will of the people is consulted, the work ethic is promoted, and foreign policy is designed to ensure domestic tranquillity. Temple then lists specific policies to improve the national welfare: strengthen and augment the navy; provide a uniform system of land registry; build more workhouses; improve the woolen trade; and abolish capital punishment for theft and robbery because it is depleting the labor force. Despite his pessimistic assumptions about the nature of man, Temple maintains an optimism that so-

cial engineering can produce peace and prosperity on a national scale.

Moving from the macrocosm to the microcosm in *Miscellanea. The Third Part*, one next encounters "Of Health and Long Life," whose major premise is that happiness is impossible without health. Temple surveys history to derive the secrets of health and long life: "great Temperance, open Air, easy Labor, little Care, simplicity of Diet, rather Fruits and Plants than Flesh." Using interesting anecdotes from his reading and from his own experience, Temple argues the virtues of each item. His style in the essay is extremely familiar and his aim unpretentious: "though I may not be able to inform Men more than they know, yet I may perhaps give them the Occasion to consider more than they do." This essay has been frequently anthologized.

Materials Temple evidently had not finished but that Swift nonetheless felt were worthy of publication fill out the volume. "Some Thoughts on Reviewing the Essay of Antient and Modern Learning" is really a rehash of his earlier essay with some jabs at critics and philologists added to counter the attacks of Bentley and Wotton. He drops the argument of the ancients' literary superiority based on the examples of Phalaris and Aesop and stresses that in the studies of lasting value—agriculture, medicine, political science—the ancients still reign supreme. The benefits and liabilities of the greatest modern discoveries—the lodestone and gunpowder—cancel out one another. The most important legacy of the ancients, however, is their understanding of the limits of human knowledge, something the moderns choose to ignore. "Heads Designed for an Essay upon the Different Conditions of Life and Fortune" outlines another exploration of Temple's favorite theme, the achievement of happiness. In essence the secret is to create an inner calm by subduing roiling passions and being content with what one has: "Man is a thinking Thing, whether he will or no: All he can do, is to turn his thoughts the best way." Temple evidently was proud of his own success in this regard and planned to quote an observation on his own life by an acquaintance who said, "If a King were so great to have nothing to desire nor fear, he would live just as You do." In his outline of an essay on conversation, Temple stresses the importance of making everyone comfortable in a social situation. Rather than specifying rules of etiquette, Temple promotes the homey pleasures of friendly talk: "In Conversation, Humour is more than Wit, Easiness more than Knowledge; few desire to learn, or think they need it, all desire to be pleased, or if not, to be easy." People talking together not only create pleasure for themselves, but also a wider awareness of the world.

In 1700 Swift published two volumes of Temple's letters. Masquerading as a third volume of Swift's edition, *Select letters to the Prince of Orange* appeared in 1701 and contains Temple's "Essay upon the State and Settlement of Ireland," which was not included in the collected works, first published in 1720. Written in 1668, the piece laments that the self-interest of many parties prevented a proper settlement of Ireland at the Restoration, making Ireland a financial sink. Temple suggests specific remedies, such as new land taxes; incentives, including broad religious toleration, to attract Protestant immigrants; and removal of the native Irish population from the counties surrounding Dublin to make that district a purely English enclave. Woodbridge argues that as draconian as this last measure sounds, it was moderate in comparison to others of the time. Indeed Woodbridge believes that as far as Ireland was concerned, "no Englishman in his time took a more enlightened view."

Claiming that some urged him to delay publication to avoid offending still-living people, Swift finally brought out "Part III" of Temple's *Memoirs* in 1709. In the preface he defends Temple against the criticisms that he speaks too much of himself in the accounts and that his style is full of gallicisms. The first criticism Swift deflects with a short disquisition on the nature of political memoirs. The second he explains by reminding the reader that French is the language of diplomacy; it would be natural that Temple, so accustomed to using the language in his negotiations, might manifest some Gallic influence in his discourse. Swift also explains why the second published volume of memoirs is called the third: the first was burned in manuscript by Temple. The third volume of the memoirs is one quarter the length of the second. Its headnote establishes the apologetic tone of the volume, which, Temple says, was "Written for the Satisfaction of my Friends hereafter, upon the Grounds of my Retirement, and Resolution never to meddle again with any Publick Affairs from this present February." Some critics of Temple, then and now, view his retreat to his garden as irresponsible, but in the third volume of the *Memoirs*, he explains his reasons. Factional bickering and pervasive duplicity defeated his attempts at constructive action. Tem-

ple discovered that he lacked the proper temperament to succeed in that climate: "the Arts of the Court were contrary to the Franckness and Openness of my Nature; and the Constraints of publick Business too great for the Liberty of my Humour and my Life. . . . And so I take Leave of all those Airy Visions which have so long busied my Head about mending the World; . . . and shall turn [my thoughts] wholly to mend my self." Typically, Temple seeks happiness by exercising control where he can and banishing the uncontrollable beyond the pale of his thoughts.

Temple's sister, Lady Martha Temple Giffard, who had been in the Temple household since the death of her husband one month after their marriage in 1662, publicly attacked Swift for publishing the memoirs without proper authority and without an authentic copy text. She evidently wanted to distance herself from the volume because it criticized certain prominent people of her acquaintance. After Lady Giffard refused to give him her copy of the memoirs, Swift used the copy in his possession. Swift responded to justify himself and his text, saying, "Nobody else had conversed so much with his manuscripts as I, and since I was not wholly illiterate, I cannot imagine whom else he would leave the care of his writings to."

It was not until 1931 that the last of Temple's writings, preserved in a holograph manuscript, were published in G. C. Moore Smith's *The Early Essays and Romances of Sir William Temple*. The romances are adaptations of those by Francois de Rosset, whose *Les Histoires tragiques* first appeared in 1615 and included nineteen stories. Temple rewrote nine of these, but four have been lost. The epistle dedicatory to Dorothy Osborne, the only letter from Temple to her that survives, reveals that he wrote these stories to pass the time when he was separated from her: "I found it to no purpose to flee from my thoughts, and that the best way was to deceive them with the likeness of objects and by representing others' misfortunes to them instead of my own." Bearing such titles as *The Constant Desperado* and *The Disloyal Wife*, Temple's romances are thoroughly conventional. The essays, dated "Brussels 1652," are not, it seems, finished products and range from a collection of a few brief notes to expatiations of several thousand words in which Woodbridge sees parallels to Montaigne and Sir Thomas Browne. The characteristically personal tone and conversational style typical of Temple's best essays are evident in these apprentice pieces.

Books and editions of Temple have appeared at a rapid rate in recent years in part because of the light that his works can shed on Swift (most of the scholarly articles on Temple pursue this theme), but in part because of a renewed appreciation of Temple's attractiveness. Samuel Holt Monk justified his new edition (1963) of Temple's essays with his belief that "they can please and instruct twentieth-century readers not only because of the charm of their style, but because to a considerable extent they reveal the temperament of a very human writer." Many of Temple's individual works are being republished, and in 1968 Greenwood Press reprinted the last edition of Temple's collected works (1814). Clara Marburg Kirk's study of Temple's epicureanism (1932) was reprinted in 1977. General books on Temple's life and works by Robert C. Steensma (1970), Hester Chapman (1977), and Richard Faber (1983) are quite sympathetic. Temple's career in government service is the focus of K. H. D. Haley's *An English Diplomat in the Low Countries* (1986). Earlier, A. C. Elias's *Swift at Moor Park* (1982) stirred up controversy by depicting Temple as an egotistical mediocrity whom Swift did not respect. Elias also comes to the conclusion that Temple doctored certain passages in his letters to make his actions look better. In appendices to their books both Faber and Haley strongly defend Temple against Elias's accusations. Various judgments and interpretations of Temple have appeared, but in the end, as Lady Giffard points out, "S[ir] Wm Temples character will be best knowne by his writeings & to that picture of him I leave those that care either to know or imitate him. . . ."

Letters:

Letters written by Sir William Temple during his being ambassador at the Hague, unauthorized edition, published by D. Jones (London: Printed & sold by A. Baldwin, 1699);

Letters written by Sir W. Temple, Bart. and other ministers of state. . . . Published by Jonathan Swift, 2 volumes (London: Printed for J. Tonson and A. & J. Churchil, 1700);

Select letters to the Prince of Orange (now King of England,) King Charles the IId and the Earl of Arlington upon important subjects. Volume III: To which is added an essay upon the state and settlement of Ireland. All written by Sir William Temple, unauthorized edition (London: Printed for Tho. Bennet, 1701);

Letters to the King, the Prince of Orange, the Chief Ministers of State, and Other Persons: Being the Third and Last Volume Published by Jonathan Swift (London: Printed for Tim. Goodwin & Benj. Tooke, 1703).

Biographies:

[Abel Boyer], *Memoirs of the life and negotiations of Sir W. Temple* (London: Printed for W. Taylor, 1714);

[Lady Martha Temple Giffard], *The Life and Character of Sir William Temple, Bart. Written by a particular friend* (London: Printed for B. Motte, 1728);

Thomas Peregrine Courtenay, *Memoirs of the life, works, and Correspondence of Sir William Temple,* 2 volumes (London: Printed for Longman, Rees, Orme, Brown, Green & Longman, 1836);

Hester Chapman, *Four Fine Gentlemen* (Lincoln: University of Nebraska Press / London: Constable, 1977);

Richard Faber, *The Brave Courtier: Sir William Temple* (London: Faber & Faber, 1983).

References:

A. C. Elias, Jr., *Swift at Moor Park: Problems in Biography and Criticism* (Philadelphia: University of Pennsylvania Press, 1982);

K. H. D. Haley, *An English Diplomat in the Low Countries: Sir William Temple and John De-Witt, 1665-1672* (Oxford: Clarendon Press, 1986);

Clara Marburg Kirk, *Sir William Temple: A Seventeenth Century "Libertin"* (New Haven: Yale University Press / London: Oxford University Press, 1932);

Samuel Holt Monk, Introduction to *Five Miscellaneous Essays by Sir William Temple* (Ann Arbor: University of Michigan Press, 1963);

G. C. Moore Smith, ed., *The Letters of Dorothy Osborne to Sir William Temple* (Oxford: Clarendon Press, 1928);

Robert C. Steensma, *Sir William Temple* (New York: Twayne, 1970);

Homer Woodbridge, *Sir William Temple: The Man and his Work* (New York: Modern Language Association of America / London: Oxford University Press, 1940).

Papers:

Papers concerning William Temple, his family, and his diplomatic missions can be found at the following places in the United Kingdom: the Public

Record Office; the British Library; the Bodleian Library, Oxford; the Wren Library, Trinity College, Cambridge; the Staffordshire County Record Office; the Hampshire County Record Office. In the Netherlands, papers can be found at the Rijksarchief, The Hague; the Gemeentearchief, Amsterdam; and the Koninklijke, The Hague. In Paris, Temple manuscripts can be found at the Archives du Ministère des Affairs Étrangères and in Brussels at the Archives du Royaume. A fuller listing can be found at the front of Haley's *An English Diplomat in the Low Countries*, from which this information was taken.

Books for Further Reading

Anderson, Howard, Philip B. Daghlian, and Irvin Ehrenpreis, eds. *The Familiar Letter in the Eighteenth Century*. Lawrence: University of Kansas Press, 1966.

Battestin, Martin C. *The Providence of Wit: Aspects of Form in Augustan Literature and the Arts*. Oxford: Clarendon Press, 1974.

Becker, Carl L. *The Heavenly City of the Eighteenth-Century Philosophers*. New Haven: Yale University Press, 1932.

Black, J. B. *The Art of History: A Study of Four Great Historians of the Eighteenth Century*. New York: F. S. Crofts, 1926.

Bredvold, Louis I. *The Brave New World of the Enlightenment*. Ann Arbor: University of Michigan Press, 1961.

Bredvold. *The Natural History of Sensibility*. Detroit: Wayne State University Press, 1962.

Butt, John. *The Augustan Age*, third edition, revised. New York: Norton, 1966.

Clifford, James. *Eighteenth-Century Literature: Modern Essays in Criticism*. New York: Oxford University Press, 1959.

Damrosch, Leopold, Jr. *Modern Essays on Eighteenth-Century Literature*. New York: Oxford University Press, 1988.

Engell, James. *The Creative Imagination: Enlightenment to Romanticism*. Cambridge: Harvard University Press, 1981.

Engell. *Forming the Critical Mind: Dryden to Coleridge*. Cambridge: Harvard University Press, 1989.

Fussell, Paul, Jr. *The Rhetorical World of Augustan Humanism: Ethics and Imagery from Swift to Burke*. Oxford: Clarendon Press, 1965.

Gay, Peter. *The Enlightenment: An Interpretation*, 2 volumes. New York: Knopf, 1966, 1969.

Greene, Donald. *The Age of Exuberance: Backgrounds to Eighteenth-Century English Literature*. New York: Random House, 1970.

Humphreys, A. R. *The Augustan World: Life and Letters in Eighteenth-Century England*. London: Methuen, 1954.

Jones, Richard Foster. *Ancients and Moderns: A Study of the Rise of the Scientific Movement in Seventeenth-Century England*. Washington University Studies, New Series, Language and Literature, no. 6. St. Louis, 1936.

Lovejoy, A. O. *The Great Chain of Being*. Cambridge: Harvard University Press, 1936.

Marshall, Dorothy. *Eighteenth-Century England*. London: Longmans, Green, 1962.

Monk, Samuel Holt. *The Sublime: A Study of Critical Theories in XVIIIth-Century England*. New York: Modern Language Association of America, 1935.

Moore, C. A. *Backgrounds of English Literature, 1700-1760*. Minneapolis: University of Minnesota Press, 1953.

Pocock, J. G. A. *The Machiavellian Moment: Florentine Political Thought and the Atlantic Republican Tradition*. Princeton: Princeton University Press, 1975.

Pocock. *Virtue, Commerce, and History: Essays on Political Thought and History, Chiefly in the Eighteenth Century*. Cambridge: Cambridge University Press, 1985.

Price, Martin. *To the Palace of Wisdom: Studies in Order and Energy from Dryden to Blake*. Garden City, N.Y.: Doubleday, 1964.

Richetti, John J. *Philosophical Writing: Locke, Berkeley, Hume*. Cambridge: Harvard University Press, 1983.

Rogers, Pat, ed. *The Context of English Literature: The Eighteenth Century*. London: Methuen, 1978; New York: Holmes & Meier, 1978.

Sambrook, James. *The Eighteenth Century: The Intellectual and Cultural Context of English Literature, 1700-1789*. London & New York: Longman, 1986.

Sherburn, George, and Donald F. Bond. *The Restoration and Eighteenth Century (1660-1789). A Literary History of England*, volume 3, edited by Albert C. Baugh, second edition. New York: Appleton-Century-Crofts, 1967.

Stephen, Leslie. *History of English Thought in the Eighteenth Century*, 2 volumes. London: Smith, Elder, 1876; New York: Putnam's, 1876.

Turberville, A. S., ed. *Johnson's England*, 2 volumes. Oxford: Clarendon Press, 1933.

Willey, Basil. *The Eighteenth-Century Background: Studies on the Idea of Nature in the Thought of the Period*. London: Chatto & Windus, 1940.

Willey, *The English Moralists*. New York: Norton, 1964.

Williamson, George. *The Senecan Amble: A Study in Prose Forms from Bacon to Collier*. London: Faber & Faber, 1951.

Contributors

Paula R. Backscheider ....*University of Rochester*
Lillian D. Bloom .....*Research Scholar, Henry E. Huntington Library and Art Gallery*
Martine Watson Brownley...*Emory University*
Isobel Grundy ....*University of Alberta*
William C. Horne ....*Salisbury State University*
Ann Cline Kelly ....*Howard University*
Brian McCrea ....*University of Florida*
E. Pearlman...*University of Colorado at Denver*
Irwin Primer...*Rutgers University*
Cedric D. Reverand II...*University of Wyoming*
G. A. J. Rogers...*University of Keele*
Peter J. Schakel...*Hope College*
Claudia Newel Thomas ....*Wake Forest University*
Edward Tomarken ....*Miami University*
Robert Voitle...*University of North Carolina, Chapel Hill*
David Wheeler ....*University of Southern Mississippi*
Kenneth P. Winkler..*Wellesley College*
Calhoun Winton ....*University of Maryland, College Park*

Cumulative Index

Dictionary of Literary Biography, Volumes 1-101
Dictionary of Literary Biography Yearbook, 1980-1989
Dictionary of Literary Biography Documentary Series, Volumes 1-7

Cumulative Index

DLB before number: *Dictionary of Literary Biography,* Volumes 1-101
Y before number: *Dictionary of Literary Biography Yearbook,* 1980-1989
DS before number: *Dictionary of Literary Biography Documentary Series,* Volumes 1-7

A

D

F

G

Cumulative Index

H

K

O

T

Y

Z